TESTIMONY OF THE TWENTIETH CENTURY

Before and After the Berlin Wall

Text and Photographs by
Marie Ueda

Western civilization is the history of
human struggle in times of war
and in times of peace.

This book, which investigates the meaning of
the twentieth century as revealed in the war of
National Socialism, is dedicated to the generations
who will live in the twenty-first century.

Published by M.I. PRODUCTIONS, San Francisco, USA

Text: edited by S. P. Marchant
Photos: edited by Marie Ueda

Cover design: Mark Soldini
Cover introduction: edited by Michele Navarrete
Book design: Marie Ueda
Introduction: edited by Jim Jacklich
Assistants: Catherine Goggins, Jennifer Dhillon, Kevin Links
Typesetting: WordRunner

Library of Congress Catalog Card Number: 95-095142
ISBN: 0-9650299-0-5

To order the book: Send check or money order for $70.00 (postage and shipping included; in California, $75.04 with tax) to
M.I. PRODUCTIONS, P.O.Box 642219
San Francisco, CA 94164-2219.

Table of Contents

Table of Contents

Acknowledgments

I thank all interviewees who were gracious enough to give me their time. I gratefully acknowledge the following individuals who have provided information and materials for this book. For historical research, I thank the following institutions and libraries in these countries:

GERMANY: (Bonn) Anna Tomforde, British journalist for *The Guardian* of London; Liz van der Muelen, embassy secretary, Joachim Wegener, economist. (Berlin) Dr. Rainer Hildebrandt, director of the Checkpoint Charlie Museum; Margit Miosga, journalist; Heinz J. Kuzdas, photojournalist; Burkhard Schröder, author and journalist; Michael Teichmann, architect; Günther Grosser, theater producer; Charlotte Swienzinski, nurse; Bettina Stirl, student; Jewish Community Center; National Library; Magistrat von Berlin; Amerika Haus Berlin. Turkish Community Center; Büro der Ausländerbeauftragten von Ostberlin; Ausländerbeauftragte — Senatsverwaltung für Gesundheit und Soziales. (Munich) Hans Krüger, journalist.

AUSTRIA: Federation of the Jewish Community in Austria.

THE UNITED STATES OF AMERICA: (San Francisco) Ron Patterson, entrepreneur; Richard Raack, professor; Elgy Gillespie, journalist; Lani Silver, director of the Holocaust Oral History Project; Michael Thaler, formerly president of the Holocaust Center of Northern California; Gloria Lyon, Holocaust survivor; Renée Duering, Holocaust Survivor; Hideo Nakamine, WW II veteran. Goethe Institute; The City Library. (Stanford) The Hoover Institute Library at Stanford University. (Vermont) Thomas Powers, author and journalist. (New York) Simon Wiesenthal Center; (Washington, DC) The Library of Congress.

ENGLAND: (London) Rhodrick Sharp, foreign news editor for BBC; Michael Simmons, editor of *The Guardian*; University of London Library; Wiener Library; Loyal Air Force Museum. (Oxford) Nicholas Goodrick-Clarke, professor and author. (Sussex) Veronica Gillespie, writer.

JAPAN: Keinosuke Miyagawa, entrepreneur.

Furthermore, I could not have completed this book without material support from: Ed Rogers, owner of Photographers Supply, San Francisco, who contributed photographic materials; Iyetomi Ueda, engineer, and Kyoko Suzuki, English teacher, both members of my family who kindly loaned me money to produce this book.

Finally, my deepest gratitude to John Sweeney, journalist and information specialist, Los Angeles, who not only gave me valuable advice on its content but also helped me to produce this book; and S. P. Marchant, who edited this book, for her professional assistance and encouragement.

Marie Ueda
San Francisco

Introduction

As one fascinated by the study of Western civilization, I have written this book to document the personal, social and political consequences of the Second World War in Europe. This is a book of interviews and photographs of people who were affected by the rise of National Socialism, which threatened to alter the course of Western civilization. The interviewees are people who were personally involved in the events of the war, people who suffered in its aftermath, people who studied its history, and members of the post-war generations who grapple with the legacy of the war today. By focusing on the Berlin Wall as a symbol of the massive changes of the twentieth century, this volume documents an inside look at National Socialism, the Third Reich and the Holocaust narrated by over eighty individuals of different nationalities — Germans, other Europeans, Americans, Japanese — and addresses many haunting questions: Why did this war happen? Why could the world not prevent it? Why did we fight? For what did so many people die? What was the meaning of the Second World War? What did we learn about it? This book is a human document of the most wrenching war and troubled time of our century.

It has been half a century since the end of that dreadful war. As time passes, the aging witnesses of the war, survivors of the Holocaust and other victims are dying, many without having told their accounts. By the turn of the next century there will be hardly anyone alive who can give a first-hand testimony of those events. In the past several years alone, four of the most important witnesses in the book have already died: William L. Shirer, Willy Brandt, Louis L. Snyder and Heinz Galinski. As members of the postwar generations, we are still linked to both, the 'war generations' and the 'new generations' who will rule the twenty-first century. It is our responsibility to investigate and transmit true accounts of this history. The sensational interpretations of this war depicted in movies and TV are more fictional than factual. Unless we understand the complex causes of this war, as well as its nature and consequences, history will repeat itself.

I have reported the story of each interviewee objectively. All interviewees were given the equal opportunity to convey their experience and express their opinions on this tragedy. These people include liberals and conservatives, radicals and extremists, nationalists and internationalists, Holocaust survivors, politicians, intellectuals, historians, authors and journalists, professors and students, as well as ordinary citizens of all ages. From 1988 to 1995, I interviewed approximately 300 people. The book reflects the broad spectrum of human experience and it has been left to readers to make their own judgment based on the material I have compiled.

HISTORY OF THE PROJECT: I felt that the Berlin Wall was the symbol of both war and peace in this century. In 1984, when I made my first visit to Berlin, then the divided city of West and East, it appeared to me a "forgotten city." It was a short visit of nine days, but I discovered many issues which hadn't been covered in the world media since the time of the Berlin Crisis in 1961, which led to the construction of the Berlin Wall. I saw people in West Berlin surrounded by barbed-wire and tightly controlled borders, ruined railways, bombarded stations, damaged buildings, bullet holes, Allied soldiers in tanks, border-patrol guards with machine-guns and dogs, and the Checkpoint Charlie Museum where the records of escapees from Communist East Germany were displayed.

In addition to its peculiar geopolitical setting, Berlin seemed haunted by 'something' not visible, 'something' which affected the thought, feelings and behaviors of Berliners, but was never spoken about. My impression was that as long as the Wall was standing in Berlin, memories of the war and a divided Germany would never end. How did the war bring about such human ruins? Who bears the guilt and responsibility for it all? I began to reflect on the forces interacting between war and people, politics and nation, and how politics inevitably shapes our individual lives. As a photojournalist, I decided to interview West Berliners to make a book, which would be a human document of the historical changes in Germany and the world during the twentieth century. In the summer of 1988, I returned to West Berlin to pursue this project. During my one-month stay, I interviewed many individuals of all ages and different backgrounds. This segment of the book is called "Life with the Wall — Interviews with West Berliners," which became Chapter IV in this book.

In the following year, on November 9, 1989, the Berlin Wall unexpectedly fell. The world was astonished and perplexed. Berlin suddenly became the center of world media attention. Shortly afterwards, Germany's political situation changed rapidly, hastening the unification of the two Germanys. It seemed my project was suddenly out of date, and I thought I had missed the chance for publication.

While witnessing the fall of the Berlin Wall as a 'revolution without a revolution' and a new emerging Europe, I observed many significant historical developments. I decided to follow those events. In 1990, during Germany's reunification, I lived in Berlin for four months and interviewed over one hundred Germans: West Berliners and East Berliners, democratic West Germans and communist East Germans. These interviews are titled "Reunification" in Chapter V.

While Germans were joyously celebrating their new state, the rest of the world reacted differently. People who had long memories of Germany's past raised their voices, particularly Holocaust survivors and some contemporary Germans. Those who had been victimized by the war of National Socialism expressed their fears about its possible reoccurrence, and opposed the reunification of Germany. During the years 1991 and 1993, I traced some of those individuals in the United States, Great Britain, Germany, Austria and Japan. These interviews comprise Chapter II entitled "History Speaks Out." While listening to their stories, I realized that this book required accurate historical data to support these testimonies. For Chapter III — "Lessons of Nazism," I interviewed people who studied the history of the Third Reich, National Socialism and the Holocaust. They were historians, scholars, social scientists, authors and journalists.

As a consequence of reunification, the long tabooed Nazi ideology resurfaced. The number of young Germans attracted to neo-Nazism and latent racism quickly became manifest in violent rampages. People feared a resurgence of the street fighting of the Nazi era. I was particularly concerned by this matter and interviewed some of these individuals who may possibly be leaders of the future Germany. I also interviewed post-Holocaust generations of Jews in Germany and in the United States. What did a German learn from Nazism and what in the Holocaust is the lesson for Jews? In Chapter I — "Towards the New Century," these highly provacative questions are addressed. I discussed the issues openly in the form of a dialogue and sometimes I argued. I believe silence on both sides causes an inversion of emotions which can explode again in the future. Although these interviews were conducted at the end of my research, they comprise the first chapter in order to give primary importance to these issues.

Marie Ueda
November 1995
San Francisco

CHAPTER ONE

Towards the New Century

*New generations of Germans,
Americans and Jews*

(Interviews conducted between 1991 and 1995)

"The second coming of Nazism in Germany."

BURKHARD SCHRÖDER

German, author and journalist on neo-Nazism. Born in 1952 in Holzwickede, former West Germany. Lives in Germany.

How did you become interested in writing about neo-Nazism, and how has neo-Nazism spread in the newly united Germany?

I have a few points to bring out about my involvement with this subject. My father was a priest and I was brought up in the environment of a traditional German Protestant sect. I was oppressed by my parents and forced to attend all church events. It was a strange custom and I hated it. Because of this particular personal experience in my childhood, I understood the meaning of religious sects very well. In the Catholic world, they have the Vatican, cathedrals and popes, but in the Protestant world they have sects.

At the age of 16, I left my hometown for West Berlin to study German history and philosophy, and then joined a group of Maoists. But after the Maoist party broke up, I became interested in writing as a career. While I was working on my first book in 1988, I accidently happened to meet Arnulf Priem, a leader of a West Berlin neo-Nazi group. He helped me to make contact with East German neo-Nazi groups. East German Nazis have their own roots, but after the fall of the Berlin Wall, West German neo-Nazi activists, which had no influence in the West, had immediately campaigned in East Germany to find new blood. They were the ones who spread the "Nazi virus" to young East Germans today. Within the first 6 months they succeeded.

How many different extreme right-wing parties or neo-Nazi groups are there in the new Germany now, and what are their activities inside and outside of Germany?

There are at least 4 or 5 small neo-Nazi groups in the new Germany: Deutsche Alternative (mostly East Germans: 700 members), Nationalistische Front (West German leaders: 400 members), NSDAP/AO (Nationalsozialistische Deutsche Arbeiterpartei: a small illegal group backed by Americans), FAP (Freiheitliche Arbeiterpartei: 500 members). Beside these, there are a lot of local groups like Gubener Heimat-Front or Nationale Alternative.

Today, two years after the unification, there are a total of about 3,000 neo-Nazi members (2,000 in East Germany and 1,000 in West Germany), and this number has been rapidly increasing. Furthermore, there are extremely important rightwing parties such as REP (Republican), DVU (Deutsche Volksunion), and NPD (Nationaldemokratische Partei Deutschlands).

These parties are ideologically similar. They all hate foreigners and want to keep Germany for Germans, and emphasize German nationalism, but they are separated by different leaders.

The most outstanding and most active party among them is the National Alternative. But after the party leader, Michael Kühnen, died of AIDS recently, it has been pretty quiet. He was homosexual and his party was divided into two parties, because some members were anti-homosexual. They call themselves "National Socialists" and are engaged in terrorist activities. The party follows the example of Hitler's NSDAP and is supported by the German-American Gary "Rex" Lauck, founder of the American neo-Nazi Party who lives in Lincoln, Nebraska. Lauck is prohibited to enter Germany, but together with his co-leader Frank Collins, a leader of "National Socialist Headquarters" in Chicago, they supply neo-Nazis in Germany with propaganda materials such as Nazi books, newspapers, bulletins, Hitler's videos, Holocaust denial publications, badges, buttons, flags, etc. They are all printed and produced in

3

the United States and shipped to Germany. The operation of neo-Nazi activities is an international network and bigger than you can imagine. Large distribution organizations exist in England, France, Austria, and many other countries.

All neo-Nazis are active and militant in both the former West and East Germany, except REP members. The Republican Party is nonviolent. And, according to East German criminal investigators, currently there are a total of at least 15,000 to 20,000 Nazi sympathizers in greater Germany, mostly in East Germany. There aren't many in West Germany because of its postwar democratic education, but in East Germany many of those Nazi youths don't believe what happened during Nazi Germany.

Do you think those several neo-Nazi parties may join forces to become a single and more powerful party?

That's quite possible. If they ever reconcile their differences and become one united power, they could get power, many votes and supporters and it could grow like a snowball becoming bigger and bigger. Remember that in the early stages of Nazism in the 1920s, Hitler got only 3 or 4 percent of the vote in elections, but within five or six years, after other right-wing groups joined together, one big party was formed. But today is different, of course. Because German industry is an international operation and they do not support neo-Nazis. And even though neo-Nazis are different from Hitler's Nazis in the 1920s, some political analysts say that neo-Nazism may grow without the help of industrial corporations. Then a different kind of party might arise, bringing a new form of fascism which is not backed by industrial, corporate or government power. Theoretically, it could become quite normal to live

with such a party, because other European countries have similar nationalistic movements. This could become a new form of German fascism.

Who is financing neo-Nazis and how do they support themselves?

The newspapers, magazines, and TV journalists from the European, American, and Japanese media pay them for interviews. Everybody is interested in neo-Nazis today, and reporters all over the world like to report about them and sensationalize them, and of course, the neo-Nazis like publicity, they like world attention. The National Alternative Party, for instance, got paid 2,000 DM by one interviewer recently and the group made a propaganda film from this payment for the last election. Those neo-Nazi members are unemployed youths and live on social welfare. Some parties get enough payments to buy guns, ammunition, knives and uniforms. And some other parties are supported by former Nazis who live in Bolivia, Argentina, and other South American countries, who fled after the war and are still alive. They also make profits from sales of Nazi propaganda items. For their headquarters, they occupy empty apartments and buildings which were abandoned by people who fled from East to West Germany.

German people are divided by blood. People who were born and raised in Germany are not German citizens because their parents aren't German. Could you explain more about this ethnic theory and the origin of nationalism?

It's governed by German law, the law which was made by the Nazi government and hasn't changed since the end of Nazism. It wasn't only made by the Nazis; it's German tradition. The Nazi regime made it stricter and the law still exists today. You are German by blood, which means your parents must be German. If you are born in Germany from French, Italian, British or American parents, you can't become German automatically. If you want to become German, you have to apply to go through a long bureaucratic process and have to pay lots of money to get a certificate as a German. Therefore, for example, so-called Russian-German ancestors who come to Germany can get privileges because they had German grandparents by blood, even if they lived thousands of miles away from Germany. We still count them as German. But Turkish parents who were born in Germany and who have worked in Germany for many years and paid taxes to the German government can't become German. They are Turkish forever. This hasn't been discussed in Germany, because we Germans have lived under this system of law for centuries and are used to it.

Also, East Germans were isolated from West Germany and didn't have any contact with other democratic nations. Therefore, one of the reasons that neo-Nazis can grow easily in Germany is that they have not lived with non-German people such as Vietnamese or Mozambicans. They only know Germany for Germans. I think that anti-foreigner and anti-Jewish sentiments are emotional matters, and people can't fight against human emotions.

And for conservative Germans, nationality and cultural tradition are the same thing. For neo-Nazis, they're proud to be German but they can't understand Turks being proud to be Turkish. Blood, cultural tradition and passport — the national identification must be all the same for the Germans. Postwar West Germany has a democratic tradition and has close ties with the Western states, but East Germans were forced to be with the former USSR, and after the collapse of the communist regime, they feel insecure and lack their own identity. Their old identity was completely crushed at the end of the war, and this identity of nationalism brings a new self-consciousness for them. For their common identity, they choose nationalism, but it went in the wrong direction, toward anti-foreigner campaigns and the resurgence of Nazism.

Most West Germans are ashamed of Nazism, and one way or another, they express a kind of war guilt over the acts committed by their parents and grandparents. East Germans have a different attitude. Why is that do you think?
Postwar East Germans haven't really been educated about Nazi fascism. First, in school textbooks, there was no mention of the Holocaust. Parents lied to their children and the communist government lied to the people. Parents may think they know what happened, but they think it has nothing to do with them. The postwar generations of East Germans were taught that Nazis killed a few Jews and some Communists, but nothing more. The point is, fascism is more than just good or bad. German fascism is a cultural structure. It's a tradition which exploits the traditional German penchant for obedience. This bad authoritarian cultural tradition is still practiced in East Germany. Basically, the structure of socialism isn't much different from the structure of fascism; dictatorship, goose-step militarism, and people going in one direction like sheep, and individual social behavior or opinions are not allowed. People are used to a hierarchical political system. They still like to live in group-oriented social systems. The only thing that changed since the Third Reich was the color: brown-shirt Hitlerism to red-shirt communism. Philosophi-

cally, their basic totalitarian orientation hasn't changed at all.

Today's younger East Germans don't trust their teachers or older people any more, because their communist government had been lying to their citizens for so many decades. So, now they think the Holocaust could be a lie, too. East German neo-Nazis now believe that the Holocaust never happened; that it was made up by Hollywood movies and American propaganda.

You were once a member of a neo-Nazi party yourself for a short time. Why did you join them?

I was interested in writing about neo-Nazis and what was going on with these dangerous groups that we don't know much about. My main reason was to get first-hand information from them. In order to get that, the best idea was to become a member. I was a spy. I joined the Republican Party around the time the Berlin Wall fell and stayed with them for 6 months. Also, as I have mentioned, I was curious because of my childhood experience when I was mentally oppressed by my Protestant parents. I wanted to learn about group-oriented religious activities. People who quit the Protestant sect or the church community became insecure and felt lost, because their working connections and social activities were all within the church circle. Once they're out they lose everything. Once you are involved it's hard to give up. I was perhaps looking for a dangerous situation to test my identity. I wanted to demonstrate my individuality to see if I could get out without any difficulty. Also, I intended to convince other neo-Nazi members that they, too, should quit the party like me.

During the time I was a member, other members never asked me any question, whether I was committed to the party or not. And, my registered official job was a taxi driver. Nobody knew that I was a journalist; they never distrusted me at all. By the time they found out who I was, it was too late. A number of articles about the party were published in local magazines and all the inside information about party activities were already known to the public. If they wanted to do something against me, I would get more publicity, so they knew it was too dangerous for them. And now, they don't even know where I live.

Besides neo-Nazi information, what else did you learn from them?

It was fascinating to learn that this kind of fascism has been growing bigger and bigger each year, and I really wanted to watch it grow. This could be the second chance for fascism to be reborn in German history. It was a strange feeling for me to be with the party colleagues, because if you talk to them, they are very ordinary people, like your neighbors or colleagues who have cats and dogs at home, and girlfriends, play piano and sing happy songs.

One neo-Nazi might not be dangerous; but when they are a group, then they feel strong and become aggressive and dangerous. We have learned from the atrocities of Nazi Germans what kind of people they were. They were all professional terrorists, monsters and mass murderers. Today it's the same. If you give them power, they will kill people. For example, if you put some of those neo-Nazi kids in power as leaders of concentration camps today, they will kill Jews. It would be no problem for them. If you give them power without control, they'll do it without fear of punishment.

What do you mean by "giving them power"?

If a high-ranking person appoints some of the neo-Nazi members to positions of leadership, they'll perform atrocities just the way the Nazis did in the Holocaust. It's the same as Adolf Eichmann. He had children and played Mozart at home, a very friendly person like everybody else, but he killed Jews as a duty. It's a two-faced personality. I think anybody can have such a personality in one way or another. I'm fighting against this hierarchical system where there is only one leader who is able to force a mass of people to do his will. That's not a democracy. However, this old German tradition still exists among many East Germans today. ❖

Photo by Dietmar Gust, 1990

"I'll give you no interview without a payment of 500 DM."

(Mr. Priem's response to my request for an interview.)

ARNULF W. PRIEM

German neo-Nazi leader, and economist by profession. Born in East Berlin in 1947. Lives in Germany.

(His recorded voice mail to callers:

♪ ♪♪ *Einigkeit und Recht und Freiheit für das deutsche Vaterland.* •♪♪•
(German national anthem)

"I'm not at home. Please, leave your message..., (then) Dha, Dha, Dha, Dha, Dha, Dha...." (Sounds of a machine-gun) ❖

"There are few neo-Nazis in the streets of Germany but plenty are neo-Nazis in their heart."

B. EWALD ALTHANS

German neo-Nazi, Director of AVÖ Public Relations. Born in 1966 in Bremen, former West Germany. Lives in Germany.

(Photo: B. Ewald Althans in his office with a flag of the former German Imperial Navy.)

Recently, I learned that you are one of the most active neo-Nazis in Germany today. A German newspaper quoted you as saying, "I am dangerous!" Is that true?

Well, it was not exactly what I said. I said, "I want to be dangerous." I don't know why he wrote it that way, but I guess in journalism if it's written "I am dangerous," it sounds sensational and people will pay attention. I want to be known to the public for who I am. This is the way to spread propaganda and to use the power of the media. I want people to know me, read about me or hear about me, and journalists from all over the world come to interview me, "a dangerous man." I want people to listen to me. That's exactly what I mean. So, yes, in that sense it means both. I want to be dangerous and I am dangerous.

Why are you dangerous?

Because of my beliefs. I believe politics in Germany today is democratic and for me democracy is criminal. I want the politicians in the Bonn government to be overthrown and replaced by better ones. The German politicians we send to parliament don't know anything. I want German people to be "anti-democratic," exactly the way Hitler planned it some 70 years ago. He was a true Messiah and I carry his message.

What does the term "anti-democratic" mean to you? What is the difference between Hitler's Nazi revolution and today's neo-Nazi movement?

Without the Versailles Treaty there would have been no Hitler, of course. Because of that treaty, Germany collapsed. When Hitler came with the answer to this problem, he did very important things for the German people. They really needed a man like him. Hitler was not a capitalist or a greedy man. He believed Germans needed a better life.

You may know Hitler was favored by a number of influential people in the world: King Edward VIII (Duke of Windsor) of England, Henry Ford, who published the famous book, *The International Jews,* in America, Charles Lindbergh, the first non-stop aviator over the Atlantic Ocean who was a good friend of Hermann Göring and Rudolf Hess. You know why? Because Hitler was fighting against communism and Jews. Historians all know this. Hitler was just the answer for Germany. And, by the way, that Versailles Treaty was enforced by the "democratic Allies": America, France, Britain and Russia, the same Allies who installed democracy in Germany in 1945. To me, democracy means the world is ruled by money, greed and Jews. I don't trust democracy. It doesn't work in Germany. The Weimar Republic, the so-called "Jewish Republic," was a good example. What neo-Nazis are trying to do today is to bring about the solution for our national and social problems. Old Nazis and new Nazis belong together like a big tree rooted in one large family. Today's neo-Nazi movement is the successor of Hitler's ideology. As a German, I'm always in a little boat with Bismarck, Mozart, Wagner and Hitler. They are all in my 'German boat' floating on the ocean of history, and I sit next to Hitler in this boat. Hitler may be a bit heavy for the boat. But, anyway, this is me, and I think the new National Socialist movement will be bigger.

What is your interpretation of the meaning of National Socialism, philosophically?

First of all, historically, until WW I the world was dominated by chauvinistic imperial armies, the British, French, Spanish, Portuguese, including

11

Kaiser Wilhelm. They were all fighting for colonialism and trying to rule the world by suppressing the second and third world countries. On the European continent, countries were related through royal marriages. Consequently the interests of kings and emperors were their own and not those of the people. When Hitler came on the scene, he introduced very important things to us for the future. He raised a question about Christianity and its related religions, including Islam. Historically, God was the center of human existence, the most important thing in the universe. This thinking had dominated us for many centuries. Then a second wave of thinking came at the time of the French Revolution. People found out that God is not the center of life anymore. The new thinking was that the human being is the center of the universe, with God and nature around us.

Then, at the turn of the 19th century, the thinking changed again. It's not God nor human beings who are the center of life, but together human beings and nature are what God is. We should all live in harmony, and none of these elements can be separated. National Socialism was based on this movement.

The Nazi philosophy was somewhat similar to Eastern Asian religion. This is why the SS, for example, made contacts with the Dalai Lama in Tibet because they thought the Dalai Lama had a similar solution. This is my view of history and the interpretation of National Socialism. So, Nazism is a movement which became linked with the people's interest.

Before asking any further questions, tell me about your background. How were you raised and how did you become a neo-Nazi?

My parents got divorced when I was a baby. My father, a teacher for disabled people, used to live abroad often and, as a child, I lived with him over the years both in Arab countries and Israel. I used to play with Jewish children while I was there and was taught to be sympathetic to Jews. After we returned to Germany, my father got married again and I was raised by my step-mother who is also an educator. Beside my sister, I have four younger half-brothers by my new mother. My parents made a good living, and financially I would say we were an upper middle-class family. At the age of 14 while I was in a Gymnasium (German high school) in Hanover, I joined a German-Jewish Youth Group, whose aim was to support Jewish communities. We used to take care of old concentration camps. We cleaned up the fields, cut grass and planted flowers, etc. At Bergen-Belsen camp, I even saw records of forensic research and documents of medical experiments, and I truly believed what I learned.

While I was pondering about the Holocaust, I encountered a group of German war veterans who opposed the Holocaust claiming these things were not true. I began reading books about Hitler and the Third Reich, and then I became fascinated by the genius of the Führer. I begun to doubt many stories about the Holocaust. They could be exaggerated. Some historians even now argue that the death of prisoners could be questionable. I then read a Jewish book that says Jews created Christianity to make non-Jews their slaves. As I read more things like that, I began to agree with the war veterans' group and joined them. I became a neo-Nazi at the age of 17. As I spoke about these matters openly, I was expelled from my school and barred from attending the university by the government because my thinking was dangerous and unfit for a democratic

German society. If I can't say what I believe, there is no freedom of speech in Germany. Is that real democracy?

What do you think of German nationalism and American democracy?

It's quite normal that every nation has its own form of nationalism, except for Germany. This has been controversial for a long time. For example, if a French person says, "I'm a French nationalist and I love France," there's nothing wrong with that. But for a German person to say "I'm a nationalist German and I love Germany," it means "I'm pro-Hitler and for the Third Reich," and this is the highest incarnation of nationalism in Germany. And we can't say this. That is our democracy, you see. I'm fighting against this. I want German people to be proud of being German nationalists. For the past decades, as Germans, we have been accused of being Jewish murderers, especially by Americans. And, I must say that most Americans don't understand this complicated side of our history, except through movies and television media portraying Germans as criminals; it's always "the good guy Americans" and "the bad guy Germans." These are fictionalized in Hollywood for entertainment, of course. Many Germans today are getting fed up with being blamed for being Nazis and Jew killers. In my view, Hollywood is virtually run by Jews. They make money off it. America is the country of money, capitalism and democracy, and it's a perfect feeding ground for Jews.

I traveled to many parts of Europe, North and South America, including Canada. I speak French and English. I spoke to many people in every country to which I visited. I find the Americans are the most ignorant people in the world. I'm part of the new German generation. I

didn't kill any Jews. Why do I have to bear the guilt? Is this democracy, too?

You own a publicity business which denies the Holocaust. What sort of reaction are you getting?

Since I opened this office in Munich in 1991, AVÖ (Althans Distribution and Public Relations), I was quite surprised how quickly the media spread the message: "Neo-Nazis are monsters." In fact, I've been getting upset and annoyed by how many lies about me are written by the press and reporters. The story about me in *Der Spiegel,* the widely-known popular German magazine, for instance, was totally wrong. I never thought they would do such a thing, because it has the most serious political coverage, and I read it every week and liked it a lot. The first time they reported about me, it was packed with lies. I was very disappointed. Some journalists wrote that I'm a homosexual. Again, it's absolutely a lie. I have a girlfriend and I am a heterosexual. Michael Kühnen, the leader of an aggressive neo-Nazi party, National Alternative, who died of AIDS, was a real homosexual, but not me. I was with his party when I became a neo-Nazi. He was the one who trained me how to become a good neo-Nazi. At that time, I was too young to understand what gay means. But after I found out that I am straight, I turned against him. I split from him and formed my own party called "National Socialists."

Could you tell me why there are homosexuals among the Nazis?

All Nazis were paramilitaristic during the Nazi era, and there were many homosexuals among them. Hitler purged many homosexuals, too. Today, we even have a gay neo-Nazi magazine in Germany, you know! I find there are two reasons why homosexuals are involved in the Nazis. First, they love to wear black uniforms and black leather boots; the higher and shinier the better, just like the original Nazis used to wear. This all-black outfit attracts them. Another reason is, I think, sadomasochism. "I'm correct, beat me up for that." I have many gay friends and often associate with them. I was once in fashion business and I dress well. I have nearly a hundred pairs of shoes and many fashionable clothes. So that could be the reason that people think I am gay, too. Anyway, black is the favorite color among the gays, not only for Nazis.

Black is a color of authority and death. I find color symbolizes a lot about people and a nation. The German national flag, for example, has three colors: black, red and gold. To me, that is German history. Black is the color of authority; the state-worship national policy; red is the color of fighting, revolution and blood; and gold is the color of victory; triumph and superiority; these could be obsessions for Germans. Don't you think so?

That's an interesting explanation. I never thought of that. I hate the German flag, anyway. I love the red flag with a white circle and a black swastika in the center. That is my favorite flag. It's prohibited to make it in Germany today, so it is made in Hong Kong. We are not allowed to raise this flag, either. If we do, we'll be jailed for 6 months. During Hitler's time when people abused the same flag, they went to jail. Today, if people admire it, we end up in jail. That's German politics, you know!

What is the degree of involvement in your circle? How many names do you have on your mailing lists, how many members, what is the age group, and who are the financiers?

The youngest neo-Nazi I know is a 2-year-old boy, but the average age in our movement is from 14 to 25. I don't know the exact number of the neo-Nazis though my business is to make contact with other neo-Nazi groups. I only have a few clerks working in my office, but in my own party there are 50 members and they are all active. We are the best secret service inside the right-wing movements.

On my mailing lists, I have the names of 15,000-20,000 people. But there are over 10,000 groups and parties of ultra-nationalists, extreme right-wingers, neo-Nazis and skinheads. This number doesn't include sympathizers. I have more followers in West Germany than in East Germany. So, in Germany now, there are few neo-Nazis in the streets, but plenty are neo-Nazis in their hearts. The names of our financiers are strictly confidential, but since our activity is international, we receive hundreds of checks from over 40 countries, but not from Japan or other Asian countries. Contributions come from all sorts of people, interesting enough, more from poor people than rich ones. Very often, we get money from old women who don't have enough money for themselves. They all write to me that they are happy that we exist. So, I have to be responsible about what to do with their money. Nobody gives me higher amounts because they can't get tax deductions from me. Other extreme right-wing parties are supported by corporations and middle class industrialists, but they wouldn't come to me because I am the living evil: I am the bad boy. Recently, by the way, I got a new financier in San Francisco.

Why do you deny the Holocaust?
I deny the Holocaust because I can prove it didn't happen. Many times I visited Auschwitz and Dachau concentration camps and saw gas chambers which were fabricated with wooden doors and windows. I photographed everything. You can see the sign that reads "Never used as a gas chamber"

You're wrong! Gas chambers didn't have windows. What you are showing me is the Dachau concentration camp whose gas chamber had indeed never been used. I saw the same sign myself. But in Auschwitz there were 3 camps and all separated by a few kilometers. Monowitz was the main camp, the proper concentration camp was called simply Auschwitz, and the killing factory camp with gas chambers was called Auschwitz-Birkenau. The Jews were murdered there. After the war ended, 6 million Jews didn't return. Where did they go? What is your explanation for that?
You talk like you're Jewish! Well, the Jewish population in German-occupied territories was only 3 million. Nazi Germans killed every Jew twice.

You are like Joseph Goebbels; he was a big liar and the Germans believed in him. Are you satisfied with your own media lies?
I'm like a master manipulator of the media. I like to conquer people's minds through the media. I'm not a slave of the media, the media is my slave. I don't need a weapon, I am the weapon. I'll tell you one thing. Not long ago, I sold 28 seconds of video footage of me for 2,000 DM. It's a good price. This is the price you can get when you become a famous person. So, I'll kill people with their own weapons.

So, every time you give an interview, do journalists pay you? I am not going to pay you...
No, for you it's OK. It depends. If you're writing for a newspaper, for example, you would have to pay a price. I have my prices now for interviews. It costs me time and time is expensive. I can make a choice whether I should charge or not, depending on my interest. For *Stern* magazine, another widely-known German photo-magazine, for example, I don't charge because they didn't lie about me. But if *Cosmopolitan* magazine from England comes, I don't care about that.

When Jewish journalists come to interview you, how do you react. Do you change your attitude?
No, absolutely not. I find the Jews are the best partners for discussion, because they have their own view. If Germans or some other non-Jewish journalists come over, and when I say to them the Holocaust didn't happen, they get angry at me and become crazy. But the Jews would say, "Why do you think that?" That is the Jewish attitude. They are well educated. Their perfect calmness and reserved manner come from the Jewish tradition of Torah education. So, talking to them is easy and the conversation with them is excellent, and I feel fantastic. They know who I am and I know who they are. We can talk from both sides. They are good listeners. There is no problem with me at all.

Are you sure you don't have Jewish blood in your family?
No. I have a "racial certificate" for that. My aunt worked for the Third Reich as a racial researcher, so she researched all of our family history. But, actually, I don't care much whether I'm an Aryan or a Jew, really. If I were a Jew, I would be a

Jewish neo-Nazi. I would fight for Jewish interests like Jews. But the fact is I'm white, I'm a German and I'm a male. I can't change what I was born as. That's why I fight for Germany, for Germans, and for German interests.

Despite the fact that Nazis were obsessed with Aryan races, Hitler didn't look like an Aryan. He was short, and with his moustache like a tooth brush and a weird hair style, he looked like a comedian, at least to me. Rudolf Hess didn't look like an Aryan, either. As a cripple, Josef Goebbels should have gone to the gas chamber. None of these high-ranking Nazis looked like decent Aryans with blond hair and blue eyes. Don't you think that's strange?

Hitler had gorgeous blue eyes and in fact many women thought he was very attractive. They were crazy about him in those days. But it's strange to me, too. If someone today had a moustache like Hitler's and hair like him for instance, it would look odd and ridiculous. But it's a different time. I guess it was fashionable at that time. But the Nazis weren't against the cripples. Goebbels was accepted in the government. They didn't kill cripples, deformed people or homosexuals. You are believing too much American propaganda.

No, I don't think so. Tell me, what are your neo-Nazi connections inside and outside of Germany? Do you know David Duke?

Yes, I do know him, but I don't like him. He wants to be a career neo-Nazi. I'm an anti-Klu Klux Klan and don't agree with the KKK people in America. To me, that's a stupid joke because it lacks a fundamental ideology. I don't care for him, really. I also have contact with David Irving, a British Hitlerian and author. I do know many more people in ultra right-wing circles, for exam-

ple, Dr. Gerhard Frey, a publisher of the *National Zeitung* newspaper who lives in Munich, and he is extremely conservative and reactionary. I hate him. I don't like reactionaries. Also, I don't agree with Franz Schönhuber, an ex-SS officer and now the leader of the extreme right-wing Republikaner Party which is also based in Munich. His view zigzags too much. He once had a Jewish wife. I never talk to him, either.

What are your other connections? Did you meet any former SS people or Nazis while you were visiting South America, and how do they live?

I was in Argentina, Chile, and Brazil in 1988. I was very upset when I saw them, because they were very poor and I had not expected to see them living so horribly. They were getting old and frightened, scared of being kidnapped by the Mossad. When Eichmann was kidnapped, there were some people who had been friends with him, so they are still scared to death, even today. I saw a 90-year-old former SS man just sitting and quietly waiting to die, and it was very embarrassing. Some of them are living on a small pension paid by the German government, but it's not enough money.

How about your East German connections? Before and after the fall of the Berlin Wall, have your neo-Nazi activities changed? Before you couldn't cross the border so easily, right?

I was in East Germany very often because my father came from the town of Halle and half of his family lives there. My grandmother, a lot of aunts and other relatives are still there. So I've always visited them since I was a kid. I made many contacts there while Germany was still divided. We did Nazi propaganda years before the fall of the Wall, of course. We always had youth groups there; we used to meet with them in Prague and give them Nazi propaganda materials to smuggle into East Germany. So, when the Wall came down, the Nazi virus was well-seeded among East German youths. And, during the night of the so-called Monday Demonstration in Leipzig in November 1989, which was an illegal rally, nearly 2 million East German people were out in the streets. I was there from the beginning to the end. It was dangerous to make speeches because Stasi were all over, but I did. I addressed the crowd and spoke to them about how I felt. The people liked it. I had great rapport with the audience.

Have you ever been arrested?

Yes, I was in prison for just 10 days in 1985. I may face another prison term again. This time, it will be for 5 years. If I really have to go, I prefer to be imprisoned in Auschwitz, because I like Auschwitz. It's not too bad, actually. If I could make a choice, I definitely would go to a concentration camp rather than being imprisoned in a dark and miserable small cell. In Auschwitz, I would get fresh air in the open fields surrounded by trees. I'd be able to work in nature and sun. I could plant flowers and grow vegetables, and take care of the camp nicely. And after 5 years I would come out physically strong with good muscles and a well trained healthy body. That would be nice.

At 27, you are young. I've interviewed many Germans in the past, and in my experience, they often change their minds. When I'd go back to re-interview the same people, they would have changed their views. So, I wonder,

would you do such a thing with me if I came back to interview you?

No, I'm honest. What I say is what I mean. The problem is you want to know what I will be in the future, and that I can't answer. I can't predict my future. I've already experienced a lot of change in my life. I've become more and more Nazi, but I changed my ways of dealing with it. When I was with the Kühnen group, I was uniformed, aggressive and did a lot of provocative things. We fought violently with radical left-wingers in the streets. I was a very bad neo-Nazi. But I've changed. I'm now a well dressed neo-Nazi. Every time I find a better way, better ideas, and a better situation. For example, people ask about me in my neighborhood wherever I go, people want to know who I am. "He's polite, he's friendly, he's helpful, he's neat, he's nice, and yes, he's a Nazi." This is a good image. A well dressed, respectable and smart looking man. It's an important thing to do if I want to be supported by many people and win. What I want to say is that although my style may change in the future — I may get married and have children one day — but I will always be a neo-Nazi, and that will never change. This is my lifetime commitment.

I once told a reporter from the *Washington Post* when he asked me about my future. I said, "I don't know how I will be if I ever seize power." You see, very often, power changes the situation, which forces one to be dishonest. I know from history that many dictators were honest when they started the revolution. They entered politics convinced they were creating a better society. But as they became powerful in their later years, they abused their power.

Since you couldn't study at a university, I guess you basically educated yourself with books. Is that true?

Over the years I bought 2,500 books of all kinds. I'm interested in science, art, technology, literature, religion, mythology, world history, and eastern cultures. I find the Japanese author Mishima interesting. I also read Chairman Mao Zedong of China, and a lot of others. I go to all bookstores. When you take any book off the shelf, for example, I can tell you what's in there. The books on Hitler and the Third Reich are my favorites, of course. In Germany today, it's forbidden to read *Mein Kampf* and we can't buy it in a book store. But I know how to get it. Funny thing is that I got mine in Taiwan. It's in German. You can buy it there in any language.

Would you like to be Führer of the future Germany?

No, I don't want to be the new Führer. A lot of people say that and I hate that. My future will be a family life. I'd like to get married and have children. One day my blonde blue eyed kids will be going around the neighborhood, smiling, and handing out National Socialist propaganda flyers: "Hitler's spirit still alive in Germany today!" Everybody would look at them and say, "What a beautiful family! What a nice neighbor! How friendly! But they are neo-Nazis!" That is the way I will be. I'll give a good example every day of my life. Everybody will hate me because they'll have to like me. That would be funny. If somebody likes me but they find out I'm a neo-Nazi, they hate me for that. As long as there is one National Socialist in the world, I, Ewald Althans is alive, National Socialism is also alive. If there is one, a second one will be there, a third one, then twenty, a hundred, a thousand, ten thousand will

be coming. And this is what is happening now. And this is what we are fighting for. This is what we keep doing, and this is why we will win one day. Right now, we are just a little machine for the big idea.

What is your view on foreigners in Germany?

I'm not anti-foreigner — I like foreigners. But I'm against the current immigration law in Germany. The American media says, "Germans are racist and neo-Nazis are rising." Germany is a small country and if foreigners keep flooding into our country looking for a better life, we Germans will have chaos, because we don't have enough land. There will be a housing shortage and unemployment will rise. America criticizes us for not letting them in. But when Haitian refugees entered the United States, the government sent them back, even though America is a vast country.

What do you think of Jews in Germany today?

There are too many Jews. It's more than enough. I don't want the Jewish influence in Germany. Remember the "Jewish Republic"; I don't want it to happen here again. Political history shows that in a democracy, Jews move in, and there will be Jewish domination in our life. That's the reason I don't like democracy. I want to stop this. The whole world is divided into two camps: Jews and non-Jews. That means I have to fight against this Jewish influence in Germany. That's all I want and that's all I'm interested in. As long as they don't live in my country, that's fine with me.

But there are only under 50,000 Jews in Germany today. Do you mean to say to them to go somewhere else?

Yeah...! ...Treblinka.... Well, I'm joking!

Now, within several years the 20th century will be ending. What is your perspective on the new century based on today's world situation?

I think the end of this century will be a horrible one. I am sure of that. I don't mean there will be another war, but I hope people will think more seriously about the reality of the world today. I think there will be great migration problems all over and a worldwide flood of refugees. What I mean is that if this kind of world is an example, then maybe one day millions of Africans will come up to the European continent, or Russian politics may worsen, or even communist China may break down. We'll never know what comes next. If that happens, millions of refugees may "float around" the world looking for places to settle. My point is that the problem is one of mass human migration. Just imagine, millions of refugees from all over wanting to enter America, for example. I'm sure the Americans, even though they're proud to be the most democratic nation in the world, will panic, you know! I do hope that world leaders acknowledge this problem and solve it. In a way, I'm certain that there is still time to think about it, so we could all live together on this planet in a better way. I really do hope people think about each other before it becomes too late. ❖

Since 1994 anyone who denies the Holocaust publicly goes to prison in Germany. Mr. Althans has been arrested, sentenced and is currently serving 5 years in jail. This interview was conducted in the summer of 1991.

"Assimilation of all Jews is out of the question in Germany."

DR. SIMON SNOPKOWSKI

German Jew, chairman of the National Association of Jewish Communities in Bavaria, Germany. Born in 1925 in Myszkow, Poland. Lives in Germany.

What is the situation of Jewish life today in both Munich and Germany as a whole?

In Munich, after the war, Jewish communities were gradually rebuilt by Holocaust survivors like myself. Over the decades, more Jewish people came back and traditional Jewish life slowly flourished again. Today, there are 4,000 Jewish inhabitants in Munich, 7,000 in the Bavarian region, and about 40,000 in all of Germany. After Berlin and Frankfurt, Munich has the third largest Jewish population in Germany. In Munich alone, we have three synagogues, a Jewish elementary school, some traditional organizations, a lot of cultural promotions and social activities, whose chairwoman is my wife, Ilse Snopkowski. Religiously, we observe the weekly Sabbath and Jewish holidays. Some Jews speak Yiddish. Besides one national newspaper called *Allgemeine Jüdische Zeitung,* we also have regional newspapers and bulletins. The maintenance of the communities is financed by synagogue taxes, donations, and subsidies of the Bavarian government.

Munich is the mecca for both old Nazis and today's neo-Nazis. How do you see that?

During the Nazi era, conservatives were linked to groups of anti-Semites, and liberals were close to pro-Jewish groups. But today, anti-Semitism is not necessarily connected with any political party. It exists among both conservatives and liberals. What we need to fight is the extreme right-wing people whose goal is to destroy democracy. Historically, anti-Semitism is related to certain religious aspects. When Johannes Paul XXIII was pope, he revised his attitude towards Jews. We hope, for the future, that the old attitude will be replaced by a fair relationship.

Regarding Jewish assimilation into the Gentile world, Jews suffered for centuries and today they still bear the pain. Is Jewish life worse without assimilation?

Jewish assimilation in Germany, I regard as an exception because of the fundamental attitude of Jewish people and because of the burden of history which has had a painful effect on them. Jewish assimilation into German society depends on tolerance of the social environment and, one way or another, it also depends on individual attitudes. But assimilation of the entire Jewish community is out of the question. In my view, this question should be addressed by the German people. The reason why Jews still exist after so many centuries is because of the history of persecution. In peace time, there are a few Jews around, but in the time of economic and political crisis, there are many Jews all over, and they become a target or scapegoat.

How do you deal with Holocaust denial propaganda and neo-Nazi activists in Munich? Why don't you have a dialogue with them?

There is no guarantee for Jews that what happened in the past will never happen again in the future. We do protest against neo-Nazis activities, but as a leader of a Jewish community, I don't meet personally with leaders of neo-Nazi parties and talk to them. I don't sit with them at the same table. The problem is much more profound. They lie to build up a new theory. As time passes and witnesses die out, it's easy to change the story and deny the fact. The Holocaust denial campaign has been widely spread all over the world now, and more so in America. The fight against this propaganda must be strengthened especially by American Jews. There are 6 million Jews in America, and we are only 40,000 Jews in Germany today. ❖

"It's not enough to cry about the Holocaust."

CHAIM EISENBERG

Austrian Jew, Chief Rabbi of the Federation of the Jewish Communities
of Austria. Born in 1950 in Vienna, Austria. Lives in Austria.

Rabbi Eisenberg, how do you teach Nazism, WW II and the Holocaust after the fall of the Berlin Wall?

Since the unification of the two Germanys, new wars are happening all over the world and we have to work hard against racism and hatred here. We have now learned that crimes of hatred never end. I want to educate the younger generations. They should know what happened historically, not just during the Holocaust, but also what happened before the Holocaust. My educational program is to give them the ability to think positively. I would include the history of Jews, Europeans and the integration between them. In Austria, for instance, before WW II, the entire culture was influenced by Jews: 50 percent of the medical doctors, professors, writers and musicians were Jews. We need to teach people that Jews contributed important humanistic principles to mankind such as the Ten Commandments and the need to love your brothers, and these things are important for our life. In return, we didn't always get what we deserved. Before Hitler, Jews in Vienna were thrown out and came back again and again, and this was repeated for centuries. But we shouldn't give up. Today, in educational textbooks for Austrian children, it clearly states that western civilization was based on Jewish values which shows the progress we've made. I hope that young people will be different in the future.

Some American youths think that the Holocaust is a Jewish holiday....

That's terrible! Shocking! I'll tell you one thing. I don't think we have to build Holocaust museums in every corner of the world and spend billions of dollars. Instead, money should be spent for education. We should never forget the Holocaust, of course. But it's not enough to cry about the Holocaust. It's more to help Jews today. For ex-

ample, we should provide housing and work for Jews who are coming out of Russia to Germany today. When it comes to the Holocaust, the Germans feel more guilty than the Austrians. They try much harder than the Austrians to make up for the Jews. They have paid more money and provided more activities for Jews.

What is the lesson for Jews from the Holocaust?

During the Holocaust while Nazi Germans were killing the Jews, other nations didn't help the Jews. Americans could have bombed the trains that went to Auschwitz or could have done other things to help. Jews learned that lesson. Lesson number one is, don't expect others to fight for you. If you are in danger, don't cry and seek sympathy. Don't run away, but protect yourself. The second lesson is, education for humanity. Jews have learned that they should be strong. We Jews have to be united and to work together. The State of Israel has a strong defense today, and unfortunately they've had war with their Arab neighbors, but I hope there will be peace.

Anti-Semitism and neo-Nazi activities are widespread today. How do you fight against them?

I'm a rabbi representing the entire state of Austria. I often give speeches on television and radio in Vienna, Salzburg and Tirol to address the people. My subject is not always about anti-Semitism but more about Judaism: Jewish culture, missions and morals to bring understanding for all. Anti-Semitism and neo-Nazism are an international problem. We discuss this in the Jewish Congress, but regarding the matter of Jewish hatred, Jews in every country have their own way of dealing with these problems and must find their own solutions. Lately, the government of Austria launched a tough law against neo-Nazi activists, so they receive jail sentences when they commit criminal activities. ❖

Questions to a Rabbi: Jews, Jewishness, and the Messiah.

IRVING GREENBERG

American Jew, Orthodox Rabbi in New York and author of the book
The Jewish Way and a monograph *Auschwitz: Beginning of a New Era.*
Born in 1933 in New York, USA. Lives in New York, USA.

Within a matter of several years this century will come to an end. It will be the fourth millennium for the Jewish calendar. You are the most influential orthodox rabbi in New York, where the world's Jewish population is centered today. To begin with, Rabbi Greenberg, what is the meaning of the twentieth century to you?

Jewish life is tightly bound with the experience of the 20th century. Two of the most important events of our 4,000 years Jewish history happened in this century, during my lifetime. One is the Holocaust and the other is the birth of the State of Israel. Both happened in the past 50 years. I was born in the year that both Hitler and Roosevelt took office, in January, 1933. Often I feel that my life is bounded with the history of the 20th century. These were the two dominant men of our century: the war-maker Hitler, and the peace-keeper Roosevelt. By the way, the two men also died in the same year and even in the same month, in April of 1945, just a few weeks apart from each other. It's really an amazing coincidence.

Could you tell me about the origin of the Jews, the history of Jewish migration, and how such a unique people were formed?

In a way, learning the history of the Jews is learning the history of the world. It's written in the Hebrew Scriptures that the origin of the Jews began with Abraham and Sarah, husband and wife who came from an area of ancient Mesopotamia, today's Iraq, around 1,800 BC. They were the first settlers who created the roots of the Jewish family in Israel. Their story was not officially recorded as history, but just by tradition. This tiny family became a large group; they formed several Hebrew tribes hundreds of years later. They are the patriarchs from whom the tribes of Israel

were descended. There is no record as to what kind of race these prehistoric Jews belonged to. Some say they were originally black but nobody knows for sure; it's hard to determine. I presume that they were like the people in the Mideast today, with olive colored skin. From the hindsight of the entire Jewish history, however, the Exodus — the liberation of the enslaved Jews in Egypt led by Moses in 1250 BC and the later return to Israel — is probably the greatest adventure of all and the central event of all of Jewish history. The Jewish religion predicted that experience, that the Jewish people would leave for Egypt and would become slaves, would get out into the desert, but eventually would become free in their own land. This Exodus event and its implications become the basic central teaching of Judaism. The Jewish religion says that what happened to the Jewish people, freedom after a life of slavery and then developing their own independence and dignity, would someday happen to the whole world. All of humanity deserves freedom and to be treated with full dignity.

During the centuries after the Exodus, the Jews created an Israelite kingdom; the great King David reigned over the country in the 10th century. Then, in 586 BC, they were defeated and left Israel for exile, according to the Bible. But they came back and resettled again in 516 BC, and began a new life there. This settlement lasted until the year 70 AD when the Romans destroyed the second Jewish commonwealth. This time was the longest exile for Jews; it lasted nearly 1,900 years until Hitler's persecution and the reestablishment of the state of Israel. Although Zionism, a movement that supported the return of the Jews to their homeland arose in the last century, it didn't accomplish its goals until the Holocaust. Historically speaking, Jews were thrown out of their homeland twice and returned twice; they spent almost two millennia wandering around the world until the current century. Then, after the Holocaust, in 1948, the nation of Israel was born and the political Zionism movement was created.

Today, because of their historical experiences, the Jewish people includes people of all races — Whites, Blacks, Slavs, Asians, Mid-Easterners, Latins and Africans, and they are scattered in every corner of the world. As a result, Judaism is a universal religion because Jews exist worldwide and have influenced the whole world over 20 centuries. A majority of the Jews have lived outside Israel and survived, which is another unique aspect of Jewish history. Today, the total population of the Jews worldwide is about 13 million: 4 million in Israel, 5½ in America, 2 million in Russia, and the rest elsewhere.

It seems to me that, historically, the Jews like to move around instead of staying and defending their homeland. For any nation, land is everything. It's vital for survival, it brings unity to its people, its culture and formation of its nation. I don't understand why Jews left so many times.
Well, they were driven out, but the majority have stayed despite this exile. That extraordinary achievement doesn't mean that Jews are not attracted to the land. They draw strength from it. But they don't absolutize the land. Their loyalty to God transcends their loyalty to land and rootedness. That helped them survive in exile. It's true that some Jews left their land voluntarily, seeking a better life. There is some evidence that even in biblical times, some Jews left to seek better opportunities. However, the Bible stresses that they were driven into exile by the oppressors and this

is the main cause of Jewish wandering. Still, the Jews were pioneers in immigration. Like the tremendous number of immigrants all over the world, the Jews moved from the poorer countries to seek better opportunities. This combination of push and pull is the reason that Jews are found everywhere. Today, the vast majority of the Jews who live in Israel are staying there because they love the land.

So, this time do you think Israelis will stay?
Yes, absolutely. I think Israel will continue to grow. Between birth and immigration, Israel has a high population growth rate today.

When I study the history of the Jews, it seems to me they tend to live with the past, by the past, for the past, and when it comes to the future, they aren't certain what the next 50 years will bring, because their future depends on the political situation of the country in which they live. Am I wrong?
I disagree. I think the amazing thing about the Jews is their dialectics. You have two contradictory forces working together. The religion is very strongly based on past events. For instance, the Exodus from Egypt is the key to the religion. But there is a very strong future orientation such as the belief in the coming of a Messiah. Normally, you might expect that one has to choose one element over the other, but I think it's really both together that create the Jewish religion. America is a very future-oriented country and not much interested in the past, but the Jews combine both outlooks. For example, Zionism looked back to the ancient biblical world, but it certainly looked forward to creating a new state and eventually Jews did it. Judaism looks backward to the Exodus and to the great events of Jewish history

which happened thousands of years ago, but it also looks forward to the future, to the Messiah, to returning to Israel, and so on. In the community there have been a lot of attempts at participating and planning for the future.

As I understand it, the Zionist movement was more of a dream about the Jews going back to Israel, the promised land. But practically no action was taken. However, after the Holocaust, the British finally agreed to make their occupied-territory in Palestine available for the Jews. It was a turning point for Jews. The world was shocked and sympathized, and was gravely concerned about the future for the Jews. So, without Hitler there would be no Holocaust, but without the Holocaust there would be no Israel. And, overall, without Hitler there would be no state of Israel, which means Hitler was, to put it ironically and indirectly, the Messiah for the Jews...

I think that is a clever statement, almost cruel, but not true. Hitler was a war-maker; and the meaning of the Messiah is someone who brings peace to our world, not war. Furthermore, if Hitler hadn't come, there would have been a Zionist State based on natural growth, not one stimulated by mass killing. The Holocaust certainly contributed to the birth of Israel, but I wouldn't exaggerate the sympathy toward the Jews. Hitler unintentionally contributed to the creation of Israel, but frankly the demographic blow which he inflicted was so devastating that he almost destroyed the survival capability of the Jews. So, I don't think it's fair to say that Israel is the result of the Holocaust. Zionism long preceded the Holocaust. The people who settled modern Israel first also preceded the destruction. 600,000 Jews settled in Israel before the Holocaust. The Holocaust was a stimulant and only a contributory force.

Some Jews try to say maybe this is the way God operates and the sacrifice of European Jewry made possible the state. I say that if that was the price, it wasn't worth it. I don't think that was a good deal. Besides, it's not fair to blame the Holocaust on God. The Jews suffered terribly. This made them insist on creating the state of Israel immediately. But the state would have come to be created in a much more constructive fashion without the Holocaust.

I think the last century was a remarkable period in our history; there were all sorts of liberal movements, including Zionism. It produced many influential intellectuals, philosophers, authors and artists. Among them was the American author Mark Twain. He lived in Austria in the time Hitler was born and wrote an essay titled *Concerning the Jews*, in which he criticizes the behavior of Jewish people in central Europe at that time. This was, in fact, written 50 years before the Holocaust. Why didn't Jews pay attention to it? (This book was published by Running Press in 1985.)

I am not familiar with Twain's criticism of the Jews. As I recall it, he wrote: "If the statistics are right, the Jews constitute but one percent of the human race." But their contributions to the world's list of great names in literature, science, art, music, finance, medicine and abstruse learning are way out of proportion to the smallness of these numbers. In retrospect, however, Jews didn't take threats of anti-Semitism seriously enough. As a result, Jews weren't prepared to resist mass murder and Europe wasn't prepared, either. Even during the Holocaust, many Jews didn't believe what was going on. Afterwards, the Holocaust was taken to heart by the Jewish community. The Jewish people learned some lessons; Israel is a part of that learning. Jews decided that they should have some place to go, a safe place of their own. Israel made the pledge that any Jew in the world could come to Israel and would be accepted even if he or she was old, poor or sick.

There are many Jews in prominent professions, but not many in the creative arena, lifestyle-oriented professional fields, or athletic, military and farming careers. For example, among influential inventors or discoverers, great painters, remarkable opera composers or world adventurers, we see hardly any Jews. Are Jews traditionally engaged with practical, conventional, and financially secured professions?
You would have to do a scientific study to answer that question. There have been a disproportionate number of Jews as Nobel Prize winners in science and medicine. I'm not sure about percentages of inventors or discoverers or artists. In the 20th century, American Jews have been disproportionately influential as leading writers and also in film and on stage. The obvious answer to your question is that you are dealing with just 13 million Jews. This is one third of one percent of the world population. I suspect that Jews make up more than one third of one percent of inventors, discoverers, etc. Of course, I can't account for specific numbers in specific fields except to say that people who created masterpieces during the last centuries are so rare that typically if you have one in a million, it's a lot. So I don't think that Jews are necessarily better at business than at being artists. Proportionately speaking, the number of Jewish bankers and millionaires may not necessarily be more than the number of doctors or

artists in Jewry. Also, let me stress that I don't think that Jewish accomplishment is just the effect of the Jewish experience of persecution. The people have been strongly influenced by religious ideas and religious models as well.

Having lived for 2,000 years under pressure, persecution and displacement, when the modern world opened up to accept Jews, a lot of Jewish energy which was bottled up came out. That's probably what you are referring to. Jews have flocked into new areas and into new opportunities because they were closed out of old ones. If a person is open to a new approach, particularly in business, the person is more likely to be successful. That may be why Jews have been visibly successful in business. But I don't think there is a proven pattern that Jews are better in business than they are in science.

Another interesting phenomenon I find is that Jewish people, as long as they live among Gentiles, are well off and successful. They have lived for so long in a society ruled by a Gentile majority, being discriminated and persecuted, in order to survive, they study and work very hard, they stick together and help each other like in tribalism. And, over the many centuries this has been Jewish tradition which created certain powers. How would they live in an all-Jewish society where nobody discriminates against anyone because everybody is a Jew...?
To answer that, Israel is an example. Israel is a Jewish society and provides a new experience for the Jews. It's of course too early to say, but it will be interesting to see if there is more or less creativity, or more or less innovation in Israel. I'm afraid we were not going to have an answer in our lifetime because it takes time to establish such a pattern. We have to wait a hundred years until we

can tell. We can speculate that for centuries, Jews have suffered and tried harder under the threat of persecution. The persecution caused something like survival of the fittest; only someone more vital and more dynamic can survive. It isn't clear whether Jews will try harder only living among Gentiles, or if they will try harder among themselves. You are right about not being persecuted when they are in the majority. But Israel has struggle in terms of the many hostile nations around it. All in all, it's still too early to give you the answer you are looking for.

Martin Luther, the 16th century religious reformer who liberated Germans from the oppression of Catholicism, in fact, tried to get Jews to participate in his movement but failed. Then he became bitter against the Jews. How do you interpret his actions?

Yes, Luther turned very hostile and brutally anti-Semitic. That left a tragic legacy which later influenced the Nazis. Luther didn't forgive the Jews for not accepting his Messiah. He is a classic example of the would-be redeemer who loves people if they follow his vision, but if they dare to resist his plan for salvation, he will stop at nothing to destroy them physically. My response to Luther is that if you want the Messiah to come, you have to be responsible. If you are overeager to have the Messiah, you will destroy the whole world in order to save it, then you make a mockery of what you stand for. In other words, the Messiah is not just an individual coming, it's the world made perfect. If in the name of making the world perfect, you start hating opponents and murdering them, you are destroying the world. Luther's anti-Semitism foreshadowed his cruel abandonment of the German peasants as well. So you see, liberators can be judged the same way as the would-be Messiah. You will know when you are making the world perfect, when there is no more war and people treat each other with equality and with dignity.

The Messiah theory is very idealistic, not realistic...

Well, that's true, but one must not give too much weight to being a realist. I think over the course of history there has been some raising of standards. Judaism started as a religion to teach the idea of one God. At the time it started, there was one Jew in the whole world preaching about one God. Now, there are millions of people who believe in one God. So, the answer is that you can't be a total realist because otherwise you surrender to the status quo. On the other hand, you can't be a total dreamer because then you are out of touch with reality. But if you blend realism and dreams, you can transform the world. This is the strong point of Judaism.

Judaism has dreams, very ambitious dreams: to make the whole world perfect. But it also has very realistic goals. I will give you one example. In Jewish tradition, you don't start to save the whole world at once. You start with your own family, you start with your own people, then you extend beyond to other people. You may end up saving nobody. But if you can save one city or one nation, that is a big step forward. So the Messiah is very idealistic; but if you take a Jewish approach, a step at a time, then it's a realistic and achievable dream.

But among the Jewish people themselves there are Orthodox, Ultra-Orthodox, Conservatives, Reformed, Secular, and they don't agree with each other on many issues. It's very confusing for us non-Jewish people.

First of all, by lumping them all together, the outsiders show that they don't understand. With every group, it's easy to lump everyone together and believe the stereotypes. One of the keys to a better world is to learn to treat people as individuals and to respect the fact that they have tremendous differences. I hope, eventually, as these stereotypes break down, people will realize that as close as Jews are to each other, there are also a lot of differences. Furthermore, racially, the Jews are not only white; we have Blacks and Asians as well. It's beautiful to have multi-colored people. We are challenged to learn not to lump people together and not to treat another race as a threat or inferior. We have to learn to respect diversity. This is part of what a peaceful world is all about.

One of the great accomplishments of the 20th century is pluralism. For many centuries, there have been cruel and devastating wars and persecutions in the name of unity. The most important new development is the emergence of pluralism, which means you don't have unity based on an identity of one race or the same thinking, but instead you respect variety. Instead of seeing difference as a threat, you see it as a treasure.

Since Jews never had a government of their own, the state of Israel is a new experience and there are great expectations. But, I can imagine that in a Jewish-only state, people may return to a biblical society. You often visit Israel; what is your opinion?
Israel is a modern society. I don't believe that it will return to a biblical society. If anything, Israel is more modern or even secular than most countries. Though the majority of Israelis have some respect for tradition, it's certainly not an orthodox society. From what I've seen the religion has flourished, but so have other forms of life. For

example, Israel has a tremendous book buying population; people read many more books per capita than Americans. So, I don't think the biblical world will be revived. But when you are in Israel, you do feel that history is present. Also, as a result of freedom of religion, religious groups feel free to express themselves and you get more dynamic expression of religion. It may seem that the orthodox are more visible in an Israeli society. In a Jewish only society they are not persecuted, so they become more visible. But the majority of Jews in Israel aren't orthodox. At one time, the majority was secular. Now, I would say the majority is traditional, not secular. As to how Israel will develop will depend on the peace process, and if peace comes, how long it lasts.

For the past 2,000 years, Jews have been hoping for the Messiah to come, but He never appeared. Since He didn't, I don't think He will come in the next 2,000 years, either. However, if He is really due to come to save the world, what nationality will He belong to, what language will He speak, will He be a man or a woman, white or black? Will He be a Jew again?
Well, literally the Messiah means the "anointed one." You know they used to anoint kings with oil so it literally and originally meant a king who would represent this perfection. I don't really think the Messiah is just a person; it's really a vision that the whole world is made perfect. The core idea of Judaism is that the perfect world is a world filled with life. The Bible predicted that, the whole world reaches toward that level: the termination of war, the end of persecution, and the end of poverty. This is not only for Jews but for everybody on this earth. As a Jew, I surely believe in the Messiah. However, I'm sorry to say

we are not there yet. Jews believe that God and humanity together are going to make a world of peace that we can all share. So, humans have an obligation to participate in the process of perfecting the world. Jews have an obligation to lead and guide for them.

Although the Messiah has been delayed, I still believe the Messiah will come some day. There is a Hasidic statement that if the Messiah came and he was an opponent of Hasidim, the Hasidim would still accept Him or Her, because they want the Messiah to be here. I, too, want the Messiah to arrive already. If the Messiah turned out to be a "Japanese woman" or any other surprise, I have no objection. The issue isn't gender or race or religion, but rather accomplishing the goal of perfection. When the Messiah is with us, it doesn't mean we will be all powerless, either. Jews don't believe the way Christians believe that the one who changed the world does so out of a state of powerlessness.

I think the Messiah missed the boat. If He was really due to come, He should have shown up during the Holocaust...
That is a very profound statement. In fact, Elie Wiesel, the 20th century Jewish writer and a Holocaust survivor, says in one of his books: "If the Messiah is coming and could have come on the Messiah's own power before the Holocaust — then it's too late to come now." However, says Wiesel, since it's too late for the Messiah to come, we will have to bring the Messiah. In other words, after the tragedy and suffering, the idea of a magical Messiah who comes and does it all for us is just not credible. If a magical Messiah were to have come at all, then was the time to come. So what's left? What's left is the possibility of a Messiah who can't come until the world is made

perfect. Then, everyone of us can have a share in bringing the Messiah.

For the Christians the Messiah has already come. What would Christians think when another Messiah comes? It would be confusing for them...
Well, Christians speak of a second coming. By the way, pointing to the world was the standard Jewish answer when there were debates between Jews and Christians. Christians say the Messiah came and the Jews say "not yet." So, a standard Jewish answer or proof is to look around. The world at war, how can the Messiah be here? When the Messiah comes, my personal guess is that all the religions will continue but with a new understanding. When I was a child, I believed the Messiah would come when everybody in the world became Jewish. I no longer expect that and I don't think it's necessary. The Messiah could mean that Christians would still be Christians, but they would respect Jews. They would not persecute Jews any longer and would learn from Jews. And not just Jews, but every religion. So, from my point of view, every religion would continue, but with a much greater understanding and mutual respect. Each would teach peace, not war or persecution, and teach responsibility for each other.

We, the postwar generations, grew up with lots of information about WW II, particularly about the Holocaust. We expressed our sympathy for its victims and survivors, however, sympathy is an emotion but not a solution, and human emotions are not reliable, because they change from time to time, and will not be transfered to the next generations. It will fade away as time passes and there is no guarantee

that the truth about the atrocities will be transmitted correctly. Some people even deny the Holocaust. In the next 20 years most Holocaust survivors won't be alive anymore. I think it's our responsibility to inform new generations. For instance, people should know more about Jews. Jews are not simply a minority, but also a very influential group of people in the world. So, education should include not only teaching about the Holocaust, but also an overview of all of Jewish history, and this should be included in textbooks for high school curricula. What do you think?

It's interesting that you say that, because the United States Holocaust Museum in Washington D.C. which opened in the spring of 1993, is packed with thousands of visitors everyday, 7 days a week. The museum organizers can't handle the crowds. They are telling people to make reservations in advance or not to come for a while. Amazingly, the majority of the visitors are non-Jewish people. This clearly shows that people want to know more about the Holocaust than we originally thought. I'm involved in education. Until now the average public school would not include Jewish history in its curriculum. The new inclusiveness is a big step in the right direction. There are large groups of Asian minorities today in the United States who are not familiar with Judeo-Christian religions and their history. They need to learn and to be included in the curriculum planning. There is some pressure to try to make sure that there is some inclusion of Jews. But it's not easy to achieve. If you are a minority, it's hard to get attention. But Jews are working on getting the history of all American minorities included. This is good for them and for everybody.

Today, you have a Jewish population of 6 million in the US, the biggest Jewish community in the world. Do you think the establishment of Jewish life in the US is successful? I ask that because the United States is a country in which Jews are treated equally. It's a final frontier particularly for Jews.

There is a crisis in American Jewry today. People are nervous about Jewish assimilation. Today, 50 percent of American Jews are intermarried and many are assimilated. You said earlier Jews are used to being pressured and they stick together. The American society treats Jews nicely so that they don't have to stick together as much. America is a very attractive society but it's not easy to be a minority. So, there has been a lot of assimilation. Right now the Jewish community feels it's in a crisis. But I am an optimist. I think Jews will learn how to live in freedom, and religions will learn how to communicate. But Judaism has to go through a lot of development to communicate with itself. When the Jews were living in one neighborhood, it was easy to be a Jew. But when you are scattered and accepted everywhere, then you have to really work hard to keep Jewishness going.

Assimilation can be a good thing for Jews. Are you afraid of being assimilated?

Assimilation is a mirror of good treatment, good social acceptance of Jews. Still, I don't think assimilation is good. Society is better when you have mixes of groups and religions. Assimilation will be damaging for Jews, but it will be destructive to American culture as well. Society is much better when it has diversity. Assimilation is a threat to Jewish society. I personally am not totally pessimistic, but many Jews are loosing their identity. Being Jewish is a culture; it involves a mental energy and an identity for Jews. Assimilation is like having plastic surgery of a mental kind. If you remove your brain or your memory and just live in the 20th century without remembering the Holocaust, it's a mistake. Life without suffering or without struggling would make a pretty shallow person. Struggle between cultures has developed Jewish intellectuals and brought Jewish thinking to a higher level. If Jews lose their Jewishness, they will not be as deep anymore.

But, I think learning lessons is more important than just remembering. We must always ask, what did we learn from the Holocaust? Because we can't do much about what happened, but we can do something for the future. First of all, we must pass on the correct information to the next generations; we can do

that, as we discussed, through education. What is your view on that?

We can organize to assure that the lessons are learned so that never again will such a destruction be possible. Some of the lessons are: the need for all potentially persecuted minorities to achieve power or protect themselves; the sacredness of life, the importance of ethical responsibility for others. The bystanders were the key factor in the extent of Jewish life lost in the Holocaust. The failure of the bystanders to resist Nazism condemned the Jews to death. We now know that all humans must show solidarity and resist oppression for each other. This is the only way to prevent the triumph of evil. As the Bible put it: "You shall not stand idly by (as someone spills) the blood of your neighbor." (Leviticus 19, 16). ❖

Questions to a liberal Jewish professor.

MARK MANCALL

American Jew; history professor of Jewish Studies, Bible, Indian and
Southeast Culture at Stanford University, director of Stanford Program
in Structured Liberal Education. Born in 1932 in New York City and
lives in California, USA.

The questions I am going to ask to you, Professor Mancall, will be sensitive for some Jews, but as a journalist, I feel it is my work to explore controversial issues. I believe that open communication is important for an understanding between Jews and non-Jews. If you feel uncomfortable answering my questions, please do say so.

I used to believe that anti-Semitism originated due to the rise of Christianity which became a very powerful religion. But some evidence shows that it existed in the pre-Christian world. Jews were already scattered around the Mideast before the birth of Jesus Christ. This would make the history of anti-Semitism 4000 years old, not only 2000 years old. Is this true?

In the ancient world there were two issues. Ancient Palestine, the area which Jews inhabited, was located between two great imperial centers, Egypt and Mesopotamia, and the whole area was the battleground for the two great centers of civilization in Western Asia. The area was constantly involved in war, the kind of war which was characteristic of the ancient world, and people were often carried away as slaves and prisoners, so I would not characterize this as anti-Semitism at all. What is interesting in the ancient world was that, especially after the times of the Greeks and Romans, a lot of Jews lived outside Palestine. There were very large Jewish communities in Babylonia; today's Iraq, Iran and Egypt. At the time Jesus Christ lived, probably one quarter of the Jewish people lived outside of Palestine. In addition to that, in the Roman Empire one tenth of the entire population was Jewish. We think that is a large number but the Roman Empire was not densely populated. So I think it's hard to

characterize the pre-Christian attitude toward this particular group as anti-Semitism.

With the development of Christianity, a profound and rapid change followed. The Christian church believed itself to be the successor to the Jewish people. Jewish people were chosen by God, then the Christian church said this is a new testament, a new government and a new law. Saint Paul was particularly responsible for this. The Christian church believed that it was the successor to the Jewish people, so Jewish people were no longer legitimate. If the Christian church now has legitimacy based upon governance of God, Jews are no longer needed. Within 200 years, the Christian church began developing a very negative attitude toward Jews, because the Jews rejected the Christian message. This was the first phase of one of the conflicts in the history of Jewish and Christian relations. So, anti-Semitism as we think of it today is not the same thing as it was in that Christian period, but it is related. I think we must make a distinction between the ancient world, which was an ethnic tribe of people and didn't have any concrete religion base, and the modern world which has a powerful religious driving force.

The Romans invaded the land of Palestine and the Jews failed to defend their land, but they didn't have to leave their territory; they could have stayed there. Why did they leave? Because they left, Jews never had a national experience until this century. As for the Jewish tribe, how did Jewish nationalism and patriotism stand in those ancient times? For example, Spain was also invaded by the Muslims, but the people didn't flee their land, and after nearly 800 years of struggle, Spaniards eventually reconquered their land from the Moors.

35

The Roman Empire had a very powerful army and the Jews were defeated. When the Romans invaded Palestine, there were tremendous internal conflicts going on there. To make the statement that Jews failed to defend their territory — that was true of everyone in the ancient world who was defeated by the Romans. It was not a failure militarily. They were defeated. Jews migrated all over the Mediterranean area and lived, particularly in the city of Alexandria, Egypt, even though they had a strong attachment to Jerusalem and used to go there for pilgrimages. Palestine was a very small and poor land, and as the population grew, people had to emigrate in order to survive. So, Jews left for economical reasons, just as people do today. Some Jews were taken away as slaves or prisoners by the Romans, some left to find a better life in commerce as merchants. All different kinds of people lived around the Mediterranean cities in those days. They lived in a multi-race, multi-national and multi-cultural environment. The ancient world was really an international and cosmopolitan world. There was no such thing as nationalism or patriotism in ancient times. Spain, on the other hand, the land of Iberia was fertile, so people didn't need to leave their territory in order to survive or to find a better living.

Jews carried their own Book everywhere they went, and they were the ones who implanted a belief in the Messiah in many places. Without Judaism there would be no Christianity, is that right? Otherwise, what is the origin of Christianity?

Certainly, Christianity came out of Judaism originally, but no Christian would admit that. Because if there was no Jew it would have to be somebody else. If you are saying from a historian's point of

view, yes, the Christian religion probably came out of one of the sects of Judaism around the time Christ was supposed to have lived. The biography of Christ is the story of Jews of a very particular area, the frontier zone between the Greek and Jewish worlds. Now, from the Christian point of view, if God wanted to send His only begotten Son to save the world, if there were no Jews, He would have had to send someone else. From God's point of view, who it was doesn't matter. Historically, yes, I think Christianity came out of Judaism. But to express the theological point of view, it's not clear that Jews were not necessary. The Judeo-Christian tradition is, first of all, a historical view, not a theological view. Secondly, it is a view which is more Christian than Jewish. Many Jews don't believe that, historically, there was a Judeo-Christian tradition from the Jewish point of view. The Christian church was required to legitimate itself in some way. Since their founding myth concerns the Jews, therefore, they have to have a Judeo-Christian tradition.

The idea of a Messiah was very weak in Jewish thought until about 100 years before Christ. Originally, the idea of a Messiah was simply the idea of a hero, probably something like a hero from a royal family who would come back and save the people nationally, not save them religiously. There was no religious element. Around the time of Christ, various groups of Jewish people emerged who believed in a Messiah as a religious figure. But that was new in those days, not profoundly a part of the Jewish tradition at all. It was talked about among small groups of Jews and it was not a very widely held idea. You have to remember that it was not Jesus Christ who established the church, it was Saint Paul, as I mentioned earlier, who was a Jew himself.

In those days, throughout the Roman Empire there were significant groups of people — some poor, some rich — who were very attracted to Judaism as a religion. In Rome, at that time there were many different religions being practiced next to each other, and one of them was Judaism. And, a lot of people were attracted to the Jewish religion for various reasons and they wanted to become Jews. But, becoming a Jew was very difficult. First of all, if you were a man, you had to be circumcised no matter what your age, and that was very painful. It was not at birth like today. So people didn't want to do that. On top of that, if you were a Jew, you couldn't eat pork which was a common food in those days. When Saint Paul began to say there was a new way to be a Jew without circumcision and without many restrictions, presenting a new law and a new testament, it attracted a lot of people. There were already many people who wanted to be Jews and didn't want to undergo the necessary rituals. So, it was a kind of basis built up already for the spread of Christianity and that made it easy to become a Jew. So, Saint Paul was one who was responsible for the birth of Christianity.

In the beginning, those original Christians were in Jewish synagogues practicing together with Jews, not in churches. In fact, churches hadn't appeared until 100 AD. In the years around 90 and 100 A.D., however, there was a split between Christians and Jews, and Christians were separated from Jews and out of synagogues. They built churches instead of synagogues.

Historically speaking, who was Jesus Christ? It seems He was a revolutionary man, who preached only 4 years...?
No, only 3 years. Well, certainly there are people who believe that, in fact, according to the story,

he came from a part of the country which was the frontier area. Many uneducated people with a full range of social problems came from this region, and certainly many social revolutionaries. So he may have been one of those kinds of people. There was nothing in the story of Christ up through the point of resurrection, that is particularly different from the story of many other figures at that time. Where the Christian story becomes different is that He rose again from the dead. That is very different. As far as we know, nobody else ever rose from death. And we don't even know He really did.

One of the problems which Christianity has is that it has this fundamental contradiction from the beginning. It claims to be a historical religion, that is to say the Messiah was a historical figure at a specific time, and yet, there is no historical evidence to support the existence of the figure. The real evidence was only the story from the Bible, which was not really evidence. That is why Christianity has to rely on faith. I think this is the problem for Christianity as a whole. To believe there is only one God who is responsible for everything is a very difficult burden.

Let me ask you about the "Dead Sea Scrolls." According to a documentary video film entitled *The Secret of the Dead Sea Scrolls* which was aired on public television in 1991, an English scholar by the name of John Strugnell, an editor in chief of the research team who has studied the Dead Sea Scrolls for over 35 years, made a stunning remark. In November 1990, an Israeli newspaper quoted Mr. Strugnell as saying, "Judaism is a horrible religion. It should have disappeared." Shortly after that

he was dismissed from his position. Do you know the story?

I'm not familiar with that particular story and don't know about him. There are all kinds of strange people in the world making strange statements. The Dead Sea Scrolls are extremely important, of course, both for Jews and Christians, but what he said is not important. His opinion was only one of many views. The Scrolls are the ritual remains of one of these groups who believed in some kind of teacher or messiah. There were many groups like that at that time and this is one of the few groups from whom we have actual, literal materials. That makes it very interesting and fascinating.

Some Jewish people are able to recognize some words of script in the Dead Sea Scrolls, which were written in ancient Hebrew about 2,000 years ago. This makes it very special to them. They feel they are close to their past. As non-Jews we have no such thing. For most of the nations of the world, it's difficult to trace the origin of words we are using unless we're scholars or specialists. I find the difference between Hebrew and other languages is that the Jewish language has no evolution in its development. Because it is an unused language, like Latin, it didn't evolve. In the history of any nation its society developed during many different periods, and the language has a parallel development. The English language, for instance, has evolved so much from mixing with other languages because of England's history and its colonialism. As Jews had no national history, Hebrew as a language didn't develop. Could that be the reason?

That's right. Hebrew stopped being a spoken language around 500 B.C. Instead, it was replaced by Aramaic, the language which was largely spoken in the Mideast. Hebrew functions like Latin, but then it was revised again in the 20th century, but Latin never was. Hebrew remains an intellectual language among Jews throughout history. So, Jews could write and read Hebrew, especially men, not so many women. It was accepted only in intellectual circles. Although it did not evolve until this century, there were some small changes throughout its entire history. The scripts of the Dead Sea Scrolls are very archaic and difficult to read, but most educated Jewish men who study the Bible and Talmud are able to read the ancient Hebrew.

Since the Messiah hasn't come yet for Jews, who is the spiritual leader for Jews? Most religions have a spiritual symbol — Christ for Christians, Buddha for Buddhists, Mohammed for Moslems. Is there a spiritual guide for Jews?

There is no such figure for Jews, really. What there is is Moses who is the lawgiver, not a spiritual leader, and that's all they have. Jews live by law. Judaism and Islam are basically religions of law. For them, what is important are the rules for living life here "now" today. For Christianity, it's more spiritual with regard to one's soul and salvation. Mohammed is not a spiritual leader, either. He is a lawgiver who tells people what God's law is. Moses doesn't say. Buddha himself is enlightened and Jesus Christ is the Messiah, so that is very different. No one is like Jesus in Judaism. The important thing for Jewish life is the law based on moral value. Unlike Christians, Jews don't have anything like spiritual communication at all. There are only a few very religious Jews who believe maybe a Messiah will come for Jews. They are some Jews in New York and a few in

Israel. But not so many. As for the rest of the Jews, they don't believe in such a thing. Jewish spiritual life is an internal life; it's part of community. Jews don't distinguish between the life of spirit and the life of community. They are very closely tied to each other and don't need a leader. Jews lived through 4,000 years of very stormy history without having leadership. They survived the Holocaust without having leaders. Jewish people helped each other and survived without leaders. So, maybe they don't need leaders in the future, maybe not, because they have a strong sense of community spirit among themselves.

How do Jews regard their ancestors, their spiritual heritage and their future?

For most Jews today, if they are concerned with Jewish things at all, it has to do with how you live your life "now," that is the important thing. They don't concern themselves with their ancestors or future life at all, and certainly they would not communicate spiritually with the past. What is the important thing for Jews is that, I live my life "now" properly. Concerning our ancestors, we can't do anything about how they lived their life because they're dead and they're gone. We don't communicate in our mind with dead creatures. Death is death. From the Jewish point of thinking, what our parents or great-parents did was a different matter. What matters is if we are leading a good life: if we relate to the present in a good fashion, that's all that matters. For us, the present is all we have: the moment of our birth and the moment we die — that is all we have. For modern Jews today, we aren't sure we even have a soul. You have to understand from the modern day Jewish point of view that our ancestors are historic and we remember them, but we don't communicate with them.

Many Jews die without a coffin, and for us it seems a terrible way to die. Most European Jews don't have a family cemetery because they were either expelled, fled or were displaced from one place to another. And, if they have three generations buried in the same cemetery, they are proud of it. What do you think?

Surely, that means they stayed in one place for that long. It's true that a coffin is not customary for Jews, but for us, the body is dead and his or her life is terminated. All you do is wrap it up and put it in the ground. What does it need a coffin for? Jews are more practical. We have seven days in which to cry and mourn, and then we go on about our normal life. That is the tradition. Our Bible says about the burial ceremony — "… for dust thou art, and unto dust shalt thou return." According to the story, God created man out of the dust and that will be what we become when we die.

Jewish cemeteries often get vandalized. How do you feel about that? It never happens to other minorities, only to Jews. Jews are hated even after they have died.

That is a silent hatred. But remember that vandalizing the cemetery doesn't hurt bodies in the cemetery. They don't feel it. It only hurts us. I will suffer if I want to. But people who do such things are uneducated and extremists. They are not typical people in society. In Western culture, minorities are basically Jews and Gypsies. It's ugly and painful, but not that uncommon. But on the other hand, look at America today, California keeps out illegal immigrants. It makes it important if I take it seriously.

From the Gentile's point of view, we feel responsible for our future children and we hope

they will not suffer because of what we did, and we wish they'll have a better life even 100 years after. Some Jews say if you are a Jew, you were born to suffer. For us, that's a terrible way to live. Is that the correct theory for Jews?

No, it's nonsense. A lot of American Jews want to paint their history and their background of great suffering. It's the way they are constructed because they become fixated by the Holocaust. They think all Jewish history is like the Holocaust. That's absolutely nonsense. Historically, it's totally incorrect. You have to distinguish between what is Jewish history and reality, and what some modern American Jews think. American Jewish children were born in the land of America, they enjoy their life in the same way as any other American citizens.

About the Jewish relationship with Christianity, Jews tend to look down upon Christianity, because of its complicated mother-son relationship. Although Christianity is not a perfect religion, it has great value. It teaches moral responsibility and social obligation, it brings people and community together, all because they share the same spiritual leader: Jesus Christ. It created Christian civilization in the Western world and it's a great civilization. In fact, I don't think it is that important who Christ was. Spirituality is the most important factor after all. Do Jews respect Christians?

Jews think Christianity is a different religion. Christians may see Judaism as the source of Christianity, which is historically and only partially true, but Jews don't really care too much. They simply see Christianity as another religion. They don't look down upon Christians; it's absolutely not true. The problem of Christianity for the Jews has nothing to do with Christian belief.

It's everything to do with Christian behavior toward Jews. From the Jewish point of view, Christianity is a different religion, and so is Buddhism, Islam and all others. The question is how other people behave toward Jews, that is what influences how Jews think, not what other people believe. It's social and historical conflicts, but not religion, except to the extent that social conflict has roots in religion. Otherwise, yes, Jews respect Christianity, of course.

You've been a professor at one of the most prestigious universities in America for nearly 30 years. When your students ask what is the lesson from the Holocaust for Jews, how do you answer them?

From my perspective, it's very much idiosyncratic, very much my own point of view. The major lesson to learn from the Holocaust is about the degree to which human beings can misbehave toward other human beings. That is the lesson which you as Germans, Chinese, Russians, Japanese, French, Spanish, or anybody else should also learn. So, from that point of view, there is not much to learn from the human point of view. It is about how debased we are capable of becoming as human beings. From the Jewish point of view, I think there are two lessons to be learned. The first is the small people in the world, minorities and small nations like Bosnia-Herzegovina, should know that the larger powers will not protect them in times of danger. Each people has to find their own form of defense, whether that form of defense is through the United Nations or some kind of national existence. The fact is that the great powers do not defend small powers and vulnerable people in times of crisis, unless it's in their interest to do so. The second lesson for Jewish people to learn is from the aftermath of the

Holocaust, not the Holocaust itself, and that is that you have to start forgetting certain points of history in order to build a future, not to become fixated on the past. And, I'm afraid that many Jews have become fixated on the Holocaust as the only source of meaning of contemporary Jewish life. And I think that is a very important thing. The future requires that we understand that the past is the past, and that we will reconstruct a new future. That's what's really important. This is my answer when my students ask me what lessons to learn from the Holocaust. In addition, as a Jewish person, I don't think the Holocaust is everything Jews have. The Holocaust was an event and we should learn from it how to understand that past, but not to change the course of the future for the Jews. We have to think of the future for Jews, not the past. But unfortunately, too many Jews think only of the past.

Jews are people of the Book. Literally, they are well educated. They are connected with written materials that were their traditional means of communication from one generation to the next. The greatest book buyers and the greatest book readers are Jews. Over centuries, it's a quite natural thing that the publishing industry has flourished with the involvement of Jews. That includes writing, editing, printing, production, manufacturing and distribution. They are experienced in these fields and know how to run the business. Now, Jews are often accused of being in control of the press. What is your comment?
The issue of media control really is modern media control, not about the Book. It's about television, film, radio, magazines and newspapers. Jews don't control the media. That was one of the accusations that happened not to be true. There are

a large number of Jews in those industries by and large, and more in the film and entertainment industries in Hollywood. In television and radio fields, not so much in commercial stations, but some in public stations. I don't know what it means to control the media anymore. In America today in the last couple of decades, it is estimated that some 80% of the news is announced by the federal government. To make another distinction, who owns the press is different from who makes the news in the press. Editors are the ones who control the news and the owners simply own the publishing companies as business. In newspapers, for example, a Jewish family owns the *New York Times,* but its editorial board and journalists are mostly not Jews. It's an accusation which was made but not supportable statistically. There was an accusation that was made that Jews run banks, but there is no Jew as president of a bank in America. I don't think there is anyone. You don't find many Jews at the top levels of management or CEOs in corporations, either. If you look at public broadcasting, Jews give funds to support educational programs and there may be some production members, reporters and editors. But proportionally, no more than others, I don't think. Probably not.

In a way, I do think Jews are good at handling the media. They raise sensitive and controversial issues.
It happens to be something Jews run into. It happens to be an industry they are involved in. I would not make a particular distinction about Jews, but many issues they raise are sensitive, I agree. Jews are very concerned about these issues. If you are of a group which has traditionally been persecuted, then, you are naturally going to become more sensitive to these things, far more

than non-Jews, of course. Media happens to be an industry in which Jews are active.

Why are there so many Jews involved in the movie industry?

Yes, Jews are very active in Hollywood. Why? Because when Jews came to America in the 1920s there was no industry developing, and since there was less competition in new industry than old industry, Jews moved into some of the new areas, and one of them was the movie industry. So, naturally some immigrants went into that. It was very reasonable to do in those days. The early generation of the movie business in America was run almost completely by European Jews: Germans, Poles, Russians, and all kinds of Jews.

Hollywood today produces too many violent films which disturb many youngsters in America, and that may be responsible for the rise of crime. My question is that since a significant percentage of Jews are involved in the movie industry, could they partially be responsible, perhaps?

Violence is a characteristic of American life. It's characteristic of all people of America. It has nothing to do with Christians or Jews, Chinese or Latin Americans, whoever. There are Italian mafia, Chinese gangsters, Korean mobs, Japanese murderers in America, and crime of all kinds. This is American life today. It's a recent social phenomenon as well. When you look back to the old days in Hollywood, they used to produce good movies, not in this way. It has to do with changes in American society. People are responsible for this as Americans, not as Jews, French, Chinese, or anything else. The fact is that it's of very much consequence for America. It has very

little to do with the particular ethnic group we are talking about.

I find Jewish people often tend to mix-up anti-Semitism with criticism. No nation is perfect; Germans are not and they know it, Americans are naive and they admit it, and Jews are not perfect people, either. I understand, of course, it's extremely sensitive but I think every group needs to live with self-criticism in order to develop a better understanding of each other, don't you think?

That's true. There is no question that a lot of Jews feel that criticism of Jews is anti-Semitic. It's a sensitive point of view but you can understand why. Given a history of such fatal persecution of Jews in this century, you can understand why Jewish people are sensitive about it. So, one may think it's not a valid point of view but nevertheless you can understand intellectually and psychologically why that will be the case. But it doesn't mean it's correct. It simply means you can understand why Jews react and respond in that way. Even so, in some societies there is anti-Semitism without Jews. It's a part of the culture. It is very hard to determine exactly which is which, if it's a critical or an anti-Jewish remark.

Today in the State of Israel, Jews live collectively in one nation. Because Jews lived in every corner of the world for so long, I would imagine it would be difficult mentally to be united as one nation?

It takes a long time, there's no question about that. But it's happening. Gradually and steadily, as people learn to live together again in one place they are developing a new personality, a new identity and a new mentality. It doesn't happen overnight. It will take more time for Israel to solve many of the problems which they are facing now. It may take another 50 years or more. It's a tiny nation, a population of 4 million, but already there is a very distinctive Israeli personality and culture. Israel has three generations already. Israel's colonial history is part of Israeli history. There is a long history there. Jews living outside of Israel are of many different kinds, and the Jews in Israel are another kind. Israel is Israel, it's the country of Jews and Arabs, and others. The two are not synonymous. Israel is not Jewish people and Jewish people are not Israel.

In Israel, I was told, people identify themselves as Israelis, not as Jews. For them, Jews are those who returned after the State of Israel was born. They don't even talk about the Holocaust there. Is that true?

They don't talk about the Holocaust so much. In Israel, people's identity arises from the land of Israel. But in America, Jewish identity arises more from the Holocaust. It has become a "Holocaust industry." You have to understand that the Holocaust took place, but it became a symbol for identity, particularly for American Jews. The Holocaust was a terrible event but you must remember that average Jews didn't take their identity from the Holocaust. It was after the 1960s and 1970s, because of various reasons that the Holocaust became a symbol. And, now, we have the Holocaust Museum in Washington, D.C. which functions the way a shrine does and people go there like on a pilgrimage.

Some American Jews say today that they can't survive without the State of Israel. Is that so?

That's nonsense. I mean it's true Jewish people survived 2,000 years without Israel. What is true, in my opinion, is that if Israel were to be defeated

in a war and suddenly disappeared, the psychological and emotional blow to the Jews would be very heavy, indeed; that would be true. For the first time in 2,000 years you have a new state and if it's destroyed, it's naturally understandable. It would be a terrible blow to bear for the Jewish people everywhere in the world. But it doesn't mean that Jewish people wouldn't survive.

Let me ask you a question of national loyalty. For example, supposing in the Olympic Games, Israelis and Americans are competing against each other, as an American Jew, which side do you support?

I could be excited for the Americans, or I could be excited for both. It's a kind of nationalism. One may have more than one loyalty and it doesn't have to be fifty/fifty, it could be forty-nine/fifty-one. I may have more than one loyalty inside of me. I will be much more excited in soccer games, for example. If it's America vs. Brazil, I prefer Brazil to win, because I like them. I don't care about America. In other words, this question of loyalty, it has to do with identity. What is my identity, and that is the real question. Loyalty is not an interesting question. What am I? Many people in the modern world are a little confused about their identities, and we have more than one identity, everyone who lives in America.

Most citizens who were born in America, after a few generations, generally become culturally American. The country you are born in is the country you love, dedicate your life to and die in. They have no problem with that. Their soul and mentality are one. Why can't the Jewish people decide?

Why should we decide? For the moment, they can live as Jews in America, which is the way they have been living. They define themselves as Jewish, whatever definition they use, and they are living happily in America. I was born in America and I am physically here, and I know I have a special relationship with this country and my mind is here. There is not going to be a war between Israel and America. Maybe there will be some disagreements, but not in our lifetime, I don't think. So, why do I have to make a choice?

Many Americans today are not very happy that they have to keep paying their tax money to support Israel. One day the United States may run out of money and not be able to do that any longer. How can it guarantee that?

There will be small problems, but I don't think it is going to be a major crisis in Israel's relationship with the United States. Whether foreign aid rises or falls has nothing to do with whether there is going to be a major crisis. Crisis means a major issue which could lead to a break in the relationship. Ultimately, it will be a relatively small problem. The question is, whether or not you have a state that would defend Israel in case of war, and whether or not Israel will cooperate with American foreign policy. So far, every indication is that they will continue to cooperate, in spite of anything that goes on around the world. In the long run, when you look at the Mideast, Israel is the only thoroughly stable country in the region. All the other regimes depend upon the personality of their leaders, whether dictators or presidents. Israel is a relatively stable capitalist and democratic state. From that point of view, there is a basic common ground on which America and Israel can stand. They need each other for their vital interests.

Today, I see there are numerous Christian movements in America. People are even talking about prayer in school. Christian religion is interfering in the political arena. As we approach the new millennium, people are feeling insecure about the future. As Christianity becomes more powerful, my concern is that it may cause religious anti-Semitism to rise again, and move toward political and social anti-Semitism. How do you see this?

I think Jews generally oppose school prayer. This issue has been an old issue. In fact, in the 1960s the Supreme Court said it's not legitimate. I don't think it's going to pass because the only way to do so is to pass a constitutional amendment, and that is a very difficult thing to do. So, this law has very little chance. It's good propaganda by Republicans and right-wing Christians, but there's not much reality to it.

Concerning a rise of anti-Semitism through the Christian movements, ironically, most of the right-wing religious people are "pro-Jewish." The reason they are is because they believe that God, Jesus Christ, will come for the second time when all the Jews return to Israel, and they want to see it. That is one of their beliefs. This doesn't mean that people would simply send all the Jews of the world to Israel; it wouldn't happen. But they would like to see the second coming of their Messiah in His homeland. For Jews, the truth is they don't care about such a thing because they are not Christian.

Throughout history, in the European countries as a whole, the areas densely populated by Jewish people had problems. But that is not the case anymore because not enough Jews are there now. Today, they are in America. I think the Jewish establishment in America is success-

ful and safe. But, on the other hand, when I question non-Jewish people about their views, nobody says "safe." How do you see that?

Yes, it's absolutely safe. I think Jews are very successful in America. There is no question about that. It won't happen again to Jews. If it happens, it won't be the Jews. You see how careful we are now. We are very sensitive to these things nowadays. Today we worry about Serbs, Bosnia and former Yugoslavia, although we don't do anything for them, but we talk about them.

Jewish participation in America has been good for the country. Jewish social contribution is vital. One day in the future, do you think the United States of American may have a Jewish president? When Kennedy was elected people reacted because he was the first Catholic president, and Irish.

Yes, one day. We should also have an African American president and perhaps a Latin president. Of course, anybody may be elected. Theoretically, we should have these kind of presidents. Whether we will or not, who knows? We should have a woman president, too, some day. That would be the future of America. ❖

The voice of a German revisionist.

ERNST ZÜNDEL

German revisionist and extremist; German-Canadian human rights activist, president of Samisdat Publishers Ltd, TV producer and radio talk show host. Born in 1939 in Calmbach near Pforzheim, Germany. Lives in Canada.

(Photo: Mr. Zündel preparing the text for his broadcast in his studio.)

You are the most scandalous man in Canada, known as "Mr. Holocaust." Everybody knows you as an outspoken revisionist. Regarding what you do here, you sound like "Mr. Freak" to me. As I understand it, you do research on the Holocaust from your point of view. Do you deny the Holocaust?

I don't deny the Holocaust. Jews were interned and they really suffered, and died; I know that. I deny the Holocaust "made in Hollywood," which has been exaggerated, distorted and dramatized. The term "Holocaust" only became popular in the mid-1970s when a movie called *Holocaust* aired for American television. This was a mini-series based on a book of the same title written by Gerald Green. The story was partially true and partially fiction, and that really blew my mind. This film had a really devastating effect on the world and totally changed me and my thinking. And, since then, it has led me emotionally to revisionism.

Every few years since the end of the war, Jewish producers in Hollywood have produced this kind of film for the consuming public, the Gentiles, who might begin to doubt the Holocaust or not perceive it with empathy. Through Hollywood films, Jews penetrate the viewers' minds. I call it "psychological reinforcement." A recent example is *Schindler's List.* Usually films are based on novels, not archival historical materials, and are made to look like documentaries. Until I saw the movie *Holocaust,* I thought the Holocaust was a bad chapter of German history and history goes on; Jews and Germans were going to heal the wound, live side by side, do business together and work with each other. But that was not the way it worked out. I realized that Jewish leadership, even the new generations of Jewish leadership, were unwilling to let it be bygone and to establish normal relationships with German people. If that is the Jewish attitude and with Jewish control of large segments of the Hollywood media—they write books without researching for historical accuracy, and so on—these people are at war against me and my people; then, I respond to Jews. That was the real reason that I seriously began to dig into the background of the Holocaust.

All I want, as a German, is to tell my version of history. I was 6 when the war ended and for wartime generations it still hurts to talk about these issues. In my youth I believed in the Holocaust, what the Germans did to the Jews, and I was totally pro-Jewish. I hated Hitler; I used to scratch the picture of him every time I saw it in magazines or books. I was very ashamed and felt guilty about the Jews. That was the main reason I left Germany. I emigrated to Canada at the age of 19. I believed that the Germans, my parents' generation, had murdered Jews for no reason. After I came here, I had access to better books and better information than in Germany. That's because Canada didn't lose the war and is a democratic state; the press is free and open, and they have a better system of libraries and universities. I began to doubt the things I learned in Germany. They were illogical. Since then, for the past 30 years, I have been researching and studying the issues, and I am heavily involved with this period of history.

In recent years when *glasnost* came, the former USSR began opening up WW II archives and they became available to the public. I personally contacted Mr. Mikhail Gorbachev to release documents about Auschwitz, which were confiscated by the Russians because they were the first ones to enter the camp. I received a package of information released by Gorbachev to the International Red Cross. I learned of new evidence unknown to the western world. I believed 4 million people died at the hands of the Germans, but the actual number of deaths in Gorbachev's documents was terribly different — 78,000. I realized that we, the postwar generations, were not educated properly. Instead, we were totally indoctrinated by the Allies — Americans, British, French — through our school textbooks. My generation of Germans today is a product of an intellectual indoctrination culture that was set up by the American government and backed by wartime Jewish leaders. As a result, I concluded the Holocaust is a criminal conspiracy against the state of Germany and a tool to benefit Jews. As I raised my voice in public, I was sued by a Jewish woman, a Holocaust survivor. I went through a total of nine years of court battles.

I believe in the Holocaust and I do not promote your propaganda, Mr. Zündel. In North America we have freedom of speech, but it must be "with responsibility" for whatever you say. My interest is in the cause of the Holocaust and its consequences. Could you tell me the historical and political background in Germany between the two world wars, and the Jewish influence on German society?

On November 9th, 1918 when WW I ended, there was a civil war in Germany. Many areas were involved in Marxist-Bolshevik revolution and some areas in socialist revolution. But later, many of those socialists turned out to be Marxists and Communists, and many of them were Jews. In Berlin, for instance, there were an ardent pro-Marxist Jewish woman named Rosa Luxemburg and a radical Jewish lawyer named Karl Liebknecht. Both were leaders of the Spartakus League which was a political and revolutionary terrorist underground organization operating in-

side and outside Germany. By then, they were already responsible for the murdering of millions of Russians, Poles and Hungarians. Their Marxist-Bolshevik movement was the scourge of Europe. In Munich, there was a man named Kurt Eisner, a radical Jewish writer who was briefly minister president of Bavaria. He overthrew the aristocracy of Bavaria, proclaimed a soviet Republic in Munich and declared a revolution in Germany; he even declared war against Switzerland because the Swiss government refused to sell locomotives he needed. He took dozens of hostages and murdered them in cold blood. Eisner was a crazy man! In the time of the Weimar Republic there were these types of anarchies everywhere in Germany and all over Europe. In Hungary, there was a Bolshevik revolutionary called Bela Kun, a Jew himself and most of his commissars were also Jews. He led a reign of terror in Hungary like Eisner did in Bavaria. In Russia, there was Lenin; he was apparently not a Jew but was surrounded by many Jewish revolutionaries such as Trotsky, Kamenev, Kanganovich, Sverdlov, Goloshchekin, and more.

Historically, what had happened was that European society was basically a monarchial hierarchy, Christian by religious persuasion and tradition. In 1789 when the French Revolution came, in which civilians overthrew aristocrats, it changed everything upside down. Since then, this revolutionary spirit was carried out throughout Europe and we had occasional uprisings like the 1848 Revolution in Germany or the Paris Commune, the first communist revolution in 1871-72. In Germany, what we call a *"Kulturkampf"* (struggle of culture) was taking place. And, each time, Jews were emancipated. They were coming out of ghettos, had German surnames and access to better education and profession, and officially they were accepted by the government and gained equal opportunities in German society. They intermarried with Germans and many Jews looked like us: they spoke German like us, dressed like us, went to Wagner festivals like us and sang German songs like us, and socially they were assimilated to the German way of life, but not in their minds; mentally, they were still Jewish. So, German society was like a state within the state. Then, many different streams in Jewish thinking were developed. There was Zionism — returning to the holy land of Israel — and all other kinds of sects within Jewry developing. Some Jews in fact became patriotic Germans, without giving up their Judaic thinking. They, too, harbored some kind of revolutionary upheavals within themselves.

In 1848 when a son of a rabbi, Karl Marx, published the *Communist Manifesto,* that impact was enormous on the Jews and that was an outbreak of revolution for European Jews. The early Communists and Marxists who were directly involved with Marx, however, never thought that Marxism could work in an agriculture based country like Russia. That was the reason why Jews concentrated on Germany, because this newly created class should be based in industrialized nations. The communist ideology spread to the rest of Europe and Russia through the international Jewish networks. These Jews were those who abandoned Judaism and turned themselves into revolutionaries, denouncing the system of capitalism, proclaiming the death of monarchy, and searching for political and social solutions for better living for the proletariat and working class. Russia at that time was a member of the European community linked to the nations by royal intermarriages. It had an autocratic government, oppressed society, high taxes for civilians, and poverty was worst for the peasants. As for Jews,

they were a suppressed minority, totally outcast religiously and socially, deprived of most civil rights and treated worse than anyone. When WW I broke out, it was a turning point for Jews to revolt. So, you must understand that after the October Revolution in 1917, the communist Russians turned themselves into anarchists, radicals, destroying orthodox Christian churches and cathedrals, committing terrors on the middle class, arresting and sending them to concentration camps and murdering them, including the Imperial Romanov family of the Tsar, the last emperor of Russia.

All over Europe, there were millions of white Russian emigres who fled communist Russia, including Russian Jews who were dispossessed by revolutionary Jews. They were telling people what was going on inside Russia. So, all nations of Europe were terrified because they didn't want communism in the heartland of Europe. Among Gentiles there was a strong resistance against this thriving horde of Jewish world revolutionaries who were extremely powerful in Bolshevik communist international connections. Europe had to protect itself from this invasion of communism. Europeans had their own survival instinct and organized themselves outside their very weak governments. This fear of communism led civilians to arm themselves in Germany the group called *"Freikorps"* — a volunteer private army of WW I veterans and patriots — like today's militia movement in America. Within less than 10 years there were military governments in Hungary putting the Bolshevik revolutionaries and the radicals down. Also in Bulgaria, Romania, Poland, and everywhere in Europe the forces of law and order were fighting against the forces of communism. Not all, but many of these socialists and communists turned out to be Jewish who were religiously secular and atheists.

So, in my view, Jews have to answer to history. Was it our problem as ethnic Germans? No, it was a Jewish problem! What made them so miserable and malcontent that they were the only minority to take action against the order of the whole country? They are unhappy living as a minority, so they tried to destroy the entire nation? The reason why Hitler had such an easy time convincing the German people, and was supported by almost all of Europe, was that they wanted to join him against Bolshevism. Collectively, Europeans had had bad experiences with Jews. In France, for example, there were 50,000 white Russian immigrants. They were telling their friends about Jewish Bolshevism and it spread by word of mouth all over France, so-called *couchemar* (nightmare). When Hitler began his military campaign against communism on the eastern front, 55,000 young Dutch men volunteered to fight against the Bolsheviks to defend Europe. These men all knew they were going to die. In Denmark, double the number of SS-men were recruited than were in the regular Danish Army. They all fought in Russia as volunteers knowing they would die.

This was the reason Hitler arrested many Jews. There was a reasoned policy against Jews. They were perceived to be the potential enemy, like in the case of the internment of Japanese-Americans by Roosevelt. The Roosevelt Administration considered them enemy-aliens, including even the innocent children born in America. England, too, did the same thing to their enemy-aliens; they even interned Jews along with Germans living there. Hitler said many Jewish intellectuals and ordinary people were associated with international Bolshevism, therefore they must be

regarded as enemies of Germany. Not because he had a crazy idea to kill European Jews for no reason. Today, we can prove from documents in the archives that this policy was justified and that it worked. When the invasion occurred in France, Hitler had the French round up virtually all Jews overnight and the system of sabotage and treason ceased for the time being, because the French communist network without Jews was paralyzed. Many Jews were underground activists for the communist group called the Maquis (guerrillas), and Hitler grabbed many of them. The Maquis was severely weakened. We know this today from evidence and classified documents in the archives that came out during my court cases in 1985 and 1988.

So, what I want to say to you is that history continues. History didn't start in Auschwitz or *Schindler's List*. Long before Schindler's List there were active Jews who were intellectually and actively engaged in a reign of terror against the peoples in Germany, Holland, Belgium, France, Hungary, Czechoslovakia, Italy, Spain, and other countries. That eventually found expression in a reaction against this Jewish tribal aggression in what was called National Socialism or similar movements, and all the dictators in Europe led movements like that from Horthy in Hungary to Mussolini in Italy, from Franco in Spain to Salazar in Portugal.

In Weimar Germany, the Jewish population was only 500,000, which was less than one percent of the entire German population. How could they influence German society? What can you say about the Jewish intellectual influence before Hilter?

I have a book called *A New Germany and Jewry.* This was written in 1933 in Berlin, its original title was *Germany's Fight for Western Civilization.* It describes why Germans did what they did. It tells of Jewish involvement in German society at that time. Throughout greater Germany, 73% of the Jewish population lived in large cities. For example, in Berlin at that time, Jews were the leading ethnic group particularly in the fields of law, medicine, entertainment and welfare. I'll give you precise data: 48% of doctors were Jewish, 54% of lawyers were Jewish, 43% of professors were Jewish, 68% of welfare managers were Jewish, 45% of hospital directors were Jewish, 38% of dentists were Jewish, 80% of the theater management was Jewish, 50% of medical professors were Jewish and 25% of philosophy professors were Jewish. These statistics alone tell us many things.

Today, for instance, in Canada we have a quota system in many professional fields. We have a quota system for football players because we don't want the national football league dominated by Americans or foreigners. Otherwise, Canadians would lose these high-paying jobs. On Canadian radio stations we also have a quota system which calls for Canadian content, because we don't want to be culturally dominated by Americans or any other national groups. Now, this is in democratic, peace time Canada, not in Nazi Canada. We have had this system for decades out of self-protection dictated by a survival instinct. So, Canadian artists are not going to be supplanted or replaced by Hollywood. This is, I think, a natural and healthy human reaction for anybody who wants to live in a democracy and to share the equality. It's a very normal thing to do. In reaction against this Jewish domination of many facets of life in Germany and Austria, Hitler declared, "No. This is Germany, not Judea or Israel! Germany for the Germans!" I'll give you another

example. I can show you a telephone book in Toronto today and point my fingers at the many names of Jewish lawyers, and you will have to admit that the legal profession in Toronto is dominated by Jews, like the legal profession in Berlin was some 60 years ago. This is true even though the number of Jews in Toronto is only 150,000 out of 3 million people, and the entire Jewish population in Canada is only 350,000, which is one and a half percent of the entire Canadian population. And yet, I'll guarantee you, sooner or later, they will dominate the legal profession by 60%, 70% or more. America is exactly the same.

Why do you think Jews predominate in these specific professions?

I can give you a subjective analysis based on my personal observation and study. They are always in professions of the mind; not professions dealing with groups, heavy machinery or land-oriented labor work such as farming or blue collar jobs. You find a small number as corporation executives, but hardly anyone in military careers or sport heroes. They are in the diamond and jewelry business, for example, and in "transportable" trades, law, espionage, medicine, banking, money lending, movie making, writing, journalism, theater, publishing, or music, etc. It's always something easily transported that they can leave anytime. There is something like a nomadic spirit in these people. It's almost like they have a suitcase packed permanently. Because of the tragedy of their history, whatever the reason, over the centuries they adopted and developed this and it became their tradition. Jews have a revolving door policy; one Jewish person leaves, another Jewish person comes in. Canadian Jews leave for the USA and Russian Jews come in, for example.

Being a German and a controversial person, do you think you are treated fairly by the media about the things you say?

In the world of media and journalism, being a German, I'm an outcast. Occasionally, I get interviewed by journalists. In fact, I was in *60 Minutes* on CBS in 1994 and on and off in *The New York Times* and other major newspapers in America. The reporters who come to interview me are usually Gentiles, but the directors, producers and editors those who are behind the scenes of these programs or articles, are usually Jewish. And, that is why I get lousy publicity. More recently, I was interviewed by a reporter from NPR (National Public Radio) and we had a wonderful discussion, but the piece was never aired. These groups of people abuse their privileges of media control. Now, you may argue with me that this is nonsense.

If you live in America today, you should know how Jewish people operate with each other and how they organize themselves. You just have to look around. The Jewish population in the USA is claimed to be less than 6 million, which is less than 5% of the entire population; however, in the legal professions, politics, news media, law and Hollywood, you find a disproportionate number of Jews. I don't interfere with anyone who is telling the fairy tale of the alleged Holocaust of the Jews. I just want to defend myself and Germany, and tell people our side of that story, and this is my right. But, as I see it, Jews want exclusive rights controlling the world's history in their own way — the "Judeo-centric" way. The situation in court is exactly the same. If you are a WASP — white, Anglo-Saxon, Protestant — you may not get fair deals, because too many judges, prosecutors, attorneys are Jews. Do you think we are justified in thinking in this way?

What do Gentiles think about this?

There are two Jewish professors, one from Israel and another from Canada, who came to the conclusion that, in Canada today 15% of Canadians are anti-Jewish. But in America, the number is higher: 22% of white Americans are anti-Jewish. According to *The New York Times,* 32 -35% of African Americans are anti-Jewish. Now, why are they anti-Jewish? Jews would say because they are bigots or racists. I say to you that the anti-Jewish people I have met are mostly white, well-educated, middle-class and hard-working males. They have intellectual, educational, historical, financial, cultural and moral reasons for their belief. I found only a small group of people that you can call bigots, those who just hate Jews out of some instinct without logical explanation.

But my point is that the Jewish political elites have to bear responsibility for the cause of the anti-Jewish feeling, because they don't give fair access to the media for Gentiles and their point of view. Not so much in commercial networks, but public TV and radio stations. It's not the person who holds the microphone, but the people who are behind the curtain, editors, producers and directors. They are the ones who make the final decisions, how to edit a story or which part to censor, whether it should be aired or not, at what time of day it should air, and so on. They have the ultimate power. Today's anti-Semitism in the world is due to a lack of understanding about Jewish people who control the political culture of the western world; America, Canada, Germany and elsewhere. They are the ones who are responsible for the decline of western civilization, because of their control of the media. They want an exclusive right because through their religious books and indoctrination by rabbis, they consider themselves better than everybody else on the planet. When they are blamed, they say "We're not responsible. You must be an anti-Jew." And, their justification is always the "Holocaust." That's why I say the Holocaust story is benefitting mainly the Jews; and the "Holocaust" has become a new religion for Jews. Compared to European people, North Americans are naive because of their lack of history and national experience in dealing with the Jews. But they are not blind; they know about the problem. They just wouldn't say anything about it yet.

Today in our society there is a decline of public morality. We have the decline of law and order, a sky-rocketing crime rate, teenage pregnancy, one third of American children are born out of wedlock, child abuse, child pornography, children killing children, etc. It all means that those people who give us our perception of our culture via the media, namely Hollywood, are responsible. Culture is largely created by the media, including Hollywood movie productions and press, and those who are the writers, teachers, thinkers and philosophers. Look at the Berlin scenes during the Weimar Republic. There were homosexuals, lesbians, heroin addicts, live stage sex-shows of humans and animals, and child pornography, and it was called *Schmutz* (filth) City. Berlin was the worst pornographic capital in civilized Europe at that time. People are forgetting that! And, these cabarets and night club owners were Jews and the pornography industry was also run by Jews. So, Hitler began to focus on these public morals and on social issues, and ultimately he disliked those people who were breaking down German society and took action against them. Now, today, after over 50 years, the American and Canadian societies are experiencing a very similar social situation to the Weimar Republic before Hitler.

I remind you that 25% of the professors of philosophy in 1933 in Germany were Jewish. In America today it's the same. The reality is that nothing has changed. That's why it's very important to study the issues that had their origin in 1914, 1918, 1933 and 1945. Today, we live with the responsibility to research and find the true reasons for the tragedy of WW II, and to find the origins and eliminate the problems so that we can provide the next generations with at least as good a place as we inherited. If we don't think like that, society will suffer a terrible fate in the future.

If that is the case, why don't you talk to Jewish leaders regarding these matters. Or, are you an anti-Jewish person yourself?

No, I'm not anti-Jewish. I'm a militant pacifist. Being an ethnic German I understand their situation very well, so I would like to help them to resolve these problems in a democratic way. We need dialogue. I have a file cabinet full of correspondence with city mayors, government officials, political leaders, human rights commissioners, rabbis, Jewish leaders, making offers to meet and to discuss these differences I have outlined to you. I would love to talk to them, but they are not interested in having intellectual public intercourse or even just a private meeting. You know why? Because they are in power. Why discuss anything with a man without power like me. Not only that, after I contacted the Jewish community center here, I was threatened with phone-calls and harassed day and night by Jews calling me a "Nazi." The Jewish leadership knows the problems. The Jewish citizens are trapped. They are trapped by the system of the international Jewish operation and there is no way for them to get out of it.

I'm a militant defender of civil rights and human rights, and I'm the only person who can face a very unpleasant fact about history regarding the gas chambers of Auschwitz. There is a reaction to it among many Germans today and I'm presenting that German reaction. I have a good long record as a pacifist and I'm a good vehicle to connect Germans and Jews. However, when I raise my questions, I'm treated as a "freak" like you called me. If you want to know the future of North American society, I'll tell you something truthfully. If Jews don't change their attitude, if their behavior remains the same, if their method is going to be the same, the result will be more of the same.

But we must understand their history of persecution.
Persecution and anti-Semitism only develop if there is Semitic striving or aggression. Anti-Semitism is a reaction to something. Jews are not innocent victims. They always say that they have been the poor victims of Gentiles. But they brought retribution on to themselves and their own people by their own voracious and rapacious behavior, which was implanted by the preceeding parental generations. It's like "karma," and I believe in karma for Jews. When you read their Bible of Jewish law, the Talmud, it tells you that Jews are superior to the *goyim* (Gentiles), all the non-Jewish populations of the world. It says: "Jews can rob, cheat and torture Gentiles, and Jewish men can have vicious sex with Gentile women," just because they are superior and we Gentiles are inferior. If a thousand-year-old Jewish official statement says Gentiles are only created to look like humans so that they don't offend

the people they serve, what does that portend? If we live in the same society with this kind of people with this kind of concept in their minds, it's tailor-made ready to cause an inter-ethnic disaster, of course! It's obvious by that line of thinking that the world is automatically divided into two sides: masters and slaves — Jews as superior and Gentiles as inferior.

Jews are an egocentric group of people. They are Judeo-centric: they largely think of themselves that's all that matters to them. Only Jews think that Germany had a fixation with Jews. When Hitler defeated the Jews, that was it for him. He had millions of other tasks to be done for his own people. Jews are only important to Jews. They think the world is revolving around them, but the simple fact is that it doesn't. The great majority of Jews are the most brainwashed people on the earth, next to postwar Germans. What they need is psychiatrists and psychoanalysts, not historians. They are mentally the most complexed group of people and most Jews know this instinctively. That's why they can produce a man like Sigmund Freud, whose patients were mostly Jewish. What I want to say is that if we want to live in a better world, Jewish people have to re-examine their own behavior, not just accusing others constantly all the time. They also need to examine themselves and should begin to treat others equally, not look down upon them arrogantly.

Every group of people is egocentric, whether Americans, French or Catholics. Jewish egocentrism could have something to do with religious belief, perhaps?
Their heaven is earth — living today. That's why they want to have a luxurious life; owning the biggest Cadillacs, living in the nice houses and taking big gambles in business, for they want to

make a heaven "now" while they live. For them, heaven must always be in the present. They are not promised like Christians or East Indians: a life after death, another incarnation, another joy and another happiness. They don't think much of the future, how their children and grandchildren should live, and how to make a better world for them. They don't think of such things. Even in their biblical history, it shows it. Moses said to his followers, "I'm going to lead you to the promised land." While he was out on a mountain talking to God, what did the Jews do? As soon as he was out of sight, they got themselves a new god and danced around the golden calf. Moses came down and he got so angry that he took the tablets and smashed the golden calf, their new god, to the ground. They didn't wait for Moses to bring a new code of law. You don't need a new book to learn about the Jews. It's all there. Nothing has been changed since. They cannot think of the future; Jews want to have something "now." They want instant gratification of their every wish or desire. So, their mind is very different from ours.

The reason the history of Jewish people is one of turmoil, of rising, peaking, of repeated tragedy and falls, is that they are great tacticians, but very poor in "strategy." They are excellent in developing something, exploiting opportunity and tactically very clever, but when it comes to strategy, they are only concerned with themselves — me, me, me — I and myself. They don't have ears to listen, eyes to see, hearts to touch, fingers to feel, that other people's lives and destinies are affected negatively by their actions. Just look at their behavior towards the Palestinians in Israel, for example. And, each action will produce an opposing reaction. All in all, ultimately, we are all human. What separates us is "ideology," "teaching" and "thinking," which are based on religion and philosophy. These teachings for the past 4,000 years are largely why things keep happening to the Jews in Europe; like segregation, inquisition, expulsion, pogrom, persecution, massacre, murder, one after another; and these were committed by Spaniards, Russians, French, British, Portuguese, and finally by the Germans in what they like to call the "Holocaust." It must be examined how and why do these things happen and what did the Jews do wrong? Take the case of the Jews in Germany. They created the greatest Jewish power there in the early part of this century, but they couldn't maintain it. Why not? In the end they were cast out disastrously and dispersed all over the world!

So, in your view, what can be done?
Jews need a revolution in thinking among themselves. They need to clean up their own act. I associate with many Jewish intellectuals, historians, academics, authors, professors, and they are mostly brilliant people. They understand the problems very well. The Jews should listen to these Jews. I tell Jewish communities in Canada "Let's sit down at the same table and discuss the issues." But they are not willing to participate. They stubbornly refuse to bring up the issues. All they do is present what happened in the past — the "Holocaust." I say we need to re-examine it and re-evaluate it. Controlling the media, censoring the international news and blocking out the voices of revisionists are not the solution, and the Jewish leadership knows it. But my point is if it continues this way, the division between Jews and Gentiles will become deeper and deeper, and one day it will explode. I'm sure of that. This sort of frustration will be carried on to the next generations, and the children or grandchildren of Jews will become the next target. If Jews feel responsi-

ble for their next generations, they should do something about it today, before it becomes too late. If you want to know about Jewish religion and teaching, I would recommend you read a book called *Jewish History, Jewish Religion,* which was published in 1994, written by Israel Shahak, a Polish-born Israeli Jew and a long-time human rights activist. His criticism in the book is that contents of the Talmud and the talmudic literature are specifically anti-Christian and anti-Gentile. And he also warns, "Israel as a Jewish state constitutes a danger not only to itself and its inhabitants, but to all Jews and to all other peoples and states in the Middle East and beyond." When you read this book, you will understand what I'm telling you.

Since many Jews were involved in the Bolshevik Revolution, what do the Russians think of the Jews who still remain there today?

If you want to see the Jewish operation, we should look at the former Soviet Union, that was run by Jews for over 70 years. It's a good example and we should study the system. Do you think there is a cause without effect? Do you think Soviet Jewish commissars and Jewish Bolsheviks, KGB, NKBD and GPU could murder millions and millions of Russians of all ethnic groups, and not one day be taken to account for those mass murders by the relatives and descendants of these victims? Of course they will. Do you think the Russians would say simply it was a bad time in their history and simply forgive them? The Russian people will one day take exact punishment for what happened to them, and all intelligent Jewish people know it's coming. So, right now, every morning at 4 o'clock, a big jet packed full of Russian Jews leaves Moscow for Israel or the United States. The population of Jews in Russia

used to be reportedly 4 million, but hundreds of thousands of them have already left the country. So, I tell you one thing. If I were a Jew, I would get out of there immediately.

Now, I would like to know about Hitler's beliefs about religion. He was anti-Christian. He raised questions about the Christian religion for the first time since Martin Luther, the father of Protestantism. What did Hitler really plan for the new Germany and for the future of Europe?

The Christian religion is not natural to Europe. It's an alien religion and we Europeans have been rebelling against it since day one; it was forced upon us. Christianity has been desperately trying to make itself into a European religion. The Europeans were forced to become Christians by their rulers and to become Crusaders who went around killing non-Christian enemies in military expeditions with swords and armies. In other words, the Europeans had Christianity imposed on them and then tried to impose it on others. Jesus Christ was a foreigner to us and Christianity as such doesn't belong to European culture, and Adolf Hitler's movement was a rebellion against this alien concept of god. But you have to understand that Hitler was a politician, not a religious reformer. If you want to know what Hitler thought of Christianity, religion, race and culture, you should read a book entitled *Collective Speeches of Adolf Hitler,* written by Howard Fertig. It was used, believe it or not, as a textbook in unversities across the USA before the war. What he said about Christianity was: "Leave the people alone. The German people don't need another religious war between the Catholics and the Protestants, Christians and non-Christians. We have shed enough blood in religious strife, we don't need another war based on religion." According to *The Manchester Guardian* report on June 7, 1937, he said "God didn't divide us, only human beings did." He also said "... and the world will know I was right." What he said is significant to me. He said that National Socialists in Germany will dry up the source of Christianity at "its roots," and we will bring all the people of Germany together and we will celebrate the Aryan race through our movement. He claimed the religion of Europe is "race." The purity of race, blood and soul in German soil!

Hitler was a politician and he knew very well that many European problems originated in this religion. So, he knew that a religious revolution must come from the political arena. He knew all these things, because he was a powerful political leader who understood the psychology of the masses, and he knew how to use people for change. He knew the truth of the role of religion in Germany and that it was very much a part of the political and geographical nature of German culture, and that their root is linked to their own myths, sagas, legends and gods of their own land, not to the Man from Israel. In spite of this, Hitler reached an agreement with the official churches called the "Concordat." Germany before Hitler was the only state which had imposed a church tax that had made the church immensely wealthy, and it had become corrupt and its spiritual values had deteriorated. I'll give you another example. When he made the "Concordat" arrangement with the Vatican, he stated, "If the church sticks only to what the church is supposed to do, which means looking after the soul needs of people, comforting the distressed, registering and recording birth, marriage and death, then I will protect the church." He protested against the politicization and corruption of the organized churches of

Christianity, that's why during the war many priests turned against his movement.

How do Germans think of Christianity today?
As to Christianity, German churches have been losing their memberships at an alarming rate for the past 10 years, and in East Germany, church attendance is far down and many churches are empty. Seminaries cannot get priests so they have to bring them in from other Eastern European countries like Poland because they cannot get German men to become priests. In Canada, in the province of Quebec, for example, every monastery you name is empty. People practice birth control even though the church prohibits it. The Christian church is irrelevant like the steam locomotive and it will be gone in another generation.

I disagree. History shows that in times of peace people are secular, but when there are social crises or decline of morale that threaten the course of western civilization, people feel insecure and go back to the church. It has been this way for the past 2,000 years. You cannot take Christianity away from Christians. Your thinking is too far out, Mr. Zündel.
Well, I can argue with you. First, Christianity and church-goers are two separate things, and second, religiosity doesn't have to be Christianity. In fact, there was spirituality and religion in Europe long before Christianity was ever known. Many non-Christian people of the world are far more spiritual than Christians have ever been. In the western world what you are saying is absolutely correct. During the Weimar Republic, in fact, many German people went back to the church. In the past half a century alone, we have experienced times of super-radicalism, a decline of mo-

rality, and then a rise of fundamentalism again. There is always a segment of these types of people in western society, and who are those people? They are looking for a simple answer. When I talk to Christians I find it very frustrating. In a way I feel it's awesome that these people have such terrific faith in what's spelled out by the words of the Bible. What they need is self-drive and self-reliance and that can be found within. We don't need "the imported Jewish saviour" as a role model from Jerusalem for that. We can find simple answers within ourselves in our own minds. The Europeans had thriving religions and great civilizations since the times of Greece and Rome, long before Christianity. Who deprived us of it?

Christianity is a copycat of Judaism. The tendency of Christianity was Jewish and modern Christianity does not tire of telling us of its Jewish roots from the Pope on down. And we can prove it in the way people celebrate Chanukah and many other rituals. In fact, the day of Christmas, Christ's alleged birthday — so a learned rabbi wrote, is a Jewish holiday because Jesus Christ himself was a Jew. If we want to have a religious renaissance in the western world, we have to overcome the influence of this spiritual and mental occupation force called "Christianity". It's, in fact, becoming a mental disease and we have to sweep it out, and only an organized political culture-body can get rid of it by replacing it and going back to our roots. Can we find our way back to our own spirituality by exploring our inner selves? What do we need? Right now we don't have an answer nor a new religion for the western world — not yet! We have all kinds of cults all over the world and you know why? Because people are searching. Right now, millions of people who formerly adhered to Christianity

are looking for an alternative, the old Indo-Germanic religion or something, almost similar to Shintoism, the philosophy of ancestry worship and reincarnation, the pre-Christian European idea of soul and spirit.

It may take another 2,000 years...
You are still a prisoner of the past. We know today, for instance, that a program called "miniaturization" was introduced at NASA. Within five years a big cassette became a mini cassette, and now we have a micro cassette. Today, we no longer even work with cassettes because computerized memories store millions of things. This technological revolution took place in less than 20 years. So, the Bible had to be printed on paper and carried around, but now what people do is just talk in front of a microphone and that can reach around the world instantly. In my talk show, which I do 8 times a week, people pick up my voice and make copies of my message and pass it on to other people. It's fantastic! So, it means the change will come much sooner than you think. The thing that used to take 2,000 years can today be done within one, two or three generations. And, perhaps, by the next century Christianity will be irrelevant and we may find a new expression of our spirituality.

Why do you think Hitler allied with Japan? Japan is a nation of one religion, one race, one ruler, one language, one culture, and a homogeneous state. Do you think Hitler favored it because of that?
That's correct. Hitler referred to Japan as "the Prussia of the east" and the Japanese were a nation of Aryans in Asia. His generals first recommended that he should ally Germany with China, but he refused because at that time China

was militarily inferior and Japan was not. To me, Japan is a unique but boring nation. I'll tell you positive things. Japan is very fortunate because of what you just said — it's a homogeneous nation, but unfortunate because it doesn't have to struggle against outsiders and strive to defend itself. In fact, Japan today is more vulnerable than Germany, because Japanese people have not had enough historical experience dealing with the western world and do not understand the political and economic international structure and its complications. Japan also has no inkling of the power of secret societies and the Jews in the west.

As a result of WW II, the Allies defeated Germany and Japan militarily, but geographically, politically and economically, it changed very little. Both Germans and Japanese rose from the ashes, went through generations of hard work, strong discipline, dedication, self-reliance and self-control that resulted in having powerful economies in the postwar world. It's always easier to build from the ashes than to repair something. On the other hand, the Allied nations won the war only militarily, but they couldn't stand their economic competition. So, Germany and Japan are benefitting physically and economically from their military disaster. But here comes the Jewish problem: the Jews defeated the ideology of National Socialism, but they exported many of its adherents across the world, the so-called diaspora, to the United States in particular.

Now, I'll tell you something that will blow your mind. To tell the truth, economically and culturally, Japan is still relatively untouched by Jews. So, Jews, with their worldwide financial, political and intelligence networks, will dominate them. Unless the Japanese realize it and do something about it, sooner or later, in the end, Jews will destroy Japan. I'm sure of that, and we will

live to see it. Just look at Sony in Hollywood which lost over 80 million dollars because they didn't understand how Jews operate business without scruple. The Japanese don't understand the Jewish mind and I'm afraid Jews will win over Japan. Japan is strong in its economy, but vulnerable because of its insular mentality. They have ignored Jewish power and its influence in America and the West, and don't realize that America and the Western world are really occupied territories, like Palestine and the Gaza Strip. The Japanese are about to learn it at their peril.

What do you think of Jewish-Americans today? I find that the prominent American-Jews are mostly of German background and their influence on American society is enormous. They are successful and leading citizens in America; and intermarriage is popular, don't you think?

In America, one of the most dangerous things for the Jews is the success of Jewish Americans because Jews have been intermarrying with Gentiles at an alarming rate. For most American Jews, second marriages are almost always outside their own ethnic groups. So, Jews as a people or a "race" are beginning to disappear and Jews as a religious-ethnic group are evolving more and more into a ruling class. They are economically, politically, culturally and intellectually so successful that they've become a part of the leading hierachy. They are frequently absorbed by the overall population. You know what this means? It means that the American elite is partly becoming "Judaised." The concept used to be to remain exclusively Jewish, but now there's horizontal expansion in their thinking: Jewish thinking has permeated American society. Jews are becoming the victims of their own policies and their own success. In the age of multi-media, it has penetrated the diaspora without anyone realizing it. This phenomenon could be characterized as similar to what happened to the Romans. The Roman Empire absorbed too many alien ideas and concepts, too many alien populations, too much of everything and collapsed in the end. This is why Werner Sombert, an American economist, was quoted as saying that Americanism is becoming the distilled essence of Judaism. In *The New Yorker* magazine, an article called it the "Yiddishization of American culture." It talks about *schmuck, schlock* etc., and the Yiddishization of American humor.

Most Gentiles in North America today no longer think of a concept like that. They don't think of ethnicity and culture or history. They are apathetic about what is going on in today's world. They are already being "intellectually disarmed" because they have received a "liberal" education at college, which is an indoctrination of largely Jewish concepts of intellectualism; they have been educated by the information which was "filtered" through Jewish thinking and Jewish minds. The Jewish leadership can claim that they have succeeded, as they have said in their own books, beyond their wildest dreams that America is really the new Jerusalem. They only need the State of Israel for the moment as insurance. For example, when Jews commit economic crimes in Europe or America, they flee to Israel; it's like a safe haven for them.

Looking at the whole picture, as the consequence of Hitler's war, it seems that the Holocaust resulted in giving moral advantage to Jewish intellectuals, do you think?

Yes. But Jewish success is only temporary, and not forever. Every time a child is born, a new universe is born. This human being, regardless of race or ethnic background, has a chance to change the world. How do we know, she or he could not one day be a great inventor, a great philosopher or a military leader, another Mozart, Beethoven or Gandhi? Otherwise, what is life for? There is always hope of renewal. We, who are living, have to make sure that all people have access to the means of communication in this great exchange of ideas, opinions and concepts that I call "renewal and regeneration." This is why I'm against all dictatorships. Although I admire Hitler because he did many good things for German people, he had negative aspects such as controlling the media and the incarceration of people merely for dissident ideas, and he also abused his power.

All I'm saying to you is that we have to purify ourselves in order to improve some of our old ideas and concepts, and make sure that we do not repeat the mistakes of the past. That's why I recommend that people should research history freely and thoroughly, re-examine, re-evaluate, reassess and reformulate the historical materials we have found in the archives. Today, there are war archives coming out of Russia endlessly and very soon we will find out more of the truth. If their materials and ours in the western world are different, how did that happen? What are the reasons for the discrepancy? We should question and find that out. Overall, the most twisted part of the history of the 20th century is the long era of the Cold War. Because of that, we didn't have any access to the information of WW II from the former communist countries. And, now we are learning the truth of "the war" some 50 years later. So, in the western world, sooner or later, we will need to amend the school textbooks.

A nation that is ruled without ethics and morals can no longer survive. Look at the USA that has become a moral quagmire. It has become a sewer, exactly because it no longer has any national honor, no national morale, no national pride, no national identity and no national confidence. And, today the media pundits in America are moralizing others without having their own morality. They go around moralizing about the guilt of the Germans for Auschwitz and Japanese for the infamy of December 8, 1945. I mean this is a sort of substituting expediency in place of morality. Nations without morality will not endure very long. If you allow what has taken place in Western societies, which has corrupted everything with its Jewish concept of situational ethics, very soon you are going to see the fatal disintegration and decadence of American society.

Regarding genocide and human destruction, we cannot do much about what happened in the past, but we can do something for the future. My question is, "will it happen again?"
You mean to ask can the Holocaust happen again? Meaning, will certain ethnic groups be singled out for persecution and possibly extermination? The answer for that is absolutely "yes." What the Americans did in the 1800s to Native Americans! They nearly succeeded. In this century alone how many genocides have we recorded: Turks slaughtered millions of Armenians, the alleged "Rape of Nanking" by Japanese, there is Stalin's genocide of 40 million Russians, the Killing Fields of Pol Pat in Cambodia. And more recently, "ethnic cleansing" in Bosnia-Herzegovina, Rwanda and Burundi. The world has been doing nothing to stop these holocausts! So, the answer is already there. It's not only possible, it's happening right now. Even with all the propa-

ganda Holocaust information, the world has not been changed much, really.

As far as the Jews are concerned, I don't see any immediate attack from anywhere against them right now. They, however, are constantly attacking Palestinians, stealing their land and dominating them. They disenfranchise them, they break their bones, they paralyze them with police forces and tear gas, they beat them up, they exile them and bulldoze their houses. Who is attacking Jews? Only Palestinian teenagers with their *Infatada,* and they have a hard time defending themselves and don't get meaningful help from Americans or from anywhere else. If Jews are getting attacked today it is as a reaction because they themselves are very aggressive and dominating. They should examine their own attitudes and activities, their style of behavior and their methods of operation, and, if they continue what they are doing, there will be a backlash against the Jews like karma. One day they will reap a holocaust, for god or nature does not rescind his eternal laws for the Jews.

How do you analyze the result of the 1994 mid-term election in the USA, in which the Republican Party won by a landslide?
The American people are finally thinking. As far as I'm concerned, the Republican Party is not part of the solution but is still part of the problem for the American people, although the majority of them voted for a Republican Congress. Both Republicans and Democrats are responsible for what is happening in the USA today and what has befallen America over the last 100 years. Morally, economically, militarily, politically, both parties are to be blamed equally. This sort of election result is a sign of political immaturity. If Americans want to say something and change the sys-

tem, they have to find salvation outside the circles of their own power structure of those who created these problems in the first place. That was the first sign that the "two-political-party" system is the problem. I think many Americans were disappointed with Ross Perot, an independent presidential candidate in 1992. It is clear that there has been a direct backlash against the Clinton Administration. He promised each group of people in the so-called "Rainbow Coalition" the same portion of pie before he was elected, but instead, he appointed too many Jewish politicians in his top cabinet: over 50% of his appointments are Jewish. The US Jewish population is only 5% and this is far out of proportion, and most mainstream Americans know it. The white majority was reduced in representation in his administration to the influence and status of a minority population. I think this is an insult to the Gentile majority and the other minority groups. Americans would never say it publicly and they are frustrated. So, the result of the last election was mostly a protest against the Clinton government and his pro-Jewish policy.

Look at the system of communist Russia which was tightly controlled for the most part of this century, and yet it changed. As Abraham Lincoln said, "You can fool some of the people some of the time, but you cannot fool all of the people all of the time." It was 150 years ago when he said that. It's absolutely true. One thing that I was not clear in explaining, is that we have a segment of our political culture that belongs to secret societies, and these secret societies in the USA are very entrenched and amazingly powerful. And I'm against secret societies of any kind.

So, Americans may experience their own revolution, either social or political, like Russians and Germans did?

Sure, absolutely! But it will be in a different form, of course, because the number of minorities are so diverse in America today compared to Nazi Germany when Jews were the only minority.

I like American people. I like their traditions of self-reliance and free enterprise. They're hardworking, no nonsense, simple-minded and uncomplicated thinkers. For me, they are a wonder and I have a lot of respect for them. I admire their patience and I am surprised they allow themselves to be cheated, conned, manipulated and taken advantage of by others. This honest nation has been screwed and tattooed by the most inferior scum called "politicians." When the American people see that the Republican landslide is not going to change anything substantially, America is either going to have a revolution with guns, or possibly they will turn back to the old political culture and will renew themselves the only way they can, under the American system of throwing everybody out. We should not forget that America has a history of governmental change by revolution — by the people and for the people. This is a wonderful and a dangerous mixture, you see. If the government doesn't respond to the needs of the people, the people will say they are going to take over America because of the oppressive regime. If they get disappointed by the Republicans, within years, we are going to see either a powerful ground swell evolution, which will lead to electoral revolution or political revolution, whatever. If it doesn't go this way, I believe America is going to break up into a state of "war lord run areas" like Latin America financed by drug money, or like the broken-up

Soviet Union. This could easily happen on the soil of the United States of America.

So, is this the reason why Americans cannot give up the guns?

Yes, this is one of the reasons that Americans will not give up their guns and why the citizens of the United States of America are still arming themselves, because they no longer trust their own government! ❖

(On May 7th 1995, Mr. Zündel's residence was set afire by an arsonist and partially destroyed. Ten days later, he received a unabomber parcel. Mr. Zündel survived both incidents. The two incidents are still under investigation.)

"If you want to understand Jews,
you have to study Gentiles."

SEYMOUR MARTIN LIPSET

American Jew; author of *The Jews and The New American Scene, The Power of Jewish Education,* and numerous books on history; Hazel Professor of Public Policy Institute at George Mason University; Senior Fellow Hoover Institution at Stanford University. Born in 1922 in New York City, lives in Virginia, USA.

You are one of the many leading Jewish intellectuals in America today. The answers I would like to get from you, Professor Lipset, are about Jewish experience before and after the Holocaust. Some of my questions may be considered taboo, perhaps because of the "don't ask, don't tell" policy between Jews and Gentiles. But after 6 million Jews perished in the Holocaust, 50 years later today, social conflicts between Jews and non-Jews still exist. My wish is to bring about the mutual understanding between two groups of people, please do not take offense at my words.

What is the secret of Jewish survival? For the past 2,000 years this people has existed without their own land, without a shared national experience and government of their own, and without a military or army of their own?
Well, on one hand, this is a mystery, something that nobody can completely understand. But another point of view is simply that Judaism is a religion. The secret of Jewish survival is Jewish religion. Christianity, Islam, Buddhism and all other religions survive because people believe in God, rituals and so forth. Jews have survived as a religious community, not as a national entity or ethnic community. They have been able to stay together and remain religious in spite of many thousands of years of persecution. When people stopped practicing Judaism, they stopped being Jewish. In addition, persecutions by the Christians made Jews stick together to defend themselves from outside pressures. Without persecutions, there would be fewer, maybe no Jews. In America today that is a problem. In China, for example, there was quite a large Jewish community once, but Chinese people didn't persecute Jews so they assimilated.

My understanding of Jewish survival is the education derived from Jewish books, primarily the "Torah" and "Talmud" — teaching and learning of these books. That is also the reason that Jews kept their tradition going, isn't it?
That's right. Traditionally and historically, every Jewish man was expected to study the Bible, Talmud and Torah, and many of them did. The Jews were the first literate people in Europe because they had to read, otherwise they couldn't be Jewish. This kept the Jewish tradition going. Jewish women used to work while men studied the Books. In Medieval Europe, in a Catholic society, Jews were not allowed to own land; only Christians could, so many Jews became traders. Also, the Catholic church ruled that the Christian Bible prohibited charging interest on money, which meant Christians couldn't become bankers or money lenders. Jews couldn't be landowners but someone had to be lenders, so Jews moved into money lending, trading and commerce. In order to pursue these businesses, they had to live in urban areas, cities and towns. They were pushed into urban ghettos and lived with walls surrounding them. They also became artisans.

Jews were better treated in the medieval Muslim world than in the Christian world. In Islamic Spain, for example, there was a large Jewish community. Many Jews were fairly well educated and held important high ranking positions such as doctors, philosophers and governmental officers. But they were thrown out in 1492, the year Columbus discovered America, and after the Christians took over the entire Iberian peninsula. They fled to Turkey and Greece and other Islamic countries.

Jewish people have had different attitudes about money. Money became an important survival tool for Jews — during the Holocaust, for example, many wealthy Jews survived and many poor Jews died. Jews studied money seriously and learned about its value from the time they were children at home. Isn't that true?

They had to earn a living in a limited number of occupations and lending money, which the Christian authorities wanted them to do, was an urban cultural activity for Jews. But if you read the Jewish Books, there is very little about money and trading. The Talmud is a religious document dealing mostly with God and religious laws, analyzing the 626 laws which Jews have to obey. The Talmud contains interpretation and discussion of the meaning of those laws by various rabbis.

Did the Jews really kill Jesus Christ?

Well, first of all, historically we don't know what really happened to Jesus. What seems to have occurred is that Jesus opposed the Roman occupiers of Palestine and their Jewish collaborators, the corrupt ruling elite and high priests. Jesus opposed them. The New Testament (the Christian Bible) was written long after Jesus died by four different writers — Matthew, John, Luke and Mark — and they were all Jews. Each man wrote his own interpretation of the story of Jesus. They couldn't have said their own people killed Jesus. But some Jews were involved in the killing and one of the four writers was anti-Jewish. Many centuries later as the Christian religion became a powerful institution, some people and church leaders interpreted the story in an anti-Semitic fashion. But the New Testament doesn't say that Jesus was killed by Jews.

Jesus never traveled to Rome, so the story of Jesus was spread outside Israel by word of mouth by Jews around the Mediterranean area, and people never stopped talking about him how he lived and died. The Jews were the ones who needed the Messiah because they had lost their land and lived miserably as slaves. So, the idea of the coming of the Messiah was a Jewish desire, not a Gentile one. It could have been implanted to Gentiles by the Jewish diaspora, I suppose? Non-Jews could have lived without having the Messiah. What were the origins of the Messiah and religious conflict between Jews and Christians? And, without the Jews the course of western civilization could have been different. How do you comment on that?

The notion of Messiah goes back long before Jesus to times when the Jews were still ruling Israel, not after they lost their land and began suffering. It's in the original religious teachings that Jews believed, that the end will come, everything will be finished and everybody will die. The Messiah will appear and everybody will be resurrected, all peoples will follow him, and that will be the end of time. This idea developed while the Jews were living in Israel. But when the Jews were in exile they wanted the Messiah to come to rescue them. Meanwhile, many false Messiahs arose, many men claimed to be the Messiah. When the story of Jesus as Messiah emerged, his Jewish followers — they were all originally Jewish and believed all Jews would understand him as Messiah and welcome him as a new Lord— like Paul (originally Saul) preached to their fellow Jews that Jesus was the long awaited Messiah. But most Jews refused to believe him, so Paul got fed up with them. He began converting non-Jews to become followers of Jesus and to accept him as Messiah. That was the birth of Christianity.

In much of the Roman Empire there was a sort of missionary competition between Judaism and Christianity to convert the pagans. Judaism is no longer a converting religion, but up to the 3rd century common era, it was. Jews lived in most of the Roman cities and supplied the first converts to the new religion, but most people were pagans. Then, the idea of one God began to appeal to many people intellectually. Emperor Constantine, who was the first Christian emperor, ordered that Gentiles who converted to Judaism must be killed. He said that Jews could practice Judaism as they wished, but must not convert others. The religion became a political issue. As a result, conversion to Judaism and competition between Christians and Jews stopped. The rabbis ruled that it was illegal to convert Gentiles. This was the beginning of the separation of Jews and Christians.

Until around the 10th century, at the end of the first millennium, Jews lived by themselves and Christians accepted Jews as a different religious group; the people of the Bible. The Jewish Bible was accepted as a Holy Book and Christians believed that Jews were studying the Bible. Then, around the year 1100, some of the Christian friars discovered that orthodox Jews were not studying the Bible; they were pouring over the Talmud. The Talmud, as I explained earlier, contains interpretations of the Bible and debates by rabbis. The monks said the interpretations were fallacious; they said the Talmud was not the Bible and that it was an heretical work. They then began persecuting the Jews because they were heretics. Jews could not understand why Christians were reacting in this way.

The Crusades also stimulated anti-Semitism. When Christian armies mobilized to regain Palestine from the Muslims, on their way to the Holy Land, they killed Jews and destroyed their communities all around the Mediterranean areas, so many western Jews moved to Eastern Europe and Germany, and then formed the base for what would become the large population of Jews in Poland and western Russia.

Now, a question about the Talmud. Some extremists who studied its contents say that it says, "Jews are superior to Gentiles, that they can rob and cheat Gentiles, and Jewish men can have vicious sex with Gentile women." I thought these phrases were anti-Semitic propaganda fabricated by Nazi Germans during the Nazi revolution to provoke anti-Jewish fervor in German society. The contents could be misunderstood by Gentiles, or does it really say that?

No, it doesn't say such things. People made up such anti-Semitic phrases to attack Jews. The Talmud was written not about the Gentiles; it mainly refers to the debates of rabbis about Jewish laws and the Bible. There are English versions of the Talmud and anyone can read them.

Another thing is about the number "six." The Bible says "The world was created in six days," six pointed the Star of David, the Six-Day War, six million Jews were murdered in the Holocaust, and today's Jewish population in the USA is six million. Does the number six has a special meaning to Jews?

No, the number six has nothing to do with Jews. It's a satanic number. You have a good point, but I've never heard about such a thing before.

Jewish people developed their "survival philosophy" based on their experiences and it de-

pended on which country they lived in, didn't it?

Yes, they had to vary. Jewish experience in Constantinople, for example, was very different from the Jewish life in Berlin, London, Paris, or Eastern Europe. Heinrich Heine, a German poet/writer, a Jew who converted to Christianity, once said "If you want to understand Jews in various countries, how Jews vary from country to country, you have to study the Gentiles." He meant that the Jews adapted to the dominant Gentile pattern, e.g., English Jews are like English Christians, American Jews are like American Christians. So, there is not one type of Jews. They have common elements because they all study the Talmud and the Torah (the Bible), and are always a minority everywhere. They differ, for example, in their organizational structures. In America, most of the Protestant sects are congregational, self-governing, not subject to a hierarchy. American Jews are also congregational, in the same way as American Protestants. Catholics, Anglicans and Lutherans have hierarchical structures, the Jews in countries in which they dominate have chief rabbis; where Christians are orthodox, Jews are too.

In America today, as I wrote in my book (with co-author Earl Raab), *The Jews and the New American Scene,* there are different Jewish denominations: traditional Orthodox and modern Orthodox), Conservatives, Reform, and Reconstructionists. But each group is different in thinking and culture. Half of American Jews don't fit into any of these categories; most of them are secular.

In any case, Jews need Gentiles, particularly Christians, to survive, I think.

Well, I don't know, it's difficult to say. Take the case of Israel. Jews now have their own country. Like any other country, if the country survives,

the inhabitants, the culture, the religion survive. Your question is, can you conceive of Jews without Gentiles, but what does it mean? In what sense would there be Jews without Gentiles?

For example, we Gentiles can live without Jews...

Yes, that's true. But Jews can live without the Gentiles, too, as in Israel.

Yes, today, after the Holocaust. But in the past 1900 years this was not the case. This is what I want to point out — that Jews have no national unity of their own historically.

Yes, Jews were a religious group, much like any other religious minority, much like Muslims living in America or France.

Traditionally, I find Jews are not patriotic people: they don't want to go to fight in wars, which is understandable because of the oppression and rejection they experienced in the countries where they lived.

If you are rejected by the country in which you live and citizenship is denied, you cannot love the country. But the question for most of western history was not whether Jews would fight, join the army, but rather whether they were allowed to fight or not. They could not do so until recently in most of Europe. In America, Jews took part in the revolution and had high ranking officers in the Civil War; there were Jewish generals and many commanders. In Europe, after the French Revolution and Napoleon's liberation of the Jews, they were accepted by each government and society. Many Jews have participated in wars and revolutions. In Russia, Jews were persecuted until the end of the Tsar's regime, but Jews were allowed to become soldiers and were conscripted.

The Russian government tried to make Jewish conscripts give up Judaism and to force them to serve in the army for 25 years. So, many Russian Jews left for America at the turn of the century to avoid conscription. In Germany, many Jews were assimilated and fought in WW I. It was a shock for Jewish war veterans when the Nazis rejected and expelled them.

But some people say that the liberation of Jews led them to have civil rights and they got social equality with the Germans. But they were still Jewish mentally, and that was not good enough to be a German citizen in Germany. How do you respond to that?

I would say such comments are anti-Semitic, because they aren't true. In Germany before Hitler, there was a great deal of intermarriage between Jews and Gentiles. Berlin had a large community who came from mixed families, half-blooded Jews; others had Jewish grandparents and great-grandparents. Tens of thousands of Jews married German Gentiles, and they were accepted. During the Nazi time, Nazis treated Jews badly all over Europe; in Poland, Russia and other eastern countries, but they were somewhat less vicious to German Jews. Before Hitler, the upper class nobility who didn't have much money would sometimes take Jewish wives. So, quite a few aristocratic German families have Jewish ancestry.

Without patriotism, how can people go to fight in a war? Do Jews fight for their fatherland?

In America during the Civil War, as I noted earlier, there were many Jewish soldiers and some Jewish generals; the record indicates they were very good fighters. My father was in the American Army during WW I and there were plenty of other Jewish soldiers in the army. American Jews have had equal rights like anybody else and could be very patriotic. As a result, American Jews were different from those in Europe. They have been patriotic and expressed love of America. In most countries in Europe, Jews couldn't be citizens, so they didn't want to go to fight. If you are not a citizen you can't be patriotic. In the countries in which Jews were denied their rights, they could not be good soldiers.

About question of intellectualism. I find Jews are different from non-Jews in so many issues: religion, philosophy, history, politics, cultural experience, mentality and thinking, due to their suffering over the centuries. I think, psychologically, the development of human intelligence is different among these two groups. And, usually, Jewish intellectuals are more dominant than the Gentiles in American society today. I think Jewish intellectuals and non-Jewish intellectuals should be differentiated; it cannot be the same. How do you comment on that?

Jewish intellectualism is derivative from the emphasis on learning the Bible and religious study. Religious Jews gave prestige to scholars and rabbis, to Talmud interpreters. They emphasized religious learning. But, as the western world opened up for Jews, they became liberated intellectually and non-religious. Their emphasis on learning changed. They began to stress secular learning, higher education in general. As I said, Jews were the first literate people in Europe who could read and write. The Jewish men all went to religious school and the emphasis in learning continued even after they became secular, and were no longer religious. The proportion of Jews in secular higher education is much higher than among non-Jews. Today in America, for example, close to 90% of Jews go on to higher education, college and university, which is the highest proportion of any ethnic group. So, Jewish intellectualism in this country is a natural thing .

Those who go to university and study literature or sociology, whether Gentiles or Jews, will absorb the tradition of the national experience of the country in which they live. But Jewish intellectuals will vary according to background. Many Jews have written about the Jewish experience, much as African Americans do about theirs. There are quite different literatures within America, which flow from various streams; regional, religious or ethnic experiences. Canadian Jews write about their life in Canada, which is different than in America. Gentile Christians also differ among themselves; religiously they are Protestants, Catholics; regionally they are northerners or southerners. As a result, their views are different from one another.

But Christian Gentiles don't often think much of the Jewish experience, Jewish thinking or the Jewish mind, and most of them don't read books about Jewish themes.

It depends on what subject is being discussed. They may understand the Jewish point of view on the Holocaust. Take a look at what has happened to the Holocaust Museum in Washington, D.C., for example. When Jews built it, they expected to have 500,000 visitors each year. They are getting 2 to 3 million each year, and most of them are non-Jews. Jews never expected this. I would say Gentiles are interested in learning about Jews and their experience.

But Jewish survival and Gentile survival are different.

Yes, the Christian majority doesn't need to worry about survival as Jews do. The majority can live without thinking of a concept like survival. Given their past experiences, Jews think about all sorts of possibilities, Jews have reacted strongly to "ethnic cleansing" in former Yugoslavia. They sense this could happen to them.

What did Jews learn from the Holocaust?

The Holocaust and the creation of Israel interlink: Without the Holocaust there would probably be no state of Israel. The Zionist movement emerged in the late 19th and early 20th centuries, but most Jews were not Zionists. The Nazi Holocaust precipitated the creation of the state of Israel. Although western Jews, particularly American, British, Canadian, French and Latin American, those who have had freedom to do whatever they want to do, have refused to emigrate to Israel. However, Israel is still a haven for them. The Holocaust intensified their Jewish identity and led many Jews to believe that they cannot trust Gentiles. Many, perhaps, most western Jews now see the Jewish state as a safety valve in case mass anti-Semitism arises again. They remember that Jews once did well in Spain, Poland, Germany, yet they were killed or expelled. The Holocaust reminds them that no matter how much status or influence they achieve, there is always danger for Jews. No matter how free a country is, social crises re-occur, economic depressions return, and anti-Semitic beliefs have not totally disappeared. Given Jewish history, Jews feel they cannot trust the Gentiles. You have to watch yourself. That was what Jews have learned from the Holocaust. It's necessary for Jews to remain vigilant, to be organized in self-defense organizations like the Anti-Defamation League. They keep their eyes on anti-Semitic groups who propagandize against Jews. There are Jewish Community Relation Councils in every American city.

Today, 50 years after the Holocaust and the rebirth of Israel, such concerns have declined among younger Jews, because for them Israel has existed since they were born. It's not the miraculously reborn nation for young Jews that it has been for their parents and grandparents. The Holocaust is history; an old story. For most young Jews the experience of the Holocaust has declined in its importance. They see America as a different kind of society than old Europe; it has many minorities, particularly African Americans, Latinos and Asians. Jews are no longer even counted as a minority. Jews are never mentioned when minorities are discussed. Socially, they used to be outcasts, but no longer.

In Germany today, there's the law about "Holocaust denial": anyone who denies the Holocaust could go to jail. But not in America. We know why, but it confuses new generations — one nation is allowed to say but another is not allowed to say, yet we're talking about the same events, right? It should be controlled, otherwise it doesn't work, does it?
America's position is very simple. We have the Bill of Rights. You cannot legally prevent people from saying whatever they want, no matter how abhorrent. In Germany, Canada, Britain, they don't have a Bill of Rights. In Canada people go to jail if they deny the Holocaust. In Germany, there are laws outlawing anti-Semitic racist propaganda. But in America we cannot do this because the Constitution forbids restrictions on free expression.

Does this mean that Germany and Canada have no freedom of speech?
Well, freedom is somewhat more limited in those countries. We have different legal systems. We cannot do anything about German behavior and the Germans cannot do anything about American behavior. Holocaust denial bothers Germans because it implies anti-Semitism, approval of Nazism. Anti-Semitic materials are distributed in Germany, which were published in the USA and originally produced in America. But the United States has had a Bill of Rights since the beginning of its system. It's unconstitutional to infringe on freedom of speech.

Despite intermarriage between Jews and Gentiles, in many cases the Jewish tradition continues, even in America. I wonder, why is that?
Yes, but most Jews who have become assimilated now accept intermarriage. There are millions of Jews by ancestry, who are no longer practicing Jews but still feel Jewish ethnically and culturally. There is little pressure not to marry non-Jews today in America: most Jews marry non-Jews. Americans accept the Jews socially and culturally, but the Jewish community worries that intermarried families will give up Judaism. If a family of Jews doesn't maintain Jewish traditions, doesn't raise their children as Jews to still think of themselves as Jews, the children will be even more likely to marry a non-Jew.

Now, there is a new phenomenon today in America. When you go to synagogue you see Black or Asian kids, too. They are half blooded Jewish children and some have parents who were converted to Judaism. When Chinese marry Jews, their children retain Asian characteristics.

Today, the Jewish influence in American society is big in every arena; politics, media, culture, entertainment, and Jews are a leading group of American citizens. As far as the future is concerned, what kind of society will

American Jews lead for us? Idealistically, what kind of nation can American Jews provide us?
Well, first of all, I think that Jewish influence in culture has peaked; more than a decade ago a very large portion of American novelists were Jewish. Many Jewish scientists have contributed to American prestige by winning Nobel Prizes. But the highest point of Jewish intellectual influence in America is over and the proportion of academics who are Jewish has fallen. As I noted, there has been a decline of Jewish influence in literature. The novelists who were active during the 1960s were largely from the second generation of Jewish immigrants who came to America. They were involved in activities like the anti-Vietnam war movement. The next generations of Jews are less intellectual. Today's young American Jews are well assimilated and more interested in politics than culture. They are different than their parents. Many of them were still liberals and leftists in politics. Young Jews are less interested in business, and Jewish fund raising agencies are worried that Jewish big money contributors are declining, because Jewish youth who have graduated from the best colleges and universities are less involved than their parents in community activities. Regarding Jewish influence in the media, it's hard to tell what the direction is; Jews are still very important in TV and motion pictures and the elite press considerably. But I think this influence will go down as well.

Most Jews are still politically on the left and they are liberal Democrats. Today, the country is dominated by Republicans and religious Protestants. There are some important Jewish Republicans but basically when Republicans are in power, which also means the conservatives, Jewish influence is reduced. There were about 40 Jews in the Congress before 1994, but now there

are only 27. The politically powerful Christian Coalition is more important than ever. Religion in politics, the Christian Coalition, has become powerful and Jews are worried about this fact. They prefer a secular nation in which the state is not involved with any religion. But this Christian Coalition is growing.

I should note that orthodox Jews and politically conservative Jews welcome the growing influence of the Christian Coalition. They also prefer a more religious moralistic nation, one that is concerned about family values. To illustrate the complicity of America, there are Jews who are also active in the Christian Coalition. And though only a minority of Jews, less than 20% are Republican conservatives, a very much larger proportion of editors and writers for conservative publications or scholars in conservative think tanks are Jewish.

(Second Interview)
In the last interview, you said anyone can read the Talmud in English, so I've read some parts of it. In the contents I found words like "A grown-up man having intercourse with 3-year old girl; intercourse with beasts, animals, dogs and relatives, incest or having sex with dead women; sodomy, virgin intercourse and blood." "A woman who had intercourse with a beast is eligible to marry a priest." These sound disgusting and grotesque to me...
Yes, I know. Well, those things were discussed by rabbis before medieval times to define what is right in the law; what people could do or couldn't do, and lots of the stuff is very crazy. Today, certainly, nobody pays attention to such discussions. It's hard to understand why they would have had such discussions. I cannot answer you. You should ask rabbis for better explanations.

The Talmud also quotes the Emperor Hadrian, who lived 76-128 AD. He said, "As long as the Talmud existed, there was little hope for the assimilation of Jews and other nations." Do you know about this?

I don't know about that, so I just don't have an answer for you.

For Christian fundamentalists Jews are the 'chosen people.' They love Jesus who was a Jew, but don't like people who are Jews. They have 'love and hate' sentiments toward Jews. As far as the future is concerned, as long as Christianity continues, Christians and Jews are destined to live side by side forever, as it has been for the past 2,000 years. So, religion-wise, after the experience of the Holocaust, nothing has progressed much between these two religious groups after all. What do you think?

Well, that's true. But in most advanced Christian countries in Western Europe today, Christianity is declining; religion is regarded as old fashioned and few people go to church, and most people don't believe in the Bible or God. The same is true for Judaism. Where Christianity is weak, Jewish belief is also weak. Christianity is obviously not going to disappear and Judaism won't go away, either. But the growth of secularism affects both Christians and Jews. Today, the western Christian world is multi-religious. The growth of immigration produced this result in the United States and Europe, and it's now in the situation where religion no longer means the Christians and the Jews, but also Muslims and Buddhists.

In the United States, however, it's important to recognize that Christianity isn't declining. Americans are the most religious people in the civilized world; many go to church and believe in the Bible. This emphasis on religiosity affects American Jews. On the average Jews are less religious than Christians; there has been a growth of traditional Judaism among Jews, but a decline overall. Many have reacted to the Holocaust as a demonstration that there is no God. On the other hand, a famous rabbi said, Jews prevent Hitler from gaining a posthumous victory. Therefore, in order to defeat Hitler, Jews must stay Jewish, marry Jews, have Jewish children, and keep their religion alive.

About Louis Farrakhan, the leader of the nation of Islam who led the Million Man March in October, 1995. Jews and African Americans used to be close to each other, but not anymore. Farrakhan is ferociously anti-Semitic. He accuses Jews of participating in the Black slave trade during America's colonial era. Jews need a dialogue with him. How should they deal with him?

In the past, Jews supported the Civil Rights movement and gave money. Jewish groups are now telling African American leaders, if they want to continue to associate with us, they have to split with Farrakhan. Farrakhan is a good speaker and appeals to many African Americans, but he is also anti-Christian and anti-White, which creates problems for Black Muslims. Another situation which creates problems between Jews and African Americans is that, although both have suffered discrimination, on average Jews are much wealthier while many African Americans are poorer. ❖

73

Reconciliation between post-Nazi Germans and post-Holocaust Jews

RUDI RAAB AND ELIZABETH ROSNER

Rudi Raab (left in photo): German-born American, born in 1945 in Nonnewitz, Germany. Son of a Nazi officer. Police officer. Lives in California, USA.

Elizabeth Rosner: American Jew, born in 1959 in New York State, USA. Daughter of Holocaust survivors. Writing teacher. Lives in California, USA.

Tell me about your family background and how were you raised in Germany, what things did you learn about the war in your school, Rudi?

I was born on May 16th, 1945, 8 days after the unconditional surrender of Germany. During my childhood, I grew up seeing Allied soldiers in uniforms with jeeps all over Germany, and it was nothing unusual to me. I once saw a man wearing a skirt. I asked my mother about it and she said he was a Scottish soldier. If I saw a man with chewing gum in his mouth I knew he was an American soldier. They were all Allied soldiers, but to me they were foreigners. My father was a *Hauptbannführer,* which was an SA rank similar to that of an American brigadier general. He was also the administrator of the Adolf Hitler Schule in Sonthofen, where leaders of future generations were produced. All of the instructors there were indoctrinating German Aryan children, that was the purpose of the children for the Third Reich. My father was 33 years old when the war ended. He was a POW captured by the American army. After the war, all Germans had to go through "denazification." My father was required to report for the process; he just simply didn't show up and the Allies apparently had no records of him and no means of enforcing the requirement.

In school, in our history class, teachers usually started with the time of Charlemagne and generally ended in 1918. This was repeated year after year, and at the end of the term there was never enough time to deal with WW II until social studies, which was in 12th grade. Then we saw archival films of the liberation of concentration camps, bodies scattered around in the compound. We also saw them on television. So, at home, my father had friends, "old comrades" — they called each other — and these old Nazi bud-

dies were high-ranking officers. They were really the "super-Nazis," which I found out much later. For example, our family physician was one of the genetic experts who used to judge Aryan purity by measuring a citizen's skull to identify German racial characteristics.

At home, the way I learned about the war, National Socialism and Hitler was in bits and pieces, mostly. As children, my older sister and I knew we were not supposed to ask questions about the time because as soon as we started talking about it, my mother always said, "I don't want to talk about old politics!" She shut down, and we children were out of the room immediately. For her it was the old politics, but it's history for us. Because she was always shutting down any conversation of the war, it was a clear signal for us that those specific subjects were off limit, taboo, and that made me suspicious. When I was 13 while we were on vacation in Italy, I heard my father telling my sister that he considered the cause of WW II to be, of course, "the international communist Jewish conspiracy." I remember him saying that. Those were the only words we heard from my father on the subject and nothing was ever discussed again.

I had an uncle, a younger brother of my father's, and his personal history was not clear. According to my mother, he was either homosexual or criminal, in and out of jail all his life, and died of a disease. But later I learned the truth, he was a political prisoner, socialist and imprisoned in the Buchenwald concentration camp. We believe he was probably beaten to death by the Gestapo in Dresden. We can prove it now because we found his I.D. card. So, actually, my father and my uncle were enemies fighting against each other in their own country. My mother also had a brother, who was 17 years old when the war ended. He was captured in Berlin by the Russian Army. He wrote a letter saying "I had the honor of being liberated in the Reich capital by the Soviet Army at the age of 17. Then I had to start my long horrible march on foot to a Soviet POW camp. My wish for the present youth in Europe will be "to shake hands across the graves of their fathers and grandfathers, so that never again can a dictator blind people and mislead them..." This message has significant meaning for me.

Why did you come to America and how did people react when they saw you were a German?

I met my ex-wife, an American, while she was an exchange student studying in Germany. We got married there and we came to America together in 1967; I was a 21-year-old "war groom." We settled in Berkeley. I started wondering seriously about my country's past after I came to America. Berkeley is a liberal city and I didn't know anyone, except my ex-wife who had a lot of Jewish friends. And I didn't know how to react towards Jews because I'd never met any Jewish people in Germany. Some people looked at me as if I had done something wrong. I didn't know how to react because I didn't do anything wrong other than being a German, which was not my choice, but it's a fact. When I got my first job, I got promoted immediately. In the work place people were telling me, "You're German, great nation, brilliant people," and they trusted me as being a "superior white man." A man who promoted me was a WW II veteran, a bomber pilot who flew over Germany and destroyed many cities. He even apologized to me for that. So I used to say to him, "You did your job, so did my father. Let's forget about it!" That was my attitude at that time, and it stayed pretty much that way until I

met a Jewish woman, Julie, whom I met 7 years ago and live with now.

In 1989, together with her, I attended a project called "Acts of Reconciliation," a group that brings the generation of post-Nazi Germans and post-Holocaust Jews together for dialogue and healing. The group was founded in the same year by a drama/psychotherapist, Armand Volkas, a son of Holocaust survivors himself, who lives in Oakland. A few dozen of the children of perpetrators and victims often held meetings to deal with their family legacies and for open discussion.

Now, Elizabeth, you were born in postwar America with Jewish parents who were Holocaust survivors. Can you tell me your story?

I grew up in a small town in upstate New York. My upbringing was not as a normal American child because my parents were observant Jews living in a non-Jewish neighborhood. My father was from Hamburg, Germany; he was deported to the Buchenwald concentration camp and liberated by the Allies. My mother was born in Vilna, Lithuania, and survived the Vilna ghetto with her parents. They met in Sweden after the war, emigrated to Israel together, got married and came to America in 1951. Their circle of friends were mostly European Jews, who were either Holocaust survivors or emigrants around the time of WW II. I have an older sister and a younger brother. Both my parents were very much committed to Judaism; my father was particularly observant, and strongly believed Judaism has to be practiced in daily life. But my mother was more culturally Jewish. We belonged to an orthodox congregation and observed quite strict rules and regulations, and every Saturday we attended synagogue. There was a country club nearby, and it had a reputation for having no Jewish members.

We used to walk through its parking lot on our way to synagogue.

I have mixed feelings about my own Jewishness. As a child I was confused and very conscious of being different, because young children often don't want to be different. For example, every Friday night I had to stay home with my family and that was uncomfortable with my non-Jewish friends. I felt that I was establishing myself as not like everybody else. But as I grew older, my pride in being Jewish increased; I felt that I liked to be different. I liked not blending with others, like everybody else.

Although I always knew that my parents were survivors of the Holocaust, I don't really remember exactly when I heard their stories. It was not verbally communicated at first. My father, for example, had kept a star of David and the numbers that he was wearing while he was imprisoned in his camp, and he had very vivid memories about his experience. He also had photographs from the camp with his head shaven at age 15. And as I grew up he would visit my Hebrew school classes to give his personal stories of survival, which was a great contrast to what I was learning in my own public school. With school textbooks we would learn about WW II in a few pages that wouldn't really explain the stories. I remember, as early as the 5th grade, a homework assignment was to name the countries that Germany invaded. Since my mother was Polish and her relatives were killed there, she used to tell me her stories. So I knew much more about those things than learning from school teachers. I remember I was asking questions nobody else was asking. So regarding the Nazi war we knew a lot of things, much more than other average children. Finally when I put all the pieces of stories together and got a clear vision of the sequence of

the war, I was 15. Mostly I was learning at home from my parents, and from our circles in the Jewish community. However, while many other families of survivors I knew were extremely depressed, and their entire home life felt like a funeral going on all the time, that was not true in my family. My parents were still able to develop as human beings beyond that experience.

Rudi, how did you learn and feel about what Germans did to Jews?

In our school, we learned how 6 and a half million Jews were killed, about the locations of concentration camps, about the Nazi fascist empire, and how WW II began, although teachers were uncomfortable with it. We were taught that as Germans we have a collective guilt. We felt guilty, although it was an intellectual concept that I didn't really understand until I went to a foreign country. In my teenage years, I went to Holland with my family. People looked at us as Germans. When you are in Germany you don't see many foreigners, so the concept of guilt is something that doesn't exist, and nobody knows what it is exactly. I learned this is history and history is the past. I didn't come to terms with it, to be honest, until I came to America where I was confronted with it with people saying "You are guilty!" Then I said to myself, well, I was born after everything was over, so I certainly have nothing to do with it personally. That is, one way or another, I couldn't change it. So, am I guilty or not? Am I guilty because of the color of my passport? If it's yes, what am I going to do about it? I guess I can't do anything because I cannot change history. So, now, the interesting thing is that you don't become a real German until you are a part of the "German diaspora" in foreign countries. You really don't become a Jew until you learn "no Jewish members in the country club." Then, you are confronted with your differences and you have to live with it; either you are proud of it or uncomfortable with it.

Through the meetings with all the people at the "Acts of Reconciliation" and of my relationship with Julie, I've lately come up with a different interpretation of collective guilt. I did come to believe I have responsibility. I say that as a German, particularly as a son of a Nazi officer who was one of the movers and shakers of the Nazi empire. Living with a Jew, I have a responsibility to help make the slogan, "Never Again" a reality. So, I have to talk to people about what it is to be a German and what it is to discriminate against someone because of his or her nationality, ethnicity, race or religion, whatever. That, in my opinion underlies the whole thing. You marginalize some groups of people, you discriminate against them, and exterminate them for whatever reason. So the responsibility of every German is to prevent any reoccurrence of the holocaust. I'm not saying of The Holocaust; any holocaust in the future. We, as people, have to learn about each other from this catastrophe and live with each other. That means not only Germans and Jews, also Americans and Vietnamese, Hutu and Tutsi of Rwanda, and others as well. My uncle said in his letter to "shake hands across the graves of their fathers and grandfathers..." This, of course, meant he was indicating that we have to take responsibility for the Holocaust which was committed by the Germans, who, through democratic elections, elected Adolf Hitler to be their leader.

For me, being involved in the "Acts of Reconciliation," I learned to be comfortable with Jews. I learned that my peculiar misgivings of being German were shared by lots of other Ger-

mans, and also by lots of Jews. Many Jews feel uncomfortable with their Jewishness and uncomfortable having parents who are Holocaust survivors. They feel uncomfortable in American society and particularly uncomfortable with Germans. But as human beings, we have to deal and live with each other, so we have to work together to make ourselves comfortable and live with each other in spite of being different. You have to accept differences and appreciate differences.

Do you agree with him, Elizabeth?

Yes. Another thing is that when you are no longer confronted with the subject, you don't deal with it. Many Germans I've talked with say they never met Jews in Germany. They had to come to America to meet Jews. Once it's gone, it's past, eradicated, and all you are dealing with is reading and texts, and there is no reason to come to terms with the Holocaust anymore. So, I think this is another reason that Germans are more likely to confront themselves only when they come here, because as much as you capture the evidence, it seems to take a living presence to remind them of it.

How do you see the Jewish attitude towards non-Jews, being married to a non-Jew, and how do you find the differences?

I grew up with a very discriminatory attitude towards non-Jews. For instance, I was prohibited by my parents from having non-Jewish boyfriends. Among Jewish circles when someone marries a non-Jewish person, they go into *"schiva"* — mourning. The parents would say their daughter or son is dead. My uncle, also a survivor, married a non-Jewish Swedish woman after the war. Another uncle in Israel has never acknowledged their marriage, even though the wife converted to

Judaism and became a Jew, and their children are Jewish. She was the one who gave a Jewish education and Jewish identity to her children, but that is still not good enough because she was not a Jew by birth, and nothing can be done for her. According to Jewish law, only if the mother of the children is a Jew can the children become Jews, unless one converts to orthodox Judaism, which is quite elaborate. Jews welcome converts but very religious Jews don't. It varies, but that is a big question. I think there is some sense that this is a tribal association and, at some level, it's very much in your blood or genes, not about a superficial quality that you take on. And that is the dilemma; it's not how you act, it's about who you are.

Outside my family, my closest friends were mostly non-Jewish. I still resisted being trapped in a solely Jewish world. Ironically, I think, my father had mixed feelings about that himself. As a survivor he felt deeply that it's his obligation to perpetuate Judaism. But he wore a *yarmulke* only at home; he never wore it in public. When I told my parents I was going to marry a non-Jewish man, my father threatened to disown me. For hours, he tried to convince me and my boyfriend not to marry, saying it would be a fatal mistake, we would be unhappy or our children would be confused, and he made every effort to stop us. But we did marry in the end, anyway. At my wedding, people expected to see my father wearing a black armband for mourning. In contrast, I was overwhelmingly welcomed by the family of my husband; they looked at me as an individual and treated me in a much more open manner. My husband is a Christian, a Protestant, but he was not raised in a religious way and doesn't feel it's a part of his identity. He rejects lots of things about religion. For example, he believes lots of

crimes have been committed in the name of religion and is angry about that. He lived in many countries around the globe and is quite critical of almost all religions — except Buddhism — and believes they are responsible for some kind of repression against other groups of people in the name of God. And, I agree with him. My Jewishness isn't all of what I am and his Christianity is not all of what he is. We can actually be very connected on a spiritual level regardless of that fact, and that's very important to me.

Intermarriage and assimilation are things even Hitler failed to stop. But today, there is fear among the Jewish community that Judaism will be destroyed through tolerance and kindness by non-Jews, not by murdering the Jews. Being accepted into a non-Jewish world, mingling with the non- Jewish world would ultimately kill Jewish people in a tribal sense. Ironically, now it seems that Jews are the ones who worry about purity and contamination.

So, psychologically your life is somewhat ambivalent? Mentally,, you have a double life?
Well, I retained Jewishness on one hand, and was like everybody else on the other. I attended public school, went to Hebrew school at the same time, observed Jewish holidays, performed well academically in college and tried to succeed in society. I struggled all the way into my adulthood, and in some sense I still struggle with where exactly my Jewish identity fits with the rest of my life, if we have children, how we shall raise them and what identity I want to them to have, and when Jewish holidays come how do I observe them. Passover, for example, is something very meaningful to me. For my Jewish friends I'm like a Jewish encyclopedia. They all know I'm educated and have all the information, and they

come to me to learn how to do a *seder.* Passover is the Jewish holiday I really love, because it's about the celebration of freedom. My life is very much a search for me to figure out my identity. My father still struggles with his own relationship with Germany and Germans; my mother is the same, still struggling, and I have my own struggle to discover myself. Working with Armand Volkas in "Acts of Reconciliation," I feel that comfort is a big part of what I'm learning, just having to be with one another as human beings without all the ghosts following us and surrounding us.

In family life among intermarriages, do you think the Jewish side of tradition is more prominent than the non-Jewish side?

In my experience, often it has been the case, yes. Some couples struggle but it depends how strongly Christian the non-Jewish spouse feels about his or her religion. In my case, most of my friends who have a Christian wife or husband would say, "We don't want a Christmas tree in our home, but we want to celebrate Passover." Things like that. Jews feel they want to have their home life be Jewish, a Jewish sense of family to be Jewish. Speaking on behalf of Jewish people, not all but for some, that balance of retaining our identity makes us special, and feel different, and yet, we want to live in harmony with other people. We want to live peacefully side by side along with other groups of people regardless of our differences.

Since you are a Jew, your children will become Jews, too. How will you raise them? If your children, for example, want to have a military career, how would you react?

That's a very uncertain question for me. The rabbi who performed our marriage actually insisted that if we have children, we raise them as

Jews and my husband agreed with it. So, our children would learn Jewish history and tradition, and practice Judaism. But I think I will leave it to them to decide who they are when they become a certain age. I can teach them as much as I can, but I wouldn't impose their identity on them. I would teach them about the world and all religions, and what religions have in common for better or worse. But I will have a hard time if any of my children becomes a soldier or has a professional career in the military. I'm against violence in general. I would hope that I would raise my children to believe that this is not the best way to spend one's life.

If I can speak spiritually for a moment, one thing that was very much missing from my religious education was spiritual issues. What Judaism has to do with is pure human goodness and the ways humans treat one another. It finally didn't concern me that the man I married is non-Jewish, because we share the same spiritual values with the so-called religion like layers on top of that. I want to stress something about human beings that isn't about tribal values at all, even though I feel very strongly connected to my tribe. That is a great puzzle for me.

Because of your ambiguity, mainstream America is a different matter for you, right? Let me ask you more. Every year when it comes to July 4th, the day of American patriotism, when you see the American flag in the sky and American people singing the national anthem, what is in your mind? Do you feel you are fully American? Or, looking at the American flag and the Israeli flag, which one is your flag, do you feel?

I'm not terribly patriotic, and I don't think it has to do with being Jewish. I think it has to do with not being completely convinced that America is great, and I question American values. I feel very different from mainstream Americans, not only because I'm Jewish and liberal, but because I'm open minded and tolerant. The mainstream American values, I think, are not those that I share in general. I'm also critical of Israel. I think Israel is becoming more and more of a scary place to me. Until a few years ago no one dared to criticize Israeli politics. It's very controversial to do it, but the truth of the matter is that Jews need Israel. The cliche, that Israel exists because of the Holocaust, I happen to believe it is true.

I wouldn't say I'm half and half. I don't know how to quantify my patriotism. I feel strongly about Israel because it gives me a sense of security knowing that there's a place in the world where Jews can find refuge, and knowing Jews can protect themselves, and are willing to defend themselves. I've never been discriminated against for being Jewish and never felt unsafe in America, but knowing that Israel is there, I think it provides a really deep sense of security for Jews all over the world. But I don't' know when I look at the flag of America. I mean I want to say that I was born in America and I'm an American citizen, but it's nice knowing that I can move to Israel tomorrow and become a citizen with no questions asked. That is a powerful notion to think I could immediately find a new home in another country and be completely embraced by that country, and surrounded by other Jews. So, frankly, I don't feel I'm divided.

Same question to you, Rudi. How do you see flags, either German or American, and the question of patriotism?

After the war, the defeated nations of Germans and Japanese had one thing in common; We both were taught in our schools not to be patriotic. Because patriotism leads to national pride and national pride leads to fascism. So, patriotism is, so to say, a gateway to fascism. While I was in Germany, when we saw German flags in the sky, we thought who cares? Many times I didn't even notice it. But when we were on a family holiday in Sweden, we saw Swedish people put their hands on their hearts in the presence of their flag. I thought what's the matter with them? Then, when I visited East Germany in the mid-1960s, I saw uniformed soldiers wearing leather boots patrolling with machine guns and dogs, the watch towers, tight security, and all over were East German flags with the emblem at its center, worker's symbols, and I even heard marching music. I thought what is all this, a Nazi movie? It reminded me of an old movie I saw when I was a kid with Nazi flags all over. I said to myself "Gee, this is a time capsule of the 1930s! Just different flags! The workers' state had nothing to do with the Nazi state, but to me it was a symbol of fascism, communist fascism. Since I was educated not to be patriotic, that was my impression, anyway. Then, after I moved to America, I saw American flags all over, even in gas stations, at least until the late 1960s. In a stadium everybody stood up, took their hat off and put their hands over their hearts, and people sang the national anthem because they were going to play a baseball game. I said to myself, it's OK because this is America. Anyway, the German flag doesn't represent anything for me other than a little nostalgia. That's all it is to me.

I'm an immigrant. I was born in Germany not by choice, but by accident. I emigrated to America by choice, then became an American citizen by choice. My family and my education were all in Germany. So, no matter how many passports I carry, I have a heavy German accent and people recognize me and say, "You are a German. You sound like one." I can't get rid of it.

I have a son with my ex-wife. Now, I'm responding to your question about how I should raise my child, whether he should be raised as an American or a German. He was born in Germany but educated in the USA. As a boy, we taught him both English and German. When he became 16, I took him back to Germany and showed him his German heritage, where his roots are. He then continued studying German and now writes letters to his grandmother in German, which is good, I think. As a father, I believe he should know where he came from, at least half of his blood. But whether he wants to be American or not is entirely up to him to decide. I don't care. Though, he is already American mentally.

Do you find Americans are anti-Semitic, Elizabeth? And why do you think African Americans don't like Jews?

I teach in a school with lots of African American students. When I bring up the subject of racism and discrimination, they often relate to Jews because both share a similar kind of historical context. Like Jews, African Americans also feel they were oppressed for a long time. Even the most optimistic African Americans believe that they are always seen as different from white Americans, because they are so visible and are immediately recognizable, unlike Jews. People say I don't look like a Jew, for example, and nobody could tell I'm a Jew unless I say so. I think this is actually one reason which creates hostility between Jews and African Americans. Theys feel like Jews can pass into white American culture through intermarriage and that, in fact, Jews are succeeding in society. And African Americans are prevented

from having success, and sometimes they see Jews as keeping them down, as being part of the oppressive system. But there's that sense of connection, for I know how it is to be seen as less than human. I know what it's like to be treated in a degrading way, and that is very powerful. That's the message I really like to share with my African American students, because I want to stress the connections and not reinforce differences or mistrust.

Anti-Semitism is alive and well in America, absolutely. When I talk to my students about my family history, some of their first reactions are, "Jews are rich, Jewish bankers control world finance, Jews control Hollywood, Jews control media, and Jews are in the government. So, no wonder the Germans did what they did." They accept this information as fact, and they don't think they are being racist when they say that. They don't think they are prejudiced. They have been taught these are facts about the Jews, and that is anti-Semitism.

Have you experienced prejudice or been discriminated against being a German in America, Rudi?

Well, yes. I have been a police officer for 10 years in Berkeley. First, I was a part-time officer, and to become a full-time officer, I had to take examinations 3 times every year. I always passed physical, oral and written examinations, and my score was always among the top three out of 125 examinees, but I was never hired. Year after year, I applied to become a police officer with our local police department, but year after year, I was turned down. I had reason to believe it was because of my German accent. The department officials didn't want to hire a man who looked like a "movie Nazi." So, I sued the police department, that was more than 3 years ago. The case was settled and I was hired by them.

What other things did you learn from Jews that enlightened you?

One of the funniest that happened to me was that, after having met Julie, a journalist and writer, I learned something new from her that never came to my mind before. After I came to America I studied medieval German literature, and the Yiddish language is directly linked to medieval German. I noticed that, historically, Germans and Jews have lots more in common than separates us; I learned we have common roots and a common history. And, when she started cooking meals for me, it was almost traditional German cuisine like my mother used to cook for my family. As her ancestors were Eastern European-Jews, her parents spoke Yiddish, which has medieval German roots, and they maintained Yiddish culture, including the same sort of cooking. So, meeting a Jewish woman in America, I met a "traditional German housewife." We have more in common to share with each other. The truth is, I've never been confronted with my Germanness until I was confronted with the Jewishness of Julie. So, we should look at those things too, and should go forward from here. We have to reconcile, we have to talk about it, we have to keep up the memories of the Holocaust and discuss it openly. And we should make sure it won't happen in Germany again, not in America, nor anywhere else in the world.

I believe that Americans are the most tolerant people towards Jews. So, I think, assimilation is very possible here. What do you think, Elizabeth?

Maybe so. But the irony is that in Germany and many other countries in Europe before Hitler, Jews were mostly assimilated. Many German Jews thought they were Germans first and Jews second, and suddenly that was taken away. So, even in America today, some Jews don't trust in assimilation anymore. It's varied of course, but I remember when I was in college I met a Jewish woman talking about what it means to be Jewish. She said to me, "If there is ever another Holocaust, I will go as a Jew. I will remain a Jew." What she meant was, if she is put into a group of Jews as victims, instead of saving herself by pretending to be a non-Jew, she will go forward as a Jew. That was her ultimate definition. I thought it was such a victim identification and such a limited way to see herself. But to me, if I had to choose between being a Jew and disguising myself as a Christian in order to survive, which many Jews did during the Holocaust, "What would I do?" I don't know how I would react in such a circumstance. I would like to believe I have the courage to remain true to my Jewishness, but who knows what the will to survive can inspire in us? I hope never to be faced with that kind of choice. ❖

CHAPTER TWO

History Speaks Out

*People who were directly involved
in the events of the Nazi War*

(Interviews conducted between 1991–1993)

> ## "After the Berlin Wall, how quickly things changed;
> ## it's like WW II never happened."

MICHAEL THALER

Polish Jew, Holocaust survivor of a Polish ghetto. President of the Holocaust Center of Northern California. Born in 1934 near Lwow, eastern Poland. Lives in California, USA.

(Photo: Mr. Thaler in his office at the Holocaust Center of Northern California in San Francisco.)

On the first day of September 1939, Hitler invaded Poland, triggering the outbreak of WW II. At almost the same time, Poland was also invaded by Stalin from the east; it was a sandwich attack by two mighty armies. Dr. Thaler, you were only 5 at that time, but can you talk about the things you remember?

I remember very well because of the bombs and the shooting. Air raids came from Germany, and within days my hometown was occupied by Russians. I was raised in a family with an orthodox Jewish grandfather and a secular Zionist father whose ancestors had been settled in Poland for 350 years. Modern Poland had been created after WW I when the Austro-Hungarian Empire collapsed. During WW II, Poland was divided between Germany and Russia and disappeared from the world map. Germany occupied western and central Poland, and Russia took over the eastern part, which later became part of the Ukraine, and also occupied Moldavia, Lithuania, Latvia and Estonia.

As soon as the Nazis marched into Poland, a Gestapo office was established in each community, and they immediately began terrorizing all Jews in various ways — by arrest, torture, murder, public execution and random seizures of people for deportation to death camps. Polish Communists and some Catholic priests were sent to labor camps, and many Polish men were also deported to Germany for slave labor, but most non-Jewish Poles were unharmed. The killing of Jews was carried out throughout the occupation until nearly 98 percent were dead.

Can you tell me about Jewish history in Poland and the political and social circumstances of Polish Jews before and after the Nazi occupation?

The earliest Jewish settlement in Poland dated from the 15th century; Jews who were expelled from Spain, France, England and Germany fled to Poland, because the Polish king needed their skills and let them in. The Jewish community in Poland grew rapidly and by the 19th century, during the period of European industrialization, it was the largest in the world. In the 20th century, it was second only to America, which became the home of many Jews fleeing from pogroms in Poland and Russia. Warsaw was the capital of Polish Jewry, an important center of Jewish social, cultural and commercial activity. Jews lived all over the city, but worked predominantly in crafts, industries and financial enterprises owned by Jews. Apart from doctors, professors and school teachers, there were hardly any Jews in official government posts. In fact, Jews were generally barred from such positions. There was profound anti-Semitism among Poles. However, both Poles and Jews were unprepared and helpless in the face of the German war machine that was about to engulf them. The social situation became even more intense — Germans enslaved Poles, Poles hated Germans, but both, Germans and most Poles, hated Jews.

The Holocaust in Poland was a somewhat different story than in other places because of the large Jewish population. Before the war, there were 3.3 million Polish Jews, 11 percent of the total population. More than 3 million perished in the Holocaust. Many recalled the German occupation during WW I, which was orderly and relatively tolerant toward Jews. But this was nothing like that. Jews were immediately targeted for attack and discrimination; their property was confiscated, they were deprived of jobs, food and shelter, and their lives were paralyzed overnight. Then the Nazis quickly organized ghettos to isolate Jews from the rest of the population. All Jews were imprisoned inside the ghettos.

Can you tell me about your personal story and life inside the ghetto?

My parents and I, then 6 years old, were forced out of our house into an old, ruined and terribly overcrowded building. There were many hundreds of ghettos throughout Eastern Europe, mainly in Poland, Ukraine and Byelorussia. All were very similar and each ghetto was situated near the center of town. In Poland, the largest ghettos were in Warsaw, Lodz, Cracow, Lublin, and Lvov (Lwow). In Warsaw, as soon as all Jews were forced into the ghetto, the deportations began to Treblinka, an extermination camp northeast of Warsaw. Professional people such as academics, university professors, lawyers, business executives, journalists and doctors were the first to be deported. In our ghetto, Brzezany, a registration was ordered; every Jew in the ghetto had to be registered at the Gestapo office. My father didn't trust the Germans and was suspicious of what they were doing. The day of registration he pretended to be sick and stayed in a ghetto hospital instead. This was the first of the many miracles by which my parents and I survived.

The white collar workers, teachers and professionals who reported for registration were loaded on trucks by Germans and Ukrainian police, and driven to an unknown destination. Some weeks later, Ukrainian peasants described mass executions in a nearby forest and brought clothes they found at the gravesite for resale to the wives and mothers of the murdered.

The situation in the ghetto became worse day by day. There was a severe food shortage and hundreds of people, many children, died of starvation every day. The streets of the ghetto were

like a graveyard with bodies all over. Everywhere I saw lame, crippled and blind people, or people too weak to move. Every day young men came through the streets and piled the bodies on wagons and pushed them to mass graves. For my sake, my parents decided that I should live outside the ghetto. In the winter of 1942, I was taken to a Polish couple, friends of my parents who were childless. I was then 8. They kept me indoors, with the windows covered. They were very fond of me and educated me as a Catholic. But after 8 months, I was recognized by a neighbor. They became extremely anxious because anyone who hid Jews in their homes was shot to death on the spot. I went back to the ghetto to my parents. A few weeks later, the Gestapo took my father away to a labor camp. My mother and I were left alone. The ghetto was shrinking every day. We thought it would soon be destroyed, so decided to escape. I found a small window facing to the outside that had been nailed shut. It was possible to open it. One night, my mother and I made it; we were able to jump outside and escaped the ghetto.

There was only one place we could go; we went back to the Polish couple. Since they loved me, I instinctively felt they wouldn't mind us hiding there. We could stay in a loft with chickens and goats underneath. They allowed us to hide under the straw and left food for us in the barn. Then, a few days later, we heard sounds of shooting, people screaming and horrifying cries from the Jewish cemetery nearby. We could almost see them through the cracks in the wooden barn wall. The Germans and Ukrainian police murdered the last two thousand Jews of our ghetto that day in June 1943. Around Passover of that year, the Germans also tried to finish the Warsaw Ghetto, but ran into armed resistance from a few thousand young Jews, the famous Warsaw Ghetto Uprising. It lasted for four weeks.

Between 1940 and 1943, hunger and epidemics killed 85,000 people in the Warsaw Ghetto alone; 20,000 were children. Most of the half million Jews there were transported to Treblinka to be killed in the gas chambers. In the rest of the ghettos throughout eastern Poland and the Ukraine where we were, the Germans did not even bother to transport them to death camps to kill them in the gas chambers. Children, women, and elderly and sick people were left in the ghettos until they starved to death or were taken outside of town, executed, and buried in mass graves. Men were sent to forced labor camps and when they became too weak to work, they were shot. The killing was conducted by the method used earlier by the *Einsatzgruppen* — mobile SS killing squads in eastern German-occupied territories — the victims were forced to dig their own graves and lie down in them and then they were shot. Every ghetto was the site of mass killings and it went on throughout the war. And, eventually, by the fall of 1943, most ghettos were completely destroyed; except for the Lodz ghetto which lasted until November, 1944. After the destruction of the ghettos, some remaining survivors who were young and still fit to work, were deported to labor camps. My father encountered one of them, a Jewish policeman who knew everybody in my ghetto, and learned that nobody saw me or my mother arrested and taken away by the SS. He was encouraged by this information to think that we might be alive. He knew where to find us. Within the next few days he escaped from the camp and arrived at the house of our Polish couple. We were reunited. After that, we hid in barns and forests. Our fugitive life contin-

ued for another year till we were liberated by the Russians in the summer of 1944.

How do you account for the rise of Christianity and anti-Semitism in Europe? Why was it that this time conversion was out of the question as a way out for Jews?

There are obviously many factors involved. Firstly, Jews are a religious minority in the continent of Europe which already makes them vulnerable. Secondly, there is the special relationship between Christianity and Judaism. Judaism is the mother religion of Christianity. This made the Jews even more vulnerable, because Christianity behaved like any child who wants to grow up and replace the parent. So, as long as Jews persisted in denying the truth of Christianity, Christians had the strength to suppress Judaism. Because of this father-son relationship and Jesus Christ himself being a Jew, which was a big problem for Christianity, they had to believe that the reason for Christianity was that the Jews were unregenerate sinners who killed Christ, and they had to be replaced.

Obviously, one way in which you can replace a religion is by conversion. Until the last century the Jews were forced either to convert, to stay behind walls in their own district or to leave the country. They were forbidden to mix with others and to interfere in the Christian world. The big change in the 20th century was that instead of forcing them to convert or to leave, they were going to be physically eliminated. When the Nazis came to power, they no longer forced the Jews to convert; they simply forced them into ghettos and concentration camps to die. So in addition to religiously based anti-Semitism, there was an additional form of anti-Semitism, political anti-Semitism. Hitler quickly made anti-Semitism into an official government policy and the Holocaust was ordered in the name of state law and order, and rapidly spread to every German-occupied European country. For the first time in nearly 2,000 years of Jewish exile in Christian countries, Hitler's Holocaust was an entirely new dimension on an enormous scale. As a result, from 1938 to 1945, 6 million European Jews were murdered, and European Jewish civilization was effectively destroyed. For centuries, as I said, many Jews were forced to become Catholics; they were baptized and they raised their children as Christians, and often parents never even told them about their Jewish background. During the years of the Holocaust when the Gestapo showed up to arrest them, that was the first time that many people discovered that they were racially Jews. Many Jewish Christians were killed that way. For Hitler, conversion was out of the question. The "Total Extermination of the Jewish Race" — that was his Final Solution.

In political terms, how did anti-Semitism escalate in Nazi-occupied Poland?

In Poland, anti-Semitism was much deeper than in Germany. The average German didn't like Jews, but Jews in Germany numbered only 500,000 which was less than one percent of the entire German population. So most Germans, in fact, hardly met Jews in public. Whereas in Poland Jews made up 11 percent of the entire population. So there were Jews everywhere and for Poles it was easy to recognize them. Their hatred of Jews was based on religious, economic, cultural and social grounds, but it was especially supported by Catholic church doctrine. Poland was and still is, devoted entirely to Catholicism and Poles blamed Jews as Jesus killers and foreigners; their general attitude toward Jews was very negative. Although Germans and

Poles disliked one another, both had a grass-roots hatred of Jews, which made it easy for the Germans to conduct a destructive policy supported by the majority of the Polish people. When it came to the Jewish question, both agreed in principle with the official order of genocide against Jews. Therefore it was an easy task for Germans, assisted by the majority of the Polish population, to find and kill the Jewish population in Poland.

Let's take an example. The case of the Jewish minority, actually, applies to many other minorities as well. It is a social question of a minority among a majority. For instance, besides Jews, there are other minority groups in America today: African Americans, homosexuals, Hispanics, Asians. In normal social and economic circumstances, the majority can tolerate living with minorities even if they don't like them. However, if a government has the power to do something against a minority, that changes everything. When politicians decide what they want to do about them, arrest or kill them, they can succeed if they are supported by a majority of their own citizens. And, in that case, you can't effectively resist an order by the state whether you personally agree with it or not.

How can you distinguish between Aryan and Jew? German Jews look like Germans, Russian Jews look like Russians, French Jews look like the French, and who is a pure Jew or pure Aryan? In the 20th century, nobody is "racially pure." My question is why were Germans so obsessed with it?

Racially, it's very difficult to tell Jews from Aryans. In Poland, it's physically easy because most Poles have a slavic look: blue eyes, blond hair, wide features, straight noses. In general, most Jews have dark or brown eyes and dark hair. So, many times you can be identified as belonging to a certain racial group, but not always. For instance, I had brown eyes and red hair, and in Poland, I was easily recognized as a Jew, racially. But in Germany, I was like anybody else because many southern Germans look like me. Germans cannot tell I am a Jew unless I say so. With men it's easier to tell by physical examination because of circumcision. But that's not definite proof because many American and Anglo-Saxon males are also circumcised. So who is a Jew in that context? Someone who believes in the Jewish religion or identifies with that culture, or someone who thinks he's a Jew. As Joshua Heshel, a famous rabbi said: "A Jew is someone who suffers as a Jew." But it becomes even more complicated than that, because Judaism isn't a religion like Christianity. Christians had countries of their own, like England, France, Germany, Spain, Poland, Russia, Italy, etc., where they developed distinctive national cultures. The Jews had only religious customs. On this basis, the Jews developed a distinct civilization of their own in every country they lived in. From their own history, they developed a language, literature and tradition. Even Nazis realized that there was no such thing as pure Aryans. What they planned to do was to eliminate the "bad blood" that had been mixed into the Aryan race for centuries and to purify it. That's why they made laws to prohibit Jews marrying Aryans in order to breed pure Aryans for future generations. That was one of the first things they did. Therefore, even if only one of the grandparents was Jewish, they couldn't marry an Aryan because the children would be contaminated with Jewish genes. That was the basic plan for the Third Reich. Originally, Jews were supposed to be distinguished by religion, not race. But Nazi ideology irrationally mixed race and religion; once you were born as a Jew,

that was forever. You can be a Frenchman or an Englishman and be Christian at the same time. But if you are Jewish, you can only be a Jew. A Jewish Pole was not a Pole according to the Poles. Only a Christian Pole is a Pole. So there was more to being Jewish than the religion. But the only difference between Jews and other people is that the Jews lost their land base; they hadn't had a country of their own for 2,000 years.

How did the Nazis use their racial theories in support of Hitler and the Third Reich?

Nazi ideology contended that Germany's defeat in WW I and the resulting order to pay reparations, the state's decline and its oppression by other people, were all because the Germans had lost their original racial purity. They blamed intermarriage and alien cultural influences. The whole concept of the Third Reich was that Germans would be purified into one nation and one race again by getting rid of everybody else. Suddenly, there was a man telling people, "You Germans, you are the best people in the world: the reason you're starving, poor, oppressed, miserable and sick is not your fault, but the fault of others. I'm going to make you strong again. You are the super race and you will be the leader of the whole world. I'm your ruler, follow me. I'll take you there!" That was Hitler. Of course, that's all nonsense. But people believed that. And the real question is some Germans still believe that. Germans didn't support him just because he was a charismatic and magnetic speaker. They really believed him because he expressed their innermost feelings and provided simple solutions for their problems. The economic situation at that time made Germans believe him. It's just like the message put forward by David Duke, a former KKK member, Hitler admirer, and a former Louisiana candidate for governor. His theory is that white people are superior, yet are forced to pay higher taxes to support African Americans, the poor, and have to pay for welfare. He carries the same methods and same message as Hitler.

The interesting thing is that Germany is a highly industrialized nation; people are well educated, logical, intelligent and perfectionist. Everything is exact, precise and scientific. They believed this mythology which was totally irrational. Let's take another example. Besides Jews, Gypsies, homosexuals, political prisoners, POW's and many others, they also killed 300,000 mentally retarded German children and adults. They also considered people with inherited diseases or chronically ill people to be inferior. So, after terrible medical experiments were performed on these people by "perfectly logical" Nazi scientists and doctors, they were gassed and incinerated just as the Jews were in Auschwitz. Germans were killing their own people because they wanted to implement their theory and "purify" the race.

If Nazi Germany had been successful in achieving a *judenrein* (ethnically cleansed of Jews) Germany and Europe, what would the next move have been for the Third Reich?

Here I have my own opinion, which is not so unique, but it's not so common either. I think that the Nazi movement, which was meant to establish a Third Reich, was essentially an anti-Christian movement. It meant to replace God with the Führer; they were very focused on the pagan period in the Gothic era, the Valkyries and all that Wagnerian mythology. Since Judaism was the foundation of Christianity, Jews were the first to be disposed of. The next step would have been to suppress the Christian leadership and the Christian religion, and replace it with a state religion replacing the cross

with the swastika and the Holy Bible with *Mein Kampf.* But before they could get rid of the Christians they had to kill the Jews. Jews were the first target because they carried all the ideas that were taken over by Christianity; the whole ideology of man being an image of God, of human life as being important in its own right and not merely as part of a people or a nation — all those ideas ran counter to the ideology of the Nazis. Also, the Jews were much easier to kill. They were relatively few and everybody wanted to get rid of them. Once they eliminated the Jews who carried the germ of that ideology, then they could pursue the Christians. Their goal was rule by the "superior" Aryan race. That's why they introduced the concept of race on top of religion. They wanted to build a race of supermen based on an Aryan concept which is not Christian in nature but rather a pre-Christian concept. Hitler called Christ an "effeminate Jewish God." The whole idea of loving others as oneself and turning the other cheek was basically a Judaic idea. It was something the Nazis couldn't stand because, to them, the strong should survive and the weak should die. Their idea was that might is right, whereas the Judaic concept is that "the meek shall inherit the earth."

In terms of military expansion, Nazi Germany was to take over the whole of Europe and Russia, and eventually conquer the entire world. After occupying the central European countries, which Hitler called "pygmy nations," they intended to make slaves of the Slavic people, and to transform the most Aryan-looking children into Germans. They saw the Slavs as *Untermenschen,* lower forms of human life. But Hitler somehow miscalculated. Attacking Russia before destroying England may have been his fatal mistake. If England had fallen into his hands, then the establishment of the Third Reich might well have been successful.

Compared to Germans, why was there a relatively higher percentage of Jews in the prestigious professions?

The whole Jewish tradition is one of learning. The Jews are the original people of the Book. There is a heavy emphasis on education, particularly the study and learning of the Scroll of the Torah. When you stop studying the Torah because you no longer believe in God, the scholarly tradition remains in force. And Jewish parents traditionally encourage this. Their goal is to produce highly qualified professional people; Jewish parents prefer their children to be teachers, doctors or lawyers rather than athletes. Germans and Jews are similar in many respects. The main difference between them, I find, is that Jewish culture is rooted in a profound moral tradition which was developed over 4,000 years of Jewish history, whereas German society has rewarded physical strength and beauty, the Hellenic heritage. The Germans tend to emphasize esthetics over ethics and Jewish tradition is precisely the contrary. As a result, there was too much focus on racial superiority, which Germans believed they personified. Of course, the German people also produced intellectual giants, a people who developed the most advanced western culture and produced superb composers, musicians, great poets, scientists, philosophers etc., but my view is that without the moral basis, you can turn into a mass killer. Without humanistic ideas, great people can become primitive barbarians very quickly. The lack of a moral foundation caused a collapse of German intellectuals, I would say. The Nazi regime was, in a way, a good lesson for Germans; that truly showed up their problems. The ultimate Faustian bargain, the devil's dues, was the Holocaust.

What do you think about the reunification of Germany that followed the fall of the Berlin Wall, and the future for Jewish people?

Jews as a community have been nearly destroyed by the Nazis in Europe; European Jewry is finished, especially in Germany. So, today it's a different situation for Jews, but not for Europeans. German reunification is no longer a Jewish problem because, Jews now have the state of Israel. As long as Israel exists, Jewish people can survive. But Germany's neighboring nations have a new problem: they must wonder whether the "New Germany" will try again. After the Berlin Wall came down, how quickly things changed, amazing! There was an immediate resurgence of neo-Nazism and the border question with Poland, all of which go back to a half century ago to the prewar atmosphere. It's as if WW II never happened. The well-known cliche is that "history repeats itself" nevertheless, the return to the past happened shockingly fast. It really indicated that the Berlin Wall and a divided Germany had a real meaning for Europe and world peace. Nazi war crimes and the Holocaust must be openly discussed and reexamined in the New Germany. It was many decades ago, but it simply cannot be pushed away as old history. Germans are still Germans; their roots are still deep underneath — it all came from inside. The majority of young Germans haven't learned about any of that in school or weren't told about it by their parents at home. Those post-war generations have entered a new chapter of German history without really understanding their past. It's not only sad but also dangerous for their own future. ❖

"My tale of survival from the horror of the Einsatzgruppen.*"*

YAFFA ELIACH

Lithuanian Jew, Holocaust survivor of *Einsatzgruppen.* Judaic history professor, author of book *Hasidic Tales of the Holocaust* and curator of Holocaust Memorial Museum at Washington, D.C. Born in 1937 in Vilna, Poland. Lives in New York, USA.

(Photo: Prof. Eliach showing her childhood photo with her father. The same photo is displayed at the Tower of Faces and Life in the United States Holocaust Museum in Washington, D.C.)

Professor Eliach, could you tell me about your background and how the Holocaust affected your life?

I was born in Vilna, the capital city of today's Lithuania, though I spent the early years of my childhood in Eisysky, a small town some 70 km southwest of Vilna. Lithuania was Polish when I was born, and it was Russian when my parents were born. Eisysky was founded in 1073 and was one of the oldest Jewish settlements in Lithuania. My family roots were traced back 900 years to one of the well-known founders of the town. My father was an owner of lands, properties, factories, and well respected by many people and everybody knew him. Besides, he had many trusted friends in the region — Jews and non-Jews, employees, and business associates and partners.

When German troops invaded Russia in June 1941, at the same time, *Einsatzgruppen* entered Eastern Poland (now Lithuania), and immediately began killing Jews moving from one town or village to another. Between 1939 and 1941, the people in Eisysky assisted 15,000 refugees to pass through the *shtetl* (small town). They were escaping Nazi occupation in Europe and western Poland. The people of my town learned from these refugees of the ongoing Nazi atrocities.

When the Nazis troops marched into my town, my father instinctively felt that they might have terrible plans against Jews. He said we should escape and procured some money. We knew from the reports given to us by the Jewish refugees who were fleeing from Germany to Eastern Poland that Polish Jews were gathered in Warsaw, Lodz and other ghettos. But nobody had mentioned the mass killings of Jews yet. Everybody still had a good memory of WW I when many Jews fought along with Germans. My grandmother, who was a photographer, remem-

bered it very well. She said that Germans were a civilized people; we had no reason to believe they would do terrible things to us. She and my mother said that my father was overreacting. There had been many pogroms in Europe over the centuries, but Jews always survived them. So, we all thought it was just another difficult time for Jews, and nobody imagined it was that serious. When WW II began, therefore, the majority of Jews thought it would follow the pattern of pogroms during previous European wars and expected that some Jews would be killed, but Jewish life would continue. That was the reason why many Jews remained rather than running away. They simply didn't imagine that it was going to all end with the total destruction of the Jewish race in Europe. It all happened very suddenly. The *Einsatzgruppen* arrived in Eisysky on the 24th of September, 1944. All the Jews were arrested and taken to a local synagogue and an old Jewish cemetery. They were forced to dig deep ditches. Then, they were ordered to undress and line up by the ditches. Then *Einsatzgruppen* began shooting them. Men were killed on September 25, 1941 at the old Jewish cemetery and women and children were killed on the next day near the Christian cemetery. The *Einsatzgruppen* simply started shooting at their heads until they all fell dead in the ditch. In two days from September 25 to 26 of 1941, during the time of Rosh Hashanah — the Jewish New Year — 3,446 Jews in my town were massacred; 236 members of my extended family were among them. Some 6,000 Jewish communities, villages, towns and cities in Poland, the Baltic states, Eastern Galicia, White Russia, the Ukraine and the Soviet frontier met the same fate as Eisysky. Half a million Jews were slaughtered by the *Einsatzgruppen* before the full scale killing of Jews in gas chambers of the Holocaust began.

My father, mother, with my two brothers, and I, then 4, however, escaped and went into hiding. My parents and my baby brother went to my grandmother's house. My older brother and I were separated, and had to stay in two different houses which belonged to my father's Gentile friends. I was sent to the home of my nanny. I started crying because I was afraid of missing my mother. While I was crying by the window in her house, I saw a carriage passing by loaded with our household — furniture, tables, chairs, clothes, everything including my toys. My nanny covered my eyes with her hands and told me, "Don't look." I kept crying because I wanted to be with my mother. Meanwhile, my grandmother and parents and the other Jews were taken to the synagogue by the *Einsatzgruppen* with the assistance of Lithuanian guards. That was why our house was confiscated and looted, and everything was carried away by Germans. My father somehow escaped through the synagogue window and came home. He paid money to his employee to rescue my mother and her baby, who were about to be executed. The employee successfully returned with them, but they were found out by a nasty anti-Jewish neighbor and chased by the Nazis. My mother jumped out of a moving carriage and went into hiding on her own. My father arranged with a Gentile farm boy to pick me and my brother up, and we were to meet in the forest outside the town. We three were luckily reunited there. We walked toward a small town named Vasilishak that the Nazis hadn't yet entered. When my father told people in the village what had happened to us and the Jews in Eisysky, nobody believed him. Everybody thought my father was in a state of shock. They simply didn't believe

what he said. A few weeks later, while we were staying at the house of a Jewish friend of my fathers, Lithuanian police arrested my father. A few days later, the police came and took me and my brother to the jail where my father had been in custody. They asked us to identify a man who had been badly tortured. His eyes were swollen, his tongue was sticking out and his hair was gray. We replied that he was not our father. But later we learned that man was our father. We just couldn't recognize him because of his hair: he was a 32-year-old man but his hair had turned totally white within two days. He looked like a completely different man to us. That night, he escaped from the jail and came to pick us up. We ran to a Christian cemetery and hid in an open grave ditch and then escaped into the forest. We later learned that the *Einsatzgruppen* had entered that village a few days after we left and killed all the Jews in the exact same way as in Eisysky.

German soldiers and the *Einsatzgruppen* were operating two different campaigns, then?
That's right. German soldiers were to fight against the Russian army on the front, and the *Einsatzgruppen* was a special mobile squad of executioners of Jews. As soon as the German army occupied Eastern Europe and Russian territories, the *Einsatzgruppen* quickly moved in and turned the territories into killing fields. They murdered Jews prior to the establishment of the ghettos and while ghettos were already in existence. That was happening all over the German-occupied Eastern Territories before the Final Solution was launched in January 1942.

We hid during the day and kept on walking during the night because the *Einsatzgruppen* were all over looking for Jews. We ate wild mushrooms, vegetables, berries, and whatever we found in the forest. Then we came to another neighboring town called Radun, Byelorussia, 8 km south of Eisysky, where my father had a close Jewish friend. We were hoping my mother would be there if she was still alive. Luckily, we found her there with her baby. We were all happily reunited. But again, people still didn't believe our story of the Jewish massacre. Shortly afterwards, a ghetto was established in Radun. 16 people of all ages, both men and women, were squeezed into one room. Secretly people managed to set up a kindergarten in an attic of the ghetto and children were able to learn there. I remember my teacher taught us how to know the times of the day by looking at shadows. There were gallows with Jewish corpses hanging in the main square of the ghetto that we could see through the attic window every day. They were killed by the Nazis after being tortured for various reasons; caught smuggling food, illegally leaving the ghetto, wearing a Star of David on the wrong side, or not taking their hat off when German soldiers passed by, etc. We watched them all day and learned how to tell morning, noon, and afternoon as the gallows shadows changed short to long.

In May 1942, Germans made an announcement that all people in the ghetto would be relocated and were free to leave. My father said it was a trick: they were going to liquidate the ghetto and kill everyone. Within days, the ghetto was surrounded by hundreds of Gestapo and new guards in addition to the ghetto policemen. They came to the front of our building and started marching. While my father counted, they marched 14 steps up and another 14 steps down again repeatedly. We decided to jump out the second-floor back window into the courtyard one by one between every 14 steps. I did it first, my

brother second, then my mother with the baby, and my father last. There were no people in the garden, but in an attic above a carriage house and loft, there were already other people hiding with the same plan. The problem was our little baby. My mother carried cooked poppy seeds, expensive in these circumstances in the ghetto, to keep the baby asleep as though drugged. The other people didn't want us to join them because the baby might cry. At the back of the garden there was a loft so we went there, but it was already full of people, and they also didn't want to take us for the same reason. Then, my father got upset and threatened them, "I'll scream loud so the Germans outside can hear us, then we'll be all killed!" They eventually agreed to it, but took the baby, me, and my brother as hostages. We three children were grabbed away from my parents. They held our necks and threatened my parents: "If you don't give up your baby, you'll lose all three! If any of your children makes any noise, the same for all three, O.K.?" While we were hiding there, we heard a massive sound of shooting outside. All the Jews who had been taken out to the streets were executed by the SS. Through a little loft window, we saw two soldiers with motorcycles down the street. Their machine guns were decorated with the Lithuanian national flag; it was like a festival for killing Jews. While we were watching them, the men sitting next to my mother put their hands on our baby's face; he was suffocated. The killing outside the building didn't stop. We heard crying, screaming, and the sounds of machineguns, and by the late afternoon, every Jew in the streets had been slaughtered: they were shot in the head and fell into the ditches. A total of 2,000 Jews of Radun were murdered in one day, May 10, 1942. In the aftermath of the bloody shooting, 60 men were left alive to remove the blood and the messy corpses and bury them. Those who were allowed to live were given a slashed "X" mark like cattle on their back. Since my father didn't have it, he took his belt and asked my mother to slash the mark into his back. She refused to do it saying, "I sacrificed my baby to save others. A wife beats her husband, a husband beats his wife, parents sacrifice their children to survive. I've had enough, I don't want to be part of it anymore." So someone else did it for him.

Eventually, SS men found us and took us out to the marketplace and the gallows, which I used to watch from the kindergarten window. While our parents were working, the children were lined up face down on the ground for three days. After they finished with the corpses, my father knew that the SS men would kill us all, because they didn't need us anymore, and also to hide the evidence of the massacre. He said we must run fast.

We discovered that my father's brother and his daughter had survived the massacre. They came out to the marketplace, too. The six of us escaped, running into the forests again to hide. There, we met a group of Russian partisans fighting against the Nazis, and among them there were some Jews. They wanted my father to join them but without the children. My father got an idea. He offered some money to his old Gentile friend by the name of Korkucz in the nearby town to make a sort of cave shelter in his backyard to hide us. It was dug into the dirt of a farmyard, with a small hole for fresh air and pigs and chickens above us, a very tiny burrow that I, then 5, couldn't stand up in. There, my mother used to teach me how to write while my father was away with the partisans. Korkucz's family delivered food to us. After hiding there for 9 months, one sunny Sunday morning at the end

of 1943 while the Korkucz family were attending Mass, we came out of our cave to get some fresh air and sunshine. During that brief moment, a neighbor saw us. They reported us to the Gestapo, because anyone who did that was rewarded with kilos of salt. Therefore, every citizen was collaborating with the Nazis. Korkucz got terrified and told us to leave, because anyone who hid Jews would be executed on the spot along with his family. So, on a snowy night, we were thrown out into the forests. While we were running we were attacked by wolves. All six of us were bitten, but we managed to keep walking. We came to a different village where my father had another non-Jewish friend, Fredick.

While we were hiding in his house, there was an incident. A neighboring Polish woman was hiding some Jews in her home. Her son was a member of the Polish Partisans and betrayed his mother. He reported her to the Polish Partisans. They captured the woman and all her Jewish friends, locked them in the house, poured gasoline around, set it afire and burned them alive. We saw the flames and smoke, and could smell the burning flesh in the air. It was really a tragic story. Fredick then got scared and shouted at my father, "Enough is enough! Don't come back to me anymore!" After we left his house, we went back to the house of Korkucz, where we had stayed in the cave before. This was in early 1944 and the Germans were losing the war, but the Jewish manhunt still continued. The anti-Jewish people in the region were eager to catch Jews to get their reward of salt, so it was not safe for us to stay there for long. My father tried every possible friend and, as a last resort, he tried one more man who lived on a nearby farm. He begged him for shelter. "You are my last hope. We have no place to go. If you can't help us, then kill me, please kill all of us!" My father still had money buried in the backyard of our house in Eisysky, so he went back that night and returned with it. He said he would take the risk. In exchange for money the man allowed us to stay in his farmhouse.

In May that year we had a new problem. My mother became pregnant. She gave birth to her baby boy in the stable surrounded by cows, sheep and horses, just like Jesus. But we didn't know what to do with the baby because he cried, and we couldn't take him with us. My parents decided to give him away to a priest who took care of orphans. We placed the baby in a basket safely covered with clothes, and the man's shepherd took it and left it in a Catholic church in Vilna with a message: "This baby was born to a prestigious Polish family, however, unfortunately he has to be raised in an orphanage." We had to conceal his identity that the baby was a Jew. Then two months later in July 1944, the Russian Army moved in and we were liberated. Our region became free finally. We returned to our hometown, Eisysky. There had been 3,500 Jews before the war, but we found only 29 had survived and returned home. Our house was destroyed, so we went to our grandmother's house; but it was occupied by a Gentile family. After uneasy negotiations we got it back and moved in.

But Jewish hatred was still strong and we never felt safe resettling there. We heard things like, "You Jews, go back to the grave. We want Poland as a *judenrein* state. Jews are our enemy." In October 1944, as we started our new life there, my father got the baby back from the church. The baby was given a Jewish name and circumcised. My father invited a few Jewish survivors like us and we had a traditional Jewish celebration in the house. During that night, despite our house being protected by Russian soldiers, a grenade was thrown at the house. The house guests who were sleeping downstairs managed to flee, but my parents with the baby, my brother and me, were all stuck upstairs. Quickly, we ran through our bedrooms into an attic storage room where we could hide. My father moved a cupboard to hide the storage door and the five of us squeezed in. Within minutes we heard the sound of voices speaking Polish downstairs. We were liberated, so there were no more SS men or Germans around, but it was Polish partisans who were now hunting down Jews to kill. They came upstairs and saw a scratch mark on the floor. What had happened was that when my father moved the furniture, he made a scratch. The storage door was opened. Three Polish partisans were standing there. My mother who was standing by the door with the baby was first to be seen. She pleaded, "Kill me first, kill me before my baby. I don't want to see my baby dying!" They shot the baby first and then fired at my mother who was hit with 15 bullets. She fell down backward on top of me, my brother, and my father. The inside was totally dark so they couldn't see us, and they left. That was how the rest of us were saved.

The next morning we buried my mother and the baby. My father was arrested by the Russian KGB and put on trial. Among the accusations against him was the false accusation that he forcefully took a coat from a Christian. The coat actually belonged to his murdered brother. He was sent to Siberia for hard labor for eight years and released when Stalin died, then he emigrated to Israel. My brother, then 12, decided to stay on in Vilna to await our father's return. At the end of the war, Russia did permit Polish citizens to leave the country, so my uncle took me with him to Israel. I got married there and came to the United States in 1955 with my husband.

Considering your extraordinary survival experiences, what do you think is the source of Jewish immortality?

The Jews are people of the Book. They are not simply people exclusively of the Bible, but people of the Talmud of post-Talmudic literature, and volume upon volume of Halakha and Responsa. These are our traditions. The Jewish tradition is our culture and we take it with us and live with it wherever we go like a portable homeland. These books are a great teacher and the essence of our life, and they have been the Jewish law for many thousands of years. Because Jews lost their land for 2,000 years, they developed their culture and tradition through their books they carried. Wherever they went, they established their own communities in the countries they settled in. Books are compact and easy to carry. If we didn't have that tradition, I don't think we could have remained an eternal Jewish people. We live with the tradition, by the tradition, and for the tradition; and when we die, we leave the same tradition for the next generations to continue. It all depends on each Jewish person, of course.

The civilization of Christianity is 2,000 years old, but 2,000 years before that, Jewish people had already been practicing the same valued ethical principles, so human civilization itself must have been much longer than we generally think...?

That's true. Basically, Christianity took many ideas from Judaism, but it incorporated it with many pagan practices which later became part of the popular religion. Judaism never wanted to be evangelical or convert other people or engage in missionary activity like Christianity. Christianity is a daughter religion of Judaism, as is the Moslem faith. Therefore, why Jewish people have been falsely accused as "Christ Killers" and we have been paying for those sins since the beginning of western civilization. The problem is over the matter of the Messiah. Jewish people simply don't accept that the Messiah has already come as Christians believe. Another problem is that ironically, Jesus Christ was Jewish.

What are the traditional Jewish ways of life?

For observant Jews, tradition is a comprehensive guide to their lives. As more and more Jews are becoming assimilated, there is less and less chance for the survival of their faith and culture. Because our culture becomes a part of another culture wherever you are born. The Jewish tradition that keeps Jews Jewish is fading. Jews are unique. Non-Jewish immigrants don't have such a tradition; they don't carry their culture with them. After a few generations, they assimilate with the country and culture where they are born. What they carry is their custom, not a culture. That is the main difference. The Jewish way of life dominates the whole of your life. It demands strict observance. It tells you what to do every day: how to eat kosher, how to behave, whom to marry, what to do on the Sabbath, for instance, not to drive vehicles, not to turn on gas and electric lights, not to watch TV, not to use telephones and computers, to study Torah and Talmud by daylight, etc. It precisely describes how human life and behavior should be even if you are living in a totally different social environment surrounded by an alien culture. Jewish parents sacrifice themselves for their children to give them a good education, to help them stay involved in Jewish social activities, to keep Jewish books in the house, and to marry a Jewish person. As a Jewish American, I never give up my faith. I carry the Jewish tradition with me, as Moses did in the

Sinai thousands of years ago, and I'm extremely proud of it. I'm a "tiny link" in the thousands-year-long human chain, and I try to make sure that it won't be cut in my generation. My children studied the Jewish culture, and my grandchildren as well; it's important for them to continue to learn, speak, read Hebrew, and know Jewish history, tradition and culture, and practice it. That makes us better Americans.

But those books were written many thousand years ago and the world has changed so much since. How can you adjust to that?

The same books which were written many thousands of years ago are still valid today, and we live by the spirit of the same law as our ancestors. That's why it feels so special and beautiful. There is no question that the State of Israel is the Jewish homeland, yet other Jews are able to survive outside Israel in the same way because of the books — the portable homeland. For many other nations, what makes you who you are is your homeland. What makes your national identity is your land. Once you leave your homeland, the things you take with you are your customs, which fade away after a few generations, not your tradition. That is the whole difference. The Jews take their entire tradition with them, minus the land, whenever and wherever they go, and that's why they can survive despite having their own land. What makes someone Jewish is nothing racial or in the blood. As for being the most hated minority, Jews are not only able to observe the tradition, but they are able to find a way to survive amid a hostile and hateful environment. I believe the Jews are one of the oldest peoples on the face of the earth, but we lost many people over the centuries in the Crusades, in the Spanish Inquisition, and, of course, in the Holocaust in which 6 million lost their lives. I don't agree the Jews were chosen people. If we were, we would have privileges, but the truth is we don't. In my view, the Jewish people were chosen to carry the burden of faith, tradition and humanism. It's a burden but it doesn't make us the chosen people. ❖

"Living in terror in the Warsaw Ghetto."

NELLI CESANA

Polish Jew; Holocaust survivor of the Warsaw Ghetto. Born in 1935 in
Warsaw, Poland. Nurse. Lives in California, USA.

(Photo: Ms. Cesana at the photo exhibition, A Day in the Warsaw Ghetto, taken by a
German soldier in 1943.)

What kind of city was Warsaw was before the war, and how did Jews live among the Polish people, Mrs. Cesana?

Warsaw was recorded as a settlement in the 13th century, and became the capital of Poland in 1596. I was too small to remember prewar Warsaw. But my mother used to take me around the city and talk a lot about the city. It was a relatively small city, but very modern, a cosmopolitan and cultured capital city in Eastern Europe. There were great museums, opera houses, ballets and music halls, theaters, movie houses, and open-air concerts on the weekends, etc. The city was surrounded by beautiful parks and rivers and used to be called a "Little Paris."

At the time Poland was invaded by Germans, we had a weak government, both economically and politically, and Ignacy Moscicki, the state leader, was afterwards blamed for the invasion. The population of Warsaw was 1,300,000. A half million were Jewish inhabitants, more than a third of the population, and that made it the biggest Jewish community in all of Europe. The majority of the Jews lived in one particular quarter of the city. Many were well educated and in legal professions: doctors, lawyers, professors and all sort of business. My family, grandparents, parents, brother and me, were all born and raised in Poland. We'd lived there for many generations as an average working class Warsaw family and we had a relatively peaceful life. Despite all that, however, there had been deep anti-Semitic roots among the Polish people for centuries. Traditionally, Poland was, and still is, an orthodox Catholic state and the prejudice was based on its religion and its ignorance.

After the invasion Poland had fallen to the Nazis; within weeks, Warsaw had fully surren-

dered to the German Army. Destruction of Polish Jewry commenced immediately. Were you too young to remember what was happening?

In the summer of 1939, everybody was talking about what was going on in Germany; we knew it was soon going to be war. My father, a business merchant and Zionist, always talked about it and wanted to emigrate to Palestine, but we couldn't. It was in early September. I was 4 then, but I remember it because of the fear of bombing. There were huge factories near our apartment building and the Germans attacked with an air raid in the night, and a piece of shrapnel landed near my bed in our 4th floor and we all panicked. I looked down the street and saw fires and people screaming in panic and running away. Right away, we knew that the Germans were in Warsaw. Then, within a short time, persecution followed and eventually, 500,000 Warsaw Jews became the victims.

Within days, there were bulletin boards in the streets announcing that every Jew must take their luxury items, such as diamonds, gold rings and chains, fur coats, watches, silver plates etc., to the Warsaw SS Headquarters. All Jewish children were banned from attending school. Jews couldn't enter public libraries which had been built by Jewish philanthropists. Every Jew had to wear a Star of David armband in public, even babies, and if they didn't, they would be punished either by being beaten or killed. People were fined for wearing a dirty or wrinkled armband. Jews were not allowed to travel in streetcars or trains, and deprived of all human rights. When German soldiers walked in the streets, Jews had to step aside like dogs to let them pass ahead, otherwise they were abused or killed. One day I saw German soldiers grab an elderly orthodox Jewish man in the streets and start abusing him, kicking him and pulling him around by his traditional plaited beard as he screamed in pain. The persecution got intense in the time before or during every Jewish holiday.

When the Warsaw Ghetto was built, Jews were to relocate. Can you tell me about life inside the ghetto?

After one year of living in fear with riots in the city, in November 1940, construction of the ghetto wall was completed. All Jews were moved into the ghetto. No one was allowed to carry in furniture or anything else except a handful of personal belongings. The Ghetto was sealed off and totally segregated from Poles and life for Jews began inside the ghetto. My parents and grandparents, three aunts and cousins were all inside the ghetto. Then the blockade started and we learned any Jew who tried to escape would be shot. No Jews were permitted to leave the ghetto. They were cut off from work. In the beginning everybody kept quiet and calm, and they started opening up shops, schools, theaters, workshops, and tried to bring their life back to normal.

My brother, then 14, hated it and refused to live there saying, "It's like being caged animals." He sold his bar mitzvah suit, which was expensive at that time, and bought a false Christian Polish identification card through the black market, and he managed to escape from the ghetto. He had connections with the Polish youth resistance organization, as we learned later. After he left, the living conditions in the ghetto got worse. The food supply was cut off and there was not enough to eat. Polish children came to the ghetto through the sewers and smuggled food in exchange for valuables from Jews. But, the ghetto soon ran out of money and goods, and gradually the economic system collapsed. My brother used

to come to see us through the sewers and brought food like bread, eggs or milk, and this kept us alive for some time.

Meanwhile, we saw bulletin boards all over the ghetto saying, "Please be prepared to be relocated. We transfer Jews to another place for labor work. So, be ready!" Then shortly afterwards deportation had started. The trucks loaded with thousands of German and Ukrainian soldiers with guns and dogs unpredictably entered the ghetto, and they randomly grabbed any Jew in the streets, loaded them to the trucks and deported them to Treblinka, the extermination camp northeast of Warsaw. One day, grandfather and my aunts came to my mother and said, "We can't live like this any more, so we decided to go with them voluntarily. We will get bread and jelly at least." That was the last time we saw them: we never saw them again. Then my parents and I went into hiding. We were moving from one place to another and sleeping in different locations every night, and we managed to escape from the Nazis' hands. Then we lost contact with my brother.

Our survival story in the ghetto was beyond a miracle and beyond luck. My mother, 40 then, was a woman who had a strong instinct for survival. Once she discussed the situation with a friend and got an idea of how to avoid being taken to Treblinka. She knew German soldiers took Jews to the station first and lined them up, and loaded them into cattle trains. If it happened to her, she advised, while thousands of people keep moving to get into the trains in the loading process, don't follow them. Instead, walk backwards step by step and let others go forward until the train fills. That way she might have a chance to get away. Which really happened. Once my mother and I were caught in the streets and taken to the station. German guards were chasing people with dogs and shooting. I got scared and started crying. But my mother was calm and saying to me don't cry. She was holding my hand very tight, she walked slowly backwards while others moved ahead of us, and gradually the train filled up. Then another train arrived, but she repeated the same trick again, and there were no more trains after that. We and a few others were left in the station and eventually the Germans soldiers released us. That astonished my father who was in despair thinking we had been taken.

One time, my father got a carpenter's job for a housing project. He found a little hiding spot in the ceiling of the building where nobody could see it. So we went up there in hiding. There were already 30 people hiding there, including one baby. We joined them. Shortly afterwards, thousands of German soldiers appeared with hundreds of trucks and dogs in the streets, entering every building, breaking down each door with rifles and banging on the walls to hunt down Jews. We were all terrified. But we kept hiding there, squeezing against each other for hours. Then suddenly the baby started crying. We got panicked. We were all scared and afraid of being heard by the German soldiers who were below us. But we didn't know how to stop the crying baby, whose father and mother were both absent. It was held by their friend. Someone had a piece of cucumber, so we gave it to the baby to suck. We were a group of over 30 people and luckily one piece of cucumber saved all of our lives. Then a fatal thing happened to my father who was hiding in the same building, but in a different room. Abruptly, his name was called out in Polish by someone outside asking him to come out. The German soldiers knew there were 10 Jewish carpenters in the building and they had

captured 9 of them, but one man was missing, that was my father. Shouting voices threatened him that if he refused to come out, his 9 mates would all be shot instantly. He gave up hiding and surrendered to the Germans. We never saw him again. After that, survival in the ghetto was extremely hard because the ghetto became small, and it was difficult to hide and no food was around. At 7, I was very skinny and always hungry. My mother never left me alone anywhere all those years.

Another time, we were captured and taken to the station again, but this time her method didn't work because there was a "selection" process at the station. A German officer was standing there dividing people into two groups, and my mother and I were separated. She swiftly grabbed me from the chaotic crowds of people and hid me underneath her long raincoat. She began to run. No Germans were watching but a Jewish policeman was. She was stopped by him. She panicked and started a fistfight with him, holding me underneath her raincoat and shouting, "Please leave me alone, I won't go without my daughter!" At that moment she could have easily been shot on the spot. She was ready to die for me. She was determined. No matter what came next, she wouldn't go without me. In the end, the Jewish policeman stopped fighting with her and left her alone. There were big crowds around and nobody cared what was going on. Overall, the luckiest thing was that no SS guard was watching. After that incident, we used the same trick in the station, walking backwards while others were loaded onto the trains until we were left behind. In the same station, we saw Dr. Janusz Korczak, a well-known Jewish philosopher who was running an orphanage house in Warsaw. He was a prominent writer among Germans and the Nazis tried to save him from the persecution. But he chose to be transported and to die with his 200 orphaned children. We saw him taken away with his children to Treblinka. His children were under 10 years old. My mother pointed him out to me.

When we came back to the ghetto, the streets were totally deserted like a ghost town except for a few German guards patrolling on motorcycles. Most apartments were vandalized, households scattered all over, smashed windows, broken doors, and it was hardly livable. But the Jewish hunt never ended. So we kept moving and sleeping in different locations every night. In the winter of 1942, it was freezing cold and we had to burn furniture from the streets to keep warm. I had lice in my hair because I couldn't wash it for months. It was awful. Somehow, a few Jews were still left and hiding, and my mother luckily found a job. It was potato peeling in the soup kitchen of a workshop for sewing soldiers' uniforms, which was run by the Germans. She worked for 12 hours a day, which was the luckiest thing for us because she was able to steal food. Hunger was our greatest problem and the potatoes were like gold; they really saved our lives.

In the early spring of 1943, life in the ghetto became desperate. There was hardly any food around. People started dying of starvation or typhus, and by early 1944 the death toll had reached a few thousand. There were hardly any children alive. We saw an increasing number of corpses covered with newspapers left in the streets and German soldiers were everywhere. Again, every day the Germans kept saying that they provided work and better living conditions for us in the countryside, and that they would transfer us there. So clean the clothes, pack the suitcases and get ready. My mother, who was exhausted and desperate by then, believed what they said and

decided to follow. While she was washing our clothes preparing for deportation, suddenly, a Polish girl, a black market trafficker, came and asked my mother, "Do you have anything to sell?" My mother said, "I have things to give to you free if you do me a favor." My mother thought of her son, my 16-year-old brother who lived outside the ghetto under an assumed name with whom we'd lost contact for years. She wrote a letter: "Dear Mr. Marian (his Polish false name); My daughter and I are alive. I lost my husband. We are in a desperate situation. Please come to help us." In exchange for a tablecloth, she asked the girl to deliver her letter to him and the girl agreed. She never said to the girl that he was her own son. That was the last hope for my mother. By the evening, my brother came to see us. Since he knew about the ghetto conditions, he was astonished to see us alive: he cried like a baby. He obviously thought we had perished in Treblinka. It was a very emotional reunion. He immediately arranged to get us out of the ghetto.

There were smuggling businesses inside the ghetto. Within days, my brother returned with a false I.D. for my mother. His plan was to separate the two of us, so we could escape over two nights. I was the first to go aided by smugglers. I had to climb over the ghetto wall as my brother waited on the other side. When I reached the top of the wall and was about to jump off, suddenly, gunfire started inside the ghetto. The smugglers and my mother were horrified and got panicked. They ran away and disappeared in the dark. I was lost. "Jump, jump, hurry up, Nelli!" said my brother who was waiting for me. So I did. I jumped into his arms.

Before my brother took me to his place, the first thing he forced me to understand was that we were good friends, but "we were not family." His I.D. identified him as Polish, not a Jew. He even taught me that if someone stuck a knife on my neck, not to tell the truth. He was a tall, handsome boy who looked older than his age and didn't look Jewish at all. He took me to his apartment where he lived and introduced me to his Polish landlady, who never suspected he was a Jew. He and I acted like strangers.

The next night was my mother's turn. I anxiously waited for her in his apartment. She was supposed to escape through the barbed wire wall at the back side of the ghetto. It was in the early dawn when my brother came home with my mother. I was so happy to see her safe. The landlady was a widow with two young daughters, one of whom my brother was dating, who was taking a fatal risk for accommodating my mother and me, knowing that we were Jews. Anyone who hid Jews in their home would be shot on the spot. Jews living outside the ghetto would be recognizable easily by Poles, so we couldn't go out anywhere. It was only a few days that the landlady allowed us to stay at her place. My brother was convinced it'd be too dangerous for us to stay in Warsaw and said our only chance of survival was to escape to Germany. That shocked my mother, of course. It sounded to her like suicide. But his idea was that many people were dying in Germany and that was causing severe labor shortages; they needed foreign labor workers very badly. Besides, Germans can't distinguish between Jews and Aryans, so it was easier for us to stay there.

My mother's first step was to fill out a job application form and personally go to the Gestapo headquarters in Warsaw with her fake I.D. This absolutely terrified her. She kept refusing, "I can't do it, it's just impossible for me." It took him two days to convince her. With his strong

encouragement, after three attempts, she made it; she was accepted and got labor work in Berlin. As a child, I was innocently excited by the train trip to Germany. My mother spoke Polish, German and Russian besides Yiddish, and in fact, this played a key role in the last part of our survival. Our new journey as foreign labor workers under false identity began as a Polish Christian mother and her daughter, not as Jews. My mother had to remember her false birthdate and place, including the name of the church she supposedly attended. In the station, my brother handed to her the Christian Bible to read in the train and a cross pendant to wear on her chest.

How did things go with your new life in Berlin?

The first job assigned to my mother was to pick up rocks and clean up a huge farm field outside Berlin. It was physically heavy labor and too hard for a city woman like her. Then a new job turned up. A German retired couple was seeking someone to work on their farm outside Berlin. My mother being fluent in German was hired by them; her knowledge of German history and culture impressed the couple. Their farm was a few hours drive from Berlin, on acres of land surrounded by beautiful trees, a river, ponds, chickens, geese, turkeys, goats, vegetable fields and flowers. There was plenty of fruit to eat. For us it was like heaven. Only one man, a young Pole, was in charge of the entire farm. My mother was assigned to work in the vegetable field. The couple, Mr. and Mrs. Müller, were in their 60s and didn't do much work. They had a son who was in the German air force. Mr. Müller was a retired government official and wealthy; they even had a motorboat with a kitchen, dining table and bed. From time to time, boats arrived through the river from Berlin carrying goodies such as paintings, alcohol, almonds, and many other things which were confiscated from German-occupied territories. We unloaded them and stored them in two huge warehouses on the farm.

They provided for us a barn. During the day, while my mother was working, I used to go swimming in the river. Being a Polish labor worker's daughter, I was not allowed to attend German school and many German parents kept their children away from me. But I found a few neighborhood German children anyhow; I learned German very fast from them. That was, in fact, the first time I was able to be a child and mingle with other children of my own age. But, we had some problems with the Polish man on the farm. He suspected us of being Jews. Not my mother, because she was tall with blonde hair, but me. I looked very much like my father's side and didn't look like my mother. So, he thought I was a bastard born from a Jewish man with whom she'd had an affair. Every time he got drunk, he came to accuse us in our barn and we were very scared of him. Suddenly, one day the Gestapo showed up at our farm. We were terrified, but they arrested him, not us. We learned later that he had been stealing farm goods and selling them to Polish people in Berlin. He was gone! We were saved, yet again.

My mother became acquainted with Mrs. Müller. She came to the farm to talk to my mother all the time; they discussed German history, literature or art, and that pleased Mrs. Müller. She also talked about the war. She told her that if Germany was defeated by the Allies, and if Russians occupy Germany, they would commit suicide. One day she showed us a piece of soap. She explained to my mother that it was manufactured in one of the extermination camps. It was called *"Judenseife"* (Jewish soap made from

Jewish corpses) and distributed all over Germany. Can you imagine, how my mother felt about it. She almost fainted.

Meanwhile, bad news came to us. We had been corresponding with my brother in Warsaw since we settled at the farm. We learned he had been killed. He was a member of the Polish resistance fighting against the Nazis for a free Poland. He was shot to death by the Nazis in October 1943, 6 months after the Warsaw Ghetto revolt. According to his closest friend, he died like a hero for his motherland. That shocked my mother so deeply that she almost committed suicide; she lost her will to live and totally despaired. She was never the same person again.

In the spring of 1945, the Allies were bombing more and more, and the sky of Berlin was like a Christmas tree every night; we saw it from our village. Leaflets were scattered from the sky written in Polish and Russian, "War will be over soon! We will come to liberate you!" So we knew the war was ending finally, and the Russians were coming to Germany. Shortly after that, Russian soldiers came to our village and sought a Russian-German interpreter, so my mother volunteered. They were pleased to find her, but my mother still concealed the fact that she was Jewish. She didn't trust anybody, neither Russians nor Germans in such a situation. They gave us a lot of looted clothes and shoes. They were all young soldiers and wild and coarse, like peasants. They got drunk with stolen alcohol and raped young German women in the village. But they never touched my mother. They needed her because of her language skills. However, she was never relaxed with them.

After the war ended, how did your mother manage life?

At the end of the war, we went back to Warsaw hoping we might find someone alive there. The city was totally ruined by the bombardment and so devastated that we couldn't recognize it. We found no Jew alive, not our family, none of our relatives — nobody. My mother cried in despair and fear that we were the only Jewish survivors in the city. We ended up in the Red Cross outside Warsaw. There my mother met a man who also lost his entire family in the Holocaust. Most Holocaust survivors were young, not many even in their 40s and very few children. By then she had lost the energy to live on her own, and married him. In 1950, the three of us moved to Israel and started a new life.

I was then over 9 and had never been to school or had any decent childhood. Living as a fugitive in terror and fear during my childhood meant I had to catch up on my education very quickly in Israel. Despite a hard life there, I felt happy and at home because for the first time in my life, I was surrounded by other Jewish children. I learned to be strong and independent. I became a nurse at the age of 17 and started working in a hospital. There, I fell in love with an Italian Jew who was living in the United States, and I got married. I came to America with him.

Over all, the whole story of my survival is my brother. The hero is my brother. Without him, we could have never survived. He is the real hero for us and I can never forget him; he lives in my heart forever. ❖

"Non-German SS men were more savage than the German SS."

LINDA BREDER

Slovakian Jew; Holocaust survivor of Auschwitz concentration camp. Retired from home business. Born in 1924 in Stropkov, formerly Czechoslovakia. Lives in California, USA.

(Photo: Ms. Breder showing her tattoo numbers and wearing a replica Star of David for a demonstration.)

From 1933 to 1938, what was the social and political atmosphere like in Czechoslovakia?

I know that in 1933 my country was the most advanced industrial nation, with the highest standard of living in Eastern Europe. I was then under 10, and I understood nothing of what was going on, but as far as I knew, we had a free society and we had nothing to with Hitler. We had freedom of thought and religion. As Jews, we were not living in ghettos, we were relatively assimilated. Historically, Czechoslovakia is a very young nation. It was born in 1918 after the fall of the Austro-Hungarian empire, as three republics: Bohemia, Moravia and Slovakia. I was from Slovakia. The next 20 years were the most peaceful era until 1938 when Hitler occupied my country. Until then, I personally didn't even notice anti-Semitism. My family had settled in Stropkov, my hometown, in the 17th century, and my ancestors were all born and raised under the Austro-Hungarian empire.

After 1938 your country was controlled by Nazi Germany. How did things change and how were you arrested?

It was an overnight change. Everything in our life suddenly turned upside down. At that time my country had a coalition government of church and state led by Dr. Monsignor Joseph Tiso, a Catholic priest and an extreme nationalist. He supported Hitler's ideas of persecuting the Jews. He was a puppet of Hitler. He immediately broadcasted anti-Semetic propaganda over the radio, in newspapers, on public billboards and in loudspeaker campaigns in the streets. First, the Nuremberg Racial Laws were introduced in Czechoslovakia, the first state to accept them outside Nazi Germany. Then, I personally began to experience anti-Semitism. Before the war, there

were 375,000 Jews out of a population of 15 million, less than 5 percent of all of Czechoslovakia.

Many of the Jews in my community had converted to Catholicism. Everyone was like a neighbor or a friend because we had all known each family for generations. But as soon as Jews were forced to wear the Star of David in public, everybody changed their attitude toward Jews, even long-time friends. They were totally brainwashed by the right-wing government and church propaganda.

In October 1938 when I was 14, our school class was suddenly interrupted by an emergency siren and we heard on the radio that Hitler's troops had entered and taken over the Sudetenland, the western part of Czechoslovakia. Within days, Jewish children weren't allowed to attend school anymore. Then the government ordered Jews to turn over their valuables; diamonds, gold rings, silver and watches to the authorities. Every Jew was then relocated to another part of the city, where we were forced to live with several other Jewish families in one house. Then, a curfew was instituted and we were not permitted to go outside for more than a few hours daily. Our freedom was completely taken away.

We were a family of five. We had a house on a main street downtown until all our property was confiscated by the government. My father, a school teacher, lost his job. He didn't have much savings but he was able to bring a small amount of food home from farm work. Our family survived that way, day by day, hoping that Hitler's domination would soon come to an end, and everything would go back to normal again.

Early in 1942, as soon as the Final Solution for Jews was ordered in Nazi Germany, the Hlinka Guard was formed in my country. It was a national party, the equivalent of the Nazi SS with the same black uniforms. Meanwhile, anti-Jewish propaganda had been intense, from morning to night every single day over loudspeakers throughout the city blaming everything on Jews and calling us "Christ Killer." One night in March 1942, Hlinka Guards suddenly showed up in every Jewish home to hunt down girls between the age of 14 and 25. At 16, I was taken away by a truck to a railway station with many others. There were one thousand girls. We were told that we were being sent to Germany for factory work. But the truth I learned much later was that, in fact, Tiso paid Hitler 500 marks for each girl, and asked him to ensure we would never return alive. Tiso wanted to expel every single Jew from Slovakia, and that was his first policy; we were actually traded to Hitler. As a long cattle train approached the station, Hlinka Guards shouted at us "Hurry up and get in, you Jewish whores!" and they pushed us in. Inside the carriages there was one bucket of water for us to drink and another bucket for sanitary use, but nothing more, no window. Each carriage was loaded with 80 girls squeezed up against one another, overcrowded, no fresh air, and no food. After an overnight journey, the train stopped in the middle of a field and we were unloaded. We learned that we had arrived at Auschwitz, not Germany.

You were in the Auschwitz death camp for longer than anyone else, from 1942 to 1945. Can you tell how you survived there?

Life inside Auschwitz was hell, it was a war for survival every minute. It was such a tragedy in my life that even today, a half century after, I still cry from the painful scars deep in my heart.

After we got out of the train, we were lined up in the field like soldiers. The first thing we saw there was a Jewish doctor who had accompanied us, being beaten to death by SS guards. We were all terrified. It was the first shockingly brutal murder scene I had ever witnessed. After that everybody became quiet and followed orders. We were forced to march in the snow for hours until we reached an area of flat endless land surrounded by barbed-wire. Then we saw a tall chimney, so I believed it must be the factory that we were to work in. Then we arrived at the gate of the camp, an entrance arch with the big sign that read "ARBEIT MACHT FREI" — Work Makes You Free. Inside were ten brick barracks, each one barricaded with a barbed-wire fence. We, one thousand Slovakian girls, were the first Jewish females to enter Auschwitz. There were 82 rooms in our barrack. Each dormitory was about ten square yards without mattress or blanket. There were only ten toilets for one thousand girls and very little drinking water. On our first day in the camp, we were suddenly awakened by women screaming "Out! Out!" It was 4 o'clock in the morning. We saw another thousand women in striped uniforms. We quickly learned that they were criminal prisoners from Germany who had been given life sentences, and they were in charge of us at the camp. They were savage and violent, always shouting, yelling at us, whipping us like animals because we were Jews. Being Jewish was our sin. Our first day in the camp started with roll call. We were lined up, five in a row in front of the barracks and kept standing there throughout the icy morning.

While doing that, SS women took gold rings, earrings, necklaces from anyone who had them, and next they checked our mouths to find gold teeth. Then they cut off our hair and shaved our body hair including pubic hair. Next, we were completely undressed and plunged into icy water to be cleaned. Then everybody was tattooed with a number on their left arm. After that, we were given Russian uniforms from the 75,000 solders who were killed by the German army. Most of them were covered with blood stains, filthy, smelly, and full of lice, and too large, but we had to wear them without any underwear. We were given only a pair of wooden shoes, so we couldn't escape. Then we were handed a red bowl and one spoon. Our daily meals were a cup of black tea for breakfast, a bowl of soup for lunch, and pieces of bread with margarine for dinner, nothing else. The nightmare of life in Auschwitz had begun. A few days later, one of the girls committed suicide by jumping out of the barracks window. She couldn't bear it anymore. Indeed, no one could have lived more than a few months in such conditions. But it was just beginning.

As you may know, Auschwitz was the biggest camp in all of occupied Poland. In an area covering 20,000 acres of flat country land, there were 3 separate camps. Auschwitz-I: the main camp; Monowitz: the labor camp for German industrial corporations such as I.G. Faben, Siemens, AEG (German Electricity Trust) and all manufacturing war materials or related items; and Auschwitz-Birkenau: the camp for extermination where gas chambers and crematoriums were operating. More camps were added, and they expanded constantly as more and more people arrived. All prisoners, men and women, were separated in different camps and labor works. And, very soon, 4 more chimneys were built by newly arrived prisoners. I was in the Auschwitz-I camp. For the first month, I was assigned to do farmwork. We were all hungry and always desperate for food.

In early 1942 when the Final Solution to the Jewish question was established, Heinrich Himmler, SS Commander and State Police Chief of the Third Reich, ordered Rudolf Hoess, a commander in chief of Auschwitz, to expand its mass extermination facilities. Within months, more trains started arriving at Auschwitz, two or three daily from all over Europe bringing Jews, Gypsies, homosexuals, political prisoners, and others. In my women's camp, there was a drastic increase of prisoners from 1,000 to 45,000, and it became extremely overcrowded.

Then, a lucky opportunity came to me. The camp needed some 300 girls to sort through the clothes and personal belongings of new arrivals, and I was appointed by SS men to be one of them. It was called a "Kanada" unit. Shortly afterwards we learned that children, the elderly, and anyone who wasn't fit for labor work were sent straight to the gas chambers on arrival. Everybody was undressed before being gassed, so the Nazis needed people to go through the belongings. Our job was to sort out those tons of clothes, personal items, bags, jewelry, money, and so on. My particular job was to clean the clothes by hand, fold them neatly, bundle them together and ship them back to Germany on the trains which had brought people to Auschwitz.

The reason I survived and walked out alive from that death factory was because of this job. We were able to eat stolen food hidden in those bags or clothes. I was 18 then. We were all young, but we never had enough to eat so starvation was the main cause of death in the camp. If I had stayed on that farmwork detail, which was 12-hours a day of hard labor without extra food or water and lice eating my body, I would have died within months.

By that time, more prisoners were dying, and seeing dead bodies had become routine in the camp. Besides those who were gassed, more died from starvation, overwork, malnutrition, di-

113

arhea, disease, and many committed suicide. When prisoners fell sick and became too weak to work, SS guards enjoyed torturing them sadistically, and then shot them to death on the spot.

After working there for a year, I felt we must do something. The outside world must know what was going on there. I wanted to tell everybody outside to stop the killing there. A few of us in the Kanada unit wrote messages: "Nazis are killing Jews. Don't come to Auschwitz," and put them between the clothes shipped back to Germany.

Every Sunday was the day for the selection process in our camp, the day that the notorious Nazi doctor, Dr. Joseph Mengele, came to decide our destiny — death or life — gas chamber or slave labor. I passed every single selection throughout those years, because I was decently fed compared to other prisoners. That's why I survived. Of the one thousand girls originally from Slovakia, only twenty survived, and I was one of them. Overall, I was extremely fortunate.

During those years, what were the things you remember that still traumatize you?
One day in my Kanada unit, 300 girls were transferred to the Auschwitz-Birkenau camp, which was the most advanced human extermination factory of all the German death camps. We were assigned to work very close to the gas chambers where new arrivals were sent directly to be gassed. The sky was permanently covered with deep and dark smoke from the chimneys. The smell of burning flesh hung in the air. In there we saw everything. Nazi Germany's genocide industry was efficiently operated at full speed. With 12 hours shifts, it ran non-stop 24 hours a day, seven days a week, burning up to 10,000 people per day. We always saw thousands of the latest arri-

vals, children, old people, and women holding towels and soap in their hands believing what they were told, that they were to "take a shower." They stood naked in line, naively waiting, not knowing they would never come out alive. Our work site was only seven or eight meters away from them, and we knew everything that was going on, but we couldn't inform them. There was an electric barbed-wire fence between us. There were SS guards with machineguns and dogs, and watch towers surrounding us. We had no way to communicate with them. We knew that we would be gassed because I knew that the Nazis would destroy all evidence of the Holocaust. I myself was totally convinced that if I ever came out of Auschwitz, it would be in smoke through that chimney. Living in fear every moment made me feel apathetic about being dead or alive. It's very painful to remember that.

One very hot summer day in 1944, we were all thirsty and needed water. As usual, there was a long line of innocent victims standing for hours waiting their turn. They became impatient in the heat and started begging for water. One of our girls threw a small container of water over the fence to them in sympathy. I saw a little boy run to get it. Suddenly, an SS guard moved in. He grabbed the boy and tossed him in the air and as the boy fell, he caught him on the point of his bayonet, and then smashed him down beside the crematorium. The boy was instantly killed. His mother screamed and cried, but no one could do anything. I watched it all the way through. We were all helpless.

SS guards were not only Germans. They were also Austrians, Rumanians, Poles, Hungarians, Latvians, and other German-occupied nationalities. They loved shooting any Jew alive. The most exciting amusement for them was to shoot anyone who stood up to stretch by the marshes in the camp field. It was like a shooting game and they enjoyed watching them drown. At the end of the day, the last rows of the camp commandoes had to haul the dead bodies back to the barracks for evening roll call. By the time they got back to the barracks, there was hardly skin left on their backs. Then in the evening, an official announcement would be made; "One prisoner was shot today while trying to escape." I witnessed what those brutal and sadistic SS did. The SS were really barbarians.

You were on the "death march." Can you tell about it and how did liberation come to you?
In January 1945 the Nazis knew the Russian Army was coming. They planned to put mines and dynamite around the camps to kill all the survivors including us, the Kanada unit, so as to destroy all evidence of the Holocaust. But the Russians were advancing so fast that they had no time for their plans. They decided to take the remaining prisoners with them. There was a serious labor shortage in Germany and they needed us. All the Auschwitz extermination camps were evacuated, over 70,000 prisoners, of which thousands were women and one-third of the total were Jews. We were forced to march towards Germany at gunpoint by about 40,000 SS guards on horseback. The death march was beyond any human conditions. We had to walk in the middle of the winter, climbing up the snowy mountains to avoid civilian areas, with no food for a week. Death after death, the roads were piling up with bodies as we marched by. Many lost their toes, fingers or ears in the icy cold. We survived by eating snow. About two-thirds finally made it to Germany. And again, I was one of the survivors.

After surviving that death march, for the last months of the war I was in Ravensbrück, a women's camp north of Berlin. I saw destroyed Germany; devastated cities, towns and villages totally ruined by the Allied bombardments and, most of all, dead German bodies lying everywhere. Our job was to clean up Neubrandenburg air field, which had been badly damaged by the Allied bombs. While we were repairing the fields, the Allied forces kept bombing Berlin, the last city to fall.

One morning at the end of April 1945, we woke up and found no SS guards around. They knew the Russians were approaching and the fall of Berlin was a matter of days away, so they disappeared during the night as fast as possible. We saw tanks coming towards us, but we couldn't tell whether they were Russian or American because both had star marks on them. Eventually on the 5th of May, we were liberated by Russians. When I returned home, I found that all of my family had perished in Auschwitz two months after I was taken away. Nazi Germany ruined my life. I was a victim of the Nazi Germans.

As a witness, you have often testified in trials of former Nazi SS guards. Can you tell me how did the hunt for Nazis operate and how is the prosecution of former Nazis carried out?
During my 3 years of incarceration in Auschwitz, I was between 16 and 18 years old. Working at the sorting site, I was very familiar with the faces of SS guards. The Simon Wiesenthal Center, the Nazi criminal hunting center in Los Angeles, is working closely with German councils in the USA. When they caught men suspected of being SS officers who worked in Auschwitz during the time I was there, they contacted me to identify them when they stood for trial. From 1971 to

1991, I did this four times. To tell you the truth, besides Germans, the majority of the SS guards in Auschwitz were German Allied-soldiers from German-occupied countries, who volunteered to work for the SS and cooperated in the killing of Jews and others. In fact, they were much more cruel and sadistic than the German SS. I never knew their names, but I certainly remember their faces because I saw them all the time every day, and because of their accents, I could also recognize their nationality.

Since it all ended a half century ago, you may wonder how can I remember accurately? First, German council officers showed me old photos of many former SS men during the time they were working there; straight portraits, both front and in profile. My memory is very clear and I could spot them straight away. How could I forget the faces of those killers? The former SS men I testified against were two Austrians, Franz Wunsch and Otto Graff, and two Germans, Godfried Wiesse and Heinrich Kuhnemann. In the case of Godfried Wiesse, for example, as I entered the court room, he looked at me and I looked at him, and we immediately recognized each other. While many other former SS men changed their names and even physical appearance, he was obvious, because he had only one eye and was a cripple. He couldn't hide that. The testimony was too emotional for me. My heart was shaking and I cried during the whole trial. Judges always asked me the time of the events. My answer was always "I don't know. There was no sun in Auschwitz because the sky was permanently covered with deep flesh burning smoke. Auschwitz never had daylight." I also said in each trial "If he had killed me, no one would remember him and there would be no one to accuse him. He is not lucky." As a result, Wiesse, the German SS, was sen-

tenced to life in prison, but I don't know what happened to Kuhnemann, the other German SS. The two Austrians were set free. I think that the Austrian government never wanted to help find their own criminals. Anti-Semitic attitudes among Austrians remains unchanged today, and I believe it will be this way in the future, too.

After the war, since you lost all of your family, your children didn't have uncles, aunts, grandfathers, grandmothers or cousins. How did you explain to them when they were still too young to understand the whole story?

It was the most painful part of being a Holocaust survivor. My husband was also a survivor of Auschwitz, and we have one son and one daughter, both born in Czechoslovakia. When they were children, they wanted to know the meaning of my tattoo numbers, and always wondered why we don't see our relatives in the cemetery. Because beside my husband, no one else had tattooes. It hurt me every time I tried to answer them. Little by little, I had to teach them about history and Judaism, and as they grew older, I started explaining about the Nazi Germans. When my son was in a kindergarten, all the children had to take a shower. Some kids recognized that he was circumcised. One day he said to me that he was insulted by his classmates, "You, dirty Jew!" Even after that horrifying war and after so many Jews were killed, hatred of Jews has never ended in my country. People are still hostile against Jews. That was the reason we emigrated to America. I'm Jewish in heritage but don't practice now. Because of my very tragic experience, I occasionally question myself about God. Everything I was taught could not be true. How could this have happened to me and to so many Jews if there were a God for us? Was he absent during those years of Jewish genocide? I have great-grandchildren now. I never forced them to become Jews or educated them in the Jewish way of life. I believe that whether they are Jewish or not is their own choice.

Recently my 16-year-old granddaughter accompanied me on a visit to my homeland. After seeing the Jewish Museum in Prague, she wrote an essay about me entitled "Ashes."

"Memories of Jewish people and children I have never met, places I have never seen and pain I have never felt. Memories of my grandmother aimlessly wandering through the graveyard, reading the names on the tombstones, her hand probing the Hebrew letters, searching for a recognizable name, trying to touch the past, looking for answers to questions that have long been unanswered.

"I am filled with haunting memories of my grandmother weeping, touching the numbers tattooed on her arm. My memories are of seeing how tragedy can turn the strong to weak, how pain never really leaves. She needed to be protected, from Nazi soldiers, from SS guards, from the past, from the memories. I stood, confused and angry in front of her. I placed my hand on her arm, but she felt no touch, she felt nothing but sorrow, hate, and pain." ❖

"Kuwait's oil-burning smoke reminded me of the smoke of Auschwitz-Birkenau."

GLORIA HOLLANDER LYON

Czechoslovakian born Jew; Holocaust survivor of Auschwitz concentration camp and 6 additional concentration camps. Born in 1930 in Nagy Bereg (Beregi) (later Hungary, now Ukraine). Lives in California, USA.

(Photo: Mrs. Lyon with a map of Europe, pointing out the town where she was born.)

How did things change in your country in the late 1930s and early 1940s? Did the Holocaust come to you suddenly or did you have any kind of information?

I remember a particular incident when I was a child. It was in the summer of 1943 before the Nazis came to arrest us. A strange Jewish man from Poland came to my rural hometown. He was shot and injured, and carried an important message for the Jewish people: he came to inform us of something we'd never heard. "Nazi Germans are killing Jews in Poland and elsewhere in German-occupied territories. I escaped from it. I'm telling you it's going to happen here soon. Everybody must be aware." He went from street to street, village to village, and town to town across the Carpathian mountains telling Jews his story. I remember him very well. He was in his early 30s and had huge eyes with bushy eyebrows, and was a little overweight. The people he talked to in my town thought he was a lunatic and had lost his mind, poor man! At that time, in my quiet town with a Jewish community of just a few hundred, nobody paid attention to him. Nobody took his words seriously. We were ignorant, not ready to accept such shocking news. During the war years, there were many rumors which drove us into confusion, but people didn't believe it until it really happened.

Nagy Bereg, my hometown, 8 km from Beregszasz in eastern Czechoslovakia, was a beautiful scenic border town surrounded by Hungary, Romania and Ukraine. As a result of the Munich Agreement in 1938, it became part of Hungary, and we were suddenly coerced into speaking Hungarian. Since Hungary was allied with Nazi Germany, racial laws were gradually enacted. My family; my parents, 3 brothers, one sister and I, were a traditional middle-class Jewish family who

had lived in this town for many generations. My father was a wine maker/businessman and farmer. We lived in a big house with a grocery store in front and grape arbor in the side yard. We had a relatively happy life until the Nazi Germans occupied our land.

At the age of 8, I was in a Czechoslovakian elementary school, but after 1938 I was transferred to a Hungarian school. My class was mixed with Hungarian and Czechoslovakian pupils, Christians and Jews, but the instructions were in Hungarian. Besides, I privately studied Hebrew and Jewish history. Anti-Semitism didn't start immediately in the class but did later among the teachers and my peers. My parents occasionally talked about politics at home, but I'm sure that they were unaware of what was going on in Germany and German-occupied countries. The news was censored by the Hungarian government and to own radios became illegal. The Nazi racial laws were adopted by the government, and eventually reached our community. School was segregated; contact between Jews and Gentiles became illegal. Above all, the anti-Semitic laws directly affected my father's business. In the fall of 1939, one of his business associates, a Gentile friend, quit working with him; my father was deprived of farm equipment such as the wheat-threshing machine. His main income with which he supported our family of seven was cut off. Preparing for the worst, we preserved agricultural products in our attic, basement and wine cellar: corn, wheat, potatoes, etc. We also secretly hid a radio to keep up on censored news.

How were you and your family arrested and where were you taken?

The night before SS soldiers entered our town, a Christian friend came to inform us that the Jewish people would be "rounded up" so that we should be ready. We immediately notified many of our Jewish friends. Then my parents hid our family valuables: silver candelabras, silver plates, diamond rings, gold watches and necklaces, under one of the floors. My mother prepared smoked meats and matzos to take with us. At five o'clock the next morning on April 15, 1944, SS soldiers and the Hungarian police knocked on our door. They ordered us to leave within a half-hour. Each of us packed some personal belongings. When all my family members were out of the house, our neighbors and my schoolmates came out to watch us in the streets. The SS man locked the front door of the house and sealed the lock with a brown liquid wax with a swastika imprinted on it. Our house was confiscated; it became Nazi property. As we watched helplessly, I saw tears on my father's cheeks.

It was the day after Passover, an important Jewish holiday. The Nazis intentionally made their plans for that day. We were taken to a brick factory and held there together with other Jews from the entire region for four weeks. It was filled with about 15,000 people. Then we were loaded into cattle cars and transported. We were simply told that we were to be resettled in a more comfortable place. After a journey of 4 days, the train stopped. My father looked out the cracks of the box car and said, "I don't like what I see, rows of long barracks surrounded by electric barbed-wire fences, huge chimneys and watchtowers with searchlights." That was Auschwitz-Birkenau. We were kept in the train overnight. On the following morning, on May 19th 1944, we were unloaded with shouts of, "Out, out, hurry up, hurry up!" There were dozens of SS soldiers with guns and dogs. Many children screamed in fear. They shouted at us to leave all our belongings on the train.

What did you see in Auschwitz when you arrived? Can you describe the details of the selection process by Dr. Mengele?

At the ramp of the Auschwitz-Birkenau camp, the selections started. I noticed a tall man in a black SS uniform, black hat, black boots and white gloves on his hands. He was standing and quickly pointing at everybody to go left or right. The man was Dr. Josef Mengele, the notorious Nazi doctor. He was called "the Angel of Death" and was entirely in charge of the life and death of new arrivals, about 10,000 people every day. First, he divided us: the men and the women. My father, 51, and my two brothers were sent with the men, and my mother Helen, 48, my younger sister and I, then 14, went in the other direction. Then, in the women's section, there was a further selection. Old women, children, young mothers with children, pregnant and disabled women were all sent off to a different direction. That crowd was much bigger than the other one, so we naturally presumed that the healthy young women were going to look after the children, older or sick people. When our turn came, my little sister, age 12, was separated from me and my mother: she was ordered to follow the bigger group. She panicked and started crying, but an SS soldier pushed her to follow them, so she did. At that moment, we didn't know that the larger group was walking toward the gas chambers and would be murdered immediately.

A few minutes later we saw a horse-drawn wagon carrying luggage and bundles from the train passing by, and we saw my sister riding on the back. When she saw us, she looked around and while the SS men were not watching, she jumped off swiftly and joined us. There was an uncountable mass of people, children crying, screaming, chaotic scenes, and SS men were everywhere. But fortunately nobody saw what she did. We were so happy to be united. We then conjectured that we had been chosen to work, perhaps at a labor camp. We were taken to change into gray cotton uniforms. Our heads were completely shaven bald and our arms tattooed: A-6372 for my mother, A-6373 for my sister and A-6374 for me. The luckiest thing was that we three were always together.

Our first assignment was to sort clothes and other belongings. We saw people leave their clothes on the lawn, they went into the building, and after that, we never saw them come out again. We had strong suspicions because of the putrid smell, the odor of burning human flesh in the air. The smell was unbearable. Another sign was the huge black smoke clouds constantly spewing out from the chimneys. The smoke clouds of the Kuwaiti oil fire during the recent Gulf War reminded me of Auschwitz. Then, our worst fear became a reality. We realized that our work site was next to the gas chamber and crematorium No. 4, a part of the giant killing center. Several times we saw a mass of people, men, women, children and old people together undressing on the lawn by the so-called "shower room." It was an absolutely shocking scene, the worst thing I've ever seen in my life. We were deeply disturbed and horrified. This was in the summer of 1944. We learned later that it was the peak time for the killing of the Hungarian Jews and for the industrial gassing operation. Over 10,000 people were arriving in Auschwitz every day, and the gas chambers and crematoriums were over-burdened. They couldn't handle so many people so fast and they were running behind on the gassing schedule.

Periodically, additional selections were made by Dr. Mengele. He was in his late 30s, tall and handsome, and he never smiled nor said a word. He was always impeccably dressed; his black leather boots were always shiny and spotless even in the filthy ground of Auschwitz-Birkenau. His black uniform and SS hat were immaculately clean. He always wore white gloves on his hands during the selection. He stood in the middle of the barracks and pointed left and right deciding who should live and who should die. He had remarkably soft eyes, and when one looked in his eyes, one couldn't imagine him to be a mass killer. In his cool glance, one would find not the slightest idea that this man could be the hideous murderer of millions. He was particularly fascinated with genetic experiments on twins. He was obsessed with discovering a fool-proof method for every German woman to bear twins or even triplets. When he found twins during his selections, he became gentle and gave them chocolates. Afterwards he performed horrifying experiments on them; when he failed, he shot them and burned them in the crematorium. Many twins became his victims and only a handful survived. I remember the twins very well because next to our work place, "Kanada," was the laboratory where he did his experiments. We saw twin children, they were always starving. My mother used to throw food, which she found from among the new arrival's clothes, over the barbed wire fence. Once she was caught by an SS man and beaten, but narrowly escaped from being executed.

You went through a total of seven concentration camps: three death camps and four slave labor camps. How did this happen?

After working several months sorting clothes in the Auschwitz-Birkenau extermination camp, one day at the end of December, 1944, I failed the selection. I was separated from my mother and sister. Along with 30 other women, Dr. Mengele picked me to die in the gas chamber. I was the youngest. He ordered us to undress completely, supposedly for a medical check up. It was in the night. Those of us who worked in Kanada knew that this was our death sentence. We were taken to a dark barrack. A truck arrived to take us away. There were two SS guards. One of them ordered us to get into the truck. The other, a Hungarian-speaking SS, was someone my sister and I had often seen at the clothes sorting site. He recognized me and murmured to me, "You, too?" Then, he said to all of us, "You're all going to the gas chamber. If anyone would like to jump off the truck on the way, you can do so. But if you are found, you are not to give me away for I may be able to save other lives yet. But if you do give me away, both you and I will be killed." Then, he closed the canvass curtain of the truck and started driving. The truck slowly moved towards the gas chambers. It had to cross through two electrified wire gates before reaching the forested area where the gas chambers were located. The gas chambers and chimneys were surrounded by young birch trees and invisible to the outside, covered by beautiful green grass on the ground. Unless you knew, you wouldn't feel that you were in the death factory zone. I was familiar with the area because I passed it every day on my way to work and back. I also remembered a deep ditch by the narrow road on the way. I said to myself, "If I jump off, I may save my life. If I don't, I'll be gassed and cremated within hours."

I suddenly broke my silence: "I'm going to jump off. Who would like to join me?" Most of the others were like zombies, either totally exhausted or too weak to attempt to do anything. They gave up hope. Nobody replied. I was determined to take the deadly risk. The truck was still moving slowly. "I must do it now... alone... quickly... now!" I thought, and jumped off. I slipped down into a deep ditch next to the road. It was pitch black; I couldn't see anything. I crawled and touched a culvert with a little water running in the bottom. So I quickly squeezed myself in like a shrimp. About 15 minutes later, I heard the sound of sirens go on and soon the voices of SS above. My absence had been discovered. But after a while the commotion died down.

So, you hid in a culvert of Birkenau, stark naked in the middle of winter? You were only 14 years old. In normal circumstances, I can imagine, you would have frozen to death.

I was alone and probably terrified. I kept thinking of my mother and my sister mourning for me. "They think I'm dead already. I must survive to see them again." I don't recall feeling cold or having any sensation except the great feeling of triumph — I felt that I had defeated the entire German army. I don't recall much after that. But I certainly remember that I didn't move from the culvert all night and the next day. During those long hours without food or drink, without clothing, hiding in the icy culvert, I must have been cold, hungry, thirsty, tired, scared to death, but all I was thinking was that I wanted to see my mother and little sister to let them know that I didn't die, that they shouldn't grieve for me. I would see them again... Many years later, I was amazed by what I did. That experience taught me a lot. Human beings can endure much more if one has someone to live for and has a strong will to survive. One doesn't know until one is tested under extraordinary circumstances in a life and death situation, what one is capable of doing.

Approximately 24 hours later, I climbed back up to the road. In total darkness, I saw a tiny light like a tiny star in the distance. I followed it slowly. The camp field was under complete blackout and totally silent. I could see no one around. I lost my sense of direction and I had no idea where I was heading. As I got closer to the light, I said to myself, "I'm taking a deadly risk, I may end up in the SS headquarters, and I'll be savagely beaten or sent to the gas chamber after all." I took the risk. I entered a building. Luckily, it was a women's barrack. I climbed up to the third tier of a bunk. A woman inmate screamed because I was cold or seeing me naked in the dark, but she quickly understood my situation, gave me her overcoat and allowed me to sleep there. The next morning there was a roll call. Since many inmates were dying everyday, the SS didn't even notice me: one exchanged for one dead. I melted into this group. The Russian Army was approaching Auschwitz and the SS were evacuating the barracks and transporting a group of several hundred women by cattle car to Bergen Belsen, Germany. I happened to be in that group. That was how I got out of Auschwitz alive.

It took three days to reach the Bergen-Belsen camp near Braunschweig and Hanover. We were assigned to move dirt and stones for a few weeks. There were no gas chambers there, but there were crematoriums. The camp was terribly overcrowded. The diseases carried in by evacuees from various camps caused typhus to spread rap-idly. Many thousands of people quickly died from malnutrition and starvation. More and more bodies piled up. Then, we were relocated to a subcamp in Braunschweig. This was an industrial city east of Hanover where we cleared the streets which were damaged by Allied bombing, so that German military vehicles and artillery could pass through.

Then, I was transferred to a labor camp in Hanover to work on an assembly line making gas masks at a factory named Continental Gummi Werke in Linden. Toward the end of the war, Hitler had feared Allied poison gas attacks in response to Germany's V-1 and V-2 rockets. The poison gas attacks never materialized. The prisoners at the factory were of different nationalities: German civilians, political prisoners, Jews, Poles, Hungarians, French, and resistance fighters from various occupied countries. There, for the first time, I saw a sort of humanity; whenever emaciated prisoners were beaten, German civilian workers protested to the SS. There were selections, too. The SS were still shooting slaves who became too weak to keep working 12-hour days. Rations of food were meager: I was hungry all the time. At my age, 15 by then, I was still supposed to be growing, but I was instead suffering from malnutrition, vitamin deficiency and serious weight loss. I was constantly in fear of being selected for execution.

To protect the Nazi armament industries from extensive Allied bombardment, Hitler moved the major war related industries to underground tunnel locations. I was shipped out to the Beendorf slave labor camp, near Magdeburg. With other prisoners there, I worked in an abandoned salt mine 1,200 feet underground, in a factory which manufactured precision instruments for the V-1 and V-2 rockets, a top Nazi secret.

Huge elevators went down into the mine shaft. Then we walked through a salt-tunnel into the factory, the interior of which consisted entirely of white salt. There were 4,500 men and 2,000 women slaves who worked in the belly of the salt mountain. During the air raids above the ground, the Nazi officers, scientists and engineers ran to their bomb shelters; we had to keep on working. Many years later I learned that, in fact, my father and one of my brothers were working in the same area. They were in the Dora/Mittelbau camp in the Harz Mountains, the main underground factory for Nazi rocket production to which my factory was linked. They were dynamiting silos and tunnels. They were imprisoned there along with thousands of other slave workers. It was very dangerous and extremely hard labor, especially because the dynamite blasts killed many each day, as they were buried alive under falling debris; so no gas chamber or crematorium was needed for them. Prisoners who could not keep up there were sent to Auschwitz.

How were you liberated?

Towards the end of the war, there was a serious manpower shortage. More people were needed to produce war materials in Germany, and we, the slave workers, were constantly relocated from one place to another. We were totally cut off from the news so we had no idea what was happening in the outside world. After a few weeks of working in the rocket factory, we were shipped to Ravensbrück, a women's experimental camp, and from there again transported to an unknown destination. There were thousands of slaves on the train. After three days in the cattle train without food or water, half the prisoners were dead. We pushed out the corpses and left the sick people behind in the cattle cars. We heard the Nazis outside discussing our fate: "We kill them all here."

We were ordered to line up in a huge meadow. So I knew that I was going to be shot. The line was very long. Then, from the end of the line, instead of shooting us, someone was giving out a handful of raw macaroni and sugar to each of us, one by one. I had no idea what that meant. When my turn came, I held up the skirt of my dress to receive my ration, but I failed to receive it because there were holes in my dress and the food fell on the grass. I bent down to pick it up. Because of this, I was beaten up wildly by an SS officer with his wooden club until I fell unconscious. Many hours later when I woke up, I was in a regular passenger train surrounded by women inmates. They told me they had dragged me into the train, and said, "We're free! We're free now! We'll be in Copenhagen, Denmark soon." I simply couldn't believe the news. But when we arrived at the Copenhagen station, we were given an overwhelming welcome by the Danish people waving their flags in their hand. First, we were given a brown bag with food like chocolates and boiled potatoes, and everybody was smiling at us. I was confused because no one had smiled at me since the day I'd been arrested with my family. Then, I finally believed that the war was coming to an end. I was very weak but my mind was firm. Psychologically, I still couldn't trust anyone immediately; it took me some time to adjust to a normal way of thinking. From there we were taken to Sweden on May 3rd, 1945, five days before the surrender of Nazi Germany. In retrospect, the Swedish people were impressively brave. The thousands of women prisoners from Ravensbrück carried all kinds of dreadful diseases: typhus, tuberculosis, or pneumonia. But they took all of us in and nurtured most of us back to health. Still many died en route to freedom and during the months of liberation.

Since I had no memory of what had happened to me after I collapsed unconscious in the open field, I later researched the background of our rescue. During the German occupation of both Denmark and Norway, Sweden maintained diplomatic relations with Nazi Germany. For humanitarian reasons Sweden provided a haven for many Jews. Among these was the entire Danish Jewish community numbering about eight thousand. The Danes, under the courageous leadership of King Christian, saved many citizens from arrest by the Nazis. For example, every Danish civilian wore the Jewish yellow Star of David in order to confuse the SS so that they couldn't tell who was a Jew. They rescued nearly all the Jews and secretly shipped them to Sweden in fishing boats. The Swedes sheltered them for the duration of the war. In the spring of 1945, Count Folke Bernadotte, the head of the Swedish Red Cross, negotiated with the SS Chief Himmler for the release of the Scandinavian concentration camp prisoners. Himmler, hoping to use Bernadotte as a go-between to negotiate a separate peace treaty between Germany and England, agreed toward the end of April to release all prisoners from Ravensbrück. This rescue mission caught up with our train and liberated us.

I was asked to be adopted by a Swedish family in Landskrona. I went to a high school there and was happy with them. But my fear never ended that I might be the only survivor in my family. With their help, however, I found an aunt and uncle who lived in St. Louis and Kansas City, Missouri, and emigrated to America in April 1947. Then I learned more facts of the Holocaust, its scale and intensity, and I was terrified. I realized that my survival was no small miracle. I often ask myself, why did I survive? Why me? Months after the war's end, I learned that, except for one brother, age 17, my immediate family survived the Holocaust and returned home. After all, we were the luckiest family.

After a long silence, recently you began to speak out about your experience of the Holocaust in public. How did it happen?
In the mid 1970s while I was working for a financial institution as a research analyst, I found a brochure with a swastika on it saying, "The Holocaust is a Hoax." I was shocked. Then I learned that there are some people who create propaganda by denying the Holocaust ever happened. "My God, I must do something about this!" So, I decided to go public. I have spoken in high schools and to university students about my experience. And, now I'm writing my autobiography for future generations. I also produced a documentary film, *When I was 14: A Survivor Remembers,* in order to leave a legacy for future generations. A holocaust can happen anywhere, any time and to any people, unless we eradicate prejudice and discrimination among all human beings. ❖

"I was a guinea pig for the unscrupulous Nazi doctors."

RENÉE DUERING

German Jew, Holocaust survivor of sterilization experiments in Auschwitz concentration camp. Retired seamstress. Born 1921 in Cologne, Germany. Lives in California, USA.

(Photo: Ms. Duering standing by the Holocaust Memorial adjacent to the Legion of Honor Museum in San Francisco.)

How did Nazi Germany come into your life? When were you caught and what happened after that?

After Hitler became Chancellor in 1933, anti-Semitic fervor rapidly grew in Germany. My family — my parents, one brother and one sister and I — all left Cologne, my home town, and moved to Amsterdam, Holland. As refugees we were hoping that the political situation might calm down in Germany so that we could return home. My father, a businessman, never believed that Hitler would become powerful or would kill Jews. While living in Amsterdam, one day, I heard the BBC radio saying, "The Germans are building gas chambers to kill Jewish people in the occupied Eastern European territories." I was terrified and warned my father, but he didn't believe me. He simply said, "When a war is going, on the news media lie to people. I believe Germans are smarter than that. It cannot be true. The British are lying to us. It's all war propaganda, my dear!"

I became fluent in Dutch, and learned English, Spanish and French at the Berlitz language school. I became a professional dress maker and earned a daily living in Amsterdam. I got married there to a Jewish man who was a car dealer. As German war fever intensified and escalated, contrary to our hopes, the situation became worse. On the morning of May 10th, 1940, the German army invaded Holland, Belgium and Luxembourg without a declaration of war. After that, our life was changed forever. We were deprived of our basic civil rights. Jewish business enterprises were stopped. Jewish people had to hand over their bicycles, cars, radios, other valuables, and we were forced to wear a Star of David any time we were in public.

My husband spoke Dutch like a native, and during the German occupation, he voluntar-ily worked as a telephone operator at Westerbork camp, which was an internment camp for Jews in Holland. Anyone who worked for the Nazi Germans in the camp without receiving any payment was supposed to be guaranteed that his or her direct family wouldn't be arrested. So, we believed that we wouldn't be taken out of Holland. Because of his language skills, my husband was able to listen to the top secrets about what the Nazis were doing to Jews in the occupied Eastern Territories. In the emptied cattle trains which returned from the Auschwitz camp, there were often written messages found: "The Nazis are killing Jews in the gas chambers. Don't come here, don't bring any valuables." He knew of those unthinkable warnings. But people in general didn't believe it. My father simply rejected such news from the beginning. Meanwhile, my sister went into hiding and my brother moved to America. But we stayed on in Amsterdam believing that because my husband was working there, we would be saved from being transported to a concentration camp.

In July 1943, my own parents and my husband's parents were arrested and taken to the collection camp. Then, the following day I was captured in the street by a Dutch man in civilian clothes who, I learned later, was a Nazi collaborator. Together with my husband, the six of us were gathered in the Westerbork camp for detention. In September that year, along with 1,005 Dutch Jews, we were loaded into a cattle train and shipped to the Auschwitz camp. The men and women were separated on arrival. My husband had deep despair in his eyes. I tried to cheer him up, "Please, keep hoping, keep your head up, we will make it!" He nodded his head desperately. He knew his fate — that there would be no hope in Auschwitz. He died there three months later.

The following year, both my parents also died. I often think of my father who refused to believe what I had said about the BBC news of mass extermination of Jews. In the last moments of his life, I'm sure he must have regretted that he didn't take my words seriously.

I understand that you were sterilized in a medical experiment in Auschwitz. Why and how did this happen to you?

In the women's section, Dr. Josef Mengele, the notorious Nazi doctor, divided us and singled out 100 married women, and I was sent to "Block 10," which was called *Krankenblock* (hospital block), like a hospital. I wasn't sick and couldn't understand why I had to be there. From other women, I soon learned that we were chosen, so sterilization techniques could be tested on us. I was told, "If you refuse it, you will end up in the gas chamber." I was shocked.

Out of tens of thousands of Jewish women from Holland, Belgium, France and Greece, a total of 500 married ones were selected for medical experiments, and I was one of them. Our heads were shaved and everybody was tattooed. My number was 62501. Then we were handed a piece of paper — a Medical Study Agreement — that we had to fill out: tattoo number, nationality, name and address, birth date, name and address of relatives, religion, number of gold teeth if we had any. That was an official agreement with the Nazi doctors. I signed it and took a chance. For me, that was the only way to survive.

Between Block 10 and Block 11, there was a black wall called the execution site. Every Thursday we heard gunshots. Our block windows were boarded up on the outside so we couldn't see. We also heard sounds of terrible screaming and moaning from the direction of Block 11. Through a tiny hole we could sometimes see it. One day I saw a truck loaded with a pile of bodies. Block 11 was known as an interrogation cellar where the Nazis tortured political prisoners and resisters. So, we figured out what was going on there. We learned we should get used to it.

Could you tell me about what the Nazi doctors did to your body to sterilize you permanently?

The Nazi doctors used various methods to sterilize us. I saw a Greek woman whose ovaries were removed and that left her with terrible permanent scars on her body. One morning, my tattoo number was called. It was my turn. Dr. Carl Clauberg, a Nazi gynecologist, and Dr. Mengele were in charge of Block 10. They were two of the highest ranking officials of the Racial Health Court of the Nazi regime. Dr. Clauberg was in charge of my operation. He was in his early 40s, a small man who looked like a dwarf. I was laid on a black glass operation table top, which was set up in the medical experimentation room. His sterilization method on me was to inject a caustic substance into the cervix in order to block the fallopian tubes. By his instructions, an assistant named Dr. Johannes Goebel, inserted an instrument through my vagina and began to work on my right ovary. As soon as he found a tube to the ovary, he started injecting a solution, a thick pink-colored opaque liquid which contained a ground pepper-like powder in it. The effect of the injection was monitored by an x-ray machine which was positioned over the operation table itself. I lay on the table for about 20 minutes. No narcotics were used. During the whole process, all that I could think of was staying alive, and convincing myself that in this way at least I wouldn't be killed in the gas chamber.

The operation was successful but afterwards I suffered from a burning pain for three days and nights. I knew I wouldn't be able to bear children after the war. If I ever lived through this war, however, I could tell the world about my story, that I was a guinea pig for the unscrupulous Nazi doctors and their gruesome crimes against humanity.

Dr. Clauberg was very pleased that my right ovary was completely destroyed. I was called again for my left ovary. There was a shortage of Nazi doctors in the camp and this time it was performed by a less-experienced assistant. He told me he was originally a barber. He inserted the instrument the same way, but he couldn't find the opening to the tube from my uterus to my left ovary. He cut into my organs causing fierce burning pain. Again, it was done without any anesthesia. When I screamed in pain, he threatened me, "Don't make a fuss, stop it. Otherwise, I'll send you to the gas chamber!" He continued for about ten minutes until I almost fainted. But he still couldn't find the tube. It was not easy, so it had to be repeated. I had to go back another time. After he tried it on me for a second time in this barbaric way, he failed again. Eventually, he gave up performing on me. Therefore, my left ovary was untouched.

As far as I know, the sterilization experiments on women in Auschwitz were conducted by Heinrich Himmler, the SS State Police Chief of the Third Reich, and carried out on 500 healthy married Jews between the age of 20 and 30. Their aim was to find biologically simple ways to eliminate certain races. The purpose of the sterilization was to stop the production of the future Jewish generations after the war ended. The Nazi gruesomeness was unbelievable, it was a world of total madness. Dr. Clauberg was so de-voted to his research and so absolutely convinced of his scientific experiments, that in fact, in order to keep his experimental subjects alive, he actually paid 50 Pfennig for each woman out of his own expense to the camp administration.

Were you treated differently than other prisoners because of the experiments? What else did you do in the camp?
We didn't get any special treatment. We got the same portion of food as other prisoners. But on a regular basis, we were ordered to donate our blood. We were told it was for wounded German soldiers who were fighting on the Russian front. In return, we got an extra bowl of soup for that day. I was forced to do it three times.

One day, I was walking around the camp fields near Birkenau, looking to find wild grass to eat, and I came across some muddy ground covered by dark yellowish brown soil. My feet were soaked. Among the hollow grass, I found a few white mushrooms growing. I picked and ate some. Later that day, I learned about the area; it was human ashes from crematoriums scattered on top of mass graves. I was stunned. There were several crematoriums and a few gas chambers nearby exterminating over a thousand of people a day. It reminded me of a quotation from the Bible, "You are made of dust, and you become dust when you die."

What else did you see or experience in the camp?
In September of 1944, Block 10, my group of women from the sterilization experiments, were moved to Block 1, which was near the SS officers building. At the end of 1944, Auschwitz was attacked by Allied bombs. We heard an emergency siren, then a sudden huge blast that felt like a big

earthquake tremor. The target was the SS building. It destroyed the building and killed 125 SS officers. Every prisoner thought the war was over. Someone cut a barbed wire fence, so I quickly started running towards the outside of the camp. Then, suddenly, someone shouted at me, "Go back, return to your station, if not, I'll shoot you!" When I looked around, there was an SS guard aiming his gun at me from a foxhole nearby. I reluctantly returned to my block. I was very disappointed.

Around the same time, a public execution was held in the barracks courtyard. Four women were hanged. There had been an unsuccessful revolt against the SS in Auschwitz; this was unknown to the world. It was a sabotage of the gas chambers; someone attempted to destroy the gas chamber building of Birkenau and ammunition was carried in. A total of six women were arrested. All of them were from Slovakia of ages 18 to 24. Four of them were convicted, but the other two never admitted that they did it. A few hundred male prisoners were also involved in the plot and they were all executed.

As Russian troops were advancing toward German occupied territory, on January 18, 1945, all Auschwitz prisoners were evacuated and forced to walk towards Germany. It was the infamous death march. As we were leaving the camp, I saw flying ashes and smoke. To destroy the evidence of mass extermination, the Nazis had burned documents, the records of the genocide, and lists of the deaths etc., and then blew up the gas chamber buildings. For this reason, I presume the numbers of the Holocaust victims in Auschwitz couldn't be accurately determined; it could have been one and a half million or four million. Nobody could tell for sure. When the Russian troops entered Auschwitz, there were 5,000 sick prisoners left behind. Although the Nazis knew they were soon to be defeated by the Allies, they never gave up on the prisoners, even at the last moment of the war. My memory of the death march was an experience of hell. We walked in the snow for three days. If anyone sat down on the ground, that meant death and the SS immediately shot them. I saw the snow turn red with blood. Then, we were transported by cattle train. I had to keep standing up in the snow for four days and nights, and as a result, my feet became frozen and turned black. No food or water was given to us for the entire seven-day-journey.

My group of women who were in the sterilization experiments were joined with other women prisoners in Ravensbrück, the women's camp north of Berlin. There were politics, criminals, Russian prisoners of war, and even nuns from several other camps. While the Allied bombardments intensified every day, we were again transported to various other camps in a short period of time. Once our cattle train got hit during an air raid near Leipzig. I hugged a woman next to me tightly and shared the fear of death with her. I wanted to die with someone rather than alone, but luckily we survived.

How were you liberated and where did you go after that?

On the 5th of April, 1945, while marching through a town called Riesa, I walked away from my group while SS were not watching me. I escaped from them successfully and I finally became a free person without realizing the war was about to end. After that I walked through villages looking for a job and things to eat. In such a chaotic time, nobody suspected who I was, but still I concealed my identity. At the end of the war, my weight was 32 kilos down from 65 kilos before the war. I was a living skeleton. I could touch my ribs and heart.

While I was seeking a job, a German woman invited me to stay in her vacant house in the suburbs of Dresden. I stayed there until I recuperated. It was two months after the fatal bombardment by the Allies. I remember Dresden because my father used to tell me about it; it was called the "Florence of Germany" and how beautiful a city it was. The Dresden I saw was a city of death. It was totally devastated. The destruction of the city was really dramatic, like a science fiction ghost town. The streets were deserted and I was the only person out walking. I saw not even one bird flying, because all the trees were burned down. Rubble was piled everywhere, and the only paths around it were the damaged streetcar tracks. There was the smell of dead bodies buried alive under the ruins. It was like the smell of cheese.

In very early May, 1945, the Russian troops entered Dresden and liberated the city. While I was there, I met an innocent-looking teenager, a German-speaking soldier who was on his way home. In a such a devastated time, people were kind and helped each other. We became passing friends for a little while and I offered him shelter. We talked about our experiences during the long years of the war. When he told me what he had been doing, I was shocked. He told me that he had worked in the Auschwitz-Birkenau extermination camp. He was the one who dropped "Zyclone-B," a powerful poisonous gas, into the gas chambers that caused instant death by suffocation. He had to watch people dying inside through a peephole until the screams stopped, and then he had to examine all of them to make sure they were dead. He said the gas chamber looked like a large communal bathroom

with imitation shower heads which hung from the ceiling. It took 12 minutes to kill everybody inside.

He continued talking, describing in chilling detail how people died. Suffocating victims crawled around until they became a pile of corpses toppling over each other in the corner of the gas room. Many died with their eyes open. I felt speechless imagining that he could have killed my husband as well. When I finally told him the truth, that I was a Jewish survivor from the same Auschwitz camp, he was stunned. I thought how ironic life is. After that insane war, people met each other in such a way. For me, it was the most traumatic meeting I ever experienced. If it had happened under normal circumstances, I would have felt a different way, of course. At the age of 24, I understood about war and Hitler and of being a soldier under such a dictator, at least more than he did. So I kept silent. Then he showed me a small "B" mark tattooed on his left upper-inner arm. He explained to me that was his blood type, that every SS man had a similar tatoo in case of medical emergencies. Then, he expressed this fear, "If the Russians find this mark, they will kill me because they know it means I am SS. They are looking for the SS." Then, he handed me his handgun and said, instead of being killed by the Russians, he would rather get shot by my hand because he had murdered so many Jews. He showed me his remorse and guilt. I answered, "The war is over." I still remember his face. His name was Karl Gruber, 19 years old, from Vienna, Austria. I wonder what happened to his life after Dresden.

How did you decide your future?
I already knew my husband was dead while I was in the camp. If I ever survived this war, I knew I

had to start my life with another man, even though I knew I wouldn't be able to bear children. After Dresden, I went back to Amsterdam to find anyone I knew who survived the war. There I met a Jewish Brigadier General and fell in love with him. Having agreed that, between us we wouldn't be able to have children, we got married. After long years of suffering from the many centuries of the Jewish catastrophe and the horror of the Holocaust experience, as a dedicated Jew, I strongly believed that Jewish people throughout the world needed a land of their own to settle in. I saw that Palestine must become a Jewish state. With my new husband, I moved to Israel to participate in the development of our new country and we started our new life there.

After 7 years of marriage with him, something totally unexpected occured that suddenly turned my life upside down. I learned that I was able to become pregnant after all. In the sterilization experiment in Auschwitz, my right ovary had been successfully destroyed, but the Nazi doctors had failed to destroy the left side. It remained untouched and I learned it was functioning perfectly. According to a prominent Israeli doctor, it was confirmed that I could bear a child. The reason I never got pregnant by my husband was that he was carrying dead sperm. What an ironic twist, I thought. Until then, I was totally convinced that having my own child was out of the question for me. It was like a dream and that changed everything in our life. It meant a lot to me. Since I had lost my first husband and both of my parents in the Holocaust, my desire to reproduce for their sake became the most important issue in my life. I was 31 then, and never wanted to give up this opportunity. We had a house and ran a restaurant business together, but I was unhappy with him. I sought a sperm donor. My

husband was upset with my decision and our relationship deteriorated.

For him, it was a shocking discovery that he carried dead sperm. We discussed having a foster child, but it wasn't really the right idea for me, and an artificial insemination wasn't the right choice, either. If I ever had a child, he or she might like to know who the father was. I was concerned about that. So, rather than getting the sperm from a stranger, I chose a man to whom I was attracted. He understood my circumstances, and there was no personal involvement. When I got pregnant, I was the happiest woman in the world. I was very excited, but not my husband. He divorced me and cut me off financially. When my daughter was born, I had no financial aid from anyone and I had to start a new life living in a Kibbutz with my baby. Being a single mother and raising a child was hard, but despite that, I believe my decision was right. I'm glad about it. I moved to America with my daughter in 1958, and now I have two beautiful grandsons.

Tell me why did you erase your numbered tattoo?

The Holocaust happened nearly a half century ago and things have changed since. However, my memory of the incarceration in the Auschwitz will never go away. It's deeply inflicted on my mind and I can't get rid of it. Every few months, I still suffer from nightmares of my first husband who died in the gas chamber. It's as though he is waiting for me. My life after the Holocaust was never the same. While many millions of other Jews died, I survived. I feel a deep painful sorrow for them, of course, but being a survivor is more than pain. I was bothered with public reactions over the tattooed numbers on my arm. In Israel, when people saw my tattoo, they reacted because it was an identity that I was from Auschwitz. They stopped talking to me and didn't want to associate with me anymore. They refused to know about Auschwitz and me. Even my own sister and brother, who had also survived but in a different way, didn't wish to know about my life in the death camp. Because I came back from the hell of mass human extermination, for some people that meant I might carry a contagious disease. I was open about my experience, but most people walked away from me. I was isolated. As long as I had the tattoo, everywhere I went, people reminded me about Auschwitz and, psychologically, I couldn't deal with it. That was the reason I removed it. I remember my mother used to tell me when I was a child, "Once you are a Jew, your life is to suffer." I understand this very well now, but this pain is beyond words. Nobody can understand my pain and the pain can't be transferred to someone else. I have to live with it for the rest of my life. It's too simple to say that I was born in the wrong place at the wrong time in history. It's extremely important to leave the words of my Holocaust experience for future generations to come.

Why did you come to America?

After I got divorced, I lived in a Kibbutz near the city of Hadera and supported my daughter as a seamstress. When I removed my tattoo, I was accused by people in the Kibbutz of being ashamed. They said that I didn't have any Jewish pride. They couldn't understand my pain. Also I had a problem with communication. I couldn't speak Hebrew well enough and talking in German there was like being a stranger. They didn't like it, but I couldn't give up my native tongue. Besides, I had to follow their rules and regulations, and I felt it was too much pressure. I didn't feel I was free there. I really wanted to participate in the birth of the State of Israel, but the reality was different. On top of that, there were border conflicts with Arab people one after another, and I didn't feel safe living there. After surviving Hitler's bloody war, I didn't want to live in danger and fear anymore. I had enough of it in Auschwitz. I wanted to have a normal and peaceful life with new friends in a new country. That was the reason I came to America. ❖

"I was a victim of the Nazi racial policy."

JACK ORAN

Polish Jew, Holocaust survivor of sterilization/castration experiments in Auschwitz concentration camp. Businessman. Born in 1924 in Sierpc, Poland. Lives in Texas, USA.

(Photo: Mr. Oran with his family photo taken in the 1930s.)

Before you were arrested, what kind of child-hood and family life did you have in your hometown?

The town where I was born and raised was Sierpc, 130 km northwest of Warsaw, with a population of a little over 12,000, and half of which was Jewish. Even though 50 percent of us were Jews, we were regarded as a minority. The two communities, Catholics and Jews, lived across the river from each other. The town was made up of quiet working-class neighbors: shopkeepers, shoemakers, tailors, merchants, business people and landlords, etc. We got along by ourselves without much outside intervention. The Jews were peaceful and didn't bother anyone. There were three synagogues, each holding over 400 people and every Sabbath morning they were fully attended. The Catholics, on the other hand, had their own customs. The two religions practiced separately, not interfering with each other, and they coexisted in relative harmony.

We were a family of 8; my parents and 6 children, I had four older sisters and one younger brother. My father was a coach man transporting passengers from the railway station to downtown. Financially, we never had enough money, but we were relatively happy. At the end of the day at the dinner table, my father used to speak to his family and bring us the news of what was going on in the city. One evening, his face was serious as he said, "A report just came over the public radio… Adolf Hitler has been appointed as the new Chancellor of Germany." It was January 31st, 1933. I was 8 years old.

When I turned 13 I had my barmitzvah, the official day of reaching manhood in the Jewish faith. There was a Hebrew school in town which I attended. Occasionally the subject of anti-Semitism in Poland was brought up and discussed in class, but we

never found satisfactory answers. The teacher would say, "Suffering and oppression is a way of life for the entire 2000-year history of the Jewish people." There had been some incidents in which Polish Gentiles had ambushed Jewish children and had thrown rocks, but no one talked openly about the Jews' defenselessness. The animosity of the Gentiles towards the Jews in Poland seemed innate and there was little contact between the two communities. The mistrust and dislike, and the acts of violence against Jewish children were a way of life. Every year during Passover, the highest of the Jewish holidays, Gentile children were told to stay close to their parents because the Jews would capture them, slit their throats, and use their blood for Passover *matzos*.

How did the Nazi invasion come to Sierpc and Poland?

It was in the fall of 1939 and I was about to enroll at the Jewish seminary in Warsaw. I wanted to be a Hebrew teacher and was very excited about it. I was 15 years old. One day, with a clear September sky, all of a sudden, I saw a plane above Sierpc. It was the first time we had ever seen an airplane over our town. The plane dipped lower and its single engine grew louder, and within seconds something was dropped from the wing, then, a few moments later, there was a thunderous explosion on the ground and debris was scattered in all directions. Everybody was in a state of shock and stunned into silence. Then, people panicked. They began screaming and running all over. Shortly afterwards, another plane appeared and dropped more bombs and more powerful explosions followed. The streets of Sierpc were filled with confused people, and the sounds of crying everywhere, then I heard the bells and sirens of fire trucks. There were some casualties among both Gentiles and Jews and the wounded people were taken to the hospital. The following day more planes came, and this time they were targeting the hospital. When the bombs hit the hospital, an entire three-story-building was flattened and the doctors, nurses and hospital workers, as well as the patients who had been wounded in the previous attack, were all instantly buried in the rubble. The public radio was repeatedly broadcasting an announcement from the Polish government, "We are strong. We will never surrender. We will never fall."

Later, we woke to the sounds of the ground shaking. It was dawn. We heard the noise of engines and heavy equipment. I looked outside and said, "Oh, my God!" There were trucks, tanks, heavy artillery, and soldiers moving through the streets of Sierpc like a parade, and it continued for hours. I had never seen such an awesome display of power in my life, nor had anyone else in town. That was the Nazi German invasion of Sierpc. It was a fast, quiet, and peaceful occupation. There was no resistance or aggression from either Gentiles or Jews. That morning I went to take a closer look at them. The German soldiers were resting in the main square. They seemed to be regular people, no women were raped and there had been no violence against civilians. The local people lined the streets watching in silence, but they stayed away from the invaders. Some soldiers started walking around the streets. Out of curiosity, I followed them. They walked into a store to do some shopping and I saw they were having trouble with the language; the Polish shopkeeper couldn't understand German. I understood German, so I walked in and interpreted for them. The Germans seemed polite and pleased at what I did for them, and they paid me tips. More soldiers came in and I helped them in the same way, and I got paid more. I hadn't planned it but my pockets were full of coins. I was very excited be-

cause I could pay the fee for the seminary school I was scheduled to attend. But, when I came home my parents weren't pleased. My mother said, "Did they know you were Jewish?" I said, "They didn't ask and I didn't say." But my father said that I shouldn't do it anymore.

For the next few days, both day and night, more troops and transports kept moving through town. Then, without any announcement or explanation, the soldiers were lined up and marched out of town. Hundreds of trucks, motorcycles with sidecars, heavy artillery, military vehicles, cars, and mobile kitchens, etc., had all gone. We were awed and a little confused. But within days several open cars carrying officers arrived in the town, then they were joined by three trucks filled with heavily-armed SS troops. These officers were different. Their uniforms were black and the insignia on their peaked caps was a silver skull and crossbones, and they wore swastika armbands. Their attitude and conduct were different from that of the soldiers. They made an announcement that the town was now under their control. They were the highly-trained and intensely-dedicated Gestapo, the secret state police. The officers met with the town mayor and occupied the largest and nicest buildings in Sierpc for their headquarters. The families who lived in these buildings were evicted without notice.

The next day regular life somehow continued. But that evening I heard sounds of screaming in the streets. When I looked outside, there was a reddish-orange glow in the sky. The oldest and largest synagogue in town was ablaze. Jews were panicking, screaming, crying, some were praying with tears in their eyes and knees on the ground for a miracle. Behind the crowd, I saw the Gestapo and the SS men were smiling. When fire trucks arrived, the Gestapo didn't let them near the fire. They halted the drivers at gun point. The synagogue was doomed. Both Gentiles and Jews watched helplessly as the synagogue burned down. And then, a Gestapo officer stepped forward, grabbed one of the pious Jewish men who was standing by with his wife and children, and began viciously trimming his side beard. Then, he yelled at the Jews to make a circle and dance around the fire for celebration. We were stunned. An SS man moved in and fired bullets in the sky saying, "Faster! Faster!" Another SS man walked forward and shouted to the eldest man in the crowd, "Take your pants off!" The man pretended not to understand German. The SS commander walked directly over to the old man and slapped his face, knocking him to the ground. The old man began to unbuckle his belt and slowly lowered his zipper. "Faster!" the commander shouted again, and this time he violently ripped the trousers and underwear down to the old man's feet. The old man was left standing naked in front of the entire crowd. The Nazis were laughing at him. Their cruelty wasn't at an end. More gunshots were fired. Another Gestapo ordered the other Jewish men standing nearby to follow the old man, and soon dozens of men were crawling around the smoldering synagogue. It was a bizarre sight. I had watched the whole scene. I felt humiliated and shamed by the agony of Jewish weakness for the first time in my life.

The next morning the Gestapo made a demand of the Jewish community: "Your cooperation will guarantee the safety of Jewish citizens in this town. We command you to deliver to us the equivalent of 10,000 Marks in gold and silver." When the items were delivered to the headquarters, no written document was exchanged between the Jews and the Gestapo; the Jews were robbed. Furthermore, another order followed,

"Within the next two days, raise the equivalent of 20,000 dollars in cash. Otherwise, we will transport the entire Jewish people to a concentration camp." This time the Jewish community couldn't raise the money the Nazis demanded. The two-day deadline passed. Tension reached a high and intensified every time a Gestapo car passed through town.

On the third day at dawn, I heard the sound of rumbling trucks that shook the ground like mighty destruction. Then the next thing I heard was screaming from the streets: "Raus! Raus! everybody must pack and come out on the street in ten minutes!" Anyone who stays indoors will be shot!" Surprisingly, there was no panic among the people, nor in our family. Everyone moved rapidly and packed their own belongings. My mother went to the kitchen and took a few pieces of bread and some chicken. When we all got out of our house, we were forced inside large trucks. The trucks started moving out of my hometown. That was the last time we saw Sierpc. We were taken to a ghetto called Stzegonovo, 120 km north of Warsaw. We were detained there for two years. My father and I were forced laborers doing plumbing and highway construction.

When you were taken to Auschwitz, what happened there?
It was in December 1942, on a freezing cold winter morning. My entire family was shipped to Auschwitz. When we got off the cattle train, the first thing I noticed was an aroma in the air that I never had experienced before. The cold wind carried this odd smell into the area and I couldn't figure out what it was. It wouldn't go away and I felt sick to my stomach. Over 3000 Jews from our ghetto, however, remained remarkably calm and quietly walked towards the camp. The SS

gunman separated women and men and yelled, "All men between ages 18 and 40 turn to the left, others move to the right." Children were crying and women were sobbing and hugging their husbands and sons. I hugged and kissed my mother, older sisters, grandparents, younger brother and infant niece. Huge black trucks with red swastikas on the doors arrived and more SS men appeared. They violently loaded the women, children and old people into the trucks and drove away. I watched them until the trucks were out of sight. I saw tears in my father's eyes.

There were about 600 men chosen to work and my father and I were among them. The SS man started questioning us one by one about our age and occupation. My father whispered, "Say you're a gardener, OK!" and I did. "Age?" I answered "18!" The SS man said, "Pass!" Our heads were shaven, and after we took cold showers, everyone was tattooed. My number was 80629 and my father 80630.

We were given uniforms, worn-out black and blue striped garments and matching pants, a woolen cap and a pair of clogs, no socks or underwear, and a metal dish for food which we had to carry with us all the time. Afterwards I was separated from my father: he was taken away to a different block along with several other men. The rest of my group of new arrivals was taken to block number 14 to join the senior prisoners. There were slogans in German in every barrack. Beside Polish, I was fluent in German, Hebrew and Yiddish, so I understood them: "Respect your superiors." "Be clean!" "One louse — one death." "Be a hard worker and obedient." "Your block is your home." At that time I simply thought it was a labor camp and that we were there to work. I believed that eventually I would be brought together again with my mother and

the rest of the family. Senior prisoners were whispering, murmuring, and words began to spread: ...something to do with gas... or burning of something.., smell...., but I couldn't catch the exact words. An SS man entered the block. "Caps off!" someone shouted. All prisoner were ordered to take their cap off at every presence of the SS, if not, we would be punished. The SS man said, "This is Birkenau. You're prisoners in a concentration camp. Escape is impossible. Death is inevitable. Every SS recruit is your commander." That was my first day in Auschwitz.

There were rows of wooden bunks in each barracks and we had to share one bunk with six prisoners tightly squeezed against each other without a blanket or pillow. The block was shared by about a thousand prisoners. The latrine was set outside and the toilets had no seat or paper, and its walls were covered with vomit from the people who had thrown up from the foul smell. Then I soon learned the unthinkable information from the senior inmates. They were again whispering about the reddish glow in the sky and the smoke of chimneys in the distance. "The Nazis are burning our families and the smell in the air is their flesh burning..." I was horribly shocked.

What sort of work did you do in the camp?
During the next two years of my incarceration, I worked many different jobs which were all bizarre, dehumanizing, and unthinkable in a normal life. The day began with roll call every morning and selection was carried out randomly. The *Kapos* brought work assignments for the day. 30 men, 50 men, or sometimes 100 men were chosen, it depended upon the work.

The first job I was assigned was to remove the dead bodies from the camp compound. We had to pick them up and carry them in a wagon to the mass graves. These dead bodies were of prisoners who had committed suicide by throwing themselves against the electric barbed-wire-fence, who had died from starvation or disease, or escapees who had been shot by the SS men. I had never touched a dead body before in my life, and felt eerie and sick to my stomach just looking at the piles of the corpses. I hesitated to do it. But if I wanted to survive this mad world, I realized that total submission and obedience would be the only way. So, I did my duty silently. While I was doing this job, I saw a large crowd of people in the distance. They were women, children and elderly people wearing the yellow Star of David, guarded by the SS gunmen. They were heading towards the chimneys. The old-timers looked at me and warned me, "If you yell at them to tell them where they're going, they'll panic, break rank and run away, and they'll be chased and bitten by the dogs or shot by machine guns. And you'll also be dead right here."

Every prisoner suffered from hunger and starvation. How did you manage to get food to stay alive?

Three meals were given to us, but they were hardly anything: thin coffee for breakfast, a bowl of soup for lunch, and again a bowl of soup plus one slice of hard brown bread for dinner. Many prisoners kept the bread crusts for next morning's breakfast. We were permanently hungry. I soon learned various ways of survival watching how the old-timer prisoners combatted starvation. While working on the job of removing the corpses, they ripped through every pocket in the limp garments of the dead and often found small pieces of bread crusts. Those were very hard to chew but better than nothing. We shared every piece with each other. Many times the bread crusts were covered with lice but I shut my eyes and swallowed them. I was able to make contact with my father who was forced to perform *Sonderkommando*, which meant he pulled corpses from the gas chambers and carried them to the crematoriums. He got more portions of food doing that. We met secretly at night. He bought me food. There was another way I stayed alive. Believe it or not, there was a black market almost every night between Block 18 and 19. Nearly everything was available: clothes, underwear, socks, blankets, soap, watches, cigarettes, liquor, and all sorts of food, which were all collected from the new arrivals or smuggled in by some prisoners. Because of the Geneva Convention, the Nazis often used the Auschwitz concentration camp as a model showcase. And, whenever visitors from the Red Cross International Organization were present in the camp for inspection of facilities and treatment of the prisoners, we were ordered to answer their questions, "Yes, I'm getting plenty of food," or "Yes, the Nazis are taking good care of me."

You were a victim of the castration experiments by Dr. Josef Mengele. How did this happen to you?

Six weeks after my arrival, along with 30 other men in my block, I was assigned to a new job to dig ditches in the women's compound and lay the water pipe lines for the latrines and washrooms. This job was to last a certain period of time. One morning during roll call, my block *Kapo* made an announcement, "We need some volunteers for physical examination — ages between 18 and 24. Anyone who participates, you'll get a full day off work." My first thought was that I could get out of the hard work in the freezing mud for at least one day. I couldn't think of any thing else. I raised my hand. A total of 25 youngsters in my block volunteered. We were taken to a camp clinic and introduced to a doctor named Schumann who was in charge of us. Our tattoo numbers were recorded. As my turn came, I entered the surgical room. There was a large upside-down pyramid-shaped thing suspended in the room from the ceiling by a stainless steel post. It had pedestals and small chrome covered-wheels. I was anxious about what would happen to me next. All doctors spoke German. Dr. Schumann said to me don't worry, it won't take too long. His two assistants turned the chrome wheels and adjusted the machine so it was pointing at me on the square table just below waist level. Then, one of the assistants suddenly grabbed my penis. I was a virgin. I was humiliated and pushed his hands away. The doctor said that he wouldn't hurt me, he just wanted to place my penis and testicles on the table in front of me. So, I did it by myself. He then told me not to move. He asked me to do the same on other side: both right and left testicles. It was painless, harmless and absolutely nothing. I learned later that the x-ray machine was for sterilization experiments: I was sterilized. I said to myself, "Oh, my God!"

Six months passed. One morning at roll call I was selected along with a few others and transferred to Auschwitz-I, the main camp, which was cleaner and had better accommodations, and better food than Birkenau. The Nazis needed to build more buildings for new prisoners and 200 prisoners were chosen as students for the bricklayer's school, and I was one of them. We had to learn how to lay bricks, construct barracks and long-lasting chimneys. Anyway, one afternoon at the end of the class, my tattoo number was suddenly called. I was taken to Block 28, which was a hospital.

The room was small. There were a single-bed sized table in the center with surgical instruments. Three male prisoners stood there. I was ordered to strip and lie down on the table. I had no idea what for, but obediently followed the order. Two of the men gripped my arms with their hands. The another man held and squeezed my buttocks. Then, he touched me there with something raging hot like fire followed by something raging cold like ice. He repeated hot and cold, and then both at the same time, again and again. The pain was intense and unbearable. I screamed out. The man shouted, "Shut up you fucking Jew! If not, we'll kill you right here on the spot." Then he jammed a large instrument into my rectum. I almost passed out from the pain. The purpose of this exercise was to create an erection and ejaculation, and to examine the potency count of my sperm. The operation was successful and the result was positive.

Another prisoner entered the room holding a large syringe with a three-inch needle. A doctor named Doering entered the room. I was ordered to bend over the table. The doctor injected the needle into my arching back. Within minutes everything from my waist down was paralyzed. Then all the men left the room and assistants in white dress entered. When I saw them my heart nearly stopped. Their faces were covered by surgical masks and holding surgical instruments in their hands. Dr. Doering stared at me and told his men, "This won't take long." He raised a knife and incised about two inches between the center of my stomach and the tip of my right pelvic bone. Blood was dripping on my belly from the opening, the assistants held my body tightly and dabbed the blood away. When the outer skin was open, Dr. Doering quickly began cutting underneath, but something went wrong. I felt a small tingling sensation at first, but it intensified to an alarming pain as I felt each cut in my body. Even if I screamed, I knew they wouldn't stop it and could kill me. So I suppressed my voice. He kept slicing but exhaled and shook his head and said in an annoyed voice, "It doesn't matter, he's just another Jew, anyway!" Then, I felt his fingers searching deep inside my body reaching, grasping veins, tubes and arteries. I couldn't see what was being done but felt every move. I felt an agonizing pain directly from my right testicle. He placed his other hand on the right testicle and squeezed hard. The testicle was being pushed a half inch at a time through a tube and into my lower stomach wall. "Cut it off," he said. More pain and more squeezing continued. I heard him saying, "Scalpel!" I saw the shiny object moving toward my stomach. I was being cut again, but this time was inside. The pain was sharp and quick. "It's out. Suture!" he announced.

Weeks later I was called again. The same room, the same doctor, it was the same procedure and exactly the same pain, but this time it was for the left testicle. Both my testicles were completely removed. I soon learned the truth of my surgery: I would never be able to have a child. I also heard a new word "castration."

Despite having such a gruesome experience, you have married three times and divorced three times. How did your marriages work?
During the Holocaust, to sustain life was the most important matter. But after the liberation, I discovered that I was impotent. Since then my life has never been easy. I was in love with women but the sexual part became a problem. When I told them about the truth, they walked away from me. However, three Jewish women understood me and we got married. I have 3 children — one adopted and two from my former wife's previous marriage. With a doctor's advice and special injections, I was

able to have erections. Although it wasn't normal, it worked. So I believed my wives were satisfied with me sexually but they weren't. They pretended. All of them eventually found "sexually capable men" and dumped me. It was painful and hurt me deeply.

After those experiences, psychologically, how did you manage?
I was a victim of the Nazi racial policy which caused the most horrendous genocide of Jewish people in history. Gentiles don't understand our pain, our experience and our history. I tell my children to marry Jews, not non-Jews. I would like to have many Jewish grand-children and to perpetuate the Jewish race. Regarding my personal suffering, I have to take my pain to my grave. But one day I came to the point where I decided I must speak out to the public, not for my own sake, but for the children and grandchildren to come in the future. If people are ignorant of their own past, they may face the same tragedy that I went through. At an early age, I was deprived of all my family, I was deprived of my education, I was deprived of my youth, I was deprived of my sexuality, and in the end, I was deprived of my entire malehood. Being born a Jewish male wasn't my fault. I didn't do anything wrong. There are people who believe the Holocaust never happened — Klu Klux Klan, neo-Nazis and skinheads. They are dangerous xenophobics. That was the reason I decided to tell youngsters who were born after the war. When Gene Church, an author and a friend of mine, wrote a biography of me titled *80629 — A Mengele Experience,* I was released psychologically. This book is my mission to educate people of the world. ❖

".. suddenly smoke came out. Everybody thought it was air..."

YANINA CYWINSKA

Polish, Catholic and Holocaust survivor of the gas chamber in Ausch-witz-Birkenau. Ballet dancing instructor. Born in 1929 in Warsaw, Poland. Lives in California, USA.

(Photo: Mrs. Cywinska with a newspaper article of her story with photos taken in Dachau at her liberation and later as a professional ballerina.)

Of all the Holocaust survivors I have interviewed, your story is the most extraordinary. First of all, you are Polish, not Jewish, and besides you were a child. Why and how did this happen to you?

When the war started I was 10 and when the war ended I was 16, and many things happened between those years. I don't recall exactly what year or precise dates like many Jewish survivors, because my entire family was killed in the gas chamber, and I'm outside of the Jewish community, but I do remember what happened to me very well. My father was a medical doctor and my mother was a violinist, and I had one brother, a year older than me. We lived in Warsaw. Since I was little I wanted to be a ballerina. At the age of 10, my parents sent me to a ballet school in Leningrad, Russia. While I was there I suddenly received a telegram from my parents asking me to come home urgently. It was December.

When I returned, my father was serious. He told me that we weren't celebrating Christmas this year — no Christmas tree or gifts. Instead, he said, we were going to help Jewish people because they needed our help. We would collect jewelry, fur coats and valuables from Jews, and sell them to Polish people to buy food, clothes, medicine, and to help fight against Nazi Germans. After Poland was invaded the Nazis immediately began persecuting Jews. As a doctor, my father had many Jewish doctor friends, so he knew what the Nazis were doing to the Polish Jews. He couldn't ignore what was happening.

After the Warsaw Ghetto was built, my father was summoned by the Nazi Germans to work for them in the ghetto. He refused. While Nazi atrocities were still in the early stage, my father went to the Catholic church for help but he was turned down. Then, he organized an un-derground network to help Jews. He gathered all our relatives: uncles, aunts and cousins. A total of 25 family members were involved with smuggling goods through the sewers to the ghetto. But after a year of the operation, we were caught and arrested by the Nazis. Our houses were immediately blown up by grenades.

We were classified as "dirty Jew-lovers" and taken to a detention building among many Jews. One day, a Nazi soldier came to our compartment and grabbed me and took me outside. I was forced to march with other people toward the woods outside Warsaw. When we came to a flat area where there were pine trees, the Nazis handed us shovels and ordered us to dig holes in the ground. When we had finished digging rows of ditches, they ordered us to line up. Then truckloads of Jews were brought in and forced to march toward the ditches. Along with the Jews, we were also forced to follow in the same direction. Then, I heard a lot of popping sounds like firecrackers. The sounds got closer and louder. At that time I didn't know what they were doing. We were all forced to line up by the ditches. There was a Jewish woman next to me holding her baby up in her hands. She was playing with the baby and the baby was laughing. I was looking up at the baby. I noticed that the woman's shoes started sinking in the dirt and she was losing her balance. So I turned to her back to support her. Then, the gunfire went off. The lady and her baby were shot, and I was thrown into the ditch by their bodies. The Nazis kept shooting, and I was buried by more bodies. Those bodies saved my life: I wasn't hit by a bullet.

I became claustrophobic. There were pools of blood all over and I saw legs, arms and intestines scattered around. When I managed to push my head out through the bodies and look up, I

143

saw the Nazis were still shooting their pistols at anyone who was moving, breathing or moaning. So I quickly pretended to be dead; I didn't make a move. Eventually, the shooting stopped and they left. Shortly afterwards, in the distance I heard the Nazis playing harmonica and joyfully singing. All I was thinking was how could I get out of here and to go back to my parents. I tried to stand up but couldn't because I was covered with heavy bodies. There was so much slime, and it was very slippery because of a pool of the blood. I waited till it got dark. I took clothes from the dead and wiped the blood off, so I wouldn't slip and fall back in. After many hours I finally managed to climb out of the ditch.

It was night. I looked around. The Nazis had a fire and were still singing. I started running in the opposite direction. I can't remember how far it was, but I came upon a haystack. I crawled inside and fell asleep. The next morning a farmer came and stuck a fork into the hay. I screamed. He grabbed my hair and asked, "Who are you?" I screamed loud and hollered. He kept saying, "Are you a Jew? Are you a Jew?" I have blonde hair and blue eyes: I don't look like a typical Jew. I had no idea what this Jew business was all about. I asked him, "What is a Jew?" He said, "It's a religion." I told him I am a Catholic. Then, he put me in his wagon and took me to his home. When his wife saw me in the blood-stained clothes, she started hollering that I might be lying. She told him he better get rid of me, because anyone helping Jews would instantly be shot along with his or her entire family. He took me to Warsaw. He dropped me off at the detention building. My parents were in tears to see me alive. Then, my father paid the Nazis a lot of money to get my brother and me out of the detention and sent back to school. But my parents were still detained

there. After that, my brother joined a resistance group for Polish youths. I was left alone. I didn't have any money. I roamed the streets, riding the trolleys for free during the day and sleeping in sidewalks at nights. One time while I was standing in the trolley, the Nazis suddenly came on board and took a dozen men out into the street, lined them up against a ghetto wall and massacred them. They shouted that the same thing would happen to anyone helping Jews. Another time, through the trolley window, I saw a building on fire and Jewish women with their babies jumping out of the apartment windows to the ground. It was right behind the ghetto wall. The wall had wire and sharp broken glass on top so that Jews couldn't climb up. The Nazis were shooting them on the ground. They died on the spot.

There was a lot of chaos all over the city, and nobody gave me any food or clothing. I was filthy and starving. I ate rotten food I found in the garbage. Eventually, I returned to the detention center to be with my parents. We were reunited again. I think this might have been in the spring of 1942, because I remember my mother was saying that Easter will be coming soon and she was sewing a dress by hand for me. She said, "Yanina, we're going to have the most beautiful Easter holiday this year, and you're going to wear this pretty dress." The next morning, the Nazis came in and shouted to us, "Raus! Raus! Raus!" They pushed us out of the building and forced us to walk towards the railway station. My parents and I were holding hands tightly so that we wouldn't be separated. My aunts, uncles, and some cousins were also with us. We were all packed into a cattle car together. Through a peephole I watched the train leaving Warsaw. My father was a diplomat doctor and used to make trips often to neighboring cities like Leningrad,

Budapest, Vienna, and he used to take me along. I remembered the train trips with him very well. But this time the train trip was totally different. Some people died on the way to our destination.

You survived the gas chamber, which I've never heard of. Tell me what happened after you arrived at Auschwitz?

When the train stopped, the Nazis yelled at us, "Raus! Raus!" When we got out of the train, they started to grab people. I didn't know what they were doing. My father tried to keep us together and my mother kept saying, "Hold my hand tightly so that they can't grab you from me." We walked for a while and we could see the gate that read, "ARBEIT MACHT FREI." Besides Polish, I knew a few German words and some English because my father used to teach me. He also taught me some Russian and French words. My father consoled me saying, "Don't worry, we're going to be working here." We kept walking. We crossed a green area where there were tall trees that looked nice with vegetables growing on both sides. So, we thought we'd be working in the garden growing vegetables and planting flowers. But we passed through it. Then, we went downhill, and there was a concrete building built under the green park. We were forced to stop. There were piles of clothes on the ground here and there. They ordered us to take our clothes off. Some people refused and were shot to death. So, we realized that we better not refuse. I felt ashamed and embarrassed standing naked with other people. I told my father that I was cold and didn't want to be naked. He told me to be quiet and have faith, then everything would turn out alright, and tried to cover me up.

The next thing I recall was a rolling iron gate that was opened. We were all pushed inside with a lot more people, squeezed very tightly together, and I lost my mother. I couldn't find her hand. The gate was shut. Inside it was totally dark. The ceiling was extremely low which made me claustrophobic. I got very scared and started screaming for my father. There was no window and we badly needed fresh air. I looked up to find my father. There were a lot of holes which looked like sprinklers in the ceiling. Then, suddenly, smoke came out of there. Everybody thought it was air. I heard a man saying, "We're supposed to have a shower, where is the water?" Then, people started collapsing while standing up because they were packed so tightly, but there was no room for them to fall down. I don't remember anything after that.

When I woke up, I had been given mouth-to-mouth resuscitation by a woman. She slapped my face very hard and told me not to talk, not to cry or not to make any sound. She quickly let me stand up, gave me a uniform which she took from a dead body and told me to pretend that I worked there. Her name was Gerta. She was a Jew and her job was to drag the bodies out of the gas chambers and carry them into the crematorium to burn or bury them in ditches. She explained to me how I was saved. When she was dragging the bodies out of the gas chamber, she saw I was still breathing and moaning. When the gas went on, I was choked and fainted, and was stuck between the collapsing bodies. Then, a large body had fallen on my face so I hadn't breathed in enough gas to be killed. Gerta had saved my life. Since then, I lived in the same barracks with her working at many jobs in the camp. I stayed in Auschwitz-Birkenau until we were forced out for the death march.

I looked for my father, mother, and relatives all over the camp hoping that some of them had survived like me. But no one did. After the war I went back to Poland and searched for them, but found nobody. I was the only survivor of my entire family of 25 members. When the Nazi women cut my hair, I pretended that my parents were still alive and would come to fetch me. They spat in my face and said, "You're no different than the Jews. You're a dirty Jew-lover, aren't you? You get no privileges." I learned later that in the earlier years the gas chambers weren't functioning properly, and it was very rare but sometimes people were found still breathing, and out of thousands, some survived, particularly children who were stuck between the bodies. I wasn't the only survivor of the gas chamber.

Can you tell me about the gas chamber, how did it look?

The building which housed the gas chamber was fully covered by green plants and trees so that nobody could tell that a killing factory was hidden under the ground like a cellar. There was a beer garden for Nazi soldiers next to it. They had food and pretzels, and I even saw young Nazis with their girlfriends playing there, singing, dancing, drinking beer and having a good time. The size of the gas chamber was about 30 square meters. There were water drain holes in the floor to wash out the room each time they used it, and a little peephole where the Nazis could examine the inside to see if people were dead or not.

What else did you experience in the camp?

I became friends with a Polish girl who was my age, who had been arrested with her family like me. She told me that she had decided to go to a "pleasure house": it's a prostitute's barracks of women who offered sex to the Nazi soldiers. She was deeply depressed. She said to me that we had

no hope of getting out of this hell alive. We decided that if one of us died and the other survived, she should tell the world what the Nazi Germans were doing to the Jews and to us. We made a promise to each other. One morning during the roll call, she walked up to a Nazi guard, spit in his face and kicked him in the groin. She was gunned down and killed instantly. One time, with other women I was assigned to work in the "pleasure house" doing laundry. I had to wash dirty sheets and put clean ones on the bunks. There were rumors there that if women got pregnant by the Nazi officers and gave birth to boys, they would take them and raise them as Hitler's children in an orphanage. But if the babies were girls, they would put them straight away in the gas chamber. That was what women were saying, but I couldn't vouch for that. One time, I was given a different job in a factory making briefcases, lampshades and pillows. My job was to stuff hair into pillowcases. Not until we were liberated, did I realize that the leather was made from human skin.

In the women's barrack, I met a woman who said that she knew my father. She was specifically very nice to me and started chasing me all the time. So, Gerta, the Jewish woman who saved my life, got annoyed and tried to get rid of her. One day, we found she had hung herself in the barrack: she had committed suicide. Later, I learned that she was a lesbian. All the inmates were starving. They tore her body apart and started eating her flesh. It was the most shocking scene I had ever seen in my entire life in the camp. I tried to stop them but they laughed at me saying that I didn't understand the reality of survival.

The Nazis kept prisoners moving from one job to another all the time. Once I had to clean black leather boots for the Nazi officers. One time I had to work washing dishes in a kitchen for the Nazi soldiers. It was good for me because I could steal food; bread, sausages and vegetables. I stole some food for my starving inmates and I was caught by a Nazi woman. She savagely beat me up with her whip and kicked me with her boots until I couldn't move. For punishment, I was transferred to a different working site, in a medical experimental ward where Nazi doctors performed various surgical operations on Jews. They tied them up to the chairs and opened up their skulls without using anaesthesia. The purpose of the experiments was to find out how much stress the human body can take. When doctors opened a big circle in the skull, the brain was exposed. My job was to watch for bubbles. The doctors said that when the bubbles came out, that meant the man had taken all the stress he could take. It was a horrible scene to watch because they operated without any medication, so the experimentees were screaming, moaning in horrifying pain, twisting their bodies, fainted and eventually they died. I couldn't help them.

While I was doing this job in the laboratory, I met a young German Nazi soldier named Hans. He came in the room one day with the Nazi doctor. He had blond hair, blue eyes and was handsome. By that time, I was maybe 15. He stared at me and was attracted to me. Then, we flirted with each other every time we met. I remember it was kind of a chemistry working on us. Although I didn't trust him I really liked him. That was my first love. He secretly started bringing me crackers, candies, tin food, etc., and told me to eat alone and not to tell anyone else. He continued doing this for me for a while, but one day he disappeared. Around the same time, I found myself bleeding between the legs. I was shocked and panicked to see my own blood. I

screamed, "I'm shot!" The women in my barracks just laughed at me and made jokes about me. That was my first period. I became a woman. I was very emaciated and loosing weight each day and always starving. Meanwhile, I was sent back to the medical experimental ward again, but this time my job was to feed prisoners who had already been experimented on. They were in concrete cells with iron doors, and I had to feed them through holes: I gave them water and cleaned their excrement. While I was doing this Hans appeared again. This time we became closer. He said to me, "You speak very good German. You're truly believable in German. I want you to get out of Auschwitz and be with other German girls." He brought me a nurse's uniform and arranged for me to work with other German nurses. He then firmly warned me to conceal my Polish background. I began working together with them. Shortly afterwards, a chance came to me. We nurses were driven out of Auschwitz by truck. It was a great moment for me: I felt that I finally got out of that hell alive.

When we reached a small town, Hans told me not to follow the German nurses. We made an arrangement to meet at an inn, in the outskirts of Auschwitz. He wanted to take me to his parents' house in Heidelberg and was going to prepare a German citizen identification card for me. I waited there, waited and waited for hours, but nobody showed up with the I.D. Then I got bored and became impatient, and I walked out of the inn to the streets. Then, nearby I saw a pretty dress in a boutique window. My parents used to buy plenty of beautiful dresses for me when I was a child, and it suddenly reminded me. As a grown up girl then, I got a little fantasy. I walked in to the boutique shop. I wanted to try on the dress I liked and started taking my uniform off. Then a woman in the shop looked at me: she saw the tattoo numbers in my arm. She screamed, "You must be a prisoner, aren't you!" I said to her I'm just a nurse. But she didn't believe me and called the Nazis. And, I was taken back to the camp.

The situation in the camp this time was different because the Russian Army was near. The Nazis were killing the people as fast as possible; more gassing, more shootings, destroying the gas chamber facilities and the records of the mass killings to hide the evidence of the atrocities. It was an extremely chaotic scene. There was no time to burn the bodies fast enough, so we just piled them up outside the camp fields and left. That was the infamous death march, as you know. During the march I kept humming music fantasizing to myself that I survived Auschwitz. To me, it was a personal triumph. I felt I finally made it through. I didn't recall how many hundreds of kilometers we walked, but after days and nights, we arrived at a place called Dachau concentration camp.

How did liberation come to you in the Dachau camp?

I found myself near Dachau sitting on the train track starving. There were piles of bodies here and there, and more in a ditch. The ditch had some water in it and there was a duck floating. I was watching it and imagining that I would be a ballerina one day and would dance Swan Lake some day. While I was thinking that, a little Jewish boy came up to me and asked me who I was, and where my parents were. I couldn't answer him, because I couldn't remember anything. After having so many traumas over the years, I realized I had lost my memory completely: my own name, my father and mother's name, where I came from, where and when I was born, and how

old I was. Then, he said, "Please help me, I don't want to go in a gas chamber. I know where I'm going, I'm going to die in a gas chamber." I said, "I survived the gas chamber. If you don't breathe enough gas, you won't die. Don't worry." I consoled him. While we were talking, the Nazis came and grabbed both of us. With other prisoners, they took us to the concrete wall which was covered with blood and bodies scattered in front of it. Jews, non-Jews, children, men and women, the Nazis lined all of us up against the wall. They put blindfolds on us. So, I prepared myself. This will be the end of my life: within minutes, I will be dead. By then, I knew I had had enough. I truly wanted to get it over with. I didn't die in the gas chamber but I now am going to die here. I was resigned to it.

While we were standing there blindfolded and waiting to be executed, we heard sounds of people screaming and running, but heard no sounds of shooting, no cocking of guns, no pounding of boots. It was taking too long. Then we heard an awful noise. I kicked a woman next to me and said, "Gee, they drive us crazy with this squeaking sound. Let's run so they shoot us." Suddenly, someone was pulling off my blind. Then, in front of me, I saw a Japanese man in a uniform. It had a U.S. sign on it, but I started telling him, "Now, you Japanese people are going to kill us, right? Let's get it over with!" The woman next to me kept blabbering about the Japanese joining the Nazis — because of the Japan-Germany allied connection. The man bowed his head down, smiling at me and said, "We're Japanese-American. We are not going to execute you. We are your liberators!" Then, his mate gave a Hershey's bar to the woman next to me. She ate it. The next moment she collapsed. Then, an announcement was made, "Don't feed prisoners." I then realized those soldiers were talking about feeding us, not shooting us. Then shortly after, I saw Jewish male prisoners grabbing the Nazis, beating, kicking and torturing them. That scene was just unbelievable. I myself felt I should do the same but I was too weak for that: I was skin and bones, as you can see from my photo here. Instead, I grabbed the American flag and said, "We're free, we're free, we're free!"

After the liberation, having no parents and no relatives, how did you put your 5 years of nightmares behind you, mentally and psychologically?

It was a very sad time for me because I lost my memory completely: for a long time I couldn't recall my own name, my parents' name, where and when I was born, and I had no place to go and no one would come to get me. I was transferred to a D.P. camp by French liberators. But my tragedy didn't came to an end. I met a young French woman there. One night she asked me to accompany her for a walk. While we were walking in the forest, a group of French soldiers appeared, and they grabbed me and she disappeared. They tied me to a tree and began raping me. It was a gang rape by ten men. I was a virgin. When they finished, they laughed at me and thanked her. She had traded me for money. It was ironic in a way, because I wasn't raped by the enemy, the Nazis in Auschwitz during the war, but by liberators after the war. Then I got pregnant and gave birth to a daughter while I was in the camp. I was 16. I had a nasty marriage with my first husband; he told my daughter that she was a child of rape. After that she quit school and was a runaway. She didn't come home for 13 years. I was in deep despair and almost committed suicide. She is a sociopath now. So, my Holocaust saga never ends...

How do you feel about your unfortunate past today?

My father helped Jews on account of our guilt. I would say he was a humanitarian. I believe that we all have a responsibility to rescue other human beings no matter what price we have to pay. I have many Jewish friends because I helped Jews. But I've also had a Jewish man call me a Catholic bitch. Some Jews say I'm a liar. A few years ago, a TV station interviewed me, but it was boycotted by a Jewish man and the piece was never aired. I want the world to know that we Polish people also suffered and died in the Holocaust. I would like Jewish people to accept me more. I don't know why they don't like Catholics. After having such an experience, I don't believe in God anymore. If God really exists, why didn't he give Hitler a heart attack? I was involved with this mad man for six years. When people talk about their family, it hurts me because I lost every single one of mine. However, while other Holocaust survivors still suffer from their nightmares, I have now recovered from it. I went back to ballet since I came to America. Ballet always drew me. I was determined to dance since I was a child and I never lost my dream even during my years in Auschwitz. Everybody has only one time to live on this planet. I fill up my life with beauty and avoid sad connotations. I turned my scars into stars: I don't carry them with me. I feel I'm lucky. I have a wonderful second husband who helps my ballet production: We are very happy together. Despite having the worst experiences, after all, I feel that life is still beautiful. ❖

The Final Solution — the world knew about it but didn't believe it.

WALTER LAQUEUR

German Jew, professor of history at Georgetown University in Washington, D.C. and author of the book: *The Terrible Secret: The Truth about Hitler's Final Solution* and numerous other books. Born in 1921 in Breslau, Germany. Lives in Washington, D.C., USA.

Professor Laqueur, I would like to know about your background: after you left Germany, where did you live during the war?

I lived in Nazi Germany until the *Kristallnacht* when many people left the country. People didn't feel any immediate danger or threat, but we didn't feel free anymore and things were uneasy. I felt there was no future in Germany. At 17, I had just finished high school. I was more interested in sports than politics, but I was not stupid either. Everyone knew what Hitlerism meant: there would be a war and it could bring something unpleasant. Why didn't more Germans leave the country? The problem was all other countries closed their doors to immigrants. German Jews could leave Nazi Germany but couldn't enter other countries. Only a few countries were accessible — Manchuria, Shanghai and Bolivia. I went to Palestine instead. Luckily, I got permission to study at the University of Jerusalem. So I stayed there during the war. I did many things to survive financially. I was a farm worker, tractor driver, and once I was a soldier, too. And in 1944 I became a journalist. My parents stayed in Germany during the war and both died in the Holocaust. I was an only child. During my six years in Palestine, news of the war and information was available to everybody, so we knew something was going on in Germany and in the German-occupied Eastern Territories, but not what exactly. The Nazis kept the Holocaust secret from the outside world, and details didn't reach us until 1944. That was when I started writing for newspapers and other publications.

Germany was badly defeated in WW I, but within a matter of only 20 years, there arose a new militarism and nationalism, which led to WW II. How would you analyze that?

In some ways, WW II was an extension of WW I. Germans simply couldn't give up their territorial ambition. In my view, the WW I Allies made a mistake. At the end of WW I, there should have been a more severe punishment of Germany. Either they should have taken everything away from Germany, or left it alone. The settlement was something in between. As a result, Germans thought they were stabbed in the back because they didn't completely lose the war. "The next time, we will win," they believed. After WW I, if the Allies had hit harder than they did, Germany couldn't have tried again.

You have written a book entitled *Hitler's Final Solution — The Terrible Secret*. Can you talk about your research. When were the concentration camps established, and how did the Nazis develop ways of systematically killing people?

When Hitler first started terrorizing people in Germany, as early as March 1933, the first concentration camp was established in Dachau, near Munich. It was for political opponents of the Nazi regime including Jews, socialists, communists, the clergy, as well as social criminals such as homosexuals, prostitutes and beggars. But the real persecution against Jews started with the *Kristallnacht* in 1938 in Germany and in occupied Poland after September 1939. And it spread to one country after another in Central Europe as the Nazi occupation continued. When we look at the chronological study of the Final Solution, it was in January 1939 that Hitler announced the destruction of the Jewish race in Europe. But at that time there was no clear policy or specific plan about how to do it. A plan to concentrate the European Jews in Madagascar, a southeastern African coast island, was proposed in 1940, but it never materialized. Meanwhile, Polish Jews were put into ghettos — Warsaw, Lodz, Lwow, Lublin, Chelmno, Sobibor, and many others. In December 1940, Hitler signed Directive 21, *Barbarossa,* and soon after he prepared the Final Solution for the Jewish question. It was not only for Jews in the Nazi-occupied countries, but also the Jews in Britain and Ireland. Meanwhile, in the Polish ghettos, thousands were dying of sickness and starvation. But up to June 1941 and the German invasion of the Soviet Union, there were as yet no gas chambers for systematic mass extermination. In May 1941, the *Einsatzgruppen,* firing squad action groups, were organized. They were divided into four groups and operated in four different German occupied regions — northern Russia, central Europe, southern Ukraine, and the rest of Ukraine, Crimea and the Caucasus. They were to cooperate with auxiliary police, field security, local civilian volunteers, and Nazi collaborators. After Germany invaded Soviet Russia on June 22, 1941, they immediately started their operation for killing Jews, executing and shooting children, men and women and old people, burning down their houses and villages, and burying corpses in pits: 2,000 at Bialystok, 7,000 in Lwow, and 600,000 in Romania. But shortly afterwards the Nazis realized the killing methods were limited. The new techniques of mass massacre were introduced by Hermann Goering. Installations were built in various locations in occupied Poland. For this latest killing technique, Jewish people were collected in certain locations in German-occupied Eastern Territories and deported by railroad to extermination camps in Poland. At that time, it was the most high technology mass slaughtering method. Deportation had first started from the ghettos, and the first extermination camp was operating in Chelmno by December 1941.

The following month, on January 20th, 1942, a meeting took place in Wannsee, Berlin, known as the Wannsee Conference, to exchange technical information and discuss the solution for the Jewish question. It was concluded that the "Final Solution to the Jewish Question" was total destruction of Jewish civilization in Europe. And then, full-scale mass killing began. But, in fact, *Einsatzgruppen* had already killed over a half million Jews in eastern central Europe before the Wannsee Conference and continued killing throughout the war.

The second extermination camp started operating in Belzec in March 1942, killing Jews from Lublin, and the third camp was opened in Sobibor in May. Many German, Dutch, Slovak and Polish Jews were killed. In the early stages, victims were killed with carbon monoxide and poison gas in fixed airtight wooden chambers, and later those were developed into massive stone buildings. In July 1942, Treblinka, one of the biggest camps located northeast of Warsaw, began killing primarily Jews from the Warsaw Ghetto. Those camps were built only for extermination purposes. There were two types of concentration camps: labor and extermination. This caused great confusion and misunderstanding for people as the years went by. The Auschwitz and Majdanek camps were mixtures of both labor and extermination. Auschwitz was the biggest extermination camp of all, but it also supplied the workforce for various factories: AEG and IG-Farben, as well as the German railway system connected with war production.

The original Auschwitz camp was called Auschwitz Camp-I, which was established in May 1940 mainly for Poles. But later in October, a second camp was added to it. It was called Auschwitz Camp-II or Auschwitz-Birkenau. This was notorious to the world. Technologically, it was the most advanced mass murder factory and the worst extermination camp of all. "Zyclon-B" was used to speed the killings and they had the biggest gas chambers to kill a large number of people at once. Also, various kinds of medical experiments were performed. The first killings took place there in September 1941, but mass transportation didn't begin until March 1942. People then arrived without interruption. First Slovak Jews, then French, Dutch, Belgian, Yugoslavian, Czech, Norwegian, and German; the rest came in 1943 up to the end of 1944. Altogether between one and two million Jews were killed in Auschwitz.

According to some survivors, there was a terrible smell of flesh burning and heavy smoke from the Auschwitz camp during the killings. How could it fail to be noticed by neighbors? When did news of mass killings first reach Germany and elsewhere?
Hundreds of German and local Polish civilians worked at the Auschwitz camp from morning till evening: plumbers, electricians, engineering technicians, truck drivers, and many others. People went in and out of the camps all the time. Conductors of the deportation trains came and went. Some SS officers' families lived there, too. The railway station was covered with the smoke from flames which was visible from miles away, and there was also an all-pervasive sweet smell which spread for miles. At the Nuremberg Trial after the war, one of the former German camp workers described it: "The smell was simply intolerable." A number of employees talked about Auschwitz and what was going on inside the camp and when they returned home Germans often were reported as saying, "quite horrible." So, actually, very often, by word of mouth, news did spread to

Germans and created more and more rumors. People talked about it, but each story was "too patchy," people only heard about parts of it, but not about the whole scene, and no one could explain the whole event. Some believed that it might be happening in only one place. In a situation like war, everything was chaotic, bombings all over, many people were killed, soldiers, civilians, children and Jews. So, the value of human life became less important. So, no one defended Jews anymore.

How about the news media? By the end of 1942, the Final Solution and gas chambers were known by the public. Why didn't people do anything about it?
Despite the secrecy of wartime information in Nazi Germany, in fact, the Final Solution was an open secret almost from the beginning. The turning point was the Wannsee Conference. It was a question of "to know it" and "to believe it." The question was, what was known and why was it not believed? There was a denial of reality, psychological rejection of information which for one reason or another, was too unacceptable to believe. It was beyond the human imagination. Clearly, it was a question of judgement rather than intellect. Judgement can be affected by a great many factors. Ideological prejudice may be so strong as to exclude all unwelcome information, and such human behavior was still thought too unimaginable to be true. In November 1941 and September 1942, Thomas Mann, the great anti-Hitler German novelist, made a broadcast over BBC in London. He spoke in quite graphic detail of the gassing of Jews in Eastern Europe.

In June 1942, the *Daily Telegraph* of London was the first to report that 700,000 Jews had been gassed. The general inclination was to disbelieve information about the manufacture of soap from Jewish corpses. A majority of people remembered that when WW I ended, they had learned many wartime news items had been either invented or grossly exaggerated. No one wanted to be misled for the second time in one generation. They thought that they had learned the lesson from the previous war. So, you could say, it was a story of a failure to comprehend among Jewish community leaders inside and outside of Europe, among non-Jews in high positions as foreign diplomats, and among the Allied countries who either didn't care or didn't want to know. On the other hand, if the world had accepted the facts of the mass murder earlier than it did, no one knows how the situation would have been handled. Quite likely, it would not have made much difference. Jews inside Europe couldn't escape their fate because Germany was militarily still very strong. The nations outside were too weak to help them. In any case, even had they tried to rescue them, it would have done very little.

About the story of Jewish human soap made from Jews, was it true? According to one of the Auschwitz camp survivors, Jews were forced to donate their blood for German soldiers. Was that true, too?

Both were untrue. The story of the Jewish soap was a wartime rumor. The rumor that human hair was used for mattresses and war efforts was correct. But no evidence was found that soap was manufactured from human corpses in the camps. Same with the blood donations. The Nazis never took blood from Jews, because as a part of the Nazi ideology, they believed that Jewish blood was poisoned and carried vermin. Therefore, that would be wrong. Jewish blood was used for medi-

cal experiments for Jews and Russian prisoners of wars, but not for Germans. It has been 50 years since the Holocaust and the subjects have been studied and researched since, and thousands of books have been written. So, I'm telling you the truth, you can trust me.

How do you analyze the total obedience of the German people and their attitude during the war, as the Nazis said, "I'm following orders'?

You find it in many countries, not just in Germany, although obedience had always been a strong part of the German national character. It existed in Japan, too. For example, in wartime Japan when the emperor gave orders to citizens, everybody had to follow him and that obedience had to be absolute. Japanese soldiers had to obey and fight even if they hated to do it. For centuries, Germans were raised to believe that the state was more important than the individual. They were educated that the state of Germany's always first, that you had to trust your leader and to follow him. Their social order was authoritarian. Total commitment to law and order was the most important directive to a German — to obey your parents when you are child, to obey your teacher in school, to obey your boss where you work, and to obey your state leader if you are a German citizen. The tradition of democracy was weak in Germany. They liked having a leader, and when they had one, they liked to obey. And by definition, Hitler was a very powerful leader. In England or France, for instance, individual thinking exists and self expression is more common. You can question something if you don't agree before obeying. Discussion is more common than in Germany and the sense of individualism is stronger. However, I believe the German situation is different today: the new German generations have changed. West Germans are at least educated about their past. They won't repeat it. They can teach young East Germans. Although those younger Germans don't know much about the Holocaust during the war, at least they still know something horrible happened. ❖

"I was totally convinced that Germany would become a communist state."

WOLFGANG SZEPANSKY

German, communist political prisoner and survivor of Sachsenhausen concentration camp. Retired artist. Born in 1910 in Berlin, Germany. Lives in Germany.

You were born and raised in Berlin between the two world wars. What were the times like when Hitler came to power?

At the outbreak of WW I, my parents, both artists, were active Social Democrats and they were very much against the war. During the war, there was no food and people died of hunger. It was a really hard time for everybody. Then, the Russian Revolution sparked, Germany lost, and the Kaiser was abducted, it was chaos. After the war, my parents joined the Communist party, so I grew up with the party.

My mother was a devout Communist and was also a poet. She wrote the following poem titled "Woman Communist — *Trotz Alledem!*" (Despite of it all) in 1923 and it was published in newspapers in Germany.

Even after you outlaw us, you cannot beat us.
We will raise our wings just like eagles.
Even if you pronounce us dead, we will still be
*   fighting.*
You cannot outlaw us!

Even if we are silent, your sins will cry out loud.
If you imprison us to get rid of us,
whatever you do,
the hardship of the people and the children will
*   cry for bread.*
You cannot outlaw us!

We are the storm of fire, we are the people's voice.
We are storming water like a flood.
Despite all your hatred, we are the people's re-
*   venge,*
that will finally cut you down.
You cannot outlaw us!

This poem was also printed in America, in a worker's union newspaper, and as a reward she received $2.00. In the midst of the Great Depression, this was an enormous sum of money for us, not like our worthless inflation money. My mother was able to buy enough food and gifts for our whole family, and I remember, we had the most wonderful Christmas that year.

Before 1933, Berlin was in a state of civil war, the National Socialist Party had become stronger and they often clashed with socialists and Communists. I lived in the Mariendorf district and in the building where I lived, on the ground floor, there was a bar that was a regular meeting place for Communists. I remember that one day SA storm troops suddenly entered and raided the place and it turned to bloody fighting. This kind of violence was very common in many parts of Berlin during the Great Depression. There was a lot of unemployment and many people who couldn't pay rent were evicted from their apartments. These people ended up joining political parties, not only the Communist party but also the Social Democrats and Nazis. They were looking for political solutions to resolve social and economic problems.

I was 22 when Hitler seized power in Germany. I was a freelance painter working in the theater. When the National Socialist Party took charge of Germany, the city of Berlin was covered with swastika flags to demonstrate Nazi power. Socialists and Communists couldn't go out in the streets anymore. They were beaten by SA brownshirt mobs. The first thing Hitler promised people was to secure jobs for workers. The Nazi Party got a substantial amount of money from their big supporters — industrialists, bankers and business corporations. They provided jobs for people and Nazi uniforms, so this attracted most youths who were not politically conscious. Within a very short period, many people ended up joining the Nazi Party. This was one of the factors in the rise of German fascism. These people brought an unimaginable military power to Germany.

The following month, the Reichstag was set on fire and the arsonist was never found. How do you recall that incident?

It was on the night of February 27th, 1933, 8 days before the Reichstag election. The fire was started inside the Reichstag building. 10 minutes after the fire was discovered, Hitler, Göring and Goebbels were in the front of the Reichstag. They immediately declared that the fire had been set by Jews and it was a communist conspiracy backed by international Jewish communities to make revolution in Germany. The same night, SA storm troopers went out into the streets blaming all Nazi opponents. Pacifists, communists, socialists, liberals and Jews were all beaten. A Dutch anarchist was arrested and taken into custody, but he had a strong tie to the Nazi Party. The Reichstag was connected to the residential palace of Goering by an underground tunnel like a bunker and a whole arsenal of incendiary materials was found there, but no questions were raised about it. Historians are today still discussing who really set the fire. The following day, the Nazi government changed the law so that they could search private homes and properties without the owner's permission.

How did things in Berlin get worse as the years passed?

By the middle of 1933, Jews were blamed as the cause of all the chaos and the Nazis began campaigns for people to stop buying goods from Jewish shops. The Nazis painted Star of David signs on the windows and doors of the shops owned by Jews, and every customer who came out of the shop was beaten up by the SA troopers. Non-Jewish people who defended Jews were badly persecuted, often more savagely than Jews themselves. Jewish attorneys were allowed to work only for Jews, they couldn't work for non-Jews. People were afraid of helping Jews. Jewish doctors were fired from hospitals and barred from practicing; Jewish artists, writers, journalists were taken away and put in Sachsenhausen concentration camp in Oranienburg. Only small Jewish shops and businesses were left pretty much alone.

I don't know how strong the Berlin Jewish community was at that time, but I remember there were 12 synagogues and 11 of them were burned down during *Kristallnacht*. Before everything occurred, the Jews stuck to themselves. Berlin traditionally had the strongest workers' unions in Germany; during the 1920s and 1930s it was called the "red city." But Hitler immediately banned unions and political meetings. All their headquarters and office buildings were destroyed by the Nazi mobs. Union members and political activists went underground and began resistance movements; they printed leaflets, circulated them and communicated with each other.

As a communist, what did you do against Hitler?

I was one of the underground anti-Nazi activists. I was printing secret leaflets and distributing them to my communist colleagues in my district. My area was predominantly working-class and the Nazis had name lists of the Communist Party members, so we stopped having meetings and everybody called each other by fake names. I was with a group of a dozen comrades, but I never knew their real names or where they lived. One night I went up to fourth floor of a department store building in Kreuzberg and threw leaflets from a toilet window down to the street, and people picked them up. Then, I went down the streets and wrote graffiti on the walls, "Down with Hitler!" and "Nazis Out!" Then, SA troopers showed up and shouted at me, "Stop it!" I was arrested on the spot. This was in July 1933. I was taken to the Gestapo headquarters and tortured, interrogated and beaten, but I never confessed about any of my activities. I saw some Jews there looking haggard because they couldn't eat German food, they kept kosher.

As a communist and opponent of the Nazis, my trial was set for January, 1934. However, while I was in custody in the detention center, I escaped. I was penniless but through my Communist connections I was able to get out of Germany and managed to enter Amsterdam, Holland, without an ID or passport. The underground communist groups were well-organized internationally and were able to help their members leave Germany. Most of the time, I was helped by anti-Nazi sympathizers, both German and Dutch; they gave me food and provided me with accommodations. While I was living there illegally, I fell in love with a Jewish girl who was also involved with communist underground activities. I wanted to marry her but it wasn't possible because I was living without identification. I worked illegally doing small jobs but I couldn't survive, and I was supported financially by her parents. We lived together there for five years. On May, 1940, however, after the Nazis invaded Holland, I was arrested again and shipped back to Germany.

I kept corresponding with my girlfriend throughout the war. The day after I left, she went underground totally. She kept hiding, moving from one place to another every day, and escaped the hands of the Nazis. But her parents were deported to Auschwitz and never returned. People in Holland were generous. The first day all Jews had to wear a yellow Star of David, they held a National General Strike, every flower shop sold only yellow tulips and all Dutch citizens wore them on their chests to protest against the deportation of Jews by the Nazis. It was a peaceful protest.

You were in Sachsenhausen concentration camp. Could you tell me about your life there as an "Aryan" political prisoner?

After I was taken back to Germany, I was incarcerated in various prisons and camps. The first one was Dortmund where 12 prisoners were squeezed into a room that was only 15 square meters. There was an air raid by British bombers and while the camp building was jolted with a big tremor, we prisoners had to stay in our cells with trembling fear. There was no way to get out. In the autumn of 1940, I was transferred to Sachsenhausen camp. After 10 months of imprisonment there, my personal relationship with a Jewish woman was disclosed. According to the Nazis that was against the Nuremberg Racial laws and for that crime I got a two-year sentence in Tegel prison in Berlin. Then, after I completed my term, I was sent back to Sachsenhausen to serve as a political prisoner again. There was every kind of anti-Nazi prisoners there: political opponents, criminals, Christians, resistance people, POWs, Liberals, homosexuals, Gypsies and Jews. My block number was 26, known as "red block" because it was for communist political prisoners. Beside the yellow cloth badge for Jews, other prisoners had to wear color-classified badges as well: red for Communists, green for Social Democrats, pink for homosexuals, black for Gypsies and yellow with red marks for Jewish Communists and with pink marks for homosexual Jews. All prisoners had to get up at 4:00 every morning, and after roll call at 6:00, we began working at 7:00. My job was working in the kitchen for SS officers, peeling potatoes, delivering bread, cooking meals and serving coffee. So I never starved because I was able to steal food. I was lucky in many ways.

I had to work together with other inmates; many were extremists and criminals. They often abused me saying that I was present when Rosa Luxemburg, a writer, and Karl Liebknecht, a lawyer, and both were the founders of the German Communist Spartakus League, were brutally murdered by reactionary mobs in Berlin in 1919. I was only 9 years old at the time, but I was already committed to communism, so they used to make such jokes about me.

Among all the different kinds of prisoners, I noticed that there were many orphaned Jewish children in the camp. The Nazi doctors used them for all sorts of medical experiments which usually ended in death. I remember one example. Five healthy children were injected with hepatitis virus and fell sick. The doctors were hoping to discover a specific effect. They all died like human guinea pigs. There were a high number of homosexuals and some of them were among the army officers and SS men. They were executed by the SS as well. I was told at least 50,000 homosexuals were known to be incarcerated there but I believe it was more than that, because it was said that there were 30,000 homosexuals in Berlin alone. In the theater where I worked as a painter, for instance, I remember many of the actors, musicians, singers, performers, and directors were homosexual. Anyway, the homosexuals who were housed in my camp were brutally assaulted and

sexually abused by the SS: they were given extra hard labor, and those who became weak perished. But in later years, the Nazis introduced a special rehabilitation program for them. They were tested in SS brothel houses and if they performed "heterosexually" with female prostitutes, they were discharged and released from the camp and sent off to civilian labor. If they didn't perform correctly, they were castrated and released for heavy labor. It was because Germany needed manpower toward the end of the war.

The cooking was done by a group of prisoners and next to the kitchen there was a pig farm to supply the SS feasts. We were supposed to feed the pigs with the left-over potato peels. One Sunday, we stole them for our inmates and were caught by the SS. For punishment, we were forced to stand outside the freezing barracks for a whole day without food, drink or toilet access. As a result, I became terribly sick with a heavy fever. I was taken to the camp hospital and treated by an SS doctor. I stayed there for three months without attending roll call and work duty. The hospital meals were terrible but I was quite comfortable and recuperated there.

Did you have any idea what was happening to Jews while you were there?
I didn't know about the industrial mass killings of Jews until years later, the last part of the war. However, I can recall that there were some rumors that indicated the truth of what was happening; a little piece of a story by somebody here, and another piece there, but not all of it. But when I re-entered the camp in 1943, I remember that people clearly knew that 20,000 Russian POWs had been murdered there. I also knew that sick people were moved away somewhere and gassed while I was there.

How were you liberated?

On April 21st, 1945, the Russian Red Army crossed the eastern German border and their gunfire was almost heard from the camp. In the final days of the war, Himmler made a quick deal with the Swedish Red Cross: he decided to evacuate this camp and turn it over to them. So, he ordered all sick prisoners to be shot and the rest who were able to walk, were forced to march toward Lübeck, 350 km northwest of Berlin. That was the Sachsenhausen Death March. He planned to ship all prisoners who could walk to somewhere in Scandinavia. 40,000 starved prisoners were forced to walk in the rain for many days. We received three slices of bread or pieces of potatoes each day during the march. Those who couldn't keep up were shot to death by the SS and left in the roads or ditches. I saw corpses all over. When we neared the city of Schwerin during the night of the 29th, the SS suddenly disappeared. By that time, half of the prisoners were dead. On May 2nd, the Soviet Red Army arrived and liberated us. We, Communist prisoners, were all treated specially. I was taken back to Berlin. The Berlin I returned to was a dead city; the destruction was just unimaginable. Beautiful Berlin was completely ruined and I couldn't recognize it anymore. I was shocked and cried. I thought it would be impossible to build the city up again.

Do you still believe what you did then?

When the war ended I was 34 years old. Therefore, intellectually, I was mature and as a political prisoner, I understood why I had to stay in the camp during the entire war years. At the time I was arrested, I was very aware of my choices. I had to decide either to cooperate with the Nazi regime, which meant I would have to be a soldier and kill people, or I could keep fighting against the regime until the last day of the war. These were two options and I chose the latter. I took my own risks. At that time, to tell the truth, I was dedicated to communism and was totally convinced in it as a political system. I strongly believed that Germany would become a communist state. ❖

"Austrian anti-Semitism is more profound than that of the Germans."

HELEN ROSENAUER

Austrian, Viennese in wartime Vienna. Housewife. Born in 1925 in Vienna, Austria. Lives in Austria.

In March 1938, Hitler marched into Vienna. How do you remember these events?

A few days before the *Anschluss* (accession), the streets of Vienna were littered with leaflets dropped from planes about the coming plebiscite. Dr. Kurt von Schuschnigg, the newly-elected Austrian Chancellor who was anti-Hitler, had ordered an urgent vote to prevent Nazi takeover. The plebiscite was in the form of a question: "Are you for an independent, socialist, Christian, German, or united Austria?" Every citizen had to vote YES or NO, and election day was set for the 13th, Sunday. There were posters on the walls all over the city saying "Vote YES for an independent Austria," and groups of patriots were shouting *"Heil Schuschnigg!"* While the Austrian government was preparing for the election, on the 12th of March, German troops crossed the border and entered Austria at four o'clock in the morning. Despite the Chancellor's struggle to save Austria from falling into Hitler's hands, Austria was occupied. Compared to the German Army, the Austrian army was powerless. Austria ceded to Hitler. The last words we heard from Dr. Schuschnigg on the radio were, "God bless Austria!" Then he was sent to a concentration camp.

There were many "little Hitlers" in Austria. The day the Nazis entered, the streets of Vienna were decorated with thousands of swastika flags and portraits of Hitler, and members of the Austrian Nazi Party flooded the city wearing Nazi armbands. There were tremendous crowds in the main squares: 200,000 pro-German Austrians enthusiastically welcomed Hitler and the German troops with Nazi salutes as they marched into Vienna. There was a lot of noise. People were singing, *"Deutschland über Alles"* and shouting "Sieg Heil! Sieg Heil! Heil Hitler! Heil Hitler!"

and "Hang Schuschnigg! Hang Schuschnigg!" *"Ein Volk! Ein Reich! Ein Führer!"* (One people! One state! One leader!) There was no resistance among Austrians and no European country interfered with the occupation.

After the *Anschluss* how did things change?

Before the *Anschluss,* the economy in Austria was devastated. The population of Austria was 6 million and there were 600,000 unemployed, so there were many homeless people and beggars on every corner of Vienna. However, the fact was that after Hitler came to power, the domestic economy improved. Hitler called Austria "Ostmark." As many Austrians got back to work, Hitler soon became the most popular man in Austria. His name had become symbolic and many parents named their newborn sons "Adolf" and streets and squares in many cities were named "Adolf Hitler." After all, Hitler was an Austrian and very soon many Austrians adored and admired him like a new Messiah.

When I was young, I wasn't interested in politics at all. But somehow I got excited about this man and went to see him in the parade when he came to Vienna. I saw him twice: once when he was in an open black Mercedes-Benz passing the Ring, in the center of Vienna, and the other time when he was at the Hotel Imperial addressing a crowd of hundreds of thousands of people from the balcony. I must say he was an impressive orator. People said that what he was saying was not very bright, but his style was very charismatic and powerful. After that I liked him, of course.

Did you see any Jewish people persecuted?

Jewish people immediately became the primary target for Austrian Nazis. For centuries, Austrians had been profoundly anti-Semitic, much worse than the Germans, but it got even worse. There were all types of Jews in Vienna. They were quiet people living in their own communities. But Orthodox Jews were recognizable in public because of their clothing. I used to see them all the time in the streets especially in the district of Leopoldstadt. But it seemed to me they kept to themselves and would not bother to mingle with Gentiles. As soon as Hitler's Austria began, pogroms were immediately carried out by members of the Austrian Nazi Party. All Jews had to wear a yellow Star of David, and rich Jews were specifically chosen to scrub away anti-Nazi slogans and graffiti. They were forced to use toothbrushes on the walls and pavements. I actually saw Jews doing that in the streets and the Jews were humiliated. Then very soon, I began seeing anti-Semitic caricatures and posters everywhere in the streets. Wealthy Jews were able to flee to America, South America, or elsewhere, but poor Jews who had no money to buy train or ship tickets, couldn't get out of Austria. The American Jewish community could have helped those Jews, but they didn't. They were the ones who were later deported to concentration camps.

Before the *Anschluss*, how do you remember social relationships between Gentile and Jewish people in Vienna at that time?

Before 1938 there were about 3 million Jews living in Vienna, about 10 percent of the city population. The Jewish influence was large, as in America. They were all kinds of Jew: Orthodox, Reformed and secular; high-ranking professionals such as doctors, lawyers, professors, intellectuals, financiers, business men, and Jews who were not financially well off such as clerks, craftsmen, small business employees, shopkeepers, artists, etc. They all spoke Yiddish. There were over 40

synagogues in Vienna at that time, and Judaism dominated every professional field. In Vienna alone, over 50 percent of doctors and lawyers were Jews. Besides the Jewish newspapers, there were other publications but most Viennese liberal newspapers and magazines were either owned or edited by people of Jewish background, and many journalists were Jews, as well. They were educated people. In the University of Vienna, over 30 percent of the professors and students were Jews. Not only that, in the arts, many of the theaters and the advertising companies, movie and music production houses were also owned by Jews. And these Jewish connections were strong. They stuck to themselves.

During the recession, I was a student at the Academy of Music. Many senior students needed part-time jobs. I remember many of them were saying that they couldn't get jobs because they were not Jewish. For example, in our government, the Minister of Culture who funded the Academy of Art was a Jew. He favored Jewish students over Gentile students. The management was done by Jews and they hired only Jews, and many of my friends said, "If I were a Jew, I would get a job." We were not happy about it. Thinking back, it was reverse discrimination and I thought it was not fair. But these were just minor examples. Anyway, I personally never had a Jewish friend. But I want to say that the Jews are the same as we are; there are good Jews and bad Jews, friendly Jews and nasty Jews everywhere. Basically, it is a minority problem. If there is one bad Jew, people tend to think every Jew is bad. It is called "stereotype," and every society has it. I remember a Jewish doctor who treated his patients, Jews or Gentiles, without charging any fee if they were poor.

Did you witness the Jews being taken away?

Yes, I did. It started right after the Nazi occupation in March. One evening, I saw a big car in the streets. The Austrian Nazis arrested some Jews in their home, pushed them into the car and drove them away. Before Hitler came, nobody said anything about Jews openly and did anything against Jews, but everything happened very quickly after the *Anschluss*.

Some wealthy Jews sent their children abroad. Young Nazis were shouting in the streets "Heil Hitler!" all over Vienna. With the *Anschluss*, it was hard to tell who was in charge of the arrest of the Jews. Although many people felt this was not right, nobody did anything. If people did something against Nazi authority, they would get killed. Then, 8 months later, there was the *Kristallnacht*, the outbreak of total destruction of Jewry in Germany, Austria and Eastern Europe. In Vienna, I remember, in Tabo Street there were two synagogues which were burned down, and I saw books and many Jewish items were vandalized and piled out in the middle of the street.

Under nazified Austria, were all Austrian men drafted and sent off to war?

All boys and men over age 18 had to go to war. Nobody could refuse. It was tragic for every family. My father had died when I was little, but I had two brothers and both went to fight on the eastern front. One died and one returned without a leg. In combat, Austrian men were good fighters. In the Battle of Stalingrad, for instance, many soldiers were Austrians. During the war, Austrians believed in what Hitler was doing. We listened to the radio, read the newspapers and tried to learn from the soldiers who returned home, but they didn't talk much about what was going on in the war. We relied on them because we were not allowed to listen to the BBC or other non-German radio stations. After the war, we learned that much of what we had heard was incorrect. It was war propaganda and lies. After the defeat by the Russians at Stalingrad, one of the greatest battles of WW II, over 20,000 German Allied soldiers died and 90,000 were captured and sent to Siberia for hard labor. For some German and Austrian POWs, it was 10 years before they came home.

Could you tell me about the air raids in Vienna?

During the war, Vienna was bombed several times by both Russians and the Western Allies. The heaviest air raid was in 1945, in the final months of the war. The Russians bombed the St. Stephen's Cathedral, but luckily it didn't destroy the whole structure. They also bombed the Opera House, the State Theater and all the bridges over the Danube, except the main one which they needed for their own army transportation when they landed.

I remember one time, a bomb hit the bomb shelter near where I lived and 800 people, including children, died at once. In the subsequent attacks, hundreds of thousands of Viennese were killed. It was a most catastrophic human tragedy.

Toward the end of the war, Vienna was seized by the Red Army and then the city was controlled by the Allies. Could you tell me what happened?

Vienna was surrounded by the Red Army. The Russians ordered curfews; we couldn't leave home after 10:00 o'clock at night or before 6:00 o'clock in the morning. I lived with my mother and some woman friends in central Vienna. We were sleeping in a cellar together because of the bombings. We knew that the Russian soldiers might move into Vienna, so we painted our faces with black ink and put on filthy clothes. We disguised ourselves like boys. We looked really ugly which wasn't hard because during the war there was nothing to wear anyway. On March 13th, 1945, Mongolian Russian soldiers first entered our cellar. They saw our radio. They shot it immediately and kept moving. Then, shortly afterwards, several officers and more soldiers came in. One of them seemed tired and sat down in the cellar. We looked at him and he stared at us. My mother spoke a little Czech, so she was able to communicate with him. He said that he heard that Viennese women were supposed to be pretty, stylish and elegant. When he saw us, he was disappointed. But there was resistance among our neighbors. Someone fired shots against the Russian soldiers through their house window, and in revenge, they began shooting at our cellar. Luckily, as my mother was able to communicate with them, she immediately shouted at them to stop shooting. That was how we were saved. Then their commandant demanded we give them some valuables instead of the girls. We had to give up our cameras, sewing machines, watches, bicycles, clothes, records, and anything of value. Hundreds of Russian soldiers came with a row of carts pulled by horses and confiscated household goods from every Viennese house. They loaded them into their carts and marched away. The luckiest of all was that nobody was beaten up or raped. We were saved.

After that, Western Allies entered Vienna. Then, Vienna and all of Austria was placed under four-power occupation and each took control of a zone until 1955. But we had our own government and didn't lose our freedom; we had our own elections. Right after the war, there was a severe food shortage in the city and the Viennese people were starving. The American government supplied us with canned food. I already understood English quite well, and I remember the labels of these tinned food; they were for dogs. But since we were so hungry we ate them.

After the war, people learned about the horror of Nazi atrocities. What did you think of the Holocaust?

It was in June or July of 1945 that we began hearing such stories and seeing the photos. Many Austrians simply didn't believe it. When the war was going on, there were lies upon lies, rumors upon rumors, and propaganda upon propaganda, so when we learned about it, we felt that we had been betrayed by our own government. Therefore, quite frankly, we thought that it could be some sort of postwar reverse propaganda, which could have been set up by Jews. Because they suffered so much under the Nazis and Hitler, we thought Jews were telling us such things to get something out of Gentiles. I would say that the killing wasn't right, of course. Jews are all human being like us. I have seen a Jewish woman with tattoo numbers on her arm, so I believe they were in the concentration camps and the Holocaust happened. However, even today, not many Austrians are sure that the Nazis really used the gas chambers to murder Jews.

How do Austrians in general think of Jews today?

Many Austrians acknowledge that the persecution and the pogroms against Jewish people were carried out during the Nazi period. As I mentioned to you earlier, Austrian anti-Semitism is something else. It's more profound than that of the Germans. Austrian means "anti-Semitic." It's never an easy task to wipe it out from the people's minds. Many people say that they feel sorry for Jews for what happened to them, but they still say that they don't want Jews to be in Austria. They wish Jews would go away. Let me tell you something more; some people go even further. Some Austrians say that Hitler didn't finish his job properly, or they even say that Hitler didn't kill enough Jews. ❖

"When I saw Hitler, it was like I saw a Messiah."

ELMAR GUNSCH

Austrian-born German, Hitler Youth leader. Currently television and radio talk show host. Born in 1931 in Tyrol, Austria. Lives in Germany.

Hitler took over Austria very easily in the _Anschluss_. Can you explain why, Mr. Gunsch?
In March 1938 when Hitler took over Austria, the majority of the Austrian people didn't protest because they wanted to be united with Germany. They liked the idea. At the end of WW I, Austria was cut away from the Austro-Hungarian empire and, as you know, that had been a successful empire for centuries. Austria was left like a body without legs, arms, head, and this body would not survive. A rich part belonged to Italy and the good agricultural land went to Hungary. So because it had no industry of its own, Austria became a poor nation. When Hitler raised the idea of the _Anschluss,_ Austrians were happy because with Germany, prosperity for the future would be ensured.

The Austrian people immediately started persecuting Jews, even before the Germans. Why did they want to get rid of Jews?
The _Anschluss_ and Jewish persecution were different matters. In Austria at that time, Jews had been well integrated culturally and socially, and the Jewish influence had a long tradition: Vienna was particularly a center of _Ostjuden_ (eastern Jews). Austria produced many good Jews — doctors, authors, engineers, physicists, musicians, artists, and famous names such as Sigmund Freud, Gustav Mahler and Arnold Schoenberg. Although Austrians were, and still are, well known for being anti-Semitic people, their intellectual elite were strongly powered by Jews. Therefore, they were not against Jews and didn't want to get rid of Jews. Hitler occupied Austria without any authority and most Austrians didn't know what he would do after the _Anschluss,_ and what things would follow as a consequence. _Mein Kampf_ was available to read but nobody discussed its contents seriously. People didn't know what would come next, except, I would say, in the Jewish communities. Austrian Nazi thugs began humiliating, harassing and arresting Jews almost the day after the _Anschluss,_ but until _Kristallnacht,_ people as a whole really didn't realize that Hitler was fighting against the Jews.

In your childhood how were you educated and what was the social environment?
Although I was born in Austria, my grandparents were Germans. They lived in Nuremberg. So as a child I used to stay with them all the time, and because of the _Anschluss_ it was easier to move between the two countries. As you know, Nuremberg during the 1930s was the place where the Nazis held annual rallies called _Reichsparteitag_ (Day of the State Party), and the foundation was formed that created the most powerful political party in Germany's history. The first time I went to see a Nazi rally was in 1937 or 1938. I was perhaps 6 or 7 years old. During the rally, the city of Nuremberg with a population of 400,000 inhabitants was filled with nearly one million German youths of the SS, SA and Hitler Youth. They were all in uniforms, hats on their heads, shiny boots on their feet, and marching in perfect goose-step order. There were bands playing, demonstrations of athletics, and torchlights at night, and Hitler addressed the enormous crowd with charismatic speeches. As an innocent little boy, I was very impressed by that. It was the most exciting event of the year for German kids, like an important festival. I saw Hitler stepping out of his limousine. I was really fascinated to see his face. It was like I saw an image of a Messiah, truly!

How were you taught the Nazi ideology?

In my youth, I was completely surrounded by Nazi propaganda. During the Nazi rallies, all young people were indoctrinated to believe that the Germanic race was the best in the world, and Nazism was the best way to govern the German people and to protect Germany. When I was in school, all children were taught that Jews were the worst people in the world and our dangerous enemy. When we listened to the radio and read newspapers, they also announced that Jews were terrible vermin. Then at home, my parents warned me that I shouldn't go out alone in the streets because Jews would capture Gentile children and slash their throats to get blood for their ritual ceremonies. I was raised in this kind of social environment. When you are a child, you believe what you are told by your teachers, your parents and your leaders. If this occurs in your childhood, before you develop your own thinking and your own judgement, you end up believing easily. It happened to me. And it happened to many people of my generation during the Nazi period. It's called "brainwashing." This brainwashing was definitely the method for Nazification of the people. It led people in one direction and, of course, it did indeed mislead the nation very dangerously and it almost destroyed Germany.

During the 1930s, Hitler reformed many social programs and that made him a heroic figure in Germany. Could you give me some examples?

His achievements were truly impressive. Not only did he curb unemployment and lift the German people from the Depression, but he also developed a massive system of transportation. *Autobahnen* (highways) were built all over Germany

and the Volkswagen (people's car) was manufactured. It was an inexpensive compact automobile which the average German could afford to own. And in large cities, he built underground parking lots and traffic-free zones, and he also planted anti-pollution devices. He increased public parks, recreational green areas in each city. Factory and office buildings were required to build windows and design less crowded work spaces, and clean washrooms to improve working conditions and to create healthy environments. Furthermore, for workers, he provided better leisure facilities and cultural programs, and increased holidays, etc. He really accomplished many things in a short time. He planned for the prosperity of the German people over a very long future. In another view, if Hitler had died at that stage, before invading neighboring countries and before killing Jews, I would definitely agree that he could have been seen as a real hero in Germany history, even a Messiah.

During the war, you were a leader of the Hitler Youth. What did you do?

The Hitler Youth was to recruit German children from ages 10 to 18 to be trained in preparation of future duties for the Reich. The entire German youth had to participate. Apart from family and school, they had to serve the nation and *Volksgemeinschaft* (community of the people) in the spirit of the Nazis. In order to enter the elite membership, they had to pass all sorts of tough examinations. First, a racial examination was required: your family had to be Aryan for at least 3 generations. For physical fitness you had to perform an athletic test, such as jumping off a high tower to show you were brave.

An IQ intelligence test was done so you could be brainwashed to follow Hitler's worship and his command. Finally, an essay was required about the military situation in Germany. One needed strong self-discipline and lifetime commitment to the Führer. I passed all of the tests. In the Nazi Youth camp, all children sang Hitler's songs, learned how to think and behave in German ways, and I lived with this Nazi propaganda until the end of the war. Because I had a very high score in the camp I became a leader. A total of nearly 10 million boys and girls were in the Hitler Youth.

When you are young you can't decide what is right and what is wrong because you don't have a clear perspective. You are influenced by your friends and environment, as I said already, which is based on the political situation. At the time, we didn't realize we had the wrong leader. Nazism clearly stood for the destruction of human civilization and we all can understand that today. During the war, I knew that people were sent to concentration camps because my father, a civil engineer, was incarcerated as well. But I didn't know what was going on behind the camp wall. I really didn't know many things at that time until the war ended.

What happened to the Jews after the "Nuremberg Racial Laws" were enacted, and what were you told about Jews who were taken away and never returned?
German people were divided into two categories, Gentiles and Jews, and that caused social segregation and many problems between the two groups. Jews who were working in the government, at universities, in schools or in other public offices, were dismissed. After that, people didn't want to marry and many people who were married to Jews got divorced, because if you had a Jewish

spouse you got into trouble. It was difficult to find work or to progress in your career.

While my father was imprisoned, my mother and I moved to the house of my grandparents in Nuremberg. Next to our house was a synagogue and there were a few Jewish neighbors. I used to play with one of the Jewish boys despite being warned by my mother about the Gentile children's blood thing. As a boy, in fact, the story made me more curious than afraid. I felt it would be exciting if the Jews really performed such a ritual. I wanted to watch it. Anyway, they were deported one day. Nobody knew where they went. Some people said that the Jews had to be eliminated and were evacuated during the war because they were enemies of the German state. But they said they would return after the war and would get new houses in German-occupied land in the East. So we simply believed that. When I think back, however, I would say that older people knew more or less what was going on. But they never said anything openly about it especially to children, because children talk and they might end up in a concentration camp themselves. I remember there was a joke, "If you don't keep your mouth shut, you'll be sent to Dachau!"

How do you remember the bombing of Nuremberg?
Nuremberg was bombed several times by Western Allies between 1943 and 1945. I was a teenager by then. I remember it very well. Every time bombers crossed the German borders and headed in our direction, announcements were made on the radio. Then sirens went on for more than an hour before the air raid began. Every school and many buildings had bomb shelters so we had to run into a nearby shelter. When the bombing started, if we were outside, we could see hundreds

of bombs falling from the planes: it was like a rain of huge black bullets. When they hit the ground, there was a jolt like a big earthquake. Two bombs hit our street one time and exploded, and the front of our house was destroyed. That was done by American bombers. During one attack, half the city was completely ruined and some 5,000 people were killed. Among them were two of my schoolmates. The biggest air raid was on the 2nd of January, 1945, at 7:00 in the evening. As the danger of air raids increased, school children, women and elderly people in the city were evacuated to the countryside. I was in a train leaving the city on my way to a children's home in the countryside. When the train reached the outskirts of Nuremberg, it was stopped by emergency sirens. It was dark. There were hundreds of bombers in the sky; we could see them because of the red flashing lights of the planes. All passengers quickly got out of the train and had to lie down on the ground. The target was Nuremberg. When the attack began, the night sky became like a Christmas tree; it was like the bombing of Baghdad in the recent Gulf War. This went on one after another, the attacks lasted for one and a half hours, and they continued the next day and night for two days. The sky of Nuremberg was burning for three days. We could see the burning red horizon from the place we lived, some 40 km away from the city.

According to Nazi propaganda, Germany was supposed to be winning the war. As a brainwashed boy, did you ever wonder why German cities were getting attacked?

Propaganda on the radio said, "It doesn't make any difference that the enemies are attacking us, because Germany is developing a powerful top-secret weapon that will destroy the entire Euro-pean enemy. It'll be ready soon. Be patient!" Nobody knew what kind of weapon it was, but it was said that they didn't need to fly it out for bombing, that they could shoot it from Germany. It could be a rumor, but I assume that German scientists were researching an atomic bomb at that time, just as the Americans were.

After the war when you learned of Hitler's war crimes and the true story of the Nazi atrocities, what was your reaction?

Until the last moment of the war, I was fully brainwashed by Nazi ideology. I believed in Hitler. When I learned that Germany lost, I couldn't believe it. Then the next thing was that we were shown something that was absolutely unbelievable — a documentary film of the Holocaust which was an undeniable evidence of the Nazi atrocities to human beings inside the concentration camps. But my first reaction was that this must be impossible. How could my people commit such horrifying acts? I thought this could be some kind of mistake. I was totally confused. All of a sudden, I had to switch off my mind and change my mental attitude completely. Then, step by step, I began to believe it. It took me some time to recover from that shocking feeling. Very slowly, I began to understand the Nazi government was a dictatorship and the wrong regime. And, as a result, the whole nation had gone on the wrong track. Hitler, the man I adored was, after all, an evil leader.

When you are young everything is exciting and everybody has a good time. My youth had been engaged with the Nazi activities and that was all we had at that time. It was an extraordinary situation and, of course, something I'm not proud of. Occasionally, when I see Third Reich propaganda in documentary movies on TV today, it reminds me of my past and how we were during those years. I tell myself that wasn't reality, it was the imagination of my youth, it was a bad dream, it did not exist. Because of my own experience in the Hitler Youth, I don't accuse other people of my generation who were members of the Nazi Party. My point is that justice should be fair on this matter. It depends upon each individual, how much he or she learned and was able to adjust himself or herself after the new democracy was introduced in Germany. If the person still carries the Nazi mentality, that is a problem. ❖

"My transvestite attire saved my life."

LOTHAR BERFELDE

German, homosexual youth during the war. Today, known as "Charlotte von Mahlsdorf," and owner of Gründerzeitmuseum. Born in 1928 in Berlin, Germany. Lives in Germany.

(Photo: Mr. Berfelde with the furniture collection in his museum.)

Can you tell me your story as a child growing up in Berlin before the war began?

I was born in a little village called Mahlsdorf, on the outskirts of eastern Berlin, and I have lived here my entire life. I have experienced the myriad changes of Berlin and Germany. When Germany started the war, I was 11, and as you know, children from age 10 to 16 were obligated to join the Hitler Youth. However, there were some private schools in which you could somehow elude this governmental obligation. My uncle arranged for me to enter one of those schools so that I wouldn't have to become a Hitler's boy. He and his wife, my aunt, used to own an antique shop in Kreuzberg, and from the time I was little, I was fond of antique objects. I loved to collect them. In my after school hours, instead of joining the Nazi children's activities, I worked in their shop moving furniture. While I worked at their shop, I remember many Jewish people were leaving Berlin and they used to come to the shop to sell their furniture. After the *Kristallnacht,* the number of Jews who came to our shop increased dramatically, and my uncle used to buy lots of furniture from them: tables, chairs, cupboards, dressers, sofas, chandeliers, lamps, clocks, radios, paintings, books, collections of grammophone records of Jewish songs, and all sorts of things. Many items were centuries old, of high quality and valuable for collectors and museums. I used to remove them out of the Jewish homes to the shop. I had to clean and polish them, and sometimes repair them, and took care of them for sales. In the early 1940s, when the Jews were deported to the eastern German-occupied lands, Nazis confiscated their property and belongings and sold them to private citizens to finance the war industry. I witnessed many Jewish children and adults being arrested by the Gestapo and taken away from Berlin.

As a transvestite since your youth, you are publicly known as a "girl." Tell me about your survival story during the war in Berlin?

Since I was a child I never felt I should have been a boy. I liked to be with girls playing with dolls rather than playing war games with boys. I was always fascinated with and attracted to pretty female dresses, and I used to wear them in the closets of my mother or my aunt. When they saw me with their dresses on, they used to comment how pretty I could be. I had clear blue eyes and curly blonde hair when I was younger and women's clothes did fit me beautifully. I loved to wear them all the time. With lip stick and make-up on my face, I turned into a perfect girl. While doing it, I was occasionally caught by my father. He was outraged and used to beat me up. He wanted me to be a strong German soldier. But I felt that what my father demanded of me was against my nature. I hated to carry guns or wear uniforms. At the age of 12, I already knew I was a homosexual. I never needed to come out. I soon found a boy who also liked to dress up in female attire like me, and we became good buddies. During the war when we were 13 or 14, we "disguised" ourselves that way and roamed around the streets of Berlin. At that time we were too young to realize that such odd behavior in public could be dangerous. When I recall it now, it was sheer madness, actually. I was caught many times but escaped each time.

As the air raids intensified, there were curfews night after night, and after 9:00 o'clock in the evening, children under 14 were not allowed to walk in the streets. If you were caught, you could be sent to the concentration camp of

Sachsenhausen, even though you were underage. But we ignored the order and went out in drag in the deserted streets anyway. Once we got into trouble with a Hitlerjugend (Hitler Youth) patrol in civilian clothes. They thought we were prostitutes. We were taken to a district office for questioning. Without any doubt, they thought that we were girls. The officers didn't believe us when we said we were not girls. Eventually, they grabbed us and put us on the table, pulled our skirts and stockings off, and after they confirmed it, they gave us a severe thrashing with a belt. After a long night in custody, they acknowledged that we were not involved politically, so they released us the next morning with a strong warning to our parents.

By the spring of 1945, every German knew that the fall of Germany was just a matter of time. All men from ages 17 to 70 were drafted and had to take up arms, and be ready to fight against the Russians. Due to wartime martial law, those who didn't carry weapons would be executed immediately without a trial.

At the age of 17, I was again captured wearing a girl's dress and questioned by an SS commander as to whether I was a girl or a boy. I answered that I was a boy. Then, because I didn't carry a gun, I was arrested. The penalty for being an unarmed man was death by firing squad. I was taken with a dozen other men to an execution wall. We raised our arms. When the executioners raised their guns ready to shoot us, by accident, an army officer walked by. He looked at me with curiosity because I was the only "girl" among these men. He questioned me about my age. I answered that I was 16. Then, he said to the executioners, "He is still just a kid, save him! We don't kill children." I was discharged. In fact, at that time, actually I had turned 17, but I com-pletely forgot that my birthday, March 18th, had already passed two weeks before. Because of the wartime chaos, my mother had forgotten to have a birthday party for me. My transvestite attire saved my life in the end: if I had been wearing boy's clothes, I would have been dead. I was lucky.

Could you describe the things you saw in the final months of 1945 in Kreuzberg? What happened after the Russian soldiers entered Berlin?

In March and April, during the last two months of the war, Berlin was totally chaotic and paralysed. Allied bombardments had turned the buildings into ovens, explosions, ruins; and rubble and debris were all over. No street trams or buses were running. Berlin was completely *kaput*, or broken. Beautiful Berlin became a dead city. Dead bodies were piled up on the street corners, and there was no food, nothing to eat. People were eating dead animals: dogs, cats or horses that had been killed by the bombings or by falling debris, or whatever they could find. Many water pumps were also destroyed by the air raids and in many areas of the city, the water supply was rationed. There were long lines of people waiting for water. Allied bombers had flown very low and deliberately targeted civilians with carpet bombings. I saw many people killed that way. There were several types of bombs. The fire bomb was an ordinary one, but a splinter bomb exploded in all directions after it was dropped, so we had to run away as fast as we could. We used to recognize them by the sound. While the city was under attack, I was running all over to find food, and my pretty dresses were covered in dust from the bombs and explosions, but luckily I was never hit.

Even during such a confusing time, the SS officers were still hunting and executing any man who refused to join the army. In the Kreuzberg area, I saw a gallows of men with a sign posted: "I have deceived my fatherland. I am too cowardly to defend my country." That was to give the message to people who had no wish to fight — you would be next! Every man had to go in the army. Women were also shot for different reasons. Looting was very common in those wild times. I saw a few women coming out of a bombed liquor factory with looted bottles of liquor in their arms. An SS soldier shot them on the spot and they died instantly. In mid-April I received a draft notice: the Nazi authorities found out that I had turned 17. It said that if I refused, the SS would come to get me by force. I went into hiding. I found a cellar in a building where no one could see me. I only had water and a small amount of bread, and I lived there for weeks. I was really starving. Then, I heard sounds of heavy artillery and tanks from my cellar. The Russian Red Army had entered Berlin and surrounded the city. Suddenly there were Russian red flags all over Berlin. On April 26th at 2:30 in the afternoon they marched into Kreuzberg. Shortly afterwards, a Russian soldier came down to my cellar with an interpreter. They found me, a "girl," hiding, and told me that the Kreuzberg area would become a battle zone between Russian and German soldiers, so every civilian must be evacuated. And then he gave me food. That saved my life. The Russians liberated the Berliners. If they had arrived days later, I would have died of starvation. By God, I was saved by the Russians!

Afterwards, the streets were barricaded by tanks. Ground battles had begun between the two enemies. During the next several weeks, heavy fighting went on for days and nights in every corner: Berlin was turned into a city of atrocities and horrors. The streets were dangerous because there were snipers, grenades and explosions; many people were hit and wounded by them, and there were no medical supplies and no doctors. It was a horrifying experience. In the Mariendorf area some people hung white sheets in their windows as a symbol of surrender to the Russians: they were shot by the SS firing squad for treason to the Fatherland. Then we heard on the radio that Hitler had died in his *Führerbunker*. Suddenly, the Russian soldiers seemed to be everywhere, firing their machine guns in the air like barbarians, drinking vodka or German wine, and looting anything they found including women. They were looking for women to rape. They quickly learned two German words, "women out!" They broke into the houses and grabbed them. Being a transvestite, I felt I was not safe anymore. They might capture me for rape as well and I was scared to death in the last weeks of the war.

How did you start your Gründerzeitmuseum?
At the end of the war, Kreuzberg was unlivable because of the destruction. I returned to my parents' house in the village of Mahlsdorf, and started a new life — I ended up on the communist side. In the village, there was a manor house called Mahlsdorf, which was used for social programming for children before the war. After the war, it was abandoned and not inhabitable: there was no roof, no window, no gas, no electricity or water. The manor was owned by the city government. In 1959, it was about to be demolished, so I got it for a small price. I moved into the cellar. I worked at a farm during the days and every weekend I repaired it by myself: it took me 13 years to restore the entire manor to livable condition.

Then, little by little, I installed my personal collection of *Gründerzeit* furniture — *Gründerzeit* is the Bismarck period, an era of rapid industrial expansion in Germany — and other collectors' items which I bought from antique shops during the war, including the world's first grammophone and lots of record collections of Jewish songs, and other items which I found in flea markets after the war. It became a small museum of 18th and 19th century collections. In the early 1960s, I opened only a part of it to the public: I just wanted to show people my private collections of beautiful furniture. Under the communist regime, I wasn't allowed to charge any fee to visitors. Therefore, financially, it was hard for me to manage it. However, occasionally, Defa, East German TV movie productions, used it as a location, and I was also often in the movies as a transvestite actor, which helped fund my museum and kept it going.

During the communist regime, what was people's attitude toward homosexuals?
In 1952, the East German government prohibited gay and lesbian meetings, and bars, restaurants and theaters where they used to meet were closed down. In Germany there has been an anti-homosexual law called "Paragraph 175" since the Nazi era, and that was enforced in East Germany. Homosexuals had nowhere to meet each other. To find their mates, they begun contacting each other through newspapers and magazines using special codes. I made announcements in it myself. Many people contacted me. In 1973, we founded the homosexual and lesbian association of Berlin, and occasionally, we even had homosexual conferences and the participants used to give their speeches here. Then, on the weekends, my museum turned into a homosexual social

club. In the cellar, I set up a replica of a 19th century Berlin *Kneipe* (pub and restaurant) with everything authentic of that period. We used to have many parties here and had a wonderful time, actually. Then in 1978, the police found out about us and I had to close down the meetings. But we never gave up the meetings entirely: we went underground. The meetings took place in private homes. But we were observed by the Stasi, the East German spy operation.

Through my movie appearances and this sort of craziness, I became widely-known in the former East Germany as "Charlotte von Mahlsdorf" or the "Queen of Mahlsdorf." Some people came to me and said, "Hitler must have forgotten to kill you!" For many years I was labelled as "undesirable" or some kind of a crank. But being a queer, I have never been arrested and I have never hidden my nature. I would say that, in the former communist world, I was a pioneer of homosexuality. And today, over 30 years after I opened it, I still live in the museum, and I have many visitors from all over Germany.

Recently, you were honored for your dedication to the museum. Could you tell about it, and how you look back over your years in wartime Berlin?
I've been awarded the "Service Order" for my work with this museum by the Federal Republic and I'm certainly happy about it. I'm the first transvestite and openly homosexual person to be honored in Germany. During the war, two friends of mine were imprisoned in the concentration camp for being homosexuals: one survived and one died. But for me, the most painful memory of the war is about the Jewish people, and what happened to them. I used to watch them being taken away with my own eyes. That

was a terrible crime against humanity and that is painful to remember. At that time I didn't even have any idea what was happening to them, but because I was removing the furniture from their property, I felt deeply sorry for them. As a personal remembrance to them, I wear a Star of David pendant on my chest although I'm not a Jew. ❖

"My husband was murdered by the Nazi state not for what he had done, but for what he had thought."

FREYA VON MOLTKE

German, widow of Helmuth James von Moltke, co-founder of the Kreisau Circle, anti-Hitler resistance group, and contributor of material to the book *Letters for Freya*. Born in 1911 in Cologne, Germany. Lives in Vermont, USA.

How did National Socialism come to you and your husband's life, and how did German people react when Hitler came to power?

I met my future husband, Helmuth James von Moltke, while I was still a student. I married him in 1931. He was the great-grandnephew of Field Marshal Helmuth von Moltke, one of Germany's nobility, and a lawyer. I was 20 years old. In the early years of my marriage, I continued to study law and got my doctorate in 1935, although I never became a practicing lawyer. We lived in Berlin. At that time, Germany was politically in a civil war. There were semi-military from the left to the right and the center, and each had a private army. There was constant fighting in the streets between Communists, Socialists and Nazis, and our government was constantly changing administrations. It was a very rough and chaotic time, but it didn't affect us personally very much.

Then, the Nazi Party won lots of votes and Hitler was appointed as Chancellor of Germany by the aged Hindenburg, who was nearly senile by that time. We were terrified. In the beginning, a lot of German people supported National Socialism because they believed it was national which seemed patriotic, and they were thinking socialism meant that the labor and factory workers might have their share in the government, and their life would get better. They thought this National Socialism was just what Germany needed.

My husband, however, disliked Hitler and National Socialism, even before Hitler took office. On January 30th, 1933 when a friend of ours said, "Well, it's a good thing the Nazis have come to power because the German people are getting tired of all these changes in our government, and now the Nazis have a chance to govern our country." Helmuth was very upset. He said, "How dare you say such a thing! This is a catas-

trophe! It's a terrible thing for all Germans. It's the beginning of the end of Germany." From the beginning he knew that having Hitler as our leader meant war. He immediately warned all his Jewish friends to leave the country because Hitler was going to do what he had written in his book, *Mein Kampf.*

After he finished his studies in Germany, Helmuth studied international law in Austria and England. His goal was to become a judge, but not under a dictatorial regime such as Hitler's. He was not a nationalist; on the contrary, he was an anti-nationalist. He was a liberal and a very free-thinking person. He wanted Germany to be a democratic nation like England, France or America. That's why he could stand up against a man like Hitler. He clearly foresaw the whole picture of the Nazi regime from the very early days.

How did the name "Kreisau" come about, and how was the resistance movement formed while the Nazis government was creating such a powerful state?

First, Hitler destroyed all his opponents completely: Communists, Socialists and all other political parties. Within a matter of weeks, he arrested people and sent their leaders to concentration camps, and after that the Nazi became quite systematic. That created a horrifying fear. People became more and more afraid to say anything against Hitler, and opponents became isolated. People who didn't like Hitler felt they were lost and out of touch with others, and they didn't know what to do. They went underground eventually. So, it began very slowly. In 1939 my father-in-law died, and being the first son, Helmuth inherited the family estate in a town called Kreisau, then in Silesia, now Poland. It was a family farm with a 19th-century castle-villa.

Someone had to take care of the household, so, the obvious thing was for us to move there. But, being a lawyer — by then trained at London's Inner Temple and in Berlin — my husband had to be in Berlin for his practice, so we kept our apartment in Berlin. He lived in both residences, in Berlin during the weekdays and Kreisau on weekends. I used to visit him in Berlin all the time, but stayed mostly in Kreisau until the end of the war.

In the mid-1930s, meanwhile, lots of positive things happened to the German people and Hitler's popularity had risen. Hitler told the people that they were going to have a better life with socialism in human form and nationalism in patriotic terms. It sounded attractive to many people and they believed in him. They were happy with his idea and the majority supported him. What could we do? We could hardly do anything. The real criminal side of Nazism was that people lost all of their human rights, and in the end, Hitler's gangs could rampage through Germany and do anything they wanted. It was a truly monstrous regime. Even today, it's still difficult for me to think that really happened. Although most Germans didn't want war and the war was not popular when it came, until the war, they believed Hitler was doing a fine job. As private citizens, we couldn't do much, but we could help victims, for instance, Jewish people. My husband thought that all his Jewish friends and their families should get out of Germany. Being a specialist in international laws and having many connections with England and America, he was able to help them leave the country and go somewhere safe. At the time of *Kristallnacht,* in particular, he aided many Jewish lawyers and people whose property and business were taken over by non-Jews.

During this time, anti-Hitler sentiment had grown, mostly among the young and well-educated professionals: civil servants, academics, lawyers, journalists, intellectuals, professors, army officers, conservatives, liberals, socialists, aristocrats, Catholic and Protestant activists, even some members of the Nazi Party. It was a slow process to bring people together by word of mouth, and it was led by Helmuth and his friend Peter Yorke. A circle of people met frequently in Berlin and occasionally at our house in Kreisau. By 1943, our circle had increased to about 20 people. In the same period, there were other anti-Nazi groups, and some of our people were connected with them as well. Such activities were a great risk for anyone. The leading activists were Adam von Trott zu Solz, a Rhodes Scholar and a diplomat, Peter Graf Yorck von Wartenburg, a lawyer working in the War Office in the Bendlerstrasse. The members of the Kreisau Circle were not a homogeneous group of people. Politically they had different views and ideas. They focused on how they could change to the post-Third Reich Germany, or Germany after Hitler. They often argued, but they learned to compromise with each other to create a new Germany after the Nazi regime was overthrown. They planned a democratic government with different political parties based on Christian principles. In order to pursue the plan, everybody agreed that Hitler had to be assassinated. The big question was how could the German people learn to be democratic, something that Britain and France had been for centuries. When you study German history before the Nazis, you find that Germany has always been governed by Kaisers and in the hands of civil servants, and has much less experience with democracy. Democracy never worked in Germany. The meetings, by the way, never took place with everybody together at once — it was always a few people at a time. In fact, until the July 20th 1944 attempt on Hitler's life, this way of meeting continued. But after the failure of that plot, because some of our members were involved with it, they were found out by the Gestapo. It was the Gestapo who used the name "Kreisau Circle."

Quite a number of church people were involved in the resistance. Hitler planned a "Thousand-Year Reich," and suppressed Christianity. Did that mean that Hitler became the new national figure for Germans?
Hitler's nationalism would have become a kind of new religious symbol for Germans. Hitler was anti-Jewish, therefore, in terms of the Judeo-Christian tradition, he was fundamentally an anti-Christian as well. He rejected Christianity as an alien idea saying it was part Jewish and oriental in origin, and had originated 2,000 years ago. He attempted to implement his "racial purity" theories of German origins, and tried to restore a new paganism in Germany. But he was careful because he knew that there was lots of power in the church. After he made the "Concordat Agreement" with the Catholics, he then tried to put in a nationalist bishop at the head of the Protestant church. But that caused a great uproar, so he left it alone and decided to wait for a chance in later years. Anyway, he didn't like the church and always wanted to annihilate both Catholic and Protestant faiths. Under Hitler, the church was not to have any power, and all young people were pressured to join the Hitler Youth, not church organizations. On the other hand, the German church as an institution was not totally anti-Nazi. But many individual Christians in both denominations stood against Hitler. They were very brave to do so. Hitler banned religious proces-

sions, closed monasteries, the Catholic press was banned, and some priests, clergymen, monks and nuns were harassed, jailed and even killed. They fought back and struggled to keep their traditional church in order.

During the war as an active anti-Nazi resistor, what did your husband precisely do and how was he arrested?
When the war began, all German citizens, young and old, men, women and children, had to participate in the war effort in one way or another. Everybody had to work either in the military or in some way that was related to the job they were doing at the time. Since my husband had expert knowledge in the field of international law, he was drafted by the Reich to be an advisor on the rules of law in warfare. Even war had certain rules to follow and it was worth keeping them, because otherwise it could affect our own people. So, as the war started, at the age of 32, he held a position as the legal adviser in the Foreign Office of the German High Command in Berlin. In this capacity, he tried to communicate with the Allies and used his office to help hostages, prisoners of war, forced laborers and Jews.

But in January 1944, an acquaintance of his was arrested, tortured, and confessed that there were anti-Nazi conspirators among the Nazi high rank officials and he named Moltke, my husband. He was taken into custody. It was terrible because, by then, we had two small sons who were 7 and 3 years old. Although I had been well aware that this might happen because he was involved in such serious matters, when it did happen, I was very upset. He was first imprisoned in Ravensbrück concentration camp as a political criminal. I was able to visit him once a month and was allowed to talk to him for two hours. We talked about many private things. He knew Germany would lose the war and was optimistic about it. He said Britain would never give in, and America would eventually join the war. Inside the prison, he was treated better than other inmates, he didn't have to do any work, and most of the time he read books or wrote me in his cell. When July 20th came, and the Gestapo learned that he was not involved with the plot because he was already in jail, the Nazi authorities almost discharged him. He was supposed to be transferred to an ammunition factory labor camp. But then, the Nazis found out that at that time he was connected with the conspirators of the plot.

How did you manage life with your little children, and why was he executed in the end?

I continued living in the Kreisau farm on some income I had from my family. During the war people didn't need money, anyway. I had enough to eat because of the products from our farm. It was a huge farm which employed 60 people, and it was also valuable for the state because it produced grains, potatoes, vegetables, sugar, beets, eggs, chickens, pigs, etc. As for my children, I told them their father was dead. They didn't understand what death meant, but they were happy attending the local school and playing at the farm. After the July plot, Moltke was tried in Tegel for treason for failing to report the activities of his associates. After one year of incarceration, he had to stand trial and was condemned to death. On January 23, 1945, he was executed. He was 37 years old. In the end, he was murdered by the Nazi state not for what he had done, but for what he had thought.

In retrospect, although we did not spend every day together, we were a very close couple. I respected him and loved him very much. One of the reasons for our closeness was that we always wrote letters to each other. During those long years of his struggles with the state, he wrote me constantly, telling me all the details of his life and activities in the resistance, about his friends and conspirators, secret information, and everything else. These hundreds of letters from my husband became a great treasure for me. The days before his execution, he wrote the final one to me and our two boys:

"...Throughout an entire life, even at school, I have fought against a spirit of narrowness and unfreedom, of arrogance and lack of respect for others, of intolerance and the absolute, the merciless consistency among the Germans, which found its expression in the National Socialist state.. Ever since National Socialism came to power, I have done my best to mitigate the consequences for its victims and to prepare for a change. I was driven to it by my conscience, and, after all, it is a task of a man. From 1933 on, I have therefore had to make material sacrifices and to run personal risks. In all these years, Freya, who was the one who suffered most from these sacrifices and who always had to be concerned that I would be arrested, imprisoned, or killed, never hindered me in what I considered necessary, or made it harder in any way. She was always ready to accept everything; she was always ready to make sacrifices if it was necessary. And I tell you that is much more than I did. For running risks oneself, which one knows, is nothing compared with the readiness to let the person with whom one's life is joined run risks one cannot gauge. And it is much more, too, that the wife of a warrior accepts, for she has no choice; one word from Freya might have held me back from many an undertaking."

Throughout the Nazi regime, Germany lost many valuable young people, including my husband. He was an inspiring intellectual who carried a deep moral conscience. That's why I think it was a great loss for Germany to have killed him. ❖

Within the exhibition photos:

JOURNEY TO SAFETY

Adolf Hitler came to power in Germany in 1933. The build-up of the dictator's fanatical racist policies, directed mainly against the Jews, came to a head on the 9th – 10th November 1938, later referred to as "KRISTALLNACHT" (night of the broken glass).

Jewish shops were smashed and looted, homes were destroyed and synagogues burned. 20,000 Jews were immediately sent to Concentration Camps.

Fearing for the safety of Jewish children, the British Government of the day promised to allow 10,000 unaccompanied Jewish children to enter Britain. Operation "Kindertransports" started on the 2nd December 1938 and ended with the outbreak of war on the 3rd September 1939.

This exhibition tells the story of their journey.

• 50TH ANNIVERSARY YEAR •

REUNION OF KINDERTRANSPORT

EXHIBITION

20–21 JUNE 1989

50 YEARS AGO WE ARRIVED IN BRITAIN FROM NAZI GERMANY, AUSTRIA AND CZECHOSLOVAKIA.

CHILDREN AGED 3 MONTHS TO SEVENTEEN YEARS, ALONE AND BEWILDERED.

"After my experience, I can now tell you that Jewish persecution never ends."

BERTHA LEVERTON

German Jew, Holocaust survivor through *Kindertransport*. Born in 1923 in Munich, Germany. Lives in England.

(Photo: Ms. Leverton at the 50th Anniversary exhibition of the "Reunion of the *Kindertransport*" with photos of Jewish children arriving in England.)

How do you remember Munich in 1933 when Hitler came to power, and how did things change for the Jewish people afterwards?

I was a ten-year-old schoolgirl. There was a big Jewish community in Munich at that time, perhaps tens of thousands of inhabitants. There was a Jewish quarter, but many Jews lived in other parts of the city. It was not a ghetto like the one in Warsaw. There were about 10 synagogues: secular, Reformed and Orthodox, a few Jewish retirement houses, a hospital, a school, and newspapers. My parents were originally from Poland and we were classified as Polish Jews in Germany. Germans never naturalized Jews to become German citizens. Although my father fought for Germany during WW I and I was born in Germany, we were still Polish Jews. My father was in the leather goods business. I had a younger sister and brother. Until 1933, school education was open to any Jewish children. Parents were able to choose if they wanted a Jewish school or a German school. My parents were Orthodox so we three children attended the Jewish school called Die jüdische Volksschule and we studied a German curriculum in addition to a Jewish curriculum and took Hebrew lessons. But most of the secular Jews sent their children to the German schools.

There were Nazi teachers and after 1933, Jewish children who attended the German schools were often taunted or beaten by Gentile classmates. Between 1933 and 1938, many of those children were expelled from their schools and Jewish schools had to accept them. I remember the children who came to us from German schools had a higher standard of education and soon became the top of the class. But they had problems adjusting to Jewish studies, because they were raised as non-Jews and their parents had never told them they were Jews or about

their Jewish heritage. It was a big culture shock for them. In the same period, there were book burnings all over the city. Many books related to Jewish matters and Jewish Bibles were taken from libraries and book stores to the streets and burned by Nazi mobs, SA and SS men. When the Nuremberg Laws were launched in 1936, Jewish publishers were shut down and Nazi newspapers increased. The most well known anti-Jewish newspaper was called *Der Stürmer*.

After that, we weren't allowed to go to swimming pools, ice skating rinks, movies, theaters, anywhere in public where there were Germans. It got worse and worse year by year and finally resulted in the *Kristallnacht*. That night we were in the streets and didn't go home because we heard a rumor that there was going to be a pogrom against Jews. We knew that some weeks before some Polish Jews in Germany like us were sent back to Poland, and they had been stranded in the no man's land between Germany and Poland. So, that night we felt it would be dangerous to stay home so we walked through the city for a whole night. During that night the Nazi thugs smashed many Jewish homes, broke up their furniture, confiscated their valuables, and dragged men out and took them to concentration camps. Many synagogues, holy books, Jewish stores, shops, restaurants and schools were set afire and destroyed. We lived in an apartment building where there was only one other Jew among all the units, so the SA and SS men didn't bother our home and left us alone. The following day, the Jewish schools and publishing houses were closed down. At that time, although the Dachau concentration camp already existed near Munich, the Nazis weren't killing the Jews yet. However, we didn't have the slightest idea of what would come next in our life.

About the *Kindertransport*, when did this begin and how did you come to England?

It started in England after the *Kristallnacht.* After that shocking violence against Jews in Germany, European Jews were well aware of it and Jewish people all over the world began to feel threatened. Jewish communities in Britain immediately petitioned their government and funds were raised. The government announced that they would permit an unspecified number of Jewish children up to age 17 to enter Britain. While nearly every country had closed their door to the Jews, Britain started taking child immigrants. One day, my little sister found out from her friend that she was going to England. As there were many more children than places in England, the whole thing was kept rather quiet by the *Gemeinde,* which was the Jewish organization that dealt with welfare and Jewish affairs in the Jewish community in Germany. My father made arrangements with the officials. They agreed to take me, aged 15 then, and my brother, aged 12, for transportation. We were told not to talk about this to our friends, because they only had a small quota that was primarily for orphans or those whose fathers were in concentration camps. My parents and my sister stayed behind.

On the 4th of January 1939, seven weeks after the *Kristallnacht,* I left my home with my brother. I carried one suitcase with clothes, my most precious photographs and my favorite books. We joined a group of 60 children in the Munich railway station. On our way to Hamburg, more children got on board, and we were gathered with many hundreds of other children. Our train went to Holland, then we were transferred to a ship and arrived in Harwich, Dover Court, England.

How many children were transported to England altogether? How was your new life in a new country, and what happened to your sister and parents?

The *Kindertransport* had begun at the end of 1938 and continued until the outbreak of war in 1939. During nine months of operation, about 9,500 Jewish refugee children came safely to England and were saved. The youngest one was a three-month old baby. They were from Germany, Austria, Czechoslovakia and Poland. Britain provided homes for all of them. British Jewish committees found foster homes by making announcements in the newspapers throughout the country and people, both Jews and non-Jews, responded. My brother and I were adopted by a Christian couple who had no children. Our foster father was a house builder and he and his wife lived in a nice house in Coventry, but after the Blitz on the city, they moved to Yorkshire. Six months later, they also allowed my sister to live with us, so all of us were taken in by them and we learned English from them. However, their treatment of us wasn't great. Though they were receiving money from the Jewish Refugee Committee for our care, they treated me like a maid. I wasn't allowed to go to school. Not only that, as the oldest, I was sent to work in a cotton mill and they took my wages away as well. My brother, too, worked in a factory. Only my sister, the youngest one, was allowed to attend school: she had a good education. At least I wanted to read books, but since they were working class people, there wasn't any book in the house. Of all things, though, the most difficult custom we had to adjust to was the Christian way of life. Apart from that, I had the task of avoiding the unwelcome "friendly" attention of my supposed guardian.

We were raised to be fairly religious by our parents. We celebrated all the Jewish holidays and we kept a kosher diet, and so, everything outside our tradition was totally strange and a tremendous culture shock. We used to celebrate all of our wonderful festivals both in synagogue and at home such as Passover, Rosh Hashana, Yom Kippur, Hanukkah, and then, every Sabbath, of course. Being children we missed these festivities very much. We weren't familiar with Christian festivities, and we never celebrated Christmas or Easter. Besides, all we had to eat was English food which was not kosher, although we never ate pork at all. Meanwhile, my parents successfully escaped from Germany and we were reunited. In 1944 we started a new life in England.

How did your parents get out of Germany? Didn't immigration become very difficult as the war began?

From 1933 until 1938, it was easier for Jews to emigrate to America, Australia, Canada, England, and elsewhere. They had quotas. But after the *Kristallnacht,* they turned down Jews. While every European Jew wanted to leave, President Roosevelt refused to take even Jewish children. He didn't want to overload America with Jews. When war started in September 1939, there was a big scare here because people thought Hitler might invade England as well. Then, England suddenly announced that they didn't want spies here, and the German Jewish men could be spies, too. They took the *Kindertransport* boys over 16 and shipped them out to Canada, Australia and New Zealand. On the way one of the ships called "The Arandora Star" carrying 1,200 men was hit by a German torpedo and sank. A lot of lives were lost and it was a terrible tragedy. Those boys who were sent to the Commonwealth countries,

joined the army in later years and came over to fight for the Allies against the Germans.

Besides the *Kindertransport,* England accepted more Jewish refugees than any other country. There were also other Jewish refugees who entered England on the quota. However, as the war intensified, Winston Churchill's government interned German and Austrian men aged 16 to 60: they categorized them as "enemy aliens" and that included Jews as well.

How my parents arrived in England was a unique story. After we left Germany, the situation worsened for them. My father was taken to a concentration camp but released shortly after because he was a WW I veteran. But their business had been closed by the Nazis, and they worked and lived in the Jewish hospital which was still considered the safest in Munich. Geographically, Munich is in the south and borders Austria and Switzerland, it was much easier to escape from there than from Berlin or Hamburg. One day, they walked toward the south carrying only money. They hired a guide who lead them to the border. They went to Yugoslavia first, today's Croatia and Slovenia, then entered northern Italy. Germany had made a pact with Italy but the Italians were different. They weren't Nazis and my parents were fairly safe there. My father then became ill in Rome and was hospitalized, but the Italian hospital took care of him. Other Jews from Germany and Italy were taken to internment camps, but because my father needed intensive care, he got special permission from the Italian government to stay in Rome.

My mother was, in a way, a smart woman: she went to the Vatican and begged priests for help. During the war the Vatican was officially not helpful to Jews, but my parents were an exceptional case. They successfully received official stamps on their false identification papers. With these fake papers they were able to enter Spain, and then it was easy to get through to Portugal because these two countries were neutral during the war. They weren't allowed to work there but, by that time, American Jewish organizations were contributing money to save European Jewish refugees who escaped to these two countries. The Jewish Committee in Portugal gave them some cash, provided accommodations and social services. There were a few hundred Jewish refugees in both countries. So they lived in a relatively nice flat in Lisbon for a whole year. And then, from there they took a ship and arrived in England while the war was still going on. So, in the end, my whole family was saved. I must say we were just lucky and one of the very few cases.

During wartime, how was the attitude of the English in general toward Jewish refugees?

A lot of English people couldn't tell between German Jews and German people, and they treated us as Germans. That was the most peculiar thing. They didn't understand that we were refugees from Hitler and having a hard time. We couldn't blame them for that. But many of them were very gentle and kind to us: there was no hostility or violence against us. Once, a BBC reporter called us "miniature enemies" because we were children. But after the war they understood better what was happening to us.

You and your family were saved in such a miraculous way, but your friends and many other Jews died in the Holocaust. You must have felt pain for them...?

It was really shocking, of course. Most parents of the *Kindertransport* children died in Auschwitz. Perhaps 10 or 15 percent of the parents survived.

We felt a speechless sorrow for those who lost their parents. At the same time, we also had a guilt complex because our parents survived. While every single English citizen was celebrating the victory, we were in deep mourning because those children became orphans. We even felt ashamed because we had parents. Towards the end of the war, many Jewish boys joined the British Army, changed their names and fought in Germany. They looked for their parents and relatives, and then saw what had happened there. Many of them never recovered from that trauma, even nearly 50 years later. It's something, psychologically, that never left them. Some of them even live in mental hospitals today.

After the war some *Kindertransport* children remained in England and the rest of them emigrated to America, Canada, Australia, New Zealand and Israel. In fact, the year 1989 was the 50th anniversary of the *Kindertransport* and I organized a reunion. A few hundred of the ex-*Kindertransport* children who are now grandmothers and grandfathers, reunited in London. It was a very moving gathering. Then, I compiled the stories of 250 reminiscences called *I Came Alone*. This book was awarded a prize in 1992.

You went to a Jewish school as a child and you obviously studied Judaism. Before everything happened, did you ever think another Jewish persecution might occur in your lifetime? And how did you raise your own children after your personal experience?

By the time we were sent to England, I was a teenager and I knew the history of Jewish life and of the many pogroms in Poland. Although I was well aware of it, I didn't think anything like it directly would come to me in my life. But after my experience, I can now tell you that Jewish persecution never ends. I was raised religiously and I carry my own belief, so when everything happened, I was less shocked than the secular children whose parents were assimilated and who lived a non-Jewish lifestyle. Those children suffered the most. Many of those Jews knew that they were Jews and celebrated Jewish holidays, but they didn't have the intense Jewish grounding that we had. So there was a division between religious Jews and non-religious Jews, and in a way, religious Jews were ready mentally. Many Jews today don't know anything and don't want to know. Perhaps, it's because their parents went through hell in concentration camps and they don't believe in God anymore, and who can blame them? It's very difficult to evaluate what happened to us.

During the postwar years, I straightaway joined a Jewish congregation and married a religious Jew. We have three children all brought up to be religious with the traditional Jewish education. We were afraid that if we didn't, they might marry a person from a different religion. In fact, they are more religious than I am. It happens quite often. After 6 million Jews perished, we felt we couldn't afford to lose any more. A lot of Jews assimilate and intermarry, far more than we want. Throughout the 2,000 years of history of Jewish persecution, there were "many Hitlers" who attempted a total extermination of Jewish people, but we survived. I believe Jewish people will never be extinct. ❖

"The British were anti-Nazi rather than anti-German."

VERONICA GILLESPIE

British, veteran of the Royal Women's Force and a secretary for the *Kindertransport* organization. Retired writer and journalist. Born in 1914 in Durham, England. Lives in England.

(Photo: Mrs. Gillespie holding a leaflet from the "Reunion of the *Kindertransport*.")

How did you become involved with the *Kindertransport* organization and what kind of work did you do?

In 1938, at the age of 24, while I was a student at a London college, I met a Jewish girl who was working for an organization which was set up to help Jewish children persecuted by Nazi Germans to get out of Germany. Later this spread to Austria, Poland and Czechoslovakia. At the end of my school term I needed a job, and a secretarial position with this organization was available. That was how I started with the Movement for the Care of Children from Germany. I believe it was jointly organized by the Council for World Jewry and the Quakers who were the only people who could enter Germany and make deals with German officials who wouldn't speak to Jews. Originally, the "Movement" dealt mainly with German Jewish academics who had been expelled from their universities in Germany and their families. After the Nuremberg Laws were passed, more German Jewish families entered England with temporary visas. But after *Kristallnacht* and by the end of 1938, the Movement was growing so rapidly that a bigger office was set up in Bloomsbury House, and the name was changed to Movement for the Care of Refugee children. This was funded by the Baldwin Fund, an English charity, and by American Jewish funds.

In England, every major town had a Refugee Committee to find families willing to offer this hospitality and the children were given free hospitality with British families. I worked in the Aftercare Department corresponding with members of the local committees, and sometimes with foster parents or the children themselves about all sorts of complaints and problems. For example, many refugee children had better clothes than the English children in their foster families. In Germany, the Jewish parents had made colossal efforts to send their children away in good clothes that would make them look attractive. So, I had to help the foster parents to understand that in spite of the smart clothes the child had been deprived of the most important things a child needs — family life, a happy home, education and the hope of a future. I was paid three pounds and ten shillings a week.

As the situation for Jews in Germany became critical, how did British immigration rules change, and since the Jews couldn't deal directly with Nazi officials, who really did the negotiating?

Six months before *Kristallnacht,* regarding Jewish immigration, there was an international conference in Evian, France. Britain was concerned about the future of the Jews. The suggested solution was that all Jews could go immediately to what was then called Palestine, British-occupied land at that time. At the same time, Britain thought it would be unfair for Arabs, so they limited Jewish entry into Palestine. As an alternative solution for Jews, they decided to accept the Jewish children into England after *Kristallnacht.* These negotiations were carried out by a Dutch lady named Mrs. Gertrud Wijsmuller-Meyer, who was a social worker and the wife of an important banker in Holland. She was a Gentile. When she heard that the British government was willing to take 10,000 Jewish children, she personally went to Vienna to see Adolf Eichmann, an SS captain who was in charge of Jewish affairs in Austria, and made a deal with him that big parties of children would be gathered at the main German railway stations, and they would go to Holland and then by ship to England. Eichmann permitted this and the Germans actually paid for the trains. The children were put on special trains, usually at night. A funny story was that when Mrs. Wijsmuller-Meyer met Eichmann in his office, he doubted that she wasn't a Jew. He asked her to pull up her skirt. He stared at her legs for a long time and said, "Hmm... they aren't Jewish legs! I'll talk to you."

By April 1939, it was pretty clear that we were going to be at war with Germany very soon. The British government said it needed a guarantee to protect these children, so they started collecting 50 pounds of security payment on behalf of each child when they arrived in England in order to avoid spending their own citizens' tax money. But this was mostly covered by the American Jewish Fund. All these children entered England without passports. If their parents applied for passports in Germany, the procedure would have taken forever, and the German officials would change the boys' names to Abraham and the girls' names to Sarah. Some British foster parents wanted to adopt these children but they couldn't, because in British law it is prohibited to adopt a foreigner. Some children wanted to be naturalized, but again because of the immigration law, they couldn't before they turned 18. However, as a matter of fact, Britain temporarily changed the law in the end. There were some adoptions when the Jewish children's parents were dead, or by special agreement.

During the war, the British government put Jewish refugees into internment camps under the suspicion of being spies. Why did they do this?

It wasn't only Jewish refugees who were interned. By the summer of 1939 when war with Germany became inevitable, there were a lot of refugees besides Jews in this country: Poles, Czechos-lovakians, Austrians as well as Germans. They were either political refugees seeking asylum or intellectual exiles who opposed Hitler's Germany and fled their countries. When England entered the war with Germany, people in England were panicked and all these refugees over the age of 16 were interned. They had to face a tribunal which divided them into three categories: friendly aliens, doubtful aliens and enemy aliens. I thought it was unfair, in a way, because everybody was fighting against the Nazi regime. Among the three the best category was friendly alien, and they were released shortly afterwards. Most of them were middle-class Jews who came over with their families. The enemy aliens were German or Italian prisoners of war. The doubtful aliens were somewhere between these two. All of these aliens, anti-Nazi refugees and pro-Nazi POW's, were interned together in camps in the Isle of Man, Liverpool, and Huyton. Besides these foreign refugees, the British government interned some of their own people as well. There was a pro-German faction called the British Fascists and when war was declared, Sir Oswald Mosley, the leader, was interned as being a dangerous man.

Could you tell me about the early stages of the war when the Germans started bombing London?

At the beginning of the war, it was the time we called the "phony war" because we could still go to work and our life was fairly normal. But shortly after, the Germans began full-scale bombing of London. It was scary. My flat was in South London, and from the window I could see the German bomber planes fly in from the south and east along the Thames River. There was a bomb shelter in my block of flats which was lucky, so I used to run down quickly every time I saw planes in the sky or heard the sirens. It was the time of the Battle of Britain in 1940, after the fall of France. Britain was really fighting alone against Germany. Most people didn't have bomb shelters in their houses and were sleeping in the underground railways during the air raids. When sirens went on everybody started running down below with bundles of bedding.

Often the bombers came in the evening and attacked constantly until dawn. It shook the buildings terribly. As soon as bombers sheared off, people could get some sleep before they went to work. This went on day after day, night after night. The next morning there would be bomb craters in the streets and a big notice saying "Diversion"; all traffic had to detour. In such chaos, people helped each other. Bus drivers sometimes took people to the door of their home. British people were quite stoical. There were many casualties, of course, but on the whole, people were almost excited about it. It was a strange new experience, I would say.

During one of the worst air raids in London, my flat was bombed and I lost everything, and all of a sudden I became homeless. I never saw so much broken glass in the streets before. London was really devastated. I was still working in Bloomsbury House at that time. I became head of the Shipping Department which was engaged in trying to send the refugee children on to countries out of the war-zones. But by now the Atlantic crossing was too dangerous and there was nothing much to do at the office. So I decided to join the Women's Forces. I first volunteered in the navy, but I faced a problem that had never occurred to me before. I had a German surname, Holzaffel, that was questioned. My grandfather was a German and I happened to be a quarter German. I thought it was ridiculous

because I couldn't speak a single word of German. I felt, suddenly, like an alien. It tells how people were paranoid during the war, actually. The navy officer said it was necessary to investigate my background and it would take weeks. Since I lost my flat, I was sleeping in a bomb shelter every night and didn't want to wait. I gave up on the navy and joined the army instead.

As a woman, what kind of duty did you do in the army?

Women over 18 were conscripted and could either go into the army, navy, air force, nursing, land work or war factory work. When I volunteered for the army in 1940, I was 26, and I was made an officer because I was older than the others. Women weren't allowed to fire guns, but they could be put in non-combatant jobs in an ordinary infantry regiment. I was put in a searchlight battery. There were about 35 women there all doing things like cooking, cleaning, driving army vehicles, working as clerks and plotters. Plotters were the people who plot the planes on the big-gambling-like table which showed where the enemy fighters were, and then their officers decided where to send our fighters. There were perhaps 70 searchlight regiments in the whole of England, and only one of them was entirely manned by women. The only men we had were a radar and a motor-mechanic. I was at a house called Swakleys, on the northwest edge of London. This was a seventeenth-century house which had a platform and tall chimneys with little ladders that went up it.

So, when attackers came, I had to hastily get dressed in the Khaki uniform and trousers, get my binoculars and headphones, my tin hat, and rush up the ladder right up this chimney. At the top of the chimney, there was a little platform and then you saw the six lights all around you. Orders were given to the plotters over the telephone. You could also hear messages from the sector headquarters and it was almost always: "Raid approaching from the south and east, height 20,000 feet." Then, suddenly one night we got raids approaching from the same direction, the height was 4,000 feet. We suddenly realized these must be the pilotless motorized planes that the Germans were sending over and, in fact, we saw explosions near the battery. They were what we called "doodle bugs." Germans called them V-1 rockets, the most high-tech missile at that time. They were launched from a rocket launcher on the French coast carrying a big load of high explosives. They sounded "boom, boom" like a motorcycle, and then the engine would stop abruptly after flying about one hour, then hit the ground and cause a lot of damage. They came on fixed routes during the day or night, but we got wise to the fact they were not going to hit our site. The fighter planes used to fly out to shoot them down, and sometimes, they could be captured by spreading a huge net in the air suspended from barrage balloons. After a while we got used to it.

The German propaganda made a big deal that the British people were extremely terrified of these rocketry weapons, but in fact, we weren't as terrified as they expected because it was easy to work out what the trajectory was going to be. As I said, they could be exploded in the air by fighter-planes as they travelled steadily along on their fixed course. They aimed at Paddington Station a few times, but failed to hit the station each time. Then, a year later came the V-2 rockets, enormous bombs which the enemy shot into the stratosphere. They suddenly appeared in the sky and came straight down without any warning,

and landed on the ground and everything around you suddenly exploded.

In the winter of 1944 to 1945, Germans weren't sending ordinary planes over at all, and we didn't need searchlights anymore. So my group, the women's searchlight battery, was moved to Blackheath, southeast of London, an area where more V-2 rockets were landing. We were encamped on the grass of the heath and had a small searchlight on a lorry. Every time these V-2s landed, we had to get on the lorry, drive as fast as we could to the site where the damage was, and illuminate the place with the searchlight while bomb squads dug wounded people out.

Before and during the war, what was the British people's attitude toward Germans?
Before the war most British liberals in my circle thought that the Versailles Treaty was scandalous and unfair for Germans. We thought that the French had been terribly mean to the Germans and blamed them for all their difficulties. Many people were quite sympathetic to Germans really, as far as I know. In fact, in 1938 I was in Austria for the Easter Holiday. I remember many Austrian and German youths were out of work and the situation seemed hopeless. After the war began, since we had fought against Germans in the previous war, we thought Germans were our natural enemy, I suppose. However, I personally believed that the Germans and the Nazis were different. I recall for instance, that wherever Winston Churchill did a pep speech to get people's courage up, he always said the Nazi hordes; he never said we were fighting the Germans. So, we always thought that there was a terribly bad group of people in Germany rather than saying all Germans were terrible.

I think, in general, British people were anti-French rather than anti-German. Because we thought the French had let us down at Dunkirk because they were defeated so soon, and we had to carry on standing alone against Germany, you see. The Nazis were anti-Semitic — that was the main thing. There were also some anti-Semitic groups here, and they were probably sympathetic to the Jews being thrown out of Germany, but I would say there was certainly very strong anti-Nazi feeling in this country, but not much anti-Jewish feeling. Mind you, let me tell you something. I was in America in 1936. I saw a sign written on the gate of a golf club, "NO-JEWS PLEASE!" I was shocked, actually.

At the end of the war when the world learned of the Nazi atrocities, what did you think?
In April 1945 the war was about to end, and the British Army insisted that everybody in the army had to know what we had been fighting against, and showed us an army documentary of Bergen-Belsen concentration camp. There were over 10,000 unburied corpses piled up ten feet high and British soldiers pushing this mass of emaciated corpses into a pit with a bulldozer. We were terrified. That was the first time I learned about the gas chambers and the Holocaust. My first feeling was for the Jewish children of the *Kindertransport* where I used to work. By then, many of them were grown up and had joined the army. But some of those corpses could be their parents. I felt it would be awful for them. For years after the war, I know a high proportion of them have been treated in psychiatric hospitals. It was more dreadful than the human psyche can take. ❖

A story of young German heroes of Munich.

FRANZ J. MÜLLER

German anti-Nazi activist, participant in the "White Rose," student resistance group against Hitler. Director of the White Rose Foundation. Born in 1924 in Ulm, Germany. Lives in Germany.

(Photo: Mr. Müller by the White Rose Memorial at the entrance of the University of Munich.)

How do you recall your 12 years under the Hitler regime, Mr. Müller?

I was in high school when Hitler started taking over Austria, Czechoslovakia, Poland, and attacking Jews. To tell the truth, in the beginning, in the early mid-1920s, Hitler didn't seem important. I couldn't finish reading *Mein Kampf*; it was written in bad German. When you read *Der Stürmer,* the Nuremberg-based anti-Semitic newspaper published by Julius Streicher who was Hitler's fanatical anti-Jewish associate, the front pages were, for example, covered with graphic cartoons of Jewish men having sex with blond Aryan women, or they ran reports that said Jews are like rats and rats harm people, so they had to be persecuted, and so on. At my school there were both pro and anti-Nazis among the professors, lecturers and administrators, as well as among the students. The majority was "brown."

I understand that you were associated with the "White Rose." Could you tell me how it began and who was involved with it?

The White Rose resistance originally grew out of a circle of friends who were medical students at the University of Munich between 1942 and 1943. The members were Sophie and Hans Scholl, who were sister and brother, Christoph Probst, Alexander Schmorell and Willi Graf. This group of 5 — all in their early 20s and from a middle class background — were not revolutionaries. While all young Germans were obligated to join the Hitler Youth, they stayed away from the Nazi activities and learned more of Nazi ideology; these students got into conflicts with the members of the Hitler Youth. Instead, they became engaged in their own circle of friends. They gathered together with their professor, Kurt Huber, and they started writing anti-Hitler leaflets. The

first four written by Hans Scholl and Alexander Schmorell were sent out in June and July 1942, the last two in January and February 1943.

Since 1939, except for Sophie, all these youths had been drafted into the army and in 1941 and 1942 were sent to the eastern front. They heard of Nazi atrocities, their friends had seen the Warsaw Ghetto, and they returned home with the horrifying information of what the Nazi Germans were doing. When they were reunited in Munich, they held serious meetings and discussed ideas about how to resist Hitler and stop the war. They concluded that direct mail to individuals would be the best way to get their message out. Between June 1942 and February 1943, they secretly printed leaflets called "Leaflets from the White Rose" on their manual printer. They distributed them by mail inside and outside of Munich. Sophie and other members of the White Rose travelled to other major South German and Austrian cities to mail them out.

At that time I was 17, and I was drafted for National Labor Service, but I had an accident so I had to stay home in Ulm. Afterwards Hans Scholl needed someone for mailing work and contacted my friend Hans Hirzel. I agreed with him, so I decided to take the risk. I secretly got hundreds of envelopes and postal stamps. I got names and addresses from telephone directories, specifically names of professors, educators, restaurant owners and other people who deal with the public. Hans Hirzel and I posted these letters. It was an extremely dangerous task because there were Nazi and Gestapo security men all over, and buying stamps in the post office was monitored and I risked being reported as a suspicious person. But we managed it successfully. Over several months we mailed out about 900 mailers. But shortly afterwards, I was drafted and sent to France.

What were the contents of the texts? Could you read a short excerpt?

They printed a total of six leaflets and each one was about one or two pages. The first of the four leaflets reads "Leaflets from the White Rose." Here is an excerpt: "...It is certain that today every honest German is ashamed of his government. Who among us has any conception of the dimensions of shame that will befall us and our children when one day the veil has fallen from our eyes... Goethe speaks of the Germans as a tragic people, like the Jews and the Greeks, but today it would appear rather that they are a spineless, will-less herd of hangers-on, who now — the marrow sucked out of their bones, robbed of their center of stability — are waiting to be hounded to their destruction.... by means of gradual treacherous, systematic abuse, that system has put every man into a spiritual prison....every individual, conscious of his responsibility as a member of Christian and Western civilization, must defend himself as best he can at this late hour, he must work against the scourge of mankind, against fascism and any similar system of totalitarianism.

" ... It is impossible to engage in intellectual discourse with National Socialism because it is not an intellectually defensible program.... Now the end is at hand. Now it is our task to find one another again, to spread information from person to person, ... and to allow ourselves no rest until the last man is persuaded of the urgent need of his struggle against this system... since the conquest of Poland three hundred thousand Jews have been murdered in this country in the most bestial way. Here we see the most fright-ful crime against dignity, a crime that is unparalleled in the whole of history.... All Polish male offspring of the nobility between the ages of 15 and 20 were transported to concentration camps in Germany, and all girls of this age group were sent to Norway, into the bordellos of the SS men! ... Why do the German people behave so apathetic in all these abominable crimes? ... until the outbreak of the war, the larger part of the German people was blinded because the Nazis didn't show their true faces... but now we know them for what they are, and it must be the first and only duty, the holiest duty, of every German to destroy these beasts... We have no great number of choices as to these means. The only one available is "passive resistance" .... we must oppose National Socialism,.. we must soon bring this monster of a state to an end. A victory of fascist Germany in this war would bring immeasurable and fateful consequences... All Germans, all fellow citizens, we must protest. It is not too late!

"...the best way would be through passive resistance or SABOTAGE. Sabotage of armament plants and war industries; sabotage of Nazi gatherings, rallies, public ceremonies; sabotage in all areas of science, scholars and researchers who are processing warfare materials: universities, technical schools, laboratories, research institutes or bureaus; sabotage in the press, publications, newspapers; sabotage in all cultural institutions which could enhance fascism among people. Every word that comes from Hitler's mouth is a lie. When he says peace, he means war, and when he blasphemously uses the name of the Almighty, he means the power of evil, Satan. ...Please do try to convince all your acquaintances, especially those who are in the lower social classes. Please duplicate this leaflet and distribute to as many people as possible!"

When and how were the members of the White Rose arrested?

The following year, 1943, on the 2nd of February, it was in the "Battle of Stalingrad," that the German Army lost its military initiative to the Russians. It was the beginning of the end of the war on the Eastern front and the first crucial defeat of the German Army, and it was the turning point of WW II. The German people were perplexed. The members of the White Rose decided to take this chance and they launched a resistance campaign to take emergency action against the Nazi government. They urged the public for support. During the nights of mid-February 1943, Hans Scholl, Alexander Schmorell and Willi Graf went out on the streets and in the university compound, and they painted slogans, "Down with Hitler!" and "Freedom!"

In January and February 1943, they printed the fifth and sixth leaflets titled "A Call to All Germans!" And, this time, Sophie and Hans Scholl decided to distribute the copies of the leaflets inside the center hall of the campus. On the 18th of February, in the late morning hours, they entered the university and placed the leaflets in the atrium, classrooms, and hallways. Its contents were:

" ... The war is approaching its destined end.... Hitler is leading the German people into the abyss. Hitler cannot win the war, he can only prolong it! ... Retribution comes closer and closer!... Germans! Do you and your children want to suffer from this aftermath? ... Do you want to be judged by the same standards as your seducers (the Nazi gangsters)? Do you want Germans to be hated and rejected by all mankind all over the world? ... Make your decision before it becomes too late! ... A criminal regime cannot achieve a German victory... a terrible but just judgement will be meted out to those who stayed in hiding who were cowardly and hesitant. ... Freedom of speech, freedom of religion, the protection of individual citizens from the arbitrary will of criminal regimes of violence... Support the resistance, distribute the leaflets!

" ... In the Battle of Stalingrad, 330,000 German men have been senselessly and irresponsibly driven to death. The day of reckoning has come. ... Students! For us there is but one slogan: Fight against the (Nazi) Party! Get out of the Nazi organizations! ... Get out of the lecture rooms of the SS corporals and sergeants and party bootlickers! We want genuine learning and real freedom of opinion. ... Hitler has been destroying all intellectualism and all moral substance among the German people.. Up, up, up, my people, let's take action! — "

While they were dropping the last copies from a balcony onto the atrium ground, a janitor saw them. Shortly thereafter, they were arrested by the Gestapo. Then, all the university exits were blocked. All the students were instructed to assemble in the atrium, and every student who had taken a leaflet had to turn it over to a specially-designated collector. Sophie and Hans Scholl were immediately taken into custody for interrogation. The arrest of their friend Christoph Probst followed shortly afterward. He was the one who had written the text, and he was married and the father of three young children. The three were incarcerated in the Gestapo headquarters in Bavaria. Then, four days later, on Monday February 22, 1943, at 10:00 am, the trial against them was held in the Munich Palace of Justice. In reference to the leaflet activities, Sophie stated, "What we have said and what we have written is what so many German people believe today. Only they don't dare to speak out." In response, the President of the *Volksgerichtshof* (People's Tribunal), Roland Freisler, became hysterical and kept shouting, raging, screaming and indicted them for "treasonable aid to the enemy, preparation for high treason and demoralization of the German troops." He sentenced the three friends to death. During the trial, not a single objection was raised for the defendants. Then, they were taken to Munich Stadelheim Prison. Three-and-a-half hours after the trial, they were executed there by guillotine. "Freedom," was the last word Sophie left and Hans shouted the same standing before the guillotine.

How were you arrested?

At that time, I was doing my army duty in German-occupied France, so I knew nothing of this trial. On the 16th of March, 1943, I was suddenly arrested there. I was sent over to Munich, to the same Gestapo headquarters in Bavaria. I was interrogated for a week by a Gestapo man who had worked on Sofie Scholl. They had already arrested the other members of the White Rose group: Kurt Huber, Willi Graf, Alexander Schmorell, and there were another ten men and women friends arrested, including myself, who helped with the distribution to the other cities. On April 19th, the trial against us was opened. The same President of the *Volksgerichtshof* sentenced Kurt Huber, Willi Graf and Alexander Schmorell to death. I was lucky not to get the death sentence. I got a five year prison-term.

As a result, how many leaflets were sent out and what was the public reaction?

From the beginning to the end of the resistance movement, they had printed about 10,000 copies. In the summer of 1942, they printed only 100 copies of the first leaflet, which were mailed

in the Munich area. 35 of them were turned over to the Gestapo headquarters. There were a lot of Nazi supporters of course, so it was a quite normal reaction, I would say. The last issue, however, went through another resistance group and reached England. As a result, on the nights of July 3rd and 24th, 1943, the British planes dropped hundreds of thousands of copies over Germany. It was called, "A German leaflet: Manifesto of the Munich Students." England was trying to get Germans to stop fighting. Today, if you ask people who received the leaflets at that time, they say they were happy about the whole operation. It was a sign of courage, hope, and the dignity of mankind. On the other hand, many people say they thought it was silly and unsuccessful; they sacrificed and died for nothing.

Could you tell me about your foundation?

The White Rose Foundation was established in 1987 to commemorate these six courageous youths who fought and died for free Germany. Their movement was not successful in the end, however, we must remember their spirit forever. That is the purpose of our foundation. During this time of extraordinary crisis in German history, they took the most fatal risk. In retrospect, Munich was the birth place of the Nazi movement, the city where Hitler launched his Putsch. It was Hitler's city and a center of the Third Reich, after all. At that time this city was inundated by reactionaries, conservatives, radical right-wingers and ultra-nationalists. On the other hand, the University of Munich was an intellectual center in Bavaria, and during the 1920s, Heinrich Wieland and Richard Willstatter, both Nobel Prize-winners, taught there. The city is now known for the White Rose as well, and the memory of Sophie and Hans Scholl and the other members are extremely significant to Germans. Since we founded the office here, we have been supported by the city of Munich and officials, and by the Ministry of Culture and private donations. We organize exhibitions in Germany as well as internationally. We give political science lectures, panel discussions for school children, students, educators, public audiences, to educate them about the story of the White Rose and other German resistance movements, and about the people who fought against the Nazi gangsters. We have recently made a memorial site in the university campus. They are stone leaflet-papers on the pavements of the entrance where the leaflets were actually once scattered. ❖

"Whether or not they were Jews, my husband still would have helped them."

YUKIKO SUGIHARA

Japanese, widow of Sempo (Chiune) Sugihara, Japanese diplomat who saved 6,000 Jews, and author of the book *The Visas For 6,000 Lives*. Born in 1913 in Iwate-ken, Japan. Lives in Japan.

(Photo: Mrs. Sugihara stands by photos of her late husband Sempo Sugihara and herself at the the age of 28.)

During the prosecution of Jews in Europe, your husband, Sempo Sugihara, issued 6,000 visas for Jews. This was unknown to the public until recent years. Can you tell me how it came about, Mrs. Sugihara?

It was in the summer of 1940 while my husband, a Japanese consulate general, and I were posted in Vilna, the capital city of Lithuania. We lived in a quiet residential house overlooking the city. The consular office was on the ground floor of the building with our family residence on the second floor. My husband worked downstairs during office hours and came upstairs after work. At that time Lithuania was occupied by the Russian Army and the Russian government had just ordered that all foreign nationals and diplomats leave the country as quickly as possible. And, in fact, we were preparing to leave for Berlin. It was on the morning of July 27 that my husband and I saw a crowd of people at our gate. Many of them had dark hair and were not tall. My husband explained that they were Jewish people who escaped from the Nazis and had come to beg for visas to get out of Europe. In the beginning there were hundreds of people, but he said he expected thousands more to come.

Since Hitler held office in Germany, the Jewish situation in Europe had become graver year after year: the Nuremberg Law, *Kristallnacht,* the *Anschluss,* the Invasion of Poland, and many European nations were anti-Semitic, certainly all the Baltic states. Because of his diplomatic access to information, my husband was well-informed that the Nazis were persecuting a great number of Jews in Germany and in Poland, and he knew many of the Jews were desperate to leave Europe. Their hope was to get visas from foreign embassies but there was no country which was sympathetic to the Jews; many embassies turned them

away. Since Japan was allied with Germany since 1936, we knew very well in political terms what this meant: Japan couldn't issue the visas for them either. If one did, what sort of consequence might one face? My husband was of course aware of the consequences. At that time, he was 40 and I was 26, and we had three boys who were 5 and 3 years and 1 month old. Also, my sister was living with us as a housekeeper.

Within days, as my husband predicted, our building was fully surrounded by thousands of Jews, including many children. They stood by the fence for days and nights demanding visas from the consulate general. It was awkward for us to get in and out of our house: we couldn't go out to do shopping. For us, it was painful to ignore those desperate Jews. As we watched them through the window, my sister took a few snapshots of the crowd. My oldest son said to my husband; "*Kawaisoh!* (How pitiful!) Let's help them, Daddy, can you?"

Finally, my husband decided to talk to them. He selected five persons from the crowd for negotiations. According to their story, they had come all the way from Poland because they had heard that their only hope would be crossing Russia by the Siberian railway and entering Japan by transit-visa. Then they would go elsewhere. They wanted my husband to give them this special visa. Later, we learned the Dutch Consulate in Vilna had hinted that the Japanese Consulate might be helpful to them. As he listened to them, my husband realized that he had to be sure that they wouldn't stay in Japan but would just pass through Japan. He contacted the Dutch Consul, Nathan Goodwill, who had sympathy for the Jews. As the final destination, Mr. Goodwill agreed to use the Dutch colony of Curacau. It is a tiny Caribbean island on the northern coast of

Venezuela. He said the island had no customs, so anyone could debark there and walk in from the shore. The idea was great. But my husband couldn't decide on his own; he had to confirm his decision with the Japanese government.

My husband was fluent in Russian; he was like a native when he spoke it. He also spoke German, English and French. At the time, among the Japanese there weren't many linguists like him, and in many ways, his skill was extremely valuable during the war. To be honest, he was officially a diplomat, but he was working for an intelligence service in Vilna. In wartime Europe there were many people like him, particularly among foreign diplomats, journalists, professors, even among students. One of his duties was to listen to the top-secret government information that was being sent from both Russia and Germany, and inform the Japanese government by sending cables. Although Japan was on Germany's side, I believe our government wasn't fully confident in Hitler. Counter-intelligence is one of the most vital tasks for any nation, and Japan was no exception. And Vilna was a particularly excellent listening post.

Regarding the issuing of the transit-visas for Jewish refugees, he confidently sent a cable to the Foreign Office in Tokyo. The answer from Japan was "NO." But he didn't give up. Russia at the time was not fully anti-Semitic yet and he knew it would be possible for the Jews to travel through, and eventually make it to Curacau. He made a second proposal to Japan asking for 50 transition days. But again the response was the same: Japanese policy would not allow Jewish refugees to pass through Japan. There was not much time left, but he couldn't ignore the desperate people and leave the consulate. How could we do that? These thousands of people depended on

us for their lives. My husband was gravely concerned about them and he couldn't sleep for two nights. After his third proposal was rejected, finally, he made up his mind. He ignored the government order and decided to issue the visas for them. I clearly remember what he said to me: "I will take the risk. If I'm fired by the government and lose my diplomatic position, I will become a civilian. Since I'm good in Russian, I'm sure I will be able to find a new job, perhaps as a translator, and I will be able to support you and our children." I agreed with him and said "I understand. Let's help them."

Early in August he made an announcement to the crowd, "I will issue the visas for all of you." Everybody was happy and excited by his decision. In order to issue the transit-visa to Japan, what was required were the final destination, which was Curacau, the railway and boat tickets, money for travel expenses. He had to interview them one by one to confirm everything before issuing the actual visas. Then, he begun writing the visas. There was no Japanese typewriter, so it had to be done by hand and he had to do it all by himself; there was nobody in the office who could help him, except myself. But he was very cautious and never allowed me to help him. I was to keep away from his office. His words were, "As you know, I'm taking a deadly risk against my own state and Germany. If the Gestapo show up, I will take the entire responsibility. I do not want you to be involved in this matter. We have three under-aged children and if both of us are arrested, in the worst case, our children would become orphans. I don't want that to happen. If I am executed, you are to raise our children without me."

According to a historical document, Mr. Sugihara issued 2,000 visas, but he actually issued 6,000 visas. Can you explain the difference?

Each visa had to be written out by hand, and in the beginning he was copying every name of the refugees very carefully, double-checking the spelling, and then he had to register the visa numbers. It was a long process for one man alone. Since this particular consulate was set up primarily as a counter-intelligence service, there were not enough visa forms and we had to print our own. Stamping the documents was done by one of the Lithuanian clerks who worked in the office. At first, my husband estimated he could write 300 visas a day. Day after day, from early morning to late evening, he kept writing. And by the end of each day he was totally exhausted. I used to give him a massage after all this heavy work; that was the only thing I could do for him. Meanwhile, Lithuania officially became an annexed state of Russia and we were again ordered to leave the country immediately.

He realized that the process was not going fast enough and that thousands of refugees were patiently waiting their turn. There was a park across the street and they slept there during the night. At the same time, we got an order from the Japanese government to close down our consulate and to leave for Berlin immediately because the border would be shut. They warned us but my husband ignored the order. We were the only foreign diplomatic family left in the city. So he needed to speed up the process. Therefore, after visa number 2,000 he quit recording the numbers, and at the same time, he also quit collecting the small service charge. He thought it would be better if there were no official record. He had been doing it for a total of four weeks until the end of August. Finally, on September 1, while we

were ready to set off for Berlin, we were met by more Jews at the Vilna station and my husband issued more visas for them through the train window until the last moment when the train started moving. In the end, he issued approximately 6,000 visas.

Why did your husband save the Jews and what was the reaction of the Japanese government to what he did?

Whether or not they were Jews, my husband still would have helped them. What my husband did was for moral reasons and he never expected anything in return. Our case was totally different from the "Schindler's List" story because Mr. Schindler made a profit at the outset. Nazi conduct against the Jews was a crime against humanity and every foreign diplomat knew that Jews were murdered, but they ignored it. My husband took the matter seriously and he did something significant to save them. For him, money was absolutely out of the question. When we were in Berlin, two Japanese ambassadors, Saburo Kurusu and Hiroshi Oshima, who was renowned as being pro-Hitler, knew what my husband did, but they didn't comment. In any case, my husband and I always believed that saving human lives is not a crime. In fact, my husband wasn't the only Japanese man who saved doomed Jews. A man named Major Onodera, stationed in Sweden as a military diplomat in the same period, also saved a number of Jews, but in a different way. The Nazi activities were really terrible and from the beginning of the war, my husband told me that Germany and Japan would be defeated.

Besides this matter, what other things did you experience during the war?

In fact, I was almost killed many times. In the autumn of 1944, we were transferred to the Embassy in Bucharest, Romania. At the time, the country was occupied by the German Army and there were many German soldiers around. At the same time, the Russian Red Army entered Romania. Shortly afterward, the Allies began attacking the cities which were occupied by Germans, including Bucharest. The air raids continued day after day. Their target was the oil field which was the main energy supply for the Germans. For our family's safety, we moved to our summer house in Brasov, a two-hour drive from the capital.

Before Vilna we lived in Helsinki, and I had some very special mementos from that time that I didn't want to lose in the bombing. They were record albums of Sibelius, my favorite Finnish composer, who I met while I was living there. The records were autographed and given to me, so they were very precious. I had left them in our Bucharest residence and wanted to save them, so I decided to return to Bucharest. Our chauffeur drove the car for me. On the way, the car broke down. The area was fully surrounded by German soldiers, and I was offered a ride by one of the military vehicles passing by. The driver was a young German soldier. When we came closer to the capital, it was burning. The city was a battleground between Russian and German armies and we were told that the Germans had begun retreating, so no one could enter the city.

There were hundreds of German military vehicles and tanks, and thousands of soldiers retreating. The scene was a fantastic chaos like watching a movie. The only way to get out of there was to drive through a forest nearby, so we did. But it was already filled by Germans and we couldn't move forward or backward; we were trapped. Hours went by, but nothing could be done. I got out of the car and walked around the woods. Then, I came across a young lieutenant there. He said we were fully surrounded by Romanian partisans waiting to attack the Germans, so it was dangerous to move. When I explained my status, that I was the wife of a Japanese diplomat, he said it was safer for me to stay with him, and he offered me his automobile for shelter. In the evening he brought me a hot meal and a blanket. We talked for hours; he showed me courtesy and treated me respectfully. Every soldier knew he was lost and doomed, and no one was saying "Heil Hitler!" anymore. After being trapped there for two days, food was running out, so the young lieutenant ordered his men to go toward the German border. He came and told me that they didn't have enough ammunition to fight the partisans, and he warned me we might be shot. He told me to prepare myself. He showed a strong sense of responsibility for me; he was very polite and diplomatic. As we moved, a staggering number of partisans started shooting at us. Everybody had to get out of their vehicles and lie down on the ground, and so did I. The partisans were not as well trained in shooting as the Germans, but eventually the Germans were hit and died one by one in front of me. The young lieutenant covered me with his body to protect me from the bullets. Suddenly, I heard a powerful explosion and I lost consciousness. After the rain of bullets was finally over, it became quiet. When I awoke, the lieutenant was not on my back. He had been thrown to the ground nearby. When I got close to him, his body was already cold. He was dead. It was so sad that he died for me. Without him I would not be here today. He saved my life. He must have felt that it was his duty to protect me. That experience taught me something about the Germans. They have two extreme sides at the same time: they are totally cruel and absolutely loyal.

After that, the close calls didn't end. The next morning as the surviving soldiers walked toward Germany, I walked a country road toward my summer house. No one was around. I came across a cabin. I was so exhausted and I knocked on the door. Someone opened it with a gun pointed at me. I was dragged in and surrounded by several men with guns. They were Romanian partisans. At that moment I though I would be shot on the spot. They didn't believe that I was a Japanese. When they got close to me, I was really scared to death. Finally, I shouted at them "Shoot me! Kill me now!" in Japanese. They were surprised by my voice and withdrew their guns. Then, they brought a German-speaking interpreter. I told them my story, who I was and why I was lost in the forest. They understood me and smiled at me, and in the end I was released.

As to the whole scene, while my husband saved Jews, I was saved by a German. It's all a human tragedy. In the beginning, the German soldiers were very excited, all enthusiastic for Hitler marching up and down in their beautiful uniforms, but in the end, it was all too pathetic and miserable. ❖

"We are Americans, we fought to defend American democracy."

WALTER INOUYE and NEIL NAGAREDA

Japanese-Americans, 442nd RCT veterans who fought in Europe against the Germans. Inouye: born 1915 in Hawaii. Nagareda: born 1924 in Hawaii. Both retired and live in Hawaii, USA.

(Photo: Mr. Inouye, right, and Mr. Nagareda wearing T-shirts from the veterans' reunion of the 442nd Combat Regiment Team.)

When Japan attacked Pearl Harbor, what do you remember and how did things change for Japanese-Americans in Hawaii, Mr. Inouye?

Inouye: That Sunday morning when Pearl Harbor was attacked by the Japanese, I was living outside the harbor by the Honolulu airport. Because of the sounds of the airplanes and the shooting, I turned my eyes to the sky. There were warplanes streaking towards the harbor. Following their path, I saw black smoke bellowing up from the harbor. Some long torpedoes were quite visible under the low-flying planes making their final approach to attack American battle ships. Watching and wondering about all these activities, and seeing the rising sun emblems on their planes, at that moment, my mind refused to believe they were Japanese, and the fact that the Japanese did indeed attack the United States thereby destroying my belief in the moral code of the Japanese.

Being second generation of Japanese ancestry, a Nisei, I was not only shocked but disappointed that Japan had failed to maintain their honor. By the evening of that day, Japanese premises, particularly by the airport which was a sensitive area, were raided by FBI agents. The next day, President Roosevelt declared the day of the attack "the day of infamy." After that, all we Japanese-Americans were classified as "4-C enemyalien Jap" and forced to discard our cultural identity. In February 1942, Roosevelt issued Executive Order 9066, which meant the arrest of all AJAs (Americans of Japanese Ancestry), and many were sent to the mainland to relocation camps.

I was from a family of ten children and my parents were immigrants from Japan. Our house was searched. My mother had a portrait of Emperor Hirohito in our home. She hid it in the bottom of her sewing machine before the FBI

agents arrived in our house. They didn't see it and left. But a handful of Japanese-Americans were arrested, some were POWs actually, and were shipped to the mainland for internment. But in Hawaii, most of the Japanese-Americans didn't lose their jobs because they were the main work force and America needed laborers for the war industry. So they remained in the islands, and went on throughout the war. However, as the war developed in the Pacific, discrimination against Issei and Nisei was heightened.

Could you tell me about the Japanese-American volunteers, how they ended up fighting in the war against the Germans in Europe, Mr. Nagareda?

Nagareda: After the attack on Pearl Harbor, Issei and Nisei people in Hawaii didn't resist: there was no sabotage, no spying for Japan or anything against the US government. Three months after the attack, among the Nisei students at Hawaii University, a labor unit called Varsity Victory Volunteers (VVV) was formed. It was a group of 1,500 boys to offer military service to protect the islands of Hawaii as a part of their loyalty to America. The US Army Chief of Staff, General C. Marshall, ordered the establishment of a provisional all-AJAs battalion. In early 1943, this unit was activiated as an infantry combat team and shipped to Camp Shelby, Mississippi, for military training. The unit was named "100th Battalion," and it was the first Japanese-American Combat Team Battalion. In June they were shipped to North Africa and then moved to fight against the Germans in Italy. They were attached to the 34th Division there, the unit of Caucasian Americans from the Midwest known as "Red Bull."

As the war became more intense in Europe, many Nisei boys, both in Hawaii and on the mainland, volunteered for US Army service. In Hawaii, for example, though there was a quota of 1,500, over 10,000 men of Japanese ancestry applied. They were all willing to fight to defend America. Eventually the Hawaii quota was increased to 3,000, because the proportion of Japanese-Americans in the population was much higher than on the mainland. In the end, the total of Nisei boys who volunteered in the entire country was over 4,500, including some volunteers from various internment camps on the mainland.

I was 18 years old. It was a difficult decision for me because of Japanese family tradition; I was the oldest son in my family and I might never return home alive. But I was born and raised in America, so it was a natural thing for me to fight for America, even though being of Japanese ancestry, our freedom was deprived by our own country. But I strongly supported American democracy and believed what democracy stands for. I passed the physical examination. Our motto was "Go For Broke!"

While we were still in Camp Shelby, we knew our fighting destination would be Europe, not the Pacific. In June 1944, we, the 522nd FA Battalion debarked in Brindisi, Italy, and were reunited with the 100th Battalion which was already fighting there.

Inouye: I was first with the 522nd Field Artillery Battalion, and later joined the 442nd Regimental Combat Team. The whole combat team was formed by groups of infantry, engineers, medical people, a music band and artillery. I was in the artillery. Our campaign was to recapture territories which were occupied by the German Army and to liberate civilians, cities and villages by pushing the German army back to the north, and we had to cross the Rhine River to get to Germany. Between the periods of fighting, we were attached to the Texas Battalion. We Nisei battalion teams participated in eight major campaigns in Italy, France and Germany.

Nagareda: I would like to tell you a funny story. I worked as a command and reconnaissance truck driver. In Hawaii, we AJAs talk a pidgin language at home: we speak English, Hawaiian and Japanese all mixed together. When we made radio communications with other combat teams, we Hawaiians talked to each other in pidgin slang in a Japanese accent. For instance, we called the 100th Battalion "One puka puka" (puka means a hole in Hawaiian). So, if we said, "We are One puka puka," it meant "We are 100th Battalion." A funny part of this pidgin English was that, for the mainland AJA GIs, it was understood as "make puka in the hole." It was hilarious. Or, when one said, "You go stay go. We going stay come," which meant, "You go ahead, we will join you." This sort of message, of course, made it confusing for the enemy Germans who were monitoring our communications all the time. The Germans had no ida what we were saying to each other, you know. So in the end, it was a great advantage for us; our pidgin language worked out very well during the fighting in Europe.

The 100th/442nd Battalion was the most decorated combat unit in US military history during the war. Out of the many campaigns you were in, which was the toughest battle?
Inouye: We were in a few major battles. The so-called "Hill 140" campaign was one of them. It was the first major battle with Germans. In early July 1944 while we were marching toward northern Italy, near a seacoast town called Livorno, the Germans were heavily armed and fortifying the

top of a hill where they were able to look down on us. Our infantry men had to approach them from the bottom of the hill. That was very frustrating because they were in a vulnerable fighting position. The enemies were watching them and waiting for them to come close before firing at them. We could see the enemies during the day, but we had a problem at night. We couldn't see the Germans even though we knew they were there. We had to fire at them randomly without seeing them. The Germans were strong fighters, too. They were firing down at us constantly. This non-stop battle continued for several days and nights without anyone getting enough sleep. The infantries were all tired, exhausted and totally devastated. There were massive casualties. Finally, the lieutenant called in the 522nd Battalion, which I was with. We had sophisticated artillery to attack the enemies with air bursts. We were told to fire according to directions given by the forward observers. We fired as close as possible because our infantry men needed coverage from us. Normally, we didn't fire less than 100 yards away from our infantry, but we were on a hill and saw the Germans surrounding our men, so we had to protect them. In the end, we wiped out the Germans. It was a very messy end with hundreds of destroyed corpses all over. As a result of this bloody battle, many platoon colleagues of mine also died or were wounded.

Nagareda: The battle of the "Lost Battalion" was one of the most dramatic. It was in late October 1944 while we were in southeastern France during our Rhineland Campaign and after we had successfully liberated towns and villages, such as Bruyeres, Epinal and Biffontaine. The Texas Battalion — over 200 Texan boys teamed with the First Battalion, 141st Regiment and 36th Infantry Division — had been cut off from their own

troops for 7 days. They were trapped and encircled by the enemy Germans in the forests of Vosges, by the border of Germany and Switzerland. Their food and ammunition were running out, and they were unable to get out; they were considered to be doomed. Their Major General, by the name of John Dahlquist, was desperate. He assigned the Nisei combat teams to rescue his soldiers. The weather in Vosges was horrible. It was rainy, chilly, muddy, wet, foggy, and dark all the time. Being Hawaiian-born, it was miserable. But non of us "Japs" did complain, actually. We took the order. This mission was a particularly difficult battle, because if we fired straight at the Germans, the bullets might hit the Texan men behind them. The fighting was heavy; it took 4 days to rescue them. Over 300 of the 442nd soldiers were killed, and 2,000 of them were wounded.

I understand that the 100th/442nd soldiers were in southern Germany, in the area of Dachau and Munich. What did you see inside the Dachau Concentration camps, Mr. Inouye?
Inouye: We ordinary soldiers were not informed about the existence of the concentration camps or Jewish prisoners. So, we were totally unprepared to find what we did. It was in the last days of April 1945 while we were advancing toward the east that we came upon barracks encircled by barbed wire. In Dachau alone there were dozens of subcamps in the whole area. When we got there, the gates were already open, so quite a number of our men entered the camps. I couldn't tell exactly which one I went to. It could have been the main camp or the subcamps. I was there for approximately one hour looking for German soldiers. We didn't see any because they had already fled. But we saw people in striped suits,

emaciated, skin and bones with hollow cheeks and sunken eyes; they were almost like ghosts and barely recognizable. They were just roaming around the compound. I learned later that many of them were Jews. There was snow on the ground but they didn't have shoes — their feet were wrapped in burlap. The smell was awful; I could smell the stench of the dead that almost made me choke. I kept walking around the compound. I saw a building where, I also learned later, the Nazi commanders' wives were making lampshades from human skin as a hobby. There were piled-up corpses all over, and nearby I saw several ovens. Some of them were still hot. The ground was messy. The Nazi Germans must have hurried to destroy the evidence of their atrocities before fleeing. I saw some documents, notes, written records which were scattered on the ground including some photographs. I remember one particular photo. It was a scene with two men carrying a corpse in front of a burning oven. Then, I came across a warehouse. When I opened its door, I saw this time a mound of children's shoes. Then I realized what was going on there. But, why the children? At that particular moment I got tears in my eyes...

How were the wartime German civilians living? What was their reaction seeing a group of Asian men in Germany?

Nagareda: The German people who lived in villages and towns we saw were mostly farmers, and in fact, nobody was starving. They were living well. When they saw us, at first they reacted to our non-Caucasian appearance, but as soon as they saw our uniform, they understood we were Japanese-American soldiers and a part of the US Allies. We learned a few German words to communicate with them and we became friends.

Inouye: We used our helmets to carry candy or chocolates in exchange for their products: eggs, milk, chickens, etc. The people in all the places we went were either old people or young children; the young men were all out fighting. There were a lot of young women around, so, actually we had a good time with them. Some kids came to us and raised their arms saying, "Heil Hitler!" These kids were educated in the Nazi religion. But they all knew Germany was lost.

At the end of the war, what did you do? Despite having such a glorious military record, why did the AJA community keep silent about it for so many years?

Inouye: At the end of the war, many German soldiers, not the Waffen-SS, came to us. They wanted to surrender to Americans because they didn't want to be taken by communist Russians. But a peculiar thing was that they wanted to keep the guns in their hands. They told us the reason, "We'll help you to fight the Russians." When the fighting was over, there were many Russian soldiers in Germany, so the Germans believed the Americans would be fighting the communist Russians next. But, at that time, I was confused about how to understand this, politically. One of our occupational duties was to round up the displaced people and ship them back to their homeland. We also captured a number of the SS men. They bore tattoo marks of two lightning streaks on their upper left arms. They threw away their black uniforms as soon as the war was over, and when we captured them, they tried to hid the tattoos. So, we had to strip them to identify them as SS.

Nagareda: After we returned home we didn't want to talk about such horrible things, so we just kept quiet. Between the battles we also had a good time. So, we liked to remember only the nice memories such as the Champagne Campaign in Nice, or having a fun time with children and country girls, or about the wonderful people we met in many places. Because of Jewish interest in the Dachau camps in recent years, the Jews wanted to know our side of the story, so we began speaking out. And, some say we the 442nd didn't go there, which is absolutely not true. This sort of thing made us upset. That was the reason we raised our voice. Today, we can talk about it, but it's still painful. Although I am not of a career military family, my brother served in the Korean War, and my twin sons also served in the Vietnam War, all at the age of 18. For our grandchildren's sake, I sincerely wish we wouldn't have any more war. ❖

"If Hitler hadn't killed Jews, WW II would have been just another war."

WILLIAM HELLER

American; Allied bomber pilot. Retired pilot. Born in 1920 in New Jersey, USA. Lives in California, USA.

(Photo: Mr. Heller with photos of his air force team and the combat bomber.)

Mr. Heller, will you tell me why you think the world entered WW II?

I firmly believe that war happens when diplomatic negotiations fail and, frankly speaking, if the world politicians don't want war, diplomats shouldn't fail. In 1938, the Austrian Chancellor von Schuschnigg met Hitler, and British Prime Minister Neville Chamberlain made an agreement with Hitler, and the world believed there would be no fighting. Chamberlain, in fact, said, "There will be peace in our time." But at the same time Hitler entered Austria and Sudetenland, Czechoslovakia. I'd like to remind you that the United States and Japan were still negotiating in Washington when Pearl Harbor was attacked. So, what I want to say is, how much can we trust the diplomats and politicians? All the talk in Germany and all the talk in Washington couldn't stop the war. Every nation of the world knows their politicians and diplomats can't always be successful. I firmly believe that is why each nation maintains military forces. When we examine why the entire world went into flames, it was because of the Axis Power Agreement which was signed between Germany, Italy and Japan in 1936. The agreement was that if one of them went to war, the other two would follow. If one of them was attacked, the other two would join to protect him. When this was signed, America and every Allied nation should have realized that war was coming. I'm sure that was the reason Japan bombed Pearl Harbor. Otherwise, why did Italy declare war on America? We didn't attack them. And Germany declared war on America. This all happened immediately after Pearl Harbor, and in my view, it was all because these three were in agreement. That was how WW II started.

You were a bomber pilot during the war. Tell me how you became a combat pilot and about your combat missions over Germany.

Well, I had been interested in flying since I was six years old. At the age of 15 I did a solo flight, and at 17 I had my own airplane. In the late 1930s, I felt America might go into war, so I tried to join the US Air Force, but I didn't have enough engineering education. Instead, I went to Canada to join the Canadian Air Force. After that, I returned to the States at the outbreak of the Pacific War when Japan bombed Pearl Harbor. The US needed pilots, so my air career began. After years of training, because I spoke German, I volunteered to be stationed in England rather than flying over the Pacific. In early 1943, at the age of 22, I was assigned to a combat bomber B-17 and I had a crew of ten men. After I finished 20 combat missions to Germany, I became a squadron commander. In the beginning we only had to fly 25 missions, and if you survived, you were allowed to come home. But some stayed on for extra missions: it was called the "Five More Club."

Now, you must remember, every day, each time you flew out there in the sky of Germany, it meant you were facing death. Each mission was combat against the Luftwaffe, one of the greatest air forces in the world. Each morning you would have breakfast with a group of pilots, and the next day, half of them were either dead, missing in action, or prisoners of war. And this was every day of our life in combat. At that time, Germany occupied the entire European continent, and when we crossed the English Channel toward Germany, we were attacked by the Luftwaffe. We had to be high enough to be out of the German flak range.

In the early part of the war, I thought that Germany was better both in the air and on the ground. They certainly had more experience and were definitely superior. But they lacked endurance because they didn't have enough supplies and fuel. And, as the war went on, we produced more sophisticated fighter planes and better fighting methods and more highly-qualified pilots. And the Germans began to lose experienced pilots. They began to use younger and less experienced pilots. Then, it turned in our favor and we began to dominate as the super power in the air.

During that time, my younger brother also became a B-17 pilot and I wanted him to join my group. But joining the same bomb group was not so easy, because in the Pacific War near Okinawa, a US navy ship was sunk by Japanese, and on the ship there were five brothers and they all died. They were the Sullivan family. The loss of five boys in one family at once was very tragic for their parents. So, since that incident, President Roosevelt decided not to allow family members in the same unit or organization. But I really wanted to be with my own brother, so my case was arranged specially through intervention of Brigadier General Robert Travis, who was my wing commander. I soon became a colonel. At one time, I was my brother's commanding officer. We stayed together until the end of the war. Our father was a German and had emigrated to the US, so we had a number of German cousins in Germany whom we played with when we were children. Coincidentally, two of them became pilots as well. So, we were actually fighting against each other in the air. Psychologically, that was the most peculiar experience in my life. While the war was going on, members of the same family were killing each other. Can you imagine?

How many air raid missions did you fly and what was the most dangerous mission? Also, is it true that you bombed Dresden?

Between 1943 and 1945, I flew over German territory over one hundred times. I completed a total of 59 combat missions. Sometimes if you didn't find the target you had to come back. You would find an enemy sometimes, and we would fight in the sky. You didn't always get credit for such missions. Toward the end of the war, you would get credit for the mission as long as you went over enemy territory and returned, even if you didn't hit the target. Then, the number of combat missions for each pilot was increased from 25 to 35 because by then we had air superiority and the Luftwaffe had been weakened and our losses were less. I was on both bombings of Schweinfurt and the ball-bearing factory near Frankfurt am Main. These two were the most dangerous missions I experienced. To defend themselves, the Luftwaffe put up everything they had to fight. On the first mission, we sent 130 planes across to the target and we lost half of them. The second mission, we sent 225 bombers but we still lost 60 of them. But I believe these missions did turn the tide of the war.

Now, about the bombing of Dresden. Many people criticize us on that. But you must remember that before we did it, we asked Germany to surrender and said if not, we would bomb Dresden. But they didn't. Then, my crews dropped leaflets over Dresden telling the people that if they didn't stop the war, we were going to bomb the city. It obviously became controversial because it was not a military target. It was a civilian target, same as Hiroshima and Nagasaki. Well, in any war, if you notify the enemy and warn them: "Stop it, otherwise we are going to hit a certain city." Then it becomes a military target. On the 14th and 15th of February, 1945, we carried out the mission. Let me tell you another truth. I had some relatives living there, you know. But I had no compassion or sympathy for them during the bombing. War was war! My feeling was that we had to bring an end to this bloody war as soon as possible.

How did you get the secret military information about what was going on inside Germany, and how did you evaluate the accuracy of bombs you dropped?

We constantly had intelligence reports from the Office of Strategic Service, the OSS, who were our spies before the CIA. During the war, they had people on the continent sending reports back. During the missions, we dropped spies in parachutes and they would come back two months later with secret information. To evaluate the result of bombing, we had teams of bomb-evaluation survey experts. At the end of the war, they were sent to many German cities we bombed. I joined a tour to Munich with them to see the bomb damage. We knew what kind of bombs we used and what kind of formations they would make. There were many different types of bombs and we used them depending upon the military targets. The bombing strategy we used was very precise: armor-piercing bombs to go through heavy cement and armor; antipersonnel bombs to break into thousands of tiny pieces to destroy life; incendiary bombs to burn what you have already damaged; delay bombs to explode 12 or 24 hour later and blow up while people are clearing the damage and rescuing the wounded people. This was the nastiest one. As soon as we dropped them, we sent our bomb-evaluation survey team along with our spies on the ground, and also our aerial reconnaissance to take photo-graphs. So we knew the effects of the damage while we were still fighting.

Immediately after the war, I stayed in Germany and traveled all over. And I can tell you, the bombardment damage was much worse than we realized. There were some parts of Germany that were never damaged. But I can assure you and history will tell you, it was the great victory of American air power. Without it, the war might have been prolonged for many more years, and even German Luftwaffe officers agreed with us on that. They also told me of the extreme accuracy of the American bombardment. Some Americans today criticize us and I ask them, "Why did Germany and Japan quit the war then? If the bombing did no good, why did they surrender...?" I do realize that without the ground force, we couldn't occupy the territory, of course. But the ground force couldn't occupy the land if we didn't do the damage we did. History will prove that aerial bombardment played an extremely important part in the war.

How about avoiding historically important buildings?

Though we bombed factories which were producing or manufacturing war materials, we were always told not to bomb the IG Farben buildings in Frankfurt because we were going to use those buildings for our military offices when we won the war. This sounds very cocky to say, but I can assure you that the city of Frankfurt was entirely flattened, and yet the IG Farben building was standing with little damage. And, in fact, we did use it as occupation force offices. In the early stages of bombing, we were strictly told not to bomb the historically-important public buildings, but Dresden changed all that. As I said to you earlier, we asked the Nazi government to surrender, but they refused. Although everybody knew that Germany was going to be defeated soon, Hitler stubbornly kept resisting. Then, toward the end of the war, we Allies became impatient. The bombing of Dresden was really out of desperation to finish the war. For us it was the time to say, "Enough is enough! We're going to do it!"

In your case, you were fighting against your own people. Morally, it must have been a strange conflict. How do you look back on those crazy years?

Well, it was the same situation with the Nisei, the second-generation Japanese-Americans. They were born in the United States, but were fighting against their own people. I was a second-generation German fighting against my own people. But one thing was common to all of us: we were all American patriots fighting for America. When Hitler first entered the Rhineland in the mid-1930s, that was not allowed under the Versailles Treaty, but he kept on going, going, going, and it became clear that he was killing Jews on a massive scale. Until then, America hadn't done anything against him. Because of that crime alone, every American was angry at Hitler. I want to say that the Holocaust was something else: it was an unspeakable tragedy. Three days after the liberation of the Dachau death camp, I flew in to see the situation. Half of the prisoners died after we liberated them. It was the most shocking sight any human could ever see. Thousands of piled-up corpses, skeleton prisoners who were too weak to move. It was just a horrifying scene and who could forget it? You don't have to be a Jew to realize how bad it was. If the Germans hadn't killed Jews, WW II would have been just another war, I would say. No one on the earth in my generation could deny the Holocaust. If there are any, they must be liars.

Overall, how did you feel when the war ended, and what happened to your brother and your German cousins?

When the war ended, it was a strange feeling to find myself between the time of war and the time of peace. Wherever you were and whatever you were doing when the war finished, you stopped fighting. Because the war was over, there was no more enemy feeling. While we were fighting we never dreamed something like this would happen. When you fight with such tenacity against the Germans and against the Japanese, you don't think that these nations would be such firm, good friends afterward. Well, my question is why should people have a war? When WW I broke out, Americans thought it was not our war, but we went to finish it. When WW II broke out, we believed that was not our war either, but we also went to finish it. As I mentioned to you in the beginning, they were both failures by diplomats and politicians.

After the war, I worked as a captain pilot for Lufthansa Airlines. I worked with many of the German pilots who flew against me during the war. We are very close friends today. Many of them knew my cousins. How funny war could be! My brother stayed in the military and became a good career combat pilot. He was also promoted to a colonel and fought in the Korean War and the Vietnam War. But unfortunately he was killed in Vietnam. By the way, I had one more younger brother who also joined the army and became a colonel and fought in the Korean War. So, we brothers were three colonels who fought in three important wars in this century and we all served our country. Our mother was very proud of her three colonel sons. And, so was I. ❖

CHAPTER THREE

Lessons of Nazism

*Scholars and other people who studied
National Socialism, Hitlerism, the
Third Reich and the Holocaust*

(Conducted between 1991 and 1994)

"The people of Beethoven, Bach, Brahms turned into the people of Hitler, Himmler, and Hess."

LOUIS L. SNYDER

American, professor of German history at the City University of New York and the City College of New York, and author/editor of 75 books on the Third Reich, Hitler, and European Civilization. Born in 1907 in Annapolis, Maryland. Deceased in 1993.

(Photo: Prof. Snyder stands by the library in his home in Princeton, New Jersey, USA.)

You are one of the few American historians who lived in Germany in the period before Hitler. How did you see Germany at that time, Professor Snyder?

From 1928 to 1931, I studied at the University of Frankfurt-am-Main as an exchange student and Humboldt Foundation grantee. Through my historical studies and experience with the German people, I foresaw the rise of Hitlerism, Nazism and the persecution of Jews. After I returned to America at the age of 24, I wrote a book, *Hitlerism: The Iron Fist of Germany,* which was the first book on Hitler to be published in the United States. New York publishers and editors as well as the general public were very skeptical that Hitler would seize power. Even a Jewish leader in New York said to me, "Youth is often inclined to exaggerate. I'm closer to Jews in Berlin than you are. I assure you nothing will happen to Jews in Germany."

When one wants to know about the German people, politics and society, one must look at the history of Germany. In modern western civilization, the Age of Enlightenment had a strong influence: freedom, liberty, equality, tolerance, cosmopolitanism, fraternity and constitutionalism were important ideas passed on to citizens at the base of society. All those were developed in 18th century Europe, except Germany. Germany did not accept the western Enlightenment. What she took was a different direction; an illiberal national character developed. She adopted the state principle policy. The German state was more important than the German people. It became the way of life in Germany. You were forced to do what the state wanted you to do, not what you as an individual desired to do. Authority, uniformity and order; these became key words to describe German society.

Could you give me a brief history of Germany before Bismarck, and explain how Germany was formed and developed?

Geographically, Germany stands in the heartland of central Europe and has never known natural frontiers, whereas Britain can be identified as an island, Italy and Spain with a peninsula, and France with seacoast boundaries. But Germany has always had artificial and impermanent borders. German territories have alternately been expanded and diminished by wars, colonization, purchase, exchange, or royal marriages. From the Middle Ages until 1871 and into the present day, Germany has been an unfavorable geographical structure and is split apart instead of bound together. Lasting peculiarities of localism, regionalism and sectionalism have resulted from this geographical fragmentation.

Racially, there is no such thing as a "German race." In the veins of the German flows the blood of Ostrogoths, Visigoths, Vandals, Burgundians, additionally even the Mongol-Tatar Huns, Angles, Saxons, Jutes and Lombards. The "racial purity" of the German was complicated by intermarriage of his ancestors with Alamans, Franks, Swabians, Frisians and Slavs. Additionally, Jews also intermarried with Germans. All these lines helped produce a people that is ethnically one of the most mixed in Europe. The German people may be distinguished as a linguistic and cultural entity, certainly not as a "pure Aryan," Nordic, or Indo-European race. To make a comparison, Japan is an island country and has never been invaded or colonized by any other tribes or nations since the beginning of recorded history. Therefore, I would think that the Japanese are racially perhaps the least mixed people in the world today.

The history of Germany is distinguished by dualism in almost every aspect. There have been many bitter disagreements among the German people, political, religious, cultural, economic, and psychological. Historically, Germany has been devastated by conflicts from both within and outside its borders. Throughout the Middle Ages and well into modern times there were bloody feuds among the German aristocracy. The religious wars of the 16th century left a trail of slaughter and in the Thirty Years' War of the 17th century, Germany suffered great damage and a drastic loss of population. By the 18th century, the forceful overpowering of German territories came from Prussia which sought to impress itself upon German history.

Bismarck achieved the national unification of Germany in 1871, by means of a policy of "Iron and Blood." Germany's drive for "a place in the sun" in 1914 and again in 1939 were carried on in this tradition of violence. Still another fatal dualism in German history was religious conflict: Protestantism vs. Catholicism. Whereas most other European nations have one major religion, Germans are divided between Lutherans and Catholics.

In the development of modern Germany, how did German nationalism and militarism become the foundation for the country that was responsible for two world wars?

Germany was unified very late as a nation in 1871. Before that, in early 19th century Germany, originally there were 1789 different states. And, German nationalism in those days was culturally oriented. The *Communist Manifesto,* the Revolution of 1848 and a democratic and political reform, all failed in Germany. In 1862, Chancellor Bismarck made a statement: "Iron and Blood," which guided German policy. After waging three wars with neighboring countries; Denmark, Austria and France, Bismarck unified Germany into what was known as the Second Reich. Bismarck was a great politician in Germany and European history. His united Germany had democratic forms; however, its political and social formation did not follow western democracy. While England and France emerged as unified national states in early modern times, in Germany there persisted ambitious and endless pursuits of an idealistic world empire. The geographical location of the German state was such that when one looked east, there was Russian autocracy-authoritarianism, and when one looked west, there was democracy. But Germans never decided which one to take. They took neither. They went the German way; instead, they went with a state-first national policy.

Authoritarianism was established by Bismarck, then known as the "Imperial Iron Chancellor." By the end of the 19th century, Hegelian Dialectic was imposed on the German educational system; many generations of schoolmasters were grounded in the doctrine of Hegelianism. School children, university students and professors, academics and all others, were to be taught and educated that people must listen to the German state and follow its dictates. Later in his life, however, Bismarck said, "I should have educated my people in democracy, the way western world enlightenment stands." He regrettably admitted that he had misled Germans. After his death, Kaiser Wilhelm II took power. He restored militarism: he pursued policies of territorial expansion, colonialism and aggression.

The outstanding facts of German history are a polarity of development and a dichotomy of ideas and procedures that have never been resolved. The history of the Germans has been the story of struggle for a working compromise between uniformity and disruption. Uniformity was contrary to the ethnic, political and cultural divergences of the Germans. At no time in German history had either one central power been strong enough to crush the centrifugal tendencies of the component parts, with the exception of the short-lived Chancellor Adolf Hitler and his Third Reich. Here, I, specifically, would like to quote the words of a British historian, A.J.P. Taylor; from his work *The Course of German History*, written in 1946:

"The history of Germans is a history of extremes; it contains everything except moderation. In the course of a thousand years the Germans have experienced everything but normality. They have dominated Europe and been helpless victims of the domination of others; they have enjoyed liberties unparalleled in Europe and fallen victims to despotisms equally without parallel, produced the most transcendental philosophers, the most spiritual musicians, and the most ruthless and scrupulous politicians. "German" has meant at one moment a being so sentimental, so trusting, so pious, as to be too good for this world; and at another, a being so brutal, so unprincipled, so degraded as to be not fit to live. Both descriptions are true; both types of Germans have existed not only at the same epoch, but in the same person. Only the normal person, not particularly good, not particularly bad, healthy, sane, moderate — he has never set his stamp on German history.

Geographically the people of the center, the Germans have never found a middle way of life, neither in their thought nor least of all in their politics. One looks in vain in their history for a 'juste milieu,' for common sense - the two qualities which have distinguished France and

England. Nothing is normal in German history except violent oscillations."

How do you analyze those political and social consequences that affected individual Germans?

In the modern history of the German intellectual arena, Hegel has a great name as a philosopher, but in my view, he actually misled the German people. He implemented an ideology of the state principal which was the foundation of German nationalism. Authoritarianism and totalitarianism simply do not work. Democracy has many faults, but it has shown itself to be a better way of life.

There were some Germans who turned to Western ideology. Goethe was one of them. He understood that. From the viewpoint of German national character, there seems to be a striking difference between individual and mass reactions. The attitude was recognized by Goethe: "The Germans — so worthy as individuals, so miserable in the mass!." As individuals, the Germans are a wonderful people like your next door neighbor, but in mass, they are different. An American psycho-historian Lawrence K. Frank wrote this about the Germans. Here is an exerpt from his 1944 article in *Psychiatry Journal*, "Biology and Psychology of Interpersonal Relations":

"One of the major difficulties of Germany is the lack of coherence and emotionally acceptable history; the German people are dangerous, because they have no consistent traditions, but rather they reach into the past for whatever rule and sanction seems desirable or expedient at the moment. Obviously such a people alternate between Beethoven and Bismarck, between the extremes of high ethical and artistic endeavors and the worst cruelty and ruthlessness, depending upon the circumstances and the exigencies or opportunities they face."

When I was living in Germany at the time of the rise of Hitler's social revolution, I could see what would come next. An important point we must always remember was that Hitler came to power legally. What this means is that he had the power to conduct the "State First German Policy," which was originally founded by Bismarck. Hitler told his people what to do and the people were to obey their leader absolutely, because he had the authority. They knew he was a dictator but believed he was officially elected Chancellor. The Germans simply followed him. Their minds were completely poisoned. They never seemed to realize that they were making a terrible mistake. Then what happened was the people of Beethoven, Bach and Brahms turned into the people of Hitler, Himmler and Hess.

In contemporary history, Germans have had political crises, revolutions or wars about every 20 years, and peace never seems to last long. Why is that do you think?

In medieval times, Germany built the Holy Roman Empire, which was considered to be the "First Reich." Ever since, until 1945, Germans tried to re-create that empire again and again, and failed. It was a medieval concept and the world had changed. Although Germany never owned large colonies like Britain, France or Spain, she built up military power to dominate all other neighboring nations. To conquer the world in the 20th century was unrealistic. The world would not allow it to happen. At the end of WW I, after the abdication of Kaiser Wilhelm II, Germany was forced to accept the Treaty of Versailles. The Weimar Republic, a newly formed democratic government, was born. Germans went through the Great Depression but their economic recovery was a miracle. At that time, I was studying at a German university. I remember

what young German students were saying: no more militarism, no more nationalism, no more war, and they did not want to serve in the army anymore. Many Germans were not interested in buying volkswagens. Instead, they wanted to buy fashionable foreign cars.

Then Adolf Hitler, who was a WW I veteran and never believed Germany had been defeated, began to speak in public. He blamed Jews and liberals for losing the war, and insisted that Germany would win next time. He launched a new German nationalism and the idea of world domination. After he came to power, the situation rapidly changed. The transformation of Germany was incredible. First of all, within years, an extraordinarily successful industrial revolution took place: it ended unemployment. So, many Germans were impressed and thought Hitler was an ideal leader. Nazi followers and supporters increased dramatically. They hated the Versailles Treaty and did not want to pay reparations to France. They did not understand democratic agreement or democracy. Authoritarianism was so deeply rooted in the German people and society, it was simply impossible for them to reject it. They blindly believed Hitler and followed him. Britain, France and the United States were not ready to enter another war. When Hitler invaded Poland, the world was against him and Nazi Germany. In the early stages of the war when Germany was winning, Hitler praised his people for their successful battles. But in the great wars in our history, the early battles do not count. A beginning is not an end. Who won the last battle? That is ultimately the important thing.

How did you feel when the Berlin Wall came down?

It was a feeling similar to that when WW II finally ended: it was a relief all over the world. It was the end of the Cold War between the United States and the former Soviet Union. Two Germanys physically became one Germany. West Germany is a successful capitalistic state and able to pay billions of marks to take care of East Germany. It was very sudden, but a great change and a tranquil transformation. However, when the subject turns to German nationalism, one question still remains. It has been debated among historians whether national character exists; some say it does not, others say it does. My inclination is to believe that it does exist. But it can be changed according to the spirit of the times. National character can be a blessing or a curse. If it is militaristic, it turns out to be a curse. German nationalism has changed drastically since 1945. There is evidence it may be rising here, and there is also a rise in neo-Nazism, but I think it is minor. The Bonn government is controlling it. Germans today have learned much and also they feel frustrated by their past. German intellectuals have racked their brains to find an answer for their country's descent into Nazi barbarism. They obviously do not want to retain that old form of nationalism. The majority of Germans are trying to wipe out the mistakes of their past. Many still hate to talk about it openly. Above all, we must not forget the errors of German nationalism. It resulted in a catastrophe. Hitlerism was an irrational ideology based on Bismarck's "Iron and Blood State Worship." From London to Moscow, Finland to Greece, much of Europe lay in ruins. The death toll was the greatest human tragedy: nearly 60 million Europeans died. Moreover, there was the genocide of Jews; 6 million innocent Jewish children, men and women were systematically exterminated by Nazi Germans. The Auschwitz gas chambers are a national disgrace for the Germans.

German reunification was both criticized and praised worldwide. In your most recent book, *Contemporary Nationalism: Intensity and Persistence,* you have written that German nationalism has changed. Can you analyze this more specifically?

I would say that the vehemence of nationalism may change under historical circumstances. Germany and Japan, both ravaged by strong nationalistic fervor, were defeated in WW II and lost millions of their own men in the conflict. In the postwar years, both turned their aggressive behavior to peaceful economic pursuits. In the process, they moved into prosperity and set an example for other nation-states. West Germany, for example, became a leader in global economic power while communist East Germany sank to the level of the Soviet Union. However, both were careful to retain characteristics of national pride, which is the essence of nationalism. Nationalism played a vital tragic role in German history.

German nationalism was born in the darkness of Napoleonic despotism in the early 19th century. During the French Revolution, France invaded Germany, and this ignited German nationalism. Until then, Germany was a medieval mixture of peoples who were regarded as gifted and relatively peaceful concerned primarily with their cultural activities. Napoleon gave them a boost toward unity by wiping out most of the small principalities. Instead of being humiliated, Germans turned to their heroic past. They were attracted by the contemporary movement of romanticism and communal tradition such as folk songs, fairy tales, sagas, poetry, music, operas, art, and so on. According to Johann Gotfried von Herder, a German historian and philosopher of that time, the human race is a unit in which all nations could live in harmony for the cultivation of humanity. This view eventually led German intellectuals in 1848 to adopt unity on the basis of liberation. But they failed miserably. After the mid-century, Germany was then shaped by the policies of Bismarck. As I said before, he pushed his people into a dangerous milieu, synthesizing nationalism, state worship, autocracy and militarism. By the turn of the 20th century, the German people were led into the kind of national aggression which the world had to strike down.

To analyze German nationalism, another contrary aspect is symbolized by Hegel. While Herder had stressed a unity of all nations, Hegel developed his theory of the *Volksgeist* (national spirit), that the history and culture of a people can be traced to a common root. He opted for the obedience of the individual to the state and chose glorification of the state as the legal goal of the German people. He called for obedience to the state. His ideology formed an important element in German history — obedient, submissive, apolitical and militant. It was obvious that difficulties arose when those in control of the state provided the wrong kind of leadership: Kaiser Wilhelm II and Hitler. As obedient citizens, it was logical that Germans would follow those who held power. The great ambitions of Wilhelm II were followed by those of Hitler. The Germans followed their leaders into the abyss of two world wars and both times were defeated. They were trapped in a monstrous dictatorship by a barbarous Nazi regime, which was unique in the history of civilization. Since that painful experience, the Germans were clothed in misery, but slowly and surely began to recover from the evils of Nazism. Since 1945, the recovery of Germans marked another drastic change in national character; the aggressive attitude of the past was rejected. Within four decades, West Germans turned their talents to the pursuit of economic prosperity. Their political lust was put aside; to be succeeded by a policy of work, work and work. For the rest of the world, it seems their work ethic brought about an economic miracle. Indeed, it was a remarkable development in German history. There is little doubt that the Germans feel the burden of their past. There has been tremendous change since the era of Hitler when the German name was cursed throughout the world. After a long historical struggle for popular freedom, I believe the Germans are filled with a sense of shame and responsibility.

How do you see 20th century nationalism, which seemed a disappearing national force during the Cold War, and a unity of European nations?

For centuries, there has existed among peoples everywhere a consciousness of belonging together. In the late 18th century, this state of mind developed into a powerful ideology that has continually grown in importance, first engaging the attention of Europeans and then spreading to the rest of the world. Nationalism is beset by many inconsistencies, contradictions and paradoxes, and national character is a concept closely related to nationalism. I believe that nationalism in the 20th century has been an outspoken and realistic historical force. It is a global phenomenon and the accepted way of political life for nation-states scattered throughout the world. It is behind the popular flag-anthem syndrome in our time. Most do not see nationalism as disappearing, but as a most powerful and resilient force that just refused to go away. If anything, I think it would become more powerful at the end of the century than at its beginning.

Despite the persistence of nationalism throughout the continent, the post-Cold War European nations went ahead with their plans for the leap to unity. Led by Chancellor Helmut Kohl, who had pushed the drive for German reunification, the 12 leaders of the European community met at Maastricht in a special session of the European Parliament and approved treaties that would forge common economic, foreign and defense policies. The idea was to propel Europe into the 21st century as a cohesive power able to meet challenges from the United States and Japan. The most important economic decisions were to have a single currency, a single foreign policy and a single code of laws by the year 1999. Kohl insisted that the German experience with the evils of nationalism in the 20th century caused Germans to support a vital restructuring of Europe. "The way to European unity," he said, "is irreversible."

At Maastricht the British complained that European union would include numerous contentious political questions. They insisted that only the British Parliament could make a decision to abandon the once mighty British pound. British Prime Minister John Major accepted the plan with strict reservations about British sovereignty. Whether the pact toward European unity will be successful by the end of the century remains to be seen. It will have to overcome the powerful consciousness of nationalism still existing in Europe. ❖

A psychological study of Hitler and the origins of Nazism.

DR. NICHOLAS GOODRICK-CLARKE

British, historian in German studies at Oxford University, Hitler scholar and author of *The Occult Roots of Nazism* and other books on German philosophy and culture. Born in 1953 in Lincoln, England. Lives in England.

Dr. Goodrick-Clarke, you have extensively researched the mind of Adolf Hitler and studied his psychological analysis. To begin with, I would like to examine Hitler's upbringing. He was the fourth child and only surviving son of a young mother and an older father who had been married twice before. As I understand it, infant death was common in those days, and while his elder brothers died, Hitler survived. So, Hitler was a special child for his mother, and she perhaps spoiled him, and he had an unhappy relationship with his father. Can you talk about this?

That's true. Klara Polzl, Hitler's mother, had lost three children before Hitler was born. There is no doubt that she made a great fuss of him because this infant was the first of her children to survive, so that Hitler was a very special child for her. She indulged him fiercely and allowed him to do whatever he wanted rather than encouraging him to concentrate on a vocational career as his father Alois, an Austrian civil servant, obviously expected of him. For this reason, there were many disputes and arguments between the young Hitler and his father. His father worried that his son wouldn't have a firm grasp on a career and would not be able to consolidate their family in the ranks of the middle class as opposed to his own background in the rural peasantry. His father was very strict and violent, and had high expectations of his son's achievement as a decent and respectable citizen like himself. His mother provided a softer side saying, "It doesn't matter that your father spanked you. You're a wonderful boy, you can become whatever you want!" In *Mein Kampf,* there is evidence that Hitler may have witnessed fighting and domestic violence between his parents.

I think Hitler aspired to get something more glamorous and more metropolitan than the type of regular provincial job held by his father. After his father died, there was no doubt that his mother had neither the means nor the desire to discipline him. She was quite willing to indulge his dreams and fantasies of becoming an artist. I often think of Hitler when he made the journey from Linz to Vienna to submit his artwork and to interview for the Art Academy. He was really determined to make it much the same way as young people today are inspired to make an exciting career in the arts. These aspirations can be clearly seen in his friendship with August Kubizek.

Can you tell me about August Kubizek?

He was Hitler's friend during their youth in Linz, and they later shared a room together in Vienna when Hitler was struggling to enter the Art Academy. He wrote a memoir of his friendship with Hitler, *Adolf Hitler, My Young Friend,* which was published in 1953. This book contains very valuable insight into Hitler's behavior as an adolescent. Kubizek was musically talented and studied music in Vienna. He described Hitler as having rather grandiose ambitions often inspired by images of heroism and epic achievement. Kubizek writes of Hitler's excitement at opera performances, particularly of Wagner's *Rienzi* — a story about a medieval Roman patriot who was a great orator and a political reformer. This figure represented a popular demagogue with the charismatic power of leadership. Hitler was deeply moved by this performance and claimed that he would one day become the "Rienzi" of the German people. Kubizek was a passive partner and good listener in this relationship. He writes in his memoir that as a teenager, Hitler was very much the awkward adolescent with dreams and fantasies of greatness out of all proportion to his actual circumstances.

I think this is again something that ties in with the point I made earlier about his mother saying, "You're a wonderful boy. You can do anything you like." This sort of infantile ego can lead to inflated expectations on the child's part that he could indeed achieve anything. That is why Hitler, very much a self-educated man, was all too ready to latch onto images of exalted leadership, inspired superiority and dominance. Hitler possessed intense imaginative ability and would have had no difficulty in imagining himself as the Wagnerian hero. In my view, the "Rienzi" figure is more important than *Parsifal*. It provided a kind of a blueprint for Hitler's career, I would say.

The relationship between Kubizek and Hitler during their years together in Vienna is also highly revealing. Hitler was somewhat envious of his roommate who was doing very well at the Music Academy, while he couldn't get into the Art Academy. After failing his entrance test, Hitler kept busy pretending to be an art student painting in their small shared room.

However, this idyll couldn't last indefinitely. After Hitler's mother died, in the summer of 1908 while Kubizek was away on vacation, Hitler just disappeared without any message or communication. Apparently, he went underground to sleep in hostels and shelters for the homeless. Kubizek lost all contact with him, which saddened him because they had been friends for years and writing to each other. They didn't meet again until 30 years later when Hitler took over Austria in 1938 in the *Anschluss*. Kubizek's memoir is absolutely crucial for our understanding of Hitler's teenage and student years.

Hitler is an unusual name. From where and how did it originate? Also, according to Walter C. Langer, the author of *The Mind of Adolf Hitler*, his grandmother was a servant for the Rothschild family, the Jewish banking empire in Vienna. After she became pregnant, she was kicked out due to suspicion that the baby's father could be Baron Rothschild. If this is true, Hitler was one-quarter Jewish. What does your research indicate?

Schicklgruber, the family name of his father, was the maiden name of his paternal grandmother. The reason for that is that his paternal grandmother was not married when his father was born. He was an illegitimate child named Alois Schicklgruber, bearing the name of his unmarried mother, which is not necessarily a Jewish name. He got the name "Hitler" when his mother later married a man named Johann Georg Hieldler and took his name. Her brother-in-law, Johann Nepomuk Hiedler, who became Alois' foster father, instigated Alois Schicklgruber's change of name to his own with a variant spelling, Hitler. The name Hitler is of Czech origin. There were many different spellings from Huettler to Hiedler during the early modern period in this province. I don't know about a Rothschild connection. But it has been alleged that Hitler's natural grandfather was a Jew called Frankenberger, in whose family Alois Schicklgruber's mother was employed as a cook.

In analyzing Hitler's mind, how do you think his childhood experiences influenced his developing personality and his character?

I think Hitler was born a natural leader. He had an extraordinary talent for leadership and always expected to be in charge of everybody else. As a child, he expected to be the ringleader saying, "You go over there, do this, do it this way," and so on. Whatever he did, he had the natural energy of a commander who expects to be in a dominant position. This is all the more remarkable because, physically, Hitler was not a big or strong boy. When we look at him in photos with his classmates, he was of a below-average size. To exert that kind of command, I think this implies someone who is more shrill, more vociferous, more bullying and aggressive, one who can raise his voice. For example, small dogs can often intimidate big dogs by being more aggressive and hysterical.

After Hitler left Kubizek in 1908, what was he doing in Vienna until he moved to Munich in 1913? What did he read during this period, for instance?

There is a lot of speculation concerning what Hitler read. Some historians have suggested that he read works by Houston Stewart Chamberlain, Paul de Lagarde, Friedrich Nietzsche and Arthur Schopenhauer, writers and philosophers of the late 19th century. However, I think that Hitler probably never read those writers. Rather, he spent a lot of his time reading magazines or newspapers. It's said that he may well have read literature by two Austrian occultists, namely Guido von List and Jorg Lanz von Liebenfels, both from Vienna. Lanz's *Ostara* magazine is a very important document in this context. It illustrates the development of an extreme dualist racism. According to Lanz, the whole world is really a battle-ground separated into a dark race and a white race. The white race is endangered and must triumph over the dark race. This sort of dualism, graphically illustrated, was found in *Ostara* magazines which were published in Vienna at that time and sold in street corner kiosks. These were very similar to today's science fiction comics.

(*Ostara* means the Easter Goddess in the Germanic pantheon). The literature of anti-Semitism, illiberalism, racism, anthropology were all discussed in *Ostara*.

At the turn of the century, there was the modern German occult revival movement, which evoked the Pan-German movement and *völkisch* nationalism in Germany and Austria. These movements were a breeding ground for paganism, German mythology, anti-internationalism and anti-Semitism. In addition to being anti-Christian, these discriminatory movements later became the essence and foundation of National Socialism.

What other ideologies contributed to National Socialism?

There is evidence of two contemporary political movements at that time in Vienna that impinged on Hitler's consciousness. One movement was led by Karl Lueger, the anti-Semitic mayor of Vienna, and the other movement was led by Georg von Schoenerer, the founder of the Pan-German movement in Austria calling for the unification of Austria and Germany. In 1871, when the new German Reich was united by Bismarck, Austria was excluded. Von Schoenerer wanted to unify the German-speaking people in the Austro-Hungarian empire with the new German Reich.

Another movement that touched Hitler was the Social Democratic movement which was essentially Marxist, engaged with raising the consciousness of the working-class people, proletarians, industrial workers and farmers united through marches and demonstrations. There is a passage in *Mein Kampf* about these. I think Hitler realized that the Social Democrats understood how to mobilize the masses. Von Schoenerer understood the ideology of nationalism, Germanism and exclusionism, and Karl Lueger understood how to galvanize people with a simple message of exclusionary groups. Hitler was very much influenced by these men in his early days in Vienna. What we really see is that Hitler's idea of nationalism was a very potent idea in unifying many people of a common ethnic origin. The Social Democrats strove for solidarity among the working-class movement and were successful. Here we see the origins of the conjunction of nationalism on the one hand as an appeal to the ethnic identity of all Germans in Central Europe, regardless of which side of the frontier they lived on and of socialism, or at least the notion of the solidarity of the people, on the other hand.

The Nazi movement thus unified socialism and nationalism. The separate ingredients of these two movements were very apparent in the 1920s when the Nazi Party struggled to achieve power in Germany.

Would you say that Nazism rose from a combination of the defeat in WW I and the strategic timing of those socialist movements?

Yes, there is no doubt that the Nazi movement was a result of postwar chaos and intense demoralization of the German people following defeat in WW I. They lost military force, national self-esteem, industrial output, money, and territories; so much was forfeited under the terms of the Versailles Treaty. It's fair to say that Hitler only came of age as a politician as the direct result of postwar shock. Without World War I, there would be no Hitler. But I would also say that Hitler's personality, already formed through his youth experiences, contributed to his eventual influence. As a war veteran himself, Hitler obviously felt something should be done. First, he was an artist at heart; his political ideas of national regeneration and reconstruction were inspired by

an artistic design. He was almost painting on a huge canvas called humanity. So, much of his behavior was Bohemian and he had a lack of regular hours, and his conduct of war was sporadic. All of this indicates that he did not have a trained mind. It suggests far more the behavior of someone who is an artist or an enthusiast. I think that his youthful ambition was the clue to the rest of his life. We should also recall his sudden desire to do something very important when he was recovering from his gas blindness in 1918. Hearing the news of German surrender while lying blind on his hospital bed struck him down, and at the same time, gave him a new mission. He became really determined to right what he saw as a terrible wrong for the German people as the vanquished of WW I.

Why did Hitler instigate his movement in Germany rather than on his own soil, in Austria?

Well, this goes back to his youth experience. When he was a schoolboy in Linz, his favorite class was German history going back to the era of Charlemagne detailing the unification of the German empire in 800 AD. Dr. Leopold Potsch, his history professor and a Pan-German nationalist, made a strong impression on him. Before his time in Vienna, Hitler had never been with non-German people. As a result of the late 19th century commercial development, Vienna, the capital city of the Austro-Hungarian empire, was a metropolitan magnet. This empire was a multiracial conglomerate. There were at least 12 nationalities in the empire. Besides Austrians and Hungarians, there were also Poles, Ukrainians, Czechs, Galicians, Slovaks, Slovenes, Croats, and more. Constitutionally, this was the only way the emperor could govern the empire. At the same time the immigrant population of the capital had grown dramatically, and Vienna was a center for colored people, hosting a melange of darker people from Eastern Europe and the Mediterranean area, as well as many Jews. The city was like London during the 1960s or New York today. This was Hitler's first experience living in a strange city with more diverse nationalities than there were Germanic people. He looked at Vienna as some form of racial infamy of multi-racial chaos.

If you recall the map of Europe at that time, Austria was a vast area with a population of some 28 million of which only a third were ethnically German. In this respect, Hitler really felt there was nothing specifically German about his own country. There was also a large Jewish population in Vienna and he saw Jews all over the city. They were typically peddlers, poor, and uneducated Jews who came from poor rural areas of Poland or Galicia. They were very conspicuous because they wore traditional Eastern European attire and many had long side beards. There is a passage in *Mein Kampf* in which he alludes to the physical appearance of Jews in Vienna and said, "I began to hate Jews."

On the other hand, the German empire established by Bismarck just across the river border of his hometown Braunau, possessed national purity and unity. In the spring of 1913, Hitler moved from Vienna to Munich. In *Mein Kampf,* he wrote tremendously euphoric descriptions of how he felt upon arriving in Munich: "Munich is a truly German city, I am surrounded by Germans and only Germans, purely Germans." There is no doubt that Hitler loved Germany as a country where Germans were only amongst themselves. The rather extreme experience that he brought to nationalism and racism is typically a function of someone who had been on the margin, and it's often the case that extreme national-ist leaders come from marginal areas. Extreme nationalism is forged in the crucible of national experience on the border of a country, and Austria was on the eastern border of German settlement in Central Europe.

Hitler was born and raised Austrian and grew up under the Austrian national flag singing the Austrian national anthem. He was already 24 years old when he moved to Germany, a mature adult. Mentally and emotionally, how did he transform himself into a good German? First of all, he was deeply disappointed with his motherland Austria, because of his sense that it was a state of confused multi-nationalism and multi-races. He saw Germans in Germany as a true community and, emotionally, felt they were a worthwhile Germanic nation. If Austria wasn't going to unify with Germany, the next logical step for him was simply to go to Germany. It's remarkable that Hitler ultimately achieved the *Anschluss,* the union of Austria and Germany, prophesied by the Pan-German movement of his youth some 30 years before. This could only really be achieved because of his strength in Germany. Until Austria had lost all of its non-German provinces and many nationalities after WW I, it wasn't really absorbable.

In this respect, Hitler was very characteristic; he was the true German nationalist seeking a solution to the German nationality question, which was a controversial issue ever since the separation of Austria from Germany in 1866. The roots of the problem began then. Before then, all Germans lived in something known as 'Germany,' yet in fact this was merely a confederation of small states. While Germany emerged to become a nation state, Austria had not yet achieved this status; it was still an imperial state of some 12 nationalities. The years between 1866 and 1938 really represent a period in which Austria was outside the German community. In addition, the Austrian Pan-German movement was very strong in Austria between the 1880s and 1918. After the end of World War I in 1918, the German-Austrians very much wanted to be part of Germany; whether the Germans wanted them to join was less certain. In any event, this was prohibited under the Versailles Treaty. The Allies were naturally concerned that it might represent a further concentration of German identity and power. Therefore, the *Anschluss* in 1938 was another challenge to the postwar Versailles international order.

How German nationalism led to Nazism is quite complicated. Considering the situation from a different angle, if Nazism had started in England, France or Italy, for example, do you think the movement would have progressed as it did in Germany?

No, I don't think so. The essential issue is the ethnic complication of a constitutional state in Central Europe. Countries such as England, Italy, Greece and Spain are either an island or a peninsula. In comparison to Germany, they have very different geographical experiences. As a result, they have different histories of ethnic interpenetration. You find a remarkable evenness and temperateness in the national character of Britain, for example, and the early establishment of Christianity is different from the survival of paganism in Central Europe. The early Germanic settlers of the British Isles in the 5th and 6th centuries had forgotten their paganism after a few generations, whereas during the 9th century in Germany, Charlemagne was killing Saxons in order to root out paganism.

Over the centuries, Western European nations successfully formed ethnically homogeneous nation states and colonized their national territories. But as soon as you enter Central Europe, you find the Germans fragmented toward the East and then interspersed with very small ethnic nations with populations of 3 to 8 million people, the Slovenes, the Czechs, the Poles, the Hungarians, the Baltic peoples, the Lithuanians, the Latvians, the Estonians, etc. This is why Germans have such a peculiar experience of being not only the people of the middle, but also the people at the border; on a colored map of ethnic settlement one sees a kind of bleeding hemorrhage of mixed races and nationalities extending into Eastern Europe.

Nazi ideology was based on the constant mobilization of hostility and enmity towards outside groups, and it was psychologically possible to identify Germanness with exclusive ideologies such as anti-Semitism, anti-Bolshevism, anti-Masonry, anti-Liberalism, and anti-Slavism. I believe it was only possible to suspend the pluralism of modern society by mobilizing this sort of energy in a people for an idea like "being German in a German nation." As a result, through a tremendous exploitation of mass media and mobilization of people into a single homogenous unit, the Nazis were trying to create something unique — to suspend the secular and mundane experience of German life. This massification of German society was first achieved under the Nazi regime. Consider the Nuremberg rallies — it was a massive display of popular theater where everyone could participate. The only way the Nazi Party could keep people in this state of excitement was by constant regimentation and focus on national identity, and a reinforcement of what they were not; they were not Bolsheviks, they were not Slavs, and they were not Jews.

But the point was, how long could Nazism have survived before it would have exploded into a form of self-hatred? There is a limit to the number of subjects you can call up for people to hate. So much of the energy of Nazism started off as very committed, positive, exuberant, and radiantly optimistic. Hitler was the symbol of the national recovery and reconstruction of Germany, committed to putting the country back on its feet by providing public works such as the construction of new motorways, dams, bridges, buildings, engineering and new industries. Everyone had a job and place to live, the economy was booming, improving every day, and tomorrow is going to be better.

So, Nazism was rather extraordinary because it gave people dreams of themselves as Germans and created a mass productive and mass consumer society similar to what President Franklin D. Roosevelt was doing in America. During the 12 years of his regime — about as

long as Mrs. Thatcher was British prime minister or the Reagan-Bush Republican presidency in America — Hitler in fact did achieve many things. But by the end of the 1930s, the dynamic of optimism reversed to arrogance and hatred.

Following the collapse of the Soviet Union, how do you see the new national disorder in the eastern ethnic states?

Given the present circumstances that surround the breakdown of party rule in Eastern Europe, we are definitely seeing again a resurgence of nationalism. The question of inter-ethnic hostility is causing great concern amongst Western observers. As I explained earlier, it's precisely the different experience of ethnic penetration, complication and confusion which may lead to a resurgence of political instability in those areas. This instability was always a problem for Germans on their eastern borders. Hitler was able to exploit this instability of ethnic identity in much the same way as Serbian warlords are doing in Yugoslavia today. ❖

"Germans should be honest with their past."

WILLIAM L. SHIRER

American, journalist, wartime correspondent and author of the book *The Rise and Fall of the Third Reich, Berlin Diary* and others, CBS radio reporter. Born in 1904 in Chicago, Illinois. Deceased in December 1993.

(Photo: Mr. Shirer in one of the last days of his life at home in his study room, Lenox, Massachusetts, USA.)

Mr. Shirer, you were in Germany before the beginning of WW II and witnessed the Third Reich from beginning to end. When Hitler came to power, how did you see the reaction of the German people?

As a journalist, I was in the right place at the right time. Truth was that many Germans jubilantly voted for the Nazi Party in a free election. Socialists, Communists and Liberals were against it all the way, but as the years passed, Hitler became increasingly popular among Germans. Most Germans don't like to admit it today, but I remember a Nazi Party rally in Nuremberg in 1934, the year after Hitler became Chancellor. In the auditorium which was decorated with thousands of swastika flags, there was a crowd of a half million people shouting, yelling, and 500,000 hands were raised in salute: "We want one leader! Nothing for us! Everything for Germany! Heil Hitler!" An immense orchestra played Beethoven's *Egmont Overture;* it was a ritual. Then, they broke into a perfect goose step. There were torchlight processions in the evenings with music to dramatize the events. It went on for seven days and nights. Those pageants made German people feel good about Hitler and impressed them especially during a time the country was in bad shape. I was amazed how enthusiastic they were for Hitler. One night during these events, I was in a crowd of ten thousand hysterical people in front of Hitler's hotel, and when he appeared on the balcony, they shouted. I was a little shocked at their faces, especially those of the women. They reminded me of the crazed expressions I once saw back in the state of Louisiana on the faces of some "Holy Rollers" who were about to hit the trail. Their faces were transformed as if they were about to see a "Messiah." Some of them almost swooned from excitement.

The fact was that, in the beginning, the majority of Germans didn't like Hitler. They thought he wouldn't become a leader of Germany. But after he became Chancellor, within years, he received a larger following and the Nazi Party rose to be the biggest party in Germany. The reason for his popularity, in my mind, was that he had given Germans what they wanted: prosperity, no unemployment, and the power of militarism. Germans at that time were very militaristic people. He gave Germans a large army which defied their neighboring nations, France, Britain and Russia. *Deutschland, über Alles* made his people very pleased.

Hitler was an Austrian. Austria and Germany share the same language and same culture, but the two states were, and still are, independent. How did he become a leader of Germany? For us, it is like a Canadian becoming a president of the United States? Can you tell me about Hitler's life, how he did seize power in Germany?

The story of the life of Adolf Hitler fascinates and repels. He rose literally from the gutter to become the greatest conqueror of the 20th century. Hitler was born on April 20th, 1889 in Braunau am Inn, across the border from Bavarian Germany. At the time of Hitler's birth, Austria was a part of the Austro-Hungarian empire which was ruled by the House of Hapsburg, the oldest royal family and one of the important empires in Europe. After WW I and the end of the Austro-Hungarian empire, since Austrians had Germanic roots and spoke the same language as Germans, they — like Hitler — thought of themselves as German. This must be kept in mind in tracing the career of the future German dictator. Though born an Austrian, he considered himself to be as German as those who lived in Germany. He believed that all "Germans" should be united into one nation.

He was disinterested in school and at the age of 16 he quit school. Then his father died. His young mother had to support him and his little sister with a small pension. He was disgusted with regular employment. He spent his time in Linz hoping to be an artist or an architect. He often spent the evenings going to heroic operas of Richard Wagner. He spent his time on books on German history and mythology, and brooded on world problems. His friends described young Adolf as a pale, sickly, shy and quiet youth, but he could also suddenly burst out with hysterical anger against anyone who disagreed with him. Since his early years, some of the aspects of his character later played a key role in his life. He twice failed entrance examinations at the Vienna Academy of Fine Arts, so his great dream and ambition was cut off. But he couldn't accept his failure. Instead, he blamed the teachers as "abnormal."

When he was 19, his mother died. Her death put an end to his plan. He left Linz for Vienna hoping to make something of his life. His life in Vienna when he was 20 to 24, turned out to be the most miserable years of his life. Since he hated regular jobs, he had to work at odd jobs like beating carpets, shoveling snow or carrying luggage in a railway station, and occasionally he worked as a construction laborer or a house painter. He managed to live with irregular wages by sleeping in flophouses with shabby clothes, his face unshaved. He was a vagabond. The future dictator of Germany was a high school drop-out and what we Americans would call a "bum." He neither smoked nor drank. Without much work or many friends, he spent most of his time devouring books. He later wrote in *Mein Kampf* of

his life in Vienna, "In this period, there took shape within me a world picture and a philosophy which became the granite foundation of all my acts."

What, then, did Hitler learn as a down-and-out tramp during his 4 years in Vienna? What were the "world picture and philosophy" on which he later based the awful deeds that almost destroyed the world? For him, peace and democracy were bad things for mankind. They made men corrupt and soft. He also conceived the preposterous idea that Germans were a super-race superior to all other people, more intelligent and more skillful than the Americans, British, French or Russians. For him, Germans were the "master race." This was widely held among Germans in those days.

How could a high school drop-out establish National Socialism as such a powerful political party?

Hitler had no education but he was a very shrewd man. If a political party was to be successful, he knew two things; it had to manipulate millions of people and use terror. It had to master the art of propaganda, which often meant telling lies to people, and bigger lies were better than smaller ones because it was easier to make people believe them. They must know how to terrorize people who disagree with National Socialism which meant arresting or killing political opponents. He knew the value of oratory in politics. Hitler practiced his preaching and began to speak in public. He soon learned that he could sway people by his eloquence. Over the years, he became the greatest orator of his time in the world. I went to many of his rallies, and I remember many of his speeches. He spoke for hours without manuscripts. Usually most politicians have speech writers, but he did it by himself, at least in the beginning. What he was saying was 'bullshit,' but when I looked at the audiences, at the fanatical eyes, the gaping mouths, I was amazed how totally they were in his spell. We had no orator in those days to match him.

Another aspect of his life in Vienna was that he developed a grotesque hatred for the Jews. In *Mein Kampf* he wrote, "Wherever or whenever I saw Jews, I get sick to my stomach. I began to hate them. I became an anti-Semite." This prejudice against the Jews became a fatal disease for Hitler which led to the massacre of six million innocent Jewish people. What is significant to this story is that he became the German dictator and had the power of life and death over many millions of people. He drove his people to invoke his own anti-Semitic "disease" and caused the Holocaust which wiped out most of the European Jews. Because he couldn't stand life with Jews and all the other mixed races in Vienna, in 1913 Hitler left for Munich, a city with fewer Jews and in the country he admired most, Germany.

When he arrived in Munich, he had no job, no friends, no home. But the following year, the outbreak of WW I offered him an opportunity. He volunteered for a Bavarian regiment. At age 25, he started a new life in Germany. Serving in the military, at least he was fed, clothed and given shelter. During the war, he served on the western front in France as a dispatch runner of the 16th Bavarian Reserve Infantry Regiment. He was twice wounded and twice decorated with the Iron Cross. In 1918 when Germany lost, he couldn't accept the defeat by the Allies. He created the legend that the German army hadn't been defeated, but they had been "stabbed in the back by the slackers at home." He blamed these slackers:

Communists and Jews. This belief led Hitler into politics.

Returning to civilian life in Munich at age 29, he had no education or skill. He had no experience in politics at all. He joined a tiny political party in a beer hall in Munich called the "Committee of the German Workers' Party," the origin of the Nazi Party. Hitler was the 7th member to join and he soon became a smart organizer and a propagandist. He designed a party flag with the symbol of an ancient swastika cross, the sign of Aryan purity and supremacy. Then he founded an army, the S.A. — *Sturmabteilung* — so-called storm troopers or brown-shirts to terrorize opponents. The most important thing of all was that he discovered that he could draw large audiences every time he spoke in public. Many came just to listen to his speeches and often left the hall converted to Nazism.

By 1921, because followers increased after he joined the party, he succeeded in making himself dictator. He changed the name of the party to the "National Socialist German Workers' Party." (Nazi is an abbreviation of *nationalsozialistische*.) Then he assumed the title of Führer (leader). Everyone in the party was subordinate to him. The sub-leaders who helped Hitler hold political power in Germany were Ernst Röhm, Rudolf Hess, Hermann Göring, Alfred Rosenberg, Gregor Strasser, Heinrich Himmler, Julius Streicher, and Joseph Goebbels. By the fall of 1923, Hitler thought that his party was strong enough to attempt a "coup d'état" to overthrow the Weimar Republic so he could make himself dictator of Germany. This was known as "Hitler's Munich Beer Hall *Putsch*."

Could you tell me how did the *Putsch* happen and how did it fail, and how did Hitler build the Nazi Party again?

The Weimar Republic was five years old then, and politically, economically and socially, Germany was still a total mess. The main reason was that the Ruhr, the raw material and industrial center of Germany, was occupied by the French army because under the Versailles Treaty Germany failed to pay a war reparation to France. Millions of German men were out of work. The value of the German mark went down: four million marks to one dollar. Many Germans could hardly buy food. Germany badly needed someone who could lead them out of this economic chaos. The Nazi Party was known only in the state of Bavaria in those days, and Hitler was still an unknown man for most Germans. Nevertheless, on November 8, 1923, Hitler decided to take over Germany. There was a political rally attended by 3,000 Bavarian government supporters in a beer hall in Munich. Hitler headed there with his armed S.A. troops, entered the crowd and interrupted. He shouted, "The national revolution has begun!" and fired his pistol at the ceiling. He herded the government leaders together to convince them to join his revolution. It was, in a way, immaturely planned. Because Hitler didn't seize the telegraph office, the news of the revolt was immediately wired to the Berlin government. By dawn, it was suppressed and the Nazi Party was ordered to be dissolved. Hitler was found guilty of high treason and sentenced to a five-year sentence in Landsberg Prison. For most Germans, this seemed to be the end of Hitler and Nazism. But as things turned out, it was just the beginning.

During the trial, he displayed his talent of oratory in the courtroom. No one else could match his eloquence and his shrewdness in cross-examination. He completely dominated the entire trial and the world news, and for the first time, he established himself as a national figure in Germany. This really drew the wide national attention of millions of Germans who hated the democratic Weimar Republic. He became a patriotic hero. In prison, he was treated as an honored guest and given an exclusive room. During his imprisonment, he started writing his notorious book *Mein Kampf* which was to shape the destiny of Germany and world history for the next 20 years. What kind of Germany and Europe Hitler wanted were all there.

With an amnesty, his five year imprisonment was shortened to less than one year. Hitler was released, but the Nazi Party was banned and he was forbidden to speak in public. He was even threatened with deportation from Germany to his native Austria. Hitler seemed to be finished. The flamboyant Nazi leader would be forgotten by almost everyone, including his supporters in Germany: Hitler was a big joke. People made fun of his "toothbrush" mustache which resembled that of the great movie comedian, Charlie Chaplin. However, Hitler was never discouraged. In his apartment in Munich, he strengthened himself and renewed his self-confidence; he completed *Mein Kampf*. The book was published by a Nazi sympathizer and became the Nazi Bible. Six million copies were sold, which made the author rich. In the book, Hitler declared that if Germany was to recover from the humiliating defeat of the war in 1918, it had to tear up the Versailles Treaty, which was imposed by the Allies, and Germany had to be free from reparation payments and be allowed to rearm. He wanted Germany to become master of the world. He was quite frank about it.

The first task was to destroy France, the mortal enemy of Germany. Then Germany had to conquer the East; Austria, Czechoslovakia, Poland, and then Russia. He didn't think taking over Russia would be a difficult task. His book gave full warning of what he would do to Germany if he came to power. He would destroy the Republic, abolish democracy, bring down the workers' trade union, and "resettle" the Jews.

When I was working in Berlin, I watched Hitler taking over one country after another and I used to wonder why the world was so surprised at this tyrant who was doing exactly what he wrote about in his book. The truth was, only a few people believed it until it was too late. Hitler picked up ideas from Germany's most learned 19th century philosophers; Nietzsche, Hegel and Treitschke. Using their books of nationalism, racism, territorial expansionism, irrationalism, he created his own barbaric ideas: the strong people must dominate the weak people. For Hitler, after the success with his book, the next step was to conquer Germany. He learned his lesson from the failure of the Beer Hall Putsch. This time, to rebuild the Nazi Party, he had to sweep voter power in Berlin and to enter the Reichstag. Hitler was not only a brilliant spellbinder, but also a good organizer. He made the Nazi Party an official party in parliament. By the end of 1925, Hitler had 27,000 followers, and within the next three years, it had increased by four times. In the national election in 1928 the Nazi Party got one million votes out of thirty million voters. But Hitler never gave up hope. Within the next five years, he built up the party to be the supreme power in Germany. As he saw himself a future German leader, he managed to get German citizenship just before he became Chancellor. This was the way Hitler legally got hold of political power; he gradually dominated the German people, and eventually succeeded in being the dictator of Germany. In many aspects, the way he misled the German people was just unbelievable. He was absolutely a genius.

In your many books, you described the men who surrounded Hitler as being like gangsters. Hitler was the ruler but the country was governed by those men. Germans were one of the most educated people in the world, why couldn't they see Nazism was dangerous?

Göring, Goebbels, Himmler, Hess, Heydrich, Rosenberg, Bormann, Ribbentrop, and others, most of them were Hitler's groupies in the Munich Beer Hall *Putsch,* and they became statesmen in the Nazi government when Hitler became Führer. As a foreign correspondent, I had to get to know them. They were regarded as a joke even by the Germans. The image of those men was similar to that of Al Capone in Chicago; they were coarse, rude, rough, arrogant and ruthless barbarians. Very few of them had a good education. I used to wonder how such a bunch of thugs could rule such an educated nation and could govern such a great country. That was one of the great mysteries of history. That this educated nation fell into the hands of a man like Hitler was a strange phenomenon to me. What Hitler was telling people was usually nonsense, but he was a charismatic speaker. He orated his most inner belief in an exceptional way, and he had great rapport with his audiences. For non-Germans like myself or anyone who was raised in a democratic society, it didn't make any sense, but for Germans it did. For them he was a Messiah who came to Germany to save Germans. That was one of the reasons that he was so successful. For centuries, the nations of Germany had been authoritarian, emperors had absolute powers and their nationalism was based on that fact. So, they didn't seem to mind that lack of freedom. Other nations like America, Britain, France had a tradition of democracy. But the Germans were suppressed by Hitler and didn't mind. Some intellectuals had a sense of decency and opposed the Nazi regime, but for the majority they didn't have any other choice. For me, I couldn't understand their fanaticism at all.

How did Hitler manage financially to enter into a war?

After he got the power, Hitler immediately broke the Versailles Treaty in which Germany was forbidden to rearm. He built up the military. His economic minister, Dr. Hjalmar Schacht, who was a very intelligent man in finance, arranged for funds to be confiscated from Jews and also borrowed money from foreign accounts and never paid them back. Then Hitler rebuilt the army adding guns, tanks, an air force, a bigger navy and heavy artillery. Germany imported many raw materials from Russia and oil from Romania. Within two years, Hitler began the draft and created an army of considerable size. Meanwhile, the armament production of war industries boomed. It ended the unemployment of five million people. It brought a miracle of economic recovery to Germany that could defy France and Britain.

What about the press and censorship during the war inside Nazi Germany? Did Hitler give press conferences or interviews?

Joseph Goebbels, the Propaganda Minister who was also a good speaker, was ignorant about anything outside Germany. He was a crippled man and had a neurotic personality. He was strictly in control of the press in Germany. In the early stages of the war, every great victory was reported in Germany, but in later years when the Germans began loosing battles with the Russian army, we weren't allowed to write about what was going on. It was wartime censorship, and German army correspondents at the battle front controlled what to write and what not to write. Then every report was censored by Nazi officers before being sent out to the foreign media, and when it came to America, it was again censored by the US government.

Hitler rarely gave press conferences or interviews. When he did, it was only for selected foreign correspondents who were favorable to him. Annually, he had a breakfast meeting with journalists in Nuremberg, but I was never invited. Dorothy Thompson, a close friend of mine and a very intelligent American journalist, interviewed Hitler before he became Chancellor and wrote a book: *I Saw Hitler*. She said, "When I walked into Hitler's salon, I was convinced that I was meeting the future dictator of Germany. In less than 50 seconds, I was sure he was not. It took me just that time to measure the startling insignificance of this man who had set the world agog." She was wrong, of course. She was expelled by Hitler after he became Chancellor. I never had an exclusive interview with Hitler. Not all but most foreign journalists who interviewed Hitler were sort of sympathetic to Nazism and since I wasn't, I never bothered to interview him in person. I thought if I couldn't write the truth about Hitler, there would be no meaning for me to do it. However, I went to most of his rallies and speeches and attended occasional press conferences. For me, it was uncomfortable and unpleasant living there knowing that Jews were being taken away and that my German journalist friends were being arrested or executed by the Gestapo one by one. But, on the other hand, as a journalist I also wanted to report good stories and to be in the place where history was being made, and that was Berlin. I was lucky to be there. So I had to be careful not to be kicked out.

Why didn't the United States join the war earlier? By the end of 1942, America knew Jews in Europe were being killed, Britain had been fighting with Germany for years and Churchill badly needed the American army. If Japan hadn't attacked Pearl Harbor, would President Roosevelt have ignored what was going on in Europe?

I think if Japan hadn't attacked Pearl Harbor, the United States might not have declared war. The point was that the American people and the US government didn't believe what was happening in Europe. I mean, I was sending daily cables to my newspaper in the US, but I had the feeling that my editor didn't pay attention to what I was writing. During the Berlin Olympic Games in 1936, for instance, the Nazis took down anti-Semitic signs, posters and slogans from the streets, and athletes, visitors and delegates wouldn't notice anything wrong. And, the Nazi officials were saying, "The reports by foreign journalists were all garbage, nothing is wrong in Germany as you see." By 1937, I was convinced that Hitler was going to war. In July 1939, a few months before the war was about to begin, I visited Washington, D.C. to see CBS news producers, congressmen and senators. I delivered my speech to them to warn them what was going to happen in Germany and Europe. Nobody believed me. As to the persecution of Jews, in fact, they got bored with me. They told to me that I was wrong; there would be no war.

How do you see the newly united Germany, Mr. Shirer?

I see the new Germany already has problems with the rise of neo-Nazis and skinheads. The collapse of the Soviet Union will turn Germany into a big power once again. That's why I opposed reunification of Germany. I'm 88 years old now. In my long life, I have seen four kinds of Germanys — the Weimar Republic, Nazi Germany, postwar democratic Germany and now reunited Germany. During the Weimar Republic, in my first visit, Germans were liberal, anti-military and hated Hitler. I was astonished how quickly they changed their minds. Some people I met years ago had changed their view completely during the Nazi period: they became pro-Hitler. I was shocked. Today, most Germans don't like to face their past. There is no future unless they learn from their past where they came from. Germans should be honest with their past. ❖

"Hitler was an evil genius of the 20th century."

LORD ALAN BULLOCK

British, historian and author of the book *Hitler and Stalin* and *Hitler: A Study of Tyranny,* Founding Master of St. Catherine's College and former Vice Chancellor of Oxford University. Born in 1914 in Trowbridge, England. Lives in England.

(Photo: Lord Bullock in his office at Oxford University.)

To begin with, how do you see the development of the Germans and Austrians at the turn of the century when Hitler was born?

When Hitler was born, in Germany it was a period of triumph. Germany had defeated France and nationalism was strong. With Bismarck's creation of the Prussian Empire, Germany had been united for the first time and Germans felt themselves to be the most powerful state in Europe. It was a country full of confidence. The Germans in Austria, on the other hand, were defeated and excluded from the new German Empire. The leaders who ruled the Hapsburg Empire for centuries, now found themselves faced with a challenge from the Slavic peoples. In Hitler's case, he was disturbed by the growing numbers of immigrants who were pouring into Austria from Eastern Europe, and Austrian Germans felt they were invaded by inferior races: Slavs and Jews. In Vienna in 1900, of the population of 1,657,000, only 46 percent was natives. They were very critical of the House of Hapsburg. So, compared to Prussian nationalism, the nature of Hitler's nationalism was very different.

Hitler saw the German people as threatened. His nationalism was a very special kind; it was Austro-German nationalism. Austrians were now not only the minority in the Hapsburg Empire facing a challenge from the Slavs, but they also had increasing hatred toward the Slavs and the Jews. In central Europe, there were millions of Germans outside Germany, of German race who spoke the German language. So, you can't identify German nationalism simply with the people who lived in the new German Empire. It's a very complicated story, but it's important to understand the whole picture.

In your latest book, *Hitler and Stalin,* you stated a different view on Hitler's anti-Semitism than other historians. You quoted Karl Marx, which I find interesting. Can you explain?

For centuries, anti-Semitism was a part of the culture in Catholic countries, not only in Germany and Austria. There were plenty of anti-Semites all over Europe. But the difference is that Hitler proceeded to actual anti-Semitism. He took action and attempted to destroy the entire Jewish race. He really meant it. To explain how he came to this point, one has to study the history of that time. As I said, a rapidly growing segment in Vienna's population was a mass of immigrants from Eastern Europe: Slavs and Jews. Proportionately, there was a much higher percentage of Jews in Vienna. They had a higher education and were in the most prominent professions; law, politics, medicine, journalism, publishing, finance, music and the arts. On the opposite side of the social scale, there were also poorer Jews in two districts, the inner city and the Leopoldstadt ghetto. They were the ones who attracted attention by their traditional Hasidic Jewish clothes and lifestyle.

During his life in Vienna, Hitler saw Jews everywhere and hated them passionately. He turned to literature for enlightenment about the Jews, anti-Semitic pamphlets and the magazine *Ostara.* As an artist-to-be, he feared modernism in art and music, pornography and prostitution, the organization of the white slave trade, and the anti-national criticism of the press. He claimed that the Jews were responsible for all of these events.

In *Mein Kampf* he says that it took him considerable time to grasp the meaning of the "Jewish problem." He discovered that "race" was to provide the master key to his view and ideology. This fitted well with another view that was the foundation of his philosophy, Social Darwinism — the belief that all life was engaged in a struggle for existence in which only the fittest survived. He confronted for the first time in his life the socialist belief in equality with his own belief in "the aristocratic principle of nature" and the natural inequality of individuals and races. The circle was closed with the demonstration that Marxism was a doctrine invented by a Jew, Karl Marx, and used by the Jewish leaders of the Social Democratic party to trap the masses and turn them against the state, that is against the German nation and the Aryan master race.

In fact, Hitler attended several debates in the Austrian Reichstag and brought this out; he denounced democracy as destructive of individual initiative and responsibility. Karl Lueger, Vienna's famous anti-Semitic mayor, was the leader Hitler most admired. Hitler felt that the German-Austrians like himself were threatened by economic and social change caused by aliens: racially inferior Slavs, the Marxists and the Jews. But he did not know how to resolve this problem yet.

So, Hitler studied politics in his own way, then? What else did you find out about Hitler after he moved to Munich?

He didn't really read books seriously; I mean he skimmed books. He took what he wanted and ignored the rest. When he moved to Munich in 1913, he registered with the Munich police as "a painter and a writer." The city at that time was attracting large numbers of artists, intellectuals, writers and other free spirits. It was a center of the modernism movement in the arts and a magnet for every form of political radicalism, both right-wing and left-wing. But Hitler kept away

from those circles, spending his time reading in libraries and in his room. According to his own account, Hitler plunged deeper into the study of Marxism's "destructive teaching" and its relation with Jewry. He criticized Germany for being allied with the Hapsburg Empire. He thought that could drag Germany down if war broke out. He was once arrested for evading military service in Austria but managed to escape, being unfit for combat because of his physical weakness. He was unable to bear arms.

A half year later, however, after the assassination of the Archduke Ferdinand at Sarajevo, he greeted with enthusiasm the news that Germany and Austria had joined in declaring war on Serbia and Russia. He joined the crowd at the Odeonsplatz in downtown Munich to cheer the proclamation of war. This moment was captured in a photo which later became famous. (It was taken by Heinrich Hoffmann, who later became the Führer's official photographer.) This war of 1914-18 brought a national unity and patriotism to Germany. Hitler not only shared in this general mood, but felt a personal sense of liberation after a long experience of failure. Hitler volunteered for service when he learned that the German Army would take him. After months of training, in October 1914, the 16th Bavarian Reserve Infantry Regiment to which he had been posted was sent to the Western Front, the First Battle of Ypres. There is no doubt that Hitler was a good soldier. He saw a lot of heavy fighting and the horror of death on the front during his 2 years' duty as a regimental runner carrying messages when communication broke down. This was a dangerous job and he had many narrow escapes, and was wounded in October 1916. For his bravery and courage, he won the Iron Cross, First Class.

The majority who experienced the horrors of war lost their initial enthusiasm, but not Hitler. He remained a super patriot with an excessive sense of duty and was accepted as a good comrade by the regiment. But he was never promoted beyond corporal. His officers almost recommended him for a decoration once, but then they dismissed the idea pointing out that he lacked the qualities of leadership. They found something odd in Hitler's behavior: he didn't smoke nor drink and was not sociable, and he showed no interest in women. Throughout his life, he showed himself incapable of forming close personal friendships.

The experience in the war provided a new revelation for Hitler. Now, living in Munich, he dedicated himself to the task of destroying Germany's enemies. For Hitler, the war turned the fantasy world of adolescence into reality, and he felt the pride of a hero ready to "prepare to die for the Fatherland." He wrote in *Mein Kampf*:

"... As a boy and a young man, I often longed for the occasion to prove that my national enthusiasm was not mere talk... Just as millions of others did, I felt a proud joy in being permitted to go through this inexorable test... For me, as for every German, there began the greatest and most unforgettable time of my life."

Many people say that the *Mein Kampf* is an awful book. How do you describe it?
It's a horrible book; it's poorly written and in very unpleasant German — ugly phrases, ugly thoughts. It's a book by someone who doesn't really understand about writing, by a man who had no education. Nonetheless, there are some parts which are of great interest. Whenever Hitler is talking about propaganda, he is brilliant. He understood how you control the crowd and how you appeal to a crowd. All that he understood perfectly. When he writes about how you should address a crowd, what time of the day you should hold your meeting, what sort of room you should use or when he says, tell bigger lies otherwise people don't pay any attention. When he is writing about these sorts of things, he writes very clearly. But when he talks about philosophy and racial views, he betrays his ignorant prejudices. When it comes to speech, Hitler was a brilliant orator and a powerful speaker. As you watch the documentary footage, you can see he was a great actor on stage. He would do tremendous shouting, raging, hand gestures, his eyes and the expression of his face are emotionally intensified, and then he just ends abruptly, smiles at the audience and leaves. Hitler's remarkable powers as a speaker were very different from traditional political speeches. It was self-dramatization and he knew exactly what he was doing.

As is generally known Hitler's private life was peculiar: no wife, no desire to have his own family or marriage. But on the other hand, the documentary footage shows how many women were overwhelmingly excited about him, acting as if they were at a rock 'n roll concert or about to greet a famous movie star.
I don't think he was very much interested in women. I did suspect that he was impotent and incapable of ordinary sexual intercourse. In his teens while he was still in Linz, he fell in love with a young woman named Stephanie, but being a shy boy, he never spoke to her. August Kubizek, his closest friend, describes Hitler: "He talked a great deal about women and love, but there was no evidence that he had sexual relations with anyone." Hitler was undoubtedly attractive to women. Throughout his career, in fact, many women were fascinated by his hypnotic power

and you can see the hysteria that affected women at his big meetings. He had an extraordinary charismatic power. Many women who met Hitler were very impressed by him and attracted to him. He himself attached great importance to the women's vote; this was one of the reasons that he remained a single man. He liked to have beautiful women in his company, actresses, movie stars, aristocrats, and he kissed their hands in the Viennese style. But if a woman tried to have an intellectual conversation or argue with him, they were never invited again. He was scornful of women with opinions of their own.

There were two women in whom he took more than a passing interest; both were 20 years younger than he was. Geli Raubal, his own niece, whom he described as the one great love affair of his life. In 1928, Geli was 17 when he began dating her, and over the next 3 years Hitler was infatuated with her and made her his constant companion in Munich. Geli enjoyed going out with her uncle, especially as his political rise from 1929 to 1931 began to bring him fame. But she suffered from his jealousy and possessiveness. There was a furious row when Hitler discovered that she was having an affair with Emil Maurice, his chauffeur. He forbade her to see any other men and refused to let her go to Vienna to have voice training. In September 1931, Geli committed suicide by shooting herself and that affected Hitler greatly. For months, he was inconsolable. As a result of the shock, he refused to eat meat for the rest of his life. He never forgot her. Geli's photographs were always hung in his rooms in Munich and Berlin and flowers were placed there on the anniversaries of her birth and death.

Now, about his next woman, Eva Braun. Albert Speer wrote in his memoir: "For all writers of history, she is going to be a disappointment."

She was a pretty but empty-headed blonde with a round face and blue eyes and she worked as a receptionist at a photographer's shop run by Hoffmann. This is where Hitler met her. He paid her a few compliments and gave her flowers, and occasionally invited her to join his party on an outing. The initiative, however, was all on Eva's side; she set her cap for him, telling her friends that Hitler was in love with her and that she would make him marry her. Failing to attract his attention, in the autumn of 1932, she attempted suicide. Hitler was particularly vulnerable to the threat of a scandal, as little more than a year had passed since Geli had taken her life. According to Hoffmann who had seen what was happening from the beginning, "It was in this manner that Eva Braun got her way and became Hitler's *chère amie*."

Braun's diary, which survived her death, showed she was full of complaints about Hitler's neglect and humiliation. She again attempted suicide in October 1935 in order to attract his attention. Hitler went to great lengths to conceal their relationship. She was denied recognition as Hitler's mistress even among the closest Nazi circle. In 1936, she succeeded in taking her place as a *Hausfrau* at the Berghof, the Führer's residence in Bavaria. She was allowed to sit next to him when he presided at lunch. But Hitler rarely allowed her to come to Berlin or to appear with him at receptions or in public. Speer writes in his memoir of how Hitler talked about his women:

"A highly intelligent man should take a primitive and stupid woman. Imagine if, on top of everything else, I had a woman who interfered with my work... I could never marry. Think of the problems if I had children. In the end they would try to make my son successor. The chances are slim for someone like me to have a capable son. Consider Goethe's son, a completely worthless son! Lots of women are attracted to me because I am unmarried... It's the same as with a movie actor; when he marries, he loses a certain something for the women who adore him. Then he is no longer the idol he was before."

Nobody knows the true story of Hitler's sex and love life, of course. But without any conclusive evidence to go on, there is a strong presumption that Hitler was incapable of normal sexual relations, whether for physical or psychological reasons, or perhaps both. I interviewed Putzi Hanfstaengl, who was one of Hitler's closest companions until the mid-1930s, and according to his account, Hitler was impotent and his "abounding nervous energy" found no normal release. After viewing such evidence, psychoanalyst Erich Fromm concluded: "The most one can guess, I believe, is that his sexual desires were largely voyeuristic." That is to say he wanted to watch women humiliating themselves in front of him, but had no interest in proper sexual intercourse. I don't think women count for anything in Hitler's life. You see, he had this obsession with his niece Geli and the things he wanted her to perform. That could be one of the reasons why she committed suicide. Fromm theorizes further on Hitler's sexual behavior, anal-sadistic sex with the inferior type of women and masochistic sex with admired women. But, overall, I think these private matters were not important to him. What interested him most was power, not sex. And, indeed, he really did create enormous power in a very exceptional way.

Do you think the Nazis abused his power?
No. I don't think anybody used Hitler. Hitler used them. I think he was always one jump ahead of people all the time. He was a solo conductor.

He was very calculating, very shrewd and very clear about what he wanted to do. In the beginning, Hitler was a small-time man and nobody had heard of him. But all the others, Goebbels, Göring, Himmler were there with him since the 1920s and they all depended on him and they took his words very seriously.

How do you describe the political relationship between Hitler and Stalin, and what did you find from your research on the Hitler-Stalin Pact?
This is absolutely clear that Hitler always wanted to invade Russia. He stated this plainly in *Mein Kampf* during the 1920s although at that time he obviously didn't know how and when he was going to do it. But he was an opportunistic, ambitious and calculating man, so it's clear that when he got power he definitely planned to do it. In *Mein Kampf* he also said that he would make allies with Britain and Italy, defeat France, then seek Germany's future in Eastern Europe and Russia with the allies. He was disappointed that Britain wouldn't make an alliance with him. So he had a problem in the West and he had to deal with that problem first. The French and British together were trying to intervene over Czechoslovakia and Poland in order to have a free hand to deal with them, and he was perfectly prepared to make a deal with Russia. He had no intention of it lasting more than a year or two. But when it happened, the world was absolutely astonished. It was, in a way, a master stroke because the British and the French could do nothing for the Poles unless they could get the Russians to act with them. Now, what about the Russians?

Well, Stalin wasn't interested in foreign policy. He was taking time to complete his domestic revolution. Two years before Hitler's attack, he had, for example, virtually destroyed the top leadership, the officer corps of the Russian Army. There were still domestic problems and much to be done to industrialize and revitalize the state of Russia. In other words, the Russian military was weak. The last thing Stalin wanted was to fight Hitler. When Hitler was anxious to make a deal with him, it was wonderful from Stalin's point of view, he couldn't have thought of anything better. This was exactly what he wanted. The Hitler-Stalin Pact was a guarantee from Hitler that he wouldn't attack Russia, and as far as Stalin was concerned, he would have been content with that for at least the next 10 or 15 years. This would give him time for preparation. But for Hitler the pact was only a temporary thing. In my book, I make it clear that Stalin refused to believe that Hitler was going to attack him, and he wouldn't allow the Russians to make any preparations. This is because he was anxious not to quarrel with Hitler and not to provoke Hitler into making an attack. He wanted more time even if he realized that Hitler would attack him sooner or later.

Do you think Hitler miscalculated Stalin's power?

Yes, I think he did. But both Hitler and Stalin miscalculated. As I said, the purges which Stalin carried out in 1937-38 wrecked the Russian Army; 40,000 officers were either shot, imprisoned or dismissed. No army has ever suffered such a loss to its officer corps in war as Stalin imposed on his own army in peacetime. Well, that of course meant that nobody took Russia seriously as a mighty power. This was confirmed by the Finnish-Soviet War, the so-called "Winter War" (1939-40), because the Russians made an awful mess in fighting with the Finns. They even-

tually did win the war but at a very high cost. I remember attending a press conference in London by the Ministry of Defense the week that Hitler attacked Russia. They were saying to us reporters and journalists, whatever you do, don't lead people to believe that this makes any difference. The Russians won't last six weeks. Hitler and everybody else believed that the Russians would crumble before him within a year. Not only Hitler, but the German army which was a very professional army, believed this and after all they had just knocked France out in under six weeks. So, Hitler obviously miscalculated.

However, they did get to the gates of Moscow and came pretty close to the oil of the Caucasus. Hitler, of course, refused to consider making a compromise peace with Stalin. He was still convinced that his luck would change and he would be able to destroy the Russian army. If he had succeeded, he would have had all the resources of Europe at his disposal and have been in an extremely powerful position, and the British and American armies couldn't have done anything about it.

Why did Hitler quit attacking Britain and turn to Russia?

It's a very interesting thing. Throughout the war, Hitler was very angry with Britain. In the beginning he never wanted to fight with Britain or destroy the British Empire because he wanted Britain to be his ally. When he realized he couldn't get them as his ally, then he decided to invade them. But he was never wholehearted about the invasion. Since Britain had airfields by the Channel and maintained air superiority, Hitler knew that crossing the Channel would be difficult. So, everything turned on whether the German Luftwaffe could destroy the Royal Air Force. They came really close but they gave up, and at that point, Hitler was very reluctant to go any further and turned toward Russia. In July 1940, straight after the French defeat, he had already ordered all the preparations for Russia. Now he said he was not going to waste any more time with England. The English are as good as defeated, they can't do anything to us. He said: We'll go on and we'll defeat the Russians within one year, then the British will just make peace with us.

Now, why did Hitler want to ally with Britain? I think he admired the English for the wrong reasons. He was always fascinated by India; he said once there were only 50,000 English people out there, but they ruled the whole Indian empire and he thought that was wonderful. Hitler said the English made a great empire and the Germans should make a great empire, too.

He said he would guarantee the British Empire. For a long time, the British government didn't believe he was a real danger. Hitler was very clever handling the British in the early years. After invading his neighboring countries and telling them a lot of lies, then the British government finally decided Hitler had to be stopped. It was clear that he was a great manipulator. He knew how to take advantage of situations which he had created.

Would you say Hitler was one of the most influential men of the 20th century?
I'm afraid, yes. He was an evil man. I would say that of both Hitler and Stalin. They were horrible men who shook the world and the world changed forever. ❖

"Without MAGIC intelligence, the war would have been prolonged."

CARL BOYD

American, military historian and the author of *Hitler's Japanese Confidant* and *Extraordinary Envoy,* and professor of history at the Old Dominion University, Norfolk, Virginia. Born in 1939 in Philadelphia, USA. Lives in Virginia, USA.

(Photo: Prof. Boyd in his office at Old Dominion University.)

Regarding your most recent book _Hitler's Japanese Confidant — General Hiroshi Oshima and Magic Intelligence 1941-1945_, as far as I know, you are the only person who has researched this subject. Could you tell me what it is all about?

This book is chiefly concerned with intelligence issues and is based largely on recently declassified cryptographic messages from WW II. The primary sources are in the National Archives in Washington, D.C. There are a few people who work on the cryptographic intelligence of WW II, but most of them emphasize the German rather than the Japanese side. And in particular, I think it's fair to say that I'm the only researcher in either the United States or Japan working specially on the German-Japanese connection in WW II. The Japanese records were either destroyed during the bombing raids on Tokyo in 1945, or Japanese intelligence officers destroyed their own materials before the American occupation was organized. The Japanese were concerned that the American forces would use these records as evidence against them in postwar trials.

Could you explain the history of this cipher system that was so important to the Americans? Basically, it concerned top-secret intelligence and diplomatic messages exchanged between Berlin and Tokyo?

That's correct. My study relies heavily on the messages of Oshima and several wartime Japanese foreign ministers. Top secret enciphered messages were sent between Berlin and Tokyo from the time of the rise of Nazi power to the fateful Nazi invasion of the Soviet Union in 1941 to the collapse of Germany in 1945. These messages were intercepted and deciphered by American intelligence agencies, also by the British to some extent,

and the information they provided was of enormous value to the Allies throughout the war. How the American government was able to do such a thing is an important and interesting story.

In 1930, a small group of code and cipher specialists began a training course in Washington, D.C.: This was the beginning of the US Army's Signal Intelligence Service (SIS). These specialists formed a unique team in the American communication intelligence community. The cryptoanalysts were Japanese, German and Russian linguists, and they had a special sense of mission. Among them was John B. Hurt, a Japanese linguist who was exceedingly knowledgeable about Japanese history, art, and cultural affairs. He was a remarkable man. By late 1930, for example, SIS knew that Japan had plans to invade continental Asia, particularly Manchuria. This happened on the 18th of September in 1931. The cipher system used by the Japanese foreign ministry in the 1930s was solved by the American cipher specialists. As the number of members in the SIS gradually increased over the years, all sorts of breakthroughs were accomplished while monitoring the Japanese secret radio communications.

Then in 1939, the Japanese changed their cipher that the SIS called RED; RED was replaced by PURPLE and the SIS was unable to break PURPLE for some 18 months. William F. Friedman, chief of the SIS, referred to these hardworking cryptonalysts who eventually broke PURPLE as his "magicians," because they brought miracles, as he said. From this experience came the cover name MAGIC for the intelligence produced in this operation. The Japanese codes and ciphers were extremely sophisticated and difficult to read, and the Japanese were so confident that the PURPLE cipher couldn't be broken that they never changed it throughout the war. And

255

the SIS was reading this high-grade diplomatic cipher starting at the end of September 1940. Moreover, Americans continued reading it straight through the war. The Japanese, in fact, changed a lot of other naval and army codes, but never the code PURPLE. This code was used as a foreign ministry code by Tokyo for all messages sent to Japanese embassies, consulates and missions throughout the world.

The Japanese opened their country to the world only in the last century around the time of Bismarck's government in Germany. What was the historical interaction between Germany and Japan?

A significant relationship between Germany and Japan goes back to the time of the Meiji Restoration in 1868. Japanese reformers realized that Japan had to modernize in order to become a strong member of the international community of nations. They learned very quickly. They were impressed by the Germans in many respects. For example, the Japanese government based its new constitution on the Bismarck constitution; medicine was heavily influenced by the German example; and the Japanese army was patterned after the German army system folloiwng the German victory in the Franco-Prussian War of 1870-1871. Furthermore, a number of students were sent to Europe and the United States for study. Although Germany and Japan fought against each other during WW I, in the 1920s, the two governments reestablished diplomatic relations and opened embassies in Berlin and Tokyo. There were seven Japanese ambassadors posted in Berlin before Oshima, who was first appointed as ambassador in 1938. It's interesting that Germany and Japan were not only different in terms of language and culture, but also their development

as modern nations was utterly different. Nevertheless, they were important allies during the war.

Who was Oshima and what was his attitude toward the Nazi government?

Oshima graduated from the Japanese military academy in 1905. He studied German language for several years in various military institutions, and he spoke it fluently. He was a son of a Japanese military family with a tradition of distinguished service to Japan; his father was a general and Minister of War in 1916-1918. Since there was a pronounced German influence during Japan's modernization, the study of German history, politics, culture, language and military affairs was common, particularly by those Japanese who sought military careers. He studied Clausewitz at the academy. Clausewitz was a Prussian general early in the last century and the author of a book *Vom Kriege* (On War). This book has had a major impact on strategic studies on war throughout the world.

From 1921 to 1923, Oshima was assigned to Germany as an assistant military attache. His tour of duty was uneventful: He later recalled that he received "an unfavorable impression — politically, economically and militarily — of the Weimar Republic." He disapproved of the fundamental nature of republicanism and the Versailles Peace Treaty restrictions that were placed on Germany's armed forces in the 1920s. Oshima was totalitarian in his orientation. In 1924, he was stationed in Vienna as a Japanese military attache working in the field of Russian espionage. By March 1934, he was promoted to the rank of colonel and reassigned to Germany as military attache. It was a year after Hitler became Chancellor and the Nazi government was hard at work introducing changes. Oshima attended the Nuremberg rally that year and became convinced that the will of National Socialism had triumphed and that German military strength was being rejuvenated. He voiced his strong approval. William Shirer, an American correspondent in Berlin during the 1930s, met Oshima a number of times. He described him as being "more Nazi than the Nazis."

What did Hitler think of Oshima? I mean, racially, Japanese are not Aryan.

It's of course difficult to second-guess Hitler. Hitler's earlier views expressed in *Mein Kampf* were not altogether complimentary to the Japanese. But after 1933, political expedience encouraged a change in his attitude. His impression was formed gradually as his own power and ambition grew. Hitler showed interest in promoting German-Japanese relations and in 1935 met the enthusiastic military attache in Berlin. The attitudes of the Japanese in Berlin, especially Oshima's, encouraged Hitler. Hitler valued Oshima's pro-Nazi mentality and any kind of racial reservations that Hitler may have had simply didn't apply in this particular instance. There were other overriding considerations.

In 1937, moreover, Hitler ordered the cessation of the German sale of arms to the Chinese with whom the Japanese were at war. German arms manufacturers had long sold weapons to the Kuomintang, the nationalist Chinese of Chiang Kai-shek. Chiang was fighting the Japanese army as well as the Chinese Communists. Hitler's order was a way of appeasing the Japanese. The previous November — in 1936 — Japan had concluded the Anti-Comintern Pact with Germany. Nothing, except the German aid to China, seemed to stand in the way of ever closer German-Japanese relations, so Hitler and Oshima believed. Earlier, in 1935, Hitler told Oshima of

Germany's intentions to split the Soviet Union into several small states. Oshima, who was three years older than Hitler, secretly discussed with the Führer how they would operate in the gathering and exchange of information about Russia, and if hostilities occurred, the German and Japanese armies would continue to cooperate. Oshima's rapport with the top Nazis was exceptional; he also enjoyed special relationships with leading members of Hitler's government — Ribbentrop, Canaris, Keitel and Himmler — and they regarded him as a comrade in the struggle against foreign enemies of the Third Reich.

In 1937, Italy joined the Anti-Comintern Pact and later this association of the Italians, Germans and Japanese developed into the Tripartite Pact, a military alliance signed in September 1940. By that time, Oshima was back in Japan temporarily. But by the time he returned to Germany as ambassador representing Japan at large in February 1941, MAGIC intelligence was prepared to play an important role.

How much did the Germans and Japanese trust each other?

Shortly after Oshima's arrival in 1934, an American assistant military attache by the name of Captain Hugh Rowan in the US Embassy in Berlin reported to Washington that there were about 150 Japanese nationals in Germany, many of whom were probably special agents. Most of the alleged informers were Japanese scholars and students registered with various German universities. Some officials in the Tokyo government distrusted Hitler. However, since the Manchurian incident in 1931, the western democracies were suspicious of Japan. Agents in Germany were not necessarily trying to spy on German activities. Nevertheless, Japanese officials in Tokyo wanted as much information about foreign affairs as possible. Fearing the rise of communism, Japan, in a state of international isolation, needed an ally. The Japanese and Germans agreed that their countries ought to unite against a common enemy, communism. For both, Japan and Germany, the alliance was a marriage largely of convenience. Who else was there? Japan was rabidly anti-communist in the 1920s and 1930s, and that condition obviously suited the Nazi Germans, who were also anti-communist. Furthermore, in Hitler's view Japan, a major naval power on the other side of the world, could be useful in a campaign against Russia, and Japan was not as close to Germany as Italy. Therefore, from Hitler's point of view, Japan would not compete with German interests. As Goebbels wrote in his diary in 1943, "The aim of our struggle must be to create a united Europe. The Führer re-emphasized how happy we can be that there are no Japanese on the European continent. Even though the Italians today give us many headaches and create a difficulty, we must nevertheless consider ourselves lucky that they cannot be serious competitors in the future organization of Europe. If the Japanese were settled on the European continent, the situation would be quite different."

It was a marriage of convenience, but what was Hitler's final goal? Goebbels called the Japanese a "yellow peril."

It's true at least in theory, that the Germans and Japanese had very tentative arrangements to divide the Soviet Union between them. That was a long-range goal, mostly in Hitler's mind. There is some indication that at first, in 1941 and 1942, Hitler was not particularly keen on the idea of sharing Russia with Japan, because he was under the assumption that Germany alone could conquer the Soviet Union. But as it became increasingly clear

that Germany could not bring about the defeat of the Soviet Union, he started to urge the Japanese to attack from the east. And Oshima, in turn, urged his government to comply with Hitler's wishes. The Japanese would attack from Manchuquo, across the Amur River, and into Siberia, as Hitler and Oshima had already discussed. Hitler needed the Japanese and to be derogatory toward them, with reference to the so-called yellow peril, would not have been politically shrewd. And, by and large, I think Hitler was a clever politician, up to 1941, at least.

On the Japanese side, however, and from a pragmatic and economic point of view, there was no advantage in attacking the Soviet Union. There was no known oil in Siberia, nor were there minerals and resources of energy that the Japanese needed to run their large military establishment. However, these valuable commodities were in Indonesia, Indochina, Borneo and other southern areas. I am reluctant to speculate about such matters, nevertheless, I imagine it would have been an enormous chore for the Germans to govern occupied territories of the size of the Soviet Union without some sort of outside cooperation, chiefly from the Japanese. The German population at that time was little more than 70 million while the Russian population was much larger. On the other hand, there is reason to believe that the Japanese and Germans couldn't have managed territories adjacent to each other. Friction could well have developed between the two governments.

So according to your research, the German and Japanese Axis relations were more serious and more ambitious than generally thought?

Yes. Since Oshima's initial contact with Hitler in the mid-1930s until 1945, the two men had met many times; Hitler met Oshima more frequently than any other foreign representatives. Soon after Germany's great success in the *Anschluss* and Sudetenland settlement in 1938, Oshima was appointed to the rank of ambassador, moving from his military post to a diplomatic post. National Socialist officials warmly welcomed him as the official diplomatic representative of the Japanese government. Oshima visited Hitler at his villa in Berchtesgaden, Bavaria. He expressed delight over the development of ever closer relations with growing sympathy and understanding between the two nations. In return, Hitler praised the spirit of the Japanese people who had made "such remarkable advancement in the last decades," and asserted that common action against communism was a further indication of the "spiritual kinship" of the German and Japanese people. Hitler cleverly quoted an old Japanese proverb which stressed the importance of wary watchfulness after success: *"katte kabuto no o wo shimeyo."* (After winning, keep the string tight on your helmet.) Hitler and Oshima held more meetings than ever after he became an ambassador. Their negotiations were always very cordial and their conversations were always candid. The interesting thing I find is that, while Hitler was meeting with this eloquent Japanese warrior-diplomat, he never showed any of his notorious short temper or outbursts. Oshima was truly Hitler's Japanese confidant.

However, Hitler's "Non-Aggression Pact" with Stalin in August 1939 angered many in the Japanese government. They rightly considered Hitler's action as a violation of the secret supplementary agreement to the Anti-Comintern Pact of 1938. For Oshima, it was shocking news and the new German-Soviet Pact put him in a very awkward position. It undermined the anti-communist premise of recent German-Japanese diplomacy. He protested to Ribbentrop. The Hi-

ranuma cabinet in Tokyo was forced to resign and a new cabinet was formed headed by Prime Minister Nobuyuki Abe. There was a mood of distrust of the Third Reich and the pro-Axis forces in Japan.

The Germans realized that they were in danger of losing their valuable Japanese comrade as ambassador. Despite Ribbentrop's effort to keep Oshima at his post in Berlin, Oshima was obligated to resign and returned to Tokyo. The Abe cabinet advocated the establishment of a balanced foreign policy, nevertheless, many Japanese high-ranking officials still had considerable admiration for Hitler's boldness and his impressive success with the German armed forces in European affairs. In September 1940, the political climate changed when Japan finally joined Germany and Italy in a tripartite military alliance. During Oshima's stay in Tokyo, however, Ribbentrop kept in contact with him through the German ambassador in Tokyo, Eugen Ott. Thus, Oshima had continual access to National Socialist officialdom. In December of 1940, as the war in Europe resulted in more victories for Hitler, Oshima was re-appointed as the ambassador and returned to Berlin in February 1941. He stayed in his position in Berlin until the defeat of Germany. During the war Japan remained pro-Hitler all the way through.

Oshima was in Berlin on the 7th of December, 1941 when Japan attacked Pear Harbor. Did the SIS find any indication of the forthcoming attack?

There was massive circumstantial evidence to suggest hostilities between the United States and Japan. Although this situation was appreciated by MAGIC analysts before the attack, several opportunities were missed to form a clear picture of the impending disaster. As a result, things didn't come together soon enough to avoid the calamity in Hawaii on December 7th. To be more chronological, in October, Japan had another government crisis and a climate developed in which war was increasingly likely. The new prime minister, General Hideki Tojo, ordered his new government to carry on their imperial government policies. The MAGIC Tokyo-Oshima messages continued to contain only limited indications of the impending hostilities. For example, on the 29th of November, Oshima wired Tokyo with a message based on a discussion with Ribbentrop: "Germany would not refuse to fight the United States if necessary." Oshima quoted Ribbentrop verbatim: "Should Japan become engaged in a war against the United States, Germany of course would join the war immediately. There is absolutely no possibility of Germany's entering into a separate peace with the US under such circumstances. The Führer is determined on that point." These communications between Berlin and Tokyo were deciphered by the American cryptologic teams and Roosevelt knew about them. But the record to date is no more exact than this, and I don't believe there was a "smoking gun," so to speak.

What other messages had the SIS successfully deciphered?

US cryptologic forces were monitoring most of Oshima's messages as well as reading the traffic between the foreign office in Tokyo and other Japanese government officials abroad. Several weeks before Operation Barbarossa on June 22, 1941, Oshima provided the MAGIC analysts with additional information about Hitler's impending campaign. "When Barbarossa commences," Hitler predicted, "the world will hold its breath." After

the invasion many American and British military analysts had doubted that the Russians could survive. Oshima was convinced that the German-Soviet war was going to end in a German victory soon and that there wouldn't be enough time for Britain and the US to come to the aid of the Russians.

Other important facts American intelligence learned through Oshima's wireless mail were the details of various German strategic plans, including the defense of Normandy in 1944. This sort of information was of vital importance to Anglo-American strategists. Earlier in the war, after Japan struck at Pearl Harbor and the German army failed to seize Moscow in the first week of December, Oshima's intercepted messages to Tokyo provided the Western Allies with information about the war conditions on the Russian front, which was otherwise extremely difficult for the Anglo-Americans to obtain. Tokyo ordered Oshima to investigate conditions in the German-occupied portion of the Soviet Union and in 1942, Oshima's report was intercepted. He reported at the end of 1941, that the Germans killed or interned 150,000 people in the Baltic states and captured the oil fields in the Ukraine, Galicia and Romania, and the Soviet Union was taking a terrible beating. His reports continued to be studied very carefully in Washington because the strategic repercussions for the western coalition would be disastrous if the Soviet Union surrendered.

In another instance, the Americans first learned from Oshima about the July 20, 1944 assassination attempt on Hitler that failed. Ribbentrop notified Oshima just hours after the attempt. Oshima's report to Tokyo was immediately intercepted by the MAGIC intelligence. In one respect the Western Allies were reassured that

Hitler's incompetent conduct of the war would continue. If German military professionals had gained full control of running the war, the end of the series of Allied gains such as D-Day in June, would probably not be far off. There were many other examples of the importance of Oshima's intercepted messages. The main thing was that the Japanese ambassador had a thorough knowledge of important German wartime secrets and reported them to his Tokyo superiors. These messages were intercepted, deciphered, translated by the American code-breakers and sent to Roosevelt. In Britain, there was a significant difference in the British intelligence effort called ULTRA. But they were also able to obtain information from breaking the German-code created by the so-called ENIGMA machine.

So, you believe that the work of military intelligence was absolutely vital to Anglo-American conduct of the war?

Yes, of course. Without cryptologic intelligence work, the war would have been prolonged. It's entirely conceivable that if the Americans hadn't had access to the Axis ciphers and codes, including the Polish and British work on the German ENIGMA intercepts, WW II could have lasted perhaps a few more years. There is no question that this type of intelligence shortened the war, saved the lives of millions on both sides, and helped to bring an inevitable victory for the Allies.

What happened to the relationship between Hitler and Oshima at the end of the war while Berlin was burning?

After the Allies began bombing Berlin, the Japanese Embassy was removed from Tiergarten to the north of Berlin. The main communication between Berlin and Tokyo was through Oshima. The Nazi government trusted Oshima more than his government, and some cabinet members in Tokyo criticized Oshima as Hitler's puppet. I think such criticism was too harsh. Oshima made mistakes of course, but he stood up to Hitler in a surprising and forceful way on several occasions. For example, when the war was going badly for the Germans in September 1944, Oshima personally visited Hitler. Recalling their friendship since 1935 and that they shared an ambition to conquer the Soviet Union, Oshima, knowing of Hitler's catastrophic failure, asked him: "Do you still expect to make it?" He had the audacity to put this bold question to the Führer. That was something that no Nazi minister did. Hitler answered Oshima calmly suggesting that such an opportunity had probably passed! So, I would give Oshima a little more credit.

Oshima got out of Berlin on April 14, 1945. He and his staff fled to the Alps. MAGIC intelligence analysts knew that. They surrendered to a unit of the US Army on May 11. They sailed to the US where they remained interned until the surrender of Japan. Oshima was charged as a war criminal and was tried by the International Military Tribunal in 1946-1948. He was sentenced to life imprisonment, but in 1958 he was granted clemency. He died in June 1975 at the age of 89. The irony of the story was that Oshima died without knowing that during all of those years when he was an important diplomat in Berlin, his messages were constantly being intercepted by the enemy, the Americans. ❖

"Hitler's burned body was snatched by Stalin."

RICHARD RAACK

American, historian specializing in German, Eastern European and Soviet history on WW II and the Cold War, author of the book *Stalin's Drive to the West: The Origins of the Cold War*. Born in 1928 in Los Angeles, USA. Lives in Germany and California, USA.

(Photo: Prof. Raack in his home in Berlin, next to a World War II propaganda poster on Russian war victory.)

Professor Raack, could you tell me about your research and your academic background?

After I retired as a history professor at California State University, Hayward, I researched the historical film representations and aspects of the history of WW II, particularly the relationship between the Soviets and the Western Allies. My main study was the history of Poland and Germany, but my research also deals extensively with the USSR and the USA. I graduated from Harvard University with my thesis on the Napoleonic period. During the 1960s, I lived in Poland and studied 19th century Polish history, then I worked on historical newsreel films about the US, Poland, Germany and the USSR. Through those documentary film materials, I've found a different kind of information about WW II, including the Holocaust. These film materials are not much known to the Western world. Based on those and written sources, I have also been writing about Eastern European history.

I speak Polish, Russian, Czech, French and German, and as a historian, my language skill is extremely useful. During the decades of the Cold War, I visited former communist countries for my research, reading war materials in archival libraries in Moscow, Prague, Warsaw or Berlin. They were all fascinating and many of them were inaccessible to many Western historians or foreign journalists. In the mid-1980s when Mr. Gorbachev came to power in Russia, his *glasnost* campaign brought a big change for historians. Because of Mr. Gorbachev's "revolution of openness," the Russian government began opening up many of its files about WW II and the Cold War.

I would like to discuss the last days of Hitler's life, which are still mysteries after nearly 50 years. To begin with, could you give me a brief story of the background that is generally known to the public?

There are a number of books already written about it. Hitler was known to have committed suicide on the 30th of April, 1945, at approximately 3:00 in the afternoon, together with his newlywed bride, Eva Braun, in his Chancellery bunker located 50 feet underground in central Berlin. According to witnesses who were in the bunker on that day, they heard the sound of a gunshot which echoed throughout the bunker from Hitler's suite, so they believed that Hitler had shot himself in the head and died. These witnesses were apparently Joseph Goebbels, Martin Bormann, Ambassador Walter Hewel, SS adjutant Otto Gunsche, bunker doctor Stumpfegger, chauffeur Erich Kemkpa, cooks, secretaries Frau Gerda Christian and Frau Traudl Junge, and generals Wilhelm Burgdorf and Hans Krebs, the commander of the Berlin garrison Weidling, and the head of the Hitler Youth, Arthur Axmann. Gunsche was the first to enter Hitler's suite. He found Hitler's body crumpled up with blood running from his head. Beside him was Eva Braun's body. Then he and Bormann wrapped the two bodies with blankets and carried them away to the Chancellery garden with a few guards who arrived with gallons of gasoline. They poured the gasoline on the bodies and burned them. To burn a human body entirely by an open fire, without an oven, takes many hours. By the evening, the cremation was still not finished.

Meanwhile, the bunker was completely surrounded by Red Army troops. There were tanks all over and a heavy bombardment by artillery intensified around the bunker. Just a few hundred yards away from the bunker, the Soviet flag was raised by a Russian soldier on the top of the Reichstag symbolizing for Stalin the fall of

Germany and Soviet victory. (The scenes later taken at the Reichstag became famous in the Soviet pictorial propaganda accounts of WW II.) Everybody in the bunker was frightened to death. They were hurrying to get out of the bunker as quickly as possible. During that night, some managed to escape. None of them saw the two bodies completely consumed. In the last chaotic days of the war in Berlin, there was probably not enough gasoline to keep the bodies burning. Goebbels, however, stayed in the bunker. On the next day, after he made a radio broadcast that the Führer was dead, he killed his six children first, then committed suicide with his wife.

Within days, most escapees from the bunker were captured. Then, on the 8th of May, Nazi Germany finally surrendered. The captured bunker group members were soon all deported as POWs to Moscow for imprisonment. Some of them died there but the rest who survived didn't return to Germany until the mid-1950s. The Soviets released them long after Stalin died. Bormann's remains were found some years later. He apparently failed in his escape from Berlin.

When the Russians entered Hitler's bunker, they found the charred bodies of Goebbels and his wife lying in the Chancellor's garden. These photographs were published. However, the Soviet government never announced what happened to Hitler's body, and right after the war, there were all sorts of rumors, and some of them spread by Soviet agencies. Hitler escaped and was still alive, he was in exile in Spain, he flew to Argentina by private airplane or he went to Japan in a Japanese submarine and took all the gold from his Swiss bank, and so on.

In recent years, however, you've found out new information. Please tell me about it.

Well, we all know that the location of the remains of their corpses has been unknown. Then, in 1968, a Russian journalist named Lev Bezymenskii published a book disclosing the long-concealed Soviet autopsy findings on the German Führer and his bride dating back to 1945. This book was, strangely, available only in the Western world. It was not printed in Russian or other Eastern countries. Bezymenskii's publication was, of course, a big surprise in the Western world and once again resurrected one of the unresolved enigmas of WW II history. His story was the finding of Hitler's and Braun's corpses, the result of the autopsy, and the reports of how they died. It was said Hitler had died by poison; he had taken cyanide. The witnesses at the *Führerbunker* had credibly testified at the time Hitler died as to Hitler's method of death — a bullet to the head. And, most Western historians believed the story. Hitler had more than obliquely promised his people this way of death, the way of a soldier. This was what we all knew as late as 1968.

Then, 23 years after the Führer's death, it was revealed that the cause of his death was poison. The visible gunshot wound to his head was reasonably explained. Hitler thought the poison might not work, and he might have asked the most trusted person to complete the work with a pistol in case he didn't die. At the last moment of his life, his hands could have been uncontrollably trembling, and he might have thought that he might fail by his own hand. His fear was to end up wounded and alive in Soviet hands. However, the autopsy reveled that the poison did kill him. But again, Bezymenskii wrote this story only in the West, and at that time most Westerners were skeptical of his report because of questionable Soviet sources. Why were there discrepancies? The hypothesized shot which explained the blood reported by the witnesses, produced no obvious wound according to the autopsy report at the time of the forensic proceedings. At the time, skepticism about Bezymenskii's story seemed fully merited. Two notable and widely-known Western Hitler scholars, Hugh Trevor-Roper and Werner Maser — at least a few years ago — had still not accepted the Soviets findings. But in this case, the Soviets were evidently correct. There was no reason for Bezymenskii to concoct the printed photos and documents he published. The significance of Bezymenskii's report is that it was the first documented Soviet account of the Führer's death published in the West. In the spring of 1945, the Red Army troops were the first to seize Berlin and the Western Allies couldn't make it. The Red Army found the body and identified it. The Soviets admitted this at last after 23 years, and Bezymenskii published the documents to prove it.

However, the truth was that Bezymenskii's report was not the first account confirming the evidence of Hitler's suicide by poison. Years before the Bezymenskii's publication, his former student-colleague in Moscow, Elena Rzhevskaia, a novelist, had published a short story. It contained what she knew was to be one of the most dynamite secrets of the century. But at that time no one in the West could read it. Russian is not a lingua franca for most Germans and Westerners, and Rzhevskaia didn't publish as a historian in a scholarly publication that might be read by many professional historians. She actually wrote the article about the death of Hitler and the forensic research on his body in 1953, the year Stalin died. But, after long delay, the study was published in 1961, and then it appeared in a book of

short stories. Not a place where historians were likely to notice. Then, much later, she again wrote a full account of the story under a more indicative title: "The Berlin Reports." The story suggested that she couldn't tell her account during the Stalin era or even immediately after his death. The fact that Bezymenskii made his revelations in the West under the dramatic title *The Death of Adolf Hitler,* just three years after Rzhevskaia's second publication, suggests a connection between the two.

In fact, Rzhevskaia was an eyewitness to many of the events. She was a Red Army interpreter and translator of German during the autopsy of the corpses of Hitler and Eva Braun, and also during the search for the dental records which ultimately confirmed that one of the bodies recovered from the Chancellery garden was Hitler's. These events were kept secret by the Russians even after Stalin's death, so the information didn't reach the West until 1968. As a journalist, Bezymenskii certainly had Western connections. He was ideally placed to put the material in the hands of a Western publisher. However, the story was originally told by Rzhevskaia.

You have recently interviewed Rzhevskaia, the translator in Moscow. What was her real account?
Yes, I found her in Moscow and visited her. She is in her early-70s. She didn't know that Bezymenskii had written a book because before *glasnost,* she couldn't get Western books. Because of Soviet censorship, Bezymenskii knew that his Western-published book wouldn't come into the Soviet distribution system. She talks to the press about the story openly, but many journalists today still know little about the background of the Nazi his-

tory. They have yet to get it straight. Here is the basic story that Rzhevskaia told me:

On the second of May 1945, the Red Army entered the *Führerbunker*. They found the charred corpses of Goebbels and his wife Magda, and nearby they discovered a brand new grave which was covered with a small amount of earth in the Chancellery garden. They unearthed the grave, and indeed they found the remains believed to be those of Hitler and Eva Braun. The corpses were burned by petrol but not destroyed. The Soviets took them and notified Stalin in Moscow. They carried them out to a hospital at the outskirts of Berlin, a town called Buch. A few days later, a group of autopsy experts and medical specialists arrived from Moscow. On the 8th of May, the day that Germany surrendered, the autopsy was performed. A sequence of photographs were taken. The autopsy finding reports indicated that Hitler's brain was undamaged; Hitler had only one testicle; the dental work of one of the corpses matched Hitler's personal dental file which they traced to his dentist. These autopsy reports were filed "top-secret." This whole operation was, of course, ordered by Stalin. Then, they buried the remains in an unmarked grave nearby in former East Germany.

But some time later, Stalin gave a new order for another autopsy. So, again they exhumed Hitler's body leaving Eva Braun's this time, and performed another autopsy. Then, after that, the body disappeared. According to Rzhevskaia, the body was "not cremated" which meant Bezymenskii was wrong in his book. She said it was "not destroyed" at least. But no one knew where Hitler's remains have gone. They could have been buried somewhere in former East Germany or shipped to Moscow. And until today it has remained unknown. Rzhevskaia speculates that

Stalin probably kept the body hidden somewhere and died without disclosing the location. This was the story she told me in November, 1989.

The fact is, a few weeks after the second autopsy, Stalin told an American diplomat in Moscow that the body of Hitler had never been found. Also, in the summer of 1945 during the Potsdam Conference, he was telling Western journalists that Hitler had escaped to either Spain, Japan or Argentina, the Nazi allied countries.

How do you analyze Rzhevskaia's testimony and how do you speculate about Stalin's behavior and his lies?

In the last days at the *Führerbunker,* everybody was given cyanide to kill themselves, and Hitler himself tested it with his beloved dog Blondi, and it worked. The dog died instantly. So he knew the cyanide could get immediate results. A few days before Hitler's death, Benito Mussolini, Hitler's ally, was killed and his body was put on public display in a street of Milan. Hitler was perhaps terrified the same thing would happen to him. I think the poison suicide theory makes sense. At that point, Hitler's promise to his people to die like a soldier — a gunshot suicide — became less important to him. While the children of the Hitler Youth were fighting against a mass of Soviet tanks outside the bunker defending Berlin, Hitler was himself committing suicide inside the bunker. Hitler knew that Stalin wanted to capture him dead or alive, and would take revenge on him. In the final hours of his death, I'm sure Hitler was totally paranoid and his hands might have been trembling. If a bullet failed to kill him, Hitler knew that he might end up wounded and alive, captured by Stalin. That was the reason that he ordered his adjutants to burn and destroy his body after his death to make sure that wouldn't happen to him. So, I believe Hitler died by taking cyanide. Stalin was obsessed by his victory over Hitler, and for many years he knew that Hitler was dead and as a result of the autopsy, but he never admitted it or announced that Hitler was dead. Not only that, his propagandists kept suggesting that Hitler was alive and, in order to keep their mouths shut, he kept most of the witnesses of the *Führerbunker* including Hitler's civilian dentist and his dental assistants in prison in Moscow. That was the weirdest thing of all. Stalin's behavior may probably be explained as follows: He was going to use it as propaganda to claim that somebody was hiding Hitler. This information kept Westerners looking for the "non-existent Hitler." According to *Der Spiegel* magazine in 1991, Hitler's body had been kept until 1970. Now, at the end of the Cold War, Russia has finally opened up some of their wartime files, so I'm hoping the world may soon learn more clear information about Hitler's body and his relation with Stalin, and what exactly Stalin had planned. The weirdest thing I found out recently is that the former Communist Russian government had preserved the brains of Lenin and Stalin. So, maybe Hitler's brain might have been preserved.

Despite the fact that Berlin was conquered by the Red Army, why did Stalin divide the city and share it with the Western Allies? What do you speculate Stalin's next territorial ambition would have been?

By mid-1943, it became clear that Germany would lose the war. In February 1945, the conference was held between the Soviet and the Western Allies in Yalta, a city on the Black Sea, South Ukraine. The three leaders, Stalin, Churchill and Roosevelt discussed the fate of Germany. The three had earlier agreed to the division of Ger-

many and Berlin, including Austria, into zones of occupation after Nazi Germany surrendered and Hitler was overthrown. Germany would become an occupied country. Stalin and the Western Allies followed this point of the agreement.

However, Stalin thought the division would be temporary and that he would get all of Germany by undermining the Western Allies. Whatever government they set up in West Germany, the Soviet Union would soon take over the whole of Berlin and the whole of Germany. In a way, Roosevelt was very foolish. He had told Stalin that America would withdraw their army in two years. So Stalin felt that once that happened he could undermine the British and the French as well. His plan was not just speculation, he was really determined to do so. The Berlin Blockade in 1948 was an aspect of this. I found a lot of documents about how Stalin had constantly intervened in the Soviet zone of Germany right after the war. He was virtually running the whole show himself, giving orders to his foreign representatives and the German Communists. Stalin eventually intended to take over ultimately all of Western Europe as he did Czechoslovakia in 1948. In the Polish archives, I also found the same: Poland, too, was absolutely controlled by Stalin. In fact, to tell the truth, this Soviet ambition began back at the time of WW I, even during the Russian Revolution. As soon as Britain and France collapsed, the Red Army would march into Western Europe and the proletariat would be "Bolshevized."

You may recall that the Red Army invaded as far west as the Vistula in 1920. Stalin was also in a rage with General Francisco Franco of Spain because he'd facilely allied with Hitler during the Spanish Civil War from 1936 to 1939. Franco proceeded to use the revolution in Spain to take over. Furthermore, on the Pacific side of Russia, Stalin wanted a share in the occupation of Japan. I have no doubt that his final goals in 1945 when he met the American and British armies in the middle of Europe were to bring the revolution as far west and east as he could. He had to wait until they withdrew their armies. But without having a major war, this was not possible and he was very cautious about getting into another war again, because of the existence of the atomic bomb. Stalin had supreme power over the Soviet communist totalitarian regime. He was the absolute dictator. In terms of territorial ambitions and his acts against his own citizens during his 29-year dictatorship, he was just as mad as Hitler. He just didn't use gas chambers to kill people, but he was a different kind of monster.

Nazism and orthodox communism were thought to be political enemies. Those two dictators seemed to hate each other. What did the "Hitler-Stalin Non-Aggression Pact" mean?

Stalin calculated at least as early as 1939 that there would be trench warfare between Germany and the Western Allies as in WW I. If Hitler attacked Poland, the Western Allies would declare war against Germany, and the Germans and Western Allies would end up fighting each other. If it happened, he thought there would be historical breakdowns in the fighting as occurred in Russia in 1917: Stalin speculated that revolutions would occur in Western Europe just the way a revolution occurred in Russia. He prepared his plan which was originally the "Hitler-Stalin Pact" or the "Molotov-Ribbentrop Pact" (Hitler and Stalin had never met personally). It was a phony peace alliance which, according to Soviet propagandists and some historians, was to secure Russia from a Ger-

man invasion. The two dictators agreed to divide Poland for their own benefit. However, Stalin's idea was further calculated. As soon as the Germans and Western Allies were killing each other and internal order began to break down, the Red Army would march in to make a Bolshevik style revolution in the Western European countries.

But Hitler easily triumphed in the West, and as a result, Stalin was afraid that the man who made the pact with him was now going to attack him. He realized there was nobody for Hitler to fight against but him. Stalin was suddenly standing alone. Although he never trusted Hitler and knew war with Germany was inevitable, he was not fully prepared, yet. He had begun arming as fast as he could, but the Soviet Union was so backward that when the Germans did attack the Russians, they were still not ready.

What was the origin of the Cold War?

One great asset was Poland's postwar territorial borders. To understand the beginning of the Cold War is to know its history and it's a complicated one. It was originally Stalin himself who fixed Poland's present borders, the Oder-Neisse Line — river borders between Poland and Germany, without completely consulting his Western Allies. He deliberately set out to deceive them by keeping secret some of his planning. This was just one of the many issues in which Stalin regularly did just as he chose. Another aspect was, of course, his secret plan to use his Moscow trained communists to takeover first his zone of Germany, and then all the rest of it, and to use them to takeover Poland, Czechoslovakia, Hungary and others. All this information has now been documented since 1989, because of the accessibility to the former Eastern Bloc archives, on which I have worked in Berlin, Prague and Warsaw. Stalin was the one who was finally responsible for the Cold War. The Western Allies were naive at that time. Their wartime trust of the Soviets eventually turned into suspicion and changed Western willingness to cooperate with the Soviet Union into enmity toward that country.

How did Stalin gain his power compared to Hitler's ascent?

Stalin was the Soviet Communist Party Secretary under Lenin, the founder of Russian Communism, and after Lenin died in 1924 without appointing a successor, Stalin usurped control of a large part of the party apparatus. He, in effect, took control of the Leninist legacy. He slowly consolidated his power by getting rid of his rivals, purging his opponents, and then he began executing people during the 1930s through 1940s. Some sources say he might have murdered over 20 million of his own people. Stalin also disliked Jews. There were many Jews in his Communist Party circles and he killed many of them. In the last years of his life while he was ill, his doctors were all Jews and he got paranoid that the Zionist Jews were going to get him. He couldn't trust them, so he executed all his Jewish doctors. A funny story was that the only doctor he could trust was a non-Jewish animal specialist. He was under the care of a man who was not even a doctor — an animal field surgeon.

All tyrannies are insane, however, the most hilarious things about Hitler and Stalin are that these two were amazingly similar in many ways. Both were foreign born — Hitler was an Austrian and Stalin was a Georgian, both were school drop-outs, both had a grudge against Jews, both were zealously popular messianic figures in their nature, both killed tens of million of people, and both were madmen. After all, these two tyrannies were running the whole show in central Europe for much of the mid-20th century, and the world still suffers from the consequences and the aftermath of their legacies. ❖

Women's role under the Third Reich.

KONNILYN G. FEIG

American, professor of history, Holocaust researcher and author of the book *Hitler's Death Camps.* Born in Minnesota. Lives in California, USA.

You are one of a very few non-Jewish persons who has thoroughly researched the Holocaust. How did you become interested in the subject, Professor Feig?

It started with my own interest after college when I began pondering man's inhumanity to man some 35 years ago. In the beginning, I wasn't intending to write a book on the matter; it came as a result of my study and deep commitment. From the 1960s to 1980s, I traveled many times to Western Europe, West and East Germany, Poland, Czechoslovakia, Hungary, Bulgaria, Romania, Russia, Ukraine, and the Baltic states. I believe I remain the only person to have spent thoughtful time in all of Hitler's 19 official death camps. During the period, I talked to perhaps 1,000 Holocaust survivors and over 200 former SS men and Nazi officers. While I was doing that, to tell you the truth, I was jailed several times in the communist states because the state authorities suspected that I was a CIA agent or a Jew.

From my years of travel to the camps, I gained an intellectual understanding of hanging blocks, torture cells, brutality, starvation, slavery, human medical experiments, mass graves, gas chambers, crematoriums, human ash fertilizer, mattresses stuffed with human hair, lampshades and gloves made from human skin, shrunken human heads for paperweight, and so on. This wasn't just genocide. People used other human beings for medical abuse before killing them, and after slaughtering them, they used their remains. In order to study further, I mastered German and French so that I could communicate with people who were directly involved, and I could read the original materials. This is not a Jewish issue; it's an issue of human abuse and destruction, and the problem applies to everybody in the world, even today. This human destruction was well-organized, deliberate, systematic, calculated, and the magnitude of the Final Solution is incomparable to any other case in 2,000 years of human history. The goal was to destroy every vestige of several groups of people from the face of the earth — the Jews, the Gypsies, homosexuals, and undesirables. One thing was clear that Hitler, the Nazis and the SS could not have done it alone. I have been studying this issue of evil and struggling to find answers about it for most of my life. The world was silent. Its people and its leaders didn't speak out. But openness and knowledge are the only way to avoid this kind of mass abuse in the future. During the early 1960s when I started teaching about the Holocaust, I was the first person in the United States to teach the Holocaust in a non-Jewish institution.

From your years of study, how have you come to analyze the Jews, the Final Solution, and the Holocaust?

The study of the Holocaust is a controversial and painful issue for many reasons. For most Americans, it is the most fascinating and horrifying event in history. As one studies it, one becomes wiser by confronting the evil, the madness, the insanity, and the death, but it drives one to a terrible wisdom that haunts one as well. It scars you. First, the Holocaust didn't erupt out of a barbarian environment. It happened in 20th century Europe in one of the most civilized countries, and it was carried out by a people who created Beethoven, Schubert, Bach and Goethe, a highly educated nation. In any event, throughout the history of western civilization, it had been fairly simple to understand cruelty, savagery, devastation and destruction. You could always find a reason or explanation for it. But the Holocaust was something very different. Its mission was the

271

extermination of every Jew from every corner of the earth. Its single goal was that the Jews must die.

Over the centuries, the people of the western world raised the "Jewish Question." It came out of frustration, impatience, fear, and at the same time, a grudging fascination with the cultural holding power of a stubborn "chosen people." The Jews refused to cooperate with the Gentiles, it was said. No man could serve two gods, a Jew could not serve both Judaism and Christianity — a conservative and a liberal religion. As centuries passed, this Jewish question created a dangerous situation for the Jews and it resulted in irrational Jewish-hatred. To resolve the problem, in medieval times, the Jews converted to Christianity. At the turn of the century, the Jews assimilated, and after 1933 the Jews emigrated. But, after 1938 the Nazis decided that the Jews must die. Hitler and his followers demanded a "solution," so the dead Jews were the only good Jews. Hitler believed he had a divine mission to purify Germany and create a true racial community cleansed of its "bloodsuckers" — the Jews. The Final Solution for Jews was the culmination of the Jewish question.

The Final Solution was incorporated directly or indirectly into the international community, including church institutions. How do you see that aspect?

In the early stages of Nazism, Hitler pointed to the Jews as an international problem and promised his followers that, "We shall not let it rest until the question has been resolved." Once in power, Hitler intensified his denunciation against the Jews, using the forceful Nazi propaganda machine, and he successfully maneuvered anti-Semitic campaigns. The outbreak of war changed

Hitler's response to the Jewish question. He was not ready to annihilate the Jews, all the Jews — yet. In order to carry on with the war, he needed to use them at least temporarily as labor.

Even many "good folks" thought "something" should be done. For example, Carl Goerdeler, one of the opposition leaders to Hitler, thought the Jews should be sent to "an appropriate territory with acceptable physical conditions, probably in Canada or South America." Why? Because a new order for Jews "appears necessary in the entire world. It is a matter of course that the Jewish people belong to a different race." Hitler was clever in his war against the Jews. After depriving them of their civil rights and dehumanizing them, he used them for the war effort. The Third Reich could not have carried on without the labor force of the Jews. Then Hitler exterminated them but he couldn't erase 6 million Jews without massive help. As he moved across the continent of Europe, he met crowds of willing assistants in his neighboring countries. In fact, some of them introduced anti-Semitic legislation even before Hitler asked. They provided railroads and manpower for the Holocaust.

While many Jews tried to flee Germany and Europe after *Kristallnacht,* the entire international community closed its eyes: They refused to take Jews into their countries. After 1941, all the Western Allied leaders knew about it, but they did nothing. Besides this apathy, the public official attitude of the churches throughout Europe mattered a great deal. Their attitudes seldom reflected genuine Christian doctrine, but more the culture and politics of individual countries. In Austria, for example, the Catholic bishops openly welcomed Hitler. In Poland, the Catholic church spoke publicly against the Jews; in Greece, the Orthodox leaders remained silent. But in Italy, the Catholic priests acted like the rest of the Italians and aided the Jews; in Bulgaria, the Orthodox church leaders spoke up for the Jews; in the Netherlands, the Calvinist church remained passive and indifferent, while in Denmark, the Danish Lutheran church made an extraordinary effort to help Jews. And in Germany, Lutheranism remained energetically subservient to the state. There were some courageous Catholic priests, nuns and clergymen who challenged the Nazi activities, but they were also incarcerated in concentration camps and died. In the Dachau death camp, there was a larger clerical group than in any other camps. The SS made a distinction and German clergymen were treated better than Polish clergymen.

During the Weimar Republic, German women had higher positions in the work force than ever before, but the Nazi regime deprived them of this. How were women affected during the Third Reich, and what did Hitler and Himmler plan for German women in order to pursue the "Thousand-Year Reich"?

To answer these questions, we need to look at the racial policy of Hitler and Himmler to see how it affected women in particular. First of all, we need to assess the Nazi philosophy about non-Aryan women and the different steps taken to meet the problems they raised for Nazi Germany. The Nazi slogan for women was: *"Kinder, Küche, Kirche,"* — children, kitchen, church. Himmler's new racial theory that was designed to promote pure blood had to be coordinated with the new women's theory. Deterioration of the German race was caused in part by the mixture of inferior races, particularly with Jews. Thus, every effort had to be made to forbid certain marriages and to require abortion and sterilization.

Hitler, Himmler and the Nazi state were concerned about Germany's population. At the end of WW I, Germany had lost population drastically. During the Weimar Republic, which was a democratic regime, women were socially emancipated and the number of professional women increased; and as a result, the birth rate dropped sharply. The Nazis believed it was essential to induce women to return to traditional domestic roles of the good German *"Hausfrau"* (housewife). Their primary campaign was to convince people that their most important mission was the bearing of children. If Germany was to conquer the world, it would need people to settle those countries and provide the manpower.

When Hitler came to power, German economic life was out of order, and he saw unemployment as an emergency. The Nazis simply removed women from the work force to provide jobs for men. Then, the Nazis began a major campaign to change women's role in society. The woman was to become the guardian of the hearth, the bearer of children. The campaign against childlessness began when Hitler spoke of emancipation as unnatural. Goebbels said, "A woman's duty is to be attractive and to bear children. The idea is not as vulgar and old-fashioned as it might seem. A female bird makes herself beautiful for her mate and hatches her eggs for him." Under the Nazis, the noblest career for a woman was wife and mother. A woman's status and social position should depend on the number of children she produced. The family was essential to the country, so they encouraged women to marry young and stay inside the homes. They discouraged employers from hiring women. They gave families financial incentives to encourage them to have many children.

There was no woman in a leading position in the Nazi government. To the Nazis, women were basically inferior to men. They banned women from judicial and public office and most other professions, and they also reduced the number of women in higher education. Once the status of woman was diminished, she was back in the home to produce large families. For that purpose, the Nazis provided benefits for childbearing. There were financial inducements in marriage, loans, child subsidies and family allowances. To pursue the program, the Nazis introduced harsh curbs on abortion, undermined the idea of equality for women, and mounted a major struggle against homosexuals. And, they relaxed the divorce laws for childless couples. When it became clear that there were not enough men to go around, and they weren't making their goal for the population plan, they initiated a campaign that gave childbearing priority. Motherhood, not marriage, was a woman's duty to the state. Therefore, extramarital sex was encouraged, and they attempted to end the discrimination against unmarried mothers. The Nazi policy considered the family the calling of the nation. Success in the "Battle of Births" became the prerequisite for victory on other fronts.

These propagandistic measures created a cult of motherhood. When that cult was joined to a campaign to raise the quality of racial selection by developing a program of human stock breeding, they began to see the results. The Nazis now had to convince each girl to bear four children at least. They also had to encourage parents to view their daughters' illegitimate children positively. Any German female who produced a baby was entitled to benefits; the more children, the more benefits. Women in Nazi Germany were ordered to commit themselves to the battlefield

of life. The birthday of Hitler's mother became the "Day of the German Mother." Hitler decorated mothers of large families with the "German Mother's Cross": bronze for 4 children, silver for 6, and gold for 8. If there were twins, triplets or quadruplets, all the better for the state. By August 1939, three million German mothers received those decorations which entitled them to special privileges. The Nazi leaders insisted publicly that a decline of the birth rate would be more devastating than war.

So, according to the Nazi Aryan birth program, what kind of nation would it be if Germany had won the war?

After the war, there would have had to be a fundamental change in the concept of marriage. Hitler and Himmler agreed that bigamy would be the answer. And, every child who would be born in Germany would have to be Aryan. For this program in the mid-1930s, Himmler and the SS established the *Lebensborn* organization. They built centers of racial selection and human stock breeding for future German generations. The organization provided a cradle for every baby, facilities for the confinement of pregnant wives, fiancees and girlfriends of SS males. Its purpose was to enable racially-valued unmarried pregnant women to have their babies, either to raise them with state financial aid or to hand them over to the SS for adoption. Himmler took a personal interest in the entire operation. He also encouraged breast feeding. Good milk producers — mothers who breastfed their babies for a long period — received awards from Himmler. He stated that every SS man had to produce four children at the minimum, and if not, forfeit his career. A childless SS leader had the duty to adopt Aryan children. To reach the goal, the Nazi state indoctrinated the boys in the Hitler Youth and the girls in the "B.d.M." — Bund Deutscher Mädel. They were only 15 or 16 years old, and inexperienced and easy to be brainwashed. The "B.d.M." girls proved very receptive to the state message. Sexual intercourse was not for pleasure, love or affection. They were just mating to contribute to the building of the new order. Himmler stated the same to SS women whether they were in barracks or brothels. Himmler's ambition was to produce 120 million Teutons for Germany by the year 1980.

Who were the women in public under Hitler?

Some in the limelight were: Leni Riefenstahl, the glamorous film producer and a star who produced *The Triumph of the Will* and *Olympia*; Hannah Reitsch, Hitler's pilot and the first woman to win the Iron Cross; Gertrude Scholzklink, the leader of the Women's Nazi League; and Emmie Göring and Magda Goebbels. In a stunning fashion, in a nation of the "Führer Cult," it is understandable that the only real opportunities for women's leadership abilities were in the concentration camps as guards and assistants. Perhaps one of the basic sicknesses of Nazi Germany was that the Aryan woman was degraded to the point where she couldn't use any of her talents without being engaged with anti-Nazi activities or incarcerated.

What did the Nazis plan for non-Aryan women and children in the German occupied Eastern nations?

For non-Aryans, the Nazis developed a program aimed at destroying foreign nations and ethnic groups by eliminating and suppressing national characteristics. They implemented their program of genocide by kidnapping children from Eastern workers; by forcing women to get abortions and sterilizations; by evacuating enemy populations from their native lands; and by the extermination of the Jews. The Nazis considered Poland to be the most inferior of all. When they took over Poland, they demanded the dissolution of ethnic groups of about 15 million people who were living there.

For the rest of the Poles, Himmler ordered the SS to select racially-valued children to be kidnapped, brought to Germany, and raised in ignorance for the purpose of assimilation. It is estimated that the Germans kidnapped 200,000 Polish children who were considered to be the most Germanic-Aryan-looking. The Nazis found them in playgrounds, orphanages and streets, and literally snatched them. The boys were raised to become SS mercenaries, and the girls between the ages of 8 and 12 were given hormone injections to accelerate puberty and then selected as breeding women or liquidated. They were the stock of *Lebensborn* for Germany. But the Jewish women, without any exception, were to be completely extinguished. For the rest of the Poles, according to the Nazi racial policy, they formulated a policy which was the opposite of *Lebensborn,* and now Poland became *Todesborn* — a foundation of death. In Norway, Himmler found the best stock for mating between native "racially pure Aryan girls" and German soldiers. It was successful and a unique opportunity for the German Reich.

As Germany had a severe labor shortage during the war, they were still gathering Polish children for labor camps. Many little girls, who were brought to Germany to be slaves, were sterilized between the age of 3 and 7; the young boys were castrated. Only about 20,000 Polish children returned to their country after the war.

It sounds like animal breeding. What would have happened if a pregnancy resulted from an SS man and a Polish woman, or a Polish man and a German woman?

Himmler prohibited sexual intercourse between Germans and foreigners. Therefore, each case was investigated by the Nazis. The SS man would be thoroughly investigated, and a court-marshal often ordered. Unless the woman was of good Aryan stock, an abortion was performed. A male foreigner who had sexual contact with a German woman would be arrested.

If the man was racially inferior, he would be sent to a concentration camp to be hung. If he was of racially good stock, he would be subject to Germanization: their baby would be raised in *Lebensborn*. By the way, I did my own research on *Lebensborn*, and I found its major leaders are still alive and free today. In 1947, a trial was held, and the court concluded that the *Lebensborn* society was a welfare organization and a system of maternity homes. *Lebensborn* had nothing to do with the kidnapping or harming of children. Therefore, all defendants were declared "not guilty."

Now, I would like to go back to our earlier discussion, when you said you have no final answer for the Holocaust. The world is silent on this issue. If we don't know the answer, what is the lesson or do we just leave it as it is?

That is probably the hardest question to answer. Why do we not know as much as we should about it? Ever since the beginning of human existence, there has been abuse in the world. People abuse everybody else for different reasons, either racially, physically, sexually, ethnically or religiously: Blacks, children, women, homosexuals, minorities, handicapped people, Jews. This pattern of abuse has never been different over the centuries. Let's look at the social history of our own country, America. Blacks, Irish, Latinos, Chinese — they have been subdued. What I can say is that human beings seem to have an abusive nature. They tend to overpower others if they feel superior and to suppress other people who are in a weak or vulnerable position. During the years of the Holocaust, Americans were silent, our government was silent, the Vatican was silent, churches were silent, the world was silent. These were all different nations, different institutions, different individuals, but they had one thing in common: they were all Gentiles. WHY..?

Well, I have no doubt that the Christian tradition, from which I came, seriously encouraged anti-Semitism. We should acknowledge that. The Bible with which we all grew up says that the Jews killed Christ; many churches take that literally and seriously. It's serious business that the Son of God was killed. I think there is no question that theological anti-Semitism is responsible. It was encouraged by the Christian background more than by any other single factor. It would be hard to resist, especially on an unconscious level. In my view, this is a major factor for the Holocaust. The real issue is knowing or not knowing that it was occuring. Leaders and people had information then and now. So why didn't they "know" then or now? If we knew about it, then all the Christian world would have to assume responsibility. We as a nation are responsible. You can prioritize the responsibility. Within the whole National-Socialist structure, the most responsible man was Adolf Hitler, of course. Then, the SS and Nazi criminals and then their followers, the Nazi-Germans. After that, I'm willing to say the international Christian community who ignored it. Great nations like Great Britain, France, and the United States were silent and thus responsible for the widespread killing. It's not pleasant to look at it, of course. We human beings seem to be unwilling to look at anything like this because we think it's all too bloody unpleasant.

Western civilization is based on Christianity, which means, as long as Christianity continues in the western tradition, anti-Semitism will continue, and so will the Jewish problem in Christian society? Is that true?

Well, certainly the churches have tried and there has been great progress since 1945, certainly. I think one has to be accurate, and things changed a great deal after the war. Even the Catholic church officially admitted that anti-Semitism is wrong. Before the war, we were not letting any Jewish people into country clubs in the US and American Jews couldn't even get into many colleges. I think that major changes have been made. Do I still think there is religious hatred in this country? You bet I do. Of all my studies, overall,

the most intriguing thing to me is that, despite the fact Japan was allied with Nazi Germany and aggressively conducted the war, the Japanese government absolutely refused to participate in the Final Solution. Instead, they saved some Jews. My question is, does it have something to do with the absence of Christianity in Japan, perhaps...?

Japan was, and still is, outside of the world's Christian community. The Japanese are not rooted in the 2,000-year Christian heritage, so they don't understand the relationship between Christianity and Judaism. When we look at the history of Japan, they didn't have any religious or ethnic wars. The Japanese religion hasn't been affiliated with politics. The state and religion are two separated entities. Therefore, for most Japanese, when they study Western history, the ethnic hatred and violence of Christianity are difficult to comprehend. ❖

A memoir of the most important trial of the 20th century.

LORD SHAWCROSS
(formerly Sir Hartley W. Shawcross)

British, jurist and chief prosecutor at the Nuremberg Trials, former
Labor Party politician and Attorney General. Born in 1902 in Giessen,
Germany. Lives in England.

(Photo: Lord Shawcross in his London office.)

Lord Shawcross, I'm curious how you came to be born in Germany. Also, you are one of the few remaining of the WW I generation. Could you tell me about your experiences during that time?

I was born in Germany of English parents. My father was a professor of English literature at an old German university, and both he and my mother were fluent in German, and familiar with Goethe and Schiller. They were very fond of Germany and were living there when I was born. When they returned to England, I was only a month old. Although I traveled a lot, my entire life was in England. I was raised and educated in London.

I remember WW I very well, indeed. I was 12 years old when the war began. I also remember some of the air raids by German bombers. They were nothing like those during WW II, but they were still frightening. Occasionally, the airplanes came in broad daylight, and sometimes zeppelins came at night. I remember seeing a zeppelin brought down in flames one night. One day I saw a squadron of 15 or 20 planes come flying straight toward my college. The big bombers were flying very low over our building. We thought we might get hit. But they turned away. It was lucky we didn't get attacked. At that time England didn't have any defense against daylight raids, there was no fighter aircraft or gunfire. So the Germans had great success and did a certain amount of damage. The air raids continued on and off throughout the war until the end. In the last year of the war, I was in the officers' training corps and expected to go into the air force if the war continued. But fortunately it came to an end.

After the war there was the Treaty of Versailles. How did you see the treaty? Was it unfair to the Germans? And during the postwar years, how was England's relationship with Germany?

The Germans thought the treaty was unfair. It deprived them of their colonies and imposed heavy liabilities on them in the form of reparations. They lost a lot of their land in Europe and this went on until Hitler came to power. It was always a source of grievance that these conditions had been imposed on them by the victors. But that's what happens in war. The Germans started the war quite unnecessarily and built up a large war machine with which they hoped to conquer Europe. They were punished for it. The Versailles Treaty was indeed very strong punishment for them. But if it had been a wiser treaty, it might not have given rise to the great resentment that helped the Germans unite under Hitler's leadership. During the 1920s after the war, however, relations between England and Germany improved a great deal. The two governments exchanged ambassadors again, and we had a perfectly normal relationship. There were more English tourists in Germany than German tourists in England, but we established a friendly connection despite the constant grievances about the harsh terms of the Versailles Treaty.

Things began to deteriorate seriously when Hitler arrived on the scene. We didn't fully realize that Hitler was not only building up the military, but that he was intent on more. When he invaded the Ruhr, which was German territory that had been taken away under the Versailles Treaty, he really expressed the sense of injustice the Germans felt about the harsh terms of the Versailles Treaty. He demonstrated Germany's military strength and when no effective steps were taken by other countries, he took it as permission to go ahead. This was a clear indication that he was intent on war and a very dangerous figure.

Before Germany entered the war, what kind of information were English journalists reporting about Hitler and the development of the Nazi movement, and what was the public reaction in England? Why did Mr. Chamberlain's peace mission with Hitler fail?

A lot of information was coming out about the growth of the Nazi regime, their increasing hold on Germany, the extent to which the Nuremberg laws were penalizing the Jews and to the extent that they realized this, the British people were shocked. But we were then, as we still are, a very insular nation. Germany was thought to be a long way away and we didn't realize the great threat the developing German policy posed for us until later. At first, we didn't realize the extremely warlike intentions Hitler had against the rest of Europe. When the crisis occurred in the Sudetenland with Czechoslovakia and the *Anschluss* with Austria, we were not militarily strong enough to oppose it.

Unfortunately, the British and the French took no adequate measures from a military point of view to defend themselves. Mr. Chamberlain made peace with Hitler in Munich genuinely believing, I think, that he had secured a real and lasting peace. He obviously realized we weren't in a military position of readiness to fight against Hitler: We had a very small air force, a tiny navy, and we couldn't possibly have entered the fighting in 1938. He knew the only way was to make the best terms he could to maintain peace in Europe. He was misled in regard to Hitler's ultimate plans, and he thought he had secured peace in our time with the agreement he made in Munich, though it was a very shameful agreement in a way. But Hitler didn't have the slightest intention of sticking to the terms to which he had

agreed, and he was simply waiting for a more convenient time to start conquering Europe.

There was no doubt that he intended to extend the boundaries of Germany, particularly to the east because he said the Germans needed more *Lebensraum* (living space), but he was really out to dominate all of Europe, if not the world. In that early stage, we didn't entirely understand the tyranny he was imposing on Germany, particularly for the Jewish people. Gradually, this came to be appreciated as refugees came over to England to seek sanctuary, which we liberally granted, although some people in England were anti-Semitic, and believed it was necessary to have a strong government without much talk of democracy. We had our own fascists in this country who supported the Nazis and Hitler, but they were not numerous. The rest of the people were either indifferent to Hitler or were frightened of him.

After the war, you were a chief prosecutor at the Nuremberg Trials. How were they carried out?

Yes, I was an official leader of the British delegation. The Allies decided that there would be a formal trial of the major war criminals. In the last stage of the war, the Allies knew that Germany would be defeated and that there would be a major change in Germany. There were discussions and debates on this matter and a great deal of disagreement about whether we should have a formal trial or not. Churchill wrote to his Foreign Secretary Anthony Eden: "There is no doubt that this is probably the greatest and most horrible crime ever committed in the whole history of the world, and it has been done by scientific machinery by nominally civilized men in the name of a great state. It is quite clear that all concerned who may fall into our hands, including the people who only obeyed orders by carrying out the butcheries, should be put to death after their association with the murders has been proved."

For a long time, Churchill was in favor of the course of summary execution. But on the other hand, President Roosevelt favored a legal process which would investigate the full nature of the Nazi regime and the guilt of the Nazi leaders. The Soviet Union claimed atrocities of Russian POWs that were committed by German troops. Moreover, in the United States, American leaders argued further over responsibility and the question of German war crimes. Henry Morgenthau Jr., Secretary of the US Treasury, was bitter at the State Department for its bureaucratic failure to save Jews. He proposed a plan of political and economic destruction and industrial dismantlement for postwar Germany: It was called the "Morgenthau Plan." This was strongly opposed within the US Cabinet as an emotional approach, especially by Secretary of State Cordell Hull and Secretary of War Henry L. Stimson. Lieutenant Colonel Murray C. Bernays and Colonel Mickey Marcus were originators of the basic trial concept. They agreed that retribution must not appear to be a Judaic act of revenge. The Morgenthau Plan was abandoned. In the end, all agreed that summary execution of war criminals could never serve as a substitute for justice. The American government firmly concluded in favor of a fair trial before an international tribunal. At first, the British statesmen had strong objections. Churchill and his Foreign Secretary, Anthony Eden, suggested execution without trial for Hitler, Goebbels and Göring when they captured them. Lord Chancellor John Simon agreed. The Russians didn't object to a trial, but they had their own ways and expressed reservations about the

form such a trial should take. General de Gaulle for the Free French also agreed to the judicial process. Eventually, in the last months of the war the final decision was reached that the Allies would hold trials.

By that time, I became the Attorney General in England. It was my responsibility to cooperate with the Americans in particular and the French and Russians in setting up these trials. In due course, very quickly, they were set up in Nuremberg — in the city where the mass rallies took place and the Nazi shrine was set up — so it was quite symbolic. The trials depended almost entirely upon documentary evidence — written materials, personal diaries, taped records, photographs, newsreel films and archives. The Germans were very methodical in keeping records of everything that happened. When war came Germany collapsed more quickly than people had expected, they neglected to destroy their archives, and the Americans managed to get most of them.

As we translated these archives, we realized they formed a very serious case against the Nazi leaders who had been captured. It not only implicated the Nazi regime but it also revealed Stalin's tyranny of this century. His tyranny led to the unjust murder of millions of people. The historical records which had been in the possession of the Russians are now being made available, and a lot more evidence is coming out. It's confirming what we have for a long time realized to be truth, that Stalin's regime was also basically an evil regime. The difference between these two tyrannies was that Hitler was more deeply inspired by insane hatred of Jews than was Stalin.

So, the trials had begun after the war and went on throughout 1946. Did you have enough time to collect all the evidence you needed?

281

How were the indictments and prosecutions conducted?

The Americans were very good at this, very efficient and had all the latest equipment. They had collected hundreds of thousands of documents, which they had processed and translated and which established the brutal nature of the Nazi regime and their crimes against humanity. The Armistice was in May 1945. The issues surrounding the forthcoming trials were discussed at a special meeting among the foreign ministers of the Big Four in San Francisco during the founding conference of the United Nations. That was shortly after Hitler committed suicide at his Berlin bunker, but at that time, the negotiators didn't know Hitler was dead, or to be precise, only the Russians knew, but they didn't tell. A total of 28 prosecutors were chosen. Among them were Robert H. Jackson, Associate Justice of the Supreme Court of the United States, Murray C. Bernays, Sidney S. Alderman and Thomas Dodd. They were appointed by President Truman — Roosevelt was dead by that time. Sir David Maxwell-Fyfe, Lord Justice Geoffrey Lawrence and myself were British representatives appointed by Churchill, and there were General Lola T. Nikitchenko, Vice-President of the Supreme Court of the Soviet Union, and Judge Robert Falco, the French delegate.

The Allies recovered all the records of Nazi high-ranking ministers, generals and governors, official and personal files, a mass of paper weighing nearly 500 tons. All this written evidence was brought together to a special center and items were sorted, screened, registered, translated and duplicated, and submitted to the prosecution members for selection and evaluation. The site of the trial was the Palace of Justice in Nuremberg, where Hitler had issued his infamous "Nuremberg Racial Laws" in 1935. The trials started in October 1945. The indictments and accusations were divided into the following sectors: *Anschluss* — invasion of Austria; *Kristallnacht* — plot against Jews; Sudetenland — assault against Czechoslovakia; invasion of Poland; violation of Hitler-Stalin Pact; Operation Barbarossa — invasion of Russia; *Einsatzgruppen* — murder of Jews; Final Solution of the Jewish Question — extermination of millions of European Jewry, Gypsies and others; invasion of France and other western countries; slave labor — violation of human labor in occupied territories; medical experiments on prisoners; murder and ill treatment of POWs both Russians and Allies; and more.

What follows are the names of leading defendants and the sentences imposed on them by International Military Tribunal:

1) **Hermann Göring** — founder of the Gestapo, Commander-in-Chief of the Luftwaffe and controlling body of the German war economy, and Hitler's successor designate. He was regarded as the most powerful Nazi leader next to Hitler — sentence: DEATH.

2) **Rudolf Hess** — Reich Minister without Portfolio and Deputy of the Führer. He shared imprisonment in the Landsberg Prison with Hitler in 1924 after the failed Munich *Putsch*. He remained Hitler's closest confidante until 10th May 1941, when he set out on his famous solo flight to Scotland which seemed to be a self-imposed peace mission — sentence: LIFE IMPRISONMENT.

3) **Joachim von Ribbentrop** — Foreign Minister, Ambassador to the United Kingdom and Foreign Policy Advisor to Hitler — sentence: DEATH.

4) **Robert Ley** — Leader of the German Labor Front, Manager of the Nazi Party Organization and Joint Organizer of the Central Inspection for the Care of Foreign Workers — He committed suicide while in custody.

5) **Field Marshal Wilhelm Keitel** — Chief of Staff of the High Command of the Armed Forces — sentence: DEATH.

6) **Ernst Kaltenbrunner** — Chief of Himmler's internal and Reich Security Head Office — sentence: DEATH.

7) **Alfred Rosenberg** — the leading Nazi philosopher, Reich Minister for the occupied Eastern Territories. He looted art treasures and property in occupied territories — sentence: DEATH.

8) **Hans Frank** — Governor General for the annexed Polish territories — sentence: DEATH.

9) **Wilhelm Frick** — Reich Minister of Interior and Protector of Bohemia and Moravia. Plenipotentiary General for the Reich Administration — sentence: DEATH.

10) **Julius Streicher** — the publisher of the notorious newspaper *Der Stürmer.* He never held a government post — sentence: DEATH.

11) **Wilhelm Funk** — Minister of Economy Plenipotentiary for War Economy, President of the Reichsbank — sentence: LIFE IMPRISONMENT.

12) **Hjalmar Schacht** — President of the Reichsbank, financial expert and Plenipotentiary for War Economy — ACQUITTED.

13) **Grand Admiral Karl Dönitz** — Commander of Submarine Arm, Commander-in-Chief of the Navy — sentence: TEN YEARS IMPRISONMENT.

14) **Grand Admiral Erich Raeder** — Commander-in-Chief of the Navy since the Weimar Republic and retained under Hitler — sentence: LIFE IMPRISONMENT.

15) **Baldur von Schirach** — Leader of the Hitlerjugend and a member of the Reich government — sentence: TWENTY YEARS IMPRISONMENT.

16) **Fritz Sauckel** — *Gauleiter* of the Thuringian government, Plenipotentiary General for the Utilization of Manpower — sentence: DEATH.

17) **General Alfred Jodl** — Chief of the Operations Staff of the Wehrmacht Command — sentence: DEATH.

18) **Martin Bormann** — Head of the Party Chancery and Secretary to the Führer (tried in absentia; he escaped from Hitler's bunker but he was believed to be alive at the time of the trial) — sentence: DEATH.

19) **Franz von Papen** — Reich Chancellor in the last year of the Weimar Republic who played an important role helping Hitler to become Chancellor, Ambassador to Austria and Turkey — sentence: ACQUITTED.

20) **Arthur Seyss-Inquart** — Reich Governor of Austria after *Anschluss,* Reich Commissioner for the Occupied Netherlands — sentence: DEATH.

21) **Albert Speer** — Hitler's architect, Reich Minister for Armaments and War Production — sentence: TWENTY YEARS IMPRISONMENT.

22) **Constantin von Neurath** — a career diplomat, Reich Protector of Bohemia and Moravia — sentence: FIFTEEN YEARS IMPRISONMENT.

These who received death sentences were all hanged on October 16, 1946. In addition to these individuals, hundreds of other names from other organizations in the Nazi cabinet were listed: the Leadership Corps of the Nazi Party, the SS men and women, the Gestapo, the SA, the General Staff and High Command of the Armed Force. Goebbels committed suicide in Hitler's bunker before being captured. Himmler fled but took cyanide at his capture. Towards the end of the war, every German leader had cyanide capsules available because they knew they would be defeated. Göring, however, stayed on and went through the whole of the trial. He made a great impression. As a man of outstanding personality, he stood above everyone else in the dock and dominated the court, which was very impressive. We all realized he was a very intelligent and powerful man, and the most interesting figure among the others. But he had obviously made up his mind. After he was sentenced to death, he, too, committed suicide a few hours before the execution.

Overall, how did you understand the minds of those Nazi leaders?

They all had different motives. Some enjoyed the power, some believed that it was important to preserve the purity of the German race, and were motivated by the belief that Jews were contaminating the Caucasian race and ought to be eliminated.

Some of them believed in the leadership of Hitler and had been inspired by Hitler. They realized he had built Germany up from being a collapsed state into a very powerful and influential nation, so they supported him. And some were simply ignorant or didn't want to know about some of the terrible things that had been done by their government, like the concentration camps. They were convicted of those crimes of which there was no doubt, but also the crimes of common murders in the camps, such as shooting Jews and prisoners and so on. I was personally shocked, of course. In Britain, people knew the basic philosophy of Nazism because Hitler had written it all down in his book, *Mein Kampf.* But we were certainly shocked at the enormity of his crimes — the concentration camps and their methods of killing people. As war went on, naturally, we heard of Jews being deported from France, Belgium, the Netherlands, and other countries where people were conquered by the Germans. However, we were astonished by the extent of the written evidence that proved it all; it made our task of prosecuting much easier.

We were convinced that the SS men and women were the most brutal thugs employed to do murderous work. There is no word to describe Nazi atrocities; it was indeed much worse than we expected. Cases of human abuse and medical experiments on prisoners went beyond the imagination. We were all shocked to see some of the evidence which was exhibited in the courtroom during the trials. For example, a preserved-shrunken-head of a prisoner was used as a paperweight at the Buchenwald concentration camp; there was a lampshade made out of tattooed human skin; tanned human-skin handbags and gloves. We were all horrified. All the defendants attempted to say that they were obeying orders. Though they did not like it they were forced to do it. But this argument no longer held legal validity. The idea of obeying orders without question is endemic in the army, but this, of course, was quite outside the rules of ordinary warfare. The defendants were either brutal themselves, or were misled by their leadership or were afraid of disobeying the orders they were given, and consequently, they did do the most brutal things.

I'm afraid that in a war on this scale, when people realize their own lives are at stake, brutal things are done on both sides, and I don't deny for a moment that some crimes were committed by the British as well. I think we were wrong in bombing Dresden and Hamburg — that's my personal opinion. But you'll find in any bitter war like this one that these terrible things can happen. We now see what is happening in former Yugoslavia. Sometimes war brings out the best qualities in people, but sometimes it brings out the worst. With war on this scale, terrible things happened.

Despite the initial disagreement at first among the Allies over whether they should have the trials or not, do you believe today that it was worth it?
Yes, I think the Nuremberg Trials were useful particularly in that it reversed the history of the war and the events leading up to it. The Germans, in their methodical way, were keeping nearly all the historical documents instead of destroying them, and the Americans had processed them efficiently. Any exploration of what had happened might have taken many years or could never have been done. In this respect, Roosevelt's proposal was absolutely right. Because of this documentation, the German people accepted the fact that the Nazi leadership had been an evil regime. As far as the German people were concerned, the trial was something of political shock therapy. How much had the ordinary German citizens known of the Nazi crimes during the war? People at least acknowledged that they are a very different people from the people they were before and during the war. I would say the trial was highly successful in forging such a unique situation. The Judgement of the Nuremberg Trial has created fundamental legal principles, which were later formulated by the International Law Commission of the United Nations in a "Draft Code on Offenses against the Peace and Security of Mankind." "Crime Against Peace" was accepted in the Draft Code to constitute specific international crimes. I think the trial, which arose in exceptional circumstances, contributed to an extraordinary degree to the development of a progressive concept of justice in international jurisprudence. ❖

"Prosecution of Nazi Crimes is a never ending task."

WILLI DRESSEN

German, director of the Investigation of Nazi Crimes and author of the book *Those were the Days*. Born in 1935 in Eschweiler, Germany. Lives in Germany.

(Photo: Mr. Dressen in his office by a poster of the city of Ludwigsburg.)

Mr. Dressen, please explain what sort of work you do here in your office?

We are in the office for clarification of Nazi Crimes. Our task is to do the preliminary investigations of former Nazi murderers, primarily to find former SS men and officers. This office was founded in 1958 and is the only bureau for this sort of investigation in Germany. This institute is funded by all regional administrations of justice of the Federal Republic of Germany to deal only with Nazi crimes. We closely cooperate with the Simon Wiesenthal Center of the United States and several other national and international organizations and institutions.

At the end of the war and after the Nuremberg Trials were over, Germany had supposedly been "de-Nazified," so Nazi murderers were no longer investigated because they had supposedly been cleared out. No German prosecutor or state attorney investigated these crimes, because after the war Germany had no full competence to do so, and most of the crimes were committed outside Germany, in the former German-occupied territories under Nazi rule, and not within the areas of German state jurisdiction. At first, nobody knew exactly what had happened. As years passed by, it became clear that serious war crimes had been committed by SS-SD, police or army members, and therefore this special investigation office was set up. We first had to trace the location where the crimes were performed, who the perpetrators were and where they live now, then we prepared a report and transmitted our records to the state attorney's office in the city and area where the accused resides.

Together with Ernst Klee and Volker Riess, you recently published a book titled *The Good Old Days* (*Schöne Zeiten* in German). But later you changed the title to *Those were the Days*. Why did you decide on such titles for this kind of book?

The title of the book came from a wartime photo album which was kept by the deputy commandant of the Treblinka concentration camp named Kurt Franz. This book is a collection of personal letters, diaries, confidential records and documents written by some of the executioners, perpetrators and bystanders during the Holocaust from 1939 to 1945. It also includes postwar court evidence and deposition from witnesses. It begins with the early stages of killing Jews by the *Einsatzgruppen* in the Baltic states and covers the SS in Auschwitz and other concentration camps in the German-occupied Eastern Territories. This is a horrible book to read. It's also illustrated by hundreds of photographs taken by German soldiers and bystanders at the execution sites. Also, there are diaries and letters of these people sent to their families, their wives, children, parents and friends, in which they describe what they saw. Such recorded evidence was strictly prohibited by the security service of the Reich at the time. This is the undeniable evidence of the massacres committed by Nazi members of the SS, SD and the Army in Poland, Lithuania, Byelorussia, Latvia, Estonia and the Ukraine. My book documents images of gruesome and grisly killings witnessed by German soldiers, perpetrators, observers, and local officials as well. These people described in chilling detail the daily executions using disturbingly sentimental words such as "achievements" or they took photographs as "souvenirs." Snapshots of the *Einsatzgruppen* executioners or camp guards show informal gatherings, musical soirees, drinking and laughing together at the end of the day after they had "accomplished" their day's work. They described their routine killing of Jewish people as enjoyable social activities, as having a good time, calling it the "Good Old Days." It's horrifying and instructive, so we won't be allowed to forget that there were times that Jews were beaten to death in broad daylight in Lithuania, and no one intervened to protect them. Furthermore, in the Eastern European countries during the German occupation, the brutality was the worst.

Following are some excerpts from my book. An ordinary German soldier who was stationed in Lithuania wrote: "Each time when a Jewish victim was beaten to death in the town square, local people clapped with excitement as if they were watching a football game and then they sang the national anthem." Another Wehrmacht soldier wrote in his diary: "While watching a public mass slaughter, I myself joined in. I borrowed a gun and started shooting Jewish children as they ran. It was like shooting birds as a sport game."

In Latvia, Jews were carried by lorry near the beach, forced to walk to the edge of a pit, and then shot by the firing-squad made up of Latvian auxiliary police. A score of German spectators were free to watch the execution. In Babi Yar, near Kiev, Ukraine, 33,771 Jews were shot dead in two days. One of the marksmen remarked: "It's almost impossible to imagine what nerves of steel it took..." Then, at the end of 1941, gas-vans were introduced as a new method of killing. A gassing specialist who worked in exterminating mentally sick and handicapped people in the Reich, for the so-called "euthanasia program," confessed: "The men in charge of the *Einsatzgruppen* in the East were complaining increasingly that the mobile firing squads could not cope with the mass shooting indefinitely. I was transferred to Riga, Latvia, as an inspector for the *Einsatzwagen* (mobile gas-

vans). I had to ensure that mass killings were done in the lorries before arriving at the pits." These killings were carried out in hundreds of cities and hundreds of thousands of Jews were slaughtered even before the full scale of the Final Solution for Jews began after the Wannsee Conference.

The uniqueness of this book is that every fact is documented by German eye-witnesses, not by Jewish survivors. This book was first published in Germany and has been translated into English, and released in the rest of the world. It reveals startling new evidence. It's a response to the revisionists, historians, and all the others who doubt or deny the historic truth of the Holocaust.

From these testimonies, what is the ultimate message of the Holocaust?

I would like to point out the statements by Rudolf Höss, Commandant of the extermination camp at Auschwitz, as the most striking evidence of all. Here are the excerpts:

"I was ordered to report to Himmler in Berlin... where he told me roughly the following: The Führer has ordered the solution to the Jewish question in Europe. There are already several so-called extermination camps in the General Government ... The efficiency of these camps is, however, poor and they cannot be expanded. I myself visited the Treblinka camp in 1942 ... in order to find out more about the conditions there. The exterminations were carried out by the following method: There were chambers the size of a small room which were supplied with gas from car engines by connecting pipes. This process was unreliable. As the engines had been taken from old vehicles and would often not start.

"For all the reasons described above, explained Himmler, the only possibility of extend-

288

ing these installations ... lay in Auschwitz; first because it was situated at a junction of four train lines, and second because the area was sparsely populated and the camp could be completely isolated. For these reasons he had decided to move the extermination program to Auschwitz and I had to set to work to carry this out immediately. He told me I had four weeks to prepare precise building plans ... He also told me that this assignment was so difficult and of such importance that he could not entrust simply anyone with it.. I thus received clear instructions to carry out the extermination of the transports delivered by the Reich Security Head Office.. there were also transports of Russian POWs coming in from the area under the control of the Gestapo regional headquarters... which, on Himmler's orders, the written instructions of the Gestapo chief in Auschwitz... had to be exterminated. As the new crematorium installations were not ready until 1942, the prisoners had to be gassed in temporary gas chambers and then incinerated in graves dug in the ground. I shall describe the way the gassings proceeded:

"Two old farmhouses which were situated in an isolated spot in Birkenau had been made airtight and were fitted with heavy wooden doors. The transports themselves were unloaded at a side entrance of Birkenau. Those prisoners fit to work were selected and taken to the camps. All luggage was removed and later taken to the stores. The others, who were to be gassed, were marched over to the gassing installations, which were about one kilometer away. The sick and disabled were taken there by lorry. When transports arrived during the night, they were all taken over by lorry. They all had to undress behind walls made out of brushwood outside the farmhouses. On the doors was the sign 'Disinfection Room.'

The *Unterführer* on duty told people, through an interpreter, to make sure they knew where they had left their things so that they could find them straight away after they had been deloused.

"In this way uneasiness was prevented right from the start. The people, now undressed, then went into the rooms. Each had a capacity of 200 to 300 people. The doors were bolted and two cans of Zyklon-B were sprinkled through the hatches into each room. The Zyklon-B was a crystalline mass of prussic acid. It took between 3 to 10 minutes to take effect, depending on the weather conditions. After half an hour, the doors were opened and the bodies were taken out by commandos of prisoners, who worked there permanently. They were then burned in trenches. Before incineration, gold teeth and rings were removed. Firewood was piled up among the bodies and when there was a pile of about one hundred bodies in the grave, the wood was lit with rags drenched in paraffin. When the fire caught, the rest of the bodies were thrown on. The fat which was collecting on the bottom of the trenches was poured back on to the fire with buckets. This helped to accelerate the burning process, in wet weather particularly. The incineration took 6 to 7 hours. The stench of the burnt bodies reached the camp itself when the wind was blowing from the west. After the trenches had been cleared the charred remains were crushed. This was done on a cement slab with wooden pounders. These remains were then taken to a remote part of the Vistula by lorry and poured into the river. After the new large incineration plants had been set up the following process was used: In 1942, once the first 2 large crematoria were ready (the other two were ready 6 months later), the mass transports from France, Belgium, Holland and Greece began. During that period the following procedure was adopted: The trains would run on to a specially-built three-track ramp exactly midway between the crematoria, the effect store and the Birkenau camp. The selection of those fit to work took place directly on the ramp. This was also where luggage was deposited. Those who were fit to work were taken to the various camps and those who were to be exterminated to one of the new crematoria.

"Once there, the latter went into a large underground room to undress. This room was fitted out with benches and facilities for hanging up clothes. Here, too, it was explained to people through interpreters that they were going to be taken to be bathed and deloused and that they should make sure they knew where they had left their clothes. Then, still underground, they went into the next room, which was equipped with water pipes and shower attachments, creating the impression that it was a shower-room. Right up to the end, two *Unterführer* had to stay in the room to prevent people from getting worried.

"Sometimes prisoners did realize what was happening. This was particularly true for the transports from Belsen, as most of them were originally from the East and knew that when the trains reached Upper Silesia, they were almost certainly being led to their death. With transports from Belsen, security measures were stepped up and to prevent mayhem, the transport was divided into smaller groups to be sent to the individual crematoria. SS men would form a dense human chain and push anyone who resisted into the gas chambers by force. However, this happened rarely as the procedure was made easier by the measures that had been taken to calm down the transport.

"I particularly remember one example: a transport from Belsen had arrived and after about

two-thirds were in the gas chamber — they were mostly men — a revolt broke out among the last third who were still in the undressing room. Three or four SS-*Unterführer* came into the room with their weapons in order to get them to hurry up and undress... As they came in, the lighting cables were torn out and they were attacked, one was stabbed to death and all their weapons were seized. It was now completely dark in the room and there was a wild shoot-out between the guards posted at the entrance and the prisoners inside. When I reached the scene, I ordered the doors to be shut and the gassing of the first two-thirds to be completed, and then I went into the undressing room with some guards with hand torches, and forced the prisoners into a corner. They were then led out one by one and shot on my orders with a small-calibre weapon in a room next to the crematorium.

"Very often women would hide their small children in their underclothes and their clothing, leave them in the undressing room when they went to the gas chambers. The prisoner detachment which carried out the incineration and was in the command of the SS would have to search the clothes and if they found any such children, send them later into the gas chamber. After half an hour, the electric ventilation was started up and the bodies were taken by hoist into the incinerators situated above the gas chambers.

"The incineration of about 2,000 people in 5 ovens took about 12 hours. In Auschwitz, there were 2 installations, each with 5 double ovens, and 2 each with 4 fairly large ovens. In addition, there was also the temporary installation as described above. The second temporary installation was destroyed. All clothing and personal effects were sorted in the effects store by a prisoner detachment which worked there permanently and also lived there.

"The valuables were sent to the Reichsbank in Berlin every month. The clothing was first cleaned and then taken to armaments factories for the workers from the East and resettlers working there. Gold taken from teeth was melted down and taken once a month to the *Sanitätsamt* of the Waffen-SS.... The highest number of gassings in one day was 10,000 prisoners. That was the most that could be carried out in a day with the available facilities."

Regarding the pursuit of the war criminals, could you tell me more about what happened after the Nuremberg Trials?

After the Trials at the International Military Tribunal in Nuremberg were over, the major Nazi leaders had been dealt with. The Americans, British, French, and other foreign courts held further military tribunals. Each of the Allies took responsibility for the trials against former Nazis in the territorial zone they controlled. Up to the middle of 1949, 12 more trials were held by the American Military Tribunal in Nuremberg. These were: Doctors who engaged in the "euthanasia program" and in medical experiments on human beings; SS Economic Administration Officers, who were responsible for running the concentration camps, exploiting slave labor and plundering foreign property; Senior executives of "IG Farben" for war aggression, indulging in economic plundering and exploiting the labor of POWs, deportees and concentration camp inmates, particularly in Auschwitz; generals who shot hostages in the Balkans; against the office of the "Reich Commissar for strengthening the German Race" in charge of the *Lebensborn* organization — kidnapping racially suitable children from occupied territories

to Germany; the ministers and state secretaries, and senior SS officers in the case of the "Wilhelmstrasse Case" — war crimes and crimes against humanity committed in their sphere of activity; and more. Also, the American military tribunals conducted the trials of concentration camp guards at Dachau, Buchenwald, Mauthausen, Mittelbau-Dora and Flossenburg.

All together, they instituted the accusations of a total of 1,941 persons and 1,517 of them were sentenced: 324 to death, 247 to life imprisonment and 946 to different terms of imprisonment. The rest were either acquitted or discharged. The trials held by British Military Tribunals tried the criminals not only in the British zone of occupied Germany, but also in Italy and the Netherlands. Besides field marshals, colonels and generals, they also tried concentration camp guards at Auschwitz, Bergen-Belsen and Natzweiler. Of a total of 1,085 accusations, 240 were given death sentences. Those who got imprisonment terms had their sentences mostly reduced later, and in 1957, the last Allied prisoners were released.

The trials held by the French Military Tribunals were carried out in the same way as the others, against the concentration camp guards at Neue Bremme and various Baden-Wurtembergian subsidiary camps of the concentration camp Natzweiler. The total number of those accused was unknown; however, 2,107 persons were convicted and 104 were sentenced to death. In addition, in French North Africa, they tried at least 1,918 German nationals.

The number of legal proceedings instituted by the Soviet Union was much higher than those of the Western occupied powers. According to Russian statements, tens of thousands of Germans, including ordinary soldiers, were sent to penitentiaries, prisons and concentration camps right after the war. Those convicted were sentenced up to 25 years imprisonment and sent to Siberia for hard labor. As of May 1950, 13,523 prisoners were serving tribunal sentences.

In former East Germany, they prosecuted more than 12,800; 118 got death sentences, 231 got life imprisonments and the others got varying prison terms. Along with the ill-famed "Waldheim-Processes," 3432 interns were sentenced; 32 received death sentences and many others had life sentences. Other trials of Germans by foreign courts were held in Belgium, Denmark, Luxembourg, the Netherlands and Norway; 507 persons were accused and 64 of them received death sentences. In Poland, by 1978, a total of 5,358 German nationals were sentenced for their involvement in Nazi crimes. We don't know the number of Germans sentenced in Yugoslavia or Czechoslovakia. In Austria, according to a publication by the Ministry of Justice (from 1945 to 1972), there were 13,607 persons convicted, and 43 of them got death sentences and 23 life imprisonment. As regards Israel, Adolf Eichmann, SS *Obersturmbannführer,* was tried by the court of Jerusalem and sentenced to death on 31st May 1962.

How many more former SS men are still at large without having been prosecuted?

Nobody can say for sure how many former SS men are alive today in the world. Those who haven't died must be 70 or 80 years of age and more. Presumably, many have died before we were able to prosecute them. We still try to find them, but as the years pass, it's not easy and the charges to find them have diminished greatly. We had addresses of suspected SS men who live in South America or in the Arab states, and they

were not extradited. When we requested the extraditions from those countries the requests were rejected or the suspects disappeared. The problem is that without cooperation of the authorities in those countries, it's impossible to proceed with the investigations. For example, we found once a man named Walter Rauff who was chief of the technical department of the main security office dealing with the construction of the gas-vans. He was living in Santiago, Chile. But the government of Chile refused to extradite him, probably, we suspected because he was an advisor for the Chilean Secret Service. Our team of prosecutors, judges and advocates flew over to Chile. Rauff testified voluntarily against his former subordinates who were condemned to long years of imprisonment. He died there in 1984. One who was extradited from Brazil to Germany for trial was Franz Stangl, former commander of Treblinka. Except for a few cases, such as that of Claus Barbie, known as the "butcher of Lyon," who was tried in France, the majority of cases were carried out in Germany.

Since we opened this office in 1958, and up to 1992, we have investigated 103,823 NS suspects. The courts successfully condemned only 6,487 of them; 12 of them were given death sentences, 163 lifetime imprisonments, and 6,197 prison terms. In many cases suspects were already dead or not identified through false information. Some changed their names and it was too difficult to trace them, and some suspects were too old to stand trial. So we had to close many cases. They were accused not only of killing Jews, but also Gypsies, lunatics, invalids, slaves, communists, homosexuals, and foreign opponents, those who were in the German Resistance. When I joined this office in 1967, we had a staff of 125, but today we only have 28 people with only 7 prosecutors. As the years pass, fewer and fewer NS-criminals are alive and more and more are old and ill, and therefore unable to stand trial.

These crimes were committed a half century ago and all the NS criminals and the Jewish survivors are getting old. The faces of the Nazis have changed and the memories of their victims have faded as well. The case of "Ivan the Terrible," misidentified as John Demjanjuk, a retired auto worker in Cleveland, USA, resulted in the most recent such controversy. How long should such hunting for aged people be carried on? Today, with the reunification, you have to deal with accusations against former Stasi members and problems with neo-Nazi youths who are active now. Punishing these people is, in a way, more important than those who committed crimes some 50 years ago. What do you think?

Yes, we have received a number of such criticisms. People say that it has been too long now, but even 5 years after the war people said the same thing. However, it's a very important part of German history and we cannot close the cases down. We

are determined to keep finding the NS criminals until the last one dies. It's a never-ending task, really. It isn't so important to condemn a man to jail who is 80 years old, but it's important to show that no man should walk away after having committed such crimes. If an SS man is convicted, we simply cannot set him free even if he is over 80 years old. He must go to jail provided that he's not too fragile and ill. What is more important is that nobody can hide himself behind the protective shield of a criminal and perverse state. But the most important fact is that in every preliminary proceeding and process the pains and injuries of so many unhappy victims come to light and are documented, and thus do not remain without history. I agree, after the Berlin Wall fell, we have more problems especially with neo-Nazis. Not all of them are young, by the way, and their activities are growing very rapidly. Extreme right-wing parties get more votes now in the elections. I never thought this could happen two years ago at the time of reunification. But, it's all part of German history and we all have to deal with it. In this connection, looking back at the crimes of the NS-time can only be helpful. ❖

Why did Japanese save Jewish refugees?

DAVID KRANZLER

German Jew, professor of the Social Science Division of the City
University of New York and author of the book *Japanese, Nazis and
Jews*. Born in 1930 in Würzburg, Germany. Lives in New York, USA.

(Photo: Prof. Kranzler in his home library.)

How did many Jews get out of Germany after 1933? What was the world reaction regarding the Jewish refugee crisis, Dr. Kranzler?

Before *Kristallnacht,* 150,000 Jews left Germany, and as the situation worsened, Jews were desperate to leave the country. At the end of 1937, President Roosevelt called an intergovernmental conference in Evian, France, to be held in the summer of 1938, to discuss German Jewish refugees. Its complete failure brought the darkest consequences for European Jews. A total of 300,000 German and Austrian Jews desperately sought refugee status, but even before *Kristallnacht,* the United States already had decided not to increase their quota and most other countries were closing their doors.

However, some 17,000 to 18,000 Jews found a haven in Shanghai, China, the only place anybody could enter without a visa. During *Kristallnacht,* 20,000 Jews were arrested and sent to concentration camps, but if they had a visa to another country or travel tickets to Shanghai, the Nazis allowed them to leave the country. The reason that Shanghai had an open door was because of the International Settlement, which was controlled by 11 nations including the United States, Japan, Britain, France, and others.

How did Jews find out about Shanghai, which was 6,000 miles away from Germany? And what was the political situation of Shanghai at that time?

Some Austrian Jews were the first to find out about it. To tell it chronologically, in 1933, the year Hitler came to power, several hundreds of German Jewish doctors lost their jobs right away because of the Nazis. At that time, China needed doctors, and since German doctors had a great reputation, the Chinese government accepted about one hundred of them. Then, with the *Anschluss* in March 1938 when Austria was occupied by the Nazis, Jews were persecuted there immediately before the *Kristallnacht* in Germany. So, some Austrian Jews entered Shanghai in August 1938. This news of the open-door policy at Shanghai spread around very quickly among the Jewish communities of both countries. At that time Shanghai was really an international city divided into three sectors — the Chinese city, the International Settlement and the French Concession. Each of them had its own laws; there were 100,000 non-Chinese and 20,000 European residents in Shanghai when the Jews moved in. As a result of the Japanese occupation in 1937, Shanghai harbor was militarily controlled by the Japanese authorities. From the end of 1938 to early 1939, 17,000 Jewish refugees got out of the ships and walked into the city. The Japanese authorities took all of them to Hongkew, the Japanese sector, without any restriction. The English and French authorities there also accepted some, but they charged $400 per person.

A year later, about 2,000 refugees arrived in Japan. They were Polish Jews who fled to Lithuania during the Nazi invasion of Poland. Lithuania was then a neutral country but was occupied by the Russians in 1940, and they had to flee again. They went east, taking the Russian Siberian railway to Vladivostok, then by ship to Kobe with their transit visas which were valid for 8-14 days. While staying there, half of them found settlements in the United States, Canada, South America or elsewhere. The rest, about 1,000, who couldn't find places to go were all sent to Shanghai in the Japanese sector. How did those 2,000 Jews get out of Lithuania? During that period in Vilna (Kovno, now Kannos), the Russian-occupied capital city of Lithuania, there was a Japanese commercial attache by the name of Sempo Sugihara. He issued 2,000 transit visas without any official order from Tokyo. With the Dutch Consul there, together they arranged their final destination for Curacao, Dutch West Indies, via Japan. After Japan, nobody went to Curacao, of course. They went to Shanghai or elsewhere. Mr. Sugihara did it in an absolute humanitarian manner. He took his own risk for doing favors for Jews.

Japan and Germany were Axis partners. Why were Japanese keen to save Jewish refugees? What was the connection between the Japanese and Jews, and what was the Japanese attitude towards Jews?

The connection between the Japanese and Jews is a long story which is intertwined with the history of the 20th century that few people know. It starts in the beginning of the century, during the Russo-Japanese War of 1904-1905. Japan required billions of dollars to purchase modern warships to fight the Russian Baltic Fleet. Baron Korekiyo Takahashi, then president of the Bank of Japan and later prime minister, went to London to float loans. European governments and their financial communities were very skeptical about Japan's ability to win the war against mighty Russia. Takahashi was unable to raise enough money. The night before he was to return to Japan, the disappointed Takahashi accidentally met a man by the name of Jacob H. Schiff, a German-born Jew, a successful financier and head of the New York banking house Kuhn-Loeb Company. He arranged for the floating of all the loans for Japan. Japan at that time was barely out of its feudal stage. Schiff's loans indeed helped Japan to beat mighty Russia.

The world was stunned. Although delighted, Mr. Takahashi couldn't understand why

Schiff was willing to gamble on Japan's success even prior to winning a single battle. Only after he and Mr. Schiff became personal friends did the latter explain his reason for such an unusual move for a hard-headed banker. He explained this fact to his astonished Japanese friend. In 1903, one year before, there was a major pogrom in Russia, in the city of Kishinev, in which scores of Jews were killed and hundreds were wounded with the aid of the Russian government. Schiff pleaded to the government to ameliorate the plight of his fellow Jews, but was refused. Then he decided to help Japan, Russia's enemy. His loans were floated not only through bankers in the United States, but also from England and Germany through his international Jewish financiers. That impressed the Japanese tremendously. After the war, Schiff was invited to Tokyo and became the first westerner to be honored by the Japanese Emperor. That was the first time the Japanese learned something about the Jews: Jews were rich and in control of world finance. That was how the Japanese interpreted the Jews. They had no idea who was a Jew and what the difference was between Gentiles and Jews. At the turn of the century, Japan had got out of centuries of isolation and entered a new era for the first time in its history. The Japanese were not familiar with western culture and society. But anyway, they regarded Jews as a powerful people.

A second factor in the Japanese stereotype of Jews had its origin in the 1920s. In 1922, Albert Einstein, the German-Jewish Nobel prize winner who was already internationally known as a great physicist, visited Japan on a peace mission. Like Schiff, he was cheered overwhelmingly by the Japanese and became tremendously popular. The world's most brilliant man was also a Jew; that was another discovery for the Japanese.

These two men were enough examples for them to believe that Jews were rich or smart because both the richest man and the smartest man in the world were Jews. That was how the Japanese interpreted it. That was their conception of Jews who control the western world, particularly in Britain, Germany and the United States. There were Jews in the world stock markets, Jews in government, Jews in media, Jews in publishing, Jews in the entertainment industry, etc. They looked at Jews in a pragmatic way.

Japan is a nation of non-Christians, and without knowing anything about Christianity, how could Japanese understand Jewish matters? What was the origin of anti-Semitism in Japan — in a country with no Jews?

Early anti-Semitism in Japan was derived from efforts by White Russians after WW I. An important element in the Japanese portrait of the Jews was this spread of anti-Semitism. After the Bolshevik Revolution and civil war in 1917-1919, the White Russians published the *Protocols of the Elders of Zion,* the Bible of the anti-Semites. This book blamed Jews for all the ills of society. They purportedly were in control of the world finance markets especially in the United States and Britain, as well as being behind the Bolshevik revolutionaries, the Jews are blamed for the downfall of the three empires — Russia's Romanov empire, Austria's Hapsburg empire, and Germany's Hohenzollern empire.

During WW I, since Japan was on the side of the Allies, a number of Japanese elite military officers who were fluent in Russian were sent to work with White Russian counterparts in Siberia. These Russians, who hated Bolsheviks and Jews, showed the Japanese officers another kind of European social disease — anti-Semitism. That

was the first major information of anti-Jewish propaganda that reached the Japanese. Among these young officers were General Kiichiro Higuchi, Naval Captain Koreshige Inuzuka and Army Colonel Senko Yasue. They had no real knowledge of Jews or Judaism but focused on the one concrete example familiar to every Japanese, the loans by Mr. Jacob H. Schiff which had saved Japan at a critical time. They verified their opinion of the influential Jewish financiers who were able to manipulate world events. In 1919, ultra-nationalists such as Inuzuka, Yasue and others like them, translated the *Protocols* and *The Essence of Radicalism* into Japanese adding their own arguments about the ills of Japan's post-WW I society, which they attributed to the "influential Jews." However, this didn't entirely influence Japanese people, because in those days they hardly knew about Judaism and most of them had never seen a Jew or known what a Jew was, because there were hardly any Jews in Japan. Besides, even if they did meet them, the average Japanese couldn't distinguish physically, culturally and mentally between a Christian and a Jew. For them, most Westerners and Jews were the same people, which in fact is pretty much the same today.

During the Japanese occupation in Manchuria and North China in the 1930s, Japanese conservatives at home were confronting the United States because of their territorial ambitions. Japan became isolated from the rest of the world community, pressured by the so-called ABCD-Power of legal nations — America, Britain, China and the Dutch. And since Jews financially "controlled" the world, including those four countries, high ranking Japanese interpreted Jews, Americans and westerners to be identical. Japanese anti-American feeling focused directly on the Jews, and they believed that the United

States, including its economy and the Congress, were controlled by Jews. Behind President Roosevelt there was Henry Morgenthau Jr., his Jewish Treasury Secretary, who was another powerful Jew. As Japan was often politically "bashed" by the United States, that created anti-Semitic sentiment among the Japanese. In addition to the *Protocols,* other anti-Semitic caricatures and numerous literature such as *Eternal Jews,* were published again in Japan. All blamed the Jews entirely. In the German version of the anti-Semitic propaganda book, *The Jews Discovered America,* the Jews were accused of wanting to make Hebrew the American national language. For most Japanese, Jews and Americans were the same people, and since they didn't comprehend the differences between Jews and Gentiles, they saw both as one and the same.

How did this peculiar Japanese perspective of Jews manifest itself during the 1930s? What would be the real reason for Japan to save Jewish refugees?

During the period of 1937-1939, at the worst critical time for European Jews, most of the western world closed their doors to Jews: The British declared the "White Paper" which greatly reduced Jewish immigration to Palestine, the appropriate Jewish Homeland, and in Shanghai, the British, American and French made it difficult for Jews to land in their sectors in the "International Settlement." On the other hand, on December 6, 1938, in Tokyo, among the Japanese highest levels headed by the Prime Minister, a special meeting was held regarding the Jewish matter" It was called "Five Ministers' Conference." They decided Japan would accept Jews and the Japanese government took a pro-Jewish policy. They would permit the entry of thousands of

homeless and helpless Austrian and German Jewish refugees into their sector of Shanghai.

As "Japan-bashing" continued throughout the 1930s, Manchuria and North China were the only places for Japan to get vital raw materials and energy sources to survive. However, in order to develop this noncultivated, endless land with its great natural resources, Japan needed capital. Billions of dollars were required to build railroads, highways, industrial factories and housing developments to bring more Japanese and Jewish settlers, both the Ashkenazi and the Sephardic Jews. There were already earlier Russian-Jewish settlers there who fled during and after the Bolshevik Revolution, and there were already Russian Jewish communities in Japanese-occupied Manchuria and North China. For these stateless Russian Jews, the Japanese government fostered "Far Eastern Conferences" and also established the Jewish Council. The total Jewish population was between 12,000-14,000. This was in addition to the influx of over 17,000 Austrian, German and Polish refugees who fled to Shanghai during the period of 1938-1941. Professional and skilled Jewish workers were employed: scientists, physicists, chemists, doctors, engineers, architects and technicians. The project committees were founded among various Jewish communities. There was no doubt that according to one faction of the Japanese, Japan's ultimate desire was to create a sort of Zionist state in Manchuria. Many refugees in Shanghai were intellectually and artistically talented and, despite being surrounded by an alien and often hostile environment, Jewish art and cultural activities flourished throughout their stay in Shanghai; there were Jewish newspapers, periodicals and radio broadcasts in Yiddish, German, Russian and English, theaters, concerts, schools and libraries, and the Yeshiva academy for scholars, kosher restaurants and other various cultural organizations. The Japanese plan was to offer the Jews an opportunity to set up their own state, "a little Palestine" in Manchuria, so they could settle and populate the barren landscape. Mr. Ishihara, General Itagaki, Captain Inuzuka and Colonel Yasue were entirely in charge of controlling the whole ambitious project as well as Shanghai City.

During this time, however, Japanese anti-Semitism, which was propagated only in theory, became part of Japanese policy. Unlike the Christian western world where anti-Semitism often resulted in persecution, violence and the killing of Jews, the Japanese gave it their "unique" pragmatic interpretation and practice of this western social plague. They believed that the Jews were very powerful in the West. Instead of persecuting them, Japan sought to make use of their alleged power on behalf of Japanese interests. For its part, Japan intended to "benefit" from the Jews under its control, and in gratitude these Jews would undoubtedly convince their "powerful" American fellow brethren in America to benefit Japan. Japan sought billions in loans from the wealthy American Jews again, like they did from Mr. Schiff during the Russo-Japanese War. High-ranking Japanese believed Jewish financial aid could further their dream. Moreover, they hoped that American Jews, who they assumed to "control" President Roosevelt, especially through Morgenthau, the influential Jew in the U.S. government, would make the President tone down his strong anti-Japanese policies. In other words, the Jews in Manchuria and Shanghai would serve to influence all the Jews of the Far East to be in favor of Japan's cause, and they, in turn, would impress the rest of world Jewry, especially in the United States. With the cooperation of Jewish brains and

Jewish money, the Japanese truly believed they could succeed.

What was Germany's reaction to the Japanese attitude toward Jews?

Germany tried to convince Japan to become an anti-Semitic state. And when Jewish refugees arrived in Shanghai, it was really confusing for Nazi officials and Japanese ultra-nationalists who were influenced by Nazi ideology. In 1940-1943, there were anti-Semitic fairs in Tokyo and Osaka which were sponsored by the German Embassy in Japan and backed by a major publisher, a department store and also the powerful Japanese Bureau of Information. They were exhibitions of anti-Jewish propaganda: caricatures, literature and graphics to show the negative characteristics of Jews supplemented by anti-Semitic lectures. These were "respectively" attended by over one million people; more than 32,000 copies of anti-Semitic brochures were distributed and 3,000 copies of a book titled *Jews, Hitler, Stalin* were sold. At the same time the old anti-Jewish propaganda books were in book stores again written by a man named Kiyo Ustonomiya.

In the same period, Captain Inuzuka, then a head of the Bureau of Jewish Affairs in Shanghai, went back to Japan. He made a radio announcement saying, "We Japanese welcome Jews, we are not like Nazi Germans. We invite Jews to Asia as long as they are loyal to us." Obviously, the Nazi Embassy in Tokyo didn't like that. While they were trying hard to convince Japanese to be Jewish-haters, they wondered who was the Jew-lover in the Japanese government. It drove the Tokyo Nazi officials into a state of confusion. The thing was that, although Japan allied with Hitler, Japan never promised Hitler to become an anti-Semitic state. Japan declared that anti-Semitism would never work in Japan, because first of all, in normal daily life, Japanese people hardly ever met Jews. How could they hate or discriminate against people they have never met? The Japanese didn't have any reason to be like Germans. That was the attitude of the Japanese. Despite heavy pressure by the Nazi diplomats in Tokyo, Inuzuka made his statement on Jews with an astonishing remark, "In our relations with Jews, we will always deal with the principle of equality as long as the Jews remain loyal to the Japanese authorities." Now, here a strange irony occurred. The irony was that Ustonomiya, the author of anti-Jewish literature, was the pen name of Captain Inuzuka, the same pro-Jew who invited the Jews to Shanghai and Manchuria. What the Nazi Germans didn't know was that Inuzuka and Ustonomiya were the same person. It sounds bizarre and crazy, but it's all true.

Why did Captain Inuzuka do such a thing? He was genuinely convinced that the Jews controlled the western world. After years of Jewish study, he concluded that Jews are a unique people; without having a country or army of their own, they were wealthy and powerful enough to manipulate or even overthrow world empires. Inuzuka described Jews as a blowfish, *Fugu,* a great delicacy in Japan despite the fact it occasionally may cause instant death by poisoning those who eat it. He said, "Jews are just like *Fugu.* It's very delicious but unless one knows how to cook it, it may prove fatal." He meant you have to treat Jews very carefully because if you handle them well, it could be tremendously beneficial to Japan. He wanted the Japanese to understand what a powerful weapon Jews could be for or against Japan. His philosophy was, "If you know how to use the weapon, it becomes your weapon. But if you don't know how to use it, it's used

against you." It was a warning to the Japanese about the power of the Jews, and yet, it was also a solution for Japan. It was completely different from the Nazis. That was the Japanese version of the Final Solution for the Jews.

After Japan attacked Pearl Harbor and entered the war with the United States, how had things changed?

In October 1941, when General Hideki Tojo became prime minister of Japan, Japan's pro-Jewish policy was still being carried out, and Japanese ministers were still trying to use Jewish international connections up until the last moment of the peace negotiations with the United States. In fact, I find that Japan's unique policy toward the Jews not only saved them, but also influenced the formation of Japan's pragmatic approach to relations with the United States prior to Pearl Harbor. Their policy was far more flexible than that of the US. Tojo tried to stop the war and was ready for peace talks with the US government, but Roosevelt demanded that Japan withdraw its army from Manchuria and North China before any talks could take place.

When Japan attacked Pearl Harbor on December 7, 1941, it changed the whole situation and the Japanese plan. Then, the "Bureau of Jewish Affairs" in Shanghai was closed and Captain Inuzuka was transferred to the Philippines. The day after the successful attack on Pearl Harbor, Japan occupied all of Shanghai. The other nations of the "International Settlement" became Japan's enemies: the United States, Britain, France, Holland, Switzerland, and others. All foreign nationalities were forced to wear armbands by the Japanese authority, and as the war became more intense, they were interned. The Jewish refugees were allowed to stay in the Hongkew section, but in 1943 under Nazi pressure, a Jewish ghetto was established. However, it was nothing like the Nazis' ghettos. The Jewish people had freedom and were allowed in and out of the ghetto every day for work, shopping or to school, and Jewish social activities still continued inside the ghetto. No Jew was killed by Japanese soldiers. Nearly 20,000 Jews, including new-born children, stayed in Shanghai that way until the end of the war when Japan was defeated in 1945. A Japanese official once asked some of the Jewish leaders, "Why do Germans hate Jews so much?" One of the Shanghai rabbis responded, "Because like you, we are also Asians."

As a Jew yourself, how do you feel about the whole Jewish Japanese affair?

I certainly appreciate how the Japanese helped Jews in such a great humanitarian manner. Although there was a military hierarchy who had certain ideas about the Jews, using Jews for practical reasons, even though their idea was complicated, oddly innovative, and not realistic, nevertheless, as a result, it turned out to be good for Jews. The fact was that tens of thousands of Jews were saved from the Holocaust by the Japanese. In the most catastrophic period of world history and while many other countries refused to help Jewish refugees, the Japanese took their own risks against Nazi Germany. If Japan had closed the doors, those tens of thousands of Jews would surely have been killed by the Nazis. Among them, 500 Yeshiva scholars were saved. That is significant for the survival of Jewish culture. It's very important that the world know that the Japanese weren't like Germans. But as a total picture, it's a good one and surely one of the brightest stories of the tragedy of our thousands of years of Jewish history. Jewish people have long lasting memories. This certainly remains as one of the better sides of WW II and the Holocaust.

Specifically, I would like to remark about Japanese people's thoughtfulness and politeness toward the Jewish refugees in Kobe during their stay in 1940-1941. For Japanese, Jews were complete strangers, but local people warmly welcomed them and treated them in an absolute humane manner like their good neighbors, which impressed many Jews, especially after fleeing from Hitler's persecution. They delivered gifts of food, money, flowers, and clothes for these stateless Jews. Although at the time the Japanese themselves had to live on food rations, some even gave up their own ration cards for the refugees. For medical ailments Japanese doctors took care of the Jewish patients free of charge. These still stand out in the minds of all those who went through Kobe as their most pleasant memory of the war. ❖

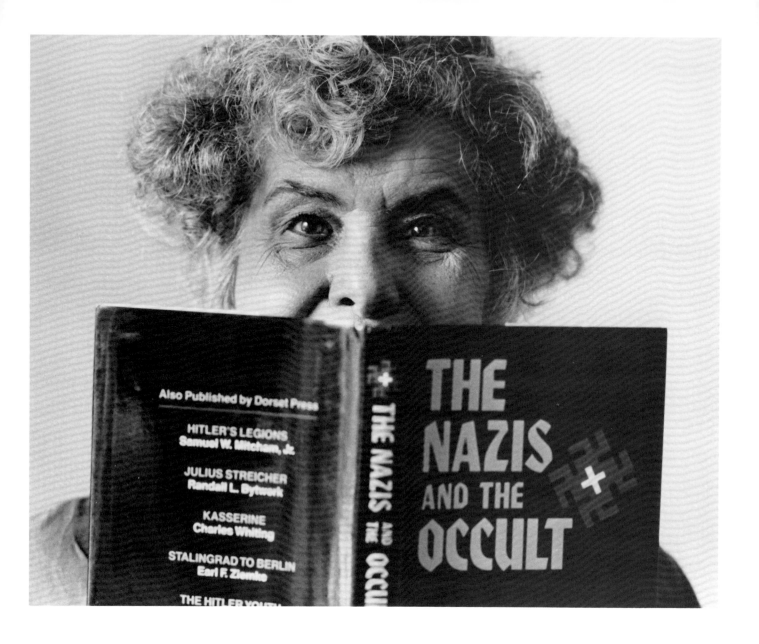

"If we believe absurdities, we shall commit atrocities."

DUSTY SKLAR

American, writer and author of the book *The Nazis and the Occult*. Born in 1928 in Sokolow, Poland. Lives in New York, USA.

(Photo: Ms. Sklar holds her book, *The Nazis and the Occult.*)

I find your book *The Nazis and the Occult* interesting. The Nazi documentary films such as *Triumph of the Will* are commonly known for their persuasive ritualistic images. Your book provides the closest analysis of the rituals of the Nazi inner circle. How did you become interested in this subject, Ms. Sklar?

To tell the truth, it was an accident. I was not especially interested in conducting research on the Nazis. In the early 1970s when the occult revival started, I began to wonder where these ideas originated and began to research their sources for my own edification, trying to trace the occult tradition back to its origins. I was fascinated by this topic — what the tradition was about and where it came from. Then, I took a course in philosophy in New York. I felt something was weird. While I was attending the class on human race, we discussed the master race, super humans, and having super human powers. The teacher suggested that in order to advance, you had to put yourself in the hands of your master and grant him your absolute obedience. That reminded me of the Nazis. I began to wonder if the Nazis were involved in something similar. It just popped into my mind. I was always interested in the occult tradition and tried to learn why people believe in it. Within a matter of months, the students in the class — well educated middle-class people — began to change. They started to say black is white, white is black, and they eventually ended up believing. I was amazed to see the transformation in these people. This reminded me of the Nazis — I'd been as puzzled as the whole world how the whole phenomenon of Nazism originated.

The first thing I found was a scholarly article researched by a prestigious German historian about the Thule Society, which was a precursor of the Nazi Party. It said that the society was studying ancient runes and symbols, but it didn't mention that this was an occult group. To me, there were signs of occult activity, such as the waving of pendulums over objects, but this was unknown to the German historians of that time, and so they'd obviously missed the occult connection.

Studying Germany's pre-Nazi history, the ground for the Nazis was already there, right?

I could hardly believe what I discovered. It was all there in the history books but simply buried. What I found was not new information. It was a question of pulling together various existing sources that nobody had touched or paid attention to after the war. I was very surprised and excited when I learned these Nazi beginnings, including the language they used, how they presented unreal self-images, and the vital elements needed to control such a civilized nation. Everything was already there in the 19th century books.

To trace this history, we must look back to the time of Bismarck's German unification in 1871, which brought a large number of Eastern European Jews to Germany. They settled in the cities and played a prominent part in their commercial, cultural and political life. Similarly, during the same period, the Jewish population in Vienna largely increased. The Jews tried to gain a modicum of social acceptance. Some Gentiles somehow felt cheated by the Jews. Slowly, a new movement called the *völkisch* — "Pan-German" — evolved in Austria. It was a cult of race based on the supremacy of the Aryans and vilification of the Jews and became part of a great popular campaign against the "foreign elements." A historical racial theory developed, and at the turn of the new century, the coming of a new Messiah was proclaimed. The mystical concepts of *Reich* and *Volk* went along with an awakening interest in occultism. Secret cults of anti-Semitism and nationalism sprang up in Vienna and spread to other cultural centers.

Who were the leaders of this movement, and how was it connected with Hitler and the Thule Society that you mentioned earlier?

Two Austrian occultists: Jorg Lanz von Liebenfels and Guido von List — known as Lanz and List, presented an irrational, pseudo-anthropological doctrine which attracted a number of wealthy backers, despite its foolishness. Their organizations boasted several influential members, among them the Germanen Orden, another group of "occult-racist-nationalists." In 1909, when young Adolf Hitler was living in Vienna, there was a comic magazine called *Ostara* which was published by Lanz, and he made contact with the occultists. The erotic language and racist rantings of this magazine were remarkably similar to Hitler's later utterances in *Mein Kampf*.

After the defeat of WW I, the German people were in a state of shock. They experienced the collapse of Kaiser Wilhelm II's regime, humiliation, reparations, unemployment, inflation and hunger. Financially and psychologically, they bore a heavy burden. The new Russian Revolution threatened to spill over into Germany. There were a high number of Communists, particularly in Munich, who threatened civil war. Conservatives and liberals were afraid to do anything to stave off communism. The Germanen Orden, which had a close tie with a Munich group called the Thule Society held meetings regularly to study the supposed occult meaning and symbolism of the ancient Germanic alphabet. It was led by an astrologer who called himself Baron Rudolf von Sebottendorf. This Thule Society soon became the political arm of

the Germanen Orden and quietly set about preparing for a counter-revolution against the Weimar Republic government. It formed an umbrella organization for many groups of racist-nationalists and enlisted unscrupulous men against the government, which they claimed had betrayed the German people. This activity also included ferocious and rabid anti-Semitic campaigns. They began to collect weapons, bought newspaper publishers, instigated terrorist activity and stirred up race hatred against the Jews. The members who played a key role in the Thule Society later became the founders of the Nazi party.

What kind of articles was Hitler reading in the magazine *Ostara*?

After his failure at the Art Academy in Vienna, Hitler lived in squalid quarters in a slum area of the city. He spent much of his time studying Eastern religion, yoga, occultism, hypnotism, astrology, telepathy, graphology, phrenology, and similar subjects which often appeal to pursuers of magical power. One day he came upon the magazine *Ostara*, which anyone could buy in street kiosks. Vienna in those days was hospitable to the formation of the occult, which sprang up with religious fervor amid the irrational atmosphere. In 1900, Lanz, a defrocked Cistercian, founded his cult group called the Order of the New Templars. In 1908, his friend List, a sort of pseudo-priest, started his occult group, the Armanen. Around 1912, members of both cults joined together and formed the Germanen Orden, which later became the root of the Nazi party. It's not clear whether Hitler was actually a member of these cult groups, but he was certainly a reader of *Ostara* and met Lanz several times.

According to *Ostara*, Lanz divided the species into the ace-men and ape-men: Ace-men were white, blue-eyed, blond-haired people who possessed everything heroic in mankind, and were superior in breeding and blood. The ape-men were colored people depicted as inferiors and threatening to contaminate the whites through interbreeding. The magazine combined the erotic and occult in an irrational blend which captured the fantasies of lost souls. According to *Ostara*, this racial struggle between the Aryan and the non-Aryan was the essence of human existence. In this cartoon magazine, Linz graphically combined race, blood and sex with ancient German occultism. This sort of pamphlet was Hitler's favorite pleasure. *Ostara* contained headlines like, ARE YOU BLOND? THEN YOU ARE THE CREATOR AND PRESERVER OF CIVILIZATION. ARE YOU BLOND? THEN YOU ARE THREATENED BY PERILS. Subtitles read, "Race and Nobility," Race and Foreign Affairs, and The Metaphysics of Race. It cost 35 pfennigs a copy and reached a circulation of 100,000 copies, selling in Austria and Germany.

Specifically, what ideology did Hitler incorporate from Lanz and List into his own racial theories?

Lanz saw a triumphal enlightenment of the higher races over the lesser races, and symbolized it in an ideology called "Arisophy." He quickly found believers and followers who supported him and he became a wealthy man, eventually owning a few castles in Austria which he converted into temples where he preached. His sign was the swastika and his slogan was: "Race fight until the castration knife." The race struggle was his major concern, but the order also dabbled in astrology, combined with Templar symbols of ritual magic, and raising a swastika flag. He made plans for world salvation and called for a racial program

featuring genetic selection, sterilization, deportations to the "ape-jungle," and race extermination by forced labor or murder. He advocated the establishment of special breeding colonies for the production of more Aryans. Exactly what did Hitler have to do with Lanz? In *Mein Kampf* the only possible reference to *Ostara* may be this one: "For the first time in my life, I bought myself some anti-Semitic pamphlets for a few heller." After Germany annexed Austria in 1938, Hitler attempted to bury all the evidence of his early influences in Vienna: he forbade *Ostara* and other Lanz publications, and to hide the evidence further, he also attempted to murder a friend who shared his shabby days in Vienna. The influence of Lanz's "Arisophy" obviously helped to poison the Third Reich.

List presented a somewhat different variation of the occultist-racist theory. His practice was paganism. The members of his secret society, "Armanen," used the *"Heil"* greeting to hark back to the pagans of an ancient Germanic race. Their holiest emblem was the swastika. To the Germanic people, the swastika was an occult symbol for the sun, which represented life. Sun worship became a pagan ritual among *völkisch* movement groups. List was a pioneer in reviving Teutonic folklore and mythology. He taught his members runic occultism and claimed that he was able to communicate with ancients possessing esoteric wisdom, similar to that of God, and he also happened to be a radical anti-Semite. His practice concentrated on the magical power contained in the old alphabet, which laid the ground for nationalism. The Armanen attracted people like Karl Lueger, the mayor of Vienna, and the well-known Austrian theosophist Franz Hartmann, as well as wealthy supporters who financed his society.

Lanz's Pan-Germanism became widely spread, not only among Germans but also among all blood-related people. He fought against all un-German thinking, including Judaism and internationalism. When the two occultist groups joined under the new name of the Germanen Orden, their symbols were runes and the swastika, and their costumes were reminiscent of Wotan and paganism. During WW I, the group was not active because most of its members were at war. However, Theodor Fritsch, one of the founders and author of a book in 1887 titled *Anti-Semitical Catechism,* published an additional edition entitled *Handbook on the Jewish Question.* It was an update of the "Catechism" and reached 145,000 readers. It wasn't until after the war that the anti-Semitic occult groups launched a mass movement.

So, Hitler copied these ideas and expanded them into the political arena?

That's correct. It was not uncommon to find occult sects espousing the politics of the conservatives, racists, and ultra right-wingers. After the defeat of WW I while Germans were in misery, they had become very radical. The Germanen Orden was reactivated in Munich in 1918 under the name of Thule Society. The group published a brochure called "Runen" to attract new members. Sebottendorff, the founder of the society, was nostalgic for the pogroms of the Middle Ages when the German Jews had been openly persecuted. He said that in his era, anti-Semitism could go further, in influencing the Catholic Church, the Protestants and Freemasonry. Also, he believed that Jews were plotting an international conspiracy under the name of liberty, fraternity and equality. Sebottendorff approached people through local Munich newspaper adver-

tisements and contacted respondees in writing, predicting, "Germany will collapse if racial inter-marriage is not halted. Only those who pass a test of racial purity can become members, which means not a drop of Jewish or Negro blood flows through your veins. Send your photograph."

What is the connection of the word "Thule" with Aryan?

Through my study in occult history, I have discovered the most northern region of the earth was called Thule, and it was believed by occultists to be the age old magic center of a vanished civilization, Atlantis. According to Madame Helena Petrovna Blavatsky, a Russian-born American theosophist who was widely known for her psychic powers in the last century, Atlantis had been swept away in the first deluge some 850,000 years ago. Her theory perplexed and inspired many evolutionists. After the war, with the rise of the German Aryan racist groups, they captured this occultist mystical speculation and developed the myth of the master race. Sebottendorff transposed Blavatsky's complicated cosmology into Aryan racism.

When did Hitler encounter this society and how did it develop in the ensuing years?

After the war, Hitler worked for the Bavarian Army for a while. He was assigned to inspect a small political meeting called DAP (Deutsche Arbeiterpartei). He ended up joining it as the 7th member of the party. He was interested in a mass political party. Through anti-Jewish newspaper advertisement the membership gradually grew. He soon took charge of the party and changed its name to NSDAP (Nationalsozialistische Deutsche Arbeiterpartei — National Socialist German Workers' Party), and held weekly meetings in beer halls. Among its members was Karl Harrer, chairman of the party. Other NSDAP members were also of the Thule Society. By that time, the Thule had a few thousand members in Bavaria, particularly in Munich. They held secret meetings regularly at the Four-Seasons Hotel. Sebottendorff's disciples were the most influential people in Munich: judges, lawyers, professors, industrialists, doctors, scientists, and even some royal family members. They viewed themselves as potential masters of the earth, protected against all dangers. Their reign would last for 1,000 years, until the next deluge. Through the occult and anti-Semitic circles, Hitler encountered the Thule Society. Its members included Alfred Rosenberg, Julius Streicher, Rudolf Hess, Hans Frank, Ernst Röhm, Max Ammann, Dietrich Eckart, Anton Drexler, Gottfrid Feder, Dr. Heinz Kurz and Friederich Krohn.

They soon found their "Führer," Adolf Hitler. It was Eckart who first introduced Hitler to the Thule Society and promoted him as the long-awaited German Messiah. They incorporated the essential ingredients of irrational programs by Lanz and List. Sebottendorff's *Führerprinzip* (leader principle) was basic to this esoteric cult: The disciple must blindly obey his master and the pupil must undergo a drastic transformation. Of course, this principle of blind obedience may operate outside occult groups as well, in everyday institutions such as the military, government and the corporate world. But, step by step, this Nazi Revolution and *Führerprinzip* led to the surrender of the will of individuals to the will of the Führer, and ultimately culminated in confessions by members like Rudolf Höss, commander of Auschwitz before his execution in 1947. He stated that he would have gassed and burned his own wife, children and himself if the Führer had asked it. Hitler surely became the most popular

leader in German history, and he certainly knew how to seize his opportunities. But at the same time, Hitler was also an occultist.

So, a Messiah named Adolf Hitler was born. How did Hitler foster the SS genocide mentality?

This *Führerprinzip* is the key to understanding the movement. It allowed for actions which violated individual conscience. Personal and individual choices were void; one just does whatever his or her leader orders, like a dog and its master. Soldiers of every army have it drilled into them never to refuse an order. This follow-the-leader syndrome and obedience to authority surely played the main part in Nazi Germany. As with other difficult periods in history, economic chaos and collapse resulted in a terrible social aftermath leading to misery, poverty and suicide. So, it was quite natural that people were attracted to occultism and the National Socialist movement which gave them hope for a new beginning. The SS mentality was thereby created.

List, the founder of the Armanen and a pioneer in the revival of pagan worship, invented an ancient race of Germanic priests of "wisdom," and claimed he was able to divine their desires through intuition and clairvoyance. His theories attracted a large audience and were studied by the Germanen Orden, and later by the SS. His documents, which were confiscated by the Allies after WW II, bear SS marks and are stamped *Ahnenerbe,* the Nazi Ancestral Research. They were apparently used in teaching candidates for the SS. We have never fully learned about all the secrets of the SS, but we do know some.

This was an occult society. This may enlighten us as to how more than a million SS men could change from ordinary citizens to mass murderers within a few years. Some of them must have participated in the Final Solution just to get by such an uneasy period. But we can't ignore the zealousness or the overzealousness with which most of them approached their tasks. Not only were they perfectly willing to perform such unpleasant tasks, but they never questioned themselves or their work's effectiveness. Fear of punishment didn't account for this. There were many alternatives: you could avoid being picked up or sabotage the SS machine without detection. But they didn't. Rudolf Höss, commander of Auschwitz, again confessed: "We were told all the time we were the elect, we were to be the Führer's and Himmler's special instrument for creating a new Reich. They became our conscience and we lost our personal morale and self-determination." The SS men truly believed in absolute obedience to the will of the charismatic Führer. They viewed themselves as a crusade of the elect, chosen to be superhuman on a special "divine mission" to take over the world.

Robert Ley, a high ranking SS officer, pointed out: "Any SS man who fails to obey or betrays the party and Führer will not thereby merely be deprived of an office, but he personally, together with his family, his wife and children, will be destroyed." It was *Kadavergehorsam* (cadaver obedience) they created through fear and religious fanaticism. The SS members were treated as a Nazi elite, secretly separated from any other parties, and forbidden to mingle with anybody else. The SS order was a state within a state. Membership in the SS seemed to present an opportunity for members to become part of a utopian society. Like the Communist revolution, I think the Nazi revolution focused on change, at least in the beginning. Instead of a class struggle, however, the movement turned into a racial

struggle. A new class would be brought to power based on the inherited nobility of the Aryan blood. This master race was to be the culmination of biological evolution. They really believed this mystical racist package.

About the Hitler Youth movement in which children and teens were brought up as heirs of the Third Reich, how were these youths brainwashed?

Traditionally, German youths in the 19th century usually belonged to religious, athletic or cultural organizations. They'd grown up with group activities which were well-organized. During the Weimar Republic, they were practicing spirituality through vegetarianism, romanticism, the occult, abstinence from sex, self-discipline and obedience. They were highly influenced in a holy war against the enemies: Freemasons, Liberals and Jews. The youth movement gradually shifted towards anti-Semitism, and little by little, Jewish youths were excluded from membership in youth organizations.

Under Hitler, the youth movement became a holy crusade. By 1934, membership in the Hitler Youth among 10 to 18 years olds had reached 6 million. They were required to be physically fit and mentally able to worship Hitler as a Messiah. Brainwashing began with literature. Even fairy tales which were read to babies instilled propagandist ideas that the Führer came from heaven to kill the enemies who wanted to eat little Aryan children. The Hitler Youth sang: "God is struggle, struggle is our blood, and that is why we were born." A book of tales published for them in 1935 included the battle cry: "No one shall live after the Leader's death." German children certainly worshipped the Führer as a god. A young daughter of a liberal professor who joined the party under pressure, later stated: "The Nazi accounts contained such fantastic plotting about world Jewry that I could hardly stop laughing as I read. It was a shock to learn how readily the children accepted these Nazi fabrications. But the most amazing thing was that after a few years of going through the routine, I began to believe the stories myself, and could no longer distinguish in my mind between propaganda and truth."

In conclusion, what are the dangers of occult thinking?

I would say that it's too simple to determine that the German soul was predisposed to totalitarianism. Generations of Germans had been submissive through iron discipline, but they had never before been genocidal maniacs. We now know how a mass of ordinary people can be transformed into automatons through massification techniques. Mass society is symbolized by modernization and "egalitarianism," and in Germany, this egalitarianism culminated in Hitler's boast that hundreds of thousands of SS men became almost one unit. These men were uniform, not only in ideas, but even in facial expression. Their eyes shone with fanatical enthusiasm and they were all unthinkably brutal sadists. We can see how a mass of men in a movement become a single type. This mass committed mass atrocities. We shouldn't forget the words of Sarvepalli Radhakrishnan, an Indian philosopher: "If we believe absurdities, we shall commit atrocities." ❖

"I hope a time will come for people to rethink what really happened."

BILLY PRICE

American, Hitler art specialist and author of the book *Adolf Hitler: Unknown Artist*. Businessman. Born in 1930 in Texas, USA.

(Photo: Mr. Price in his office, showing some sketches by Hitler from one of the pages of his book, *Adolf Hitler: Unknown Artist*.)

310

People generally know that Hitler was an unsuccesful painter before he became the dictator of Germany, but not many have seen his artwork. According to your book *Adolf Hitler: Unknown Artist,* he painted lots of watercolor paintings. What is your major reason for studying Hitler's art, Mr. Price?

When the war ended I was 15 years old. I was at the proper age to be influenced by the reality of war and violence, and Hitler often came to my mind. My quest was to learn how this illiterate man came out of nowhere and turned the world upside-down in such a short time. Hitler lived on this earth only 56 years and pulled nearly 56 million people with him into the grave; one million people for each year of his life, that's a lot of killing. When I was in school, I became interested in studying him. I wanted to know how one person could do such a thing, how this could happen, why he did it, and what caused people to follow him. I was as confused as anybody else. He was someone who was difficult for anyone to understand and I wanted the challenge of finding out about him. I studied him, not because this man was a devil for German history, but also because he was the devil for all mankind. Since I'm interested in art, it was appropriate for me to look into his artwork. I researched and analyzed his personality through his visual expressions to figure him out. I made a big circle of it and divided it up into slices of pie. I took one small slice of the pie, that was his art, and studied it. My study was to learn about Hitler as a person through his artwork. There are thousands of people who studied other sectors of the pie — his structure of the Third Reich, politics, military strategy, territorial expansionism, foreign policy, racial extermination policy, etc. — and I'm not an authority in any of these other studies. I can only tell you what I learned, and I'm a specialist only on his art.

After researching Hitler for over 40 years, I asked myself, "What is it that Hitler actually earned?" What I learned was that he killed a lot of people to earn power. He earned the right to be studied "correctly." He earned the right for historians or psychiatrists to learn about him correctly. The only thing that Hitler ever earned honestly is for people to study him without being pushed politically by the right or the left. Through the 750 of his paintings that I have gathered in my book, highly-qualified psychiatrists and historians should be able to understand why Hitler was like he was.

Many subjects on Hitler are controversial even today. While working on your study, what was the reaction of people to what you were doing?

As we all know, Adolf Hitler was not like Rembrandt or Leonardo da Vinci. He was a bad painter. You know, we see the paintings of Winston Churchill and he was a good painter, but not Hitler's. But that is not my point. I look at his work as a way to reveal his personality, and that's my primary interest. Now, in my book, it's possible some of the paintings are not authentic and I mention that to the reader. There are about 500 more paintings supposedly by him but I feel they are fake or "questionable," so I didn't include them. After working so many decades, I became an expert at detecting Hitler fakes as well. While working on this, reporters came to me and asked, "What makes you like Hitler?" I always answered that I never said I liked Hitler. I just studied Hitler. Someone even accused me of being pro-Hitler or anti-Jewish. People who saw and read my book responded with letters, some complimenting or praising Hitler and others on what

311

bad taste I have. In 1983, I published 10,000 copies of the book in German. German newspapers criticized me saying, they shouldn't allow an American to publish such a book in Germany. They couldn't look at it straight. They resented my book. I contacted several major American publishers, but it was rejected because I didn't mention that Hitler killed 6 million Jews. Well, the reason I didn't say it was because my book is not political. I just analyzed his mind through his visual work. Eventually, in 1985, I published 10,000 copies in English at my own expense in the US. Every copy was sold.

The thing is, in my book, I never wrote I'm pro-Hitler or I don't like Jews, or anything like that; not even one word. My book doesn't even have a picture of Hitler or a swastika. I didn't say the words "good painting" or "bad painting," either. I just presented it, "Here are Hitler's paintings, it's up to you to decide good or bad." Over the years, however, I learned that if you talk about anything to do with Hitler, within 5 minutes, you'll be getting into the Jewish subjects. If you want to talk about WW II German military strategy, within 5 minutes you'll be talking about the Jews. And the same thing, if you want to talk about Hitler's art: within 5 minutes, you'll be talking about the Jews again. We have to be sympathetic with Jews, of course, and we have to be sensitive in order to understand them. It's a highly emotional issue for them, indeed. So, the point I'd like to bring out is, over the years, I learned that the Jewish people are the ones who study most of the historical issues on Nazism and the Holocaust. And in my view, more non-Jewish people should research and study such topics.

Truth is that despite his evil character, Hitler painted peaceful things such as landscapes, **buildings and flowers, still lifes, and none of his work is violent or bizarre. He was just an ordinary street artist. But his drawings of humans are terrible.**

Yes, that was one of his weaknesses. But he was good at landscapes. It's possible to describe Hitler as an artist only during the early period of his life. There are some people who praise Hitler's paintings saying how great he was, and I couldn't convince them that I'm not looking at him as a painter. I'm looking at his character, his way of thinking and personality through his art. Hitler himself knew that he didn't have talent in art and he realized he wasn't an artist. But he would have loved to be an artist. He had a lot of knowledge about good art and he knew that his work wasn't good. He was even ashamed of his own artwork. He failed twice in the entrance tests for the Vienna Academy of Fine Art, as you know. Now, in the first test, he was marked "drawing unsatisfactory" and failed. Standards of the Academy were very advanced and the selection criteria was extremely high. The competition was such that only one out of every four applicants was accepted. In the following years, Hitler attempted another entrance test at the Academy. He was rejected again. This time his art exhibited more architectural skill than artistic talent. He admitted architecture was his great love, but he didn't have the high school diploma that was required to study it. He became bitter but not discouraged by the rejections. He was determined to make it on his own. During his life in Vienna, he lived in poverty, and to earn his living he painted and sold his works in various framemaking stores, and in return he was treated to free dinners by the owners. He was particularly fascinated with architecture and his work reflects this in his numerous drawings of houses, churches, public buildings, city and street scenes, all in watercolor. His style of painting was influenced by the Greco-Roman tradition and 19th century neo-classicism.

His other interest was classical opera, and in fact, he often painted stage scenery and designed costumes for opera productions for his own pleasure. After he moved to Munich, he painted around the city, and occasionally did commissioned works and also painted numerous pictures at the registry office behind St. Peter's Church and sold mass-produced works to newly wed couples leaving the Church. He earned a modest living that way. He once told an acquaintance, "I paint that which the people want to buy."

During WW I in France, he continued to paint behind the front lines whenever he had free time. In this period, the great variety of materials indicates the wide range of his interests — postcards, portraits, landscapes, and sketches of front line life. After the war, Hitler turned increasingly to politics and began devoting more time to architecture than to art.

What else did you discover about him?

In all my study, I found he had two abilities; the ability to sketch and the ability to communicate. For example, when he was having conversations with his ministers, generals or commanders about war strategy or something else, and when the discussion became complicated, Hitler would grab a piece of paper and a pencil and rapidly draw sketches of buildings or armaments, so that everybody could understand exactly what they were talking about. Albert Speer, Hitler's chief architect and Minister of Armaments, said, "Hitler could sketch things quickly, and one thing about his sketches was that the scale was always perfect." It might not be a good sketch but the di-

mensions would be correct. With his ability to sketch and communicate, he was like a cartoonist.

During his political activities, his artistic output began with NSDAP matters and urban planning. In his direct involvement with the Volkswagen, for example, he personally did a whole series of sketches for the automobile design. People who were close to him recalled that he loved to sketch and doodle drawings of all sorts of things, caricatures, furniture, interior design or monuments. Technical developments intrigued him, as well. One of his architects said that Hitler closely followed every detail of projects such as the wide-gauge railway system.

You said Hitler himself knew his own artwork had no artistic value. How did your research indicate that?

In regard to his own talents, particularly after WW I, Hitler sensed the value of his own works. He was well aware of the increasing value of his political career versus his artistic ability. Knowing the amounts he had received for his paintings in Vienna and Munich, he was very realistic about their relative value. There were certain works of which he had once been proud, but later in his political life when they were mentioned by his inner circle of friends, he was rather annoyed and even embarrassed. He was likely to dismiss them as "silly works by an amateur done as a fast way to make a living." When one of his officials purchased one of this original watercolors for a high price, Hitler was furious about the amount he paid, and asked him to return it to the owner saying, "This is obviously a fake. I never painted that!" But, later he admitted that it was indeed his work.

You were once a collector of Hitler's paintings yourself. After the war, what happened to Hitler's artwork, how did it become scattered and where are hundreds of his other paintings today?

In the USA before the war, there was once an article about Hitler as an artist in his youth which was illustrated with his paintings in *Enquire* magazine. At the end of WW II, his paintings were either plundered or confiscated by American authorities. According to reliable information, a large collection was removed from the Obersalzberg, Hitler's mountain residence, in April 1945 by the SS and shipped to Italy.

The single most important collection of Hitler's art is owned by an English art collector. The largest collection of Hitler's architectural drawings were in the hands of Albert Speer. Some others were scattered among Hitler's close associates, but when they were imprisoned, they disappeared into the hands of their interrogators.

During the postwar years, I personally collected a total of 33 of Hitler's watercolor paintings. Since I was interested in his work, I looked at private collections and went to auctions in Austria, Germany, England and the USA. I bought a few from auctions, but most of them came from individual collectors. I also kept a record of them. And after over 40 years, my information on this matter has become a master file; no one else has it. That was the reason I published the book. Now, in my book, many owners of the paintings don't want to reveal their names, so I noted only "Private Collection." People who deal with Hitler's art today are investors. I think Hitler's paintings are a very good investment; percentage-wise you'll make more profit than on a Rembrandt, for instance. But I've tired of keeping

his work. Because of the public reaction, I wanted to get rid of it, so I sold my collection.

Besides his artwork, can you discuss other things you studied about Hitler?

You're getting me off of my slice of the pie. I'm not an authority, however, I can only answer with what I think or what I've read. One thing about *Mein Kampf;* it's too boring to read and, at first, I thought it was because of the translation, but even for Germans it's boring. Albert Speer testified at the Nuremberg Trials that Hitler never read the book. I bet you Hitler couldn't even spell words right. I bet you Hermann Göring never read the book. I bet you Heinrich Himmler never read the book, either. People said they read the book to make out like they knew something. I believe absolutely that Joseph Goebbels was the liar who master-minded the whole operation of the Third Reich.

In his youth when his mother was dying of cancer in Linz, her doctor was a Jew and Hitler gave the doctor a painting. Regarding Hitler's anti-Semitism, most of his hatred of Jews began after WW I when Germany was defeated. I'd like to mention Martin Luther, a 16th century German religious reformer. When you read him, you find a ferocious Jewish hatred; he wanted to destroy the entire Jewish heritage — kill rabbis, burn synagogues along with women and children. Hitler copied the ideas of not only Wagner but many influential people like him.

Now, I said to you earlier that Hitler earned the right to be studied "correctly." After almost an entire lifetime studying Hitler, reading hundreds of books and masses of archival information, interviewing hundreds of his close friends, associates, his former Nazi and SS officers and learning German history, I've come to one conclusion. There is no sin greater than "know-ingly distorting history." In other words, if an author distorted history knowingly, that is a sin and that cannot be forgiven. If the author made a mistake about the information, he or she can be forgiven; maybe one didn't try hard enough. One may do it to sell a book to make money and to become famous, but I'm not such a contributor. In my opinion, history must be accurately re-searched and clearly written. Because as time passes and after those authors die, it becomes more and more difficult to find out what really happened, and the truth will never come out. And, people of the next generations would write books based on such inaccurate information. It is as if someone had distorted the life of Jesus Christ 2,000 years ago, or something like that. That would be a tremendous responsibility for future generations. That would be something "unforgivable."

If I didn't gather information on Hitler's art when I did, it would have been gone forever. Even in the time while I was doing it, many wit-nesses to his art were either already dead or dying out one by one. I should have started much ear-lier than I did. After the people who knew Hitler died, people created new stories about him and we never know the truth. It's said that history is cyclical. Mankind always repeats history, because people don't study history. We don't study our past, so we are cut off from it. I agree that history repeats itself, but not necessarily in the same clothes; it comes out in different clothes. How-ever, I'm optimistic. I do hope a time will come, a time for people to rethink what really happened in the middle of Europe in the middle of our century. I really do. ❖

Nazism and architecture of the Third Reich.

DR. WOLFGANG SCHÄCHE

German, architectural historian and author of the books *From Berlin to Germania* and *Architecture and Urban Planning in Berlin Between 1933 and 1945*. Architect. Born in 1948 in Berlin, Germany. Lives in Germany.

(Photo: Dr. Schäche in his home with his book, *From Berlin to Germania*.)

As a lifelong Berliner, what is your memory of the ruined postwar Berlin?

During the 1950s, growing up in the ruined city, I remember many things of a political nature, of course. Although the city was divided, the border was still open and all the public transportation was free and you could go to both sides of the city. The damaged buildings and houses were bulldozed and there was piled-up rubble on the sidewalks all over the city. Occasionally, mines exploded and people got hurt or killed by accident. Despite the warnings, as a child, I was excited to play in such dangerous areas. These sorts of living conditions were very normal for all Berliners. At home, my father, who was an actor and musician at that time, criticized a lot of things about Germany and spoke about his awful experiences in the war. So, I was aware of what had really happened and the political meaning of the Nazi war. But as years passed, people gradually became reluctant to discuss the time of National Socialism. Nobody wanted to think of Hitler anymore.

How did you become interested in the architecture of the Third Reich?

I wanted to be an architect since I was young. During the late 1960s and early 1970s, which was the peak of the student movement throughout the globe, there was a tendency for people to look at world problems as being based in society. And, when I looked at German history, I realized that nobody had really thoroughly investigated or researched the architectural history of the Third Reich in Germany, even though it was our recent past. I knew that it was such a horrible time for every German that the generation before us had tried to put it behind them. I wanted to challenge this most controversial subject in a better way, in a democratic way. I wanted to learn about the reality of this horrible era of German history through German architecture. At first, when I studied the history of Berlin architecture and town planning during the Nazi period, it seemed of the usual kind. But when I investigated it more, I found an interesting connection between National Socialism, which was a regime of mass murder, and their architectural work. Although many Third Reich buildings were bombed and destroyed, I was able to trace them back through libraries and archival records. I wrote my thesis on this subject, but I continued working on it for nearly 20 years afterwards.

Hitler's dream was to be an architect. Chronologically speaking, from 1933 to 1945, how had the Berlin City Planning Commission prepared for the creation of the Third Reich? How can you analyze the meaning of the architecture of the "Thousand-Year-Reich," and how did Hitler express his great political power in architecture?

Hitler used to tell people if he hadn't been a politician, he would have been an architect. It's a well known story. But to me, it seems like a big joke. He was surely interested in architecture, but as his regime acquired power, he really developed his vision of war and his ambition of conquering the entire world. In the early stages of the war after he conquered Europe, Berlin seemed the most powerful capital in the world, although it was only for a short time. Hitler planned to create Berlin as the center of the world and to last for the next thousand years, which is the meaning of the Third Reich. He even planned to change the name of the city from Berlin to "Germania." He carefully calculated this fantastic dream.

Until the 1920s, historically in Germany, you could find a lot of conventional and traditional architecture. During the Weimar Republic, the renowned Bauhaus style was established. It was a school of design that developed a style characterized mainly by emphasis on functional and simplified design in architecture and all types of arts. Then, in the late 1920s, there was a worldwide economic crisis, the Great Depression, so hardly anything was built. But after 1933, for the next 4 years during the first phase of the Nazi government, architectural design was mixed with the already existing styles of the 1920s. But it changed very rapidly as the Nazi regime grew more powerful. They found something new. Their plan was to support the developing system and to be conciliating. During the Berlin Olympic Games in 1936, which was a very important international event for Germany, they tried to show the world that Germany was different from what it actually was. They tried to pretend we didn't want war. In those days, I would say, Hitler was a "wolf wearing sheep's clothing."

After 1937, architectural planning entered the second phase as Nazi policy changed rapidly. It was very clear at that time that the plan was to be ready for war. The plan for a special state architecture was developed by Speer. Hitler determined to make better quality design on a monstrous scale. Originally, they planned to start the war by 1940, and after that, Germany would be the master nation of the world.

When you study the history of Europe, politics, arts, social matters or whatever, you find architecture is always a manifestation of society. And, of course, the architecture of the Third Reich is a typical example. It's an expression of its political phase; you can't divide the two. It's impossible to understand architecture without understanding the political background at that time. In other words, authors can write literature opposing the ruling power and artists can paint paintings protesting the regime, but architects cannot erect buildings against the political power. There is a big difference between the art world and world of architecture. Style can be done in a very innovative way or sometimes in a regressive way, but as I said, architecture is always an expression of power and a reflection of the political and social climate of the time. This is, of course, one of the exciting sides of this research, to look for the relationship between the Nazi regime, which was, in my mind, the politics of narcissism and the architecture of narcissism. The architecture is an important expression of this policy. And the buildings which were built during the period of the Third Reich — most official buildings — were based on Nazi power.

In order to create the new Germania, Hitler relied on his top architect Albert Speer. What kind of working relationship did they have, ideologically and personally, and how close were they?

I would say Speer was an opportunist. He was 34 years old when Hitler assigned him to work on this gigantic city project for the new Germania. He was an ambitious young architect and wanted to be the best in his class. But in reality he was a catalyst. He did everything that Hitler said. He was Hitler's master architect. Hitler dreamed of being an architect but he wasn't an architect. Hitler used this hungry young architect so that he would be able to fulfill "his dream." Speer was like a tool in his hand that Hitler could implement with his own ideas. Politically, of course, Speer strongly supported Hitler and the Nazi regime in a very active way. He was not only the architect, he also participated in the political architecture.

From early 1940, he was the Minister of Armaments and War Production, which means he was also a politician. In his autobiography *Inside the Third Reich,* he wrote, "If Hitler had any friend in the Third Reich, I was his friend." So he was very close to Hitler. You could see that for an architect who had to plan the architecture for a thousand years, it could be a very big irritation. You could also see not only a continuity in the forms, but a continuity in the planning. In 1933, for example, the plan was to stop the innovation of the 1920s modern styles and to develop something else to last to the year 2000. Speer had done drawings, made a blueprint and model for the building of the "Great Hall," which had a dome of 290 meters in height and 315 meters by 315 meters in the main hall, which was to be the center of the new Germania. It was to be the tallest single hall ever built. The height was more than double the height of the Arch of Triumph of Paris. But Hitler asked him to make it even higher, over 300 meters in height. The scale of the Great Hall could hold hundreds of thousands of people at once; it was the most monstrous building that any human ever designed. Enormous monuments normally refer to ancient Roman architecture, but it couldn't even be compared. Speer designed this most expensive building, it was an extravaganza and the most enormous building you could possibly imagine in the world. It was too static and, in my opinion, not human architecture. It was the architecture of violence, of course. For Hitler, new Germania was to demonstrate the power of Germany and be the greatest capital of the world.

Was it technically possible for German engineering to build such a monstrous building at that time?

Yes, German technology at that time was able to do it. It wasn't just an idea. All the solid construction of this monster architecture was carefully planned and the engineers were working very hard to make it a reality. Germany at that time was already a highly developed industrial country with all the power and all the high-tech systems, so for Hitler and other high-ranking Nazi ministers, it was a serious project. America, for example, had built the Empire State Building in the 1920s and the Golden Gate Bridge in the 1930s; both are magnificent engineering structures even today. Germany was also doing the same thing. Italy and Spain were also nations under dictatorship and fascism, but if the Italians or Spaniards had planned the same sorts of projects under Mussolini and Franco, they wouldn't have been able to do it. Compared to the Germans, they were, at that time, nations of farmers. In many fields, science, technology, machinery, chemistry and engineering, Germany was, since the early days of the century, ahead of all of Europe.

In my opinion, Hitler's architecture was aimed at longevity. He really calculated for the long-lasting future of the Third Reich. He tried to use his architecture as a sign of the big development of the so-called National Socialist movement. It suggested to people that it wasn't architecture on a human scale, as I said, it was architecture for Germania, to show Nazi imperialism and aggressiveness, and indeed to show German superiority to the world. Over all, this architecture was a declaration of war, like producing tanks, guns or bombs, and at the same time, it was a model for human oppression.

How many other architectural projects were designed or planned?

Beside Speer there were hundreds of architects working on city planning. In Berlin alone there were 200-300 projects: government buildings, monuments, public housing, schools, libraries, stadiums, opera houses, railways, bridges, stations and museums, and Speer was in charge of the entire operation. There were plans for many other German cities as well. Besides the Great Hall, Speer personally designed about 50 buildings and monuments. In Berlin, for example, he planned the new Chancellery and the bunker, the triumphal arch, new palaces for both the Führer and Göring, and for the Reichsparteitag Rally in Nuremberg a special stadium which had more than 400,000 seats, with special lighting to dramatize nighttime events at the Zeppelin airfield. In Munich, where the Nazi movement was born, he planned a special monument of the eagle crown, and so on. He built detailed architectural models for these works. Most of these buildings were never built as Germany entered a full-scale war. However, it was a remarkable achievement for the young Speer.

I understand you interviewed Speer after he was released from prison. What is your impression of him?

Some people portray him as a hero of the Third Reich, but frankly, I don't think he was even an architect: He was just a classic intellectual opportunist. He saw himself as becoming a big hero of the architecture of the 20th century. Because Hitler was fascinated by his work, Speer couldn't control himself. He was, at least in this field, like Hitler's puppet. He was very excited with this chance of a career as an architect and very enthusiastic about it. All I can say is that perhaps Speer worked in the wrong service in many ways. Being an architect means, in my thinking, being a human being, and making things on a human scale is one of the first principles. At the same time, any architect should be responsible for developing the structure of buildings as well.

For my thesis research, I interviewed him many times during the early 1970s, and to tell the truth, I've an impression that Speer lacked as a normal human being. He was, of course, a well-educated and self-disciplined person, and he was willing to talk with me and responded to my questions. But I saw his attitude was somewhat aloof, no deep emotions. He was very serious, always precise and a perfect gentleman, but his nature was introverted, not expressive. After 20 years of incarceration, he had plenty of time to think over the Nazi past, of course. Above all, I saw him as a man with a brain. He did it all with the head, but not with the heart. Just try to imagine, in retrospect, any person who could work for Hitler and make him pleased producing such cruel and violent work demonstrating an ugly side of human nature, what kind of human being was he? If you are a zealous believer of Nazism, it may make sense. But if you are a normal human being, it doesn't make sense at all. Anyway, to be honest with you, I can't evaluate the structures of the Third Reich without thinking of the evil man Hitler and those Nazi monsters, or without thinking of concentration camps and the SS murderers of 6 million Jews. From a historical point of view, it's impossible to separate these things. It was all in one system and it all comes together. You can't say, well, the architecture was fine but what Hitler did was wrong. You can't say that. Everything was all under one system.

Berlin has been one of the centers of political life in Europe, but the architectural history has always been affected by each change in the political climate. How did things change after the Berlin Wall was destroyed?

Before Hitler, most city planning was done by the kings of the Hohenzollern dynasty, and in every phase Berlin was at the forefront. Now, in post-Wall Berlin and after the reunification, the Berlin government has proposed new city planning and, in fact, many architects are involved with the project. I'm very skeptical that a master plan would be helpful because it's too static. Times Square in New York, for example, is a fantastic urban place. It's not pretty but it's a manifestation of city liv-ing. Piccadilly Circus of London is a demonstration of a big city. These are not the result of a master plan. What I'm saying is that you have to think about the social dimension of the city. Also, it must have some technical rules that, for example, skyscrapers cannot be built in an inner city circle. In the framework of this rule, a lot of democratic ideas can be implemented. An interesting perspective in this project is that architects of many nationalities are participating: Americans, French, British and Japanese. So, I'm hoping that when they put their ideas together, it will create a unique city structure with a lot of international flavors. ❖

The German intellectual exiles in Hollywood.

DR. HAROLD VON HOFE

American, author of numerous books on German intellectuals in exile and director of the Feuchtwanger Institute for Exile Studies at the University of Southern California. Retired professor. He lives in California, USA.

Before the outbreak of WW II a number of German intellectuals had exiled themselves in America, many in Southern California. Can you tell me about the German colony in Hollywood and Los Angeles?

During the Golden Age of the movie industry in America in the 1920s and 1930s, a number of successful German movie directors such as Dieterle, Lubitsch, Koster, Thiele, Fritz Lang and Billy Wilder, were invited to Hollywood. They came to Southern California and began new careers. When Hitler came to power, the German and Austrian elite, intellectuals, philosophers, writers, playwrights, poets, composers, artists, novelists and scientists gradually fled their fatherland. By the middle 1930s, many settled in exile in southern France, in the seaside town of Sanary-sur-Mer, near Marseilles. The number of the exodus was staggering, including the most famous people like Albert Einstein, Sigmund Freud, Thomas Mann, his brother Heinrich, Arnold Schoenberg, Bertolt Brecht, Lion Feuchtwanger, Bruno Frank, Leonard Frank, Franz and Alma Mahler Werfel, Alfred Doeblin, Ludwig Marcuse, and among them many were Jews.

When the Nazis invaded France, although the southern part was not occupied, the Nazi pressure was strong and many Jews lived in constant fear. In 1940, however, some of them managed to flee. They crossed the Pyrenees Mountains on foot, entered Spain, then went to Lisbon, Portugal, and took a boat to New York. Einstein and Freud settled in Sanarx. But many came to Southern California. By the time Europe was in a full-scale war, there was a huge German emigré colony in Southern California. The number of exiles was a magnet and thousands of people came, including British novelist Christopher Isherwood, who lived in pre-Hitler Berlin. Some of them were very poor but some were not. The INS, the US immigration authority, was concerned that they would be a burden to American tax payers.

So, Hollywood movie production companies gave contracts to German writers to write screenplays. The companies provided offices and secretaries for them, but they didn't actually expect them to write scenarios for motion pictures. They were already renowned novelists, dramatists and essayists. It was just a friendly gesture of co-operation helping them to stay in America as a haven until the war ended. Very few of them actually worked for the movie studios. But after their contracts expired, the aid came to an end. They had to struggle to survive. They needed money to pay the rent and to eat. Some successful movie directors and screenplay-writers set up an organization called the "European Film Fund." Many of the people in the movie business contributed money to support the fund. One of the most effective men was the film director named William Dieterle. The exiles eventually settled in Los Angeles — Beverly Hills, Brentwood, Pacific Palisades and Santa Monica. The warm Mediterranean-like climate of Southern California was attractive to them.

I'd like to explain how I came to meet them. My parents were Germans and I grew up with a bilingual education. After I graduated with a Ph.D. degree in German literature from Northwestern University in 1939, I became a research scholar. I had been visiting Germany since I was born and my connection to Germany was close. In 1942 I attended a German lecture given by Ludwig Marcuse, a renowned writer who was a German Jew. The topic was the German exile in America. I became acquainted with this circle of German intellectuals and I was socially involved

323

with them. I subsequently wrote articles on German writers and their life in exile. I write both German and English, but most of my work has been published in Germany.

As a German-American, how did you feel about the whole situation? And how did these Germans adapt to American life?

At that time I thought it was an intellectual crisis for Germany. When we study the history of the world, at least in Western Europe or America, such a huge exodus of prominent and important people had never occurred. It was a unique phenomenon in Western civilization. During the time of the French Revolution, for example, Victor Hugo and few others left, and in 19th century Germany, Heinrich Heine was exiled for political reasons, but the scale of this exodus from Germany between 1933 to 1939 was unparalleled. Some of the leftists emigrated to Moscow, but most of them came to America. They found it unbearable to live in a country under Hitler. Hitler's Germany was really a society of madness.

Anti-Semitism in Germany was of course responsible for causing Jewish writers to flee. Some of their families perished in Auschwitz and other concentration camps. Those who were not Jewish such as Thomas and Heinrich Mann, and Leonard Frank left for political reasons. For them it was unthinkable to live in a nation under National Socialism. Although they were refugees in America, they continued to feel they were German. They spoke German to each other and wrote in German. Marcuse and Feuchtwanger used to say, *"Meine Heimat ist die deutsche Sprache"* (My home is the German language.) Historically and politically, there is a rich humanistic tradition in German culture as you can see from Goethe, Schiller, Schelling, Kant, Nietzsche, Hegel, Schopenhauer, Fichte, Bach, Beethoven, Mozart, Schubert, Schumann and Wagner. That is still a rich part of German cultural history. The exiles were here to represent German heritage and continued to create works of literature, art and music while they were living in Hollywood.

During the intellectual destruction by the Nazis, there were book burnings in Germany. Precisely, what sort of books did they burn?

The book burning was symbolic, but there were tens of thousands of books that were confiscated. Did the Nazis burn all of them? No! The books which they destroyed had Jewish, democratic, socialist or communist themes. For example, Feuchtwanger had a book called *Jud Süss* — an 18th century novel based on the true story of a Jewish financier who chooses death rather than conversion. The novel was a huge success in Germany as well as in England and America. The volume was burned. But the Nazis knew such books were valuable outside Germany and they needed hard currency, so they sold thousands of copies in Switzerland and made a profit. For their own records, the Nazis always kept many of the names of those influential writers and books which were banned. From 1933 to 1940, hundreds of volumes of German literature were published in Holland because it was not possible within Germany, but when the Nazis invaded the Netherlands, they were confiscated and taken to Germany. Many were found in Germany after the war.

There was strong anti-German sentiment among Americans during the height of the war. What was the reaction among Americans toward those exiled Germans?

In intellectual circles people knew very well who they were and why they were here: they were anti-Nazi Germans. For instance, prominent conductors such as Bruno Walter were giving concerts and Thomas Mann and Einstein frequently gave public lectures in various cities. They were distinguished individuals. American people knew who were Nazis and who were anti-Nazis. But there was another side. At the time, I was writing articles for the *Los Angeles Times* about those exiles who were Jewish. My view was sympathetic for the Jews and I often received nasty letters from the readers saying, "You like Jews, don't you? While the Nazis are doing their work in Germany, we'll get the Jews here, too. Just wait!" There was also anti-Semitism among Americans. Although the US government didn't intern German-Americans like they did Japanese-Americans, there was a strong anti-German feeling among some Americans which was acceptable during the war. There were curfews for those German citizens living in the USA. Everybody had to be home by 8:00 o'clock in the evening and they were not allowed to leave their homes. That caused conflicts and anger.

At the same time, there were numerous anti-German books published such as the *Thousand Year Conspiracy* and *Germans Must Perish*. In the latter, it was written something like, "The Germans are such evil people that all German males should be sterilized after the war, so that by the year 2,000 there will be no more Germans left on the earth." The author's thinking was that the Germans had caused two world wars, and if we annihilate all Germans, it would mean no more problems in the future. Killing all Germans would be the answer. Then, we as mankind can live in peace and harmony, which was nonsense. Things are not that simple. Today, there are many wars all over the world and they have nothing to do with Germany.

At the time, there were already established Jewish communities in New York and elsewhere. What connection did you find between those German/Austrian emigré Jews and the New York and Los Angeles Jews?

The older Jewish community was largely of Eastern European origins — Polish, Hungarian, Ukrainian, Russian and others, and they didn't have a close relationship with German/Austrian Jews. The Jewish people were divided into religious and secular groups, and a number of German-speaking Jews were well educated and successful. Some were arrogant, snobbish and tended to look down on other Jews. Compared to Eastern European countries, Germany had a high standard of living and people had a better education. There had been prominent Jews such as Einstein, Mendelssohn, Karl Marx and Freud who were outstanding, and very few intellectuals who were of eastern origin. When Hitler began his *judenrein* campaign, most of the German Jews felt they were just like any Germans and wished to be assimilated. Many had never been in a synagogue; they had German surnames and lived scattered in many parts of German cities like any other Germans, not in ghettos like the Eastern European Jews. Therefore, no one could tell the difference between Jews and non-Jews, as it is in America today.

In the 19th century as Germany emerged as an industrial nation, liberalism and secularism emerged as well, and gradual emancipation for Jews came along with it. German society had become more tolerant and proportions of Jews were able to become lawyers, doctors and pro-

fessors, because Jews were assimilated. **German society seemed to provide a rich intellectual soil and great cultural background for the many outstanding German Jews. What do you think?**

Yes, it's true. In other words, if Einstein had been born in a small Polish town, probably he wouldn't have become the Einstein we know as one of the greatest scientists in the world. He grew up in German society, had a German education, worked in Germany at the Berlin Institute and in Switzerland. The German foundation was responsible for his career. In many ways, Germany was intellectually a breeding ground for Jewish people. The same applies to Freud. The highly intellectual atmosphere at the University of Vienna and the rich Austrian culture had contributed to his great work. Another example was Franz Kafka, a Czech-born novelist. He wrote in German. He was sustained by the Austro-Hungarian Empire which also provided a German background. If you are interested in German history, the whole Jewish situation was doubly tragic for the Jewish people, for their loss to Germany.

I discussed the subject on one occasion with a Jewish-American friend. He asked, "Do we know any great, internationally recognized intellectual Jew who is from Israel?" I answered, "We can think of some names of politicians and statesmen, but not scientists, philosophers or writers." I could imagine that the fusion of "Jewishness and Germanness," as these two chemicals interwove uniquely with each other created many great Jewish intellectuals in the German cultural area of Europe. With the Nazis, that came to an end. Today, there are only 40,000 Jews in Germany. There is not going to be another Einstein or Freud, I don't believe. National Socialism ter-

minated that fruitful fusion of Jewish and non-Jewish Germans.

What happened to those exiles at the end of the war? Also, could you tell me about the Feuchtwanger Institute for Exile Studies?

In 1943, Lion Feuchtwanger, with his wife Marta, settled at a residence named Villa Aurora overlooking the ocean in Pacific Palisades. In this Spanish-style estate he continued writing and often gave readings from his works for his close friends and guests: Thomas and Heinrich Mann, Bruno Frank, Ludwig Marcuse and Franz Werfel. Occasionally he also invited Charles and Oona Chaplin and Aldous Huxley, a British novelist. The house was big enough to accommodate a large library. He began collecting books and eventually it was filled with over 30,000 volumes.

At the end of the war, many of the German exiles became victims of McCarthyism in America. They were labeled as communists and some returned to Europe. Brecht left the US in 1947. Some German Jews emigrated to Israel, but they were reluctant to learn the Hebrew language. They continued to speak German and since German wasn't a popular language there, after a few years they returned to America or Europe. Heinrich Mann died in 1950. His famous brother Thomas Mann was given American citizenship, but he was so outraged by US government actions that he moved to Switzerland in 1952.

After Feuchtwanger died in 1958 and Marta in 1987, the Villa was left to the University of Southern California as the Lion Feuchtwanger Memorial Library. It was restored and supported by the German Friends and Supporters of the Villa Aurora and the German government. There is cooperative cultivation from the legacy left by Lion Feuchtwanger and other German intellectuals in exile by the German "Friends and Supporters of the Villa Aurora" with headquarters in Berlin, and the Feuchtwanger Institute For Exile Studies of the University of Southern California in Los Angeles. Today, Villa Aurora is a research center for American-European relations and for the German exile literature of those writers, artists and intellectuals collectively known as "Weimar by the Pacific." ❖

An untold history of a Nazi mecca in Bavaria.

ANNA ELISABETH ROSMUS

German, researcher of the history of the Third Reich, essayist, author of various books, and heroine of the movie *The Nasty Girl*. Born in 1960 in Passau, Germany. Lives in Germany.

(Photo: Ms. Rosmus with her two daughters in her home. The background painting is her own work, to teach children about civil disobedience.)

You are one of the few young German writers who openly criticize Germany's Nazi past. How did you get involved with the whole scene?

When I was in school I never saw any documentary film about the concentration camps being liberated, and no one ever told me about the unspeakable suffering of the victims of the Nazi Germans. None of the survivors ever came and spoke about their horrible experiences at my school. When I first learned about Germany's brown-shirt past, I was 20 years old. At that time, I was a student at the University of Passau, my hometown in Bavaria. It's a border town with Austria, some 180 km northeast of Munich. In 1980, I participated in an essay competition on the subject of "Everyday Life in the Third Reich." As I began my research, I encountered difficulties aimed at preventing my historical work. For the people in Passau, the way of dealing with their past was quite simple. Everything was the fault of the leader and everyone else was basically an opponent of the regime! It was a big lie. Half a century later, however, this "reality" was suddenly challenged by me. I began finding out about the history of Jews in Passau. I chronicled anti-Semitic acts committed by community members in my town. Quite a few people became anxious and hostile about their image as "opponents" to the Nazi regime and they sabotaged my research. As I pursued it further, the town authorities withheld its historical archives. I got the impression that the entire town had conspired against me. Then I was expelled from my university. Anyway, I completed my research and did a documentary on Jewish families in the town.

In 1983, my first book *Resistance and Persecution in Passau 1933-1939* was published in Munich. The following year I won a prestigious prize for this book. At that time, I also won the law suit against the town mayor and got wide national media attention. Since then, I've never stopped writing essays and books about the same subject. But the harassment against me has never stopped. When I was inquiring into the town's most recent past, for instance, I was slandered and threatened with a knife. I was getting abusive phone-calls night after night and anonymous hate-mails. For Passauers, I became a "nasty girl." I began to ask myself, is it possible to love a country whose inhabitants simply don't want to have anything to do with their criminal past? Can I possibly feel at home in a state where the entire nation committed such a barbaric crime against humanity? Some of the Passauers called me "Jew-whore" or "dirty sow" because I was simply researching the whereabouts of some Jews in my town. These people actually said that they regret we don't live in medieval times because they could hang me or drown me or burn me to death.

Can you talk about the movie *The Nasty Girl*, which was based on your experiences in Passau? What kind of response did you get in Germany and internationally? Are you satisfied with the result?

Because my first book received a famous cultural prize in Germany, it got the attention of Munich's award-winning film director, Michael Verhoeven, best known for his *The White Rose*, which covers similar ground. He decided to make a movie out of my story. His intention was to show the world an example of a young German Gentile and how she got involved in studying the history that was taboo to discuss in her society, and how she developed the civic courage to fight against authority. How just an ordinary girl like me could suddenly become interested in politics without having experienced that part of our history.

The Nasty Girl was nominated for an Oscar and it was hard to suppress, except in Germany. It was shown in major German cities but not well received. After showing only one day in Frankfurt, for instance, it was stopped because theater owners and audiences weren't interested. They felt too uncomfortable facing their Nazi guilt. In Passau, town officials had to figure out how to avoid showing it. But it was a big success abroad. It has been shown in most parts of the world: America, Australia, England, Ireland, and other European countries. I have traveled to a few of those countries and attended the premiers. I was overwhelmed and got interesting responses. For instance, in Dublin, Ireland, people came to me and said, "We see the movie as being not only you, but we also see similar problems in our country. Our Catholic church dominates and non-Catholics are minorities who are hated. The minorities are on the fringe in our society like the Jews are in German Christian society." In Australia, people felt a similar thing about what they had done to the aborigines, their minorities; it's more or less the same mechanism. People in America are reminded what they did to their original inhabitants, the Indians. I didn't expect these responses from the movie and I'm happy that the film was able to use me as an example that could explain so much about human behavior.

Through my personal experience, I've learned many things. In our media-filled society today, education simply can't be left to teachers and parents alone. Every area of culture, film, television, theater and the press, needs to contribute something. America bears responsibility for Vietnam. Towards the end of the war, the media played an important role. They showed the mas-

sacres committed by the GIs at My Lai and so they helped the anti-war movement. Also, there was the mysterious death of President Kennedy. Years later these subjects were explored in movies and have become a part of international culture. Germany bears responsibility for the consequences of WW II and for the partition of Germany into two states. Years ago when people came out into the streets of Leipzig to demonstrate their feelings, there was no armed force. Perhaps television crews were there and journalists provided cover. The media played a crucial role in bringing the "reunification." The same way in Czechoslovakia's "gentle revolution" which was originated by students at Prague's Academy for Film and Television. So, the media produces results. I believe this kind of news and coverage is what our culture needs and the state government should support films. They ought to single out movies that pose questions about the history of our past. The media, including the film industry, often mirror these expectations. In Germany, the TV mini-series *Holocaust* and documentary *Shoah* caused widespread debate on whether such films should be made and shown.

On the other hand, Neil Postman, the chairman of Communication Arts at the New York University and the author of *Amusing Ourselves to Death: Public Discourse in the Age of Show Business,* wrote about the danger of television industries "practically entertaining us to death." He warns that we shouldn't depoliticize film. We would thus be skewing information even further in the name of entertainment, especially when the subject is Germany's brown-shirts past. The German people have an obligation to speak out because we are responsible for the victims of those years. Writers try to spell out what happened through their stories and historians and political scientists pursue new details.

From your years of studying the social problems of the minority among the majority, how can you describe the psychological and social phenomenon of the Jews?

The interesting thing about Jewish study is — amongst others — learning the history of their persecution. Many Germans often used to wonder why there were such a high number of Jews in prestigious professional fields and why so many Jews possess wealth, and speak more than one language. While I was writing a book about Jews, I discovered more about them which the majority of Germans have never experienced. Since the beginning of human civilization and many centuries before the Third Reich, being the minority, nearly every generation of Jews had an experience of persecution and pogrom: of being personally abused or discriminated. Jewish life often has been a repetition of this persecution. Born to be a Jew means, subconsciously, to live with the fear of persecution. "One day I may become the next victim and suddenly have to flee somewhere leaving everything behind." As a Jew, there would be no guarantees for the future to live and die in the same place they were born. I realized that Jews live psychologically with an uncertain feeling. That's why many of them become good money savers. So, many Jewish parents give their children a higher education. They send them to good universities to study law, medicine, music or to get some other practical professions or skills, to learn many languages so that they can start a new life in any country in the world as doctors, scientists, lawyers, violinists, pianists, writers and journalists. If they speak a few languages they can practice their profession in any

place they settle. Children of Jews naturally have to prepare for that. Having a good education is a way of survival. In fact, during the Holocaust, Jews who spoke several languages survived more than those who couldn't. Compared to Jews, on the other hand, being a Gentile and a member of the majority, most of us are guaranteed to live in the same country where we were born until we die, so we don't feel a necessity to be like Jews.

After reunification, I talked to a number of the younger generation of German Jews, those of the age from 15 to 35. Germany isn't an easy country to live in for those whose parents and relatives perished at the hands of Nazis. The German government of course tries to make them quiet and calm them down in Germany, but they expressed their fear that the new bigger Germany wouldn't be a safe place for them any more. One day sooner or later, they could lose their rights. They feel they are much more of a minority now than before. In Germany, no German could have two nationalities, except for the Jews. The German Jews are allowed to have two passports: German and Israeli. For many younger German Jews today, the State of Israel is their only alternative. They have rather mixed feelings for their last retreat, whether they like it or not. The experience of persecution and human suffering explain many things about the Jews. Because of their life fleeing from one country to another from generation to generation and also being educated, over the centuries many have developed their own intelligence. Since many are advanced in aesthetic sensitivity and languages, they are able to read books in different languages and able to learn more than us. Their philosophy and thinking have developed through centuries of experiences of human pain, suffering, misery and struggle. This could be one of the many reasons why there is a high proportion of intelligentsia among the Jews.

Can you tell me about the history of the anti-Semites in Passau and the Bavarian region, and what you learned from your research?

Not many people know that here in Bavaria, which is made up of predominantly Catholic inhabitants, there were anti-Jewish boycotts 8 years before Hitler came to power. Passau is truly the Mecca of German anti-Semitism. According to my study, the history of Jewish persecution in Passau traces back to the year 1200. In the 1920s, there were 400 Jews here, but the anti-Semitic fervor was so strong that most of them fled the town, and by 1933, only 40 Jews were left. When my mother was a child growing up during the Nazi period, she said she never met a Jew. This town was anti-Semitic without Jews. Famous writers and a bishop in our region declared publicly that Jews had no rights and should be cast out from our society. And for several centuries no one spoke out for them. As everybody knows, the National Socialist Party was born in this region. Passau is known as a Baroque eden on three rivers. Adolf Hitler was born in the next town across the river and spent a part of his childhood here; Heinrich Himmler's father was a teacher at my school; Adolf Eichmann lived and married here, and he organized the deportation of the Austrian Jews here; Julius Streicher and his family lived close by; Ernst Kaltenbrunner, an Austrian Nazi, and many other original Nazi members used to get together here for meetings. They all grew up here with the deeply-rooted anti-Jewish Bavarian mentality. Local Nazis organized the party here in 1920.

Aryanization and *judenrein* were requested many years before Hitler. For instance, in the year 1920, one of the residents demanded publicly that concentration camps should be built immediately, and all Jews should be sent there or murdered. This was reported in the local newspapers at that time. So, everybody knew it. More recently in 1985, a former concentration camp guard fired on a Jew here. Meetings of the Deutsche Volks Union, the biggest gathering of European right-wing extremists, take place here every year. David Irving, a British pro-Hitler author, comes here to attend the rallies almost every year.

How do you see the Germans' attitude toward civil obedience? How has the Bavarian mentality changed since the Nazi era?

For mainstream Germans to deal with Germany's role during the war, the idea is to pass over it and not touch it. There is no thought of dealing with what has happened. For most individuals it's: I didn't know it, I didn't see it, I didn't hear it. The Germans are obsessed with law and absolute obedience to state authorities. That is the main problem. I'll tell you another example. During the war there were some German Christian civilians who helped the Jews: they hid them in their homes and saved them from being deported to the gas chambers. It was of course illegal by Nazi law. But even today after 50 years, those Germans are uncomfortable speaking about it. They feel ashamed of themselves, afraid they'll be detected as protectors because it was against the law. As the real good Germans, they feel guilty for what they did because they broke the law. For most Germans, to obey law and the state is more important than to be human beings... For me it's just incredible!

Recently, I learned about a different kind of war crime which was also committed by the Passau civilians. In April 1945, about 2,000 Russian POWs were murdered here. A few Passauers brutally shot them to death. How they did it was very cruel. Only a few of them survived. They were hidden by German families in their homes. I found one of the families and interviewed them. They told me their secret stories, but they don't want to be identified and they strictly barred me from publishing their names. Because it was prohibited to save prisoners by Nazi law, they are still afraid to be publicly known in this matter by their neighbors even today. They feel rather sorry for what they did. Killing prisoners of war was against the Geneva Convention Agreement, of course. But a few Nazis gave the order to do it. I'm afraid to say this Bavarian mentality hasn't changed too much since the end of the Nazi era.

Can you talk about the killing of 2,000 Russian POWs, how they were killed?

In the last hours of the war some Passauers captured Russian officers. They ordered the Russians to dig graves, lined them up, and quickly shot them or stabbed them to death. Then they removed the genitals of the officers and dismembered their bodies using knives. Then they buried them in the ditches while some were still alive. Two of the victims managed to get out of the ditches after the SS and the murderers had left. Several hours later American soldiers entered Passau. The two survivors told the story of their horror. The American officers gathered the people in the town aged 16 to 60 and ordered them to dig out the mass graves. They pressured them to clean the bodies, place them in coffins and rebury them in proper graves with crosses and names on them, and put flowers on them. I found all the evidence of this in historical documents in the United States National Archives in Washington, D.C. Furthermore, what I found out was that our Mayor was a Nazi himself. So, it was clear to

me why people didn't want to discuss anything to do with the matter and why I was expelled from my university. As I pursued my research, I found there were more Nazis in Passau. Some were honorable, respectable and highly decorated citizens in our community.

Besides the social relations between the majority and the minority, there is no doubt that religious hatred has fueled the problems between Christianity and Judaism. How do you see this?

I would point particularly to Catholicism. The Catholic church was extremely powerful and controlling of the people in my region. During the period of the Weimar Republic, which was politically and socially the most liberal time in Germany, many people became secular and the church lost members. During the Nazi regime Hitler put pressure on all religions, people couldn't deny the Christian God. They resisted and went back to their traditional religious life. In other words, if Hitler hadn't put pressure on Christianity so much, German Catholicism might not have become so strong.

When it comes to marriage, however, religion does cause problems. For instance, my own mother, a native Passauer and now age 64, couldn't marry a Protestant man because the two belonged to different religions. In her generation most people were concerned with their children's religious identity. So, religion split the people even among the Christians. So, when the matter comes to relations between Christians and Jews, the problem becomes deeper and more serious. For generations, the two groups hardly mingled with each other socially and had almost no desire to intermarry. There was a silent wall between them. Most German Jews married only Jews.

How did the Holocaust change the attitude of the postwar generations toward the Jews in Germany?

I can see quite a change. First, some of the younger generations of non-Jews became Jews: They converted to Judaism. I personally met about 25 German Gentile Christian men and women who married Jews. They learned Hebrew and the history of the Jews and became Jewish. But they aren't really religious. It was, in a way, out of sympathy. They felt a kind of guilt and responsibility for the Jews what their parents' generation had done to them. Their children can become Jews, especially, if the mothers were Jewish. My husband was a Catholic Gentile and so are my daughters, but since I became interested in Judaism, I understand more of the inter-connection between the two religions. Judaism is the origin of Christianity. I love Jesus as a person because he was Jewish and I believe he was a good human. In my view, what happened was that for 2,000 years his name has been taken over by Roman Catholicism.

Another interesting change I've seen among the post-Holocaust Germans is Jewish names for Gentile children. I named my second daughter Salome. She is 8 years old now. Salome means in Jewish "peace is with me" and was the name of a famous female dancer in the ancient times. I chose this name because it sounds pretty and exotic, and I wish her peace, and also because of my sympathy for Jews. Among 40 children at the university's kindergarten, I found many typical Jewish names such as Benjamin, Sarah, Salome, Simon, Rachel, instead of common German names such as Hans, Heinz, Fritz, Hermann, Siegfried, Wolfgang, Brigit or Ursula. One day out of curiosity, I asked their mothers why they chose those names. Many of them didn't know these are originally Jewish names.

The only reason I found was they liked the sound; it seemed exotic and interesting, and they wanted their beloved children to be raised with this beautiful sound. Then I found the name of Patrick which is a typical Christian name. When I asked his mother, she blushed. She told me she was a Jew and didn't want her son to be identified as a Jew. She said if he had a Jewish name he could become an outcast in the community. I thought it was very interesting.

In Germany today, despite the hostile German-Jewish relationship, every third-born female was named Sarah, many in middle names, which is a very new tendency. There are girls named Sarah all over Germany now. During the Nazi time Sarah was a name for Jews but now it's a very popular name for German Gentiles. I felt how peculiar and ironic politics are. After all, the most common names in the Christian world such as David, John, Joel, Michael, Anne, Mary, Elizabeth are Judaic names. We all live with a Judeo-Christian influence, and one way or another, people just forgot about it.

There are many issues about the Holocaust and Jews as a religious and racial minority. How should they be taught to German school children, particularly in Bavaria?

Like I said, at my school, my teacher never said anything about the Holocaust and Jews. I never met a Jew and grew up without knowing anything about them. That's because teaching the Holocaust at school has been discouraged in my region of Bavaria. I believe it's an important issue to discuss publicly for everybody. So, I teach my children about Jews and their experience of being in the minority and I bring up political, social and cultural questions at home to inform them and encourage them to think about this matter. A funny thing occurred. One day Salome, age 4, was at school with a group of pupils singing a song, "God loves all the children! God loves all the children!" She suddenly stopped singing. She asked her teacher a question. "If God loves all the children, why couldn't He stop the Nazis from sending Jewish children to the gas chambers?" The teacher was stunned. She had no way to answer and it was an awkward moment for her. None of the rest of the children knew what Salome was asking, of course, because they had never heard of it. I was so surprised a little girl like her could be able to transform it in her own little world and had developed her own mind and thinking. She was a good example. I strongly support educating our children on these matters starting at an early age. If we Germans don't speak to the children about such questions of our past, we are not providing the right educational opportunity to the next generations.

What other things did you learn from your personal experience?

This is my ideal. I would like to live with people who neither fear nor suppress the truth and who acknowledge the mistakes of the past. I would like to live in a society which regards those with different opinions as opponents but not as enemies. I would love to live with a community which can bear to be criticized and can attempt to correct their mistakes instead of denying them. I would like to live in a state whose representatives are frank about dangers and do something about them rather than pretend that they don't exist. This is where I would like to live. This kind of state doesn't exist, of course. However, I value our constitution the most because it guarantees freedom to the greatest possible extent. This is why I, even a small-town-student, was able to sue the town authorities; it took me 4 years of struggle to persuade the town to hand over the Nazi files, but in the end I won. It demonstrates that fundamentally this state is "working." And I have to say that the town is supporting me now and I have received a lot of public support from all over the country, including political prisoners who suffered from injustice. This experience gave me encouragement and a feeling of not being entirely defenseless. It gave me confidence for the future. And now, I'm able to continue working on my research on highly controversial political subjects in my town in peace. ❖

The true meaning of the Holocaust.

DR. RICHARD L. RUBENSTEIN

American Jewish theologian, professor of religion at the University of Tallahassee, Florida, author of the book *After Auschwitz* and other books. Born in 1924 in New York. Lives in Florida, USA.

My question to you, Dr. Rubenstein, is regarding your book *After Auschwitz*, which is one of the most controversial writings about the Holocaust I've ever read. First, could you discuss the remark made by a Berlin clergyman, Dean Gruber, "The Nazi slaughter of the Jews was somehow God's will, that, for His own inscrutable reasons, God really wanted the Jewish people to be exterminated by Hitler." This is very shocking. What is your interpretation of that?

My point is that it was based on a literal interpretation of Judaism and Christianity. If one believes in God, the omnipotent God of the Bible, then one must regard the Holocaust as God's will. Personally, I don't have such a belief. That was one of the reasons I wrote this book to expose that view as wholly unacceptable. And, basically for most Jews and many Christians, the idea that the Holocaust was God's punishment is unacceptable. At the same time, they didn't want to give up the basic belief in Judaism and Christianity that God works in history. And what I was arguing was that you can't have it both ways, that if you accept God as working in history, and if you accept the idea that there is a chosen people, then you have to say that God was involved in the Holocaust. My personal conclusion was that there really is no chosen people. I reject the idea of a chosen people.

This book, by the way, was first published in 1966, before the Six-Day War in Israel. At that time, there was a tremendous reaction. *Time Magazine*, *The New York Times* and *Playboy* did interviews and profiles on me. People regarded my views as very scandalous. But the interesting thing is that the book didn't die. It went from one printing to another until 1991. And more recently, I was invited by my publisher to do a revised edition. So, the last edition contains in fact 50 percent new materials. Besides, it was written in the aftermath of the unification of Germany, so it's almost a new book.

As it was scandalous, most Jewish readers were very angry with me for a very long time. But in 1987 the Jewish Theological Seminary from which I originally graduated, awarded me an honorary doctorate for writing the book. The reason was that even though it was controversial and they don't agree with my opinion, I had raised the fundamental issues about the Western idea of God and the Holocaust.

Who said the Jews were chosen people, Jews themselves?

The Christians said so, too. What Christians say is that when Jesus Christ came, those who followed Christ were the "New Israel," and therefore they are now the chosen people. So, underneath all the other disputes between Jews and Christians, there is the question "Who is the chosen people?" Now, many ordinary Christian people like to think, "Oh, well, that's just a fantasy that the Jews have about themselves." But what they don't realize is that if they study Christian theology, Christians have the same belief about themselves. The technical term for it is "supersessionary." Christianity is a supersessionary religion. Christianity doesn't say that Judaism is wrong; it says that Judaism has been superseded and its full meaning has been revealed in Christianity. I once argued with a Christian clergyman, William Sloane Coffin, who was a famous leader of the peace movement in the 1960s. I said to him that we Jews didn't believe in the chosen people because to believe in it, we had to believe in God at Auschwitz.

You mean the chosen people were to be killed...

Yes, well, exactly. He got upset. He said, "How can you give up the chosen people? — You are my roots." Because if the Jews aren't the chosen people, then why is Jesus so special? Like him, many Christians want the Jews to believe in the chosen people. For us, that is the Christians' problem, not the Jews'. This sort of deep belief has been going on for centuries and what is involved here is no conscious effort to deceive believers. I just put it differently. What you have is a way of apprehending reality. This is the Jewish way of apprehending reality, and what I have to stress is that, belief in the chosen people idea is part of the Christian way of apprehending reality. Because, if the Jews were not the chosen people, then the Messiah could not have come from Israel, you see. So, what I tried to show in the book is that there are some unpleasant consequences in believing in this, and I don't want to believe in it.

How do you contrast Christianity with Buddhism, for example, or Japanese Shintoism?

Shintoism is a purely Japanese tradition. It's got to do with family, ancestors, community, nation and the land they belong to. You don't have missionaries, though Japanese Buddhists do attempt to spread enlightenment. The difference between spreading enlightenment and what Christianity does is that in Buddhism you are not expected to say that "so and so is the source of my salvation," and that message was brought by God who was born at a certain time, lived at a certain time and died at a certain time. Now, in Buddhism, enlightenment ultimately has to come from within oneself, therefore, it's not a missionary religion. I ask why is Christianity missionary? My answer has to do with what I call the cognitive instability

of Christianity. Let me explain what I mean by cognitive instability. If my view of reality is based upon propositions that a lot of people regard as not in accord with common sense, and if even I have some doubt about my view of reality, then I'm in a condition of cognitive instability. In that case, what constitutes social, cultural and historical knowledge for me becomes unstable. Now, I do think this is true of Christianity. Incidentally, I also think it is true of Judaism which is also based on history, although a different history.

Christianity lives in a condition of cognitive instability. If you can't prove the truth of the propositions that you believe in, you try to convince other people of that truth so that you form a world where everybody agrees with you. If everybody would agree that Jesus was in fact the Messiah and this became a part of culture, then the condition of cognitive instability would go away. So, wherever there is a non-believer, the Christian world must reach out and convert that person, or if they do not convert under certain extreme circumstances, like for example the Crusades, they must fight against them and destroy them. And you know what happened in Japan in the 17th century when the Europeans arrived? The Third Shogun of the Tokugawa government declared "No Christianity in Japan," and that was a success. Because the Japanese realized that their civilization depends on their own beliefs, not on being Christianized. The point of all this is that I think this is very deeply related to the problem of Europe. Because European civilization was based upon the fact that Europe was the Christian heartland, and the expansion of Europe had a great deal to do with the cognitive instability of Christianity. And, I think it had a great deal to do ultimately with the Holocaust.

What about your other point that National Socialism was an anti-Christian movement. How do you explain that?

As Christian thinkers often point out Nazism was an anti-Christian explosion that departed utterly from Christian morality, and I think this view is undeniably true. It's the anti-Christian explosion of Christians against their own value system. It was the negation of Christianity as negation was understood by Hegel and Freud. The classic villains of Christianity, the Jews, became the prime objects of extermination for the anti-Christian Christians, the Nazis.

To study its background, one must bring out Germany's non-Christian past; the "Teutonist and Volksreligion" movements during the 18th and 19th centuries. Resentment against Christianity and its enforced displacement of the Teutonic gods has been a significant motif in German life since the Napoleonic wars. This resentment had important roots in the peculiar historical and geographical situation of the Germans. One root is in the old tension between the Teutonic north and the Latin south, from which Catholic Christianity originated. Charlemagne's forced conversion of the Saxons and Luther's break with Rome were in part manifestations of this tension. They regarded Christianity as the product and imposition of a foreign Latin culture, and it was resented in influential German circles. Nazism grew in part out of this aspect of German cultural history. Although Hitler was willing to use the Church's powers for his own purposes, he was also committed to its ultimate elimination. Once Hitler revealed his intentions to his associate Hermann Rauschning: "Neither of the denominations — Catholics or Protestants, they are both the same — has any future left, at least not for the Germans. Fascism may perhaps make its peace with the Church in God's name. I will do it, too. Why not? But that won't stop me from stamping out Christianity in Germany, root and branch. You can't be both — a German and a Christian."

This theme of Teutonic roots turned up in Hegel's early writing. He titled one of his earliest writings, *Is Judea then the Fatherland of the Teutons?* Hegel complains that Christianity has emptied Valhalla of its gods and forced the German people to accept a Jewish God and its fables in place of their own. In other words, "Do we allow an imported God in our land?" This observation presupposes the concept of *Volksreligion* in which the religion, mythology and social organization of an ethnic community or *Volk* are regarded as a single organic unity. When any element in the constitution of the *Volk* is displaced or discarded, the unity of the whole is broken. Such a breach in "Volk" unity occurred when the indigenous Teutonic gods were displaced by the foreign God and the myths of the Jews. For Hegel, the gods of a people are an objectification of the inner nature of that people. By rejecting their own ancestral gods, the Germans were in the deepest sense rejecting themselves. The young Hegel didn't carry his own logic to its ultimate conclusion in action, however, he was followed by others such as Erich Ludendorff and Alfred Rosenberg. They were more prepared than he to enter that realm. They concluded that German alienation and self-estrangement could be terminated only by an end to the Jewish God of Christianity. This yearning figured very largely in Nazi ideology. It received one of its simplest formulations in the watchword of Hitler's Reich: *"Ein Volk! Ein Reich! Ein Führer!"* The Nazis had a clearer image of what and why they were fighting than either Jews or Christians. I think what Hitler wanted to do was to introduce a kind of new German paganism, and what the Vatican saw was that they could outlast him.

What do you mean by that, precisely?

Well, the Vatican is one of the best informed institutions in the whole world, and not just about religion. They know what's going on in every country of the world. They have priests and different orders like the Jesuits who are in contact with rulers throughout the world. And I'm sure that the people in the Vatican understood the deep pagan intentions of the Nazi movement, especially Pius XII. He was the Pope from 1939 on through the war and into the 1960s, until Pope John XXIII. I'm certain, as he was the head of an organization that has been active for almost 2,000 years, he had a lot of historical experience. The Vatican undoubtedly said, "Well, we can outlast them. They're not going to do us in." But in the meantime, I'm sure that the Pope saw Hitler as doing his dirty work. Not only cleaning out the Jews, but eliminating the threat of Bolshevism which he regarded as a Jewish threat.

But if Hitler successfully completed "the dirty work" and created his own paganism, eventually wouldn't that have become a threat to the Vatican?

Yes, but the point is that you deal with the threats that are closest at hand. I mean, from the point of view of the Vatican, they saw him as less of a threat than Bolshevism. And by the way, it isn't that the Vatican plotted to destroy the Jews, or anything like that. But when Hitler began his project of extermination, the Vatican had to ask itself, "How do we feel about this?" And the answer is: "This is a terrible thing. We'd never do anything like this. Nevertheless, it serves our pur-

poses." For example, if you had asked the Vatican if they advocated exterminating all the Jews, the answer would have clearly been "No" On the other hand, if you had asked most German church leaders in 1933: "Do you want to get rid of the Jews?" The answer would have been "Yes." But, if you then said, "We'll do it by murdering them," they would have said, "No, that's not what we mean." So what the Nazis did was to ask the question, "Do you want to get rid of the Jews?" But they didn't tell the ministers and religious leaders how they intended to do it. In other words, they were saying, "You leave that to us, that's our work, not yours." And I'm quite sure it was the same thing with the German people. I believe if you had taken a vote in 1933 or even as late as 1939, and put it on the ballot, "Do you want to get rid of the Jews?," the answer would have been "Yes." If you asked the second question, "Do you want to exterminate all the Jews?" I think the answer would have been "No."

The Nazis understood that what was wanted was contradictory. The people and the Church wanted those objectives fulfilled, but they didn't want to face the fact that the only way their objective could be implemented was through mass murder and extermination. So, when the mass murder and extermination took place, there was silence on the part of the Vatican, and silence on the part of almost all German religious leaders. And the reason was very simple. They didn't want to put themselves in the position of saying, "Yes, we endorse extermination." On the other hand, they knew well that Hitler was getting rid of the Jews, which was what they wanted. That's the way I see it anyway. You have to remember that Hitler made several claims. One, he claimed that he was really doing God's Christian work. Second, Hitler was not directly threatening the churches. I mean, what the future would bring is a different matter.

Regarding Hitler's "Thousand-Year Reich," since he was anti-everything except himself, what kind of religion could the Nazis have chosen for this new nation? Would Hitler have been the next God or Messiah?

Yes, that's correct. Not a Messiah in the Christian sense. He was a charismatic leader; that would be the way to put it. And every German swore allegiance to Adolf Hitler. Not to the constitution or to the law, but to Adolf Hitler. That would be the answer.

You have been writing a new book about former Yugoslavia. Can you tell me about what sort of things you are focusing on?

The title of my new book is *Holy War and Ethnic Cleansing.* The basic idea of this book is about the reason Christianity has been a missionary faith. In May 1993 while I was visiting Serbia and Croatia, I met many officials of both sides. An influential person there informed me something that had never come to my mind, "If you really want to know why Yugoslavia was broken up, it's because of the Vatican." At that time I thought this was far-fetched. But the more I thought and the more I read, I became aware that there is not one, but several wars going on simultaneously in former Yugoslavia.

One war is between the Serbs and the Croats over the boundary territories, which are now controlled by ethnic Serbs who will not live under the Croatians. Another war is being fought in Bosnia, and this is the most important war, between the Serbs on the one hand and the Croats on the other hand, who are sometimes allied against the Muslims and sometimes against

Serbs. Now, the more I thought about what he said about the Vatican, the more I realized that history comes into play here. This is the land which was the dividing point between the Roman Catholic Church, which is the Latin church of the West, and the Greek Orthodox Church, which is based on Constantinople. The two have been bitterly separated for almost 1,000 years. One of the reasons why the Vatican doesn't want to interfere in Yugoslavia is because the dominant power of command in Yugoslavia was always Serbia. They had the army, the government and the capitol Belgrade, and it was dominated by Greek Christianity. I came to the conclusion that the nations of Europe do not want to help the Bosnian Muslims because they don't want a viable and sovereign Muslim state on the European continent. If necessary they are prepared to let the Serbs commit genocide to prevent it.

Now, why would the nations of Europe not want a viable Muslim state on the European continent? I find there are several reasons. One is that, historically, the biggest challenge that Europe ever faced was the challenge of Islam. That started in 711 when the Muslims conquered almost all of Spain. They didn't leave Spain until 1492, which was nearly 800 years of domination. They also conquered Sicily, southern Italy, the entire Balkan peninsula, Romania, Hungary, southern Russia, and even Kiev was once ruled under Muslims. The Europeans have a long memory that Americans don't have. The Europeans are determined, first, that there will be no Muslim state in Europe, and second, that the continent of Europe be the heartland of Christendom. I call it Christendom rather than Christianity because I'm talking about a cultural-historical realm. There are probably people in Europe who don't believe literally that Jesus was the Messiah. Nevertheless, all of their rituals, Christmas, Easter, weddings and funerals are based upon a liturgy which centers around him as the Messiah, which they will never give up. In that sense, what you have is a culture and a civilization which is deeply rooted in Christianity.

Now, how did they expel the Muslims from Europe originally? They expelled the Muslims under the banner of the cross. The relationship between Europe and Christianity is very deep, and I can see that what's happening in Bosnia — even the genocide — is a European refusal to allow a people with another religion and civilization to have a viable presence. They're not going to stop them from having a little Gaza-strip republic around Sarajevo, because there are too many television cameras around. Many journalists have been killed there.

I recently wrote an article in a journal called "Partners in Ethnic Cleansing: The United Nations, the European Community and NATO," in which I argue that if you pay attention not to the words of the statesmen, but to the way in which these organizations undercut every attempt to do anything to stop the genocide, then what you see is that they really want the genocide, because they don't want the Muslim state. Now, what's that got to do with the Holocaust? During WW II, no major group in Europe made any serious protest against the killing of the Jews because it was a way of getting rid of an unwanted people which didn't fit into the cultural integration of Europe. In wartime you can do terrible things, but you can't do it in peacetime. In that sense, the Holocaust was a success. It eliminated the Jews as a significant influence in Europe. It seems to me that, looking back on the 20th century, what appears to me is the final triumph of Christendom in Europe. There have been two

ethnic cleansings: the Jews in the Holocaust and the Muslims in Yugoslavia.

Do you call it, basically, religious wars?

I wouldn't say a religious war so much; I would call it a "civilizational war." For example, to explain that, if you are born in England, studied at Oxford, were raised as a Christian and attend the Church of England, even if you think Jesus is just a "messiah fantasy," you wouldn't leave the Church of England because it would hurt your social status. It's a sort of participation in the community and the society you live in. That's why I say it's not necessarily a religious war. The function of the clergy and the theologians is to continue to assert that underneath the civilization, no matter what skepticism there may be, this civilization is rooted in ultimate truth. Of course, you also have the problem of cognitive instability. That's an additional reason why you don't want to have Muslims around who'll say, "No, Mohammed was the last of the prophets, not Jesus." You certainly don't want Jews around who'll say, "Yes, Jesus is interesting, but we know him better than you." And that's the worst offense of all, because, if Jesus was Jewish, as he was, that heightens the cognitive insecurity and instability which is the greater threat for Christendom. Therefore, the way I now see the Holocaust is it's a continuation of the attempt of Europe to achieve cultural and civilizational homogeneity.

Since the time of the French Revolution, there were a whole series of challenges to European Christianity. There was the challenge of secularism that has been largely overcome. Then there was the challenge of Marxism which some people saw as an extension of Judaism. There was the challenge of Judaism. Why did the challenge of Judaism become so much worse in the 19th and 20th centuries? Paradoxically, the very ability of the Jews to adopt the language, schooling, and culture of the larger nation made them more of a threat. Because no matter how well Jews spoke German, they were still Jewish and didn't believe in Jesus as the Messiah. What's worse is that if Jews became professors, authors, journalists, commentators, publishers or entertainers, then they influenced German culture with their so-called "Jewish virus."

How do you see the future of Europe and the world in the next century?

I've heard that Germans don't even want to speak English anymore. I guess they like to stay to themselves without too much outside influence. But you know what's going to happen? The Russians and Americans will have a common interest in an alliance against Germany. I believe this absolutely. It happened twice: In WW I you had democratic France still believing in the French revolution, and Czarist Russia as allies. I don't mean it's going to come to a war between Germany and the United States again; that's not the

issue. The whole commercial world is too interwoven today and the Russians aren't going to stay down forever. The Russians were at one point allied with the West against Germany. What really set the West off against the Russians was the fear that, as they were extending themselves into Europe, they would control Germany. I don't regard the Germans as evil. I regard them as having a problem that involved the rest of the world. In that they are a talented people in many ways, so numerous, and being in the center of Europe, they're bound to affect the balance of power on the European continent. I also believe that the Americans will stay in NATO to defend the rest of NATO against the Germans, in other words, to keep Germany from developing too independently. It's going to take a long time for Europe to adjust itself to a unified Germany. It's not going to be easy adjusting itself to the civilizational conflicts which I think are there. Europe will be increasingly the heartland of Christendom and there are unresolved tensions there, especially in Germany. I think Germany will remain a problem for Europe and for the world in the coming century. ❖

German physicists and the origin of the atomic bomb.

THOMAS POWERS

American, journalist and author of the book *Heisenberg's War* and other books on war and espionage. Born in 1940 in New York City, lives in Vermont, USA.

As a journalist and author, you've written a lot about wars and nuclear weapons over the years. First of all, could you explain the meaning of the so-called "Nuclear Winter"?

Since the early 1980s, I got interested in nuclear weapons and have done a lot of research, particularly about war strategies and how we planned to use them in the case of World War III. Regarding these subjects, I have written many articles for American magazines and newspapers. I specifically studied what would happen in the event of an actual nuclear war, something which has been unknown in human experience. "Nuclear winter" was a theory that, in the event of a full scale nuclear attack, there would be so much debris cast up in the atmosphere that it would actually block out the sun for a long period, perhaps many months or even years. The effects on the climate would be a disaster: cold and dark would settle over the entire earth. As a result, it would severely disrupt agriculture and that would lead to a terrible die-off of the human race and all living animals, trees, plants, and everything else on the earth. This was a scientific theory about the consequence of nuclear war. People haven't ever experienced anything like this before so nobody knows what would happen. People were afraid that it could happen.

During the Cold War these two great superpowers, the Soviet Union and the United States, were locked in a rivalry which seemed in danger of sparking a nuclear war which would mean a terrible destruction at the end. At the peak of the Cold War, the nuclear arsenal was escalating very fast on both sides. There were thousands of missiles and rockets on both sides targeting each other. And from that point, I became seriously involved with this matter. The history of nuclear weapons — the origin of the Nuclear Age and how everything began.

So, your book *Heisenberg's War* is the result of your research. Now, who was Werner Heisenberg and what is his connection with the Nazi war? Chronologically speaking, how did things develop?

Werner Heisenberg was a young German scientist, born in Munich in 1901, who graduated from the University of Munich in the 1920s. Collaborating with his close Danish associate, physicist Niels Bohr in Copenhagen, he invented quantum mechanics and the "uncertainty principle." It's what we now call simply "quantum physics," and in 1932 at the age of 31, he won the Nobel Prize. This was theoretical physics and had nothing to do with nuclear physics. By the mid-1930s as Hitler came to power, there was a kind of falling out. Certain scientists understood that perhaps great energy was contained in the atom. If you could release it, you could make bombs with it. At that time, they weren't sure that energy could be released. However, in the later years, with the discovery of fission by the chemist Otto Hahn in 1939, it became clear and suddenly all physicists in the world believed the bomb was possible.

In the scientific world in the early 20th century and during the Weimar Republic, Germany was the birthplace of modern physics. They were the pioneers. Among German physicists, one way or another, there were many Jews involved. During the 1930s along with the rise of the Nazi movement, there was an academic squabble at the University of Munich among post-graduate physicists over the successor to the retiring professor named Arnold Sommerfeld. Anyway, it became a bitter political battle. The Nazi Party was very much against Heisenberg because he collaborated with many Jewish physicists. They considered him a traitor to German physics. Nazi sympathizers were angry at Heisenberg claiming he was a follower of "Jewish physics," by which they meant hard, difficult, theoretical physics that had been invented by people like Bohr and Albert Einstein. Some of these German physicists hated this fact and there was a big fight between the Nazis and Jews.

Between 1933 to 1940 as the Nazis threatened the Jews, many Jewish physicists were driven out of Germany, Austria and Italy. Most of them left for Britain and America. Among those who emigrated to the United States were Leo Szilard, Eugene Wigner, Edward Teller, Hans Bethe, Victor Weisskopf, Fritz Reiche, and, of course, Einstein. Others were Enrico Fermi, who was an Italian but his wife was a Jew, and Karl Lark-Horovitz, a Viennese Jew. These old friends now formed a circle of refugee scientists who settled in their new homeland, in the major cities in America. In the summer of 1939, just before the war, Heisenberg was invited to lecture at a number of universities in the United States, including the University of California at Berkeley, Chicago and Rochester. He visited his old friends, the Jewish physicists, most of whom were settled as physics professors at major universities across the country. They all discussed war as inevitable and urged Heisenberg to remain in America, but his response was, "I believe my country needs me." He was firm that he would not leave Germany. And, after a few months when the Germans invaded Poland and Europe was already at war, he returned to Germany. And he actually stayed on in Germany throughout the war.

Now, I have to make a long story short. In January 1939, as I mentioned to you earlier, the news of the discovery of fission — the splitting of

the nucleus of the atom — was announced in Washington, D.C. by Niels Bohr, who was on a visit to America at that time. That was the first stage. Every physicist in the world found out that, "Now, we're going to be able to make terribly destructive bombs out of uranium." But then they realized production of the right kind of uranium that you can use in a bomb was very difficult. How to make atomic weapons was very complicated to explain. Technically, you have to control a chain reaction and once you can do this, you can make fuel for an atomic bomb. Basically, there are two ways to make the fuel. One way is from natural uranium. It's from two types of isotope called U-238 and U-235. But the latter one will explode, so these two atoms must be separated and it's very hard to do, because both are chemically identical. The only difference is a very slight difference in weight. They needed a huge factory and a hundred acres of land. The other way to produce bombs is in a reactor. In the process of neutron bombardment, it creates plutonium which also will explode. So, as soon as the scientists could make plutonium, they knew they could make atomic bombs. Anyway, this whole operation was a very expensive project.

After the war began in the United States and Britain, the scientists were convinced that it could be done: They were excited about it and urging their governments to go ahead. They were afraid the Germans were already working on it, because fission was discovered by a German physicist in Germany, and it was known that the Nazi government was very much interested in it. They were interested in using it for military purposes right from the first day of the war. They had actually taken over and controlled the Kaiser Wilhelm Institute in Berlin. They set up a special program there for further research of fission and possible atomic bombs. So, as early as 1939, they gathered all of the prominent scientists in Germany such as Otto Hahn and Carl Friedrich von Weizsäcker. They were headed by Heisenberg. The Nazi government was, of course, enthusiastic about this program. On the other hand, the governments of the Allied countries weren't sure, because they had to persuade their political leaders and the high-ranking military that the project was going to cost a fortune, and take a long time, and so on. Therefore, the Allies feared that the Nazis could be ahead. So, during the war they were very afraid of the Germans.

As I studied deeper, right in the beginning, I found out that everybody who was involved with the atomic bomb project on both sides, German and American, was angry at Heisenberg and I couldn't figure out why. It was fear of the Germans that originally prompted the atomic bomb program in America. After all the fears we had, I discovered that the German bomb program at that time was nothing. Compared to the "Manhattan Project," virtually nothing had been achieved. The truth I found out was that Heisenberg, the head of the German bomb project, successfully persuaded his own government that the project was too difficult.

What was the reason that Heisenberg was so reluctant about the German bomb project? Did you find out he was anti-Nazi? Which side was he on politically?

He was an anti-Nazi. He portrayed himself as being essentially apolitical. His old Jewish physicist friends in America were fearful that he was a Nazi because he refused to leave Germany. They tried very hard to get him out of Germany. But the real reason they tried to persuade him to remain in America at the time of his visit in 1939

was because they were afraid he would build a bomb for Hitler. That was what they were most afraid of. But at that time this matter was strictly confidential and no one said anything to him directly. If they asked him why he wanted to return to Germany, he would say, "Germany needs me. I must stay with my country." They would say, "But your country is run by a madman. Hitler is a criminal." But for Heisenberg, Hitler was a passing thing. It was Germany that he loved and he couldn't bear to abandon it. At one time he said to a friend, "One day the Hitler regime will collapse, and that is when people like myself will have to step in." Many of his friends were very angry at him throughout the war. I learned that this was a question of great sensitivity, especially among the scientists who had worked for the Manhattan Project at Los Alamos in New Mexico, where the bombs that were used on Hiroshima and Nagasaki were built.

What was Heisenberg's wartime activity in Germany? Many intellectuals and scientists were also killed by the Nazis. He could have been killed, too?

He knew it, of course. So, he was very careful because he wanted to survive the war. He had a family: a wife and many children. He certainly avoided many difficulties but also took many risks, too. Throughout those years he was almost killed on several occasions. For example, he belonged to an organization called the *Mittwochgesellschaft* (Wednesday Club). This was an old club of people associated in academic fields: scientists, professors, authors, intellectuals, and those classes of people who didn't leave Germany during the war like him. The last meeting of this Wednesday Club was held in Berlin in July of 1944, a week before the serious assassination attempt to kill

Hitler. Many people were involved in that plot. Besides, that meeting was held at his institute and he was the host that night. Heisenberg was not a part of the plot and never arrested, but he was there. So, he knew all these people. They were engaged with various resistance groups, which meant that they planned to take over the government after they killed Hitler. He obviously knew a lot about the plot, of course. Half of his friends and colleagues who were in that meeting were executed. Therefore, he himself was living in terrible fear that he was going to be swept into it, too.

Regarding the German bomb program, what was the Führer's intention? In the research process, how did Heisenberg persuade the Führer and the other Nazi ministers?

This part is very difficult to explain and you have to understand who Heisenberg really was. This is the whole reason that I wrote my book. First of all, there wasn't any bomb program in Germany after all. There is additional secret evidence that shows that Heisenberg was taking risks to figure out how to deal with this dilemma. In April of 1941, he sent a secret message to the United States warning the Americans that there was German interest in the new bomb and he was in charge of the program: He was the theoretical director. And the message was that Heisenberg himself would try to delay the research process as much as possible. But there was a limit to how much he could resist the orders he was given by the German authorities. Therefore, the Americans should take his warning seriously. That was the essence of his message. Heisenberg, however, showed up at work in his institute every day for four years.

The year 1942 was a turning point for both American and German scientists. By then, the various German scientists and military men clearly believed that an atomic bomb was possible. Albert Speer arranged to meet Heisenberg to discuss it. Speer was an architect of city planning for the Third Reich, but as he got Hitler's confidence, he became Minister of Armaments and War Production, and by that time he was in charge of the entire German war economy. For Heisenberg, Speer was the right person to discuss the production of munitions, the war effort as a whole and the possibility of the bomb. If Heisenberg wanted to build a bomb, then Speer was the perfect ally. On June 4th, the meeting was held in his institute with Speer, Heisenberg and his scientist colleagues. Speer asked the scientists if they could build the bomb, Heisenberg personally answered, "Yes, theoretically it can be done. But it's very expensive: We would need billions of Reich Marks and it's very time consuming. Besides, it's very uncertain, we can't predict that it would be done in time for use in the war." So, it essentially shut down Speer's enthusiasm.

Speer delivered his report to Hitler. Hitler then just passed it by and didn't take it seriously. Therefore, in the end, this issue was never seriously discussed in the Nazi government. One way or another, however, theoretically Hitler understood the atomic bomb could be created because some sources say he even used to make jokes about it such as, "I hope I don't live to see the day when the scientists all blow up the world." So, he sort of knew about it. Even before the war began, there were already a lot of newspaper articles about the "superbomb," you know! There were all sort of explicit rumors throughout the war. At one time, there was a rumor that an American bomb would soon be dropped on Dresden.

In the early years, Hitler was very enthusiastic about the invention of V-I and V-II rockets that were very sophisticated and revolutionary weapons at that time. But he didn't fully understand that combined with the rockets, the atomic bomb would produce completely fatal weapons. And if Hitler had had these two powerful weapons, he would have won the war easily. Thank God it didn't happen!

Do you think Hitler was not smart enough to understand the possibility of nuclear weapons?

Hitler was smart and certainly an intelligent man. There's no question about that. He was smart enough to take seriously what the scientists were telling him. But it's a question of who's telling him and how they're telling him. I mean a man like him, he would listen to the tone of people. First of all, he needed someone he trusted to tell him, and then listened to the tone in their voice. He was not a scientist; he didn't know if one could build a bomb or not. For example, recently in the United States, Edward Teller convinced President Ronald Reagan that with the Star Wars program, we could build a very elaborate defense system in space to shoot down enemy missiles. Well, what does Reagan know? He is a politician, not a scientist. He doesn't know anything technical. He believed Teller because he trusted him. So, it was the same way in Germany. If somebody had convinced Hitler who he knew, liked and trusted, then he probably would have gone ahead. Speer could have convinced Hitler. But nobody ever did that in Germany, and that was a critical thing. The critical difference is that the German scientists didn't support the effort. They didn't push it hard and they didn't insist on it.

At the same time, this top secret atomic bomb program known as the Manhattan Project was already in progress in the United States. How did these American scientists persuaded President Roosevelt? What was the government's attitude toward the production of this fatal bomb which changed the postwar world forever?

In the United States, it was exactly the opposite. The American scientists were all fascinated about it. It was a very different story for the German scientists. They were pulling on the coattails of government officials and saying, "You must pay attention to this. This is very important, you must go ahead. You must put effort into this." And I say "the American scientists," but, of course, many of them were refugees and emigres from Hitler's Germany. You have to understand that these men had all started out life as the smartest kids in their school with a great desire to learn and challenge the secrets of nature. And they loved to talk about science and to figure out how things worked. They were worried about Germany. In particular, Leo Szilard, Edward Teller and Eugene Wigner begged Einstein, "Please write a letter to the President because he will read your letter. If we write to him, he won't read it because we're not famous. But the President will read Einstein's letter." Although Einstein's famous theory was basic to the question of nuclear physics, he didn't work on the Manhattan Project. He was simply the most famous scientist in the world at that time.

After the Allies entered the war with Germany, the American scientists such as J. Robert Oppenheimer, an American-born physicist who studied in Germany and knew many German scientists, Fermi, Bohr, Arthur Compton, E.O. Lawrence and others pushed this program very hard, and in June 1942, the Manhattan Project was launched. The operation was huge; over 60,000 workers were hired, and it was run by military men who wanted to win the war: General George C. Marshall, the Secretary of War Henry Stimson, administrators Vennevar Bush and James Connant, but especially General Leslie Groves, the director of the project, who was an absolute "monster of resolution." He was totally determined to win the war and he knew how to win it. He was going to win by dropping A-bombs on Japanese cities killing hundreds of thousands of people in a few hours, and driving the Japanese out of the war. And, he really did it. It worked perfectly. Einstein, however, expressed his remorse for what he did, but by then it was too late.

Anyway, in Germany, on the other hand, nobody was running the A-bomb program with that spirit. But they had somebody running the rocket program like that. It was the same kind of spirit; they had to build underground factories and had a hard time getting materials they needed for it, but they built thousands of rockets to attack England, and this was a huge effort, too. And they made it. However, the German A-bomb program was a different story. In fact, in June 1942 when the Americans began the "Project," coincidentally the German A-bomb project was dismissed. I would say it was a question of human motives. The question is not that they could have. It's not that the German psyche was against big programs and couldn't handle them. It was because Heisenberg didn't want to build an A-bomb for Hitler. It was very simple. In my view, Heisenberg was a true hero for human morale. He played a very important role in the whole scene. For my book, I've interviewed a key German scientist on this matter named Carl Friedrich von Weizsäcker, who was a close working colleague of Heisenberg's. He is now in his 80s

and alive and well in Germany today. He told me that Heisenberg was deeply concerned about the possibility that nuclear weapons would place a horrible responsibility on mankind. In my book I quoted the whole explanation from him.

You said earlier that many people who were involved with the bomb program, both Germans and Americans, were angry at Heisenberg. Why was that?

Many of the old German scientist friends of Heisenberg's who came to America, Hans Bethe, Victor Weisskopf, Leo Szilard, James Franck, Rudolf Peieels and many others were all angry at him, but Bohr in particular who was Heisenberg's oldest and closest friend since the 1920s. He helped him in inventing quantum physics for which Heisenberg won the Nobel Prize. It took me a long time to figure out why. The reason why they were angry at Heisenberg was, in my opinion, because of certain emotional complexities. They were very fearful that the Germans would build an A-bomb and since they all knew that Heisenberg was a pioneer in German physics, he would lead the German A-bomb program. So, they urged the US government to start an A-bomb program. And without that fear of the Germans, or that fear of Heisenberg, there would have been no American A-bomb program. So, in a certain way, their belief about Heisenberg was responsible for everything that they did. During the war their fear was so intense that they became involved in an attempt to either kidnap or assassinate Heisenberg. And they actually proposed to the American intelligence services that it should be organized. This was something that has been deeply hidden and very difficult to bring out. But it is all true. The American secret services planned to assassinate him.

In America, after Einstein's A-bomb program proposal was approved by Roosevelt, General Groves ordered the American Air Force to bomb certain laboratories associated with universities and academic institutions in Germany to try to destroy their A-bomb program facilities, and the German scientists who were working there including Heisenberg and Otto Hahn, both Nobel Prize-winning scientists. So, this was a terrible thing, you know. It forces us to think what war means, really. These bombing raids were a very personal, direct and deliberate attempt to kill people who were involved in the program. But, the thing was that when the war came to an end, they discovered that this man, Heisenberg, whom they feared so much, was not making A-bombs for Hitler after all. And, truth was, he didn't do it for moral reasons. This made the American scientists furious, including Einstein, by the way. The fear that Heisenberg was building a German A-bomb turned into anger over his attempt to explain why he didn't build a bomb. And why did Heisenberg himself never explain clearly what he did during the war, working in his institute for 4 years? His answer was always, "Of course, we German scientists understood the moral implications of building A-bombs for a man like Hitler. We agonized over what we would do if we were ordered by Hitler to build such a bomb. But, thank God, we were saved from the agony of this decision because the job was too big for wartime Germany." This was his answer. Instead of being involved with resistance activity, he acted quietly but effectively because he didn't want to be executed.

The American A-bomb project was originally designed to attack Germany, but by the time the A-Bombs were ready to use, the Germans were already beaten. So, the Americans turned them on the Japanese. Who decided how they would be used and for which cities?

Yes, Germany was the source of major concern when the program originally began. But it wasn't going to be ready against the Germans, and meanwhile they were beaten. In June 1945, after 3 years of hard work, the Americans finally succeeded with the A-bomb. On the 16th of July the world's first A-bomb test took place in New Mexico: It was a plutonium bomb. It worked perfectly and they were all satisfied. General Groves described the result: "For a few thousandths of a second the light was as bright as a thousand suns." As Japan was still fighting in the Pacific, it was intended to be used against Japan. In the last part of the war, the Americans planned to invade Japan, but its main island was difficult to invade. So they decided to use the A-bomb before the invasion. But over all, technically speaking, the final decision was made by President Harry S. Truman. Roosevelt was dead by then. But the decision to use the bomb was actually reached at the beginning — in the decision to develop and build it. Of course, they would use it! Why else did they spend all that money? It was a huge weapon; it was called the "fat-man." Groves suggested that two bombs would be enough to convince the Japanese to abandon the war. He proposed Kyoto at the top of his list. But this was strongly opposed by Stimson, reasoning that Kyoto was the spiritual and historical center of Japan. That would be an assault on the Japanese psyche that the Japanese would never forgive. Stimson also had a personal sentimental reason — he had visited Kyoto for his honeymoon, so he knew how beautiful a city it was. But Groves tried to keep Kyoto on the list until the last minute of the negotiations.

So, since those 2 A-bombs were dropped on Hiroshima and Nagasaki, the world has completely changed forever...

Yes, it has. The bomb has never been used again. Although the arms race developed between the United States and the Soviet Union, it was controlled by fear of these atomic bombs. The bombings of Hiroshima and Nagasaki were terribly cruel. But what more could we ask of such a demonstration? The bomb has never been used since and the United States and the Soviet Union never went to war. There are many small wars all over the globe today and dangers never go away. Everybody knows that it is perhaps even more likely that one or two bombs could be used by someone now, after the end of the Cold War. But nevertheless, as a whole, nearly 50 years of the Cold War has been the most peaceful time in Europe in our century, or even in any century, actually. It's all because of these two bombs. ❖

CHAPTER FOUR

Life with the Wall

*West Berliners who lived
with the Berlin Wall*

(Conducted in the summer of 1988)

Berlin's history teller

ROBERT H. LOCHNER

American journalist and foreign correspondent. Director of the International Institute for Journalism in Berlin. Born in 1918 in New York. Berliner for over 40 years.

Mr. Lochner, you've had a long career as a journalist. Can you tell me about your personal and professional background?

My father was a journalist, and in 1923 he was assigned to Germany as chief correspondent of the Associated Press. I came to Berlin with him when I was 5 years old. I was educated and raised here until the late 1930's, just before the war broke out. During the war, I was in the United States for my university studies, but came back to Berlin after the war in 1945. Since then, I have been in and out of Berlin and Germany until I retired in 1971. Altogether, I've been in Berlin for about 40 years.

My father, Louis P. Lochner, was a well-known war correspondent and a big influence on me. After college I instinctively entered into his profession as a foreign correspondent. During my forty years in the field, I did many things. I started professionally in the United States while the war was going on, working as an announcer for NBC, making shortwave radio broadcasts to Germany against the Nazi regime. After the war, I returned to Germany and started working as a radio reporter for the American occupation radio station, and later for Radio Frankfurt. I was an editor-in-chief of the *Neue Zeitung* and then served for the U.S. High Commission in Bonn as chief of the Press Division.

During the 1960's, I was head of Voice of America's European Division in Washington. Returning to Berlin, this time as a director for RIAS, a radio station financed by the American government, I served as interpreter for President John F. Kennedy, Vice President Lyndon B. Johnson, NATO Commander Dwight D. Eisenhower, and other generals, military governors and high commissioners. After retiring from government service, I decided to stay in Berlin. I founded the International Institute for Journalism and am still head of that institution. Now, I do occasional freelance work for American media.

You lived under unique circumstances and you had some interesting experiences. Could you talk about them?

I could say that I witnessed the most dramatic political dramas in the rise and fall of Nazi Germany. That was an extraordinary era of transition for Germany. I became a history teller. In the 1930's during the rise of the Third Reich, I was a teenager attending German high school. We had to listen to every speech Hitler made on the radio while we were in class. We all had to stand up and sing the national anthem and give the Nazi salute; but not being German, I was not obliged to do so.

After school hours, my father took me to many different parts of Germany to attend various political events, such as rallies and press conferences. These were some of the most fascinating experiences I ever had. For instance, in the summer of 1936 during the Berlin Olympic Games, when Jesse Owens, a black American runner, won the first gold medal, Hitler suddenly stood up and walked out. His political philosophy was such that he regarded Negroes as subhuman. He was so frustrated that he couldn't stand it. I was in the press seats a few meters away from him and can still remember the anger and hatred in his face.

In September of 1938, my father took me to the annual Nazi party convention in Nuremberg. There again, I watched Hitler as he addressed hundreds of thousands of Nazi supporters amid tens of thousands of Swastika flags. Thousands of men marched by in perfect order to triumphal music to show their force, unity and absolute control. By that time, the Nazi party was already demonstrating enormous military power and everybody — from the journalists to the informed civilians — was frightened and feared that Germany would start a war. There was no doubt about it.

Within a few weeks, the Munich Crisis occurred. In October, Hitler occupied Sudetenland, a western territory of Czechoslovakia. Under the Munich Agreement the Czechs had to cede part of their land to Nazi Germany without a fight. My father, a well-informed anti-Nazi journalist, warned that this would lead to war. He kept saying that it was just the beginning of Hitler's barbaric invasion, and war was inevitable. That year he won the Pulitzer Prize for his coverage of the event.

About the Berlin Wall, what was the situation before the Wall was built? Why did East Germany build the Wall? Was there no alternative?

I was stationed in Berlin at the time as a radio reporter. Before the Wall was built, the division between East and West Berlin was marked with barbed wire put there by East Berlin officials. There were no customs officers, and it was easy to cross over by walking right through. West Berlin was opposed to the barbed wire, and demanded that the border be kept open to maintain "free circulation within Berlin." The tension grew, and both sides became highly emotional. If West Berlin forcibly removed East Berlin's barbed-wire fence, fighting was bound to start, and it was clear that this could escalate into another war. So, West Berlin decided to let East Berlin have its way, and keep the barbed-wire division.

However, during the summer of 1961, the number of refugees from East Germany to West Germany rose dramatically: 10,000 people a day,

with 3,000 of them going through West Berlin alone. From the end of the war until that summer, 3 million East Germans from a total population of 17 million, fled to the West. It was obvious that the East had to do something about it, but nobody knew what action they would take. Then, at midnight on August 13th, they started building the Wall. After that, the flood of refugees stopped, and as a result, East Germany's economy recovered. Now, of the communist countries, East Germany has the highest standard of living and economically they're the most powerful nation. In fact, the Wall was very effective. Without the Wall, the country couldn't have done it. The Wall was their only choice, and it was the right decision for them.

John F. Kennedy was concerned and sympathetic to West Berliners and their situation as they became physically cut off by the Wall. How do you recall his visit to West Berlin? What was the atmosphere like?

Berlin was, of course, the capital city of today's divided Germany. Berlin was the center of the political, economic, cultural and social life of Germany. Geographically, Berlin is at the center of Europe, but after the war Berlin was never able to regain its vast wealth, and today, it is a totally different kind of city. Today, the cultural and economic centers of Germany are Munich, Hamburg or Frankfurt. However, from a political point of view, the importance of Berlin has never diminished. Today, West Berlin stands as a symbol of refusal to become a communist state, even though it's in the middle of communist territory. West Berlin is an outpost of Western civilization. To keep democracy and freedom alive, West Berliners have suffered, fought, endured, and survived despite constant harassment from communist Russia. This should not be forgotten. The existence of West Berlin is a big headache for Russia. But Berlin will continue as it is now. The two Berlins remain a point of direct political confrontation between two superpowers — the confrontation of capitalism and communism, between the United States and the Soviet Union. Keeping Berlin alive is necessary, not only for West Germany, but also for free Europe and for the entire free world.

How did West Berlin change or develop after the Four Power Agreement?

Actually, the Four Power Agreement has formed present-day West Berlin and, in many respects, has resulted in a triumph for the city. When the war ended with Germany's unconditional surrender in May of 1945, Berlin, an area of 341 square miles (833 square kilometers) was a city under foreign sovereignty. The western part of the city (54 percent of the total area) with a population of over 2 million, was occupied by the Western Allies: the United States, Great Britain and France. The Eastern part of the city (46 percent of the total area) with a population of over 1 million, was occupied by the Soviet Union, and divided by a 100-mile-long border (162 kilometers). That has not changed, even today. For over 40 years West Berlin has suffered many crises and pressures from the Soviet Union, such as blockades, the threat of military withdrawal by the Western Allies, and finally the Wall.

After the Wall was built in August of 1961, the threats and difficulties didn't stop. There were continuous interruptions of traffic on the access roads between mainland West Germany and West Berlin. The only free uncontrolled passage was by air. To eliminate the tension in West Berlin and to provide practical improvements for the citizens, the three Western Allies and the Soviet Union negotiated and they signed the Four Power Agreement in September of 1971. The Soviet Union agreed to provide transit by highway, railway and waterway through the territory of East Germany to allow access between West Germany and West Berlin. West Berliners, who were deprived access after the Wall was erected, were allowed to visit their families in East Berlin and East Berliners could visit West Berlin. Restrictions were eased on tourist transit and air safety has been improved. Each year many aspects of life become easier as relations improve between East and West and the existence of the Wall becomes less and less important. Recently, for instance, West Berlin began dumping its garbage in East Berlin. Of course, West Berlin pays for this service because East Berlin needs the strong West German currency. Following the signing of the Four Powers Agreement, West Berlin was gradually reintegrated politically, culturally, socially and economically into mainland West Germany. Best of all, the quality of life of West Berliners has improved tremendously, and West Berlin is no longer an isolated city.

How do you see the idea of reunification of the two Germanys? Will the Wall ever be torn down?

Many conservative Germans are very enthusiastic about it, of course. But, to tell you the truth, most European nations are perfectly content to have a divided Germany because they have suffered from German domination. Their memories of the war are still very vivid. By itself West Germany is a leading European nation, but if East Germany joins West Germany, Germany will turn into a superpower. Most of Germany's neighbors, including the Soviet Union, are psychologically quite nervous about this. I guess it has something to do with the national character and attitude of the German people. They are hard workers, highly disciplined, and very well informed. Only America and China, two big and powerful countries that are remote from Europe, can afford to be unconcerned about the increased strength of a reunited Germany. After all, neither China nor the U.S. has ever been threatened by German occupation.

As I mentioned earlier, under the Four Powers Agreement, the two Germanys are becoming closer each year. In my opinion, the idea is to be able to travel freely between the two Germanys and the two Berlins, and as long as both sides can communicate easily, their physical division (the Wall) becomes less important. "Re-unification" is not of any great significance. Both sides have learned how to live with the Wall. Tearing it down is not the answer. Before that happens, there are many things to be resolved. First, the two Germanys must work together and agree with each other politically on many issues. Realistically, if the Wall is bulldozed now, too many refugees will flee to the West and the whole situation will be out of control again. If the Cold War comes to an end, it will be a long process to normalize the two Germanys. ❖

"Within fifty years, the two Germanys will be re-united."

STEFAN GÄNSICKE

Deputy Chief Editor of Axel Springer Verlag Publishing Group. Born
in 1930 in Potsdam and raised in West Berlin.

(Photo: Mr. Gänsicke in front of photos of prominent journalists in his publishing house.)

Mr. Gänsicke, what was it like to be a young Berliner living in the city at the end of the war and how did people feel emotionally at that time?

Right after the war, living in Berlin was totally devastating. We were hungry with very little to eat, no jobs, and our houses were ruined. There was no gas or heating during the long cold winters. We were absolutely dejected and our daily lives were just miserable. And there was no perspective at all. We hadn't the faintest idea what kind of future we would face as Germans. We knew that we had proved to the Americans, to our European neighbors, and to the rest of the world that we were real jerks. We felt that we would be excluded from the family of nations 'forever.' It was humiliating, the most pitch black time, and the hardest emotional experience of all.

How long did this feeling last and how did people get out of this situation?

It lasted until 1948. The Berlin Blockade changed our emotional isolation. The Soviet Union tried to isolate us from West Germany. Stalin wanted to gain control of all of Berlin to grab supremacy over the former capital of Germany. He wanted to cut off all our supplies from the Western Zones and to force 2 million inhabitants into mass starvation. But the West Germans raised an outcry for the West Berliners. Western Allies, predominantly Americans, started airlifting foodstuffs, coal, industrial goods and other necessities and that way, they kept us alive for one year. That was the signal that the Western Allies would join hands over us and protect us from communist Russia. Because of that, we saw the light at the end of the tunnel. We felt that we were being admitted as a member of the Western Nations. We belonged to the West.

Since then, the situation has changed greatly. I have recently learned about the "human trade" between the two Germanys. How did the West German government start buying political prisoners from East Germany?

After the Berlin Wall was built, separated family members appealed to the Bonn government for help. Negotiations started between the two governments and a settlement was reached to do the exchanges for money. Since the early 1970's West Germany has been paying the East to release political prisoners. Today, they are steadily releasing about 20,000 people each year, sometimes even without receiving money. We can only guess it is because they want to get rid of the dissidents, the so-called "refuseniks," who are seen as a danger to society. Their political ideas are a bad influence. But this problem creates more problems. A wave of discontent has spread over the years and it has been growing. Most people want to come out. They can watch our western TV and listen to our radio stations, and there is no way to stop them. They can visit us and learn our way of life, and see how our society works. We have a high standard of living, but also a high tax system. The West is a hard-working and competitive society; it's no "dreamland," but looking at us realistically, our social system works better. Above all, the main thing is freedom.

What kind of people are leaving East Germany and why isn't communism working in East Germany?

They are pretty ordinary people like blue-collar workers, farmers, doctors, lawyers, teachers, and so on; young and old from all sorts of professions, not only intellectuals. The communist regime was established in East Germany at the end of World War II, and that was not by the people's choice. Communism hasn't put down any roots among the East German people; it is superficial. They have to live with constant agitation, government propaganda and political pressure. They are, culturally and mentally, absolutely German. We speak the same language, eat the same food and share the same history and traditions. They think they ended up in the wrong place with the wrong government. They believe that they belong to the West. They have been isolated from the West for so many years that, in many ways, they are more German than we are. Peculiarly enough, we've discovered that some of them have maintained views from the old Hitler era or even a 1920's-type mentality, and that stuns us. On the other hand, because West Germans are more westernized, we have lost our identity. They have not. But, finally, we are all the same people and we belong to each other.

Both Germanys have a relatively low birth rate. Could you explain why you think that is?

I think it is a temporary thing that today's young people have no great desire to have children. It could be explained by several reasons. First of all, the fear of war. In both the East and the West, the individual German is highly conscious of war. If we ever have a Third World War, the ugliest and most intense fighting will probably be right here. These young people don't want to take the risk that their children will have the same bitter experience they did, and have to grow up with those dangers. Secondly, the deteriorating ecology is a factor. Germans are very concerned about their physical environment. The air is polluted, the rivers are toxic, the forests are dying, the ozone problem is worsening, and so on. This is not a happy world for children to grow up in. I believe that is why German people are reluctant to have

children. I certainly hope that this is not forever. If disarmament continues and if this world becomes a safer and cleaner place, 20 to 30 years from now, the worry about the war will finally disappear. Then the birth rate will follow a normal historic pattern, and I believe people will regain the natural desire to have children.

What is your opinion about the young generations' plans to insure world peace?

Since 1945 there has been no major war, at least in Europe. We have been enjoying peace for many years now, but that is not a gift from heaven. For most youngsters today who were born after the war, living without war is absolutely normal. They don't realize that this period of peace was brought about by the "balance of terror" between two big superpowers, Washington and Moscow, the "equilibrium of arms." Today, the superpowers have decided to scale down their arms race, which is a marvelous development and a major step, but also a very delicate process.

How do you think Mikhail Gorbachev's policy of *glasnost* will affect the future of the two German nations?

Knowing their superiority in arms, the Soviet Union is liquidating its communist economic empire, realizing that with Mr. Gorbachev, it has relinquished its old imperial aspirations of ruling and bringing communism to the rest of the world, and must bury the great missionary dream of Marx and Lenin. The Soviets have already given up on Afghanistan; they just couldn't handle it. The USSR has acknowledged that communism does not work. We can see an earthquake happening inside the Kremlin.

Historically, when an empire comes to an end, it's a critical and sensitive time. Panic and chaos permeate the hierarchy and the outcome becomes difficult to control. The Soviet Union has had little experience building an empire of communism. It is just over 40 years old, whereas Great Britain was a 300-year-old empire before its domination of the world gradually ended. Concerning the world's current situation, if everything goes well, it will be an endlessly interesting time. I would say that the two Germanys will be re-united within the next fifty years, at least as a confederation of states. ❖

"Let us hope for Mikhail Gorbachev."

MATTHIAS FRINGS

Author of numerous books on human sexuality. Born in 1953 in Cologne and has lived in West Berlin for 11 years.

(Photo: Mr. Frings working in his home.)

Why do you live in Berlin and how are things different in this city?

For me Berlin is the real city of Germany. Hamburg is about money, Munich is for yuppies and Frankfurt is ugly. For young people this is the only city in Germany to live in. Furthermore, Berlin is not Germany, yet it is still German. It is a nation of its own, an island, an odd city. The cultural and intellectual center is here; all the important events take place in this city. But politically and economically, it is totally dependent on mainland Germany. That makes me love and hate living here. People come to visit Berlin to experience an idea of freedom and live a free lifestyle, but they go back home while their taxes keep getting paid to Berlin. Seventy-five percent of the city's budget comes from Bonn. The West German people really have to pay to support the city of Berlin.

I understand that you often visit East Germany. Despite their political and ideological differences, how would you say the two Germanys view each other?

Young people who come to Berlin are not interested in making a career in business, but they are interested in creative pursuits: writing, poetry, painting, and other arts. Since before WWII, Berlin has been Germany's most famous city for those who want to express themselves creatively, and it will continue this way on into the next decades and maybe longer.

In my view West and East Germany can't be together mentally. The two ideologies are too far apart. I think things will stay as they are, at least for the next 25 years or more. However, the two communities do need to stay in contact. This has started now for the first time since the city was divided, and there is increasing cultural and art exchange. Today, West Berlin artists, actors, dancers, musicians and movie directors go to East Berlin to make movies, play in theaters and give concerts, and so on. There's a lot of discussion about how our society should be built, and also about politics and art. We are learning the differences between each other's lives under communism and capitalism. It is very interesting and stimulating as we discover and learn about each other. During the past five years, especially since Mr. Gorbachev has come to power in the Soviet Union, many things have changed dramatically. The influence of *glasnost* has been drastic in all our lives. They have had to live with so much propaganda in communist East Germany, but now they realize they can't live with these lies anymore. We can see clearly that the East Germans seriously want change.

In the art world, what's the difference between East and West Germany?

I do believe they are very different. I think the East Germans are on a much higher level than we are, absolutely. People in the East are much more serious, and although that doesn't necessarily mean better, in many cases it does. Their artistic standards in movies, in the theater and in literature are very different from ours. For example, what we do in the West is very entertaining and it's capitalistically-oriented. But they are much more profound and more deeply concerned with social matters, political problems, women's issues and philosophy.

How much freedom of speech do they have?

In East Berlin, if you go to cafes or places where people meet, everybody is arguing and discussing heavy political issues and social matters in a very solemn way, and that's something we don't do much of in the West. But they talk and discuss openly only up to a certain point. Then they often become cautious and won't say what they truly feel.

In regard to the two fundamentally different social systems, what differences do you notice in communications and understanding about politics between the East and West?

As West Berliners, we are able to visit East Berlin easily, walk in and look around and see how people behave there. It is easier for us to understand them by observing their living circumstances. They can't come over so easily and the majority have never been to the West. They only know us by watching TV or listening to the radio; therefore they really do not know us very deeply. When it comes to communication, matters like hedonism, irony, humor, jokes or sarcasm, they do not respond like we do in the West. They lack the background. Their political background makes them think and behave in a straightforward way and that is a very basic difference between us.

If they were allowed to read our written materials, our literature and newspapers and magazines, they would understand more about our background and how capitalism works and how people live and behave in our world. On the other hand, living in the West, we are able to read books on communism, but most people don't bother. They are either lazy or they censor themselves mentally because of the Cold War. But I'm quite convinced that little by little the situation will change. Mr. Gorbachev is a man of power; he holds the key to the future of the Soviet Union and the Eastern block. I'm sure that East Germany will liberate itself gradually, and become a more open society as each year goes by. Let us hope for Mr. Mikhail Gorbachev. ❖

"I was a soldier who never wanted to be a soldier."

MARTIN HARNÖSS

WW II veteran and retired artist. Born in 1906 in East Africa. Resident of West Berlin for over sixty years.

Can you tell something of your background and how you became involved with art?

My family moved to Berlin when I was 7 years old. My father was drafted during WW I and was killed. My mother became a war widow at the age of 23, a single working mother; she raised me and my two sisters. I had loved painting since I was a little boy and my mother supported me through art schools. In 1939, I was drafted to fight in WWII, but I was a bad soldier. Instead of carrying guns, I was carrying canvasses and I painted or drew the officers and soldiers in the barracks. I never shot anybody, not even once. I was a *Woyzeck* — a soldier who never wanted to be a soldier.

What type of painting or drawing did you do and how did you manage to support yourself as an artist during the war?

I painted portraits and scenes, but specialized in modern paintings and caricatures. The Nazis disliked my work and never accepted it, because my caricatures were very politically-minded and satirical, making fun of Nazi officers and the military system. In 1941, I was wounded in the leg and hospitalized. The following year I was discharged.

Deciding to work as a professional artist, I came back to Berlin and started working at theaters and newspapers, doing cartoons and illustrations. At the same time, I displayed my work in cafes, restaurants, pubs or cabarets. But during the war, there was not enough work, and it was extremely difficult to survive. Although I was supposed to receive a military disability pension from the government, confusion arose and I could not get it.

How did your life as a professional artist change after the war?

I was living in East Berlin when the war ended and was married there. But we decided to leave for West Berlin because the East German Communist Party insisted that I should become a member. I refused. Having been based in Russia during the war, I was sick of communism and wanted to get rid of it. In 1958 there was no Wall between East and West, and the Brandenburg Gate was still open; so it was easy to cross the border. I just walked through with my wife and two daughters. In the West it was much easier to find work; I became a commercial artist, designing posters and book illustrations. While working in the city, I was recognized by the Assembly of Berlin Artists, a prestigious honor for an artist. I finally presented an exhibition and became one of the leading artists in Berlin. That was in 1968; I was 51 years old.

The history of Berlin has obviously affected your life very directly. Which time was the hardest for you?

Every five or seven years it seems I have met with one obstacle after another, either a personal or a political problem. I lost my father in WW I, then came the Great Depression, the Nazis seized power, I was drafted and injured, the war ended, we moved to the West, the worker's revolution occurred, then in the 1960s, the city was divided and we had the Berlin Crisis. As a freelance artist, these political crises had a direct financial impact on my life. I was up and down almost every day struggling. When I think back, I have never had peace in my entire life. I was never able to afford a car until I bought a Red Cross lottery ticket in the 1960s, and won a Mercedes Benz.

Could you tell me about the golden age of Berlin in the 1920s?

During the mid-1920s I was in Berlin and continued my art studies. In those days, there were over two dozen playhouses and concert halls, several opera houses, dozens of museums, major film production companies, over a hundred newspapers and other publications, and so on. Berlin was internationally known as the intellectual and cultural center of the work, and it was the most important city in all of Europe. There were also well-known major artists who lived here, for example, Kandinsky, Klee, and Nolde, and writers such as Brecht and Döblin, architects like Britz and Reinickendorf, and so on — you name it. Everything was in Berlin. As a young artist, I found it the most revolutionary and evolutionary, inspiring and exciting cultural environment I ever experienced in my life. Both physically and culturally, Berlin provided the greatest splendor Germany has ever known. Compared with that, Berlin today is a tiny village. ❖

"In order to escape, I became a soldier."

PETER-MICHAEL MADER

Construction worker who escaped from East Germany. Born in 1963
in East Germany.

(Photo: Mr. Mader standing in front of the Berlin Wall, with graffiti.)

Tell me about yourself, Peter. What finally made you want to escape?

My father is an army officer and my mother is a social worker, and both are totally devoted to the Communist Party. We lived in Hoyerswerda, where I attended a technical school. I have one sister, and my girlfriend and I have a two-year-old son. We were an average family, with a very ordinary life, but I could not agree with my parents' political viewpoint. During the year 1986 I worked in the USSR as a mechanic, and there I learned about the reality of the communist society. My view changed. Returning to East Germany, I realized that in this kind of political environment there was no prospect for the future. So I decided to escape to West Germany.

Tell me how you planned your escape and the details of the actual escape.

After thinking for many months, I decided to become a soldier in the hope that I might become a border patrol guard. I knew that a border patrol guard would have a very good chance to escape. So, I joined the army at the age of 21. I told no one about my plan, not my family or friends, not even my girlfriend, because I knew it was too dangerous to mention. I explained that I wanted to be a soldier to dedicate myself to my country. I lied.

I worked extremely hard in the army to show what a good and patriotic soldier I was, and no one in my barracks suspected anything. After 18 months I was promoted to sergeant, and attained a position with the border patrol. This was what I had wanted and waited for. How excited I was. My station was the town of Helmstedt, 90 kilometers east of Hanover. Being on the Border

Patrol involved patrolling with another guard, sometimes with police dogs. We would guard between two walls, that were 30 meters apart and 3 meters high. There were three 8-hour patrolling shifts. Each soldier carried a semi-automatic rifle on his shoulder, and we were trained to watch and shoot escapees through the Wall. One day, my opportunity came. I had a night shift, from 10:00 p.m. until 6:00 a.m., without dogs.

Painstakingly I examined the walls to find the best spot to climb over. On a quiet and cool summer night, about midnight, I was patrolling with my supervisor. The next pair of border guards were 2 kilometers away from us and there was no watch tower nearby. We were completely isolated. So, it was safe. "It's my best chance. I must do it now," I told myself. Swiftly, I pulled the rifle off my supervisor's shoulder, aimed my gun, and shouted at him to lie down on the ground. "What are you doing, sergeant? You must be kidding!" he said. "No, I'm not kidding," I told him, "Don't move or scream, or I'll shoot you." The Wall was about 10 meters away. I immediately ran to it, placed my rifle vertically by the Wall, stepped on it and climbed up to the top of the Wall, then jumped over to the West. I was finally free! The whole process took only five minutes. Once over, I was picked up on the highway by an automobile. I was safe, but, of course, I cannot tell you how scared I was, but I was absolutely determined not to live under a communist regime for the rest of my life, so there was no other choice. I had no criminal or political record, but since my rank was sergeant, if I had been caught, under military rule, I might have received the death sentence. I'm still scared to death when I think back to that time. ❖

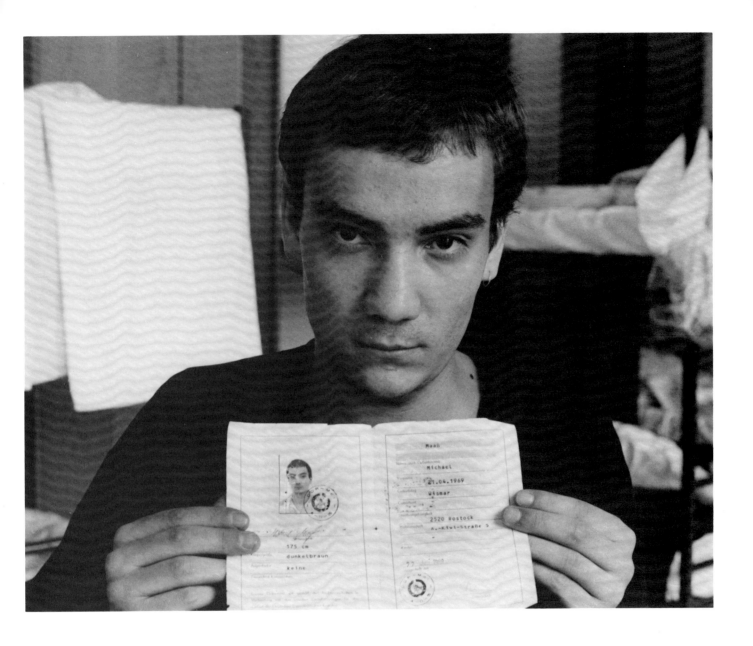

"I am no longer an East German citizen."

MICHAEL MAASS

Factory worker and former political prisoner. Born in 1969 in Weimar, East Germany. Lives in Berlin.

(Photo: Mr. Maass showing his East German identification document.)

You're one of many thousands of youths who attempted and failed to escape to the West, and were put in jail in East Germany. Tell me about your escape and why you wanted to get out.

While I was a factory worker in Rostock, East Germany, I was very unhappy about the whole social and political system of communism, with the authorities constantly interfering in our private lives. I wanted to have some freedom in my life. So I decided to come to the West when I was 17 years old. I had learned that the easiest escape route is through the Czechoslovakian border to either West Germany or Austria. So I took a train to Prague and changed to a bus to Cheb, a Czechoslovakian city that borders on both West and East Germany. At 4 o'clock in the morning on November 11, 1987, I started to climb up the border wall, but I was chased by two police dogs and caught by 5 Czechoslovakian border guards with machine guns. The police beat me up for half an hour thinking I was with other escapees. I was jailed in Cheb, but later extradited to the jail in Plzen, Czechoslavakia. I spent one-and-a-half years there, then I was transferred to Magdeburg jail in East Germany, and then to Karl-Marx-Stadt, where most of the prisoners were released to the West.

Tell me about your life in jail. Were you ever tortured?

Yes, I was tortured because I refused to work. I was beaten up and my legs and arms were chained to four corners of the bed for five days. My hands were twisted and that left permanent scars on my wrists. The food was bad and in such small portions that I was always hungry; no vegetables, no fruit, not enough nutrition. I lost ten kilos in two weeks.

We had to share a 25-square meter cell with 10 prisoners. We had no windows, no light, no fresh water, and the toilet was in the middle of the room. The shower was only cold water. People were constantly becoming sick with various kinds of illnesses. Everybody had to get up at 4 o'clock in the morning and have a shower and breakfast, and then work until 3 in the afternoon. I was forced to do some technical work on TV sets nearly nine hours a day, five days a week.

But nine months later, I was suddenly released. I received a written document saying, "You are not an East German citizen anymore," and given a one-way railway ticket to West Germany. At that time I could not fully understand why, but much later I learned from a lawyer that I was bought by the West German government for 40,000 DM (US $20,000).

What about your family? Do you have any contact with them?

I have parents and one sister; they all live in Rostock. My parents are members of the Communist Party and I never agreed with their political philosophy, so at home we had arguments all the time. I will never see them again, but I would like to see my sister one day. I never told any of my family or my girlfriend that I planned to escape. I abandoned everybody and left everything behind. I just took my jeans and the clothes I was wearing.

What are you planning for the future and how is your new life in free Germany?

I would like to be an actor. Right now I am looking for a job as a waiter, so I can support myself in acting school. Later, I want to travel the world and see the free western countries. ❖

"I escaped through Checkpoint Charlie."

FALK MÜHLBAHC

Electrical engineer and escapee from East Germany. Born in 1970 in Radeberg and raised in Leichenberg, East Germany.

(Photo: Mr. Mühlbahc standing in front of the gate at Checkpoint Charlie in West Berlin.)

When you escaped to the West, you were 17 years old. How did you come to that decision? Was it by yourself?

No, the decision was made with my family. We felt that living in a communist society was uncomfortable and we were unhappy. So, we, my parents and my brother, all agreed and decided to move to West Germany. But the bureaucratic process was very slow, and the immigration laws so strict that only a limited number of people were allowed to leave. Preference was given to those who needed special medical attention or who had relatives in West Germany. Since we had no specific reason to emigrate, it kept dragging on. We waited for 6 months without response from the immigration office. My family would have waited longer, but I didn't have the patience. Besides, even if we had waited for years, it might be for nothing. I felt we wouldn't be accepted anyway, so I decided to move alone.

First, I wanted to see the border. I took my motorcycle and a map and drove to Plauen in the southwest of East Germany, about 8 kilometers from the border. I was stopped by a police officer who asked what I was doing there. I said, "I am a motorcycle-lover making a tour of the border and I'm lost." But he didn't believe me. I was taken to Oelsnitz into custody. After seven hours of questioning I was released. This surprised me, because I thought they could arrest me for attempting escape. When I got home and told my family what had happened, they were angry about the behavior of the police officers, saying it was an invasion of my privacy. Can't a citizen of East Germany travel freely inside East Germany? They sent a letter of complaint to the city officials at Oelsnitz. About a month later, an official from Oelsnitz came to my home to apologize personally.

Since border control security is tight everywhere, didn't you think escape would prove too difficult?

No, on the contrary, my desire to be free became even stronger after that. I planned to try once more from somewhere else in mid-July of 1988. By then, I knew that I would not be shot for trying to escape, because the border guards were no longer shooting escapees. And if I were arrested and had to spend a few years in prison, I knew I'd be sent to West Germany after my release. So I decided to take the chance. But this time I didn't tell anyone.

What was your next plan?

I went to East Berlin on my motorcycle. For the next few days I looked around, observing the Wall between Friedrich Street, Brandenburg Gate and Checkpoint Charlie. I assumed that I could make an escape attempt from one of those three places. Although I was questioned by police officers, they didn't arrest me. They just warned me not to hang around in the area. I told them I was just a country boy from the southeast enjoying a sightseeing tour.

During that time, I noticed scaffolding I could climb up near the Post Museum, a vacant six-story building at the corner of Leipziger and Mauer Street. On July 24, 1988, at 11:30 p.m., I went back there. No one was around, so I began climbing up. When I reached the top of the building it was easy to move from rooftop to rooftop toward the last house that was parallel to the Wall. For hours I observed what was happening on the ground and made sure that nobody was watching me. Then I saw three pipes only a few meters away from the Wall. One of the pipes led down the side of a one-story house, so I climbed down the pipe and into the courtyard by sliding down a lightning rod.

From there, I watched until 3:55 a.m., when the border guards passed by. Then I moved swiftly to the corner of the last house right next to the Wall. I sat there for about five minutes to make sure nobody saw me, including the guard in the watch tower. Suddenly, I became scared, feeling that I would fail. Unexpectedly, a small car approached from Zimmer Street and turned into the courtyard. "Good timing," I said to myself. I assumed the guard in the watch tower would be momentarily distracted by the car, and with the rest of my courage, I jumped over a small fence about 1.5 meters high which surrounded the border control guard house, and I ran toward the West as quickly as possible.

I couldn't think of anything else. I just kept running. I crossed a wide street which was Koch Street, and then looking back, saw a car following me. Were the East German border guards coming to capture me? I didn't realize that I was already 200 meters inside the west side of the Berlin Wall! Then I saw a nearby police station. I rushed in and gasped, "I just escaped from East Berlin, please protect me!" When I knew I was safe, I cried. It was like waking from a suspenseful nightmare. ❖

"We need feminization of power in politics."

HILDEGARD VON MEIER

Feminist and "Woman for Peace" Activist. Born in 1934 and raised in Berlin.

(Photo: Ms. von Meier in her home with a display of her anti-nuclear posters.)

All wars end dramatically, and in the case of Berlin, the end of the war was both traumatic and ironic. Today, none of the politicians seem to care about Berlin; the city leads a kind of forgotten existence. And if anyone does care, what can they do about this troubled place? As a Berliner by birth, what kind of political lesson did you learn from postwar Germany?

The status of Berlin hasn't changed since 1945. In fact, the domination of the four powers in the city has never been discussed since the Potsdam Agreement. In the early postwar era, we lived under constant threat from the communist East, which gave us the impression that it was our sworn enemy: that the Russians were coming to invade us. But the occupying Allies gave us security, and we considered them our support, our defense from any invasion by communist Russia. So, we have no problem spending our tax money on the Allies for our protection, because West Berlin is a completely disarmed city and no West Berliner can be drafted. In the Cold War atmosphere of fear and during the World Peace Movement of the 1960's, it was West Germany that played the most significant role toward bringing peace to Europe. They talked about the concept of deterrence and détente, about fear, and about the catastrophe that might destroy Europe. For the first time after the war, West Germany raised the issue of the need for an alternative European peace plan.

Nowadays, even if we have conventional war, Germany and Europe cannot be defended. There are nuclear plants all over our soil, and this could have catastrophic consequences even without any bomb being dropped. For this reason, we West Berliners have a tremendous responsibility to help work out détente. We must be emphatic that all our industries should be guided by the concept of peace: war material industries, laser technology and communication industries should be prevented from bringing about the escalation of the nuclear armament competition. We must be well informed with a good worldwide communication system. We need a political human network.

You are very involved in the "Women for Peace" movement. How do you combine politics for women with the movement for peace? How can women participate and in what way can they achieve their goals?

That is the main issue. In Germany we still live with the reality that women, wives and mothers do the housework and take care of the family. That burden always falls to the women and leaves us with little time to do much else. The key issue is that women must find a new way of living. My personal goal as a woman activist is to help women find structures in which we can feel emotionally comfortable, in an atmosphere allowing us to be active in different fields such as politics, ecology, industry, and in economic issues. We need the right communication networks. We need close connections with women in parliament. We need to discuss theories that will encourage a woman to become candidate for parliament and take her place there. We need a feminization of power in politics.

In West Berlin we have the "Alternative List," which is the same as the "Green Party" in West Germany, and it works quite well. Regarding women's participation, it is equal. But this is certainly not true in other political parties. Within the Social Democratic Party (SPD), for example, women are misrepresented in a rather reactionary way. I want a broad spectrum of responsible women involved in thinking sensibly.

Like men, women need strategy, too, but for more than just power games.

Earlier, you mentioned the political and physical protection of West Berlin. What about the environmental part of that protection? In both East and West Berlin, each side has an international airport and a military airbase, which makes a total of four airports within a city of 450 square meters (800 km), and that is quite a lot. The air space must be very crowded, leading to bad pollution problems, and so on. How do you see that?

In the matter of Berlin's environmental protection, I feel growing anger at the noise and air pollution, and it worries me considerably. Concerning new plans for transportation, we need to cooperate with East Berlin. We should concentrate on providing more trains in Germany and continental Europe, not only for environmental reasons, but also because it is far more economical, safer, more practical, saves energy, and most of all, because it's more efficient and can carry more people. Currently, Berlin is in trouble on the environmental level and an alternative transportation system must be developed.

How do women view the issue of the environment and the peace movement differently from men, and what approach should women take to make their views known?

Women are born spiritual. In many aspects women have instinctive ties to their spiritual nature. Today, the nature of the earth is being destroyed, entire species of animals are dying every day, everywhere in the world. As women we are able to feel that connection inside us. Every woman wants her baby to be born safe and healthy and we are intuitive experts at motherhood. For two years after the Chernobyl nuclear disaster, the milk of mothers was contaminated at a rate ten times higher than that of the milk of cows, which means unborn babies are weakened while still in the womb, and the immune systems of babies are affected before their birth. According to doctors and scientists, these phenomena are completely new and unknown. We are facing an unprecedented ecological crisis.

Moreover, a number of mysterious skin rashes have been reported: asthma and, more recently, allergies of unknown origin. Chemical industries and pharmaceutical manufacturers are happy, of course, to produce medicines and medical supplies for treatments and profit commercially from this problem.

I believe this is a woman's issue. Now, women must say no. We need a different agenda and perspective from men. Many men possess a missile mentality, whereas women must live by a different philosophy. We must stop men's power domination. We have the International Women's Conference with Eastern Bloc socialist women every year where both sides present social and environmental problems regarding working women and mothers. We discuss and exchange ideas concerning both sides' political and social conditions, and we try to find solutions. It is vital to encourage women in the Eastern communist countries to develop independent views and to take the human rights issue seriously. ❖

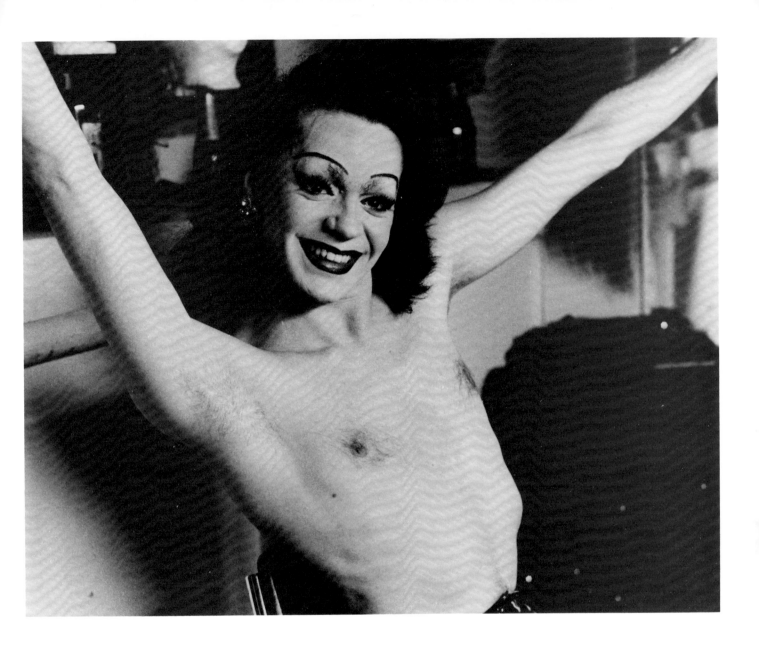

"In Berlin, we do everything Berlin style."

JOSEPH DILLON

Irish entertainer at the Dollywood Night Club. Born in 1960 in Dublin, Ireland, has lived in Berlin for 2 years.

(Photo: Mr. Dillon after his stage show.)

What was your image of Berlin before you came, and what were you hoping to find?

I had heard so much about Berlin before I came, had read Christopher Isherwood's novel, seen the movie *Cabaret,* and so on. I was intrigued and it was all true. There is no doubt that this city is exciting, wild, extravagant, charismatic and magnetic. What's more, I'm right in the middle of it. In terms of night life, this is an original and authentic place, and everyone should come and experience it at least once in a lifetime. Berlin is waiting for you.

As a nightclub entertainer, what are the advantages of living in Berlin?

I came here to establish my career and learn about nightclub management. I'm a stage dancer with 16 years' experience, and have traveled all over the world and worked in all the major cities. But to be successful in this field, dancing isn't enough. You have to be able to talk and sing and make people laugh — a complete act — to give audiences the maximum enjoyment. Historically, Berlin is known for these scenes. People think post-war Berlin has lost these values, but I disagree. It still has that tradition and originality that makes it a leading entertainment city today. Berlin's unique ambiance is hard to describe to anyone who hasn't been here. It's an utterly different type of entertainment from Las Vegas or Broadway. Here, we do everything Berlin style. That's why I'm here — to learn and develop that Berlin style.

Tell me about your night club. What kind of shows do you present and what kind of audiences do you attract?

My club is not a commercial or tourist-oriented place like many others, but rather a type of neighborhood club. We get many middle-class "Yuppies," young and old, and even families with growing children, who are into Berlin's 1920's nostalgia. Each night we have four different shows performed by seven entertainers: actors, singers, dancers, comedians. We don't repeat the same show, so the audience can stay and enjoy until the end of the night, which is about four o'clock in the morning. We present many female impersonator shows, but no imitations of famous celebrities like Marilyn Monroe. That's old-fashioned! A high quality show and professional performance — these are the priorities of our club.

This is a city of extreme contrasts — joy and fear. From a foreigner's point of view, how do you see the city's political situation?

Personally, I am not concerned about it that much. Not being German, it doesn't affect me. The city has been surrounded by the Wall since I came, so I accept it as it is. What upsets me is when young escapees from East Germany are shot at by the border patrol guards, and that occurs almost every day, and nobody can do anything about it. As far as political matters are concerned, there really is no comparison to Ireland, where I come from. Catholics and Protestants in Northern Ireland have been fighting each other for decades because of fundamental religious and philosophical differences. Berliners are entirely different. Berlin was once one city, divided by force, not by choice, and that is tremendously different. Maybe, you could call it "the fate of Berlin." In a way, I am quite sympathetic, especially to the younger people. I am not a political person, but I wish the citizens of the world knew and thought more about the reality of Berlin. ❖

"Berlin: draft-free, cheap living and a lot to learn."

MICHAEL DUBUS

Computer programmer student. Born in 1969 in Creglingen, West Germany. Has lived in West Berlin for one year.

No one can be drafted in West Berlin, but in West Germany, you have to do mandatory military service. Is that so?

Yes. I object to the idea of any military system. I don't want to become a soldier and learn how to use machine guns to kill people. I don't think people can make peace with military instruments, and I don't think the military defense system keeps the peace either.

What have you learned from living in Berlin?

After living here for a while, I realized that there are plenty of things to learn about the history of Germany which can never be experienced in any other West German city. For example, the destruction of this city reminds me that a horrible war took place in my country many years ago, and visually, we must face its reality here every day. Not only the Wall; there are still many ruins of bombed buildings and houses with bullet holes which are left untouched everywhere. I think it is very important to keep those ruins unchanged, because this daily reminder ensures that people won't forget the war and its consequences, and what happened to Germany. To live with ruins reminds us of the past and hopefully we can learn from it, and not repeat the same mistakes again. In other West German cities, there are new buildings and factories, clean parks, and nothing to remember from the war. Therefore, people are likely to forget, especially the postwar generations. Most West Germans ignore the war and their past. I think that's a shame.

What difference do you see between the Berliners and the mainland Germans concerning their attitudes toward politics?

I'm not militant or political; I never go to demonstrations or rallies. However, I read newspapers, watch TV news, and vote in elections to express my choice about which politician or political party I want to represent me. I think West German people in general are careless about what's going on in politics. The majority of West Germans are working-class people; they go to work 8 hours a day, pay taxes, come home, watch football, drink beer, play with their children, go to sleep and do the same thing the next day. They repeat that ritual every day, mechanically, throughout life. They don't think about what the politicians are doing. Many Germans have never even visited Berlin; they are really ignorant about their past. Living in this special city taught me an alternative way of thinking. Because Berlin doesn't have a population of money-oriented middle-class people, or even any huge industrial corporations, it's pretty cheap to live here. Therefore, I find two advantages in living in Berlin — no draft because of its special political status, and cheap living because of its economic condition.

Do you feel Germans will start another war?

In our schools, all German children learn history and geography. Over one hundred years ago, Germany was united with the Prussian Empire which gave it an enormous amount of territory that included eastern Germany, Poland and the western parts of the Soviet Union. After two world wars, we lost most of these territories and Germany was even divided into two countries. I don't feel sad about it. The last war was the end of it, and I feel enough was enough. No more war here, but of course, no one can guarantee that. My feeling is that, as long as the Federal Republic of Germany keeps strong ties with the United States, West Germany will not repeat history. ❖

"I can never imagine Berlin without the Wall."

SOOSIE HAUSBECK

Artist and part-time model. Born in Neuss, West Germany in 1967.
Has lived in West Berlin for eight years.

Most West German youths who move to West Berlin are looking for excitement and a new lifestyle. What is yours, and has Berlin changed very much since you came?

I am a social refugee. The reason I moved to Berlin is simply because I did not like the West German people. They are very conservative, mentally stereotypical, reactionary and boring. I love to dress in my own style, for instance, but they are aggressively against the way I look and my punk appearance. They cannot understand that different people have different ways of thinking and living. I hitchhiked to West Berlin when I was 15 years old. My family is upper middle class; my father's in the insurance business, but I never rely on them financially. I had never been to West Berlin before, but I had a feeling that perhaps I could meet more free-thinking young individuals here, with whom I could share and enjoy interesting cultural activities.

West Berlin has changed since I came, especially the Kreuzberg district where I live. It has become chic and touristic and more attractive to rich people who have money to buy condominiums and can afford higher rents than poor people, and they're trying to push us out. There has been increased property speculation and building over the past several years, and we fear that we may lose our comfortable life here. It is a pity that Kreuzberg is losing its originality. The hippie area is becoming yuppie. I'm afraid that it's like another Haight-Ashbury in San Francisco in the 70's.

You don't seem to have a regular job. How do you manage to survive and what are your plans for the future?

I work on and off as a model for photographers and painters, and sometimes I play bit parts in the movies to earn some money. I also dance on stage. There is not much work here in West Berlin, and more jobs are available in West Germany, but I hate the people there, and do not want to go back. I do want to survive and establish my life in West Berlin. At the moment I'm having a difficult time finding work and my income is not enough. But I can get social welfare; 412 DM (US $210) from the city government each month plus 250 DM (US $125) for rent support called *Wohngeld,* which helps tremendously. My apartment is 350 DM (US $180) per month, so I can live modestly. Besides, I never buy new clothes; I either get them from friends or in second-hand shops. As far as my future is concerned, I think I'll keep on in the same direction.

How do you find life in the city by the Wall? What is your impression?

Personally, I don't care much. Many West German tourists and foreigners ask us how we can live in such terrible conditions with the ugliness of the Wall. But for us West Berliners, the Wall is always there and we are used to living with it. I like the Wall and think it's great. I just can't imagine West Berlin without it. For me, it's unthinkable that politicians will unify the two Germanys and pull down the Wall. I can't imagine it. ❖

"Education is a key element in German people's lives."

ELKE STENZEL

High school teacher and lecturer at the Free University of West Berlin.
Born in 1946 in Düsseldorf, West Germany, and has lived in West
Berlin for 22 years.

Ms. Stenzel, over the years you've visited schools and colleges in the United States as a guest teacher on educational exchange programs. How do you find their educational standards compared with those of West Germany?

Frankly, educational standards in the West German secondary schools (high schools) are higher than in the United States. But that does not mean the American high schools are ineffectual. Approaches to education in both countries are different. We put much more emphasis on academic training for our high school students, while American high school and grade schools emphasize their function as social training ground for students. I think German academic training in high school is really college level, and that is the basic difference.

More precisely, the last few years at West German secondary schools are equal to the first few years of college in America. So I find American college students really have to study hard to catch up. Overall, university students in West Germany are inclined to be liberal and independent.

You also visited schools in East Germany. How do you think they compare, bearing in mind political and social differences?

Educational standards in East Germany are very good. All students must attend the same levels of school that we do in West Germany, but then, only ten percent of these students are selected to proceed into higher education, which means the university, and so that's very hard to get into. Under socialism, admission often depends on what kind of political activities the student was involved in at school, and the parents' profession. For example, if a student is a party member, he or

she is privileged and finds it easier to pursue higher education.

In your 15 years as an educator, have you found any changes in people's attitudes about education in West Germany?

In Germany, education is a key element in our lives. Generally, we Germans want to get as good an education as we can because it is the key to a good career or to a rise to a better profession, and eventually will help us to enjoy a better life and a higher social status. Whatever you want to do in life, go to college, university or into business, you need a high school diploma. You need a certificate to prove your level of education. To get that piece of paper, you must take very elaborate examinations.

In recent years, particularly, I have noticed a considerable increase in the number of students who attend middle school and secondary school. I believe, because of the more highly qualified people and the higher standard of education, required in West Berlin, you are compelled to work very hard to achieve anything academically.

How do you find the social life in West Berlin compared to that of other German cities?

I find a distinct difference between the people of West Germany and those of West Berlin. Berlin society is more open and less class-oriented with people mingling more easily than in other German cities. Furthermore, many wonderful international cultural events and activities take place here. I would never leave Berlin; it's my city.

What do you think, personally, of Berlin's future?

It is true that to live in Berlin is to become involved with politics whether you like it or not.

Like all West Berlin citizens, when I visit East Germany, I have to carry, along with my passport, a special identification card issued by the city of West Berlin. That's because the East German government considers West Berlin to be controlled by the Allies even today; it still does not accept West Berlin. Furthermore, West Berliners cannot vote in our own country, West Germany. Berlin City sends 22 representatives elected by West Berliners to the West German parliament in Bonn. That is why people here get involved in politics and often become emotionally intense. In a way, this is quite normal if you live in Berlin.

Concerning Berlin's future, it depends on what happens in the Soviet Union, and of course, other international politics. But I do not believe that the political situation will change in the near future in Berlin! ❖

CHAPTER FIVE

Reunification

East and West Germans in the Newly United Germany

(Conducted between 1990 and 1991)

ROBERT L. LOCHNER

(Second interview; see Chapter IV, p. 354)

Since our interview two years ago, the political situation in Berlin has changed dramatically. The world was astonished once again by Germany's historical transformation in this century. Everything happened so suddenly. As a veteran journalist living in West Berlin, did you see any sign of the collapse of the communist regime in East Germany?

In retrospect, I would say that Western journalists didn't see the signs of total disintegration in East Germany at all. Thinking back a few years now, Mr. Gorbachev made it clear that he would not intervene in the internal affairs of East Germany any longer, and thus, Erich Honecker, the leader of East Germany, lost his big brother. That was a signal of the coming fall of East Germany. Several months before, tens of thousands of East Germans had escaped to the West through Czechoslovakia, Hungary, and Austria, and even then, we thought Honecker would still be able to control the situation somehow. But obviously he didn't.

It became clear that the government of East Germany had to loosen up the travel restrictions on their citizens. And, in fact, in 1988 and 1989, Honecker allowed nearly two million retired people to travel to West Germany freely, though most of them returned home. There was no mass exodus or flood of people or anything like that. I think the rumors could have been misinterpreted.

On the night of November 9th, 1989, the world was stunned watching the television news from Berlin as incredible numbers of East Germans entered West Berlin, crying with joy,
screaming with excitement, dancing and celebrating with champagne in front of the Wall. That night was so unpredictable. Can you describe why the situation developed so quickly?

The afternoon of November 9th, after a long press conference in East Berlin, the announcement was aired that, starting at midnight, any East German citizen would be allowed to travel to the West without any restriction. We didn't think that was so sensational, but people didn't wait. By midnight, masses of people rushed to checkpoints and the border areas became out of control, so that the East German government decided just to let them go. That was the end of the Wall.

Who made that decision? Who held the final key to the fall of the Wall? Would you say it was Mr. Gorbachev or Mr. Honecker?

It's very hard to say. Mr. Gorbachev had nothing to do with those details. He had already decided not to interfere with the domestic problems of Mr. Honecker's regime. But Gorbachev's nonintervention led to the fall of the communist government, and eventually brought about the reunification of Germany. Honecker was ill in bed, so we still don't know who was responsible. More likely than not, it appears that it was not the decision of any one person. In late October 1989, the East German government promised it would drastically liberalize travel restrictions to the West. But a few days later, it was announced that the conversion would take time and that people must wait. Then mass protests against the government began in East Berlin and the chaos spread to Leipzig, Dresden, and other cities. Soon it became clear that everything had changed.

I don't think any individual was in charge or intended it to happen. I do believe, however, that the government was overcome by events and just wanted to avoid the risk posed by the anti-government movement, and avoid provoking popular anger. I would say the result of the spontaneous uprising was dramatic and successful and led to escalation. Tearing down the Wall was part of it. The outcome was unbelievable and unique in the entire history of Germany. ❖

STEFAN GÄNSICKE

(Second Interview; see Chapter IV, p. 359)

Mr. Gänsicke, in the interview we did two years ago, you said, "Within 50 years the two Germanys will be united." I mentioned this to some West Berliner friends. They laughed and criticized you for being too optimistic. As it turned out, your estimate was too conservative. You never thought you would see unification in your lifetime. How do you feel now?
It was absolutely unbelievable. It still is. Sometimes, I have to make sure that I am not dreaming. The dream suddenly came true and, yes, it brought great euphoria to me here in my office in West Berlin. Many people screamed for joy and actually cried.

How did everything happen so quickly? Could you give me a chronology of the key events?
The evening of November 9th was the first time the East German border guards had let everyone go through to the West. Within hours after the radio announcement at seven o'clock, West Berlin was jammed with people. Kurfürstendamm (the main avenue of West Berlin) was packed with traffic and crowds. It was truly a historical moment, as you saw on television. To explain more pre-

cisely, the actual exodus began in the spring of 1989 when Hungary cut the barbed wire border to Austria. The Warsaw Pact nations opened the borders to the West. Everyone looked to see what action the Russians would take. Surprisingly, they ignored what was going on. After that, thousands of East Germans escaped through Hungary to Austria and West Germany. Shortly afterwards, Czechoslovakia allowed East Germans to travel to the West, and Poland soon followed. By mid-summer, it had become clear that East Germany must do something to stop the terrible drain on the population. Those escapees were intelligent, educated, and energetic people of working age. We still thought that the Russians would come to rescue East Germany, but no action was taken.

On October 7th of 1989, on the 40th anniversary of the celebration of the establishment of communism in East Germany, Mr. Gorbachev visited East Berlin. The next day in a brief television interview, a reporter criticized him for his failure with *perestroika* and *glasnost* in East Germany.

Mr. Gorbachev bluntly responded; "The people who come too late will be punished." That was the signal that the mighty Soviet Union was not going to save East Germany. Exactly one month later, on November 8th, what Mr. Gorbachev said was clearly understood by all East German soldiers on the streets of East Berlin. The next day marked the end of the totalitarian communist regime and became a historical day for Germany. All in all, it was a totally unexpected and unbelievably peaceful transformation.

Now the map of Germany has been changed once more. How do you analyze the reality of having lived with the Wall for 28 years?
I have always looked upon the Wall as a punishment. A good example can be found in

Dostoyevsky's great novel *Crime and Punishment*. The crimes we committed were WW II and the Holocaust. Regrettably, we became the "bad boys of Europe" and we lived through 45 years of divided Germany and Berlin, and 28 years with the Wall. Our punishment has lasted for nearly the length of one person's life. Although I was absolutely perplexed by the sudden change at the beginning, I must admit that I feel great relief, humility, and joy now.

Now that the two Germanys have been reunited, can West Germany handle the disastrous economic situation of East Germany?

When we found out how horrible the economic situation was in East Germany, we thought "Oh, boy! Our honeymoon is over!" It will cost West Germany millions of marks, or perhaps billions to restore its industrial and productive ability. Production and manufacturing methods are hopelessly out of date. Under the communist regime, people lost their motivation, flexibility, and initiative, and those have to be brought back. The fact is that the mental part of the damage is harder to repair than the physical. I would say that economically the next three to five years will be a tough time for East Germans, but the mental education will take much longer. But West Germany still has the power, money and brain to make it work. Within a matter of ten years, the German economy will rebound. Although I don't believe we can beat Japan, Germany will at least become a powerful nation again in Europe.

Germany and Japan dominate the world economy today. However, Germans work fewer hours than the Japanese. How can Germany maintain its strong economy?

That is an interesting point. In fact, over the next few years, we will try to reduce the work week to 35 hours, but we will try to maintain our wage base and standard of living while we compete in the world market, high-technology, and industry race. Germany and Japan are both well educated, highly industrialized nations with a hard working attitude. However, I honestly believe that in many fields, Germany can't compete with Japan for some very fundamental reasons. Firstly, social conditions are different. The Japanese are willing to work harder than anyone else. Secondly, the Japanese don't have the problems with trade unions that Germans have. The unions in Japan are based in each corporation or company. The unions in Germany are nationally standardized, which results in differences. The strength of the German economy is based on the high standards of its products and industry in the upscale markets.

What do you think of *perestroika* and *glasnost*, and about the future of the Soviet Union?

We have a big problem ahead in Germany, but in comparison to the problems in the Soviet Union, it doesn't actually seem that bad. In such a gigantic state, change can't be as fast as it can be in our case. In fact, there is danger that if change comes too rapidly in Russia, civil war could break out. We are extremely concerned about this. They have different problems from ours: they have lived under a Marxist-communist regime for 73 years, far longer than East Germany. Before that, Russia was a rural nation; it has never been an industrialized country. After Karl-Marx's Manifesto was introduced in 1848, and then the Russian Revolution occurred in 1917, Lenin and Stalin tried to industrialize the country, but the whole structure went the wrong way, as we know. Now, it has almost entirely fallen to pieces. It will have to go back, and introduce a manufacturing system, and an open market-oriented economy. These are enormous political tasks: it's like trying to educate a 19th century nation in order to bring it up to the standards of the 21st century. To be honest, I have no idea that can be done. ❖

MATTHIAS FRINGS

(Second Interview; see Chapter IV, p. 363)

In our last interview, you expressed quite an optimistic view about Gorbachev and Germany. At that time, did you think that the Wall would come down and that the two Germanys would be united?

No, never. I never thought the Wall would come down so fast and neither did anybody else. Since Mr. Gorbachev became the leader of the Soviet Union and introduced *glasnost* and *perestroika*, most Germans, including conservatives, felt that he was a very special kind of politician who would affect, not only Russia but all of Europe. We started to think of him as a new type of communist leader, completely different from any leader that Russia had had before. And we seriously thought that he could be a revolutionary who might be able to bring peace. Although we never believed the Wall would remain forever, neither did we think it would come down overnight. It was truly a great surprise for everybody. To us, Gorbachev is a great man. He is a genuine peacemaker and deserves the Nobel Peace Prize.

You also mentioned in our last interview that there would be ideological problems in the communication between East Germans and West Germans. How do you find it to be now?

It has been one year since our new life began. After being a divided nation for 45 years we've come together again. I, like all Berliners, feel grateful for "life without the Wall." However, this does not mean we, the people of the West, can mentally "westernize" East Germans overnight. Things are not that simple. The people of the West must learn to deal with the people from the East. We speak the same language and communicate with the same words but our meanings are different. We have lived under utterly separate political philosophies — communism and capitalism. The two social systems and structures are completely opposed to each other. East Germans have their own ideology, history and culture to which they belong, and West Germans can't take that away from them. East Germans have been deeply influenced by their political environment. It may take more than one generation to "capitalize" their minds.

Today is November 9th, 1990, the one-year anniversary of the collapse of the Wall. Everybody should be happy and filled with relief after the long agony and stress caused by the presence of the Wall. Why aren't Berliners celebrating?

We have all sorts of problems in Berlin at the moment. The major one is unemployment. Since the East German government no longer exists, all its officials, employees, and workers were fired without much notice. For example, in the news media, which is my professional arena, many of my East German friends and colleagues lost their jobs. Television journalists and radio reporters who lost their jobs there came to look for new positions in the West, but nobody hires them because their working attitudes are different from ours. They were not trained or educated to work the way we do in the West: we are quick, sponta-neous and creative, and they are not. Those newly unemployed workers can't pay their rent, and that has increased domestic and economic problems all over East Germany. On the other hand, in West Germany, many people can't find apart-ments because of the sudden population surge of East German refugees. All these factors cause peo-ple to feel tense, insecure, and unhappy. That is why we are not celebrating the fall of the Wall. Of course, the politicians knew that if the gov-ernment changed quickly from one system to an-other without careful planning, it would mean social chaos which would directly affect every East German citizen, but they did it anyway. The "fat cat" brother decided to take care of his poor little brother as quickly as possible.

Those are the main reasons why we are not celebrating today. But, to tell the truth, there are other reasons why we don't celebrate on Novem-ber 9th. Historically, it coincides with the follow-ing negative anniversaries: it's the day of the start of the German Revolution; the abdication of Em-peror William II, followed by the defeat of WW I in 1918; the day of the Beer Hall *Putsch,* Hitler's revolt in 1923; and the day of the *Kristallnacht* in 1938. Ironically, November 9th is a cursed date in our history.

Although the fall of the Wall has caused new social problems and economic crises and will certainly cause more upheaval in the future, do you still think it was a good thing for both Germanys?

Yes, of course, absolutely. For the time being, people are insecure and uncertain about the fu-ture. Some people say; "We want the Wall back!" I feel that is disgusting. Do we want that huge prison back again? No way! We are not happy at the moment because we are confronting many changes and many problems, but that will not last forever. Even so, I think we should be grateful for all the good things that have come to us.

There have been great ideological upheavals, political crises and wars in the past centuries of Germany history. German people suffer di-rectly from the political consequences. What do you see for the future of Germany?

Socialism made many people discontent over the years, and it became very unpopular. If you are a socialist now, it's better to keep your mouth shut for the time being, because people think socialism has failed. It will take a long time before we find and even talk about ideologies other than capital-ism. I'm quite sure capitalism is not the last an-swer for our history. For the moment, the West-ern world is claiming to have liberated the Eastern world from the miserable burden of com-munism, claiming that capitalism has won be-cause it's the best system. But the ideology of socialism should be remembered as a political les-son. Unfortunately, though, only intellectuals can understand that. As for how our society will change, I would really like to know what Ger-many will be like 100 years from now. ❖

Willy, the man who kept peace in postwar Germany and Europe

WILLY BRANDT

Politician; former Chancellor and Foreign Minister of West Germany, former leader of the Social Democratic Party, Mayor of West Berlin during the Berlin Crisis, Nobel Peace Prize winner and author of numerous books. Born 1913 in Lübeck. Deceased in 1992 in Bonn.

Mr. Brandt, you are one of the most influential politicians of the twentieth century in Europe and the world. I would like to know about your early life, and how you became involved in politics.

I was born in Lübeck, north Germany's port city. I was originally named Herbert Ernst Karl Frahm. My childhood coincided with WW I and the Great Depression, when German people were desperately poor. My family was also very poor, working-class, and I grew up with Social Democratic roots. It was quite a natural role for me to be interested in people and politics and how the two things are connected. At 15, I was a chairman of the Socialist Workers' Youth Union and a leader of anti-Nazi activists in my hometown. In fact, with my colleagues, I got into fist-fights with the Hitler Youth brownshirt gangs in the streets. I was wild when I was a young man! When Hitler became Chancellor of Germany in January, 1933, I was upset. The following month, I visited Berlin to make contact with a group of people holding clandestine meetings against Hitler's new order. Berlin was called "red city" then, and had the highest degree of anti-Nazi activities of any city in Germany. Shortly after that, the Reichstag was set on fire and Hitler immediately arrested members of the Communist and Social Democratic Party. I said to myself, with Germany under Hitler, what would be next? I knew it would be war.

During Nazi Germany, you were in exile and only returned to Germany after the war. Can you tell me about your life as a political refugee, and what you thought of Hitler's Germany?

As a fervent anti-Nazi activist, I felt I was in increasing danger. In late 1933, I was deprived of my German citizenship by the Nazis, and I be-

came a citizen without a state. I fled to Norway as a political refugee and took Norwegian citizenship under a new name, Willy Brandt. I established an anti-Nazi underground network. I was then 19. I attended Oslo University and worked as a journalist as well, supporting German and Norwegian resistance movements. Then, in 1936, the Civil War burst out in Spain. By that time I was a radical left-wing Socialist committed to fighting against any fascist's or dictator's regime. I traveled to Barcelona as a reporter for Scandinavian publications, and I met with the Social Democratic International Youth Organization. I was impressed by the compassion of the revolutionary young Spaniards fighting for democracy, and I learned a great deal from them.

When Norway was invaded by Hitler in 1940, my Norwegian citizenship was canceled by the Nazis. I managed to escape to Stockholm, Sweden, and kept writing for periodicals and newspapers there, and I kept close ties with international student groups. At the time of Hitler's military victory over Poland, I sensed that Hitler's fascism would escalate into full-scale war in Europe. Fascism is a collective term for right-wing totalitarianism and radicalism, the deprivation of democracy, trade unionism, liberalism and also intellectual freedom. Nazi fascism took away my homeland and my citizenship, and I had to live with a disguised name. But I've never concealed my German origin and had no reason to be ashamed of it. Although I was emotionally attached to Norway and felt it was my second home during my exile, I always hoped that Hitler would be defeated so that Germany might survive, and not disappear from the world map. I never lost my faith in Germany. I called it the "other Germany" — I was not against Germany but against Hitler's Germany. I never lost hope that the hatred of the war years would be overcome, and some day we would build a Europe in which we could live together in harmony and peace. Peace, when it comes, must be determined by the social balance of power.

You were mayor of West Berlin during the Berlin Crisis, the most critical conflict between West and East in postwar Germany, which almost led to World War Three. Your achievements then gained you international renown. How did you handle the situation in the divided city and persuade Berliners and Germans to keep the peace?

To make a long story short, postwar Germany was really unsettled; a defeated state with destroyed cities, a divided country and a divided city, a dismembered nation in the heart of Europe. At the time, the Berlin Blockade was followed by an East German workers' uprising, and in 1956 the revolt in neighboring Hungary had been brutally suppressed by the mighty communist Russian army. We'd learned enough lessons from the past. During the Berlin Crisis we knew that if we West Berliners tried to remove the Wall and fight back against East Germany backed by the Soviet leader, Nikita Khrushchev, it would mean either bloody revolt or possibly even atomic war. The West-East conflict in Berlin meant escalation could trigger another world war.

I was rather disappointed that President John F. Kennedy of the United States couldn't do much for us. There was a high degree of misunderstanding within the Four Powers Agreement in Berlin — the US, Britain, France and the Soviet Union. The Western Allies were responsible only for the protection of West Berlin, as the Soviet Army was responsible for East Berlin and East Germany. When the agreement was signed,

the building of the Wall had not been foreseen. Therefore, the western Allies didn't have the power to move the Wall. And then later, even the western superpower America, could do nothing.

When the war ended, the Cold War began: Berlin became a victim of the Cold War and a symbol of the Iron Curtain. The events of August 13, 1961, totally changed the character of the city; no more free access: communist East and democratic West facing each other across the street, with people and their families split up. As the mayor of West Berlin, I had to convince my fellow citizens that we had to live with the Wall for an uncertain length of time in order to maintain peace in Germany, Europe and the rest of the world, and to avoid another war in which tens of millions of lives might be lost. Berliners were forced to control their emotions and to think and act reasonably. I persuaded Berliners that coexistence was our only chance for survival. Peaceful coexistence was the only alternative to nuclear holocaust and global suicide. The question for the rest of the world would be, "Why should people die for Berlin?"

During the early days of life with the Wall, how did you develop your political relationship with President Kennedy, and what was your hope for the future of Berlin?

I met John F. Kennedy several times, even before he became President. Because of him, my personal and political ties with the United States were strengthened. We were of the same generation and entered political careers during WW II, but by very different routes. When he visited West Berlin in June 1963, he was welcomed by hundreds of thousands of jubilant West Berliners and it was very exciting, one of the greatest experiences in Berlin's history. He was elegant and

intelligent and could fascinate with his eloquence. The brilliant speech he had rehearsed
with me in my office went on to make history —
"Ich bin ein Berliner." Over all, what impressed
me most was his practical and creative way of
thinking. He thought ahead and looked to the
future. He once said, "History teaches us that
enmities between nations do not last forever. So,
let us persevere. Peace need not be impracticable,
and war need not be inevitable." His triumphant
visit to West Berlin confirmed my belief that a
democratic Germany and a free Europe could
only live in clear accord with America, because
the two continents were linked by vital interests.
The East-West conflict and the communist peril
still existed in Germany: Germany was interested
in détente. Mr. Kennedy taught me about the
winds of change. I was influenced by him and
later developed an idea — called *Ostpolitik* (Eastern policy) — to normalize and improve relations
with the Soviet Union and the Eastern European
countries. He gave me courage and hope for Germany. Then, five months later, he was killed. His
death shocked people all over the world, especially us, of course. My feeling was that I had lost
my great partner for peace. I still sometimes la-
ment him. Had he been alive, I could have
pushed many things earlier, the German question
of reunification, and so on. He was a few years
younger than me. If he were still alive, he would
be in his mid-seventies.

**After the war Japan was not divided. Tokyo
didn't have to live with any wall and the Japanese people were not divided. However, they
were hit by two atomic bombs and that changed
everything. That experience is still vivid in the
mind of many Japanese, and the majority believe
that to start another war would mean the end**

**of mankind. In that respect, what do young
Germans think today?**
Fortunately, we in Germany weren't hit with an
atomic bomb. But the bombardment and total
destruction of Dresden in which 90 percent of
the city was flattened and tens of thousands of
lives were lost, that was almost as bad as the
atomic bomb blast. But realistically, I can't imagine people's reactions if there were another atomic
attack today...?

At that stage the world was horrified and
we entered a new era: the nuclear age. It was
Armageddon and a turning point in our history:
terrifyingly different from the traditional wars
which mankind had fought for many thousands
of years. I think, to a certain degree, the feeling of
the German people is somewhat similar to that of
the Japanese. Besides the Berlin Crisis, there were
other crises during the Cold War era such as the
Cuban Missile Crisis, and each case was an intense, serious, and frightening experience because
of the existence of nuclear arms. Everybody was
afraid of a crisis because it might escalate and
become atomic war. The psychological dread of
the Germans was so deep that they wanted to
avoid any kind of war. The recent Gulf War was
shocking to us, because we thought such a war
would be impossible, but now we know it could
happen again today. In Berlin, Bonn and other
major German cities during the Gulf War, we saw
anti-war rallies with crowds of perhaps as many as
500,000. So, it shows clearly that today's Germans are also sensitive and panicked by the reality of war, and like Japan, refused to send military
to fight against Iraq.

**During the 20th century, two men have been
the most important politicians in Germany:
Adolf Hitler, warmaker, and Willy Brandt,**

peacemaker. From the experience of the Nazi tragedy in the 20th century, what is your message for the generations of the 21st century?

The Gulf War gave us vital lessons. We need to re-think and re-examine world politics and world peace. War can occur anywhere in the world and there are dictators that come and go all the time, not only Hitler in Germany, but in any country and in any generation. We have now faced the truth that world peace doesn't last forever. We now know that we, the people, must work hard to make peace and make our world a safe place to live.

My message for the younger generation today is that people should remain critical of those who are in power, but not in a mistrustful way. They must inform political leaders to step ahead quickly toward peace, and move against ambi-tious dictators who are endangering the future of the world.

By the middle of the 21st century, the world population will be doubled. In a number of countries, such as Korea, great progress is being made. But still dozens of regional crises exist throughout the globe, and hunger and poverty are growing in many parts of the world. My simple belief is that, wherever hunger exists, peace becomes endangered. Throughout my own lifetime, I have experienced hunger twice during the two world wars. Hunger grows out of war and, if we don't do anything to stop it, I'm afraid that war will grow out of hunger and misery. I think it would be wise for young people today, not only to be aware of those new challenges, but also to urge world leaders to move a little bit faster than they are doing now — before it becomes too late.

❖

Founder of Berlin's non-violent human rights movement.

DR. RAINER HILDEBRANDT

Berlin human rights activist, founder of the Checkpoint Charlie Museum of Berlin. Born 1915 in Stuttgart, Germany. Lives in West Berlin.

(Photo: Dr. Hildebrandt showing one of the photos in the Checkpoint Charlie Museum.)

Dr. Hildebrandt, I would like to know about your family background, and how Nazi Germany changed your personal life and your thinking?

First of all, I must say, if Germany had not had a man named Hitler, the story would be totally different. But unfortunately, we did... I was born to an art historian father and painter mother. My mother was half Jewish and I was classified as "one quarter Jew," but after a special application, I was initially able to avoid Nazi harassment. In my youth, I was relatively *unpolitisch* — an apolitical person, and in 1933 when Hitler seized power, I didn't care at all. But in later years when my father was fired from his university teaching position because of his passion for Matisse, Marc Chagall, Paul Klee and so on, whom Hitler outlawed as "degenerate" artists, Nazi totalitarianism became my personal problem. And my "non-Aryan" mother and her family, who had lived in Germany since the 16th century, were suddenly in trouble: they became dangerous foreigners.

I moved to Berlin in 1937 at the age of 23, and became a student of technological physics at Berlin University. There again, a new law decreed that all students were to be indoctrinated with Nazi views and had to be drafted for the Voluntary Labor Service. Being "apolitical," I ran away to Paris, but as France turned refugees away, I had to return to Germany and the university. While working in a factory as a craftsman and studying hard, I started thinking about life and politics, and how politics affects our personal lives, and decided to switch my studies to humanities: history, philosophy, and psychology. In 1938 when Hitler occupied Czechoslovakia, I was deeply shocked like many other Germans. I saw the prelude to a new world war and sensed great catastrophe ahead.

For the first time in my life I felt it was my duty and responsibility to engage myself in political action. We had to overthrow Hitler. We had to resist his dictatorship and totalitarianism. But what could be done as an individual, and if hundreds and thousands felt the same way, how could I communicate with those others.? I was ready to work to destroy the Nazi empire. I transformed myself from an apolitical person into a revolutionary fighter. I joined circles of anti-Nazi resistance members. One was headed by professor Albrecht Aushofer who was plotting the assassination of Hitler, and the other led by Horst Heimann who had ties with the Schulze Boysen Harnack Group — the well-known espionage network planning to kill Hitler. The year was 1942, the German armies were winning in the war. After studying the history of philosophy, I was intrigued by Oswald Spengler's books: *The Decline of the West* and *Years of Decision.* Both had an important influence on the foundation of the Third Reich, and I was also studying Walther Rathenau, a brilliant philosopher and politician who had been murdered by right-wing terrorists in 1922. Since those books were strictly outlawed by the Nazis, I had to hide them in a hotel room. But my girlfriend found them and reported me to the Gestapo. I was arrested and sentenced to death by the firing squad. While I was waiting in the interrogation room in the Headquarters to be taken out and shot, I jumped through the window and escaped. It was one of the closest calls of my life.

The military operations of the Third Reich dictatorship were notoriously effective. How did you manage to survive?

After the escape I went into hiding under an assumed name, changing shelters every night, but I was caught in a hotel raid by the Gestapo again. After weeks of investigation, I was declared an *Unpolitischer* and my death sentence was lifted. I was imprisoned for one and a half years until the middle of 1944. On July 20th of that same year, our great conspiracy to assassinate Hitler ended in failure. In retaliation, Hitler killed 4,980 members of the resistance who were connected to the conspiracy. I was arrested, too, and tortured by the Gestapo for months but, thank God, narrowly escaped from death again: I was sent to a regiment instead. While the Western Allies were bombing more German cities in early 1945, Russian troops entered Berlin. I sneaked out of the army, came back to Berlin, and went underground again. By that time, Berlin had become the central battleground between Russian and German soldiers, and bloody man-to-man street fighting continued for months.

It turned into an atrocity and total catastrophe. SS guards still combed the streets, I was caught again. But by that stage, the battles had become triangular: Nazis, anti-Nazis, and Russians against each other. In the end, the Nazis surrendered me because they were in danger of being killed by Russians. I was held by the Russians for a while, but finally released and became a free person at the end of the war. Those wartime years in Berlin were a time of living dangerously. It was just unbelievable how I survived...

During the postwar transformation years, Berlin underwent so many unexpected changes. Can you talk about those?
Postwar Berlin was originally supposed to become a miniature model city in which East and West could live side by side, but things went wrong. People in the Western sector were free while people in the Soviet-controlled sector were not. The

neighbors had great differences: rich vs. poor, free vs. slave, capitalism vs. communism. In 1948, the Soviets threatened to take over West Berlin, and I learned that old Nazi concentration camps in the Soviet zone were being re-opened by the East German government. Tens of thousands of Berliners and the East German civilians simply disappeared over the years: they were transported to these camps. I also found out that the concentration camp workers were often the same people. The ones who used to torture and hang people under the Nazis were doing exactly the same job. I was shocked. Most people paid no attention to these reports. No one knows how many people perished. I believed this was a new nationwide crime against humanity. During the war I fought against Nazis and many of my friends were murdered by them. Now I realized the Third Reich had turned into a "Red Reich" run by a new kind of totalitarian regime, the East German communist government. "Silence is suicide," I thought, and decided to fight against the communist dictatorship. I, who had fought in the resistance against the Nazis, joined the resistance against the communists.

After the war, you became a journalist and activist. What made you fight the East German communist regime, and later against the Wall?
The end of the war brought a certain "logic of destiny" for Germany by separating Berlin and Germany. By the time the Wall was built, I was already known as a writer and human rights activist through my essays and articles for *Der Tagesspiegel* newspaper and my radio broadcasts opposing the East German regime.

I became one of the experts at the Western Information Office. Through my close contacts with East German refugees and escapees, it became clear to me that a large scale escape movement was growing in East Germany. There was a possibility that East Germany would seal off West Berlin and West Germany. I was seriously concerned about it and informed politicians in Bonn, but I was ignored. At that time this idea seemed technically inconceivable because everyone thought that it would bring about the financial collapse of East Germany. After the Wall was completed and had closed off the whole of West Berlin, no one knew how long it would stand. I fought against it from the first day of its existence until its very last day: November 9th, 1989.

How did you get the idea of founding the Checkpoint Charlie Museum and the 13th of August Association?

After the 13th of August, 1961, when the East German government began building the Wall, I saw people jumping out of the apartment windows on Bernauer Street to get across. (This was in the District of Wedding, West Berlin, the area where residential buildings stick to one another and became a border substitute for the Wall between East Berlin and West Berlin.) In order to stop the escapees, the East German government started blockading the building windows with concrete, cementing one floor after the next, every day higher and higher, until they reached the top floor. Meanwhile, people kept jumping from the available windows whenever the East German border guards were absent, and it went on like that morning until night, day after day. There were hundreds of onlookers, reporters, photographers, and firemen in the West Berlin section of Bernauer Street watching the jumpers. As lower windows were sealed off, people began jumping from fifth or sixth floor windows, or even from roofs. It was extremely dangerous.

Firemen prepared fire-nets to catch them safely. But it was not always successful, especially for young children or the elderly, and some missed the fire-nets and were killed instantly or severely injured. Being an eyewitness, I had to do something to stop it, so I rented an apartment nearby where I was able to photograph jumpers, escapees, and East German soldiers every day from my window, and exhibit my photojournalism at home. This attracted wide media attention.

Year by year, visitors from all over West Germany came to me with dramatic stories of how they had escaped. Some had hidden in cars or trucks, some had come by mini-submarine through the Spree River (the border river that runs through the center of Berlin), or by balloon or hanglider, some were brought through underground tunnels (an escape for which they paid a lot of money). Many unlucky people were, as we know, shot to death by East German Wall guard soldiers, and some cases never reported. As the years passed, my documentary show became successful and in the early 1970's we expanded and moved to "Checkpoint Charlie," next to the central custom house for visitors and tourists. It was re-named; "The House at Checkpoint Charlie." We have been here ever since, and hundreds of tourists from all over the world visit us every day. This whole project was entirely independent of any political motivation. My intention was to demonstrate the injustice of the Wall strictly as a human rights matter. But there is also a historical value, to teach the people of the world about the Wall. The reason I founded "The 13th of August Association" was to commemorate the specific date on which Berlin was physically divided. At the same time, its purpose is to gather updated information from escapees and political prisoners about the human rights situation in East Germany.

Now, after the fall of the Wall, how will you carry on the human rights activities you have established?

My focus will be on commemorating the many victims: people who sought freedom and died. During the time of the Wall, 300 deaths were officially reported, and if non-official deaths were added by the East German government, the total may be nearer to 1,000 or more deaths. I mentioned to you earlier the "logic of destiny," which contributed to the lengthening of the separation of Germany — how painful it was. My point is that those dead "must speak," and we must understand the meaning of their death. If the two Germanys had been unified earlier, there would have been fewer victims and far less tragedies. From released political prisoners, I learned that there were few deep values among the East German government's leaders. False and self-interested, they used unmotivated violence against their own citizens to reinforce the power struc-

ture, which was beyond any possibility of reform. In the words of Tolstoy; "One only really gets to know a government when one has spent time in its jails." That includes me, too...

What is your view on the consequences of the Nazi regime which caused Germany to have tremendous responsibilities to the world?

Painful as the separation of Germany was, it contained a certain destiny, as I said. In recognizing the significance of this term, Hitler's war enabled communist Russia to dominate central Europe. The postwar generations were thereby made to feel tremendously responsible for resisting both the "new" communist dictatorship and the "old" Hitler dictatorship, which created the Cold War, not only in Europe but in the entire world. Now, both dictatorships are gone and the two Germanys have been united. However, this responsibility has not come to an end, but has led to Chernobyl and the mass production of nuclear armaments in the hands of uncontrollable governments. ❖

"Germans should commit to battle against radicalism."

HEINZ GALINSKI

German Jew, Chairman and leader of the Jewish Community of Germany, and Holocaust survivor of Auschwitz. Born in 1912 in Marienburg, West Prussia, and deceased in 1993 in Berlin.

Mr. Galinski, you are one of the few Holocaust survivors who came back to Berlin at the end of the war. Why did you return to the city where such horrible pogroms occurred?

I returned to Berlin to find my former wife and my mother, hoping that they might have survived, and because, being a German citizen who had lived in Berlin for most of my life, my memories were here. Berlin is my hometown, so it was quite a natural decision to return. I had been through horrible and terrifying experiences, of course, but I never felt like taking revenge on Germans, or anything like that. I was one of 1,400 survivors out of the 173,000 Jewish inhabitants of prewar Berlin. Surviving the Holocaust was miraculous in itself. I was given a second chance to live. I was convinced that the only solution for future Jewish generations was to establish a new Jewish community here. Together with my fellow survivors, we decided to reconstruct those "human ruins" in a humanitarian way.

You witnessed *Kristallnacht* which marked the outbreak of full-scale Nazi war against the Jews. Can you explain how it happened and what you remember of that day?

I remember it very well. That morning, November 9th, 1938, my father said, "My dear son, I'm afraid that today the Nazis will start arresting Jews. Leave home, leave Berlin, go somewhere else as quickly as possible!" I was 25 then, and I was skeptical that the Germans would do such things against their own people. But I took his advice. My wife and I took the subway all over Berlin to see the public mood.

In the evening along the Avenue of Unter den Linden towards the Alexanderplatz, we saw Jewish shops, department stores, restaurants and offices being smashed by Nazi thugs. Broken win-

dow glass was scattered all over the streets. Anti-Jewish slogans, swastikas and Stars of David appeared on Jewish-owned buildings. Later that night, Berlin synagogues went up in flames. Most of the synagogues, which were the religious and social centers of Jewish life, were damaged or destroyed. Among those were some of the world's largest, most magnificent buildings with irreplaceable historical architecture. That night, the fate of the Jewish people began.

Let me explain it chronologically. After the Nazi regime was begun by Hitler in January 1933, there was a rapid increase in political and social anti-Semitism all over Germany. As the years passed, Hitler's ideology also spread outside Germany, especially to the Eastern European countries. There was growing anti-Semitism in Poland which had the most Jewish inhabitants in Europe, and increasing violence against Jews. Many of them fled to Austria, but were not given permission to enter by the Austrian government, because of the *Anschluss,* and were deported back to Poland. But the Polish government refused to allow them to re-enter. That was a desperate time for Polish Jews. They had nowhere to go. Tens of thousands of Jews were stranded on the Polish-German border, in an area of no man's land.

On November 7th, 1938, in the German embassy in Paris, a German clerk named Ernst vom Rath was shot by a 17-year-old Polish Jew named Herschel Grynszpan. Two days later, on the evening of the 9th, vom Rath died. This immediately triggered Hitler's anger. Goebbels officially ordered a nationwide pogrom against Jews. That was how *Kristallnacht* began.

Why did Herschel Grynszpan kill the diplomat? His family was among those stranded on the border for months, and he had tried without success to contact his family there. This appeal to the German embassy in Paris was rejected. Impatient and frustrated, he shot the German diplomat. No political motivation was found for the assassination.

The terror of *Kristallnacht* spread throughout the major German cities: Hamburg, Cologne, Frankfurt, Munich, Dresden, Leipzig, and many other towns in greater Germany. Now, it was not only Nazi mobs and hooligans, but large numbers of ordinary citizens who went on rampages, too. They were wrecking, looting, and burning anything that belonged to Jews, vandalizing Jewish cemeteries, screaming hysterically — and this went on day and night for a week. As a result of this state-ordered pogrom, over 200 synagogues were burned down, 7,500 Jewish-owned stores, houses and properties were damaged. Hundreds of Jews were murdered and 30,000 Jews were arrested and sent to concentration camps.

My mother, my wife and I didn't want to leave because my father was old and disabled, and we couldn't leave him behind. I trusted that the Germans wouldn't arrest us, thinking things might calm down. So, we decided to stay in Berlin. We were safe, actually, until 1940. Then I was drafted for labor as an asbestos worker on the construction of an SS building. By that time, every Jew was forced to wear a yellow Star of David. Some German people were consoling and gave me cigarettes or a piece of bread, or showed some gesture of humanity. Then, my father was taken by the Gestapo to a police station and died during an interrogation. After that, I knew I could be next. One morning in February 1943, I saw 12 Gestapo men standing at our door ready to arrest us. We were taken in a cattle wagon to the East. After days on the freezing train, we arrived at the ramp of Auschwitz, and an SS officer separated us: the men and women going in different direc-

tions. The last words I exchanged with my wife and my mother were, "Do we have the right name tags on our baggage?" I never saw them again. They were gassed in the death factory.

How do you feel about the reunification and new Germany?
In my view, the unified Germany has a great opportunity to create a new kind of country in Europe, but obviously it carries a great responsibility for the future to ensure that *Kristallnacht* can never be repeated. Right now, I'm quite concerned about the violent activities by neo-Nazis taking place in the former East Germany, but I have hope that Germans have finally learned from the past.

In November 1938, during the *Kristallnacht* when hundreds of synagogues were destroyed and Jews were beaten and arrested in the streets in Germany, the vast majority of German people thought it had nothing to do with them, and looked the other way. That's why the whole European continent went up in flames shortly afterwards. The world still hasn't recovered from that pain.

Let's look at what happened in 1989 in the former East Germany. The people removed their own regime. Because they hated the government so much, they came out into the streets and took matters into their own hands. The power of the people brought about reunification. What I want to say is that if a people's mass action against their own government had taken place during the Nazi regime in Germany, WW II could have been avoided. My criticism is that when the "Treaty of Unity" was signed on the day of reunification, October 3, 1990, it should have contained some recognition of the reality of the German past, and a commitment to battle against any form of radicalism, especially anti-Semitism, racism, and neo-Nazism. Its preamble should have contained a statement by the German people accepting their guilt for what they did in the past, which resulted, after all, in the division of Germany. I wished to have a statement that Germans were truly committed to all the victims of the Holocaust. I very much regret that this was not included in the new treaty. My point is that such a fundamental fact — in the existence of a democracy should be of concern to everyone — it's not just a Jewish problem. My goal is, of course, that the events of the Nazi period should not be forgotten.

As the leader of the Jewish community in Germany, what do you think is your duty, and what should be done for a better future for Jewish people in Germany?

Since I returned to Berlin at the end of the war, my major task has been to combat anti-Semitism in Germany. It's widely known that I've been continuously involved with this in many ways. In political terms, I have kept close ties with both, the West German Parliament and with the individual German states, and have been discussing the matter in various ways. For example, what Jewish matters should be taught in schools and universities? After the fall of the Berlin Wall, I also visited East German officials to discuss these Jewish matters and the best way to ensure increasing political awareness among young scholars. The problem was the former communist education system.

Because the Jewish theme had been suppressed for the past 45 years, people never talked about it openly. And then, after the reunification, suddenly the subject emerged in a way that created a new wave of anti-Semitism and new hostility against foreigners. In terms of Jewish matters, I'm afraid that it's like the prewar period.

After the reunification, I became especially involved with public relations and media. For instance, with the help of church leaders, I organized discussions with leaders of radical and right-wing groups of young people about anti-Semitism. It's always vital to communicate with such groups in order to prevent people from slipping into reactionary racial views which eventually lead to violent activities. Although the far right won very few votes in the November 1990 election of united Germany — the first free election in 57 years — we can't ignore the fact that there are still too many individuals following ideologies linked to the Nazi past. It showed that there are invisible barriers between Jews and non-Jews, and we acknowledge that it will take a long time before a wholly normal relationship can be established. That can only be accomplished step by step. It's not easy for either side to escape the legacy of the past. Most European Jews lost family members in the Holocaust, and they are still tortured by terrible memories. On the other hand, many Germans don't want to be reminded of what happened here in this century because they know they failed to prevent the most horrendous crimes against mankind. ❖

Berlin's working class mayor

WALTER MOMPER

Politician, mayor of West Berlin during the fall of the Berlin Wall. Chairman of the Social Democratic Party. Born 1945 in Solingen, Niedersachsen, Germany. Lives in West Berlin.

Mayor Momper, since the student movement of the Sixties you have been involved in Berlin politics. What is your memory of postwar Berlin?

My father died in the war before I was born. I was brought up by my mother in Bremen. During the war many people lost their families, and situations like ours were quite common. During my early childhood in the 1950's, I remember my country as poor, destroyed, divided, and devastated, and we were always hungry. During the Berlin Crisis, I visited Berlin on and off, but didn't move here until 1964. In those days this city was still very much in ruins, and it didn't fully develop until recently. While I was a student studying social history and political science at the Free University of West Berlin, I became interested in politics and was influenced by the radical student movement. As a chairman of the local Socialist Youth in Kreuzberg, I was aware of the sensitive issues involving the Wall. I was 21 years old, but for most Germans it isn't unusual to be active in politics at an early age. Ever since, I've always been very active in my party — the Berlin branch of the Social Democratic Party.

You were the last mayor of West Berlin — from March 1989 to February 1991 — before the unification and you've since lost in the united Berlin mayoral race. Did you accomplish the things you planned for the city?

As a politician, my goal was to be re-elected. During my two-year term as the mayor of West Berlin, with my governing team, I worked hard to improve the public transportation systems and social programs as rapidly as possible. But much depended upon negotiation and compromise with the coalition parties such as the right-wing CDU (Christian Democratic Union), and the left-wing

"Alternative List" (Green Party). To begin with, I nominated women to take 8 of the 14 seats of my governing cabinet, and that was the highest proportion of women in any European state. Equal opportunity for women was my principal program.

But all our plans were suddenly interrupted by the opening of the Wall, an absolutely unscheduled and unexpected event. It changed everything; not just the two Berlins and the two Germanys, but also all of Europe.

Do you agree reunification came too fast and without enough planning?

Yes, reunification was too fast and confused the relations between many people. The whole process of change in the East and West went on at an unbelievable speed. After the Wall fell, there were clear signs that in East Germany, the economy, the internal security system, and the ruling hierarchy were falling over like dominoes. So it was necessary to speed up unity. As an acting city mayor facing one unpredictable new situation after another, I was trying hard to organize East Berliners and West Berliners into one cohesive group.

In December 1990 before the first national election in the united Berlin, there was squatter trouble in East Berlin. You used police force to control it and it turned into a big riot. As a result, you were blamed and lost your mayoral position. Do you regret that?

No, I don't. I agree our timing was wrong but I would never have changed my actions just because the election was ahead. Those young militants who occupied vacant buildings in former East Berlin were barricading themselves in, and refused to move out. We failed at negotiation.

Therefore, I had to send in the police to drag them out because those buildings were run down and needed to be demolished for reconstruction. Regarding a similar matter, for instance, before the election, Chancellor Kohl promised people no tax increases, and what did he do after he was elected? He raised taxes. That is not my style. As a political leader, I like to be honest with my people all the way.

You are renowned as mayor of Kreuzberg. Why do you like living there?
I live in Kreuzberg because the people are interesting, neighbors know each other and talk openly, and I like its cozy social ambience, with varied restaurants and bars. Also, we have convenient transportation to every part of the city. The Berlin government provides a special villa for the mayor but I refused to live there. Once there was a question about my lifestyle, but why should I move out of the place I like most? You could say I'm the people's mayor or you could call me Berlin's working class mayor. ❖

"Berlin will become a world economic center."

TINO SCHWIERZINA

Mayor of East Berlin during the fall of the Wall. Vice-president of the
House of Berlin parliament representatives. Born 1927 in Katowice,
former German territory in Poland. Lives in East Berlin.

(Photo: Mr. Schwierzina in his East Berlin office.)

Mr. Schwierzina, you were mayor of East Berlin when the Wall fell, and now you are vice-president of the united Berlin parliament. How did you adjust from a single party system of the East to a multi-party system of the West?

This political union happened very quickly, and as democracy spread, my colleagues and I found that the multi-party system could appeal to each individual's particular interest. My special political affiliation is with the Social Democratic Party. In the East we were too pragmatic, and sharp divisions between right and left didn't exist. For me, I don't concentrate on right and left, but on a whole set of questions that people are confronting now which need to be solved.

For the reconstruction of Berlin, you need many foreign investments. Are there any problems?

No, I welcome any kind of foreign investments. I was initially confronted by investors who wanted to build 200 hotels, 300 department stores, and a few hundred gas stations. We also want industry around Berlin, but nobody wanted to build a factory. So, we had to pick and choose from the investors who proposed contracts. Of course, I keep Berlin's doors open for every investor, but at the same time, they can't have whatever they want, for, as you know, Berlin has limited space: It can't grow bigger. Therefore, some investors must go elsewhere. When Berlin becomes the seat of the government, the capital city of Germany, it will attract industrialists, financiers, capitalists, and investors from all over the world, and eventually it will become a world economic center. Berlin is the perfect place for a capital that looks toward the East: Poland, Czechoslovakia, and the Baltic states. Up to the 1980s, Bonn was the per-

fect capital for the West, but in the 1990s, Berlin is the logical place.

After 45 years of separation, do you think both East and West Germans have learned the lessons of their history?

The best way to prepare for a solid future is to know the past. The end of separation of the two Germanys was a turning point for the new Germany and a visible sign of the end of WW II. Both Germanys have learned lessons from the war, and if today there is a danger, it comes from the extreme right-wingers. But I don't think there's a big danger. I believe even the smallest action by ultra-right-wingers should be exposed and confronted.

Before last year's election, politicians promised the people that taxes would be not raised, but after winning the election, they raised taxes. In this important time of political transformation, people, especially in the East, feel distrust for their government and for their politicians. How do you respond to them?

During the past year, the people in the East had to vote in elections five times. People grew tired of voting all the time during such a short period. At the moment, many East Germans feel insecure because of the sudden economic changes that resulted from this transformation. Many people lost jobs, they suffer from extremely high inflation, and they fear social unrest will create serious new problems. They've learned that it's not easy to catch up with the West German economic system and the ways of democracy. Right now they worry more about social and personal matters than political issues. If I knew how to deal with this problem, I would be a financial minister. Obviously, the two different economic systems need

413

to be equalized as quickly as possible. The government has set up a timetable of about 3 to 5 years, but it's difficult, and you can't just let the free market forces work. You have to target concrete programs. Once all reclaiming of property* is over, things will be much easier for investors or property buyers. And, then the manufacturing capacity will increase, and the economy will recover. ❖

*Germans and German Jews who fled the East German territory during the Nazi period and up to 1989 are now entitled to claim their properties back.

"Berlin is a bridge between Western and Eastern Europe."

DR. HANNA-RENATE LAURIEN

Politician, member of the Christian Democratic Union Party, President
of the Berlin House of Representatives. Born 1927 in Danzig, the
former German territory in Poland. Lives in West Berlin.

(Photo: Ms. Laurien in her office.)

Frau Laurien, I hear that many people say the reunification came too fast, and they have been hurt by the dramatic overnight change. A majority say it should have waited. What is your opinion?

The average Berliners never said that. I agree the reunification has come very quickly and miraculously, but nobody says it was too quick. After the fall of the Wall, East Berliners were flooding West Berlin, so if it hadn't been done quickly, even more people would have come to this part of Germany. Fast action was necessary. Chancellor Helmut Kohl has been criticized by some people, but now the majority agree it was a good thing he did it the way he did. The major problem is the process of reforming the ruined economic system of East Germany. Its economic status is not just depressed, it's a catastrophe. It's much easier to close down factories or shops than to save them and open new ones. So many workers were laid off from their work and can't find new jobs. That's a terrible problem, of course. A lot depends on how people view their elected officials. Some may criticize politicians and the government for being uninformed, but others have a sense that we're all cooperating to improve the situation. There are quite a variety of views on how to change the system for the new Germany.

What's the best way to right the economic balance between West and East Germany, and how long do you think recovery will take?

West Germans and East Germans criticize each other. West Germans say that East Germans want to have the good life too quickly. It took West Germany 40 years to build up today's standard of living, but East Germans want it in half a year. East Germans nag West Germans, saying they think they know everything, and all they want is

money and so on. But we politicians are doing all we can to help people grow together.

For the past 58 years, East Germans had been living with dictatorships: Hitler was a dictator and so was Honecker. People were not allowed to speak, think, and express themselves democratically. And, of course, there were no free business practices, either. For East Germans everything is completely new and many of them have no idea how to handle it. For those who lost their jobs, the government is paying unemployment benefits of 70 percent of their wages, and establishing job training courses, and increasing pensions for the elderly, and so on. It will take time. I would say for the whole process — perhaps 3 to 4 years.

The political side of reunification has been achieved, but what about the mental and social aspects of reunification?

That's another serious problem. After democracy was introduced in former East Germany, the comrades who knew only one political party system, communism, and fought together against their only enemy, totalitarianism, are now disappointed and have become each other's enemies. In the Western world, democracy means the multi-political party system: Liberals, Socialists, Communists, Conservatives, Christians, and each party has a different ideology. By learning to complement and balance each other, we can all live together peacefully. As I said, since Hitler's days the majority of East Germans have lived under dictatorships and therefore this is a completely new political experience for most of them. You can imagine what a confusing time they are having socially and mentally.

For instance, former East Germany's underground political network operation known as

"Stasi" kept hundreds of thousands of informants throughout the state. There were at least two informants per family spying on people, bugging telephones lines and informing their government. It was this way for decades. Understandably, people are still paranoid and suspicious of each other, even neighbors or friends.

The question is, should we punish those ex-Stasi members and their collaborators or not? Some say we should send them to jail or execute them. Let's look at Honecker, the leader of the state. I think he and his hierarchy should be on trial, of course. But realistically it is impossible to jail tens of thousands of informants or hang them. But we must find a solution. Justice and the law are the first answers.

People's freedom will die if it is not connected to justice. In a free democratic system where the law prevails, we must follow the law, not our emotions. In our political history, it's an absolutely new experience to deal with this kind of reform and social transformation, and of course, it takes time for discussion. It's a long task, indeed. What we need is patience. In this matter, patience is our most important virtue.

At the moment, people seem to be equally divided about the decision whether the capital should be in Bonn or Berlin. Why can't the governing bodies remain in Bonn, while Berlin would stay the cultural and social center like Washington D.C. and New York in the United States?

I'm for Berlin as the capital. It simply can't be compared to Washington, D.C. and New York, or Sydney and Canberra in Australia, because the foundation of the German state is different. Since the end of the war in 1945, Bonn has performed the role of integration with the West, so that West Germany could participate as a free country in Western Europe. This role of the Bonn government, and of former Chancellor Konrad Adenauer really shouldn't be forgotten. Both Bonn and Berlin have very important functions, and I have no intention of attacking or fighting against Bonn. Moving the capital to Berlin makes sense for a number of reasons, however. When you look at two thousand years of European history, Paris, London, and Rome dominated in the West, and Warsaw, Prague, and Moscow in the East, and we all flourished together sharing cultural experiences, social functions, and so on. Geographically, this city could play a perfect role in metropolitan life throughout the country. Besides, we must deal with all sorts of political and social problems in the former East German cities like Dresden or Leipzig, and it's much closer and easier from here than from Bonn. On many levels, Berlin is the bridge for the integration of East and West economically and socially. Berlin is the center for the future of New Germany and for the whole of Europe. Bonn is a provincial city and too far away, and it can't understand these things.

I agree Berlin will become more crowded and more expensive, but if we don't get a government lobbying presence here, then industry and corporations won't move here, and there will be no economic growth. Moving the capital, implementing much-needed social housing plans, will take between five and ten years. I'm quite convinced the majority of Berliners and Germans support Berlin as a capital, and we will get it over here. ❖

*"Germany's brutal history is my enemy:
that's why I write."*

HEINER MÜLLER

East German playwright, author of over 40 plays including *Germania
Death in Berlin* and *Hamlet-Machine,* former Director of the Academy
of Arts of former East Berlin. Born in 1926 in Saxony, Germany. Lives
in East Berlin.

You are one of the most powerful and influential playwrights in postwar East Germany and Europe. Most of your plays focus heavily on the dark parts of Germany's past. Has it something to do with your own life experience, and what is your message to the audience?

Ever since I was a child, I have been a victim of Nazi Germans. My father was sent to a concentration camp for being a socialist and an anti-Hitler activist. So, I have to deal with the history of my country because it's very much a part of my life. German brutality is my enemy, that's why I write. The terrors and horrors I write of come from Germany's sadistic history. German history goes back 2000 years — to the fall of the Holy Roman Empire, the so-called First Reich, barbarism of the Middle Ages, and brutality and misery of the Thirty Years' War, the invasion of Napoleon, the Prussian Empire's militarism, and WW I followed by the rise of Nazi Germany — it's the repetition of war after war, invasion after invasion, and revolution after revolution, and peace hardly ever lasts long. So, from this perspective, Nazism was the culmination of the cycle of our violent national history. That's the history of my country, and to me, that's my real enemy.

I don't want to let people forget our past. Using my creativity and imaginative powers, I like to express my feelings to the audience and let them confront German history and guilt. From my point of view, art must feel a yearning for another world, and I believe fear is a good teacher for everybody. My hope is that my plays, such as *Germania Death in Berlin,* could never be written again in the future.

What do you think of the West Germans of your own generation, and their attitude towards war guilt and responsibility? Also, what is your view of reunification?

In former West Germany there are many ex-Nazis who feel absolutely innocent. The majority of them think they have no responsibility at all for what they did. They believe they did nothing wrong. I don't like their moral irresponsibility. Hegel, a widely known German philosopher, said that people never learn from history. And that's true. But I can't forget our guilt. I truly feel our national guilt over what we did during the Nazi era. What shocked me most is that after the fall of the Wall and the reunification, we are facing again the rise of nationalism, racism, and anti-Semitism. I thought those seeds had been pulled out. But I now see that 45 years after the war was not long enough for Germans to learn their lesson. I'm afraid that the united Germany will be troublesome for its neighboring nations.

With the new Germany, some say your most highly regarded plays have already become outdated, and that the audience is gone. Is that true?

It's not true. After reunification, German problems became economic, not political. People have no money. East Germans have gained the freedom to do anything they want now, but at the same time nearly fifty percent of the population have lost their jobs. Therefore, they don't have the money to buy theater tickets. Righting the extreme economic unbalance between the two former states and economic recovery is the priority for everybody right now. It may take years, then, but I'm sure my work will become popular again.

419

You are a dedicated socialist. The fact is that capitalism has returned to Germany. How do you feel about it?

Capitalism doesn't give us a solution. Money represents power and capitalism interprets political freedom, but for me the definition of capitalism in the context of freedom is just a phrase. I believe that social justice should be of primary importance. I agree, although we worked hard, our socialism was a failure. But it was a very important experience for us. Everybody learns from its failure to win a better way of life for the future. And, I'm sure sooner or later people will come up with a new political ideology, and will try something else again. That's the history of Germany and Europe, after all.

How does American capitalism look to you?

America is the richest "underdeveloped" country in the world: homelessness and poverty are omnipresent, the health care and social welfare systems are outrageously inadequate. It's a violent society, with the worst crime rate, and unlimited guns in the hands of civilians. It's out of control which shocks me the most. Furthermore, it has high illiteracy and the standard of education has declined. I'm afraid America is certainly not a role model for us. ❖

"Nazism can happen outside Germany, too."

HANS-JOACHIM MENGEL

Professor of political science at the Free University (West Berlin) and Humboldt University (East Berlin). Born 1947 in Hessen. Lives in West Berlin.

During the Vietnam War in the Sixties and Seventies, there were all sorts of power movements: student power, Black power, women power, acting for human rights and freedom of speech, and demonstrating against the war in Vietnam and against South Africa's apartheid. People seemed to be protesting against almost anything. Thinking back on those years, however, there were no demonstrations against the Berlin Wall. No one protested against it throughout its entire 28-year history. How do you interpret that, Professor Mengel?

Shortly after the Wall was built, there were some protests inside West Germany, of course, but I agree with you, there was no international protest. At the time the Wall was built in the middle of the city separating Berlin residents and their families, the world was shocked. And there were feelings of hopelessness and helplessness, but no one could do anything about it. The foreign point of view, though people didn't mention it openly, was that everybody was pleased to keep Germany divided. There was fear that if the two Germanys were united, it might be dangerous for world peace again. So, why sympathize with Germany? The fact of the matter is the rest of the world — England, France, the United States — could live without a united Germany. Ms. Margaret Thatcher, prime minister of England, even argued German unification should wait perhaps another ten years.

This unification, on October 3, 1990, was in fact the second unification. The first, in 1871, was done under Otto von Bismarck, the Iron Chancellor of the Prussian Empire. Therefore, it's properly called "reunification." How do you explain the differences between the two?

The main difference between those two unifications is that this time it was organized by the people. The people came out into the streets, and they didn't have any idea of unification in the beginning. The line of unification became clear later as things developed. The unification of 1871 was managed by politicians, so it was completely different. This time it was brought about by people's power; the people took their own fate into their own hands, and that is a very rare thing in the history of our country.

Let me use Korea as an example. Its unification depends absolutely on two respective governments and their politicians. But in our case, in the beginning, the two governments were reluctant, and did not want to be united for different reasons. But eventually they had no choice: they followed the people.

For centuries, Germany has had border disputes with Poland and other neighboring countries. Do you think it will ever end?

We have to see the whole process of unification in relation to European unification. I'm deeply convinced that all of Europe, both West and East, will be united, and as the first step, the original Treaty of Rome will be changed and a new political union will develop. If so, then Germany will become a part of a larger union of different countries sharing a common economy, a common foreign policy, and a common defense with a united army, and so on. Then Germany will not be an independent state, so it will become impossible to dispute borders with neighboring countries anymore. For the moment, though, things are difficult, because we have different wealth levels and unbalanced economic standards, plus a chaotic unemployment situation in the Eastern European states. But in the long-term future, individual borders will no longer play a great role, and disputes over them will become meaningless.

There seems to be a huge gap between the mental attitudes of the two Germanys. Young East Germans seem not to feel the "war guilt" as much as the West Germans do. Is it possible that certain problems like the resurgence of neo-Nazism and aggressive nationalism could be caused by the censorship of history textbooks by the former East German government?

That has something to do with the educational process, of course. It's true that most of the young East Germans feel as if they have nothing to do with Hitler, Nazi Germany, or war crimes. I presume they feel that since they were not there at the time, they weren't involved with it or affected by it. It happened five decades ago, and they may think they're completely out of it. Most of the communists who opposed Hitler during the war were exiled to Moscow, and after the war they returned to East Germany. Perhaps they simply ignored German war atrocities, or pretended they had no responsibility, because they were absent while everything happened. They also argued they were not successors of the Third Reich, and never paid any compensation to Jews and the State of Israel, which West Germany did. I also teach at the Humboldt University in former East Berlin, and I have noticed that there are great differences among those generations who were formed by the different educational systems and social backgrounds. I estimate the gap may last for at least five to ten years before the historical and educational differences will be equalized.

I also find there is a big difference in the way the two former Germanys view the Wall. Most West Germans believe it was a punishment for the process started by the Third Reich, but East Germans believe it was to protect their socialist regime. How do you see this?

First of all, we must remember that the Wall was actually built by East Germans, not by the Russians. Mr. Erich Honecker, leader of the former East Germany, built the Wall to protect his regime from capitalism, which was the enemy. Therefore, it was their choice. That's why, perhaps, they didn't think and feel the way we do.

How do you focus on Hitler's war when you teach your political science students at the university?

To begin with, it was not Hitler's war. It was the Germans' war, because a majority of Germans participated in it and chose to follow him. Without followers and supporters, Hitler couldn't have done it. Therefore, all Germans are responsible. Hitler made it his plan to conquer Europe, expanding German territory both west and east, spreading his ideology that the future human race had to be Aryan, and targeting Jews for genocide. In any normal sense, there is no explanation. He had an absolutely mad psychological structure of his own and no one can answer for it.

Of course, there were many intellectuals and resistance members who opposed Hitler's ideology, but they were either murdered by Nazis or fled Germany. I can say one thing: the problem was that the minority became the majority. Nazi ideology was started by a small group, a minority, in the beginning, and from the intellectual point of view, it didn't make sense, and at first, people didn't pay that much attention. But it spread unexpectedly to a large number of people. The majority of people began to run in the same direction like sheep, and by the time people realized it, the Nazis had already formed a powerful party with an organized political system controlling all of Germany, and it was too late to repudiate it or to stop them. The political lesson we learned is that any time controversial political ideologies are introduced, we must examine them thoroughly, and should intervene or take action in the early stages of the process. We must fight against them. We should always be cautious and aware of the political environment, because after a certain political power is created, it's too late to stop it. It's a permanent task, not only for Germany, but also for every country in the world. It may come in different forms, but Nazism can happen outside Germany, too. Therefore, it's vital to have a democratic political education for every citizen, for every nation of the world, and in every generation, even in a country which is presently a democratic state, because democracy can't be guaranteed forever.

Currently, the former East Germans are facing an economic crisis that is worsening from day to day. What is the best solution for them, do you think?

In the West, we have to make even more of an effort to stabilize the economic situation in the Eastern European countries and equalize their economic and living conditions. There is a need for Japan, for example, to help them out, because Japan is economically the most successful country in the world today. After all, everyone is endangered by a destabilized Europe. So, I believe Japan should contribute, too, and participate in this process. The former East Germany needs considerable foreign investment. ❖

"Germany hits the highest and lowest points of human existence."

MICHAEL CULLEN

American journalist, architectural historian, and author of the books *Brandenburg Gate* and *Reichstag*. Born 1939 in New York, USA. Lives in West Berlin.

As an American, you were born and raised in New York, but you've lived in Berlin longer than in your own city. What made you become an expatriot, and why do you prefer living in Berlin?

I have a complex love-hate feeling about Berlin. New York and Berlin are both exciting cities, but in different ways. New York has social excitement, but I personally feel it's too much — it's exhausting. But the excitement in Berlin is political, social, and cultural, and that's enough for me. Berlin is never a boring city; historically, it's been very important in Europe and for the whole world. There are many problems to be resolved, and political tension has been high for many decades. But I especially like the intellectual stimulation that seems to be in the air of Berlin. I can smell it and can feel that cultural existence as a part of me. I was 25 years old when I came here.

Since my teens I had been very intrigued with European literature, music, and art, and I grew up playing music at home. I was attracted by the great German composers like Bach, Brahms, Mozart, especially Beethoven, and I became intrigued about the country from which their culture originated. My knowledge of Germany was the Third Reich, of course, because I'm Jewish, which made me naturally interested in this place where everything happened. Being in Germany I have a strange feeling, because it is the place where the greatest music was written and also where the world's worst tyrant took power. Germany hits the highest and lowest points of human existence.

You've lived with the Wall in Berlin for 25 years. As an outsider, how did you feel about it and how did your feeling change after the fall of the Wall?

I never liked the Wall. I didn't like to look at it and I hated it every time I saw it. First of all, from an esthetic point of view, it was not a good-looking wall: pretty ugly and certainly not pleasant. I believe the Wall symbolized a major crime committed by the East German government against their own people, and that repression revolted me deeply. It should never have been there in the first place.

I have good friends in East Berlin, and as an American I was often able to get through the Wall to visit them for dinner or to spend some time. But when I wanted to invite them to visit me in West Berlin, they were not able to come. Our friendship was thus affected by the Wall. My feeling was that my duty to myself and my friends was to make the Wall more and more meaningless, to overcome it, and to make sure that the "two Berlins" wouldn't become more divided than they already were. I didn't anticipate that the Wall would come down until perhaps one day in my old age or after I died. And, the night of the fall of the Wall, my first thought was that I could finally invite my friends of East Berlin for dinner — that was the nicest thing, and I really felt happy about it.

You are an author and journalist specializing in city-planning and historical architecture. What kind of work do you do specifically?

From the city-planning point of view, Berlin is rather unique and complicated, because it's a "patched city" — a combination of nearly one hundred different towns in an area of 800 square kilometers. There are about 20 city halls and each town has a different structure and over a dozen duplicated street names. For example, there are eight Berliner Streets, five Bismarck Streets, and ten Charlotten Streets and so on. Therefore, without knowing the district names, it's hard to know where you are going. Street addresses in some old areas confuse visitors because the numerical system is horseshoe style, not divided into odd and even numbers. This city-planning was done three centuries ago, hence its uniqueness. When I said earlier the two Berlins shouldn't become more divided, I meant that while doing my work as a historian researching the Berlin's architecture, I always kept the idea in mind of Berlin as one city, not "two cities."

When I investigated over 750 years of history of Berlin and wrote books or articles about it, I made sure to emphasize Berlin was one city, and whenever I mentioned locations of aged or valuable buildings, for instance, seldom used terms like West Berlin or East Berlin. I used district names so that Berliners could figure out where the building was in the city.

For the past 45 years, the majority of Germans have lived with a "burden of guilt" from their past. How do you analyze German guilt?
I don't think that all Germans are guilty. I don't agree that the children and grandchildren of the Third Reich monsters are guilty — they had nothing to do with it. There are three kinds of guilt in ethics: guilt by commission — actually doing something wrong; guilt by omission — not doing something you should do; guilt by remission — neglecting to do something. And if you were born a son or daughter of a guilty person, you are not guilty. However, you may have a certain responsibility to carry on. First of all, you can feel shame. Nothing can be done about that, because the atrocities took place before you were born or while you were too young to do anything. But if the guilt was committed under your own name, that affects your identity. Germans

also have a collective identity as Germans, and it's impossible for them to escape from their past. I always felt that Germans have the right to feel the shame of it. Shame can help you to form your life and change your attitude, perhaps becoming more sensitive and thinking about solutions. People don't need to feel guilt when they are not guilty, but shame is different. The next thing is responsibility. Today's young Germans can't be responsible for what happened 50 or 100 years ago, but they should be responsible for the future. The responsibility of what they have learned from the past should be carried on so that it doesn't occur again in the future. Guilt, shame, and responsibility are the components of my theory, and I like to differentiate between those three categories.

As a Jew, are you politically active?
I am very much involved with politics. I like to believe that being politically oriented is a healthy thing; exercising our responsibility and developing our way of thinking, educating people socially, and working to make things happen politically.

I believe nothing is impossible if one is active in this way, and that we can make a better world and improve the future of our society. And, I'm well-informed about what is going on. That's why I am dedicated to what I write.

On the matter of being a Jew, I can say that those who were not involved can feel shame, too. For instance, even though I'm far away from Israel, I feel very ashamed of what the Israeli government is doing to the neighboring Palestinians in the name of Jews, which is my collective identity, and that is my shame. But I'm not responsible and not guilty because I'm not there. But I'm responsible for trying to stop it because I'm alive and able to think, feel, judge, and consider the whole matter seriously, so I have to do something. That's why I'm a journalist and I write. What I can do for Israel is sort of limited by where I am standing right now. But my feeling is that I can educate today's younger Germans to grow up with less guilt, but with a sense of responsibility. I can teach them that we can do something for a better life. Political and social change won't happen unless we, the people, make it happen, and every person should be responsible for that. ❖

"We had a great time in Berlin with the Wall."

HIROOMI FUKUZAWA

Japanese lecturer at the Free University of West Berlin. Born in 1942 in Tokyo, Japan. Lives in West Berlin.

(Photo: Mr. Fukuzawa with his wife and daughter in their home.)

Why did you leave your country to live in Berlin?

I was born, raised, and educated in Japan. During the Sixties, as a young student, I lived in the United States in the time when young foreigners who had been living in the US for over one year could be drafted by the US government and sent to fight in Vietnam. If you fought for the US Army, you could easily get US citizenship. But if you refused the draft and left the US, re-entering the US would be difficult. Some of my Japanese and German friends were sent to Vietnam and wounded, and some even died there. To avoid this, I left the country. In 1968, I came to Germany and studied political science and the philosophy of Karl Marx at three German universities: Stuttgart, Munich and the Free University of Berlin. I have lived in Berlin ever since.

During that time, I returned to Japan for 2 years, but didn't like it there any more. The Japanese social structure and intellectual life didn't meet my personal expectations. Although I'm self-exiled from Japan, I don't feel I'm German. Even for many Germans, Berlin is such a unique city that it's like being abroad. This is my city, my choice, and I love Berlin so much that I wouldn't mind dying and being buried here, but not anywhere else in Germany. At this point, I could say I'm a "Japanese Berliner."

During the Sixties, how did the student movement and the anti-war movement begin in West Berlin and Germany, and how were German people influenced by them?

We were the "Generation of 68" or the "Flower Generation," as it was called in America. That movement had a huge impact in West Germany, intellectually pushing it towards liberalism and social change. As a result, people's attitudes changed tremendously.

Originating in America, triggered by protest against the war in Vietnam, the "Flower Generation" inspired a social revolution in West Germany and the rest of Western Europe. That social change had a strong influence on the postwar German generations, who became less conservative, less class-oriented, less traditional, more polite, and so on. Interestingly enough, many of the '68 generation, now in their 40s, have become teachers or educators in high schools or universities, and have passed on to their students ideas about peace, alternative lifestyles, and ecology. Vegetarianism was one such change.

West Berlin isn't West Germany in the real sense. It became the center of the German student movement, of course, because of the existence of the Wall. Because the West German capitalists hated the city surrounded by the Wall, there was no industrial or commercial investment in West Berlin. Therefore, the Bonn government had to support this isolated city by taxing German citizens, which took up a high percent of the state budget. And, people who moved to the city were liberals, artists, students, and politically-minded young people who didn't like West Germany, so that naturally created an unusual atmosphere. Living inside the Wall was like living inside a ghetto where you were protected from both communism and capitalism. Thinking back, we had a great time in Berlin with the Wall. Some people say life with the Wall was better than it is without the Wall. I agree that those were the good old days for Berliners.

Germany and Japan are the leading nations economically today. How do Germans look at the Japanese, and how do you compare the two societies as a whole?

In Germany, people are classified according to their education: they are divided by a class-oriented society. For example, highly cultural activities such as concerts, operas, or theaters are the luxury of middle-class people; not many working people attend. In Japan, education is also essential for a good career and a good life, but average Japanese working-class people commonly enjoy cultural activities, also.

During my 8 years of teaching at the Free University, news of the Japanese economic boom gradually became a topic in the German media. Much information comes from Japan, and many magazines and newspapers report on Japanese economic, social, historical, and cultural matters.

So, young Germans today know that *"Japanologie"* (Japanese Studies) will be beneficial and provide great job opportunities. There were only 15 students in my class a decade ago when I started teaching, but now the number has increased drastically to 350 students. Most graduates of Japanese Studies want to be employed by German corporations and stationed in Japan because they enjoy privileged conditions as German employees; for example, more vacations and holidays.

As Berlin becomes the capital of the united Germany, I would expect that, sooner or later, the political climate will change as West German capitalists move in. What do you think?

I'm against Berlin as the capital. Most West Germans don't like the idea for various reasons. First, Berlin is associated with many bad memories, psychologically, because it reminds people of the negative side of German history. Secondly, it's located next to the eastern part of Germany, close to Poland and the Soviet Union, and though this is considered good for East Germans, it's geographically too remote for West Germans. Many feel Berlin is like a foreign city, and have no emotional attachment to it. Thirdly, it will become an expensive and crowded city. Middle-class and white-collar groups will move in, and eventually people will be divided by class again, just as in other German cities. Of course, Berlin will change. I would say that the liberal tendency of Berlin will continue for the next 5 to 10 years, but after that, I'm not sure how it will go. The political balance will be changed by newcomers: conservatives and upper-class people. They will become the new Berliners and take charge of the new Germany of the future. ❖

"Hitler made many people into Jews."

VERA BENDT

German Jew, curator of the Berlin Jewish Museum Project and author of the book *Berlin Museum — Judaica.* Born in 1947 in Wiesbaden, West Germany. Lives in West Berlin.

(Photo: Mrs. Bendt displays centuries-old menorahs in her office.)

Mrs. Bendt, could you tell me about the project and what kind of research you do for the new Jewish Museum?

I have been employed by the Berlin Historical Museum as a curator since 1979. My task is to build a new Jewish museum in Berlin which will be devoted to the history of Jews in Berlin. It has been five decades since the end of WW II, and you may wonder why there hasn't been a Jewish museum in Berlin before. There were Jewish museums once, but they were all destroyed by the Nazis in 1938 on *Kristallnacht* and its aftermath. Every Jewish institution was destroyed except the Jewish hospital and cemetery. In 1943, the Jewish community administration was closed, and all the workers were deported to Theresienstadt concentration camp, and then many of them were transferred to Auschwitz to die. Before Hitler came to power, the Jewish population in Berlin was 160,000; after the Nazi persecution of the Jews, only 5,000 were left in Berlin. Most were married to non-Jewish partners which gave them some small degree of protection: at least they were not deported. After the war about 3,000 Jews came back to Berlin.

When Berlin was divided, Jewish people started to rebuild a new community by themselves, but nobody thought about a museum. It was impossible to think about such things when they needed housing, medical care, food and jobs for the Holocaust survivors who returned to Berlin, and were more important than a museum. Some time elapsed before anyone could even think about cultural affairs. But in 1971, there was a commemorative exhibition on the Jewish history of Berlin, and since then the West Berlin parliament has been planning a new Jewish museum. When I came to Berlin in 1979 as the first curator for the museum project, my main work was to bring things together — arts, crafts, paintings, literature, documents, and archives related to Jewish history in Berlin. The location of the museum has changed as the political situation changed. Originally, it was planned to be built next to the Berlin Museum. However, since then, the Berlin Wall was dismantled and Berlin's situation has changed. We hope the project will continue as planned.

Before the war, Berliners and German Jews had been well integrated. Can you give an idea of the social history of Jews and Germans in those days?

Berlin was once called the intellectual center of Europe, and the history of Berlin and the history of the Jews were interrelated for centuries. For example, during the Weimar Republic, in the so-called "Golden Twenties," Berlin was a very cosmopolitan city with an international reputation. There was a wide range of cultural activities: art, music, theater, and literature, and there was a marked Jewish influence in every aspect of the culture. Not only in the arts, but in everyday life, Jewish presence was felt to be quite normal. People were not concerned about whether a person's background was Jewish or not. People in Berlin were internationally-minded, socially liberated, tolerant; there wasn't really any racial consciousness. This social atmosphere attracted many intellectuals and liberals from all over Germany, of course, as well as any Germans who wanted to feel free and enjoy an open society and lifestyle. Berlin was truly a haven for many other Europeans and Americans, too.

This ambience naturally attracted Jews as well. More Jews from Eastern Europe and Russia emigrated and the Jewish population in Berlin increased. As a result, we've seen many Jewish industrialists, financiers, doctors, professors and government officials. Cultural life and the performing arts also flourished: there were many outstanding and successful Jewish artists, entertainers and talented comedians.

But at the same time there was poverty in Berlin and Germany — the Great Depression — which helped push Germany into war. An extreme political situation gave rise to nationalism and racism so that the Nazis came to power in Germany. At that time, two extreme elements co-existed in Berlin: radical liberalism and ultra-nationalism.

After the war when Berlin became a provincial town, cultural activities, commerce, and everything else moved away to other German cities. Then the Berlin Wall was built, and Berlin was isolated. Most Berliners who remember the old Berlin recall what a wonderful time they had in those days; they look back on that period nostalgically, and feel it was magical, a truly golden time for them. When the Nazis took power in 1933, Berlin was turned upside down.

The Nazi racist regime and anti-intellectual policies led to the destruction of Jewish life in Berlin. What do you think went wrong, and how will the new Jewish museum deal with this?

The Nazis planned to make Berlin the center of the nation, a city without Jews — *judenrein.* They began by kicking out Jews from every area of life: intellectual, industrial, business, cultural, scientific, medical, etc. In the first stage, Jews emigrated to other countries. But later, as most countries shut their doors to Jews, the Nazis deported and killed them in the German-occupied Eastern Territories. Jewish scientists, physicists, doctors, and academics either emigrated else-

where or were captured and murdered. Since Berlin was a heavily concentrated research center for science, medicine, and university projects, it was seriously affected. Berlin practically died. Then the war turned Berlin into ruins and ashes. In my view, in a very metaphysical way, the Berlin Wall symbolized the effects of the Nazi regime. During the Nazi period, there was an "invisible wall" which divided people like apartheid into Jews and Aryans. It was a system which created a wall between people by means of laws: through registration, social pressure, job discrimination and in many other ways. I think of it as the "invisible wall." The Berlin Wall was a symbol of the Cold War, as the superpowers split, dividing the world into two parts. But the Cold War was also a result of Nazi Germany, we must remember.

When I started working on this museum project 11 years ago, there was hardly anything related to Jewish tradition and religious life in my office. But later on, many items were donated by a Russian-Jewish Berliner who returned to Berlin after the war and collected things from junk shops in the 50's. There were a dozen synagogues in prewar Berlin which were destroyed during *Kristallnacht,* and lots of the items were found among the ruins. This Jewish cultural inheritance should not be forgotten. The purpose of the museum is to express this Berlin history and commemorate those Jewish Berliners. The museum building was designed with a zig-zag wall: this could become a monument to WW II which was caused by Germany's racist Nazi government, and also commemorate the ideological origins of the Berlin Wall. The Museum has been financed by the Berlin Government, by taxpayers and city lottery money. This project — the historical research and the construction of the museum —

will be completed by 1995 and then open to the public.

We talked about Jewish immigration from Eastern Europe and Russia to Germany. Centuries ago, how were Jews given family names when they settled in Germany?

In the Middle Ages when Jewish people entered Germany to settle, the German authorities wanted to give them names but not Christian names, because the Germans refused to have the same names as Jews. So they gave them names which weren't names at all. Some were invented — odd and funny ones such as Knoblauch (garlic). They also assigned names with a special meaning related to what they were doing. For example, craftsmen who dealt with gem stones: Goldman, Silverman, Feinstein (fine stone) or Einstein (one stone). In those days, Jewish people couldn't take up any profession they wanted, but skilled work with gems and precious metals was open to them. Some Jews already had names referring to the city or their ancestors, or biblical names such as "Joseph son of Abraham" or "Moses son of Abraham," or names of famous rabbis, such as Levin or Cohen. There were many Abrahams. The Jewish people preferred their names to be connected with historically famous individuals or national heroes of centuries ago.

You are a German Jew of the postwar generation. What influenced you to emphasize your Jewish heritage today?

My father was a Jew but my mother was not: I'm a half-Jew. At first, during the Nazi period, Jews who were married to non-Jews and people who had no Jewish religious connection were able to escape Nazi persecution. If your parents or grandparents were Jewish, the Nazi racial law made you Jewish. The Nazi government enforced this by means of documents tracing back to the early 19th century, such as birth certificates and registration papers. Many people whose families had converted to Christianity two or three generations before were traced back to their Jewish ancestors and killed in Auschwitz for that reason. The Nazi bureaucratic operation was absolutely insane.

My father survived the Holocaust but my parents never practiced Judaism or anything else, and I grew up without it. My parents never told me that I was half-Jewish because my father never saw himself as Jewish. In his generation, during the Weimar Republic, Jews were characterized by their religious practice, without which they weren't regarded as Jewish, including my father. But the Nazis changed German history by dividing the population into Aryan Germans and Jewish Germans for the first time. I'm of the first generation after the Holocaust.

It all happened to Jewish people of the previous generation, but had I not learned about this shocking Nazi racial ideology, I wouldn't be Jewish today. In every aspect, Hitler made many people into Jews; people who had no Jewish identity or Jewish contact anymore were forced to be Jews. This also played a role in my family. For me, being a Jew is my own, my voluntary decision, and without Hitler I wouldn't have become interested in Jewish life. I don't believe one is Jewish by blood, and being Jewish isn't my identity, either. It developed because of my family history and was reinforced by my own life experience as a human being. Many postwar German people like myself, became interested in their Jewish background more than ever, and wanted to find out about it. Let's take another example. The half-Jewish children of an "Aryan" father and a Jewish mother. Their mother survived because of her non-Jewish husband, but her own parents, grandparents, brothers, sisters, uncles, and aunts were taken away and killed in the gas chamber. Their family life was affected. This kind of tragic experience forced people to become involved in learning about Jewish life; that includes myself.

In the Jewish community in Berlin there are many such cases. Children of Holocaust survivors like myself are now grown up and in the prime of our lives. Most of us are married to non-Jewish partners because there weren't enough Jews in postwar Berlin, and we have children of our own. Our children are not wholly Jewish biologically, but they are growing up in the Jewish community, studying Judaism and Hebrew by choice. They think of themselves as Jews and want to be Jews. Before Hitler came to power, many Jews converted to Christianity to hide their origins. But nowadays, even young non-Jewish people of the post-Holocaust generations are converting to Judaism. That is a direct result of Hitler's persecution of the Jews. What an irony of German history.

How much anti-Semitism do you see among Germans?

Anti-Semitism is a kind of infection like bacteria that subconsciously remains in everybody's mind, not only in Germany but in every society. There are many products of anti-Semitism; we just don't always recognize it. Even Jews themselves can also be products of anti-Semitism, without realizing it. If you are Jewish, you always experience some kind of anti-Semitism in your life which is a negative force, and you react to it all the time. If you have never seen your own identity as something positive, you're determined by a negative

force. That has been the big social handicap for Jewish people.

You're surrounded by this special barrier and constantly feel anti-Semitic hostility everywhere you go. You're treated like a stranger. People can't tolerate this all the time and remain unaffected. Particularly, childhood experiences with anti-Semitism are also a factor. Many German families who had partly Jewish backgrounds, wanted to escape it and hide their past connections. Until recently, Jews were seen as inferior in German society, and most parents didn't tell their children about their Jewish origin. And if the family had converted to Christianity, they didn't want to talk about their old religion anymore. But children react sensitively to their own environment; in schools and among their friends. I had the same experience. I wasn't raised or educated in the Jewish tradition at all, but the first signs of anti-Semitism came to me at quite an early age.

Today Germany is a democratic state and its people are well educated. But the roots of anti-Semitism still exist and many people can't accept human equality; they are not able to overcome negative feelings towards foreigners. With all these problems, can Germany be called a real democracy?

Germans are different. First of all, the foundation of the society is different. This doesn't apply to everyone, of course, but in the society as a whole there are many who can't overcome such feelings, even after the catastrophe of the Holocaust. I'm not certain of this, but Germans seem to feel an inferiority complex of their own. They feel they are deprived of something by someone all the time; they feel insecure and want to hit back at someone. This feeling is especially deep among East German people.

Many members of the postwar German generation feel that they have been made guilty by Hitler's war which was the work of their parents or grandparents, and they're getting fed up with feeling guilty about the Jews. They feel it's enough. It's true they did nothing and cannot be blamed. And nowadays, they don't want to talk about it, or listen to it anymore. Perhaps it's psychological: they have suffered and sufferers are victims, too. But now, suddenly, after the Berlin Wall disappeared, those "victims" (such as neo-Nazi skinheads) are behaving like "murderers." ❖

"We weren't taught that the Nazis killed six million Jews."
BETTINA STIRL

Student at the Humboldt University, East Berlin. Born in 1966 in East Berlin. Lives in East Berlin.

(Photo: Ms. Stirl in her studio apartment.)

I have found there are major educational differences between East and West Germany. Bettina, what were you taught about the causes of WW II and the rise of Hitler?

I learned that during the 1920's and 1930's there was high unemployment in Germany, and that was one of the factors that helped Hitler come to power. People knew he was a crazy man but they wanted jobs. He created strong economic power by eliminating unemployment. So, people supported Hitler and thought the Nazis government was good. What he did during the war was bad, but I never learned the details, because Nazi ideology was never taught in schools, and it was forbidden to read *Mein Kampf* in East Germany during the postwar years. Students weren't allowed to discuss it openly.

Did you learn about the Holocaust — that 6 million Jews were systematically murdered by the Nazis?

No, I didn't know that. We learned that some Jews were killed, but I really didn't know it was that many. The first time we learned anything about it was when I was 14 years old in junior high-school. Our school made an excursion to the Sachsenhausen concentration camp in the town of Oranienburg, 30 km north of East Berlin. As we visited this site of Nazi atrocities, I remember that my classmates and I were all shocked and horrified. We were deeply moved. That was my first experience learning about Germany's past. What our teachers taught us was limited. After the fall of the Wall, while I was traveling in western countries, a number of people told me that the two world wars and the Holocaust were caused by Germans. I felt embarrassed and ashamed by how little we knew about it. That was a new experience for me.

What did you learn about the Wall?

When I was born, the Wall was already there. I grew up with it, so visually it was part of the normal scene for me. In school we were taught that we needed the Wall because of our capitalist enemies in West Germany, West Berlin and the Western states. At the end of the war, the Russian army had come to save Germans from capitalism because states with a socialist system were better than those with the capitalist system in the West. Capitalists were our enemy, bad people.

Did you believe that?

I personally didn't believe it, because my mother told me it wasn't true. We were able to watch West German TV programs every day and I thought Western people were the same as us. Then, in later years, I learned from books that the Wall was the result of WW II. But as a child, I didn't know that. I believed what I was taught in school for many years, until I learned differently from books. I learned the history of the Wall from my mother, who was 10 years old when the war ended. She remembered vividly what had happened in Germany: people were saying "Heil Hitler" during the war, but after the war, they had to clean out burned bodies from the ruined city and lived in hunger. During the decades of the Wall, there were escapee stories in the newspapers sometimes, but no details were reported. After the Wall was gone, I went to West Berlin, and when I saw memorials of escapees who were killed by border guards, I was shocked by the vast number. I couldn't believe it. The East German government had not told us the truth.

What differences did you see between the two political systems in East and West Germany?

Did you ever think of escaping to West Germany yourself?

The two German states lived under different political systems for 45 years. East Germans liked to enjoy a good family life, surrounded by friends and safe neighbors, and to share each other's human values. And they appreciated free kindergarten, free education and free medical care for their children. But West Germans tend to be materialistic egotists. They want money, cars, a glamorous life. With the failure of socialism, we East Germans have lots to do to catch up with the West German system.

When Hungary opened the border, several months before the Wall came down, many East Berliners went to Austria through Hungary by train, and then flew from Vienna into West Berlin. It was a distance which takes only 30 minutes on foot without the Wall. How crazy it was. I understood those young people very well. I didn't want to stay in East Germany for the rest of my life, either. Like many others, I desired a good education and a profession, to travel around the world freely on my bicycle, to learn and to develop my own ideas while I'm still young: that was my dream. People really wanted to get out of East Germany and travel in the West without the restrictions that had frustrated young East Germans. While many thousands of East Germans were flooding into West Germany, I wanted to do the same, thinking the border might shut down again and this would be my last chance to get out of East Germany. Together with a friend, I got a visa for Bulgaria and planned to go to the West.

Then, on the evening of November 9th, we heard on the radio that the Wall was open and everybody was free to go to the West. We didn't believe it. That historical night when almost everyone in East Berlin rushed to the Wall, we went to bed as usual; we simply thought it couldn't be true. Next morning I went to the university. All my friends were hung over and recounting what had happened the previous night. They drank champagne in the streets and celebrated in West Berlin. Then I believed it. I took my bike and swiftly cycled toward the Wall. It was like a dream to me, biking through the streets of West Berlin without a passport. The first place I visited was Kreuzberg, because I used to see Kreuzberg on TV and longed to be there. That was the most exciting experience for me.

What do you think of the neo-Nazis in East Germany?

It's difficult to understand those people because they know what happened in German history, and now they are doing the same thing. I can't understand them. Those youths have no idea about their own future. They do what they were told to do, and that's the problem. It's really sad and I feel bad for them. I do hope German fascism won't rise up again.

Tell me about the cost of living in East Berlin.

I live in a studio apartment in central East Berlin. It has a small kitchen, but no bath or shower, and the toilet is in the hallway on the same floor to be shared with other tenants. It has no phone. The six-story apartment building has no elevator, either. The cost of rent is 28 M (East German Mark) per month, which has not changed since the 1930's. I get student financial aid from the government of 200 M per month, and another 15 M in additional aid towards my rent, a total of 215 M. I couldn't survive on this amount of money in West Germany but it's sufficient in East Germany. Before, our government used to pay all the cost of medical care for every student, but now we have to pay 50 DM each month to the government for health insurance. Because of the political turmoil, the new government may even stop paying student aid soon. So all students have problems. At the moment, I am being supported by my father who is a construction worker for a power station. We have 50 percent unemployment in East Germany and masses of people are still losing their jobs every day. I'm really worried that my father might be laid off, too, perhaps very soon. So, I'm not sure now if I can continue my studies or not. Another problem is that my apartment building is privately owned, not government owned, and my landlady is now able to raise the rent under the new government policy. It could be increased up to 300 DM to 400 DM* per month or possibly more. I'm very concerned about that; this is my most serious worry at the moment. We gained freedom: we are free to travel anywhere we want, but we've lost jobs and we have no money. We now have a democracy, but at the same time, we are learning that the cost of democracy is very high. ❖

*DM = Deutsch Mark (West German Mark). The West German Mark was adopted as currency by East Germany in 1990 prior to unification at an exchange rate of 1 DM: 4 M.

"We East Germans are second class citizens."

ANGELIKA WEBER

East German, lecturer at the Humboldt University of East Berlin. Divorced working mother. Born 1952 in Aue, Saxony, East Germany. Lives in East Berlin with her two children, Jenny and Martin.

(Photo: Ms. Weber with her children in her home.)

When the Berlin Wall was opened, people all over the world watched on TV as hundreds of thousands of East Berliners flooded into West Berlin. But many of them returned home right away. Were you one of them, and can you tell me your impressions of the West?

I used to come to West Berlin for my university research, so I knew the city quite well. But I wanted to show it to my two children, so like many others we came to West Berlin. At Checkpoint Charlie, we were welcomed by thousands of West Berliners and each East Berliner was given 100 DM. But my children were very disappointed. There were plenty of things to buy and to eat everywhere, and attractive window displays, which we don't have in East Berlin, and it seemed exciting in the beginning. But things were surprisingly expensive and 100 DM was nothing. We went to a department store in Kurfürstendamm Blvd., but when we saw the price tags on the things my children wanted, clothes, sporting goods, shoes, bicycles, and electronics, we were disappointed and walked out. Not wishing to stay in West Berlin any longer, we returned home dissatisfied. West Berliners were full of joy, with tears in their eyes, having champagne parties by the Wall, and singing songs, but I personally couldn't understand those people. Why did the failure of socialism have to be celebrated in such a manner? Why were they so happy? For what? The standard of living in East and West Germany is so different that they call us East Germans second-class citizens in the new Germany. We are unfashionably dressed, industrially and materialistically backwards, lacking in business skills, and slow-minded. Indeed, I agree we are different. Every time I come to West Berlin, the first thing I notice is the expressions on people's faces and in their eyes. Western people move fast and think on their own, their eyes look shrewd and reveal their motivation. Something is on their minds all the time.

East Germans are mentally slower, lacking self-motivation and I find the expression in their eyes is significantly different from Westerners; they look passive. Forty-five years of a divided Germany has surely ingrained communism deeply in their minds: that's a big problem.

During the long years of communism, what do you think went wrong?

Since I'm an academic specializing in the history and political science of Indonesia, I had a few chances to travel outside East Germany, to Indonesia, India, the Soviet Union, and in the Eastern bloc as well as West Germany. It was then I perceived the negative side of our country. My family and I were Communist party members, devoted to socialist ideology, but I realized that what our government was doing to our people in the name of socialism wasn't good. First of all, most East Germans couldn't travel to Western countries freely; that was the most painful part of the communist regime. More realistically, we couldn't easily get the things we needed. We had to wait an average of 10 years to buy a simple and mechanically lousy automobile. We had to wait 15 years to get a simple telephone for a private home, and the quality of telephone service hadn't improved since the 1920s. We had limited use, couldn't get through to West Berlin, and the line was noisy. We couldn't buy fresh fruits or vegetables, and so on. People couldn't be patient any longer. We are the people and the people needed *perestroika*.

As a divorced working mother supporting teenage children, how did things change in your life after the collapse of communism?

In every communist country in Eastern Europe, 90 percent of women have a profession or some kind of job; after they are married and have children, they still continue working. It has little to do with financial reasons. They like to contribute to society. I was married when I was a 16-year-old student, and together with my economist husband it was much easier to find a flat. If you were single, it was impossible to rent or buy an apartment or house, so many people got married for the same reason. After having two children I was able to continue my university studies because our social system was good: kindergarten and health care were free. The school system was financed by the government so every child could have a good education free of charge. I used to think about what was wrong in communism and what was good in capitalism. Capitalism always divides society into rich and poor, and this two-class system isn't a good thing.

I think a mixture of the good side of the two systems would be the ideal: the capitalism of the USA and the communism of the USSR.

My personal life has changed drastically in the year since the fall of the Wall. I lost my teaching job and with two growing teenagers, I have a real problem now. Because of the political changes and budget cuts by the new government, the Humboldt University has drastically decreased the number of professors, lecturers and staff workers: 300-400 people were fired and I was one of them. The main reason was political — Stasi connections. Many of the university professors and department staff were involved with the Stasi. They were the first to be suspected. The West Germans think that almost all university employees in East Germany were involved with it, and because of my background, my socialist study, they think I'm Stasi, too. I used to earn 1,200 M per month, but

I'm now unemployed and get 600 DM (*Deutschmark*) welfare every month, which is lower than a pension. In addition, I am paid 300 DM for child support from my former husband. Before the collapse of East Germany, my house mortgage was 200 M, but now I have to pay 900 DM, and I can't afford it. I need money and a job. Since I have had one academic concentration my whole life, my educational qualification is very specialized, and there are many highly-qualified professors and educators in West Germany. The education system in our old communist East Germany has now become useless. It's impossible for me to find a working position. What can I do?

How about you, Jenny, how did things change for you?
Jenny: I wanted to study medicine and become a doctor, but I'm not certain about my future now. Everything, every aspect of our lives, has suddenly been turned upside down since the collapse of the communist regime. The lucky part was that I've found a part-time job at a local gasoline station for a small wage, and I can contribute something to my mother.

Martin, tell me about the Wall, before and after — what have you learned from your teacher in your school?
The Wall had an anti-fascist purpose. It was necessary to divide East and West Germany because we were a socialist country, wanting to live without interference from other countries. The answer was clear as to why the Wall was needed. Now, it's gone, but no student ever questioned their teachers about the reason it was destroyed. We presume people know the reason, and don't want to think about such things anymore because it's too tiresome! ❖

"The new Germany may produce the atomic bomb."

ALEXEJ SESTERHEIM

High school teacher and anti-nuclear weapons activist. Born in 1945 in
Eifel, West Germany. Lives in East Berlin.

(Photo: Mr. Sesterheim with exhibition photos of atomic-bomb victims of Hiroshima in 1945.)

How did you get involved in anti-nuclear activities?

In 1980, there was a photo exhibition of the bombing of Hiroshima and Nagasaki in a gallery in West Berlin. It was organized by a group of Japanese women who lived in West Germany. At first, I was reluctant to see such depressing photographs. But when I saw them, these photos were visually so shocking that I was terribly disturbed. They changed my thinking. There are nuclear plants and cruise missiles all over the globe which could destroy the world, and now I felt aware of it. I realized that I should pay attention to politics and become concerned about world peace. I thought people should know more about the nuclear armaments. Then, in 1983, I organized the same show in my hometown of Eifel, which has a population of a few tens of thousands. It was overwhelming; 12,000 people showed up. At the same time, we hoped that the fear visually aroused by those photos might trigger an international denunciation of atomic weapons' production throughout the world. The photos were pessimistic, but the exhibition was successful.

In Germany today, both in the West and in the East, people are still not allowed to talk openly in schools or with their families about what our parents did. But the young generation today should have the right to know the facts of history, the deeds which were committed by their parents and grandparents. As a high school teacher, I personally have a critical view of the German educational system. I believe that the teaching method in Germany is wrong because it focuses primarily on implementing systematic knowledge, and lacks the human touch — an exchange of opinion between students and teachers. Individual thinking by students is discouraged. Teachers pressure students to achieve good grades and students don't develop the capacity to think for themselves. I'm against such a system.

For instance, if students don't act the way their teachers want them to, they get kicked out of school: all students must do the same. If they please teacher, they get good grades, and having good grades is a big deal in German society. School children aren't allowed to express what they feel and think. It's an authoritarian system. As a result, children are mentally pressured by their parents at home, psychologically pressured by teachers in school, brainwashed by priests at church on Sundays, and then oppressively pressured by employers at work. That is the German way of life. In this respect, by the way, I think the Japanese educational and social system is very much like Germany's. I don't like it, and I believe it must be changed. I opposed that system and I gave an "A" to every student in my class, so I was fired by the school principal. I'm out of work at the moment.

What I want to say is that for centuries this German educational system has led to people being raised and educated like human computers rather than human beings. Therefore, during the Nazi regime when everybody followed the dictator Hitler, Germans turned themselves into machines, behaved like robots and killed 6 million Jewish people in a mass industrial operation. "I only followed orders," they claimed. They had done nothing against authority.

The atomic bomb was originally developed in the United States to attack Germany. If the atomic bomb had been dropped on German soil, can you imagine what the consequences would have been?

I know that atomic bombs were originally made to attack Germany, not Japan, but many Germans don't want to know that. By the fall of 1944, when atomic bombs were ready to be produced, there were clear signs that Germany would lose the war. But since the United States had invested so much money and so many years on research for the so-called Manhattan Project, they wanted to test it anyway. There was a dispute between scientists and the US military leaders because peace talks between Japan and the USA were imminent. But if peace negotiations materialized before they could test it, they would not be able to see how it worked. After successful tests in the New Mexico desert, they wanted to see the result on humans. Two types of bombs were dropped: a uranium bomb on Hiroshima and a plutonium bomb on Nagasaki, and more would have followed on Kokura, Yokohama, Kyoto, and other cities if Japan hadn't surrendered. School textbooks say that atomic bombs were used in order to end the war: in my view that isn't true.

When Germany lost the war, the German people were shocked. But if Germany had been attacked with atomic bombs, I think that the Germans would have been even more deeply shattered. The emotional consequences would have been different: I imagine it would have been torture. If radiation victims die as they still do in Japan today, that would remind Germans of the war endlessly. It only took one atomic bomb blast to flatten Hiroshima within a matter of minutes, and the city lost its identity completely. Many German cities were also totally destroyed by Allied air raids, and lost hundreds of thousands of inhabitants. People identify themselves with the worst crisis. The more they are crushed, the more they find out about themselves. America's atomic bomb was the powerful message that changed the history of the war.

Many Germans today want to forget their past and what they did. They refuse to talk about it. How do you see that?

There are different types of German people; some learned from their own mistakes and catastrophic events, but some go even further in the wrong direction. Many Germans today still think that Hitler was patriotic and a good man, and that the Nazi war was a good thing for Germany. I'm afraid the majority of Germans are never able to learn their lesson.

What is your view of the new Germany?

The new Germany is very prosperous, and most of its inhabitants want to forget everything about the past and look forward to a good future. The majority of them hate to look back at their negative past, which they identify with German weakness. But my point is that without studying the past, there will be no future. They think they are optimistic but, for me, there is nothing behind them but pessimism. Germany has meant war after war, and when peace comes and you examine its background, it isn't peace at all: it's a preparation period for another war. WW II led to a nuclear age. In the twentieth century, world civilization has developed to produce materials like chemical weapons and nuclear arms which destroy the entire earth: animal species and mankind. There is pollution, there's damage to the ozone layer. It's totally out of control. Half a century after the invention of atomic power, nuclear technology today has produced weapons one million-times more powerful than the atomic bombs dropped on Hiroshima and Nagasaki. I'm quite certain that the new Germany will produce atomic bombs of its own, sooner or later. ❖

I had to wait 15 years to buy a Trabant car.

ROLAND FUCHS

Student in agricultural science at the Humboldt University, East Berlin.
Born 1960 in East Berlin, East Germany. Lives in East Berlin.

(Photo: Mr. Fuchs with his "Trabant.")

How did the collapse of the Berlin Wall affect your life, Roland?

Actually, in my case, unlike many other East Germans, the collapse of the Wall was beneficial: it became easier to do my professional research and study. I'm a student in agricultural science working on a doctoral thesis, and I needed to travel to foreign countries for further study. As you know, before the Wall it was very difficult for East German citizens to make trips outside the country. However, right after the fall of the Wall, travel restrictions were lifted and, as a result, in 1990, I was invited by the United States government to study agricultural environment protection and public policy at the University of North Carolina. It was an international training program for agroscience researchers and students. Unified Germany gave me such a great opportunity and I'm glad it's happened rapidly and unexpectedly.

How do you compare agricultural study in the US with the Eastern countries?

There are lots of differences in productivity and agricultural efficiency. First of all, in the US they manage with fewer workers, use more machines and produce more products than we do. But generally the US wastes energy in the form of pesticides, fertilizer and fuel, because those are so cheap in the US. For instance, one gallon of fuel costs $1.00, while it's $5.00 or 6.00 in Germany. Moreover, you can find more processed agricultural products in the US, but it's very difficult to buy naturally processed vegetables and fruits. In East Germany, we also produce highly processed products but at a much lower energy cost. As far as I'm concerned, the US doesn't value energy efficiency like we do in the Western and Eastern European countries. The US produces good quality fruits and vegetables because high standards are required by consumers, but to produce high quality means also using a high quantity of pesticides, insecticides and other chemicals. US consumers like to buy big, shiny, perfect-looking apples, oranges, bananas, grapes, etc., and are less concerned with health issues. In fact, it's better and safer to eat small, naturally-damaged peaches than pesticide-treated perfect-looking ones. In this respect, I fear that American health will be damaged in the long run.

I understand that the principle of American capitalism is competition, and competition makes for better quality, and mass consumption means mass production, and mass production means money. Because I also deal with capitalist agriculture in countries like Canada and others, I know how the market economy works. But I still think there are too many similar products in the US — hundreds of types of cheese, milk, bread, butter, etc. In another respect, I find a huge amount of waste of resources connected with fast food: plastic, paper, boxes, styrofoam, brown bags, bottles, cans, newspapers. The US recycling industry and environmental awareness lag far behind both East and West Germany. Americans may think it's expensive to develop a recycling system; that's not true. You can achieve a balance between consumers and producers, with cooperation and community participation.

What did you think of Berlin with the Wall?

I was born one year before the Wall was built so it was quiet natural for me. I used to watch TV and listen to the radio from West Germany but didn't think about the people, who have a different way of thinking from us. I've traveled in the USSR and other Eastern communist countries, but I had never been in West Berlin or any Western countries before the Wall came down. In fact, I never thought I would have the chance to meet capitalist-oriented people such as other Western Europeans or Americans. It was just impossible to imagine. Berlin without the Wall is another world and a very different experience for me.

Tell about your car, a Trabant, which was the only automobile produced in East Germany.

I bought this car second-hand in 1988 with my girlfriend. In East Germany it took 15 years to buy a new car. One sent in an application and then waited for 15 years. That was the normal way to get a car for East German citizens. Therefore, it was much easier to buy a used one. But we had to pay more than a new car cost, because there was no competition in the economy, and the price was fixed by the government. A new Trabant costs 10,000 M, but for our 13-year-old Trabant we paid 10,000 M which was, in fact, a bargain price. People normally pay 16,000 M to 18,000 M for a 10-year-old car.

To buy a used car, people waited an average of 1 or 2 years to find one through the newspaper. Announcements usually didn't state a price, you had to negotiate with the owner. Sometimes the owner asked for 3,000 M officially, but actually the payment was 10,000 M. Official and actual prices were different. When we bought this car, the mileage was 8,000 km and the previous owner had kept it in relatively good shape; it was not too bad for a 13-year-old car. But it makes a terrible noise so that we have to shout at each other while we drive and the engine is running. It has no radio but it does have a heater. However, it only warms up the front seats, and if you sit in the back, you shiver. Its maximum speed is 60 miles per hour. I love driving and when we bought this car, before unification, we were so happy and excited about it; low mileage, in good condition, a low price. But after the unification, we didn't feel the same way anymore. We would like to buy a faster and better car. When this car dies, it'll cost us 100 to 350 DM to dump it. ❖

"Hitler's mystery should be de-mystified."

PETER GREAVES

Visiting Australian photographer. Born in 1966 in Brisbane, Australia.
Lives temporarily in West Berlin.

(Photo: Mr. Greaves stands in Kurfürstendamm Blvd. in the city center of West Berlin.)

How has your impression of Berlin changed since you got here?

Before I came here my image of Berlin was slightly different. There are many trees in the streets, no high-rises, and it looks so attractive that I was quite surprised. But when you walk around the city, you still find bullet holes in the buildings, and that's something you can't easily pass by or simply forget. I knew modern German history: WW II and the Berlin Wall. I wasn't ignorant. But I certainly got more than I expected. Because I'm a photographer I always look for something many people usually wouldn't notice, and since I'm interested in world history, it all comes together. You don't have to read books. You just keep your eyes and ears open. History forces itself on you when you are in Berlin. Growing up in Australia is really nothing like here.

During WW II, many Australian soldiers were killed in Germany and in the Pacific. Were any of your family involved in the war, and what was your primary interest in Berlin and Germany?

Two of my uncles died in WW II. One was a bomb navigator and was shot in Hamburg by Germans, and one was killed in New Guinea by the Japanese. In later years, another uncle was killed in the Vietnam War. My father was one of eight brothers and loosing three of them through the two wars was a terrible family tragedy, especially since Australia never started any of those wars. My special interest in Germany was that I grew up in a German community in my hometown. My father spoke German and we all used to communicate in German, so I was naturally intrigued to see Germany. I came to Berlin right after the collapse of the Berlin Wall, and have been here for one and a half years. I have seen a great historical change in Germany.

Recently, Hitler's bunkers were unearthed in the center of Berlin where the Berlin Wall was standing. Can you tell me about it?

I believe it was sometime in July 1990. It was while Pink Floyd, a British rock music group, was preparing an open air concert to celebrate the fall of the Berlin Wall in an area now called no-man's land in Kruezberg. As they were digging out the underground for the concert stage, they found Hitler's bunkers. Those weren't ordinary soldiers' bunkers or his personal bunker, but were probably the headquarters designed for high-ranking SS officers. I saw them on TV which was taken by the musicians' video camera. There were huge piles of bottles of French wines and some remains of human bones on the ground. Then, I saw that its interiors were decorated by murals, and I remember those images were quite frightening. One picture showed SS officers and Nazi generals standing by tanks and, in the foreground, Hitler was standing like God. Another painting showed Hitler standing in the foreground surrounded by lots of Nazi soldiers: SS, navy, army and airforce officers were holding hands tightly and giving the Nazi salute with a bright orange light behind them. The paintings were incredible, and anyone who saw them would definitely have felt that there was religious worship involved with the Nazi leadership.

What was the public reaction and what happened to the murals and bunkers then?

I thought this was a great historical discovery, and I expected to see further details the next morning in a front-page-story in the local newspapers. But there was only a tiny article on the back page with a short announcement by the city government. It was scarcely noticed by the public, and didn't even become an issue at all. The thing that surprised me most was that the German government reburied the bunkers after three days: they cemented them up and sealed them from the public. There was no historical examination or official announcement. Their explanation was the bunkers were dangerous because they were full of ammunition, and that they might attract certain groups such as neo-Nazis or skinheads, who might turn them into a neo-Nazi shrine.

Those bunkers were not ordinary bomb shelters or places to hide temporarily. They were designed to be inhabited for a long period of time so Hitler would be able to continue commanding his troops if Berlin came under attack. They were probably the most important bunkers in Berlin. I knew about Hitler's bunkers, but I'd never seen or heard of anything like those strange murals before. They almost seemed to belong in some sort of church. They were certainly religious symbols for the Nazis. It was definitely a Nazi shrine which raises lots of questions.

We learned about the Third Reich in school and I know it was a delicate and uneasy period of German history, of course. But there is a deep gap: there were no SS records or written documents in public. Many of them were taken away by the Russian Red Army in 1945 and you just couldn't find them. There are many mysteries surrounding the Third Reich. Those bunkers could have been one of the keys to resolving many things. But instead of taking them seriously and restoring them for examination, the German government just reburied them. They couldn't face their painful past. I don't think there are enough people looking into that period. There remain so many unanswered questions even Germans themselves

wouldn't know. People around the world who are interested in the subject, simply couldn't find out what was really going on. Maybe in 10 or 20 years, many relics of our history will appear. By that time, people will be emotionally detached from the subject, because people who were related to the matters will be dead. Then, I'm sure some people will start to investigate. At this time, no one knows exactly what happened to those bunkers, but if they were destroyed many people would think it a pity.

Hitler had so much control over ordinary hard working people who were really desperate. Why did this man have so much power? I would like to know WHY...? Those bunkers would provide a certain key to finding the answer. Little things add up to a big picture, and if they were destroyed, you only get half of the big picture. The bunkers really showed another side of Hitler. During the recent Gulf War, US President George Bush called Saddam Hussain a new Hitler. Who was Hitler, then...? The truth is, after nearly 50 years, we still don't know who he really was.

Besides Hitler's bunkers, what else did you see around Berlin?

I found other ruined bunkers, as well as a number of army quarters and shelters for former Nazi officers and soldiers which had been untouched since the end of the war. They are located in the middle of Berlin, 15 square kms of land south of Tempelhof airport. The area is unknown to the public, but neo-Nazis hang around sometimes. In a huge flat woodland area, there are perhaps hundreds of railway tracks that are much wider than ordinary passenger train railways. I walked around to examine everything. Since the area is by the airport, I would imagine it was used for a war material transportation quarters to move ammunition, guns, bombs, tanks, etc., by train or air. By looking around those ruined army shelters, you can tell that quite a number of officers worked, lived and slept there, because each building has ten rooms and each room has a desk, beds and shelves. Each building has a communal toilet, bath, washing room, dinning room, and kitchen, and there is a small factory in a back room full of machinery. You also saw black leather boots and gloves, pens, cups, forks, knives scattered around the floor. Each door was painted in black and red. It was weird. When you walk in, you immediately get an eerie feeling: you feel a smell of death and fear. Strangely, the color of the ceramic urinal was not white; it was painted black with a blue border. I found so many odd things like that among the junk.

Following the tracks further down, I found a few train bunkers which were built right at the end of the railways. They were obviously constructed to protect cargo trains in case of air attack by the Allies, so the Germans could move their war materials, petrol, chemicals, tanks, aircrafts, soldiers into the bunkers as quickly as possible. Those bunkers were made of a thick, solid concrete, strong and absolutely enormous, and still in good shape. Looking at those bunkers and examining other buildings, you can tell that Hitler had planned his war really further in advance than the Allies imagined. He built something that could last for more than a hundred years. Even by the width of the railway you can tell he built the biggest war train in the world. There are residential houses for officers' families nearby with little bunkers covered by bushy trees. There you can still see the remains of bloody man-to-man combat, probably between Germans and Russian soldiers. Its interiors are a horrible

mess; broken chairs, tables, couches, children's shoes, baby carts and toys were scattered all over the floors and in every room you can see bullet holes all over the walls.

Along the railway lines there are grave markers. People were buried here and there, because cemeteries were full. I imagine uncountable groups of unknown German soldiers, civilians and children killed by the battle were buried around the area. In the last months of war, Berlin was defended by old men and Hitler's youth, boys 14 to 16, fighting against the Russian Red Army because most German soldiers were in the front or killed in battle. I presume those were graves of some of those young boys and old men.

Tell me what you've learned about Hitler?
The things that Hitler did to create the Nazi devil empire were absolutely unspeakable. There is no way we could possibly talk about him as a normal human being. What is more strange to me is that I can't find any good autobiographical literature which clears up some obvious points about him, his psychological profile showing how sick and deranged he was, his irrational mind and schizophrenic side. Even Germans have no answers for that. For every other dictator in our history, way back to Caesar and Napoleon, we have a clear personal profile. But Hitler was just a face and a bunch of war maneuvers on a chess board. At this point, we actually don't understand anything about him. Maybe German people want all this swept under the carpet.

I'm in a city where 46 years ago nearly everyone was killed. I want to know why. It's unique — that's Berlin. Germans don't talk about the Nazis and they don't say a word about Hitler. If you bring it up, they think you are morbid. They avoid discussing it, especially older people. If I confront them, they say, "You must be a neo-Nazi." They seem so introverted and I don't know exactly why. They can tell me what happened "politically" of course, but it's no profound in-depth answer. As Hitler remains a great mystery, people tend to fill-in the gaps with their own ideas and make up their own theories, turning Hitler into a powerful God-like image. I think that's the basic reason that young neo-Nazis today shave their heads, tattoo their bodies, go out in the streets and frighten people. That's why the Berlin bunkers, the ones with the murals, and many other things surrounding the Third Reich should be thoroughly investigated and de-mysti-fied. I know it's painful, horrible, and embarrass-ing for Germans, but it would help everybody in the world to understand.

How about the young East Germans?

When I talk to young East Germans, many of them don't know about the Nazi era even though they have bullet holes in their houses. I end up telling them what happened. The two Germanys are now united and the real democratic German nation has finally begun. But since it has been taboo to talk about the Nazi past, now all of a sudden, speaking out about everything is confus-ing for East Germans. Many feel it had nothing to do with them because it happened a long time before they were born. They feel no responsibil-ity. The new Germany is already the top worka-holic nation in Europe. Germans really work hard: work is the most important thing in their lives. They always say "work! work! Get your job done and don't think about anything else. Work makes you safe, that's all you need." There is no doubt that Germany will be a prosperous nation

again soon. Germans are not only excellent work-ers but also the best soldiers in the world. When their leaders gave them orders, they wouldn't obey fanatically, or emotionally, or wouldn't change their minds half-way through. They would just do as they were told exactly and on time. That's really frightening — like machines missing a human aspect. Law and order are cre-ated by humans, who make mistakes and humans don't do certain things. I wonder what makes the inside of the German mind that way.

What would you think about the story of Hitler and its future?

Hitler gained all that power and abused it. Nearly 70 million people died because of this man. He was ruthless, a monster, a poisoned man who cre-ated the most horrifying empire our modern his-tory has ever known, yet, we have no clear infor-mation about him. As far as the future is concerned, one day people will become curious about their own past and want to know more about Hitler. I'm certain those generations will come some day in the future. And, when they want to read books about him and find out the truth, they'll discover there is nothing there but a huge gap. The fact is that no one can put a finger on what the neo-Nazis are doing. Hitler remains a mystery and they create more mystery; they see Hitler as a God-like figure. They continue to talk about him, admire him and sympathize with him. Jesus Christ was not a God when he was alive: his life was a mystery, too. 100 years from now, Hitler may end up a romantic war hero for many people, not only for neo-Nazis. Who knows? It's really scary. All because we know so little about the truth of this man. ❖

Why can't the painters of the Wall get paid?

THIERRY NOIR

French artist; painter of the Berlin Wall murals. Born in 1960 in Lyon, France. Lives in West Berlin.

(Photo: Mr. Noir in his art studio with some of his artwork.)

What made you move to Berlin and become an artist?

Since my childhood I wanted to live outside France: I wanted to be an expatriot. That was my dream; not London or Paris but somewhere else. While I was living in Lyon, I realized that some of the greatest rock'n roll musicians, such as David Bowie and Pink Floyd, had played concerts in West Berlin, and I thought it must be a very exciting city. It seemed as if West Berlin were an island city, but why? I was intrigued. I quit my boring office work and moved to West Berlin in the winter of 1982. I was 22 then. Shortly afterwards, I met a French artist who was painting on the streets in West Berlin and we became friends. I never thought I'd have talent in art, never having painted before. But spending time with a professional artist influenced me. In 1984, we decided to paint the Berlin Wall together. In those days, only graffiti was on the Wall; most of the graffiti comprised anti-communist messages or anti-American slogans written by West Berliners. At that time, no one was painting from the top to the bottom of the Wall. We were the first artists to paint full-scale murals.

Painting on the Wall automatically became a political or social demonstration, even a kind of human protest. The Wall stood five meters inside the actual borderline on the East Berlin side. So, while we were painting, strictly speaking, we were inside East German territory. As you know, since painting on the Wall was prohibited in East Germany, East German border guards used to come and chase us while we were painting. They claimed that we were inside their territory, and the Wall belonged to them. They shouted at us not to paint. West German police were not allowed to help us because we were in East Ger-

many. But we kept painting while the border guards were not watching.

After the fall of the Wall, pieces of the Wall were sold all over the world. I understand that you and your artist friend filed a claim to the Berlin city government about your artwork. Can you explain what your demand was?

When the Wall fell down, nobody considered what was to come next. People started cutting down the Wall, selling it piece by piece, and making money out of it. Some pieces were valued over many thousands of dollars. The Wall suddenly turned into something of historical value. As unknown artists, painting the Wall was our own choice; no one told us to do it, we did it for our own artistic expression, and we agree that nothing can be done now. However, we believe the paintings were good, colorful, pretty, had artistic value, and were too valuable to destroy. That's why people all over the world bought them. If those pieces were just gray stones, who would pay such big money for them...? The Berlin Wall was hated by every German for so many years. Who would pay money for such a hated object...? We believe it's because of our artwork. A number of photographers shot our paintings and sold them to publications. Why can't the painters get paid? We felt it was unfair. We had a hard time buying paint, and we would like to get contributions from organizations who made profits out of our work, at least a small percentage of them. There is no law or anything like that for this kind of case, of course. It's an unusually exceptional claim — just a consequence of the sudden fall of the Wall. We are waiting to hear about the results of our filing, and hoping to get a special contribution for Wall artists sometime next year. ❖

457

We Turks are the biggest minority in Germany.

M. TURGUT CAKMAKOGLU

Turkish immigrant, president of the Free Turkish-German Friendship Club in West Berlin. Born in 1952 in Ankara, Turkey. Lives in West Berlin.

(Photo: Mr. Cakmakoglu in his Kreuzberg office.)

Mr. Cakmakoglu, can you give me a brief history of Turkish immigration to West Germany?
In the late 1950s when the West German economy began to recover from war, West Germany needed foreign workers. The governments of West Germany and Turkey signed an agreement that Turkey would offer workers to West Germany. Only men under age 30, started to arrive and work in West Germany. They were all over the country, not only in West Berlin. During the 1960s, as a result of the West German economic rebound, Turkish labor became important. The majority were unemployed workers from small rural towns or villages. In the early stages, they worked here mainly in mining, steel and auto industries. Many saved money to buy land or to build houses back home, so they didn't want to spend their money in Germany. Their average income in Germany was over 10 times higher than that in Turkey. They were transferring a large amount of money they earned back home because they wanted to return home after a few years. As years passed, this caused inflation in the Turkish economy, and the price of property went up. They had to work longer years in West Germany to get the same properties. For this reason, more people began to settle in Germany, bringing their brides and families, to get pensions in Germany.

How have things developed since then, and how many Turks live in Germany now?
The Turkish population in Germany today is about one and a half million, and 123,000 of them live in Berlin. We are the biggest minority in West Germany. The problem was where to live. We didn't want to spend too much money for rent. In West Berlin, we dwelled in low-rent and working class areas, such as Kreuzberg, by the Berlin Wall. As a result, German inhabitants moved out and more Turks moved in, and gradually it became a Turkish ghetto: it made the integration of Turkish and German people very difficult.

Another problem was language. The early groups of Turkish workers didn't learn German, because they wanted to return home eventually. But later, second and third generation Turks went to German schools and spoke German better than their parents. Turkish children now are equally educated and treated the same as German children: there is no problem in schools. In recent years, more and more Turks are attending high school and Turkish students account for the largest percentage of foreign students in German universities today. But at home, the traditional Turkish education taught through the family is quite different, and that can cause problems.

More recently, after the fall of the Wall, how have things changed?
The rise of neo-Nazis has created a new problem for Turks all over the country. Some time ago, a group of skinheads, for instance, threatened to kill one Turkish child in each school in Berlin, so all Turkish parents kept their children at home. This kind of threat and violence against the Turkish community has been growing rapidly since the Wall came down and it's out of control now. We have lived with the Wall for decades, and it has been a quiet neighborhood and a cozy ghetto life for us. But after the Wall fell, almost immediately a new dimension faced the Turkish minority in West Berlin. We thought the fall of the Wall was a good thing for the two Germanys, but we never expected this kind of problem.

As president of the Free Turkish-German Friendship Club, my task is to create a good relationship and sense of community between Turks and Germans through public relations work such as newsletters, bilingual newspapers, information exchanges, joint commercial enterprises, shared cultural activities, etc. We need to understand and cooperate with each other, so the two different peoples can come together. And of course, Turks, with the strong cooperation of German commu- nities must fight against the growing power of neo-Nazi gangs and the ultra-right-wing. For this process to occur smoothly, contact with local journalists and city officials would help. But we don't want to be involved with politics or relig- ion, and we avoid political intervention. ❖

"Some police officers are also neo-Nazis: they don't help us."

CAN NGUYEN

Vietnamese worker, with his wife, Huong Tran Thinam Ainh. Born in 1964 in Saigon, Vietnam. Lives in East Berlin.

(Photo: Mr. Nguyen, center, with his wife, center left, and their roommates in their East Berlin apartment.)

Why are you in East Germany, Mr. Nguyen?

When the Vietnam War ended in 1975, my country became a communist state. Among socialist governments such as the USSR, Eastern Bloc countries, Mozambique, Ethiopia, Angola, Cuba and North Vietnam, there were exchange programs for workers and students. Personally, I was never interested in coming to East Germany, but when I finished high school at 18, the North Vietnamese government ordered me to study in East Germany. In a socialist state, state authority decides what people are to do. I was sent to a small town, 14 km north of Dresden, to study forestry. After studying German for 3 years and then forestry for 2 years, I worked in the forests until the fall of East German communism. Currently, there are tens of thousands of Vietnamese and about 80,000 foreign workers from other socialist countries living in East Germany.

After the reunification, how did things change, especially monthly earnings?

I used to earn 750 M every month before, but I lost my job because of reunification. My income was completely cut off by the government, and I had no savings. I live with my wife in one of the apartment buildings especially provided by the East German government for Vietnamese workers. We share a small room with two more married couples, a total of six people in one medium-size bedroom. Our rent used to be 90 M per month: 30 M per couple, but after reunification, it was raised to 900 DM. Now, each couple has to pay 300 DM: it's an outrageous increase. But we are able to survive because I have a business permit to sell clothing and cheap factory products in the streets.

Tell me what you remember about the Vietnam War and what happened to your country.

I was 11 when the war ended, so I remember very little. My family was living in the countryside so it didn't affect us much, but one of my uncles died because of the bombing. I specifically recall the heavy American air raids in 1972 when I was eight years old. I saw rockets in the sky and fighter planes and heard horrifying bombing noises, but I didn't see any Vietnamese fighting with US soldiers. The war was a bad thing, of course, but Americans are nice and friendly. The American people didn't start the war, the US government did. We can't blame individuals. I don't care much for politics and I could care less about communism or capitalism, either. We'd like to have a peaceful life, but American-style capitalism attracts me especially after the failure of communism. It might enable me to buy a big house or car. I'm in favor of American capitalism.

Violence against foreigners has increased in East Germany. Can you tell me about it?

People's attitudes have changed since the fall of the Wall; incidents of aggressive behavior against foreigners have dramatically increased all over East Germany. Radical neo-Nazi youths with shaved heads have been attacking Asians and black Africans randomly in public. East Germans are angry that we are here. They shout at us: "Foreigners out!" With rising unemployment, we Vietnamese have been serious targets of racial bias. Some were pushed off a moving train, our social workers' office and some residences were set afire by arsonists, and these skinheads are all over looking for foreigners. It's not safe to go out in the evening, because they attack us. There is a police station in front of our apartment, but some police officers are also neo-Nazis, and don't help foreigners. We are living in fear in an insecure situation. ❖

"Glasnost resulted in the resurgence of anti-Semitism in Russia."

ALLA AND EDUWARD LAPIZKI

Russian Jewish refugees in East Berlin. Alla (sister): medical doctor, born in 1963. Eduward (brother): student, born in 1967. Both born and raised in Kiev, Ukraine, the former Soviet Union. Both live in East Berlin Jewish Refugee Center.

(Photo: Lapizkis in their refugee center home in East Berlin.)

Eduward, why did you decide to come to Germany, in the country where the worst Jewish persecution in history occurred, rather than going to Israel?

Eduward: Because we have a friend in East Berlin, a friend of our parents, and Germany isn't too far from our county. Since the fall of the Berlin Wall, Germany agreed to accept a quota of Jewish refugees, so we left the Soviet Union illegally in July 1990, three months before German unification. Since we arrived in Germany we have been staying in a refugee center. We don't want to go back to the Ukraine again. Since Gorbachev's *glasnost* and *perestroika* campaign began in the mid-1980s, life in the USSR has become increasingly difficult for Jewish people, because of a rise in anti-Semitism. The reason we chose Germany was that it provided an easy immigration access: the bureaucratic requirements were simple. Although we didn't have any relatives in Germany we were accepted. Besides, Ukraine is much closer to Germany than to Israel so that we'll be able to visit our home often to see our parents and friends. We didn't know anyone in Israel to make contact with.

We learned about the Holocaust from our parents, who escaped persecution from the *Einsatzgruppen,* and we also studied German history on our own, about all the things that happened in Germany during that period. But I'm not afraid of it now. I was told that the young generation of Germans has learned enough lessons from that, and I don't think they'll repeat it again in Germany. I see that today's Germans are a different kind of German.

How has anti-Semitism increased since glasnost and what was your experience dealing with it?

Alla: Our problems began because of our parents' nationality: we have a British Jewish mother and a Russian Jewish father, and since we were born in Kiev, in the Soviet Union, we had to carry a Russian identification card and Russian passport. Every person who was born and has Russian nationality in the USSR, must have their parents' and grandparents' origins listed on every official document. If your parents are Jews, it's marked "J" — that is the State law. We don't know why, but it has been that way for a long time. So every time and everywhere I apply for a job, when they see the "J" mark on my I.D. card, people react. Physically, we look like Russians or anybody else — but it has nothing to do with our appearance. It's all in their mind, but I was rejected in every application. I finished my university study in medicine in recent years and have a doctor's degree to become a physician, but I couldn't get a position in a hospital in Kiev. And, especially these past years, it became obvious that anti-Semitism and job discrimination against Jewish people is the main issue in Russian society.

There is an openly anti-Jewish neo-Nazi organization called Pamyat in the USSR. It used to be an underground organization before Mr. Gorbachev came to power, but after the glasnost movement started, they came out of hiding. Because of this, Jewish Russians have now become victims of social ostracism. That is the reason that we decided to leave the USSR and come to Germany. We wanted to go to the USA but we had no connections there.

How did glasnost affect you, Eduward?

Eduward: Pamyat emerged very quickly in Russia and it targeted only Jews. There was no physical violence such as attacking Jews in the street, but there was discrimination in schools, universities, jobs and housing — many Jewish people couldn't find apartments. I started studying at the university in Kiev in 1981, but by 1984 I couldn't keep studying there anymore. So I had to quit.

How much financial support can you get from the German government, and what is the situation with regard to finding a job?

Alla: At the moment it's extremely hard to find a job because of the economic situation in the united Germany. But I speak very good German and am hoping to get a job by next year at the latest. Since we are legal refugees we can stay free of charge in the refugee center here in East Berlin, which provides us with one room for two of us. An average three-bedroom unit with one bathroom and kitchen is shared between three families, so for large families it's often crowded. We don't need to pay for electricity, gas and water. We get food stamps and each person gets 400 DM (US $260) per month from the German government. We have to pay for public transportation and buy clothes and other things. We also have our savings from home, so we can somehow support ourselves.

What do you think about the collapse of communism?

Eduward: Young people in the communist Eastern European countries have been educated under socialism since they were born, so they aren't used to living with free enterprise. Therefore, many people have found it difficult to adjust to the Western way of thinking and to understand their mentality. East meets West isn't such an easy thing: it's a sudden culture shock in every respect. Living in the West, nothing is free. The cost of living is high: rent, medical care, education, and everything else. But in the communist USSR, we also had problems: constant material shortages. We couldn't find decent food in the shops or basic medical supplies in hospitals, or simple things we needed in daily life. I believe that the political system had to be changed and, as a whole, I basically agree with the ideas of capitalism. That's why I came to the West. ❖

"The political incompetence of Russians was the reason I left."

JURI GINSBURG

Russian Jewish refugee with his family: wife Maria and son Mikhail. Book translator. Born in 1950 in Moscow, USSR. Lives in East Berlin Jewish Refugee Center.

(Photo: Mr. Ginsburg with his wife and his son in their Jewish refugee center home in East Berlin.)

Mr. Ginsburg, when and why did you come to Germany?

There has been a deep anti-Semitism in the USSR for centuries. People don't like Jews, but it was taboo to say it openly. But, Gorbachev's *glasnost* was supposed to bring political and social reform for the people of the Soviet Union, but it went the wrong way: it encouraged people to express their hidden hatred of Jews. Now in the Soviet Union, they are able to say frankly in public; "We don't like Jews". I'm of the postwar generation; born, raised and educated in Moscow, and Moscow was my city. But that's changed very quickly.

Suddenly, we became foreigners alienated in our own city. By profession, I'm a freelance book translator in Russian, German, Dutch and English, and I was doing a quite well in Moscow. But I have gradually lost my work. I felt there might be trouble if we stayed any longer. So it didn't take too long to make up my mind to leave my country, before the situation got worse. A refugee application wasn't difficult: after three months of waiting, we were permitted to enter Germany. I studied German history and literature and I speak German perfectly; so I came here to find a job. We arrived in Berlin in January 1990.

Throughout the history of Russia, as the ideology shifted from Leninism to Stalinism, communism to something else, every time there was a crisis, Jews were blamed and became the victims. It happened in WW I during the Russian Revolution, then in WW II, and now lately after the failure of Gorbachev's revolution, Jews have become the victims once again. That pattern has always been repeated and the target is always Jews. And after all with each political ideology: fascism, totalitarianism, communism, socialism, whatever, there is no harmony or compromise among the Russians. I'm really fed up with the political incompetence in Russia. That's the main reason why we left the USSR.

In Germany, and especially East Germany, Jews have also been seen as unwelcomed foreigners as we have seen from the violence in the streets. Despite that, are you willing to settle in Germany?

In a way, I was surprised and shocked that a *judenrein* sentiment still exists in Germany today. I'm not a politically-oriented person. I'm more of an academic but I can see that the political situation in Germany has shifted from one extreme to another, either left-wing or right-wing, whichever government comes to power, and no one knows in which direction it will go next. And the situation for Jewish people gets worse when there is economical instability. Since the Wall has gone, West Germans have been pressuring East Germans, and these two states have a big economic gap right now. I wonder how a united Germany can overcome with it. Nobody knows what Germany will be like in 10 years. Anyhow, luckily, we have just bought a flat in East Berlin. If everything goes well, we'll settle down in Germany. My country is where I live and feel at home. But if something goes wrong, I have no idea where to go next. I was told that Japan has a severe labor shortage these days. So perhaps, our final destination will be Japan...

What is your plan for the education of your family?

Jews are hard-working and financially well-organized people, and education is the primary issue in our life. My wife is studying German and my son goes to a good elementary school. We are on social welfare for refugees but I have enough savings of my own to support them, so there is no problem at the moment. However, I'm concerned about the attitude of many East Germans who have quickly turned into capitalists: people who used to be intellectuals and dedicated communists have now changed. They have made a mental switch and are now materialists. And, there are those people who are running to East Germany to make a fast buck. There are now many video shops everywhere in East Berlin; it's booming business. Anyone can easily buy all kind of video tapes of violence, guns, murder, drugs and sex etc. This is a negative part of materialism and a cause of social decadence. I'm afraid that it will be a dangerous influence on the young people and the future of Germany. ❖

Conclusion

I would like to remind the readers that in any war, whether political, religious or territorial, every nation and every individual becomes a loser, both victim and vanquished. Just name the Holocaust, Hiroshima, Nagasaki and Dresden. The "winning" sides are also "victims," morally and intellectually.

In retrospect, the twentieth century has been the most turbulent era of world history — the First World War, the Russian Revolution, the rise of German nationalism and the Second World War, the Nuclear Age, the Cold War, and finally the collapse of Russian Communism. When the long decades of the Cold War were over, it seemed to many that world unity might be achieved after all. Instead, new wars have erupted, some of which are characterized by centuries old, deep animosity about tribal, ethnic, territorial and religious conflicts such as in the former Yugoslavia. The world today, in fact, has become more complicated, unstable and unpredictable than ever before. In the Nuclear Age, any war might result in a global tragedy with unforeseeable consequences.

In less than four years, a new millennium awaits us and a new chapter of history will begin. However, the fundamental human conflicts, over which we have fought in two world wars to end all wars, are yet unresolved. The entire world — every nation, every citizen, every racial, religious and ethnic minority — must work harder to resolve these conflicts. We must recognize our similarities, respect our differences, and cooperate with each other if we are to avoid war, genocide and environmental destruction. Despite our best efforts, however, it is unfortunate that we must pass on these unresolved problems to new generations.

Marie Ueda
January 1996

TESTIMONY OF THE TWENTIETH CENTURY
-- M A I L O R D E R F O R M --

Price $65.00 (US) plus $5.00 shipping/handling: $70.00 (Inside California $75.04 including tax)

Your name:_____ Profession:_____

Name of institution: (if any)_____ Department:_____

Address: _____ City: _____

State: _____ Zipcode: _____Phone: (___)_____

How many copies? _____ Total price: $_____ Signature: _____

Credit card #: VISA_____or Mastercard:_____ Exp. Date__/__/__

Or send check or money order to: M.I. PRODUCTIONS, P.O. Box 642219
                                     San Francisco, CA 94164-2219 USA

Order by phone: (415) 951-2470   fax: (415) 474-1264

--✂--

-- TESTIMONY OF THE TWENTIETH CENTURY
-- M A I L O R D E R F O R M --

Price $65.00 (US) plus $5.00 shipping/handling: $70.00 (Inside California $75.04 including tax)

Your name:_____ Profession:_____

Name of institution: (if any)_____ Department:_____

Address: _____ City: _____

State: _____ Zipcode: _____Phone: (___)_____

How many copies? _____ Total price: $_____ Signature: _____

Credit card #: VISA_____or Mastercard:_____ Exp. Date__/__/__

Or send check or money order to: M.I. PRODUCTIONS, P.O. Box 642219
                                     San Francisco, CA 94164-2219 USA

Order by phone: (415) 951-2470   fax: (415) 474-1264

--✂--

TESTIMONY OF THE TWENTIETH CENTURY
-- M A I L O R D E R F O R M --

Price $65.00 (US) plus $5.00 shipping/handling: $70.00 (Inside California $75.04 including tax)

Your name:_____ Profession:_____

Name of institution: (if any)_____ Department:_____

Address: _____ City: _____

State: _____ Zipcode: _____Phone: (___)_____

How many copies? _____ Total price: $_____ Signature: _____

Credit card #: VISA_____or Mastercard:_____ Exp. Date__/__/__

Or send check or money order to: M.I. PRODUCTIONS, P.O. Box 642219
                                     San Francisco, CA 94164-2219 USA

Order by phone: (415) 951-2470   fax: (415) 474-1264